OP   30$^{\underline{00}}$

THE GOSPEL ACCORDING TO ST JOHN

HERDER'S THEOLOGICAL COMMENTARY ON THE NEW TESTAMENT

General Editors

Serafin de Ausejo, Lucien Cerfaux, Béda Rigaux
Rudolf Schnackenburg, Anton Vögtle

RUDOLF SCHNACKENBURG

THE GOSPEL ACCORDING TO ST JOHN

VOLUME THREE
COMMENTARY ON CHAPTERS 13–21

CROSSROAD
New York

1987
The Crossroad Publishing Company
370 Lexington Ave, New York, NY 10017

ISBN 0 8245 0098 9
Library of Congress Catalog Card Number: 81-22157

PUBLISHER'S NOTE

The first volume of this Commentary was published in 1968 and included certain features that were not in the original German edition: the Greek text of the Gospel, a bibliography, textual indices, and an index of authors. In the second volume, and in this third volume, we have been able to retain all except the Greek text which, under changed conditions of production, would have increased the price to an intolerable level. For the same reason footnotes now appear at the end of the volume. The excursuses have been restored to the appropriate places; as in the German edition. In essentials, however, the second and third volumes follow the same pattern as the first.

Contents

THE GOSPEL ACCORDING TO ST JOHN

COMMENTARY

Jesus in the Circle of his Own.
Passion and Resurrection (Chapters 13–20)

INTRODUCTION TO CHAPTERS 13–20

After closing Jesus' revelation to the world (12:36b) and emphasizing this with a final reflection on unbelief (12:37–43) and a summary of Jesus' revelatory discourse (12:44–50), the evangelist opens a new part of the gospel in Chapter 13. In the form in which we have the gospel today, this part begins with quite lengthy discourses by Jesus in the circle of his followers, culminating in the prayer of the departing redeemer (Chapter 17). This is followed by an account of Jesus' arrest, trial and passion (Chapters 18–19), to which the chapter on the resurrection (20) is added. 20:30f are clearly the original conclusion to the gospel. The length of Jesus' discourses and dialogues in the circle of his disciples shows that these are of considerable importance, but, from an objective theological viewpoint, the evangelist's account of Jesus' trial and passion is obviously no less important. The theological content of the resurrection stories should also not be underestimated.

Is the gospel planned in three parts: Jesus' public works, his dialogues with the disciples and the passion and resurrection? Or are there only two parts, the division between them being formed by the end of Chapter 12? This is an important question for our understanding of the literary genus of the gospel. If there were three parts in accordance with the original structure, such great emphasis would fall on the discourses of Christ, divided between those given to the world and those intended only for the disciples, that the representation of the passion would appear to be no more than a supplement attributable to tradition. It is obvious that this structure would not point to the evangelist's neglect of the passion and resurrection, because he presents these events in a way that indicates profound theological reflection, but it would show that they were not the ultimate goal of the entire gospel, the vanishing-point where all lines converge.

There are several reasons why we may assume that the evangelist wanted his whole work to point unequivocally to Jesus' passion and resurrection:

(a) Even seen only from the outside, there is nowhere else in the gospel such a strongly marked new beginning as the one at 13:1. Even if Chapters 15–16 and/or Chapter 17 were integral parts of the original gospel (a problem which will be discussed later), they are none the less closely linked to the chapters that follow by 18:1 (ταῦτα εἰπών . . .).

(b) If Chapters 15–16 and/or Chapter 17 are accretions, and if, in the gospel as originally planned and fashioned by the evangelist, 18:1 followed Jesus' call to the disciples to leave the room where the last supper was being held (14:31), the much shorter 'farewell discourse' (Chapter 14) leads without a break – inviting the reader to join in – to the event of the passion.

(c) Jesus' being together with his disciples and his trial before Pilate are bracketed together by the comment in 13:1: πρὸ δὲ τῆς ἑορτῆς τοῦ πάσχα. The theme of the passover is not of great significance in the dialogues in the upper room, but it plays an important part in the trial (18:28; 39; 19:14) and is probably also important as a background to the death of Jesus (see 19:36).

(d) The feast of the passover on which Jesus suffered death, however, forms an important link between the first and the second main parts, since, in the last section on Jesus' public life, the reader's attention is unmistakably drawn to the imminent feast (11:55; 12:1). It is not difficult to distinguish a gradual approach to the passover of Jesus' death. In 11:55, it is 'drawing near'; the anointing at Bethany took place 'six days before' (12:1); the farewell meal takes place 'before the passover'; and the day of condemnation and execution is the 'day of rest' of the passover (19:14).

(e) The inner content of the evangelist's presentation and the expectation that he encourages in the reader, however, make it obvious that a detailed account of the passion was necessary. At the washing of the disciples' feet, Jesus says to Simon Peter: 'What I am doing you do not know now, but afterwards you will understand' (13:7). At the last supper, Peter is not able to overcome his lack of understanding, which is expressed as misunderstanding, and the reader too cannot appreciate the deeper meaning of the washing of the feet until he considers the death of Jesus. The same applies to the announcement of the betrayal (13:18, 21), Jesus' discourse about his departure (13:33, 36) and the other uncomprehending questions asked by the disciples (14:5, 8, 22). Even a Christian reader, who is able to interpret Jesus' announcements, expects an explanation through the event itself.

(f) References are made in advance to Jesus' death even in the first main part of the gospel, beginning with the cleansing of the temple (2:17) and then repeated in comments about the 'Jews'' intention to kill Jesus (5:18; 7:1, 19, 25, etc.). These also continue in the references to Jesus' 'hour', the deeper meaning of which is revealed even more strongly later (12:23, 27, see also 32).[1] The second main part of the gospel begins with the emphatic statement that Jesus' 'hour' has come to leave this world for the Father (13:1). This event, symbolized by the evangelist in the 'lifting up' or exaltation on the cross (3:14; 8:28; 12:32), and indicated to the reader (12:33), also calls for a narrative report to make the meaning indicated effective. The evangelist refers back to this in his accounts of the trial (18:32) and the crucifixion (19:37; cf. 8:38).

(g) There is only one surprising element, which is that the 'exaltation' and the 'glorification' of Jesus are regarded by the evangelist as theologically so closely related that to separate them into an event of the crucifixion and a resurrection event seems hardly meaningful. The 'resurrection' following the death of Jesus is in a different category from the glorification that took place in the exaltation on the cross. In returning to that traditional category in Chapter 20, the evangelist was clearly constrained not only by the traditional material, but by the course of events themselves. He did not, however, entirely abandon the category of the resurrection of Jesus after his death (see 2:22; 10:17f). The announcement of Jesus' 'coming' and of the 'seeing' of the disciples (14:18f) is fulfilled at Easter (20:19f), as is the promise of the Spirit (14:16f, 26; cf. 20:22).

We may therefore conclude that Jesus' dialogues with his disciples in the upper room at the last supper do not form an isolated part of the gospel, but represent only a transition to Jesus' passion and resurrection. If this conclusion is accepted, it should be clear that the gospel of John is a presentation of the life of Jesus culminating in his cross and resurrection. A comparison with the gospels of Mark and Luke can also help us to understand the special nature of the structure of the fourth gospel in this second main part.

Although it was also conceived from the post-paschal standpoint, Mark's gospel has a different internal organization. Jesus' conversations with his disciples, which have the special function of instructing the community, are (with the exception of the discourse on the end of time in Chapter 13) merged into the general presentation of his public activity, but are often characterized by the presence of such statements as 'when he had entered the house', or 'in the house' (7:17; 9:28, 33; 10:10), or 'privately' (4:34; 9:28; 13:3). The revelation of the mystery of the passion to the disciples (8:31) represents a turning-point which also gives the work its literary structure, since the second part is structurally determined by the announcements of the passion, which are obviously cumulative (9:31; 10:33) and at the same time lead up to the days in Jerusalem and the passion itself.[2] Jesus' public activity and the instruction that he gives to his disciples are not separated and the controversies with his opponents continue in the second part, but the inner dividing-line is consistently drawn (in 4:10–12). When Jesus is alone with his disciples for the last time (14:12–42), he gives them a certain amount of private instruction, the most important being about the institution of the Eucharist, but no directions are given about the time that will follow his death.

The gospel of Luke is presented in a way that is different from that used for Mark, and is closer to the gospel of John in that it contains a kind of 'farewell discourse' spoken by Jesus in the upper room (22:24–38). It consists of a collection of the logia that would be important at the time when the disciples would be left alone. These words of Jesus spoken before his departure are – with the exception of the 'testament' in vv. 28–30 – concerned with the imminent time of contestation, distress and struggle, for which they contain both warning and encouragement. It can hardly be denied that this Lukan passage may have influenced John in some way. The Lukan statement 'I am among you as one who serves' (22:27) may in particular have had an influence on John's washing of the feet.

The Johannine farewell discourse (Chapter 14) is entirely subservient to the evangelist's theology. Its aim is above all to provide a basis for the disciples' (and all believers') continuing community with Jesus, in spite of the imminent separation, and to strengthen the future Christian community in its believing existence. It also points to the prospect of Jesus' return after Easter and to that of Christians' lasting community with him through the Spirit. In this way, it bridges the gap between the passion of Jesus and his earthly separation. It is precisely for this reason that it plays an indispensable part in the account of the passion that follows: light is thrown in advance on the darkness of this event and its frightfulness is diminished. The Johannine passion is therefore really a story of Jesus' victory and of the fulfilment of his work.

The structure of the second main part of the gospel is very clear. It is, however, obvious, in the light of the discussion about the farewell discourse(s), that questions of literary criticism are inevitably involved here. How, for instance, should the discourses in Chapters 15–17, which begin immediately after the call to leave (14:31), be judged? Is it possible to distinguish, within this chapter, individual discourses that should be considered separately? What is the relationship between the prayer in Chapter 17 and the original farewell discourse in Chapter 14 and the other discourses in Chapters 15–16? The theological discussion about the integrity of this chapter within the gospel of John, its structure, its origin and its nature has continued for a long time now and has recently come to the fore again.[3] The literary problem that arises in connection with the 'additional' chapter (21) and the concluding remark by an editor (21:24f) also has theological consequences. Do the literary strata, which can to some extent be established, not point in each case to a different theological understanding and aim? There are, for instance, two interpretations of the episode of the washing of the disciples' feet. The first is symbolic and theological and points to Jesus' death (13:6–10) and the second, which is centred on the washing of the feet as such, is paradigmatic and parenetic (13:12–17). These two interpretations force us to ask whether in this passage an editorial stratum based on a different view should not be distinguished from the evangelist's presentation.[4] The problem is further complicated by the introduction of the disciple whom Jesus loved into the community sharing the farewell meal (13:23–26). The question of his relationship with the evangelist and the final editor of the gospel will be discussed when the chapter concerned is considered.

The Johannine account of the passion has its own special characteristics, which distinguish it from the synoptic versions, but it also includes certain traditions that bear the mark of close contact with the gospel of Luke. A great deal of attention has been devoted in recent years to its theological character, which it owes mainly to Johannine Christology, and to its history of traditions.[5] Jesus' arrest, the Jewish trial and the denial of Peter (18:1–27), on the one hand, and the vivid presentation of the trial before Pilate (18:28—19:16), on the other, are both unmistakably Johannine in form and at the same time give rise to questions, the most important being whether the evangelist may have made use of a previously existing account. This question arises in an even more acute form in connection with the short and very strange report of Jesus' way of the cross and crucifixion (19:17–30) and the relatively extensive account of the piercing of Jesus' side and his burial (19:31–42).

The chapter on the resurrection (20) is divided into the events on the Sunday morning and Mary Magdalene's visit to the tomb, the 'race' between Simon Peter and the disciple whom Jesus loved and Jesus' appearance to Mary Magdalene (20:1–18), on the one hand, and Jesus' appearance to the disciples on the evening of the same day in the closed room (20:19–23) and his appearance to Thomas within the circle of the disciples a week later (20:24–29), on the other. Behind all these events, the evangelist's theological intention and his concern for the community that he is addressing are discernible. He also makes use of certain traditions, at least in the case of the events at the tomb.

The additional chapter (21) raises the question of authorship and the author's intentions. The 'disciple whom Jesus loved' is presented once again in quite a striking way in this chapter (21:7, 20–23; see also 24) and this makes it necessary for this figure, his significance for the Johannine community and the part that he played in the development of the gospel of John, to be reconsidered. This editorial conclusion to the gospel in its present form must always be kept in mind as a key to our understanding of the gospel as a whole.

Jesus in the Circle of his Own
The Last Supper and the Farewell Discourse (Chapters 13–14)

Chapter 1

Jesus' Last Meal with his Disciples: 13:1–30

The first section that we have to consider is clearly marked off by the departure of Judas Iscariot (13:30). It opens with a solemn introduction which is theologically heavy and linguistically even overladen (vv. 1–3) and in which the only concrete statements made are the bare comments that it was 'before the feast of the passover' and 'during supper'. It is obvious from this that the evangelist was not interested in the external event, the meal itself and the details. There are only two things to which he gives close attention – the washing of the feet, which, according to the text in its present form, took place during the meal, and the exposure and the departure of the traitor Judas. Both of these are very characteristic of the evangelist's way of thinking and his intentions. The whole presentation is subservient to his theological thought and to his intention, as directed towards the circle of his readers.

The fourth evangelist must have assumed that his readers were acquainted with the historical events that are known to us to a very great extent (although with many gaps) from the synoptic gospels. His manner of writing is expressed, for example, in his accounts of John the Baptist, in which he leaves out much that is known to us from the synoptics and devotes his attention to certain aspects which cannot be found in precisely this form in the synoptics and on which he therefore throws new light. This way of writing cannot be explained as a desire to supplement the synoptic accounts. It was clearly his intention to interpret them. The extent to which he knew them cannot be determined by this, but the most astonishing fact is undoubtedly the evangelist's complete omission of the institution of the Eucharist. This complex problem will be discussed in Excursus 15. In this case a critical analysis of the section from the literary point of view is an essential preliminary step to any exegesis and may lead to an appreciation of the fact that exegesis cannot take place here at only one level. It is, on the contrary, clear that a distinction has to be made between the parts that were originally provided by the evangelist himself, other textual accretions and even further editorial additions.

Literary Analysis of Jn 13:1–30

1. The Problem

Without literary criticism, it is not possible to understand the text of Jn 13:1–30 in its present form. Certain exegetes have not taken the existence of different literary levels into account and have seen the whole section as the work of one hand, that of the evangelist. If, however, it is accepted that the gospel had a fairly long period of development (see Vol. 1, pp. 44–74), the evangelist himself will not be held responsible for all the difficult passages in the text, all unmotivated transitions nor all tensions in the thought-content of the gospel. The following individual difficulties are worth noting in particular:

(a) Vv. 1–3 are linguistically overladen in a way that does not occur elsewhere in the whole gospel. There is a very complicated sentence structure in 10:35f and there are also lengthy sentence structures in Chapter 17, but these are of a different kind (they are ἵνα and καθώς clauses). The long sentence found in 13:2–4 consists of participle constructions and is unique in the gospel of John. In its compression of ideas (though not in a single sentence), 6:22–24 provides a certain analogy, but this passage can be explained as a later editorial expansion (see Vol. 2, pp. 33f).

(b) Both the interpretations in the passage on the washing of the disciples' feet (vv. 6–10 and 12–17) are difficult to understand, but neither is purely coincidental in its juxtaposition to the other. The first is theologically more profound and in it the washing of the feet is seen as a symbolic action pointing to Jesus' death. The second is paradigmatic and is centred on the humble service of Jesus – itself based on the washing of the disciples' feet.[6]

(c) In v. 10, the uncertainty of the textual tradition (does the phrase εἰ μὴ τοὺς πόδας belong to the original text?) shows that the passage presented quite considerable difficulties at an early stage. There is also the question as to whether v. 10b, with its change to ὑμεῖς, is not an extension *ad vocem* καθαρός. The commentary in v. 11 is also open to the suspicion that it may be an editorial addition.

(d) V. 18 also does not follow v. 17 easily. V. 18a is connected with the end of v. 10 (οὐχὶ πάντες). If vv. 10b–11 are not original, v. 18 might be the continuation of v. 10a. If the whole of v. 10 is original, an editor might have accepted the end of v. 10 with v. 18a, after interpolating the second interpretation, and then have gone on to make the statement about the betrayal of Jesus.

(e) Vv. 18f, with the Old Testament quotation and the reason for believing is, in its own way, a valid statement about betrayal by a companion at table. V. 21, on the other hand, is a duplication. If it is a clarification of the more veiled statement made in the quotation from the Old Testament, then the introduction to v. 21, according to which Jesus was 'troubled in spirit', is very surprising in view of his resolute attitude in vv. 18f.

(f) V. 20, which comes between these verses, has no real meaning at all in this context. How, then, did this 'synoptic' logion (see Mt 10:40) arrive in this position? (There is another similar 'synoptic' logion in v. 16.)

(g) The traitor is unambiguously indicated in the scene with the disciple whom Jesus loved (vv. 23–26). The difficulty that the other disciples let Judas Iscariot leave the room is apparently satisfactorily solved in vv. 28–29, but to accept this solution would be to overlook the fact that Peter prompted the disciple whom Jesus loved to ask Jesus the question and would hardly have been content to receive no reply when he saw him speaking to Jesus. Are vv. 28–29, then, simply added on the basis of reflection? (V. 30, after all, follows v. 27 quite easily.) Or should the scene with the disciple whom Jesus loved perhaps be attributed to an editor?

(h) The remark that, after eating, 'Satan entered into him' (v. 27) is, if we look back at the beginning of this section, in conflict with the other statement in v. 20 τοῦ διαβόλου ἤδη βεβληκότος κτλ., which is also linguistically clumsy. The two remarks can be harmonized only with difficulty. In this case, the second, in v. 27, has more claim to originality.

There are also further difficulties to be found in the existing text of Chapter 13, but those mentioned above are sufficient to show that a literary analysis is both justified and necessary.

2. The State of Research and Methodological Considerations

Complete agreement has not yet been reached by those who have analyzed this section from the literary point of view, but several lasting results have been achieved. The earlier literary critics were generally speaking in search of a 'basic document', but, although they perspicaciously drew attention to the textual difficulties, they were unable to agree about the scope of the basic document itself.

A clear picture of this basic document and the later additions emerges from J. Wellhausen's work in this sphere.[7] According to this scholar, the introduction, vv. 1–3, was the work of a second person, but vv. 4–5 belong to the basic document. The two interpretations of the washing of the feet are incompatible with each other. The first and 'open' interpretation takes priority over the 'historically masked' one. Judas Iscariot does not belong to the basic document. V. 15 is followed by an appendix, vv. 16 and 20 being derived from Matthew and breaking the context. Vv. 17–19 are in the same line as vv. 10– 11. Unlike the other data in the gospel of John, vv. 21–38 presuppose a passover meal, as in the case of the synoptic gospels. Vv. 28–29 are interpolations.

F. Spitta's construction of the basic document[8] is based essentially on vv. 1–10a, 21–30. He believed that vv. 12–17, 20 were taken from other literature and that vv. 16, 19 and the phrase 'whom Jesus loved' in v. 23 were the adapter's own comments.

E. Hirsch[9] has provided a different picture of the structure. He ascribes vv. 1–2a, 4–10, 12–16, 21–26, 27b and 30 (with the exception of the editorial additions mentioned below) to the evangelist. Other elements, he believes, are the work of the editor. These include v. 2 from τοῦ διαβόλου; v. 3; ἐκ τοῦ δείπνου in v. 4; ἀλλ᾽ οὐχὶ πάντες in v. 10 and v. 11; vv. 17–20; ὃν ἠγάπα ὁ Ἰησοῦς in v. 23; vv. 27a, 28–29.

Others who have examined this text base their analysis on a source that the evangelist in their opinion used.

According to R. Bultmann,[10] the source reported that washing of the feet and the account of the action (vv. 4f) was followed by the interpretation (vv. 12–20). The first interpretation (vv. 6–10) is the evangelist's. Both interpretations are extended by an appendix or by notes. Vv. 10b–11 and 18–19 are the editorial work of the evangelist. Vv. 16 and 20 form an appendix to the second interpretation, which was probably already present in the source.

A more recent textual critic, R. Fortna,[11] is rather vague in his conclusions. The source that he believes was used by the evangelist, the 'gospel of signs', can only with difficulty be discerned in this chapter of the gospel. Elements of it can, he claims, be distinguished in vv. 2a, 4–5, 12–14, 18b, 21b and 26–27.

Other exegetes have suggested that two different traditions combined to form this text and that the final form as it exists today was the work of an editor (or editors).

M. Boismard[12] thought, for example, that two originally independent interpretations, a 'moralizing' and a 'sacramental' account, were combined. Vv. 1–2, 4–5, 12–15, 17 and 18–19 belonged to the 'moralizing' text, which was, in his opinion, earlier, and vv. 3, 4–5, 6–10 (11) and 21–30 belonged to the 'sacramental' tradition.

R. E. Brown[13] has criticized this theory, calling it too rigorous, but he insists on the existence of two intepretations: the first being vv. 6–10a (with its addition, vv. 10b–11) and the second vv. 12–17 (with its addition, vv. 18–19). Brown's fundamentally new idea is that v. 1 is the introduction to the whole 'book of the glorification' and that vv. 2–3 form the introduction to the washing of the feet.

G. Richter,[14] who energetically upholds the independence of the two interpretations, also claims to be able to give reasons for the different insights. Like the first farewell discourse (Chapter 14), the first interpretation is determined by the aim stated in 20:30f. Like the second farewell discourse (Chapters 15–16), the second interpretation has a more pastoral aim. According to Richter, 'the man who added the second farewell discourse to the first also added the second interpretation of the washing of the feet to the first' (p. 313). This exegete also thinks that v. 20 was written by a third person (p. 319).

H. Thyen,[15] the exegete who has provided the most recent analysis of this text, also favours the idea of a fundamental or original scripture, which had a gnosticizing tendency. In his opinion, this original text was adapted by an editor who was motivated by the interests of his community and the pastoral concerns that predominated in that community. The second interpretation goes back to this text, as do the genitive construction in v. 2 and the corresponding vv. 10b–11 and what is particularly worth noting, vv. 20–26.

Thyen appeals to an unpublished work by Hans-Peter Otto and comments: 'All the texts in the gospel in which the disciple whom Jesus loved figures are therefore his interpolations, which he himself composed in the light of his own intention, which is fully revealed for the first time in Chapter 21' (p. 352). According to Thyen, vv. 22–26, in which the situation of a passover meal can be perceived, come from a different tradition from the one underlying the Johannine fundamental scripture. Several times (for example, in vv. 16 and 20), he bases his explanation on the Presbyter's controversy with Diotrophes in 3 Jn.

In any consideration of all this earlier and more recent research, it is important to bear in mind the existence of the two divergent interpretations of the washing of the feet. The differences that occur in the further analysis of Jn 13:1–30 are to a considerable extent attributable to the different presuppositions made in each case and to the different methods followed. These methods are, of course, at least partly determined by the exegete's presuppositions. Several methodological considerations have therefore to be taken into account.

The principle on which the earlier literary critics based their work was to examine the text carefully for gaps and seams, tensions and inner contradictions and so on. This is a very good point of departure for all textual analysis. On the other hand, it is necessary to delay going into the question of the source and attempting to define the nature and scope of that source more precisely, since it is easy to introduce questionable ideas prematurely in this process.

All available methods can be used in the attempt to distinguish possible strata. These include, for example, criticism of the style and the matter of the text and comparisons with other passages in the gospel based on linguistic form and theological content. As in the question of the possible source, it is also advisable to postpone examining the question of the author (the evangelist, the editor or editors and other possible contributors) in order to avoid the premature construction of a model. In a word, the 'synchronic' method, as used in modern linguistic and literary studies, should be followed and the 'diachronic' method should be avoided in the literary analysis of such passages in scripture.[16] In the end, however, an attempt must also be made to explain the literary genesis of the passage.

3. An Attempt at an Analysis

There are certain duplications in the introductory verses. There is, for example, the similarity between the ideas expressed in vv. 1 and 3, namely that Jesus is leaving this world to go to the Father (v. 1) and that he had come from God and was going back to God (v. 3). There is also the repetition of εἰδώς in the same two verses. Two consecutive participle constructions of the same kind are not usual in the gospel of John, but, in these verses, there are εἰδώς and ἀγαπήσας in v. 1 and the two genitive absolutes in v. 2. The same applies to the two ὅτι clauses dependent on εἰδώς in v. 3. How is that to be explained?

The repetition of εἰδώς in vv. 1 and 3 may point to a similar intervention on the part of an editor as that in the case of εἶδον in 6:22 and εἶδεν in 6:24. The other facts, however, cannot be explained simply by this and it is important to look more closely at the text. Difficulties have been encountered in the present text of v. 1 for some time now, the most serious being that the statement 'before the feast of the passover' is not in accordance with Jesus' love for his own until the end. It only fits in with the 'hour' of Jesus in the first part of the sentence. The date 'before the passover' can, however, be included in the εἰδώς clause (see the commentary).

The content of v.1b is undoubtedly Johannine, but there are certain striking peculiarities. For example, the term οἱ ἴδιοι is used differently from its use in 1:11, where it is not restricted to Jesus' disciples. It is, however, possible to point to τὰ ἴδια (πρόβατα) in 10:3, 4, 12. The term εἰς τέλος is also unique in John, but it can be compared with the idea expressed in 19:30. Finally, the only other references to an ἀγαπᾶν of Jesus with regard to his disciples occur in 13:34; 14:21 (future) and 15:9, 12. The idea of the commandment to love, which is suspect in 13:34 as an editorial addition and in 15:9, 12 as part of the same secondary stratum, may have had an influence here. Did the editor perhaps want to provide a foundation for his second interpretation (vv. 12–17)? Despite these suspicions, however, one is reluctant to dispute the authorship of the evangelist in the case of v. 1b. The whole of v. 1 may, as R. E. Brown has suggested, be a heading to the second main part of the gospel, in which the bow is stretched from the washing of the feet to the death of Jesus. This certainly also fits in with the first interpretation of Jesus' action in the upper room (see the commentary).

The statement about the devil in v. 2 is excluded by many literary critics, because of its content, from the fundamental scripture, in which no interest is shown in Judas Iscariot (see above). Even without accepting this questionable view, however, there are formal linguistic reasons for believing that this does not belong to the evangelist's original text. These are, as we have seen, that it follows another genitive absolute and that the expression is linguistically clumsy, a possible consequence of embarrassment in view of v. 27. 'Godfather' (8:44; cf. 6:70) may have stood for διάβολος (instead of σατανᾶς in v. 27).

The second εἰδώς clause in v. 3 is more difficult to assess. What is the meaning of 'that the Father had given all things into his hands'? One is driven to suspect that this is an attempt to reject a gaining of power over Jesus on the part of the devil (cf. 14:30). In this case, the statement would be a consequence of the previous remark about the devil and similarly attributable to an editor. The Semitic phrase διδόναι εἰς τὴν χεῖρα (in the singular, it should be noted) is also encountered in 3:35, where it, however, has a different meaning (that of the full power of revelation; see the commentary on this text). It can also be compared with 7:30, 44.

If the editor wanted to refute any supremacy on the part of the devil over Jesus, then the continuation of this text (the second ὅτι clause) can be easily explained: Jesus had come from God and was going back to God – in other words, he is subject to God's power and control. If this is the correct interpretation, then this sentence has a different function from the similar idea in v. 1. The entire verse (3) was inserted, formally by means of the repetition of εἰδώς, by the editor, in order to prevent a possible misinterpretation of v. 2.

If v. 2 from τοῦ διαβόλου onwards is bracketed together with v. 3, the beginning of v. 2, 'during supper', continues smoothly into v. 4, in which, after the long interpolation, only ἐκ τοῦ δείπνου has to be attributed to the editor. The editor's interest must in fact have been directed towards the traitor, Judas Iscariot, who, despite v. 19, continued to be a stumbling-block for the community.

The narrative of the washing of the disciples' feet is quite straightforward. The evangelist is above all concerned with Jesus' conversation with Simon Peter and this certainly continues as far as v. 10a. Doubts are once again raised by vv. 10b–11, in view of the difficulties involved in the exegesis of v. 10 (see the commentary). Peter is given a clear answer in the general aphorism of v. 10a and the transition to a statement addressed to the disciples (καὶ ὑμεῖς) is not in accordance with the style of the dialogue. The declaration that the disciples are clean now places the discourse on a new level. This may, however, have been the evangelist's intention in using symbolic language, in order to prepare the way for the announcement of the betrayal. It is better, then, not to dispute the evangelist's authorship in the case of vv. 10b and 11 as well. If, however, οὐχὶ πάντες is taken to be an allusion to the betrayal on the part of a companion at table (v. 18), then v. 11 anticipates this point and would seem to be an addition by the same editor as that of vv. 2–3.

The presentation in vv. 4–5 is resumed at the beginning of v. 12, so that the latter must belong to the original account of the washing of the feet. Only the following discourse, with the paradigmatic interpretation of the washing of the feet, is open to suspicion as a later addition. An investigation of its language does not, however, lead to an unambiguous decision as to whether it is the work of the evangelist or not. The words ὑπόδειγμα and ἀπόστολος occur rarely. The emphasis on Jesus as the διδάσκαλος and κύριος is something that is not found previously. Both terms occur otherwise for the most part only as forms of address, and ὁ κύριος in the narrative suggests in each instance the suspicion that it is an editorial formation (4:1; 6:23; 11:2). It would seem that the members of the Johannine community spoke of the 'Lord'. The relationship between 13:15 and 13:34 is unmistakable, even in the linguistic formula (καθώς . . . καὶ ὑμεῖς), but 13:34 is open to suspicion, in this context, as an editorial addition. The admonitory discourse can therefore be seen as an editorial formation. It is not necessary to reject in advance the evangelist's authorship of this discourse,[17] but there are two reasons in particular that make it difficult to accept his authorship. The first is the difficulty to which many exegetes have drawn attention, namely that the second interpretation seems to have nothing to do with the first and indeed would appear to be in conflict with it (attention is drawn only to the washing of the feet as such). The second is the bad connection with v. 18 – the transition from an admonition to an announcement of the betrayal is unmotivated and the transitional statement 'I am not speaking of you all' seems artificial.

The evangelist moves, then, from εἶπεν αὐτοῖς in v. 12 and ἐγὼ οἶδα in v. 18b to the announcement of the betrayal. The editor inserted the discourse admonishing the readers to imitate Jesus and created a new transition to the announcement of the betrayal in v. 18a. The widespread view[18] that vv. 12–20 should be regarded as a unity or that vv. 18–20 are at least an 'appendix' to vv.

12–17 cannot therefore be accepted. Vv. 18–19 bear the mark of the evangelist. After revealing to the disciples the prospect of the new community with Jesus, symbolized in the washing of the feet and reconstituted by the death of Jesus (see v. 8b), the narrator at once proceeds to announce the betrayal, saying that one of them, who now forms part of the community at table, has no share in that community. This may be a hard stumbling-block for the others, but Jesus has already prophesied it. The idea of election is also found in the same context in 6:70, after Peter's confession in the name of the Twelve. The quotation from scripture, which cannot have been taken from the synoptic announcement of the betrayal (Mk 14:18, 20 par.), deviates from the text of the Septuagint and is close to the Masoretic text, much in accordance with other Johannine quotations.[19] V. 19 has a direct parallel in 14:29, but it also has the important addition ὅτι ἐγώ εἰμι. This distinctively Johannine expression (used absolutely here as it is in 8:24, 28; cf. 58) is in striking contrast with the term εἰμί γὰρ in v. 13.

If the first announcement of the betrayal (vv. 18–19) belongs to the evangelist's fundamental stratum, then the second (vv. 21f) must be suspected as a secondary addition. None the less, it has a thoroughly Johannine sound – for ἐταράχθη τῷ πνεύματι, see 11:33, also 12:27; 14:1, 27; and for ἐμαρτύρησεν καὶ εἶπεν, see 1:15, 32. The announcement of the betrayal itself is also in accordance with the synoptic version (Mk 14:18; Mt 26:21) and indeed, apart from the Johannine repetition of the ἀμήν, it is the same, word for word.

Vv. 21–22 can, moreover, hardly be an independent unit. On the contrary, they form an introduction and a transition to the scene with the disciple whom Jesus loved (vv. 23–26) and it is also clear that they deal with the exposure and the departure of the traitor. The evangelist, following the synoptic account. might then have fashioned the new narrative unit in order to emphasize Jesus' knowledge of the identity of the traitor and the impulse that Jesus gave him to carry out the action. The identification of the traitor, who has for some time been indicated without any name (6:70; 15:10b, 18), by Jesus himself is clearly the end-point of a line drawn by the evangelist. The change of mood in v. 21, as the introduction to this exposure of the traitor's identity has certain analogies in 11:33 and 12:27. It is, however, important to look more closely at vv. 20–26 to see whether the introduction of the disciple lying close to Jesus' breast can be traced back to the evangelist or whether it has to be attributed to an editor.

V. 20 comes between the first and the second announcements of the betrayal and breaks the connection between them. It can probably be explained as an addition occasioned by the idea that those chosen by Jesus (v. 18b), despite the betrayal of a fellow-disciple (v. 18c), still share in Jesus' authority (cf. the ἐγώ εἰμι of v. 19) and need not trouble themselves about their reputation.[20] The aphorism used by John is not essentially different from that in Mt 10:40, although, instead of δέχεσθαι, John uses λαμβάνειν (with the stylistic criterion τίνα. A similar 'synoptic' aphorism occurs in v. 16, and v. 20 ought presumably to be attributed to the same editor.

Does the scene with the disciple whom Jesus loved belong to the evangelist's fundamental stratum or is section 21–26 the work of an editor? An important reason for regarding it as the work of an editor is the great interest taken in that disciple in the additional chapter forming an appendix to the gospel, where that same disciple is stated to be the one 'who has written these things' (that is, the gospel) (21:24). Would he, then, have called himself the 'disciple whom Jesus loved'? Even the earlier literary critics noticed, however, that the phrase ὃν ἠγάπα ὁ Ἰησοῦς recurred in v. 23. This way of describing the disciple who lay close to Jesus' breast may therefore only have been an editorial addition, but this is by no means certain (see the commentary). For the rest, there is no reason to suspect that the passage is not the work of the evangelist; indeed his authorship is betrayed in the style (see the commentary). H. Thyen's argument, then, that the scene with the disciple whom Jesus loved is, as a whole, the work of an editor has little to support it.

This author claims that v. 27 directly follows vv. 18f.[21] In that case, then, the words μετὰ τὸ ψωμίον in v. 27 should be placed between brackets, since Thyen includes the theme of the 'morsel' in the meal situation of v. 23–26 (the passover meal!).[22] Even then, however, one difficulty still remains – the further mention of the 'morsel' in v. 30. It would therefore seem that this theme originally formed part of the basic stratum, in which the traitor must have been given his name, because he is called by the short form of that name, 'Judas', in v. 29. The passing of a 'morsel' does not necessarily point to a passover meal.[23] The 'lying' on cushions (v. 23) may, like the announcement of the betrayal in v. 21, have been influenced by the synoptic account (see Mk 14:18). John also uses this word in the account of the feast at Bethany with Lazarus (12:2).[24]

Vv. 28f were attributed even by earlier literary critics to an editor whose aim was to make the unhindered departure of Judas intelligible.[25] In fact, v. 30, without the commentary, would follow more strictly after v. 27. If the evangelist in fact made the observation about Judas, the custodian of the common purse, in 12:6, then this reflection could also be attributed to him. An insertion by an editor is, however, more probable. V. 30 certainly forms part of the fundamental stratum (written by the evangelist).

I may therefore summarize the result of my analysis as follows:

The evangelist's fundamental stratum: v. 1; the beginning of v. 2 καὶ δείπνου γινομένου and v. 4 (without ἐκ τοῦ δείπνου); vv. 5–10, 12a (as far as εἶπεν αὐτοῖς); vv. 18b–19, 21–27, 30.

A longer insertion into the fundamental stratum: the second interpretation in v. 12b (from γινώσκετε) – 17, 18a.

Shorter insertions made by the editor: v. 2 (from τοῦ διαβόλου) – vv. 3, 11, 20 and (probably) 28f.

This result does not alter our previous recognition of the fact that generally speaking only fairly small additions were made by the editor. The only longer insertion is the second (paradigmatic) interpretation of the washing of the feet and this can be understood in connection with 13:34f and 15:12–17. It is still possible to ask, however, whether the insertion in vv. 2–3, the commentary in v. 11, the second interpretation in vv. 12–17 and vv. 20 and 28f are all by the same person. Vv. 2–3, 11 and 28–29 (because of the interest in Judas) are more closely related and v. 20 is related to v. 16. If the final editing expressed in 21:24 is seen as a unified group, then only one editorial process would be assumed. The editorial additions, however, did not necessarily take place all at one time. The final editing might have incorporated the earlier (and smaller) changes and approved them. The longer insertions would in any case have been the work of this final editor – in other words, the second interpretation of the washing of the feet. (For Chapters 15–17, see below.) It is also important to point out here that not all the conclusions in this attempt at an analysis can be made with the same degree of certainty. The text as we have it at present hardly enables us to provide an analysis that is beyond dispute.

It is better to postpone a consideration of a possible source used by the evangelist, since it can only be usefully discussed if the narratives of the passion and of Easter are also taken into account. It is certain that the evangelist did not have at his disposal a special source for the events narrated in Chapter 13.

Exegesis

1. Introduction and the Washing of the Feet (13:1–5)

[1]*Now before the feast of the passover, when Jesus knew that his hour had come to depart out of this world to the Father, having loved his own who were in the world, he loved them to the end (or: to the extreme limit).* [2]*And during supper, when the devil had already put it into the heart of Judas Iscariot, Simon's son, to betray him,* [3]*Jesus, knowing that the Father had given all things into his hands and that he had come from God and was going to God,* [4]*rose from supper, laid aside his garments and girded himself with a towel.* [5]*Then he poured water into a basin and began to wash the disciples' feet and to wipe them with the towel with which he was girded.*

13:1   In the way in which it is presented in the fourth gospel, the feast of the passover, when Jesus was to suffer death, is a very important focal point (see, for example, 11:55; 12:1; 18:28, 39; 19:14). This is not because of its historical interest, but because it was theologically significant. Jesus, after all, died as the passover lamb of the New Testament, of whom not a bone would be broken (see 19:36).[26] The date with which this text begins is closely related to the εἰδὼς,[27] and further reinforces the frequently stressed prior knowledge that Jesus had of his death or his 'hour'.[28] The previously determined hour of his death (see, for example, 7:30; 8:20) at the same time also leads to his glorification (12:23). It is described here as Jesus' transition from this world to the Father, because attention is drawn to his disciples – 'his own, who were still in the world' – and his time of activity in the world (9:5) is coming to an end (see 17:11, 13). The spatial metaphor ('depart'; cf. 5:24; 1 Jn 3:14) is closely connected with the evangelist's dualistic way of thinking: 'this world', as the space of the 'ruler of this world' (12:31; see also 14:30), sounds a sombre note, but Jesus' departure to the Father points to the adversary's loss of power and the glorification of Jesus (cf. 13:31f).[29]

Jesus 'loved his own who were in the world'. In 1:11, the expression οἱ ἴδιοι is found in a different context (see the commentary). Here it can be understood in the light of the discourse on the good shepherd in Chapter 10. 'His own' are those who belong to him, who listen to his voice and for whom he cares (10:3, 4, 12; see also 27). The word 'love' in this context also recalls the relationship between the shepherd and his sheep, who 'know' each other. If the aorist participle refers to the relationship up till then,[30] then the finite verb in the aorist must point to a single action on Jesus' part.[31] This single action is a manifestation of his love for his own[32] that cannot be surpassed and will take place at the end, since εἰς τέλος can have both a temporal and a specifically qualitative meaning, that is, 'until the end' or 'to the extreme limit'.[33] It is probable that the qualitative meaning is dominant here, although the temporal meaning is not excluded, as in the expression 'his hour', to which this τέλος is related. At the hour of his death, Jesus' last word is: 'It is finished' (19:30: τετέλεσται). Does the demonstration of love (ἠγάπησεν) refer to the washing of the disciples' feet that follows immediately,[34] or to Jesus' death on the cross? It undoubtedly refers primarily to the second, without excluding the first. In the washing of the feet, Jesus' ultimate giving of himself to his own (see 15:13) was, according to the evangelist, made symbolically present and the whole significance of the washing of the feet was to point forward to the death of Jesus and the whole of the community founded on him (see 13:7). This theologically very concentrated sentence, the evangelist's authorship of which cannot be disputed, is therefore both the heading of the whole of the second main part of the gospel and the introduction to the washing of the feet.

13:2 In this verse, which is closely connected (by καί) with the preceding verse, the evangelist speaks of the event that took place during a meal – the washing of the feet. This is clear because the sentence, which begins in this verse, extends as far as v. 4 and leads up to Jesus' action. It is narrated predominantly in the present historic and because of this the variant in the participle (γίνεσθαι)[35] is not very important, since it makes no difference to the time of the washing of the feet at the last supper. If, in v. 4, after the long intervening passage, the words ἐκ τοῦ δείπνου were added (by the editor), this would indicate that the editor was thinking of an interruption in the meal. This, however, would be, from the historical point of view, a very unlikely procedure, since it was usual to wash feet only at the beginning of a meal (see, for example, Lk 7:44). The evangelist (or perhaps his source?) does not stress this at all, although ἐγείρεται (in v. 4) presupposes that those present at the meal had already sat down. He had no interest at all in the historical circumstances. He does not, for example, even make it known where they gathered, either here or in 18:1. (See, in contrast to this, Mk 14:12–17 par.)

The detailed statement about the devil, according to our analysis (see above), probably goes back to an editor who wanted to draw attention, at the beginning of the meal, to this incomprehensible breach of trust on the part of a participant at the meal. While Jesus is performing a supreme and very meaningful ministry of love for his disciples, the devil, who is the opponent both of God and of Jesus (see 8:44; 14:30; 1 Jn 3:8), is also at work. He makes Judas his instrument and in 6:70 he is himself called a διάβολος. In 8:44, Jesus accuses the Jews of wanting to do the desires of their father, the devil. The phrase 'to put (βάλλειν) something into a man's heart' also occurred in the profane sphere.[36] The reading here is striking and undoubtedly original – Judas is not named in this phrase, but only in a subordinate phrase and this can be explained by the fact that his full name is given emphatically at the end.[37] The observation is none the less remarkable, since it appears to contradict 13:27, according to which Satan entered Judas after the morsel. Should it be interpreted as an intensification? It is easier to explain if we assume that this statement in v. 2 is the work of an editor who was already familiar with the sentence in v. 27 and wanted to anticipate the attack of the devil (note the word ἤδη in v. 2), but had to express himself more cautiously in order to avoid an open contradiction with 13:27.[38]

13:3   With the word εἰδώς, we have a subordinate clause which emphasizes the power that has been bestowed on Jesus and at the same time seems to vary the idea of Jesus' departure to the Father expressed in the εἰδώς clause in v. 1. The construction of the sentence is complicated by this and the account of the washing of the feet is further delayed. This second εἰδώς clause can hardly take priority over the first.[39] It does not have the function of portraying Jesus as a perfect 'gnostic' (as Bultmann suggested), or of drawing attention to the paradox of Jesus' full power expressed in the humble act of washing his disciples' feet (as Lindars thought). It is much more probable that this statement represents a counterbalance to the previous observation about the devil and that it is also to be attributed to an editor. Analogously to v. 1, he expressed this idea in Johannine language. 'Giving all things into his hands' does not refer here to the revelatory and saving power bestowed on Jesus by the Father (3:35; see the commentary, Vol. 1). It points rather to his sovereignty, which is unassailable, despite all the efforts made by his adversaries (see 7:30, 44; 10:28f) and the apparent victory of the 'ruler of this world' (14:30), because it is founded on the Father's power. The second statement, that Jesus 'had come from God and was going to God', which is a common theme in the gospel, with many variations (cf. 7:28 with 33; 8:14, 12; 16:28, 30), also reinforces this idea: namely, that the one who comes from God and returns to God is superior to God's adversary (see 8:44; 1 Jn 3:8, 10; 4:4). This 'departure from God' does not refer primarily to the pre-existence of Jesus (see 7:29; 8:42), although this certainly forms part of John's Christology, and is therefore not an intensification of the statement made in v. 1. After choosing the word 'Father', as the one who had given all power to Jesus, ὁ θεός is chosen in the second phrase, because of the contrast with διάβολος.

13:4–5   The action, which the evangelist began to describe with the words 'during supper' (v. 2), is now depicted with very simple words. Jesus rises (the addition 'from supper' was only necessary after the long interpolation), lays aside his outer garment[40] and girds himself with a linen cloth used for drying. He then pours water into a bowl and begins the action that was regarded as a very humble service.[41]

This simple narrative style and several of the details may point to a source. The article preceding νιπτήρ may indicate a Semitic influence, but it may, on the other hand, be there because there was normally only one receptacle for that purpose. ἤρξατο (used only here in John, apart from the non-Johannine text 8:9) may also be a Hebraism familiar to us from the synoptics, indicating not the beginning of the action, but the action itself. This assumption is, however, not necessary. It is hardly possible to know when it was Simon Peter's turn (v. 6). The words that occur only in this context can be explained in the light of the unique action. The question of a possible source can only be discussed in a wider context.

Since the evangelist concentrates all his attention on the following conversation between Jesus and Peter, any attempts to provide a further interpretation are out of the question here. It is, for example, not possible to construct, from the verbs used for taking off and putting on the outer garment (τιθέναι, place, and λαμβάνειν, take) a background relationship with 10:17f, where the same verbs are used for Jesus' laying down and taking up his life (see R. E. Brown). Origen's exegesis of the emptying of the Logos in the incarnation also goes much further than the evangelist ever intended.[42] His interpretation can be detected in Jesus' answer to Peter: this humble service points to the death of Jesus himself, which is, as a share in salvation, a service full of inner authority.

2. Jesus' Conversation with Simon Peter (13:6–11)

[6]*He came to Simon Peter; (and Peter) said to him, 'Lord, do you wash my feet?'*
[7]*Jesus answered him, 'What I am doing you do not know now, but afterwards you will understand'.* [8]*Peter said to him, 'You shall never wash my feet'. Jesus answered him, 'If I do not wash you, you have no part in me'.* [9]*Simon Peter said to him, 'Lord, not only my feet but also my hands and my head'.* [10]*Jesus said to him, 'He who has bathed does not need to wash, except for his feet, but he is clean all over; and you are clean, but not all of you'.* [11]*For he knew who was to betray him; that was why he said, 'You are not all clean'.*

13:6   The scene with Simon Peter, in which Jesus' action is interpreted, has a totally Johannine form in that it contains a dialogue with a disciple,[43] who does not understand Jesus' words, which at the same time point to a deeper meaning. This scene is also one of those in which Peter is not confronted with the disciple whom Jesus loved (1:42; 6:68f; 13:37f; 18:10f, 25f). Whereas the other scenes, however, are clearly connected with the synoptic Petrine tradition, this is an exclusively Johannine passage. Is it perhaps a Johannine echo of Peter's objection to Jesus' announcement of his passion, which is included in the synoptic gospels after the confession of the Messiah (Mk 8:32f), but which the fourth evangelist does not mention at this point? A personal confrontation between Peter and Jesus can be detected in the stressed personal pronouns in v. 7 (ἐγώ–σύ). As in the synoptic account, his attitude is typical of that of the disciples (it can be compared with the failure of the other disciples to understand in Chapter 14). In contrast with this, the question as to whether Jesus came to Peter first (as Augustine believed), in between, or last (as Origen thought) is unimportant.

Simon Peter (the double name is generally used in the gospel of John) refuses to allow Jesus to wash his feet out of respect for him. The form of address (κύριε) is also used by others in the gospel; here it is made more emphatic by σύ. The opening question, which Jesus opposes, enables the dialogue to begin.

13:7 Jesus' reply points to what lies behind his action, although what this is does not become fully apparent until the following answer. The barrier to understanding which Jesus sets up between himself and the disciple serves as a literary means by which the evangelist can proceed, via Peter's energetic protest (v. 8a), to articulate Jesus' statement much more precisely (v. 8b). It also has a theological basis, however, since the disciples of necessity do not understand at all the meaning of what is said in the upper room. The significance of Jesus' action and his death is not revealed to them until the Holy Spirit has been sent (see 14:26; 16:12f, 25, 29–32). In his reply, Jesus contrasts the present (ἄρτι[44]) with an 'afterwards' that is left undefined. This cannot possibly refer to the conversation that follows the washing of the disciples' feet (vv. 12–17).[45] It can only be the time after Jesus' death and resurrection, which, according to 2:22 and 12:16, the disciples would understand by 'remembering'.

13:8 Peter does not understand this and possibly even misunderstood the μετὰ ταῦτα. He now resolutely refuses (οὐ μὴ . . . εἰς τὸν αἰῶνα) to let Jesus wash his feet. In fact, however, by doing this he confirms Jesus' words (this is a case of Johannine irony) and increases his protest against his Lord. If v. 9 is considered together with this verse, however, Peter is depicted quite sympathetically from the human point of view and, compared with Mk 8:32f and 14:29 (cf. Jn 13:37), even favourably. This is an important aspect of the fourth evangelist's portrait of Peter.

Jesus' answer is a serious warning against excluding oneself from what Jesus gives to man. The phrase ἔχειν μέρος μετά τινος really means 'to have a share or a place with someone'.[46] The deeper meaning of this phrase, then, can be understood if we consider what Jesus promised his disciples after his death. The life that he was to gain was something in which they too would share (see 14:19). They would also be where he was (12:26; 14:3; 17:24) and would therefore share in his glory (see 17:22, 24). The full love of Jesus and his Father was to be revealed to them (14:21, 23).

It is for these reasons, then, that Peter could not avoid having his feet washed by Jesus. His external act has a very deep inner meaning, as Peter begins to sense, but it would be wrong to infer more from Jesus' suggestion than the fact that his giving of himself in death and the saving activity of that death are represented in this 'washing'. Interpretations which go further than this and point, for example, either to baptism or to the obligation to love one's fellow Christians as brothers, in accordance with Jesus' example,[47] are wrongly traced back from v. 10 or vv. 14f to this statement. The washing of the disciples' feet is interpreted in the Christological and soteriological sense as a symbolic action in which Jesus makes his offering of himself in death graphic and effective, not in a sacramental manner, but by virtue of his love, which his disciples experience to the extreme limit (see v. 1).

13.9 Peter is only conscious of Jesus' warning against separation from him and, because he longs for full community with Jesus, he wants not only his feet, but also his hands and his head to be washed. It is clear, then, that he has not understood Jesus' words at the deeper level and that he has even misunderstood 'washing' in the figurative sense. Johannine misunderstandings frequently arise because of such words with two meanings, which can be interpreted both purely externally and disinterestedly on the one hand and metaphorically, and in the light of salvation on the other hand (see 3:3ff; 4:10–14, etc.). These have a different function with different persons who hear them.[48] Unlike the Jews, who, in 7:34f; 8:21, are shown to be, in their unbelief, at a great distance from Jesus, Peter is seen here as unenlightened in his zeal and faith (see also 13:37). This characteristic is also stressed in 21:7.

13:10 Jesus' reply to Peter in this verse is one of the places in the fourth gospel that is most disputed by exegetes. It has been interpreted in very many different ways and this divergence of interpretation has played the most important part in the extreme variety of views concerning the meaning of the washing of the disciples' feet.[49] The interpretation is made more difficult by the textual question as to whether εἰ μὴ τοὺς πόδας is original or not. A great deal also depends on the interpretation of ὁ λελουμένος. Finally, it is important to establish whether the second part of the verse (from καὶ ὑμεῖς) was written by the evangelist himself (and can therefore be added to the interpretation of the preceding text) or whether it is the work of an editor.

1. Short or Long Text?
There is evidence of the existence of a long text in various forms in a number of manuscripts,[50] but the only examples of the short text without εἰ τοὺς πόδας are ℵ aur e Vg^{codd} Origen Tertullian Optatus al.[51] Most editions have accepted the long text. Only Tischendorf decided in favour of the short text and Nestle and Aland left the question open by using square brackets. Wordsworth and White assumed that Jerome used the short text for the Vulgate. Several exegetes, including Lagrange, F.-M. Braun, Hoskyns and Davey and Bultmann, and, in recent years, undoubtedly the majority,[52] have regarded, on the basis of internal evidence, the short text as the original one. On the basis of the text alone, there are two very powerful reasons in favour of this view: (a) the continuation of the phrase 'but he is clean all over' does not, strictly speaking, allow for the addition 'except for his feet'. 'If, after the λούεσθαι, a washing of the feet was still required', Bultmann commented, 'the one who had bathed could not have been clean.' (b) Reasons can easily be found for the addition (see below), but they cannot be found for the omission, unless it were for the sake of a linguistic logic (as in (a) above) that would be obvious to copyists. We have, however, to decide this question on the basis of our interpretation of the text.

2. The Statement about the λελουμένος

We will take as our point of departure the fact that the sentence in v. 10a is formally a general statement of the kind that occurs frequently in the fourth gospel (for example, in 3:29; 4:35a, 37; 8:35; 12:35c). Comparison with other similar statements of this type has shown that they are for the most part symbolic or metaphorical. (See, for example, the discourse on the shepherd in Chapter 10.) It is therefore unlikely that Jesus merely wanted to remind Peter that he and the other disciples had bathed and did not require any further purification (apart from the washing of the feet).[53] Such a realistic understanding might prematurely have led to the addition of 'except for the feet'. λούεσθαι, however, cannot simply point to the washing of the feet that had just taken place. Almost always, this verb is used to indicate a complete bath, whereas νίπτεσθαι is employed in the case of partial washing.[54] A return to a purely external understanding, after Jesus' statement in v. 8, is, moreover, unthinkable, since the washing of the feet has already been given a much deeper meaning.

If the general statement 'he who has bathed does not need to wash, but he is clean all over' is, in this context, intended, like the statement about the son and the slave in 8:35, to clarify a theological statement, then λούεσθαι must be interpreted not only in a factual, but in a metaphorical sense. He who has 'bathed' is the one who, by having his feet washed, has been taken into the event of the cross symbolized by the washing of the feet.[55] In Jesus' reply to Peter, the washing of the disciples' feet is presupposed as the outward sign of that event and Jesus' invitation to Peter to let his feet be washed is therefore not withdrawn. Jesus' words, however, are at the same level as those in verse 8b, in other words, they point to his death. Peter is able to recognize that. Nothing more than this is required. His wish to have his hands and his head washed is foolish. The phrase 'except for the feet' is not only unnecessary in this interpretation – it is also disturbing in the context. The addition can be explained on the basis of Peter's earlier failure to understand (see above) or of new theological concerns.

The question, however, arises as to whether Jesus' words had a further significance for the evangelist without this addition. In the light of the interpretation outlined above, it is possible to ask whether λούεσθαι is not an allusion to baptism. There is evidence in the New Testament of its use as a term for baptism.[56] The image of the one who has been bathed, however, that is suggested by the washing of the feet, can be adequately understood in the perspective of the event of the cross. The stream of blood and water coming from the pierced side of the crucified Christ (19:34) is a closely related image, as is the other image of living water in 7:38, which is in fact combined with the invitation to drink (v. 37). According to 1 Jn 1:7, 'the blood of Jesus his Son cleanses us from all sin'. Although baptism, as the place where salvation is achieved, is directly connected with the event of the cross, we cannot conclude with any certainty in the gospel of John that, in using the uncommon word λούεσθαι, the fourth evangelist was also thinking of baptism.[57] The statement that the one who has been bathed does not need to wash is emphasized in the conversation with Peter, but it does not necessarily lead to the assumption that the evangelist was also following contemporary tendencies (against Judaism, with its cultic purifications, or against baptist sects).[58] On the other hand, it would also be wrong totally to exclude the possibility of such allusions underlying these Johannine statements.

Other sacramental interpretations can be found for the addition εἰ μὴ τοὺς πόδας, since the phrase would obviously tempt one to look for them, but the image of washing is very unusual in the case of the Eucharist and very remote from this sacrament.[59] There is, moreover, no evidence of images at this early period for the sacrament of penance.[60]

3. The Statement about the Cleanness of the Disciples (v. 10b)

The statement 'and you are clean' may well follow v. 10a,[61] but it may also be an editorial addition to the word καθαρός. The transition to Jesus' address to all the disciples is not in accordance with the style of the dialogue with Peter, but it can be explained if Peter is seen as the representative of the other disciples. The pronouncement in v. 10a can be regarded as a little parable, followed by an application to the disciples in the phrase 'and you are clean' (see, e.g., Lagrange). A similar case is 16:21, followed by v. 22. If this is so, the evangelist must have been thinking of the effect of Jesus' death as symbolized in the washing of the feet. The difficulty arises here, however, that the disciples are told that they are clean *now* (and not after Jesus' death). Is it possible that they have been made clean now by Jesus' washing of their feet? Jesus' replies in vv. 7 and 8 point clearly to the future. In the evangelist's symbolic language, however, a movement back to the present attitude or condition of the disciples is not impossible; this happens, for example, where he wants to make a transition to the announcement of the betrayal (v. 18). The theme of cleanness is only rarely applied to the Jewish customs of ritual purity in the fourth gospel (see, for example, 2:6; 3:25), and the evangelist only refers here and in 15:3 to the cleanness of the disciples. In the second case, their cleanness is traced back to Jesus' word.[62] This idea may be at the root of the statement in v. 10b – that association with Jesus has already made the disciples clean, but not 'all' of them. The choice of words can be explained by the image previously used. What is meant objectively here is Jesus' community with the disciples which will be built up on a new and lasting foundation by his death. What Jesus requires of Peter and all the disciples, then, is that they let their feet be symbolically washed by him.

13:11   The commentary that follows and explains the statement 'but not all of you', may be editorial, since it discloses the meaning of the veiled allusion to the traitor prematurely. The formula contains a strong echo of 6:64 and may have been inspired by it, at least if the unmotivated reference to the traitor does not go back to the same author. In 6:64; 13:11; 18:2, 5, the traitor is mentioned with the participle and, in 18:2, 5, the name 'Judas' is added (from the source perhaps?). The evangelist was clearly aiming in Chapter 13 at a gradual and increasingly distinct characterization of the traitor and ultimately at an identification of the man by name. This is evident from the progress throughout the chapter: v. 10b ('but not all of you') – v. 18 ('he who ate my bread') – v. 21 ('one of you') – v. 26a ('to whom I shall give this morsel') – v. 26b ('to Judas [the son] of Simon Iscariot').

3. Jesus' Washing of the Feet as a Model for the Disciples (13:12–17)

¹²When he had washed their feet and taken his garments and resumed his place, he said to them, 'Do you know what I have done to you?¹³You call me Teacher and Lord; and you are right, for so I am. ¹⁴If I, then, your Lord and Teacher, have washed your feet, you also ought to wash one another's feet. ¹⁵For I have given you an example, that you also should do as I have done to you. ¹⁶Truly, truly, I say to you, a servant is not greater than his master; nor is he who is sent greater than he who sent him. ¹⁷If you know these things, blessed are you if you do them.

13:12　The thread of the narrative is resumed with the word οὖν. The action that began in v. 5 is closed – Jesus here puts on his outer garment again and takes his place at table. The evangelist's narrative is, generally speaking, continuous and the meal situation is once again presupposed in v. 18. For this reason, this transition to the announcement of the betrayal (v. 18) is undoubtedly the work of the evangelist himself. The second interpretation of the washing of the feet was interpolated by the editor after the words εἶπεν αὐτοῖς. The reader is skilfully invited to reflect once again on the meaning of Jesus' washing of his disciples' feet by the introductory question in this verse. What follows is an explanation that is directed towards the community and obliges its members to see it in this way.

The prospect of Jesus' death and the disciples' share in his glory seems to be forgotten here. In this passage, the author is exclusively concerned with the washing of the feet that has just taken place. Here we have an interpretation that is independent of the first and is concerned with the exemplary aspect of Jesus' action. It is also certainly the earlier interpretation, although it is, in the literary sense, later in the gospel of John and was added by the editor.[63] It is unmistakably very close to the synoptic tradition – according to Lk 22:27, Jesus is (in the upper room) among the disciples 'as one who serves' and, in the context (v. 26), the disciples are also invited to serve in the same way. The same tradition is also to be found in Mk 10:45 (par. Mt 20:28), outside the context of the last supper, but with a reference to the death of Jesus. It would seem to be a typical editorial feature of the fourth gospel to go back to thoughts and words known to us from the synoptic gospels (see, for example, vv. 16 and 20).

13:13–15　The interpretation is constructed very impressively within the unity of a short statement. The disciples are to understand Jesus' action as their master's deliberate act of humiliation, by means of which he aims to give them an example of humble service. Jesus therefore reminds them that they address him as 'Teacher' (and generally as 'Rabbi'; but see 1:38; 20:16) and as 'Lord' (see also 6:68; 13:6, 9, 36f, etc.).[64] 'The Teacher' (11:28; cf. Mt 23:8) and 'the Lord' (see under 4:1 in Vol. 1, p. 422, n. 4) had also become titles applied to Jesus in the community. The evangelist uses the title ὁ κύριος when he speaks of the risen Lord (20:20; see also 20:2, 18, 25, 28). Jesus confirms this form of address used by the disciples with an unemphatic εἰμὶ γάρ, which is striking because of the words ἐγὼ εἰμι that are used elsewhere (see, for example, 13:19). The evangelist also uses this formula for identification (see 6:20; 18:5, 6, 8). Why, then, does this formula not appear here? Why are the words ἐγὼ εἰμι not used here? The whole emphasis falls on Jesus' lordship (cf. v. 16a). The words 'It is the Lord' (21:7, 12) have a very special sound – a further indication that they originated with the editor. The obligation of the disciples to perform a similar service among themselves follows from the action of the Lord and Master.[65] The verb ὀφείλειν occurs in John with this moral and parenetic meaning only in 1 Jn 2:6; 3:16; 4:11 (cf. also 3 Jn 8). (It also occurs only in 19:7 in the other sense.)

The exemplary nature of Jesus' action is also emphasized in v. 15. The word ὑπόδειγμα is a late Greek synonym for παράδειγμα[66] and occurs only once in the Johannine writings. It is, however, found with the same meaning in Jas 5:10 (where the prophets are given as examples), and in a pejorative sense in Heb 4:11 and 2 Pet 2:6. The idea of the imitation of Jesus, which should be distinguished from that of following him, did not begin to develop until the Hellenistic period of the early Church.[67] Because of the characteristic καθὼς ἐγώ . . . καὶ ὑμεῖς, this passage is related to the 'new commandment' of love stated in 13:34 and made the norm of love for the disciples by the whole of Jesus' life and even more by his death (see 15:12; 1 Jn 2:6; 3:3, 7; 4:17b). From a literary-critical view, these texts look suspiciously like editorial additions (see under 13:34f), but they fit well into the evangelist's language (for a comparable καθὼς, see 10:15) and they are theologically in accordance with his intention – the presence of salvation made lasting in Jesus calls for 'doing what is true' (3:21) and his word has to be accepted, kept and followed by men (see 7:17; 8:51; 12:48). Only the direct moral application is emphasized in the letter to the community. The evangelist's disciples also interpreted the example of the washing of the feet in the 'new commandment' as extreme love, the giving of one's life or at least the giving of one's possessions (1 Jn 3:16f). In 1 Tim 5:10, the washing of feet itself (with a possible reference to Jn 13?) is assessed as an act of love and a sign of Christian hospitality.[68] It was only much later, in the fourth century Latin Church (outside Rome, see Ambrose), that the washing of feet was given a kind of sacramental significance.[69]

13:16   The evangelist here resorts to a 'synoptic' logion (see also 12:25 and 26) in order to clarify his thought, but neither Mt 10:24 nor Lk 6:40 are in accordance with the Johannine version. The Matthaean version, in the context referring to the disciples' following in suffering, would have been particularly appropriate for our text, because it contains the double image of disciple-master and servant-lord. The logion of the Johannine editor can therefore only have been known from the oral tradition or from another tradition.[70] The second part, which compares one who is sent with one who sends him, is derived from the Jewish law relating to messengers and its article: 'the one sent by a man is like the man himself'. This legal article is variously reflected in the Christian tradition (see below, v. 20).[71] The term ὁ ἀπόστολος, which is rare in the Johannine writings, has no more than a functional significance (cf. Mk 6:30) and does not point to the disciples as apostles in any specific sense. Their being sent, which is a familiar concept in the gospel of John (4:38; 17:18; 20:21), implies not only dependence on the one who sends, but also being closely connected with him and committed to him. The relationship between servant and lord is the most important one in this text and it is worth noting that only the first half of the logion is included in 15:20 (in the situation of persecution). This statement by their Lord played an important part in the disciples' memory.

13:17   Another exhortation to action in the form of a blessing closes this moral interpretation of the washing of the feet. The evangelist insists on action as a condition for coming to a knowledge of the truth (cf. 3:21; 7:17; 8:31f). What is involved here is a realization of the relationship among the disciples in the activity of love. This is also the clear intention in the Johannine letters.[72] The sharp contrast between knowing and doing is closely paralleled in 1 Jn 2:29 (cf. also 2:3ff; 3:4–8). Similar statements from the pagan environment and in particular from Stoic ethics[73] provide us with very valuable information about the thought of that period. The evangelist only uses the form of a macarism once in the gospel (20:29) and this is probably inherited from the synoptic tradition (see Lk 11:27f; 12:37f, 43; 14:14). The form is, however, also found in other earlier Christian writings (see, for example, Jas 1:25; Rev 14:13; 16:15).[74]

4. The Announcement of the Betrayal and the Strengthening of Faith (13:18–20)

[18]*'I am not speaking of you all; I know whom I have chosen; it is that the scripture may be fulfilled, "He who ate my bread has lifted his heel against me".* [19]*I tell you this now, before it takes place, that when it does take place you may believe that I am he.* [20]*Truly, truly, I say to you, he who receives anyone whom I send receives me; and he who receives me receives him who sent me'.*

13:18   This verse contains the announcement of the betrayal in the form in which the evangelist himself planned it for his gospel. The first sentence was probably fashioned by the editor as a transition from the moral interpretation of the washing of the feet to the announcement of the betrayal. This shows it to be secondary – why, after all, should one disciple be excluded from the obligation to love? It also resumes the theme of the end of v. 10. To this, the evangelist here adds the words that Jesus addressed to the disciples when he sat down again at table: 'I know whom I have chosen.' He had already spoken about his choosing of the disciples after Peter's confession of faith (6:70), and then, too, he alluded darkly to the faithless disciple among them. This announcement of the betrayal, with its quotation from Scripture, is also in accordance with the earliest tradition in Mark – the expression ὁ ἐσθίων μετ᾽ ἐμοῦ in the latter may also allude to the same text in the psalms (14:18). Matthew is content simply to say 'one of you' (26:21) and Luke throws light on the idea and its incomprehensibility: 'Behold the hand of him who betrays me is with me on the table' (22:21). The same tradition also appears in the fourth gospel, but in an independent form, in which everything that has to be said is expressed within the scriptural quotation.

The Old Testament quotation, which is introduced by a brief formula (cf. 17:12; 19:24, 36), is not in accordance either with the Masoretic text or with the Septuagint, although it is closer to the former. It deviates from that text only in its use of the verb ἐπῆρεν (for הִגְדִּיל, to make great) and its addition of αὐτοῦ to 'heel'. These are probably improvements for the Greek reader. In using ἐπῆρεν, a part may have been played by the idea of an action that was blasphemous or scornful with regard to God; cf. Ecclus 48:18; Ps 37 (36):35; 75 (74):5. The Septuagint uses different words and the plural ἄρτους μου instead of μου τὸν ἄρτον. The placing of μου in front is in accordance with Greek linguistic usage (see Blass-Debr § 473, 1). The LA version μετ᾽ ἐμοῦ, although it is powerfully attested and very early,[75] can be explained on the basis of a memory on the part of scribes of Mk 14:18. τρώγειν (instead of ἐσθίειν) was commonly used in everyday speech (cf. 6:54) as the present tense of ἔφαγον (see Liddell and Scott, *Lexicon*, p. 1832, under III). Ἐσθίω also never occurs in the present tense in John. It is therefore difficult to conclude from this evidence that there is any special connection between this verse and 6:53–58.

The Old Testament text that the evangelist quotes, with a small adaptation, for his purpose,[76] not only characterizes the action of the traitor as a breach of faith on the part of a companion at table, but also makes it possible for the evangelist to emphasize Jesus' initiative when the traitor leaves (see v. 27b).

13:19   The theme of the prediction of the event is also to be found in very similar words at the end of the farewell discourse (14:29) and the evangelist's authorship cannot be disputed. The way in which it is expressed is different from the 'prophecy' in Mk 13:23 par. Mt 24:25, as well as from the form of 16:4. Now (ἀπ ἄρτι),[77] before the event, Jesus tells them so that, when it happens, they do not go astray in faith.[78] Faith is given a Christological emphasis by the Johannine formula ἐγώ εἰμι (see Vol. 2, Excursus 8). Despite the incomprehensible fact of the betrayal, Jesus continues to be the one sent by God and, after the event of the cross has taken place, it will be clear that the disciple's betrayal and the plan devised by Satan even served Jesus' exaltation. Light is thrown on the absolute formula by 8:28 – after the Son of Man has been exalted, the Jews will know that Jesus is right to make an absolute claim – as contained in the absolute formula – to divine sovereignty and dignity. This formula is not present in 14:29, but the words that follow (v. 30) have objectively the same meaning, namely that the ruler of the world has no power over Jesus, since he is judged and deprived of his power at the crucifixion (cf. 12:31). If we add to this the fact that Satan prompted the traitor to act in this way and impelled him (13:27, 30), then it becomes clear that there is only one theological interpretation intended by the evangelist and made familiar to the readers of the gospel by the formula ἐγώ εἰμι.

13:20 Jesus' claim is also echoed in the logion that follows – he is the one whom God has sent. Otherwise, however, the connection between the ideas is not easy to understand. Why are the disciples solemnly assured: 'He who receives anyone whom I send receives me'? Does Jesus want to confirm their election here (cf. v. 18b), so that they will not go astray? Their election, however, was only mentioned in passing. We are therefore driven to suspect that, as in v. 16, an editor has added this similarly 'synoptic' logion. Even in the form of words, it is very similar to the Matthaean logion (Mt 10:40). The Johannine λαμβάνειν replaces the Matthaean δέχεσθαι and the accusative of the person is a Johannine stylistic peculiarity (cf. 1:12). It might, however, have been possible for an editor to take over the evangelist's particular way of expressing himself (5:43; cf. 3:11, 32f; 12:48; 17:8). What is expressed in this logion is the article of Jewish law which insists that the one who is sent is equal to the one who sends him. This law lay behind the second half of the logion in v. 16.[79] What, then, was the editor's intention?

It is not possible to make a connection between v. 20 and v. 17 and at the same time regard vv. 18f as a note by the evangelist (an addition to the source), that a promise made to anyone who serves the disciples in love will follow the admonition to serve in love.[80] The logion (with δέχεσθαι!) only has this meaning in the Matthaean context. It is also not possible to connect v. 20 with what follows and deduce from it an admonition that the 'disciple whom Jesus loved' and those who are connected with him should be received.[81] It is more likely that v. 20 was brought about by the second part of the logion in v. 16. There is a dialectical tension between the two logia – the one who is sent is not greater than the one who sends him, but he none the less shares in his sovereignty and dignity.

It is also possible to presume that the editor wanted to raise the status of the disciples whose standing had been affected by the traitor in their midst and to protect them against criticism, since, as those sent by Jesus, they had a share in his revelatory and salvific power. The later community ought not to be allowed to forget this (cf. 20:21ff).

5. The Exposure of the Traitor (13:21–26)

[21]*When Jesus had thus spoken, he was troubled in spirit and testified, 'Truly, truly, I say to you, one of you will betray me.'* [22]*The disciples looked at one another, uncertain of whom he spoke.* [23]*One of his disciples, whom Jesus loved, was lying close to the breast of Jesus;* [24]*so Simon Peter beckoned to him and said, 'Tell us who it is of whom he speaks.'* [25]*So lying thus, close to the breast of Jesus, he said to him, 'Lord, who is it?'* [26]*Jesus answered, 'It is he to whom I shall give this morsel when I have dipped it'. So when he had dipped the morsel, he gave it to Judas, the son of Simon Iscariot.*

13:21–22   This surprising new announcement of the betrayal, which is almost word for word the same as that in the synoptic gospels (Mk 14:18; Mt 26:21), is introduced and motivated by Jesus' being 'troubled', as he was by the evangelist at Lazarus' tomb (11:33) and at the 'hour' on the Mount of Olives (12:27). It is possible, then, that the evangelist fashioned this new scene with reference to the synoptic tradition (or possibly with reference to a source). There is quite considerable inner tension between these verses and v. 19, but if the evangelist wanted to form a new scene, after the *announcement* of the betrayal, with the *exposure* of the traitor, then a new beginning is understandable. The 'synoptic' logion, with its provoking way of addressing the disciples present ('one of you') and the following remark about the 'uncertainty' of the disciples (v. 22), which is also indicated in Mk 14:19 and Mt 26:22, with the perplexed question: 'Is it I?', provided an excellent point of departure for this. Jesus' being 'troubled in spirit' fits perfectly into this oppressive situation.

Can we decide on the basis of the style in which this passage is written whether it is the work of the evangelist or that of an editor? The evangelist uses ταῦτα εἰπών in 7:9; 9:6; 11:43; 18:1; see also 18:22; 20:14. The singular τοῦτο is also found in Chapter 21 (21:9) and in 11:28; 18:38; 20:20, 22. It is also worth noting the evangelist's use of the expression as a transition in 9:6; 11:43; 18:1. It is very much in the style of the evangelist to use ταράσσειν (here employed together with τῷ πνεύματι; cf. 11:33) and μαρτυρεῖν καὶ λέγειν (cf. 1:32), although an editor could obviously imitate this style. Instead of εἰς ἀλλήλους, the form πρὸς ἀλλήλους often appears in the fourth gospel (4:33; 6:52; 16:17; 19:24), but this usage is connected with the verb used. The historical οὖν also often occurs (although, from the viewpoint of textual criticism, this is partly uncertain). It also appears quite frequently in Chapter 21. The epic asyndeton is also a common feature in that chapter. The partitive ἐx (ἐξ) in v. 21 is also to be found in the synoptic parallels. It is also similarly placed after εἰς in v. 23. The doubling of the ἀμήν seems to have been a feature of the whole Johannine school (cf. 13:16, 20). We are bound to conclude, then, that no definite decision can be made on the basis of style.

It is certainly possible to attribute this scene to an editor, but it is also clear from a critical analysis of the text (see below) that it is difficult to demarcate the editor's contribution from the evangelist's text. The exposure of the traitor goes straight on to his departure (vv. 26–27) and can only with difficulty be separated from it. Jesus' invitation to Judas to carry out his action (v. 27b), however, certainly forms part of the evangelist's presentation. He may therefore have composed the whole scene, though it is clear that he had recourse to the synoptic tradition.

There is a relatively large number of variants in this passage. It is, for example, not certain whether we should read the article in v. 21 with ᾿Ιησοῦς or not.[82] Without the article, the text is much more closely related to 4:44. In v. 22, several manuscripts have οὖν after ἔβλεπον. There are also cases of δέ after ἦν in v. 23 – something that happens frequently in Chapter 21 (vv. 4, 6, 8, 18, etc.; see especially v. 25). In v. 24, an important group of manuscripts have πυθέσθαι τίς ἂν εἴη instead of εἰπὲ τίς ἐστιν.[83] Both the evangelist and the editor of Chapter 21 prefer direct speech and the optative is rare in the gospel of John. The article with Ἰησοῦς in v. 26a is also questionable; in P[66] W, both the article and οὖς are missing. For the variants in v. 26c (from βάψας), see the commentary below on that verse.

13:23 The 'disciple whom Jesus loved' is mentioned explicitly for the first time in this verse. The entire problem raised by this figure will be discussed in a separate excursus. As we have already seen (Vol. 1, pp. 310ff), it is doubtful whether this disciple is the same as the unnamed disciple from the school of John the Baptist (1:40). The scene in the room where the last supper took place is so significant that certain special intentions must inevitably be linked to the introduction and presentation of this disciple. He was lying next to Jesus during the last supper and indeed 'in his bosom'. He was clearly a very special confidant, to whom Jesus revealed himself more than to others, and was therefore, more than any other, called and able to present the revelation of Jesus, even in this gospel, which is attributed to him by the editor (21:24). If this scene has a symbolic meaning, the question that inevitably arises is whether the figure of the disciple whom Jesus loved is himself only a symbol. This has been assumed by quite a number of scholars.[84] This question, however, can only be answered within the context of the whole problem and even then, if this scene in the upper room does not claim to describe a historical event, the question must still remain undecided.

A. Kragerud's exceptional opinion, that the 'favourite disciple' appears here, in this text, in a situation of perplexity and uncertainty as a mediator and therefore enjoys priority over Peter,[85] is, at the most, only partly true. He does, after all, not act as a mediator either with regard to the other disciples or with regard to Peter (who is afterwards not mentioned again in this connection). He is, on the contrary, presented to the community as the intimate confidant of Jesus and the description of this disciple that is already adopted in the text – as the 'disciple whom Jesus loved' – may perhaps be explained by the scene itself. In regarding the favourite disciple, as Kragerud does, simply as a symbol of the early Christian prophetic spirit, the editorial intention, according to which this disciple is presented as the guarantor of the gospel in its existing form, is destroyed (cf. 19:35; 21:24).

The disciple is in the first place introduced very vaguely as 'one of his disciples' and later described as the one 'whom Jesus loved'. It is hardly possible to conclude from this that ὃν ἠγάπα ὁ Ἰησοῦς is a subsequent insertion, because similar more precise details can be found in 3:1; 6:8; 11:1, 49; 18:26, although they are not, as here, separated by other parts of the sentence. Closer perhaps to our present case are 6:27d (in which ἐσφράγισεν separates the words ὁ πατήρ and ὁ θεός, which belong together) and 19:26. Emphasis is obtained by the position at the end of the sentence[86] and, in relative clauses of this kind, οὖτος is not necessary (cf. 1:26, 46; 3:34; 4:18; 6:29; 10:36; 11:3, etc.).

13:24 Simon Peter's sign, causing this disciple to ask Jesus a question, may be intended to stress the privileged position of the disciple himself. It is possible to distinguish a certain competition between the two disciples in 20:2–8; 21:7, 20–22, but not to the detriment of Peter and his position (cf. 6:68f; 21:15–17). The intention is rather to give prominence to the other disciple by reinforcing Peter's acknowledged authority and his intimacy and closeness to Jesus.[87]

13:25–26   The disciple whom Jesus loved leans, from the position in which he is lying,[88] more closely against Jesus' breast, falling back, so that he can gently ask him: 'Lord, who is it?' Jesus gives him the information that he requires by describing to him the gesture that he will use to indicate the traitor. His handing over of the morsel is not the same as the common dipping in the dish described in the synoptic tradition (Mk 14:20 par.), but it may be a theme that developed out of this. The morsel is not named, but it could not have been the bitter herbs that were dipped into fruit purée during the passover meal. It might have been a piece of bread of the kind used in Jewish meals as a utensil.[90] It is probable that the evangelist had the scriptural quotation of v. 18 ($\mu o \upsilon$ $\tau \grave{o} \upsilon$ $\check{\alpha} \rho \tau o \upsilon$), in which he saw Jesus as the giver of bread, in mind. The sign that exposes the disciple whom Jesus meant arises without difficulty from this context: 'So when he had dipped the[91] morsel, he gave it to Judas, the son of Simon Iscariot.' This is a clear expression of Jesus' initiative, taken to remove the traitor, and is as such completely in accordance with the rest of the image of the Johannine Jesus (cf. his attitude at the great meal, his going to Bethany, 11:7–10, and when he was arrested).

It is better, in this case, to preserve the words $\lambda \alpha \mu \beta \acute{\alpha} \nu \epsilon \iota$ $\varkappa \alpha \grave{\iota}$, which are absent in certain important manuscripts.[92] The verb is also present in 6:11 and in 21:13, at Jesus' distribution of the bread. In 13:26, as it may well have been introduced by scribes as an addition, made in recollection of these other texts. (It is hardly possible, however, to presuppose a 'communion with Judas' here on the basis of the eucharistic overtones of the other texts.) The reading Ἰσκαριώτου, for which there is more convincing evidence and which refers, as in 6:71, to the father's name Simon, points to the authorship of the evangelist.

If the scene with the disciple whom Jesus loved has the distinctively Christological intention of presenting Jesus' knowledge of the traitor and his insistence that the action should be carried out (because he knows that his 'hour' has come; see v. 1), then it is not difficult to understand why neither Peter nor that disciple does anything. The evangelist gives the matter no thought, because they have carried out their function. This means, of course, that the scene lacks all historical credibility, but we are bound to recognize that this way of presenting theological ideas in an event of dramatic dimensions is a stylistic means used by the evangelist. The editor of Chapter 21, who refers to this scene in v. 20, undoubtedly regarded it as historical. The doubts seem to have been expressed in vv. 28f, where an attempt is made to deal with them. The editor's historical way of looking at the question focusses attention on the problem of the disciple 'whom Jesus loved', but even if the evangelist formed this scene quite freely, he could not have regarded that disciple simply as a symbol or have used him just as a fiction.

6. Judas' Departure (13:27–30)

[27] *Then after the morsel, Satan entered into him. Jesus said to him, 'What you are going to do, do quickly'.* [28] *Now no one at the table knew why he said this to him.* [29] *Someone thought that, because Judas had the money box, Jesus was telling him, 'Buy what we need for the feast', or that he should give something to the poor.* [30] *So, after receiving the morsel, he immediately went out; and it was night.*

13:27 The effect of Jesus' action is fearful – Judas, who has, up to this time, been one of Jesus' disciples, is completely subjected to the influence of Satan. This underlying consideration of the event is certainly in accordance with the evangelist's way of thinking, in which light and darkness, like God and the devil, are sharply contrasted. Jesus forces men to decide and those who are closed to him are condemned (see 3:19–21; 9:39). The evangelist regarded it as so incomprehensible that anyone should decide in favour of darkness and evil that he believed that God's and Jesus' opponent was behind that decision (see, for example, 8:44). This insight is even more prominent in his consideration of the cross (see 12:31; 14:30), an event which was, he believed, brought about by the traitor. The phrase 'Satan entered into him' is therefore surprising, firstly because the gospel usually speaks, not of 'Satan', but of the devil or the 'ruler of this world' (14:30). The term 'entered into him', which indicates complete mastery by Satan,[93] is also extremely strong – certainly much stronger than the comment in 6:70: 'And one of you is a devil.' There is only one other text in the New Testament in which the same expression is used. It is applied to the same man and the same occasion. This text is Lk 22:3 and there is clearly a connection between the two texts within the history of traditions.[94] John obviously took this interpretation of Judas' action (from a source related to Luke or perhaps from an oral tradition), but connected it much more firmly with Jesus' removal of the traitor. The morsel handed over by Jesus to Judas is, in John, the signal for Satan to take possession of the traitor.[95] Jesus, who sees through this (see also 14:30), does not prevent him. On the contrary, he urges the man, who is in the grasp of Satan, to carry out his plan as quickly ($\tau\alpha\chi\iota\sigma\nu$) as possible.

13:28–9 The statement made in these verses, which may well go back to an editor (see above), presupposes that the other disciples heard Jesus' invitation to Judas. Its aim is clearly to explain why his companions at table innocently let him go.[96] The idea that Judas had the task of buying something for the feast can hardly be taken seriously into account as an argument for or against the fact that the last supper had the character of a passover meal. According to the chronology of the gospel of John, the eve of the passover was imminent (see 18:28), but it was still possible to purchase something for it on the night of the passover itself. There is hardly a moment's reflection about the haste, expressed by the word ταχίον.[97] The observation that Judas administered the common fund forms a connection between this text and 12:6, which also contains a commentary (on a remark by Judas). If 13:28f were really the work of an editor, could he perhaps have made use of that text (or is 12:6 also the work of an editor?; see the commentary in Vol. 2). The idea of a gift to the poor is also supported in 12:5f. This explanation does not, however, as we have already seen, deal with all the difficulties and this would seem to point to the fact that it is a subsequent reflection. It also interrupts the terse and very effective presentation of Judas' departure.

13:30 Judas carries out Jesus' invitation at once, without replying. The evangelist, however, comments enigmatically: 'It was night.' This statement is also reminiscent of a text in Luke which occurs at the moment of Jesus' arrest: 'This is your hour and the power of darkness' (22:53). In this case, however, John is not dependent on the historical tradition. 'Night', after all, has its own symbolism in the fourth gospel.[98] For Judas, 'night' represents the sphere of darkness into which he has fallen and, what is more, of which he has become a definitive part. It is, moreover, the zone in which man is ruined (cf. 11:10). For Jesus, it is the hour which marks the end of his work among men (cf. 9:4). This brief statement, closing the account of the traitor's departure, gathers into itself all the darkness of this event. It is a very effective end (cf. 6:71), but for the evangelist it only serves as a dark foil to set off the words about Jesus' glorification that follow.

The Johannine Last Supper and its Problems

The presentation of the last supper in Jn 13:1–30 that I have just considered at the level of the Johannine text raises a number of serious problems, especially when compared with the synoptic accounts. We must also include the text containing Peter's denial (vv. 37f) from the following section (vv. 31–38), because this episode forms a further point of contact with the synoptic accounts. I cannot unfortunately discuss here all the problems connected with the historical situation and the events that took place in this encounter between Jesus and his disciples, and must confine myself to the most important questions. These are: (1) What is the situation with regard to the dating of the last supper and its character as a passover meal? (These two questions are closely connected.) (2) What is the result of a comparison between John and the synoptics with regard to the course of events that took place at the last supper? (3) How should we judge the washing of the feet, which is only narrated in John, in the light of the synoptic accounts? (4) What are the most probable reasons for John's failure to provide an account of the institution of the Eucharist? In these four sections, then, I shall proceed from more external considerations to the inner and theologically important problems. It is also true to say that the theologically relevant question of the relationship between the last supper and the feast of the passover is connected with the date of the last supper and that there may also be theological motives at work in the sequence of the scenes. The main purpose of this investigation is not to examine the historical credibility of the Johannine presentation, but to obtain a clearer view of its distinctive character and its aim.

1. The Dating of the Last Supper and its Relationship with the Passover

According to the fourth evangelist, the last meal that Jesus had with his disciples took place before the feast of the passover (13:1). That this expresses his conviction is confirmed by the dating of Jesus' trial. The Jews who accuse Jesus do not enter Pilate's official residence (18:28; see the commentary on that text), in order to be able to eat the passover meal. Jesus is sentenced to death on the same day, the day of rest for the feast of the passover, at the sixth hour (19:14). The gospel refers consistently to the 'meal' or 'supper' (δεῖπνον) that Jesus shares with his disciples. This is a term that is not used in the synoptics. The latter speak of preparing to eat the passover (Mk 14:12–16 par.) and if this is followed by the statement that Jesus was reclining at table with the twelve ('the apostles' in Lk 22:14), then it is clear that the evening of the passover is what is meant in the synoptic presentation. According to Lk 22:15, Jesus says explicitly: 'I have earnestly desired to eat this passover with you before I suffer.' There is therefore a clear difference between John and the synoptics. Another and related question, however, is whether this difference can be resolved at the historical level or whether we have to accept the existence of two irreconcilable traditions and finally whether we should, in this case, give preference to the synoptic or the Johannine chronology.

We do not need to discuss earlier attempts at harmonization, because almost all of them have been universally rejected.[1] Only one of these earlier hypotheses, which was developed by A. Jaubert on the basis of the calendar of Qumran and was later accepted by many scholars, gave rise to rather more energetic debate within the context of the Qumran texts.[2] According to Jaubert's hypothesis, which I shall examine in the light of the Johannine texts (see below), and which was the last serious attempt to reconcile the different accounts of the last supper historically, Jesus kept to the Essene date of the passover and therefore ate a passover meal with his disciples before the passover of the priests in Jerusalem and the other Jews. Other later scholars have preferred to base their theories on a criticism of traditions in an attempt to answer the question as to whether the synoptic claim, that Jesus' farewell meal was a passover meal,[3] or whether the Johannine tradition was right. In the last case, the contrasting synoptic accounts, it has been suggested, were based on a secondary level of traditions which conceals the historical event and for certain special reasons (the desire to stress the celebration of a new Christian passover feast) provides a theological interpretation based on the passover.[4]

Before I go a little further into this problem, it is worth considering the theological relevance of the whole question. The historical problem as to whether Jesus celebrated a real Jewish passover meal with his disciples is, in itself at least, not very significant. Its importance is increased, however, as soon as an attempt is made, as it is by Jeremias, for example,[5] to understand the institution of the Eucharist within the framework of the passover. There is no account of the institution of the Eucharist in John and we are therefore bound to ask whether there may be a connection between his silence about this and his different chronology. Various suppositions have been made about this (see below: 4), but it should be borne in mind that, if it were possible to prove that the fourth evangelist deliberately changed the synoptic chronology, this would inevitably result in certain important conclusions regarding his theological intentions. I have therefore to establish whether there are, in the traditional material that the fourth evangelist uses and presents, still traces of the synoptic ideal of a ritual passover meal, despite the obvious dating of the last supper.

My first question, however, is whether it is possible for the gospel of John to give support to the hypothesis of a passover meal on the basis of the Qumran calendar. According to this hypothesis, there is an entirely new chronology of the whole week of the passion. Since the Essene passover meal was always celebrated on the night of Tuesday to Wednesday, the last supper must have taken place on the Tuesday evening. On the same night, Jesus was arrested and the first legal proceedings lasted until the end of the Wednesday morning. It was not until the Thursday morning that Jesus was handed over to the Roman tribunal, after another session of the council of the Jews. The trial before Pilate (with Jesus' having been sent to Herod in the meantime) lasted longer than it seems to have done according to the accounts in the gospels – it went on throughout the Thursday and it was not until the Friday that Pilate pronounced the death sentence, which was very quickly carried out.[6] We cannot discuss the question of the extension of the legal proceedings here; all that we can say is that the Johannine presentation of the trial does not entitle us to assume that what were apparently two proceedings before Pilate were compressed into one.[7] What concerns us above all is the question as to whether the last supper could, according to John, have taken place on the Tuesday evening.

Increased attention is given in the gospel of John to the approach of the passover of Jesus' death (see 11:55—12:1—12:12 [τῇ ἐπαύριον]—13:1). There is a concrete indication in the anointing at Bethany: 'six days before the passover' (12:1) and Jesus' entry into Jerusalem takes place (and the Johannine account differs here from the synoptic presentation) on 'the next day' (12:12). This can be seen as a point in support of this hypothesis, since, in contrast to the impression given by the synoptic accounts, it is not necessary to imagine that there were further events in the Johannine account between the entry into Jerusalem and the last supper. The Johannine presentation, however, is not entirely free from suspicion (see the displaced cleansing of the Temple, Vol. 1, pp. 353–355). What is more, it is important to note that John, who mentions three feasts of the passover and introduces all of them with the statement 'the passover (the feast) of the *Jews* was at hand' (2:13; 6:4; 11:55), only recognizes one Jewish passover and that is the 'official' feast of Judaism. There is no trace in the fourth gospel of any Essene passover celebrated on another day. The silence about this in this context is clear proof that the evangelist knew nothing of the character of a passover meal of the δεῖπνον (in the sense of an Essene passover). The gospel of John cannot therefore be regarded as providing positive evidence in favour of this very doubtful hypothesis.[8]

Attempts have also been made to distinguish elements in the traditional material included in the gospel of John of the passover meal in the usual Jewish sense. Wellhausen,'for example, commented on 13:21–30 that 'Jesus and his disciples are at the meal here and indeed at the passover meal, that is, the synoptic last supper; in contrast to 13:1; 18:28; 19:14 – it is foolish to close one's eyes to this contradiction', but he did not attempt to justify this statement.[9] H. Thyen was of the opinion that the theme of the morsel that is known from the synoptic tradition reflected the situation of the passover meal,[10] but that the handing over of the morsel should not be related to the bitter herbs and the fruit purée of the passover board. Jeremias, who did not appeal to this Johannine element as proof that the last supper had the character of a passover meal, used Jn 13:29 to support his argument that 'last-minute purchases for the festival' ($\tau\alpha\chi\iota\omicron\nu$, v. 27) would be 'completely incomprehensible' if the whole of the next day, Nisan 14, were available for this purpose.[11] One obvious objection to this argument is that the feast had already begun on the evening of the passover, although Jeremias claims that the strict provisions for the feast did not really apply until the morning of Nisan 15. Giving to the poor was also customary on the passover night. Three things can be said about these observations: (1) The word $\tau\alpha\chi\iota\omicron\nu$ (v. 27) refers to Jesus' invitation to Judas to carry out his proposed act of betrayal; it is not a question of making purchases quickly (v. 29). (2) Here the gospel is concerned only with the considerations of the others who were sharing the meal and who did not express any suspicions on Judas' departure. (3) Vv. 28f are probably a later editorial addition, made in an attempt to deal with an objection (v. 28) which might have arisen in the minds of the readers in view of the exposure of the traitor and his unimpeded departure. As we have seen (in the commentary above), this attempt is not very successful. Historical conclusions are ruled out if this was the intention.

We may therefore conclude that there is no really convincing argument to support the contention that the evangelist had a passover tradition in mind for the last supper. It would also be wrong to assume that he deliberately changed the tradition to suit a theological intention. It is usually said that he wanted to present Jesus as the true passover lamb who died on the cross at the same time that the passover lambs were slaughtered in the Temple. Even this idea, however, lacks a firm foundation in the gospel. The evangelist does not in fact say this – it is simply a conclusion drawn from his chronology and his interest in the event of the passover (see, for example, 19:36). The situation can also be explained in a different way. If the evangelist made use of an existing tradition that Jesus was crucified on Friday, Nisan 14 (the day before the passover evening), he may have found a symbolic meaning in it in theological meditation. On the other hand, it is not difficult to see why the synoptic gospels interpret the last supper as a passover meal. Not only a passage such as Mk 14:12–17 par., which is, from the point of view of the history of traditions, both late and of secondary importance, but also Lk 22:15–18, which may go back to a much earlier tradition, and such elements as 'reclining at table' and the singing of the hallel (Mk 14:26 par.), which are very characteristic of the passover meal, can also be explained by the fact that the community transferred its Christian passover (what Schürmann called the 're-founded passover') at quite an early stage to the last supper, which took place in Jerusalem within the framework of the Jewish expectation of the passover. It is true, of course, that certain questions remain unanswered in connection with this view and that it is not possible to achieve ultimate historical certainty.[12] It is, however, most important to remove all suspicions that the fourth evangelist may have falsified the tradition. It is fairly certain that he followed a source in his account of the day of Jesus' death (see below, 19:14).

According to this investigation of the relationship between the last supper and the passover, then, John and the synoptics each followed a distinctive tradition with its own chronology. The fourth evangelist did not eliminate the character of a passover meal from his presentation of the last supper in order to suppress the institution of the Eucharist. His failure to provide an account of the last supper must be explained in a different way.

2. The External Course of Events and the Sequence of the Scenes

Neither the synoptics nor John provide a really full and objective account of the course of events at the last supper. None of the evangelists displays an emphatically historical interest and each only hands down what had a lasting significance for the later community. A comparison between John and the synoptics is worth making, however, in order to clarify the theological interests of each. Reduced to a very simplified form, the external events are as follows:

Synoptics	*John 13*
Preparation for the passover meal	–
–	Washing of the feet
–	Dialogue with Peter and first interpretation
–	Second paradigmatic interpretation for all the disciples
Announcement of the betrayal, twice in Mk/Mt (in Lk after the institution of the Eucharist; compressed)	Two announcements of the betrayal (vv. 18 and 21)
Disciples' questions	Disciples look at each other, troubled (v. 22)
Strengthening of faith according to Scripture	Strengthening of faith through Jesus' words (v. 19)
'Alas for those men'	–
Jesus' revealing words to Judas (Mt 26:25)	(cf. v. 27b)
–	Peter's question and the intervention of the disciple whom Jesus loved
–	Jesus' answer to the disciple and the exposure of the traitor
(cf. Lk 22:3)	Satan's entry into Judas
–	The traitor's departure
Institution of the Eucharist	–
Journey to the Mount of Olives (Mk/Mt); Lk, see below	see below
Announcement of the scattering of the disciples (Mk/Mt) Lk –	– (but cf. 16:32)
Announcement of Peter's denial (for Lk, see below)	Announcement of Peter's denial

Disciples' dispute about who was greatest and Jesus' statement about serving (Lk 22:24–27)	– (but cf. the washing of the feet)
Jesus' promise to the disciples (Lk 22:28–30)	– (but cf. the promises in Chapter 14)
Statement to Simon and announcement of his denial (Lk 22:31–34)	see above
The two swords (Lk 22:35–38)	–
–	Farewell discourse (Chapter 14)
Journey to the Mount of Olives (Lk 22:39)	Journey to the Mount of Olives (18:1)

The most striking fact to emerge from this conspectus is that John is very close to the synoptics in the case of the announcement of the betrayal by Judas and that of Peter's denial. Betrayal and denial within the close circle of the disciples were two dark facts overshadowing Jesus' passion which preoccupied the early Christians. The evangelists differ from one another, of course, in their arrangement of these facts. Mk/Mt and John are close to one another in the announcement of the betrayal in that this element is placed within the course of the meal in every case. In Luke, whose intention is different, it is introduced after the institution of the Eucharist. The announcement of Peter's denial is in a different context in Mk/Mt, Luke and John. In Mk/Mt, it is found within the context of the journey to the Mount of Olives, in Luke within that of the last supper and in John it is found after the departure of the traitor, which is not mentioned explicitly in the synoptic gospels.

A second salient fact is that the tradition concerning the traitor has been expanded. In Matthew, Jesus speaks to Judas directly, saying that he will be the traitor. Luke's description of the scene at table is much shorter and he says that Satan entered into Judas before reporting the last supper (22:3) – an unmistakable echo of Jn 13:27a. In John, there is the additional scene with the disciple whom Jesus loved and this leads on to the exposure of the traitor. Further references to the traitor (13:2, 11) may have been added editorially. The event in which Judas is involved is clearly a graphic instruction; this becomes obvious as the narrative and the interpretation of it are extended. A part is also played by tradition and the evangelist's interpretation. Jesus' statement at table (v. 21), the fact that the disciples are troubled or that they ask questions (v. 22), and the observation that Satan entered into Judas can also be regarded as traditional in John. He may have had a source similar to that available to the synoptic gospels at his disposal for this. The Johannine tradition of the disciple whom Jesus loved is linked to this and the (editorial) reflection about the departure of the traitor makes use of a theme that has already appeared in the Johannine story of the anointing – Judas had charge of the common fund. This results in the reflections of several of those present. In this way, traditional elements and further interpretations flow together.

A third datum that comes to light when the synoptic accounts of the last supper are compared with the external events in the Johannine account is this: Luke goes his own way with regard to his marginal references. Without going into the very difficult question as to whether written traditions of a special kind were available to him and, if so, which, it is safe to say that he arranged the material that he used for 22:24–38 in his own way. In Luke, we find that the statement about the traitor is followed by Jesus' conversation with the other disciples, including Peter, and this entire combination of logia is clearly subjected to the theme of the imminent suffering and farewell of Jesus. A movement is, moreover, clearly discernible in Luke which becomes an obvious breakthrough in John. This is the movement after the elimination of the traitor, by way of the farewell statements made by Jesus with the future of the community of disciples in view, to the departure for the Mount of Olives and the acceptance of suffering. In this, Luke is the fourth evangelist's theological predecessor. Luke's preliminary sketch is fully worked out in the fourth gospel, in which the last supper is an anticipatory interpretation of Jesus' death (his love to the extreme limit; the washing of the feet) and an anticipatory care of the disciples. At this time of farewell and departure, Jesus himself removes the traitor and, in the circle of his 'own', delivers a highly significant discourse, during which the meal situation is only externally preserved. The last time that Jesus is together with his faithful disciples is the time when the future community is instructed. The whole situation is therefore theologically orientated.

The historical interest is far less pronounced in John than it is in the synoptics and one small, but quite important comment is not out of place here. Mk/Mt name the 'twelve' explicitly as sharing in the last supper (Mk 14:17, 20, par.), while Luke speaks of the 'disciples' (22:11) or the 'apostles' (22:14); for him, these are identical with the twelve. In the Johannine presentation, only the 'disciples' are mentioned (13:5, 22f), with the result that the circle of participants remains indeterminate. Is this deliberate, with the disciple whom Jesus loved in mind? This cannot be said with complete certainty and we must rest content with assuming that the evangelist had no interest in being more precise. Several disciples come to the fore, either because they are named by tradition or because they were important to the evangelist (the disciple whom Jesus loved; Thomas; Philip; the other Judas). The main function of the disciples is to include the later community in the context of the time of farewell. It was important for them to be represented and for them to be made aware of Jesus' will, his instructions and his promise for the future.

3. The Washing of the Feet in John in the Light of the Synoptic Accounts

There is no mention at all in the synoptics of the washing of the feet, which occupies the whole of the first part of the Johannine representation in Chapter 13 and has all the theological emphasis. This silence does not necessarily mean that the incident was without historical foundation, since the synoptics, after all, do not provide a full account of the course of events at the last supper. An account of the washing of the disciples' feet as an act of humility on Jesus' part would similarly not fit in very well after the pericope on the preparation of the passover meal (Mk 14:12–17 par.), in which Jesus gives his disciples instructions in a majestic way, anticipating everything. The announcement of the betrayal which follows in Mk/Mt is also written in such a way that Jesus' dignity is preserved despite the sombre nature of the information. In Luke, the meal also opens with Jesus' statement about the present passover which is to be followed by fulfilment in the kingdom of God (22:15f). This is another theological theme, within which the washing of the disciples' feet with its particular meaning would not easily fit. Jesus' conscious and symbolic action, as reported by John, is neither historically improbable – the master of the house had to provide a foot-bath for his guests at a festive meal (see Lk 7:44) – nor surprising in the context of Jesus' behaviour, since he often performed symbolic actions (such as entering Jerusalem on the colt of a donkey) and always refused to behave in a presumtuous or arrogant way. There can therefore be no serious objections to the Johannine representation on the basis of Jesus' person and actions.

The history of tradition, on the other hand, gives rise to certain critical objections. In Luke's presentation of the last supper, remarkably enough, the disciples' dispute about who was greatest is taken up. Jesus reacts with the statement about service, handed down in several traditions, and then adds: 'For which is greater, one who sits at table or one who serves? I am among you as one who serves' (22:24–27). Surely the suspicion is bound to arise that the Johannine scene of the washing of the feet was fashioned on the basis of this statement?[13] This is quite conceivable in the light of the Johannine preference for symbolic events. On the other hand, an argument can be found against this in the presentation of John 13 itself and that is that the evangelist did not himself create this scene, but in all probability took it from a source (see the analysis above), using only the plain narrative and adding his own deep theological interpretation to it in the dialogue between Jesus and Peter. If the second (paradigmatic) interpretation in 13:12–17 was written by someone else – an editor, for example, in the Johannine circle, who may have introduced an earlier interpretation in this way – this would simply be further confirmation that the washing of the feet as such had already existed in the tradition. This additional argument, however, is not really necessary (in the case of a differing opinion about the literary development of Jn 13). Even without it, there is the greater probability, as we have seen in the case of similar problems in the gospel of John, that the evangelist did not simply invent his deep symbolic interpretations and leave them unsubstantiated, but built them on previously existing traditions.

We must, however, look more closely at the relationship between Lk 22:27 and John 13. Both generally and in this special case, we can more or less exclude a direct dependence of the fourth evangelist on Luke. The central concept of διαχονεῖν in Lk 22:27 is absent from John 13. In Luke, it means, as it does in other logia (Lk 12:37; 17:8), waiting at table – a meaning known also to John (12:2). The washing of the disciples' feet does not have this form of 'service' in mind, but a different one, performed by a slave. There is an echo of this in the logion in Jn 13:16 (δοῦλος). It is significant that, in his statement about serving, which has its closest parallel in Mk 10:43f, Luke uses not δοῦλος (as in Mk 10:44), but ὁ διαχονῶν. He also takes the dispute among the disciples about who should be greatest, which is handed down by Mark in a different place, into the upper room of the last supper, in order to instruct the later community and its leaders (ὁ ἡγούμενος) about the arrangements for the meal. He provides a statement about Jesus' example in serving (see Mk 10:45) in a different form, with no reference to Jesus' death. It is probable that he was following a tradition here in which the image of Jesus' service belonged to the tradition of the last supper.[14] The words: 'I am among you as one who serves' are striking because nothing is narrated within the context of Jesus' service – that service is simply presupposed. J. Roloff assumed that v. 27 as a whole or v. 27c at least formed part of the earliest pre-Lukan account of the meal, from which vv. 24–26 were absent.[15] Whatever may have been the case, there is certainly no direct connection between Lk 22:27 and the Johannine washing of the feet.

It is, however, quite possible that both Luke and John independently of each other followed an earlier tradition in which Jesus' serving at the last supper was reported. There may be traces of such a tradition in the parable of the servants watching (Lk 12:35–38) and especially in v. 37b of this parable, where it is said that the returning master will 'gird himself and have them sit at table and he will come and serve them'. What we have here is clearly the situation that contradicts all usual and expected relationships – a situation which is very similar to that described in John 13, in which the master assumes the task of the servant, 'girds himself' (cf. Jn 13:4) and serves his servants. J. Roloff has even suggested that Lk 12:37b presupposes the account of the washing of the feet.[16] Even without this assumption, there is an echo in both Lukan texts of a tradition narrating a humble service on Jesus' part to his disciples, what is more, within the framework of a meal. It is hardly possible to ascertain how Luke gained access to this tradition, but we may be sure that it is essentially the same one that is provided by the Johannine source in the account of the washing of the feet. Other scholars hold very similar opinions with regard to this tradition.[17]

This does not mean that the washing of the feet is proved to be a historical event, but it does mean that it is no longer open to the suspicion that it was invented by the fourth evangelist as a pure theological fiction. What we can say with some certainty is that it was a tradition that has left traces independently in Luke and John and that it would seem to be a tradition going back a long way. It is not necessarily directly related to the last supper, but it undoubtedly presupposes a meal situation in which Jesus acted as a servant among his disciples. This service of love performed by Jesus was certainly linked with the last supper in the pre-Johannine report of the washing of the feet that the evangelist used in his theological interpretation of Jesus' death. We may even assume that it is the same source that was available to the evangelist when he composed his story of the passion. The account of the washing of the disciples' feet is even more easy to understand within the framework of a story of the passion. In that context, it can be understood in the sense of a theology of the passion with the emphasis on Jesus' self-abasement (cf. Phil. 2:7f). By means of Jesus' conversation with Peter, the evangelist succeeded in adapting this tradition to his own theology (see especially 13:6–8).

4. The Silence about the Institution of the Eucharist in the Johannine Account of the Last Supper

The fact that the fourth evangelist, unlike the three synoptics, does not mention the institution of the Eucharist in his representation of the last supper constitutes an important problem, the full seriousness of which has only rarely been considered. Most commentators do not give any attention at all to this problem and many authors who have written about the early Christian celebration of the Eucharist or the Lord's Supper have dealt very cursorily with it. Quite frequently, the section 6:51c–58 has been regarded as sufficient for an assessment of the Johannine view of the Eucharist. It should, however, be borne in mind that, if the early Church celebrated the Lord's Supper from the earliest period of its history (see the account of the institution of the Eucharist provided by Paul, 1 Cor 11:20–26) or 'broke bread' (see the Acts of the Apostles; cf. 1 Cor 10:16) and if this celebration, in which the death of Christ was commemorated, enabled Christians to experience the presence of Christ and to plead for his second coming, became the central act and the source of strength in the life of the community, its most important celebration, then it is both extremely surprising and very irritating that one evangelist should pass over in silence the institution of the Eucharist that is handed down by the others in their accounts of the last supper. It is clearly often more difficult to explain the absence of a text than an existing text. Any answer that is given will inevitably be conjecture more or less well founded, but an attempt must be made to find an answer to this problem.

I shall begin by briefly reviewing the most important attempts that have so far been made to explain this absence from the Johannine text. They can be grouped under seven headings.

(a) The evangelist was inclined to be anti-sacramental and, while not completely rejecting baptism and the Eucharist, he did regard them as superfluous. The leading representative of this view was Rudolf Bultmann. In the case of John 13, Bultmann assumed that the evangelist replaced the Lord's Supper with the 'high-priestly' prayer of Jesus, which was 'unmistakably related to the sacrament of the Eucharist'.[18]

(b) The evangelist did not recognize an institution of the Eucharist planned by Jesus himself at the last supper, but traced that institution back to the multiplication of the loaves and thought that it was only possible after Easter.[19]

(c) The evangelist did not provide an account of the institution, because he had already outlined his doctrine of the Eucharist in 6:51c–58.[20]

(d) The absence of an account of the institution can be explained by the literary development of the gospel. Originally, the institution of the Eucharist followed 13:30, but, when the gospel of the passion was formed, the account of the institution was broken off and inserted in a fragmentary form into section 6:51c–58. (The leading protagonist of this theory is W. Wilkens).[21]

(e) The arcane discipline led to the disappearance of the account of the institution from John. Jeremias, the principal representative of this theory, tried to justify this esoteric element by referring to late Judaism and primitive Christianity and their practices.[22]

(f) The account of the institution was replaced by the washing of the feet, which contains the deeper meaning of the former.[23]

(g) The evangelist had a pronounced interest in cult and makes many allusions in his gospel to baptism and the Eucharist. He does so, however, in his own characteristically deeply penetrating way, by means of symbolic interpretation. He interprets the Eucharist, for example, in the story of Cana (2:1–11) as the fruit of Jesus' expiatory death, in Chapter 6 by means of the concept of the life-giving power of Jesus' resurrection and in the account of the washing of the feet through the idea of the community of love. This view of O. Cullmann's,[24] which is diametrically opposed to the anti-sacramental interpretation, has been taken up in a modified form by other exegetes, who have attributed a highly developed cultic and sacramental interest to the evangelist.[25]

All these attempts to explain the evangelist's silence about the institution of the Eucharist are open to criticism, although most of them contain good and even correct elements. Hypotheses which base the absence of an account of the institution on further hypotheses are particualry open to question. This applies above all to Wilkens' attempt (see (d) above) to base his view of the refashioning of the original gospel on the evangelist's desire for a gospel of the passion. The attempted solutions of the problem mentioned under (b) above are also based on other hypotheses that have not been proved. The celebration of the Lord's Supper in the early Church may be connected with the Jesus' communal meals with his disciples and other groups during his active life on earth, but it is impossible to find a clear indication in the gospel that the Eucharist was instituted at any other place than the last supper. All the traditional accounts of the institution are at one in this and Paul says so explicitly and not in the context of an account of the passion (1 Cor 11:23).

The interpretation that the arcane discipline was involved here (see (e) above) ought first to be established on the basis of other observations in the fourth gospel itself. Several exegetes have drawn attention to the special language used in the gospel for the community (see especially H. Leroy: by means of the misunderstanding), but is that sufficient reason for claiming that the gospel contains no account of the institution because of the arcane discipline? Certain critics believe that the esoteric impression made by the gospel of John indicates that it originated in an exclusive and enclosed community, but why should this mean that the Eucharist was not mentioned by such a community? It is in fact mentioned in a very open way – in 6:51c–58. Many exegetes would, of course, attribute this section to an editor or to editors, but then the question arises: Why did that editor or those editors, who must have been quite close to the evangelist, not have any doubts on account of the arcane discipline? Jeremias has performed a valuable historical service in pointing to the possibility of an arcane discipline (in the apocalyptic writings, the rabbinical tradition of later Judaism, the Jewish dispersion and early Christianity), since this arcane discipline is usually regarded as beginning to flourish only in the third and fourth centuries. There are, however, opposing observations, including Justin's open speaking about the Eucharist (*Apol.* 65–67; *Dial.* 117), which indicate the absence of an arcane discipline. The simple solution to the problem, that there is no account of the institution in John because of this discipline, is therefore without real foundation.

The two extreme views that are diametrically opposed to each other – Bultmann's anti-sacramental view and Cullmann's sacramental and symbolic conception – are insufficiently based. Bultmann's view, which largely rests on the hypothesis that the account of the institution is replaced in John by the high-priestly prayer in Chapter 17 (see the commentary on that chapter), is supported by an *argumentum e silentio*. In other words, the evangelist does not speak about the sacraments and whenever these are brought fairly clearly into focus (as baptism is, for example, in 3:5; the Eucharist in 6:51c–58; both sacraments perhaps in 19:34b), these texts are editorial additions. What is not explained, however, is the evangelist's attitude towards this editorial work – was the editor really such an outsider? Why did the church community, in which he lived and for which he wrote, accept him? The parallel case of his eschatology (an eschatology of the present time) is, after all, available for comparative purposes. The editorial additions in the Johannine eschatology are, I believe, easier to recognize, but we should not conclude from them that future eschatology of the kind that was common to all Christians is rejected. (See Excursus 14 in Vol. 2.) On the other hand, however, Cullmann and the exegetes associated with him also make use of symbolic allusions that are insufficiently justified and point to a presumed cultic and sacramental interest on the part of the evangelist.

The claim that the evangelist does not include an account of the institution because of the eucharistic section in Chapter 6 does not take the problem seriously enough. Is that really a reason for omitting the institution of the sacrament that is, according to 6:53ff at least, essential to eternal life? Are not other prior references, such as the 'ascent of the Son of man' (6:62) or the gift of the Spirit (7:39) made more explicit later in the evangelist's presentation? As far as the replacement of the account of the institution of the Eucharist by the washing of the feet is concerned, the important questions remain open. These are: in what sense is it replaced; and is the evangelist not really interested in the sacrament, but only concerned to divert attention from it in favour of another idea?

I have criticized these attempts to explain the absence of an account of the institution enough and must now consider how we ought to approach this very difficult problem. The only really valid method, in my opinion, is to examine the evangelist's procedure and theological intentions in other contexts. If we do this, it may be possible to make a few comments that throw more light on this obscure question, even if they are not able to clear it up completely.

(a) In the first place, it is important to bear in mind that John passes over a great deal or else silently presupposes what is narrated in the synoptics. This is true of Jesus' baptism by John the Baptist (see 1:32f), the many healings in Galilee (see 6:2) and especially the great activity on the part of the people in Galilee (see 6:66). There is no account in John of the driving out of demons or of the harsh controversies about this with Jesus' opponents (see, for example, Mk 3: 22–30 par.). On the contrary, John quite often records the accusation that Jesus is himself possessed (7:20; 8:48, 52; 10:20f). Many themes of importance to the community (Mk 10:1–45; 12:13–34) are completely ignored in John. There are also many gaps in his report of the passion (for example, the time spent in the garden of Gethsemane: John gives no hint in 12:27f that he is even aware of this). The early theory that John's aim was to amplify the synoptics (and that he therefore only provides a selection) has been abandoned now, but it is widely accepted that he presupposes a good deal of knowledge on his readers' part.

(b) It is clear, however, that John expresses what is important to him even if the synoptics have already presented it with sufficient clarity. A good example of this is Chapter 6 with the great meal, Jesus' walking on the waters and the confession of Peter. Other examples are the decision of the council of the Jews to sentence Jesus to death, the account of the anointing and the entry into Jerusalem. This becomes quite clear in the story of the passion and the chapter on Easter. Why, then, does John leave so much out and yet include other material, in even greater detail? It is obviously because he is concerned with an interpretation and indeed with his own interpretation with its deep Christological insight.

(c) It is in many ways instructive in this context to glance back at Chapter 6. John interpreted the miracle of the loaves in a lengthy revelatory discourse as a 'sign'. This sign was not, as we might assume, a sign of the eucharistic meal, but of the person of Jesus. This is independent of the controversial question as to whether the last section was written by the evangelist or an editor, since, in the main part, the true bread that has come down from heaven and gives life to the world is seen in the person of Jesus. This discourse seemed to us to be open to be applied to the Eucharist, but the Christological interpretation was obviously of primary importance for the evangelist. This Christological emphasis is also present in the Johannine version of the last supper. The programmatic opening sentence (13:1) points the direction for the whole of the presentation that follows, not only the washing of the feet, but also the whole of the passion which is intimately related to it. Jesus sets the event in motion which leads to his 'hour' – he urges the traitor to do *quickly* what he intends to do (13:27), tells the disciples to rejoice that they are going to the Father (14:28) and hands himself over voluntarily and even majestically to the band of men sent to arrest him. The evangelist's omission of other things in this concentration on Jesus and his way to the cross becomes more understandable.

(d) Would the institution of the Eucharist, however, not be ideally suited to the idea of the love of Jesus for his own in the world? However much this may be in accordance with my own convictions, we are bound to leave the evangelist the freedom to express this idea in the way that seemed best to him, that is, in the washing of the feet, which pointed to Jesus' death. Since it is obviously unlikely that he knew nothing at all about the institution of the Eucharist at the last supper,[26] I have now to consider whether he did not want to relate the washing of the feet to the Eucharist. According to his representation, the washing of the feet took place, as the institution of the Eucharist does in the synoptic gospels, during the meal and it also forms its focal point. But did the evangelist want in this way to replace the account of the institution and thus draw attention away from it? It is more likely that he really wanted to interpret it in this way and to impart a doctrine to the community that celebrated the Eucharist. This teaching undoubtedly pointed in the same direction as Paul's 'As often as you eat this bread and drink this cup, you proclaim the Lord's death' (1 Cor 11: 26). The Johannine expression of this teaching would be that Jesus loved you to the extreme limit, as far as giving himself in death, in order to give you a share in his life (cf. the words addressed to Paul, 13:8b). This cannot, it is true, be proved, but it is a reasonable conjecture. It does not reduce the washing of the feet to a symbol for the Eucharist,[27] but it does enable the participants in the eucharistic meal to understand what is taking place through the symbolic value of the washing of the feet – its pointing to Jesus' death. Did the editor understand this? Otherwise, it is very surprising that he did not provide an account of his own of the institution.[28]

(e) The evangelist provides a very deep insight into the sacrament of baptism as well, in dealing with the question of Christian initiation below the surface of the dialogue with Nicodemus. It can hardly be doubted that the external course of events is subordinate in this part of the gospel to the inner content, which relates to testimony from above and being born of the Spirit. If the evangelist is thinking principally here of faith (see Vol. 1, pp. 369f, including n. 71), then this is further confirmation of his intention to lead the community to a deeper understanding in its sacramental practice. In this sense, then, John is critical of the sacraments, but not anti-sacramental. The celebration of the Eucharist undoubtedly goes back to the last supper for John as well, but it is precisely this that reveals its real meaning – the lasting revelation of Jesus' love for his own, the commemoration of his death and a share in his life. Would the traditional account of the institution of the

Eucharist, if it had followed the washing of the feet and the dialogue with Peter, have contributed anything essentially new? Was it necessary for the evangelist to include that account, when he was writing for a community that was familiar with the Eucharist and celebrated it?

We shall never be entirely sure of this, but the evangelist's silence about the institution of the Eucharist is perhaps not completely incomprehensible in the light of his literary method and his theological intentions.

Chapter 2

The Announcement of Jesus' Departure
and the Farewell Discourse:
13:31—14:31

The departure of the traitor, which leads directly to Jesus' 'hour', also points, despite all the external darkness surrounding it, to Jesus' glorification by the Father, which is expressed by Jesus in a triumphant statement (13:31f). It is at this point that he turns to his faithful disciples (in a unique address: τεκνία, 13:33) and announces to them that he is going away himself and that they will look for him in vain. This causes Peter to contradict him and this second dialogue with Peter also contains a prediction of his denial (13:36–38). This announced departure is extremely painful for the disciples. It also threatens their faith. For these reasons, Jesus tries to prepare for it in a farewell discourse. This discourse, addressed to the disciples (Chapter 14), is closely adapted to the situation and should therefore not be isolated from 13:31–38. It was, however, composed by the evangelist not only for the disciples at that time, but also – and even more importantly – for the later community of Christians, who had to be made to understand Jesus' going away and the new communion that it gave with him, from Easter onwards. This discourse looks forward to the time after Easter, when the Holy Spirit would come, as the 'other' Paraclete (14:16), to Jesus' disciples and would teach them and remind them of everything that Jesus had said (14:26). In the light of this discourse, it is not difficult to understand why the darkness of Jesus' death was dispelled in his glory (13:31f) and his departure a positive source of joy for the community (14:28). In the same way, the apparent victory of the 'ruler of this world' becomes Jesus' triumph and the completion of the work of salvation entrusted to him (see 14:30f).

The evangelist's authorship of this clear conception cannot be disputed, with the result that this section is for the most part not called into question by literary critics. What is, however, doubtful is whether the commandment to love in 13:34f, inserted between Jesus' announcement of his departure and Peter's reaction and playing no further part in the discourse that follows, was not in fact added by an editor. In addition, the train of thought in the farewell discourse is not always completely translucent and this has led to the suggestion that certain individual words and statements are insertions.

Finally, questions have been asked about the special intentions that the evangelist may have had in his composition of the farewell discourse. I shall consider these and related questions in each case either when I deal with individual texts or in my examination of the structure and the meaning of Chapter 14.

1. The Announcement of Jesus' Departure (13:31–35)

[31]*When he (Judas) had gone out, Jesus said, 'Now is the Son of man glorified, and in him God is glorified;* [32]*if God is glorified in him, God will also glorify him in himself, and glorify him at once.* [33]*Little children, yet a little while I am with you. You will seek me; and as I said to the Jews, so now I say to you, 'Where I am going you cannot come'.* [34]*A new commandment I give to you, that you love one another; even as I have loved you, that you also love one another.* [35]*By this all men will know that you are my disciples, if you have love for one another'.*

13:31–32 This important statement about glorification, which Jesus makes after Judas' departure, is introduced by an emphatic νῦν. The time was established in a striking way just previously to mark the departure of the traitor (μετὰ . . . τότε, v. 27; εὐθύς, v. 30). There is a further indication of the time, equally stressed, at the end of the logion (εὐθύς, v. 32). The whole force of the statement is therefore concentrated in this word νῦν, but it does not point emphatically to a situation during the meal, but rather draws attention once again to Jesus' 'hour', which was mentioned at the very beginning of the whole section and which marked the time when he 'had to depart out of this world to the Father' (13:1). This is especially clear if the content of the statement is considered.

An explanation of this text dealing merely superficially with the traitor's departure[1] does not do justice to its theological content. The word νῦν also occurs in the Johannine 'hour on the Mount of Olives' (12:27) and immediately after this twice on the occasion of Jesus' announcement of judgment to be passed on this world and of the taking away of power from its ruler (12:31). There too, it meant simply 'the hour when the Son of man is glorified' (12:23). It is, in other words, the hour of Jesus' death, when he will be raised up on the cross and in this way be glorified (12:32f). If this hour has already come (ἐλήλυθεν) when the Greeks came to visit Jesus (12:20–24) and Jesus entered it when he was 'troubled' (12:27), then it is clear that it does not refer to a definite point in time, but to an event with a specific content and culminating in Jesus' 'elevation' on the cross. This hour is present and effective in all the events leading up to Jesus' death on the cross, including the traitor's departure, which results directly in that event of the cross.

The darkest hour in Jesus' life on earth is revealed to the faith of the evangelist as the hour of Jesus' glorification.[2] This insight is set out in five lines, which, taken together, form a closed whole statement of refined and almost poetic value:

(1) νῦν ἐδοξάσθη ὁ υἱός τον ἀνθρώπου,

(2) καὶ ὁ θεὸς ἐδοξάσθη ἐν αὐτῷ.

(3) εἰ ὁ θεὸς ἐδοξάσθη ἐν αὐτῷ,

(4) καὶ ὁ θεὸς δοξάσει αὐτὸν ἐν αὐτῷ,

(5) καὶ εὐθὺς δοξάσει αὐτόν.

The third line of this statement is uncertain from the point of view of textual criticism.[3] It is also no more than a resumption of the second line, but it does function as a hinge, because the movement from the Son of man to God in the first two lines goes back in the last two lines from God to the Son of man. The third line is particularly well suited to mark this turning point – indeed, it is indispensable. Without this third line, one sentence introduced by καὶ would simply follow another and attention would not be drawn to the emphatic change in statement. The fact that this line is omitted by the best textual evidence can be explained fairly easily, either by the writers' outward lack of attention based on the homoioteleuton (ἐν αὐτῷ at the end of the second, third and fourth lines) or by their belief that the third line had no new content.[4]

The assumption that the fifth line is only a later addition and, according to Bultmann, an addition made by the evangelist himself to a statement taken from the 'revelatory discourses'[5] is unconvincing. Apart from the difficulty of having to convince us that there was an original text for this Johannine logion (see below), there is also the question that εὐθύς is to some extent related to the νῦν in the first line. Just as the glorification of the Son of man 'now' is stressed at the beginning, so too is it emphasized at the end, when attention is directed to God's glorification, that he does this 'at once'. God's reaction also belongs to 'Jesus' hour'. The last line is also meaningful within the framework of the structure.

Because of the special nature of this 'hour' of Jesus, it would be wrong to explain the tenses of the verbs used in this statement – the aorists in the first two lines and the futures in the last two – strictly in terms of time. The aorist ἐδοξάσθη was undoubtedly chosen with the departure of the traitor in mind. The hour occurred precisely because Jesus was glorified. It is (as in 12:23, 31) a formulation made from the vantage point of fulfilment. The use of the future in the reference to God's glorifying in the fourth and fifth lines can be explained in terms of correspondence. It is almost, but not exclusively a logical future (cf. the εἰ sentence), since this action in fact takes place in the future and, what is more, extends into the even more distant future (cf. 17:2). The most important aspect, however, is the mutual glorification of the Son of man and God. The word εὐθύς in the fifth line therefore draws God's glorification emphatically into the hour, since the Son of man glorifies God greatly. This interpretation is confirmed and extended by 17:1–5. The Son has glorified the Father on earth and, by completing his work on earth, he takes this glorif ation of the Father into the 'hour' of the event of the cross and to the climax that embraces all things. For this reason, he is also able to expect that he will also be glorified by the Father in the same hour. This glorification does not, however, consist simply of his achieving in heaven the glorification that is due to him.

It means above all that he is glorified in mediating salvation and in giving life to all believers.[6] This orientation of Jesus' 'glorification' to those who are already entrusted to him and who will follow him in the future cannot be overemphasized. In the context of 13:31f, this is ensured by Jesus' turning at once to the disciples and the farewell discourse in Chapter 14. Furthermore, in the prayer in Chapter 17, Jesus' request to be glorified himself should not be isolated from his intercession for his disciples and the later community. On the contrary, it should be regarded as having been previously directed towards it (cf. the ἵνα sentence in 17:2).

The language of the statement about glorification has a mythical and paradoxical sound. It is mythical principally because Jesus speaks of the 'Son of man' in the third person and describes what is clearly a heavenly event. It is also paradoxical, because a future event is transposed to the present and the mutual glorification of the Son of man and God is presented as a sequence and also as an interpenetration.[7] A transcendental event that is certain to faith, however, is expressed in defective human language, although it can never be adequately described. An understanding of the fundamental meaning of the text, based on an analysis of its structure – that is, the introduction at this point of the glorification of the Son of man, with which he only wants to glorify God, and, precisely because of this, the glorification on the part of God, which corresponds to the Son of man's glorifying – leads to a solution of a number of exegetical problems.

Who, for example, is the active subject behind the passive form ἐδοξάσθη in the first three lines? Judas is eliminated at once in this enigmatic situation, since he is no more than an instrument in the event. Ultimately, it must undoubtedly be God, but to see him as directly involved destroys the tension between the first three and the last two lines, in which God is introduced in a direct and emphatic way as the subject. The tendency in the first lines is rather to draw attention to the Son's work (cf. 17:4) and, for this reason, it is best to think of ἐδοξάσθη in the first line in the general sense, that is: Now the event of glorification is fulfilled in the Son of man (in which the νῦν is stressed in particular). In the second line, God is emphasized as the one who is glorified because of this (in the person of the Son of man). G. B. Caird believed that ἐδοξάσθη in the first line was a real passive and in the second line was a medial form (used in accordance with the linguistic usage of the Old Testament and the Septuagint), with the result that the meaning was that God glorified himself in the person of the Son of man.[8] However justified this theocentric understanding may be in itself, applied to this text it results in the stress becoming misplaced, because it overlooks the change from God as the object of glorification (in the second and third lines) to God as the active subject (in the fourth and fifth lines).

Another question is closely connected with this first question: What is the meaning of ἐν αὐτῷ in the second and third lines? The preposition ἐν may point to the personal mediator (see Blass and Debr §219, 1), but this is not a use of language that can be established with certainty in John. (For the impersonal and instrumental use of ἐν with δοξάζειν, see 15:8.) A purely local conception is unlikely, but, on the basis of other texts with δοξάζεσθαι ἐν (14:13; 17:10), it is possible to think of the ἐν as local in the extended sense, that is, to be glorified in the person of someone.[9]

Finally, we must ask how the ἐν αὐτῷ or ἑαυτῷ at the end of the first and the fourth line ought to be understood. The better reading αὐτῷ[10] can have the same meaning as the reflexive pronoun (see Blass and Debr § 283, 2 and 3). According to the context and the meaning, the phrase certainly does not refer to the Son of man,[11] but to God. Just as the Son of man, according to the second and third lines, glorifies God in his person, so too will God (καὶ ὁ θεός) glorify the Son of man in his person. The ἐν αὐτῷ is chosen (instead of a phrase ἀφ᾽ ἑαυτοῦ which one might expect) because of its similar sound (cf. παρὰ σεαυτῷ in 17:5).

The connection between the idea of glorification and the 'Son of man' is already given by 12:23. In Excursus 5 (Vol. 1, pp. 529–542), I have already discussed ways in which the evangelist may have come to this. Apart from a fairly long historical tradition which, we may assume, lies behind the logia of the Son of man, there is no really convincing reason to suspect that a saying from the apocalyptic tradition or a short pre-Johannine 'hymn' previously existed as a basis for 13:31f.[12] The idea of a mutual glorification between Jesus as the 'Son' or the 'Son of man' and God, his Father, which is deeply rooted in Johannine Christology, is sufficient evidence of the fact that these five lines are a typically Johannine logion, composed by the evangelist himself.

13:33   After this statement about glorification, which provides a brief but luminous prospect, Jesus turns at once to those disciples who have remained with him, to disclose to them the painful fact that they will be separated from him. To this end, he uses the loving form of address τεκνία, which occurs seven times in 1 John, but only once in the gospel. Even though the longest epistle may not have been written by the evangelist, but by another author, the use of this word is a sign that it is very close to the gospel. The statement about Jesus' separation from the disciples is deliberately formulated in a similar way to the statement made to the Jews in 7:33f, which is explicitly recalled here. In the case of the Jews, the logion led to a 'Johannine misunderstanding' (7:35f; see the commentary) and here too, the disciples also fail to understand – this is clear from Peter's reaction (v. 36). Their faith is still unenlightened – the Paraclete, who is promised, will teach them all things (14:26). Instead of μικρὸν χρόνον in 7:33 (cf. 12:35), here we have only μικρόν, possibly with the aim of indicating a much shorter distance.[13] This neuter form is taken up again in 14:19 and, in that context, should be interpreted as indicating the time up to seeing Jesus again (after the resurrection). (This is in contrast to its use in 16:16–19). In the elucidation that follows, the first phrase 'You will seek me' is only brought about the the resumption of 7:34. The main statement is to be found in ὑπάγω – this is confirmed by Peter's question in v. 36. The full meaning of Jesus' departure is then set out in the farewell discourse. The first task is to emphasize in categorical terms the hard fact of the separation: 'Where I am, you cannot come.' This statement is then relativized in the answer given to Peter ('You cannot follow me now, but you shall follow afterwards') and finally, in 14:3, it is broken up and taken further in the declaration that Jesus will take all the disciples to himself so that they may be where he is. This developing train of thought links the farewell discourse to the fundamental statement in 13:33 and it is for this reason that its formulation is so deliberate. Its function in this context is different from that of the statement made to the Jews in 7:33f. It is also worth noting the ἄρτι at the end.[14] Because of the important νῦν in v. 31, the evangelist was able to use this word here (and quite frequently elsewhere) as an unstressed adverb of time.

13:34–35 The 'new commandment' of mutual love, which Jesus gives his disciples as a provision in his testament and as a sign of their discipleship (v. 35), immediately follows the statement about the separation and, in that context, can be easily understood and interpreted as a recommendation to the disciples to preserve their relationship with Jesus after his departure by doing as he does and directing their care to each other. As Bultmann pointed out: 'It was only by loving each other that his own could continue in the experience of his love'.[15] There are, however, many reasons for thinking that the commandment to love was an editorial addition at this point, although it is very much in the spirit of the evangelist and fits in very well.

The following reasons may be given: (1) Peter's reply (v. 36) immediately follows v. 33 and Jesus' commandment to love is ignored. (2) This commandment is, moreover, not taken into consideration in the farewell discourse in Chapter 14. It may, it is true, be contained in the ἐντολαί of 14:15, 21, but the general formulation and the context draw our attention first and foremost to the idea of 'keeping Jesus' word or words' (14:23f; cf. 8:51). Love is not reduced to a theme here (as it is in 15:12, 17). The statements in Chapter 14 may, on the other hand, have provided the editor with a reason for inserting the commandment to love in 13:34f. (3) The 'new commandment' is only treated as a theme in 1 Jn 2:7f (cf. 2 Jn 5). This theme preoccupied the thoughts of the community or the members of the Johannine circle, to which the author of 1 John must have belonged. (4) γινώσκειν ἐν is a typical linguistic usage of 1 John (see, for example, 2:3, 5; 3:16, 19, 24; 4:2, 13; 5:2), whereas it occurs nowhere else in the gospel of John. This is objectively connected with the fact that the author was concerned with criteria with which to confront the teachers of false doctrine. (5) The construction used in v. 34 is striking. It can best be compared with those found in 13:15 (ἵνα καθὼς . . . καὶ ὑμεῖς) – this is the second interpretation of the washing of the feet, which, in my opinion, should be attributed to an editor – and 17:21 (ἵνα . . . καθὼς . . . ἵνα καί), a text that is also open to suspicion as an editorial addition (see the commentary). (6) The word πάντες in Jn 13:35 draws attention to those outside, in a way that does not occur elsewhere in the gospel, but does occur in the epistle, in which the community sees itself in contrast with the world (see especially 4:4–6). (7) The epistle to the Johannine community is so dominated by the theme of mutual or brotherly love that it is, together with the theme of faith, a fundamental admonition (1 Jn 3:11, 23). Because of this, it is possible to understand the need to stress the commandment to love as a provision in the testament in Jn 13:34f.

This 'new commandment', which still remains important, even as an editorial addition, is made clear in the light of Jn 13:14f; 15:12ff and 1 Jn.

The 'newness' in the New Testament generally[16] and the Johannine writings in particular cannot be explained simply as an antithesis to the Old Testament commandment to love one's neighbour (see Lev. 19:18) and the interpretation of that commandment in Judaism. There is no support for this. On the contrary, it comes from the understanding that the Johannine school had of Jesus' person and work. For the members of that school, the commandment to love one another was new in that it was given a distinctive emphasis by Jesus, his service of others (cf. his washing of the disciples' feet) and his giving himself in death (see Jn 15:13; 1 Jn 3:16). God has, after all, shown us his ultimate and unsurpassable love in Jesus, the Son of God. The love of God was 'made manifest' with his coming (1 Jn 4:9) and became a tangible and obligatory reality. Since Jesus' coming, the 'true light' which banishes darkness has been present and will not pass away (2:8), neither in Christ nor in Christians, so long as they realize the love that is made possible and demanded in Christ (see 3:14f). The love that has been given to us in anticipation by God opens up for us a new living space in which we can and should love our brothers in an entirely new way. As Augustine observed: 'This love renews us, so that we are new men, inheritors of the new covenant and singers of the new song'.[17] In the light of these texts taken from 1 Jn, this 'new commandment' is not presented simply as a moral demand. It is rather expressed above all as a new possibility which calls imperiously and insistently for realization. The experience of Jesus' love acts as a prerequisite and an impetus for a love which is new and creates a new community for the sake of this new experience.

This fundamental structure of the 'new commandment' can also be found in the programmatic statement in Jn 13:34. The καθώς phrase, in which the demand of mutual love is defined more precisely, not only provides a norm for that love, but also gives a reason for it. As is frequently the case in the fourth gospel, καθώς here means not so much a comparative 'as' as a motivating 'according to the way in which' or 'because'.[18] The disciples' obligation is the consequence of the reason for and the norm of Jesus' love.

What is disputed is the interrelationship between the three parts of the sentence in v. 34. The new commandment is expressed in the first ἵνα clause epexegetically, but the formula of this clause is resumed in the second ἵνα clause, which, with καὶ ὑμεῖς also takes the καθώς clause into consideration. Is the second ἵνα clause subordinate, giving the meaning: Jesus loved the disciples so that they might also love each other? I cannot exclude this view, which comes closer to the classical grammatical structure, here,[19] although it seems to restrict Jesus' gift of himself to this one end. Comparable texts, however, would suggest that the second ἵνα clause is a resumption of the first (see the translation). In Jn 15:12f, there is no definition of aim. In the formal sense, 17:21 is also comparable, in that the request that 'they may all be one' is resumed, after the καθώς clause 'even as thou, Father, art in me and I in thee', with a second ἵνα clause 'that they also may be in us'. This also corresponds to the recapitulations and the circular motion of the thought in 1 John.

Love as the sign by which Jesus' disciples can be known points to the future of the community. Like the evangelist himself, the editor regarded the disciples who were present at the last supper as representatives of all believers in the future (for the concept of μαθητής in the extended sense, see the commentary on 6:60; Vol. 2, p. 70.). 'All men', πάντες, are to be witnesses to the disciples' mutual love and this deliberately wide perspective also includes the unbelievers surrounding the believing community (cf. 17:21, 23: 'that the world may believe that thou hast sent me'). The fact that the Johannine commandment to love is expressed as brotherly love can be explained from this perspective. This implies not a conscious renunciation of the neighbourly love that is owed to all men, but a certain, though not exclusive restriction of that love to fellow-Christians (see Excursus 5 in the commentary on the Johannine epistles). There are many patristic texts which bear witness to high esteem in which brotherly love was held in the early Church as well as the way in which it was realized.[20]

2. The Prediction of Simon Peter's Denial (13:36–38)

[36]*Simon Peter said to him, 'Lord, where are you going?' Jesus answered, 'Where I am going you cannot follow me now; but you shall follow afterwards'. [37]Peter said to him, 'Lord, why cannot I follow you now? I will lay down my life for you'. [38]Jesus answered, 'Will you lay down your life for me? Truly, truly, I say to you, the cock will not crow till you have denied me three times'.*

13:36   A new dialogue with Peter (cf. 13:6–10) follows the statement about Jesus' departure (v. 33).[21] As in the case of the washing of the feet, this disciple also fails to understand Jesus' going away. In this dialogue, the evangelist makes use of a special tradition concerning Peter, the announcement of his denial of Jesus, but inserts into it a prophecy of his martyrdom that is not traditional. There can be no doubt that the evangelist himself composed this scene. His literary style and his freedom in employing tradition are both unmistakable.

Peter asks, in concern (and not ironically, as the Jews ask in 7:35): 'Lord, where are you going?'[22] This question is a literary means by which the evangelist is able to associate Jesus' words first with Peter and then with the other disciples (14:1ff). The repeated lack of understanding, on the part first of Thomas (14:5), then of Philip (14:8) and finally of the other Judas (14:22), is not a misunderstanding. It is a phenomenon that characterizes the attitude of the disciples before Jesus' passion (see, for example, the admonitions in 14:1 and 27). It also makes the readers alert to the goal towards which Jesus' way is leading.

In his reply, Jesus presents Peter with the prospect of following him to the same goal. The logion in 12:26 is resumed with the word ἀκολουθεῖν and, in the light of that logion (see the commentary), this promise is seen to be a concealed announcement of death as a witness or martyrdom and acceptance into Jesus' community with the Father. The line connecting 12:26 with 13:36 and 14:3 may easily be recognized in the expression ὅπου εἰμὶ ἐγώ or ὅπου ὑπάγω. The goal is not named directly, but it is described clearly enough. The appendix to the gospel contains an editorial explanation that the risen Christ predicted Peter's death as a witness in figurative language and called on him to follow him (21:18f). The word ἀκολουθεῖν links the two texts together. The situation in each case accounts for the fact that Peter is encouraged to wait in 13:36 and to follow Jesus in 21:19. The statements are therefore not contradictory. Anyone who wishes to serve Jesus (12:26) must deny his own will, listen to Jesus' words (13:36ff) and let himself be led even to where he does not want to go (21:18).

13:37–38   Peter's objection,[23] which is not so fierce as his protest in 13:8 but is just as unenlightened, because he has not grasped the deeper meaning of Jesus' words, leads to the prediction of his denial of Jesus. Unlike the synoptic version (in Mk/Mt), Peter contradicts Jesus only in the form of a question and assures him that he is prepared to lay down his life for him.[24] The question betrays Peter's lack of understanding and the assurance reveals what his own will is. He does not, however, as in the case of the washing of the feet, appear in an unfavourable light, since his words show that he is impetuous in his devotion to Jesus. In contrast, his character is depicted more harshly in Mk/ Mt. Jesus' reply is carefully considered from the literary point of view – he answers, like Peter, with a counter-question expressing doubt. This is followed in the text by the announcement known to us from tradition: 'Before the cock crows, you will have denied me three times'.[25]

A comparison with the synoptic gospels shows that there are considerable differences. The scene is arranged in a different way, the dialogue is differently constructed, and the statement concerning Peter's denial has a different form of words. In the case of Mk/Mt, the conversation takes place on the way to the Mount of Olives. In Luke, it takes place in the upper room at the last supper, but it follows Jesus' admonition to Simon to strengthen the faith of his brothers, a statement that is handed down only by Luke (22:31f). In the case of Mk/Mt, it is preceded by the announcement that the disciples would be scattered and Peter's assurance takes the form: 'Even though they all fall away, I will not' (Mk 14:29 par.). Jesus' reply, that Peter would deny him three times that same night, leads to Peter's protest that, even if he had to die with Jesus, he would not deny him. This confrontation does not take place in Luke. All that Peter says in that gospel is that he is ready to go to prison and death with Jesus. These words lead to Jesus' announcement to him that he will deny him three times. All the traditional variants, then, agree only in the statement that Peter was ready to die and Jesus' announcement of Peter's denial. John is closest to the Lukan tradition both in his description of the circumstances and in his structure. This also applies to the formulation of the denial. In Mk/Mt, there is an expression with πρίν, whereas in Luke and John there is a construction with ἕως. Without going into further details, we can say that the fourth evangelist clearly relied on a tradition that was related to Luke and that he fashioned this in his own way for his own presentation. This does not necessarily mean that he was familiar with the gospel of Luke, since he may have used a source similar to Luke.[26]

Peter makes no further reply to Jesus' extremely emphatic announcement (ἀμήν, ἀμήν . . . οὐ μή . . .). His words sound extremely oppressive, but he at once begins his encouraging address to all the disciples.

3. The Beginning of the Farewell Discourse
The Statement about Jesus' Departure and his Return
(14:1–3)

14.1*'Let not your hearts be troubled; believe in God, believe also in me. ²In my Father's house are many rooms; if it were not so, would I have told you (that I am going away?) I am going to prepare a place for you, ³And when I go and prepare a place for you, I will come again and will take you to myself, that where I am you may be also'.*

The Meaning and the Structure of the Discourse in Chapter 14

The change to the second person plural shows clearly that a discourse addressed by Jesus to all the disciples begins here. It is repeatedly interrupted by questions put by the disciples, but continues as far as 14:31, the closing words in vv. 25–31 indicating that it is a farewell discourse. The literary genre of the farewell discourse[26] was very popular in the ancient world, both in Graeco-Roman society and in Judaism. The last words of great men were collected and their admonitions and decrees and to some extent even their ecstatic pronouncements were reported. Within this single literary genre, there were many widely differing forms and each author chose the one that was best suited to his aim. The original form of the Johannine farewell discourse can be found in Lk 22. In it, traditional sayings of Jesus are brought together, clearly with the existing situation of the disciples and the later situation in which the community would find itself (see above, pp. 3–4) in mind. The Johannine farewell discourse is particularly close to the early biblical and Jewish stylistic forms. In earlier texts, blessings and admonitions are combined and there are frequently theological ideas that go back into the past.[28] Ethical admonitions began to predominate later and these were often elaborated considerably in the form of 'testaments' (see, for example, the *Testaments of the Twelve Patriarchs, Testament of Isaac 5*, etc.). There were also other 'testaments' containing more apocalyptic revelations and especially descriptions of the transcendent world and the future judgment (*Test Ad, Test Abr* 10–12, *Test Isaac* 6–8, etc.). Very different kinds of elements can be distinguished in John. The gift of peace, for instance, is a blessing (v. 27). The call to believe is an admonition dominating the whole discourse (vv. 1, 10f, 27c, 29). There are also promises throughout the entire discourse, in which they appear not only as reasons for faith, but also as a revelation of the time following Jesus' departure. The interspersed dialogues help to characterize the disciples and also mark the progress of the thought. The Johannine farewell discourse, then, clearly has a special character of its own. Unlike the revelatory discourses of Jesus addressed to the world (see Volume 1 of this work), the farewell discourse is an internal revelation intended for the circle of Jesus' disciples and an instruction for the later community that is represented by the first disciples.

Different opinions have been expressed about the structure of the farewell discourse in Jn 14. Several scholars have, for example, favoured a threefold division – the first two parts under the headings 'faith' (vv. 1–14) and 'love' (vv. 15–24) respectively and the third part a concluding section (vv. 25–31).[29] Not all the difficulties of the sequence of thought in the farewell discourse, however, are solved by this division of the chapter into three parts. A particularly stubborn difficulty is the juxtaposition of vv. 16f (the coming of the Paraclete) and vv. 18–20 (Jesus' second coming). J. Becker's suggestion, then, to make a main caesura between v. 17 and v. 18, has a great deal to recommend it. The dominant theme as far as v. 17 is Jesus' departure; his return dominates from v. 18 onwards.[30] This structure is already provided by Jesus' words in vv. 2–3 and there is a further allusion to it (v. 28) in the concluding part (vv. 25–31), thus confirming this view. Becker also believes that vv. 2–3 go back to a communal tradition and that this traditional statement was re-interpreted by the evangelist in accordance with his own present eschatology, which constitutes the real intention of the discourse. This theory, however, is hardly acceptable.[31] What is more, we have no need to look for a precise sub-division of the two main sections of the discourse in vv. 1–17 and 18–24. As elsewhere in the gospel, the train of thought is circular, turning around certain concepts and ideas by means of objections, associations etc., and the only way to discover it is by detailed exegesis. The division used in this commentary is only to provide a better overall view.

Exegesis

14:1   Just as Jesus' 'soul' was 'disturbed' ($\tau\alpha\rho\acute{\alpha}\sigma\sigma\omega$; cf. 5:7) in the hour on the Mount of Olives (12:27), so too must the announcement of his departure have confused the disciples. This feeling must also have been increased by the announcement of Peter's denial. Jesus clearly wanted to help the disciples to overcome their confusion and therefore admonished them to be steadfast in their hearts. In John, the word $\varkappa\alpha\rho\delta\acute{\iota}\alpha$ only occurs (with the single exception of the quotation in 12:40) in the context of this situation (14:27; 16:6, 22) and, in accordance with Semitic anthropology (to which John keeps; see 11:33), refers to man's emotional attitude and is the seat of his will and power of decision (see also $\mu\eta\delta\grave{\varepsilon}$ $\delta\varepsilon\iota\lambda\iota\acute{\alpha}\tau\omega$; 14:27). In 16:2, 22, sorrow and joy are involved. The disciples' faith is threatened, with the result that Jesus at once admonishes them to believe. They are first and foremost asked to believe in God himself, since their faith in the person of Jesus can come to grief (cf. 13:19). It is not possible to say with certainty whether the first $\pi\iota\sigma\tau\varepsilon\acute{\upsilon}\varepsilon\tau\varepsilon$ is an indicative (as in the Vg or as many exegetes believe) of whether it is an imperative (VL, apart from f).[32] The meaning is not fundamentally different in either case, because the following clause, the call to believe in Jesus, is in one way or the other dependent on it – the disciples can and should, the evangelist is saying, also preserve their faith in Jesus by relying in faith on God. 'Believe' in this context retains its basic OT meaning of 'trusting firmly in someone' (cf. Is 7:9; 28:16) even more emphatically than elsewhere. It also points to the specifically Johannine Christological faith, which is given firm support in Jesus' words. This is clear from the fact that later (vv. 6–10), access to the Father other than through Jesus is rejected. The chiastic construction brackets together faith in God and faith in Jesus and only the sequence is changed for the situation (cf. 12:44). For John, there is only one faith and that is in Jesus and God at the same time, with the result that trust in God is shaken if faith in Jesus is not preserved.

14:2   The revelatory statement, which dominates the whole of the following passage, confirms this exegesis of v. 1. It should also be read in connection with the admonition to faith – the one to whom the disciples should cling is the Father of Jesus. In his house there are many dwellings and Jesus is going to prepare a place for the disciples. They must therefore also keep close to Jesus, because only he can take them there. Jesus' goal is also the goal of the believers and his departure is only meaningful in that it makes it possible for them to reach that goal. This is why the statement about Jesus' departure (13:33, cf. 36) is taken up again, stripped of its harshness and revealed as what it really is – a promise of happiness for the disciples (cf. 14:28). The reference back to 13:33 is made in the clauses: 'If it were not so, would I have told you . . .' It is difficult to find any other point of reference.[33] The traditional text which follows these words presents us with a very difficult problem.

The text is presented as a whole by the editors in the following way: ὅτι πορεύομαι ἑτοιμάσαι τόπον ὑμῖν. From the point of view of textual criticism, what is not entirely certain is the ὅτι at the beginning; om. P[66*] Λ Θ P many Min. Lect. a e f q Orig[lat] Chrys. The omission can, however, be easily enough explained on the basis of the difficulties that it involves in interpretation (see below) or because the copyists regarded it as a ὅτι 'recitative', which could be omitted (Metzger). To cut out the words εἰ δὲ μή, εἶπον ἂν ὑμῖν (ὅτι) as an addition, in order to preserve a smooth statement,[34] is a forced solution that is quite unjustified. The text as it is available to us makes it possible to interpret ὅτι either as meaning 'because', or as introducing indirect speech ('that'). In addition, the sentence in v. 2b can be understood either as a statement or as a question. However it is turned, it still does not give a satisfactory meaning.[35] As it stands, the remark 'If it were not so, would I have told you' seems superfluous and banal and there is no trace in the previous part of the gospel (not even in 12:26, 32) of a statement that Jesus is going away to prepare a place for the disciples. What seems more likely is that the following statement in the passage is contained in it (see v. 3a), with the result that it is possible to conjecture that the ὅτι was originally followed by a ὑπάγω (cf. 13:33, 36), which was omitted at quite an early stage because the word that followed it had the same meaning.

An acceptable meaning is given, then, by a text such as the one provided in translation above (including the words in brackets). Jesus reminds the disciples of what he has said about his departure and now goes further, making it clear to them in a question that he would not otherwise have made that hard statement to them, since he is only going away ($\pi o \rho \epsilon \acute{v} o \mu a \iota$)[36] in order to prepare a place for them in his Father's house.

The statement about the 'dwellings in the Father's house'[37] has given rise to a number of different interpretations. Most exegetes believe that these are heavenly dwellings, however, of the kind that are frequently mentioned in Jewish and non-Jewish (particularly Gnostic) texts.

The closest parallels are to be found in apocalyptic texts; see, for example, I *Enoch* 39:4f: 'Here (in heaven) I saw another sight: the dwellings of the just and the resting places of the saints. Here, with my own eyes, I saw their dwellings with his just angels and their resting places with the saints'; 41:2: 'There (in heaven) I saw the dwellings of the elect and those of the saints'. This is connected with the idea of the heavenly dwelling-place of God, who is surrounded by his court (of angels). The homes of the just are also there. Early visions of God's throne were also included in such descriptions; see I *Enoch* 14:15–23; 71:5–10. The presentation in I *Enoch* 71 is relevant here. In it, Enoch himself is greeted as the Son of man (v. 14) and at the same time the just ones following him are given the promise: 'All those who walk in your ways . . . have their dwelling and their inheritance with you and they will not be separated from you in all eternity' (v. 16). The group of believers who venerated Enoch himself as the one who had been appointed in heaven to the office and function of the 'Son of man' (see C. Colpe, *ThWb*, VII, 429) therefore believed that they would be united to him there. Good and bad dwellings are mentioned in the Slavonic Book of Enoch for the situation at the end of time (II *Enoch*, 61:2f). An even earlier idea is that of places for the just and the bad in the realm of the dead, where they are kept until the day of judgment; see especially I *Enoch*, 22 (and Billerbeck, IV, 1019f). In Lk 16:22–26, this idea is preserved, but in Lk 16:9, we encounter an expression that is related to the idea of heavenly dwelling-places: 'the eternal tabernacles' ($\sigma x \eta \nu \acute{a} \varsigma$). The precise term used for these heavenly dwellings is not of decisive importance. II (4) *Esdras* 7:80 refers, for example, to the 'rooms of rest' in which the just, unlike the unjust, will (in the intervening time) have peace and be guarded by angels (vv. 85 and 95). In *JosAs*, 8:11, Joseph prays for Asenath: 'May she enter your rest ($\varkappa a \tau \acute{a} \pi a v \sigma \iota \varsigma$), which you have prepared for your elect' and later Levi sees 'the place of your rest in heaven' (22:9).[38]

In Philo of Alexandria, who received in its entirety the Greek doctrine of the immortality of the soul, heaven is regarded as a paternal house or city of the soul, to which the soul returned after being alienated in the world. According to *De Somn.*, I:256, 'You will be able to return to your paternal house ($o \tilde{\iota} \varkappa o \varsigma$), having fled from life and unending storm abroad' and, according to *De Conf. ling.*, 78, the souls 'return to where they came from, since they regard the heavenly circle, in which they live as citizens, as the fatherland ($\pi a \tau \rho \acute{\iota} \varsigma$), but the earthly circle, in which they lived as denizens, as abroad'; see also *Heres*, 274 and *Mos*, II:288 (Moses leaves this earthly life, the $\dot{a} \pi o \iota \varkappa \acute{\iota} a$, and goes to heaven, called by the Father).

The Mandaeans also gave great emphasis to the idea of heavenly 'dwellings' (*škinas*). The gnostic redeemer (*Mandā d'Haijē*) takes souls to their heavenly dwelling; see, for example, *Mand Lit*, 139:9ff: 'You are, for each man whose measure is full, a helper, guide and leader to the great place of light and the luminous dwelling'; 160: 'Rise up, dwell in the *škinas*, among the uthras, my brothers'. In the Ginza, this original home of the souls is often called the 'house of life' or the 'house of fulfilment'. These heavenly dwellings, which are the origin and the aim of souls, were represented in Mandaean cult in a symbolic way by earthly cultic huts or tabernacles.[39] It is, however, hardly possible to speak here of a direct relationship with Jn 14:2.[40] It would be more correct to say that both have a common background, possibly of Iranian origin.[41]

The Johannine logion in 14:2 has points of contact with all these ideas, but its Christian form comes from Jesus' reference to '*my* Father's house'. The 'many' dwellings are mentioned with the disciples in mind – there are 'permanent abodes' ($\mu o \nu \alpha i$) there for them too (and for all who believe in Jesus) and Jesus is going there to prepare a place for them (in those $\mu o \nu \alpha i$). There is no suggestion here of any grading according to status or merit, in other words, of *different* dwellings.[42] Jesus' only intention is to be united with the disciples once again ('that, where I am you may be also', v. 3).

Since these 'dwellings' are only quoted symbolically, in accordance with the views current at the time, the Johannine idea expressed here does not necessarily have to coincide with the return of souls to the heavenly house of the Father. Recent exegetes have therefore suggested a different explanation which is in conformity with Johannine thinking and which transposes this view on to a different plane of understanding. According to O. Schaefer, then, what is meant is the Father's sphere of power and love embracing heaven and earth. According to J. Heise, on the other hand, it is the 'space of love' into which Jesus takes his disciples by 'taking them to himself'.[43] It is, however, not possible, if these suggestions are accepted, to eliminate the idea of death in accordance with the situation of farewell and in accordance with the context (13:36). However correct it may be that the disciples' community of life and love with Jesus is to be restored after Easter (see 14:18ff), with the result that the statement can be completely reversed and Jesus and the Father will come to the disciples and 'make their dwelling' with them (14:23), the ultimate goal can only be reached when the disciples are where Jesus is, that is, in the glory of the Father (see 17:24). In any case, it is true to say that this gives a totally relative value to the question as to when and how the disciples are to come to Jesus – at the parousia (see v. 3), at their death or especially if they suffer martyrdom. They in fact reach the goal, which is community with Jesus and through him with God, through faith and the life that is given by faith. This is the same perspective that is provided in the words spoken to Martha (11:25f; see the commentary).

Because this is a view that is very characteristic of the evangelist, it is not possible to accept the recently expressed opinion that he is here including a statement taken from the tradition of the community, which keeps to the notion of a future eschatology and a parousia in the future (see v. 3), and changes it in the discourse that follows, by re-interpreting it in the sense of his own present eschatology.[44] The most likely explanation of how the evangelist came to make the statement concerning the dwellings in the Father's house is that he formed it himself against the background of the views that were current at the time.

A comparison with Jn 8:35 gives support to this argument. Figurative language, containing the concepts 'house' and 'remaining', is used, although they have a different character (a slave does not remain for ever in the house, whereas the son does). 'My Father' in 14:2 corresponds to the 'Son', by whom Jesus means himself (see the commentary). Even in their material content, the two Johannine logia are very close. In 8:35, the Son leads men to true freedom and he is able to do this because he 'remains' and mediates lasting eschatological existence (see 8:32). In 14:2, the Son is going to his Father's house to prepare a permanent place for his disciples, even though he is, externally at least, going away from them. Both texts are very close above all in the idea that the Son mediates true and lasting existence, although the formal point of view in the second is the goal that is reached through Jesus.

The terms used in 14:2 can easily be explained on the basis of 8:35 (including μοναί, which is from the same root as μένειν), although there is no reference in 8:35 to 'returning' or 'taking to himself'. The figurative language use of 'dwellings' cannot, however, automatically be applied to the continuation in v. 3, in which the evangelist may have come to his formulations in a different way.

14:3   This continuation of the logion, extending it to include a statement that Jesus will return and take the disciples to himself, is not in itself necessary, but this statement obviously meant a great deal to the evangelist (cf. v. 28). The expression is reminiscent of the parousia, although this is not described anywhere else in the NT as a *return* on Jesus' part, not even in the editorial statement in 21:22f (ἕως ἔρχομαι). This is a sure sign that the saying does not come from the tradition of the community. The words should not, however, be in any way interpreted as referring to the parousia,[45] since this would be in contradiction to the evangelist's present eschatology (see Excursus 14 in Vol. 2). We are also bound to suspect that the evangelist wanted to take the universal early Christian expectation of the parousia into consideration, but consciously reinterpreted it to apply to the presence of Christ and his spiritual coming after the resurrection (vv. 18ff). For this reason, he repeated the last phrase with an ἐάν-clause[46] and extended the statement with the community's expectation of the parousia in mind. This inclusion and re-interpretation of the idea of the parousia can be made clear by a comparison with the earliest representation that is available to us, that found in 1 Thess 4:16f:

1 Thess 4:16f	Jn 14:3
καταβήσεται ἀπ' οὐρανοῦ	πάλιν ἔρχομαι
ἁρπαγησόμεθα . . . εἰς ἀπάντησιν	παραλήμψομαι ὑμᾶς
πάντοτε σὺν κυρίῳ ἐσόμεθα	ὅπου εἰμι ἐγὼ καὶ ὑμεῖς ἦτε

In both cases, the idea is developed in three stages: (a) the 'descent from heaven' corresponds to John's 'coming again of Jesus'. (b) In the text of 1 Thess, with its mythological overtones, this leads to a 'meeting' with the

Lord or the 'reception' of the Lord. In John, it leads to the statement that Jesus will 'take the disciples to himself'. (c) This event reaches its conclusion and its goal when the believers 'are always together with the Lord' (1 Thess) or when the disciples 'are where Jesus is' (John).

The evangelist's intention, which is also revealed in the way in which he expresses himself, can be understood as soon as this reference to the community's expectation of the parousia is recognized. He adds πάλιν[47] because he has previously spoken of Jesus' departure and, in his view, the intervening time is very short (cf. also 16:16f). παραλαμβάνειν is not a distinctive term for the parousia,[48] but the evangelist uses it because he has previously employed the image of a house and the verb can also mean 'to receive into a house' (cf. 1:11).[49] Finally, 'to be where Jesus is' also occurs in 12:26 and 17:24 and is the Johannine expression for the union of the disciples with Jesus at the 'place' of fulfilment. Nothing at all is said about the way in which the disciples reach this goal. The 'I will take you to myself' *begins* after Easter, in the existence of the believers, in so far as that existence is an experience of community with Jesus in the present, but it is *completed* only after death (or after the parousia). These words, then, should be understood in the Johannine sense and the passage that follows throws light on Jesus' departure, which is in no sense a real separation, and on his coming again, which does not simply take place at the parousia. They also give the following passage an order and a direction.

4. The Dialogue about the Way to the Goal
The Admonition to Believe in Jesus
(14:4–11)

[4]*"And the way where I am going you know'. *[5]*Thomas said to him, 'Lord, we do not know where you are going; how can we know the way?' *[6]*Jesus said to him, 'I am the way and the truth and the life; no one comes to the Father, but by me. *[7]*If you had known me, you would have known my Father also; now (already) you know him and have seen him'. *[8]*Philip said to him, 'Lord, show us the Father and we shall be satisfied'. *[9]*Jesus said to him, 'Have I been with you so long, and yet you do not know me, Philip? He who has seen me has seen the Father; how can you say "Show us the Father"? *[10]*Do you not believe that I am in the Father and the Father is in me? The words that I say to you I do not speak on my own authority; but the Father who dwells in me does his works. Believe me that I am in the Father and the Father in me; or else believe me for the sake of the works themselves'.*

14:4   After making the programmatic statement that the disciples will reach the same goal as himself and be united with him, Jesus introduces a change of direction into the discourse which is perhaps surprising, but which is certainly in keeping with the Johannine train of thought. He does this by directing attention away from the goal to the way itself. The way is made the theme even by the linguistic form of this verse, in which the emphasis falls at the end of the sentence. This emphasis is weakened by the longer version: 'where I am going you know and the way you know.'[50] We may therefore conclude that this reading is certainly secondary. As a result of the statement about the 'Father's house' made by Jesus, the goal should be obvious to the disciples, but there is still an echo of the warning: 'Believe in me!' If they are to reach the goal, the disciples must continue to cling to Jesus and remain united with him through faith, even though they may outwardly be separated from him. This intention, at the new beginning made in v. 4,[51] is confirmed in the following verses (8–11). The whole section is concerned with urging the disciples to believe in Jesus, since it is only through him that they will reach the Father. There is a certain relationship between this passage and the discourse on the good shepherd in Chapter 10, in which the general exposition of the 'cryptic discourse' (vv. 1–5) is followed formally by the special phrase 'I am the door' (vv. 7 and 9), whereas materially, within the framework of the question of salvation, Jesus is shown to be the only mediator of salvation. The closeness that exists between 10:9 and 14:6 is not purely coincidental.

14:5 Thomas, whose melancholy nature is known to readers from 11:16,[52] here raises an objection which is, on the one hand, intended to throw light on the disciples' slowness to understand what Jesus has said about his departure (cf. Peter in 13:36) and, on the other, is used as stylistic, literary means by the evangelist to provide Jesus with an opportunity to articulate this idea more precisely. It is only in this way that Jesus' failure to respond to Thomas' main objection: 'Lord, we do not know where you are going' can be explained. Knowledge of the goal is once again presupposed (v. 6b: 'No one comes to the Father . . .') and only the way is made explicit ('. . . but by me').

14:6 After Thomas' uncertain question, Jesus' answer sounds like an extremely important revelation, a unique statement that has lost none of its sovereign power even now. The revelatory formula ἐγώ εἰμι is what gives the statement its majestic sound (see Excursus 8, Vol. 2), but this impression is strengthened by the three predicates. There is a second predicate, joined to the first by καί, in Jesus' answer to Martha in 11:25, but this is the only text in which a third predicate, also linked by καί, occurs. Despite the parataxis, it is clear that the emphasis is placed entirely on the statement: 'I am the way.' This is obvious from the context: ἡ ὁδός is a repetition of the key-word in v. 4 and is confirmed as the only focal point by v. 6b (δι' ἐμοῦ). If the two extremely important concepts – 'the truth' and 'the life' – are added, the significance of this procedure can be understood in the light of 11:25. In that verse ἡ ἀνάστασις is placed first, in a stressed position, because of the context (see the commentary), but this abstract concept, which is here related to a person, is at once clarified by the added ἡ ζωή and the objective explanation that follows. The concept 'the way' is, in itself, an unusual metaphor to apply to a person, but its meaning is made clearer by the additional statement that 'the truth' and 'the life' are also incorporated into that person. It almost sounds like a justification, but it is really a clarification: 'I am the way, that is, the truth and the life' for everyone who wants to reach that goal. In other words, by revealing the truth that leads to life and mediating that true life to the one who accepts and realizes that truth in faith, Jesus takes everyone who believes in him to the goal of his existence, that is, 'to the Father'; in this manner, he becomes the 'way'.

This interpretation of the text is the one that has generally speaking been suggested by most modern exegetes, although, it has to be admitted, with many modifications, especially in the meaning of the concept of 'truth'.[53] The church Fathers interpreted it quite differently, giving special value to the second and the third predicates, for the most part as goals to be reached. There are, however, also individual differences among the Fathers themselves. Augustine, for example, regarded truth and life together as the goal: '. . . cum via cognita qua iret, restaret nosse quo iret, nisi quia ibat ad veritatem, ibat ad vitam' (In Jo. tr., LXIX, 2; CC 500). This idea is expressed even more clearly in another text: 'Primo dixit qua venias, postea dixit quo venias. Ego sum via, ego sum veritas, ego vita. Manens apud Patrem, veritas et vita, induens se carnem, factus est via' (In Jo. tr., XXXIV, 9; CC 316). The interpretation of other Fathers is again different: through the way and the truth, men reach life or, progressively, through Jesus, the way, we know the truth and rejoice in eternal life (Theodore of Mopsuesta) and 'Via est quae perducit, veritas est quae confirmat, vita est quae per se redditur' (Ambrose[54]). Like Augustine, Origen and Clement of Alexandria also related truth and life to the Logos in his pre-existence, undoubtedly as a result of their Platonism.[55] John Chrysostom and, much later, Theophylact provided interpretations that were much closer to the text, insisting that both terms acted as a guarantee of the promise that Jesus was the way; because he was also the truth, he could not be mistaken and, because he was the life, we could not be stopped on this way by death.[56]

Bultmann has provided a characteristically modern re-interpretation, claiming that 'the way and the goal ought not to be separated in accordance with mythological thinking', because redemption is an event 'that takes place in man's existence through his encounter with the one who reveals'; the believer's existence is eschatological and 'his way is already his goal' (p. 467). This existential theological interpretation is to some extent based on the fact that Bultmann derived the idea of 'way' and 'goal' from gnosticism (see below) and at the same time demythologized this idea and gave it an existential interpretation. In doing so, however, he moved away from John, who keeps firmly to man's transcendental goal (11:25f).

Jesus' self-revelatory statement, which is given a precise and absolute expression in the sentence that follows: 'No one comes to the Father, but by me', is a culminating point in Johannine theology. It forms a classical summary of the Johannine doctrine of salvation that is based entirely on Jesus Christ. In Jesus Christ, the evangelist is saying, the invisible and incomprehensible God has, in his will to save men, made himself so tangible and so comprehensible that they are able to reach the goal of their existence along this way, by accepting in faith the truth that has been revealed to them in Jesus Christ and by sharing in his life. (For the Johannine concept 'truth', see Excursus 10 and for the idea of life, see Excursus 12, Vol. 2.)

How did the evangelist come to use the metaphor 'way', which he applies in a very pointed manner to Jesus by combining it with the revelatory formula ἐγώ εἰμι? Because this 'way' is intimately connected with the goal which man is to reach, it would in the first place seem that he derived the idea from gnostic texts, since, as Bultmann, p. 466, n. 4, pointed out, 'knowledge of the way that the soul, separating from the body, has to follow to the world of light and of the guide who indicates that way can be described as the main elements in gnostic teaching'. Statements that are close to that in Jn 14:6 are to be found in the Mandaean literature especially,[57] including, for example, the following: 'You show us the way of life and let us walk along the paths of truth and faith' (*Mand Lit* 77); 'You are the way of the perfect, the path that leads up to the place of light. You are the life of eternity, towards which you went and where you had a place in (every) true heart' (*Ginza* 271; 26ff: in a psalm addressed to the *kušta*). There are, however, certain differences which must be borne in mind: (a) The way as such, the 'ascent of the soul' (going past watch-towers and so on), which plays such a prominent part in Mandaean literature, plays no part at all in John. (b) The *kušta* (truth) itself is both the way and the guide (see the second text quoted above; see also *Od Sol* 38). Man seizes hold of this *kušta*, which becomes active in him as gnosis. In John, on the other hand, this part is played by Jesus Christ, a personal part which is not in any way diminished in the gospel. (c) The concept of truth is different in John, where it is not a reality that is divine and discloses itself, but a reality of salvation that is revealed by the historical Jesus. Gnostic ideas and images may well have influenced John here, as in the case of the related metaphor of the door in Chapter 10, where the comparable material in other religions is similar (see Vol. 2, pp. 284ff), but it is certainly not possible to establish a deeper theological effect, because the typically gnostic element, the ascent of the soul to where it was before, is not present in John, in which there is no reference at all to the soul's original home.[58]

Other scholars have suggested that the idea of the way is derived from Judaism. It is, however, hardly possible to maintain that the OT expressions 'way' and 'walking', which together formed an image for practical moral behaviour in fulfilment of the Torah, are the source of the Johannine idea, even in the further development of these expressions in Qumran.[59] Quite apart from the fact that these expressions (including the absolute term 'the way' in the Qumran texts[60]) are always concerned with man's realization of his life in accordance with God's directives, there is no conscious perspective directed towards the goal in the Jewish texts. This perspective is at the most present in the background, providing motivation, either in the promises made to those who are walking on the right way or in their expectation of God's eschatological reward and new creation. In John, on the other hand, the way and the goal form a single unity, the 'way' coming into view only through the 'goal'.

The possibility of the theme having already existed in the typology of Exodus has also been considered. Following other scholars, I. de la Potterie has suggested that Jn 14:1–6 may have been inspired by Deut 1:29–33 and that an important event in the Exodus was applied to Jesus.[61] But Jesus' description of himself as 'the way' is insufficiently explained by the OT statement that God went ahead of the Israelites on their way through the desert in order to look for a 'camping place' for them (*Targ. Jer.*: 'In order to gain a place for you, a house of his dwelling'). If the close affinity with the image of the door (10:9) is borne in mind, preference must be given in this question of symbolic language to the rich gnostic material. What is more, John must also have been led by inner logic from the theme of the goal and the image of the paternal house, into which Jesus takes his disciples, to this description of Jesus.

14.7   This verse aims to impress the principal statement, namely that Jesus is the only way to the Father, even more strongly on the consciousness of the disciples and to strengthen their faith in Jesus. V. 7 can therefore be seen as the positive expression of what is said in v. 6b: no one comes to the Father, but by Jesus, but by him one really comes to the Father. A decision about the difficult question as to which reading is preferable in v. 7 is made easier by this insight. The first version is: 'If you would know me, you would also know the Father' and the second is: 'If you have known me, you will also know the Father.' The evidence is essentially as follows:

I   εἰ ἐγνώκειτέ με A (om. με) B C Θ P λ φ pl. aur Vg Iren^{lat} Tert.

καὶ τὸν πατέρα μου ἂν ἤδειτε B C* Ψ λ 33 ἐγνώκειτε ἄν A(Θ) P φ pl. aur Vg

II   εἰ ἐγνώκατέ με (or ἐμέ) P^{66} ℵ D* a b c d e ff^2 sy$^{s.pal}$ sa bo Iren^{lat} Novat Hilar Aug

καὶ τὸν πατέρα μου γνώσεσθε P^{66} ℵ D W d sy^s sa cognovistis a b c ff^2] cognoscitis e q

The *external evidence*, which would seem to be equally balanced in the case of both versions, on closer inspection provides a number of important perspectives for version II. The texts providing the most important evidence for version I have ἤδειτε in the apodosis and this may have been influenced by Jn 8:19, whereas others have ἐγνώκειτε, which is probably an assimilation to the protasis. VL differs from the other texts providing evidence to version II in the apodosis, perhaps in the light of v. 9b, but (apart from aur) it testifies to the same version II in the protasis.

Version II should be given preference on the basis of *internal evidence*. Because Thomas' question seemed to them to be incomprehensible, the copyists were aware of the reproach contained in the lack of reality in version I, and they also probably remembered Jn 8:19. The most important point in favour of version II is that there is a better connection between it and the following sentence (καὶ) ἀπ' ἄρτι (see the commentary). It would have been rather meaningless, in the light of the verses that follow (in which Jesus reproaches Philip), to attempt to eliminate this reproach directed against the disciples, although an attempted elimination may have led to this version. My decision will, however, have to be based on exegesis of the text.[62]

In v. 6b ('comes to the Father') there was an indirect promise which is made explicit in v. 7 (the second reading: 'You will also know the Father'). The condition for this, however, is that access to the Father has to be gained through Jesus: the εἰ μὴ δι' ἐμοῦ is taken up again by the εἰ clause. A criticism that the disciples had hitherto not known Jesus (reading I) would be disturbing in the light of this promise. The 'knowing' (γινώσκειν) that is under discussion here and in v. 9 (varied and reinforced by ἑωρακέναι) is more than a merely external 'knowing' (εἰδέναι): it is in fact a finding of communion with a person (cf. 10:14f). This 'knowledge of God' is able to express full community with God (cf. 17:3 and 1 Jn *passim*). Thomas, for example, was in a state of ignorance (οὐκ οἴδαμεν) with regard to the goal and the way, but Jesus speaks of the true knowledge that leads to the goal and is fulfilled: 'If you have known me, you will also know the Father', that is, you will have full community with the Father. A better meaning is therefore given by version II.

A promise is expressed in the future tense γνώσεσθε, but this promise is already made present in Jesus. This is why Jesus continues with a correction and a clarification: 'Now (already) you know him and have seen him.' This present knowledge and vision of the Father is, as v. 9 shows, in Jesus. The καί is explanatory and intensifying. It is also certainly original.[63] This means that ἀπ᾽ ἄρτι does not mean 'henceforth', as many translations have it, but, as in 13:19, 'now (already)'. This does not point to the time following Jesus' exaltation and the sending of the Spirit,[64] but to Jesus' presence here on earth. The addition of ἑωράκατε, which is taken up again in v. 9b, removes all doubt in this context. Anyone 'seeing' (6:40) the earthly Jesus in faith also 'sees' the Father (cf. 12:45, with the synonym θεωρεῖν). That is why nothing else is required, in order to come to the Father, than faith in his Son, Jesus, who is present.

14:8   Philip's request: 'Lord, show us the Father', like Thomas' objection in v. 5, has a literary function. It makes it possible for Jesus to express the essential idea of 'he who has seen me has seen the Father' more precisely, so that the believer can understand that Jesus is in the Father and that the Father is in him (vv. 10f). The phrase 'and we shall be satisfied' is to some extent ironical, because this disciple is evidently not very satisfied. Is it pure chance that this word ('to be enough') only occurs in one other place in the gospel and that is in Philip's comment on the occasion of the feeding of the five thousand (6:7)? Ought the reader perhaps to be reminded by this echo (which is purely external) that Philip experienced that great sign and know that he was not satisfied with Jesus' revelation? Otherwise, Philip is depicted quite sympathetically as a man who is ready to believe and to lead others to faith (cf. 1:43–47; 12:21f). It is possible that he seemed, for this reason, a particularly suitable disciple for the task of throwing light on the defective faith of the other disciples by asking to see the Father, a request which otherwise displays a lack of comprehension.

The request itself is directed towards an immediate revelation on God's part. 'Show' is, for example, related in 5:20 to Jesus' direct relationship with his Father, in 2:18 to the Jews' unbelieving demand for a sign and, in 10:32 to the many works that Jesus has shown to the Jews as good actions that have come from the Father. It is, then, for John at least, a term that occurs in the vocabulary of revelation – a use that can be established elsewhere.[65] The visionary in Revelation is 'shown' what will take place at the end of time (Rev 4:1; 17:1; 22:6) and finally he is also shown the wedding of the Lamb and the future Jerusalem (21:9f; 22:1). The evangelist probably wanted to indicate that Philip was hoping for some kind of theophany comparable to the one for which Moses asked God: 'Show me (Septuagint (LXX): δεῖξόν μοι) thy glory!' (Exod 33:18). A secondary, historical tendency can be suspected here, since Jesus rejects a direct vision of God in 1:18; 5:37; 6:46. It is hardly possible to say, however, whether the allusion is directed against Jewish mysticism, the Christian gnostics (cf. 1 John) or simply against a general longing for a direct experience of God that was widely felt at the time.[66]

14:9   Philip is, in this verse, sharply corrected by Jesus. Jesus' reply makes it clear how it is possible to come to the Father through him. He reminds Philip of the long time that he has been one of the disciples and of the words and works (see v. 11) through which he must have known him. Jesus is referring here to the knowledge, made possible by faith, that he is sent by God (cf. 17:8, 25) and that the Father speaks and acts in him, in other words, that the Father is 'visible' in him. Philip should have come to a lasting and firmly established knowledge through this (the perfect tense ἔγνωκας; cf. 6:29), since it is fundamentally true that anyone who sees Jesus in fact sees the Father. Although the perfect tense is used here, it has a present meaning (cf. 12:45). As in v. 6b, the sentence is formulated in such a way that later believers will feel that they are also being addressed. Jesus' criticism of Philip also warns them not to look for special visionary experiences of God or any form of direct union with God, but to be content simply to believe in Jesus and his word.

14:10   The key-word 'believe' occurs again in this verse. For the believer, it is certain that Jesus is in the Father and that the Father is in him. This 'reciprocal formula of immanence' is a linguistic way of describing, not, it has to be admitted, in a graphic way, the complete unity between Jesus and the Father. Every analogy, after all, breaks down here. The term is known to readers of the gospel from 10:38; the context in which Jesus used it then was that of an encounter with the faithless Jews (see above). Here, however, Jesus names himself first (as he does in vv. 11 and 20). This may be connected with his criticism of Philip: 'You do not know me?' Jesus has to be seen above all with the eyes of faith. If he is seen in this way, it is possible to know the hidden depths of his being and his complete bond with the Father, resulting in his being totally 'in the Father'. The Father is similarly in him and reveals himself perfectly through him, expressing himself, as it were, in him. Jesus' words are therefore not his own words, but words that he has heard from the Father (see 8:26) and that the Father has commanded him to say (see 12:49f).

Jesus also refers to 'works' and, in v. 11b, it is clear that he is thinking here of the visible works that bear witness to him (see, for example, 5:36), in other words, of the great 'signs'. The statement in v. 10c, however, is strangely expressed: 'The Father does his works', because he is constantly in Jesus (μένων[67]). The sequence of clauses gives the impression that Jesus' words are the works that the Father does. There are, however, strong objections to this interpretation.[68] Firstly, it is clear both in 10:37f and in 15:22, 24 that there is a difference between Jesus' words and works (ἔργα). Secondly, an ἀλλά would be normal if the two concepts were so closely linked. This appears regularly elsewhere (7:28; 8:28, 42; 12:49; 14:24). Here, however, we have a δέ. Thirdly, ἔργα can hardly have a different meaning from the following verse. It must therefore be an abbreviated expression – Jesus' words do not come from him and, in the same way, the works that he accomplishes also come from the Father. It is probable that the formula 'I in the Father and the Father in me' led to this sequence of clauses (see W. Bauer), with the aim of illustrating the reciprocal action of Jesus and the Father (hence the word δέ), which takes the form of co-operation and interaction, and at the same time, of providing a basis for the statement.

14:11   Jesus now turns urgently, almost imploringly, to all the disciples. The faith which he reveals to the Father in his activity and enables the Father to be effective is expressed in the same formula and is also of such fundamental importance that the disciples should, whatever happens, have this faith. If they do not believe Jesus himself,[69] that is, his words, they should at least believe for the sake of the works.[70] According to its meaning, it is the same demand as that made to the unbelieving Jews in 10:37, although it is, in accordance with the different people to whom it is addressed, differently formulated (see above). The same formula used to describe the unity between Jesus and the Father occurs both here and in 10:38 and it cannot therefore be simply coincidental that the two texts are so similar. The disciples – and later believers – endanger their faith if they do not interpret Jesus' activity in this way. The admonition is, moreover, contained here in the farewell discourse and it may have been occasioned by that particular situation in the faith of the community. It is, however, clear evidence of the evangelist's deep and radical reflection about the words and works of Jesus as well as his entire activity on earth and his appearance among men. Jesus' words should have been sufficient for men to recognize him as the bringer of eschatological revelation and salvation. His works or actions, however, can be seen as additional visible signs and testimonies, which may be supportive and helpful to those whose faith is weaker.

5. The Promises made to Those who Believe
The First Saying about the Paraclete
(14:12–17)

[12]*'Truly, truly, I say to you, he who believes in me will also do the works that I do; and greater works than these will he do, because I go to the Father.* [13]*Whatever you ask in my name, I will do it, that the Father may be glorified in the Son;* [14]*if you ask anything in my name, I will do it.* [15]*If you love me, you will keep my commandments.* [16]*And I will pray the Father and he will give you another Counsellor, to be with you for ever,* [17]*(even) the Spirit of truth, whom the world cannot receive, because it neither sees him nor knows him; you know him, for he dwells with you and will be in you'.*

Jesus here makes a new beginning (with the solemn, emphatic formula ἀμὴν ἀμήν), although still within the framework of the demand of faith (ὁ πιστεύων), and makes certain promises to his disciples for the period following his departure. In this way, he justifies and strengthens his demand for faith. There are two promises which belong more closely together: the promise that the believer will do works of the kind that Jesus has done and will even do greater works, and the promise that requests made in his name will be granted. The promise of the 'other' Paraclete should, however, also be included among these promises, because it is also linked to them in its content. Jesus with the Father will help the disciples here on earth by granting their requests. In the same way, another 'Paraclete', the Spirit of truth, will also lead and support in an intimate way that will remain hidden from the 'world' in their community on earth, in which he himself has, until now, been the leader and supporter.[71] V. 15, which intervenes, should not be seen as unmanageable 'flotsam' and eliminated from the original discourse.[72] It can be interpreted as Jesus' condition for his disciples, so that he can continue to be active and effective on their behalf.

14:12 Continuing with the theme of the 'works' that he has already mentioned (vv. 10c and 11b), Jesus promises the disciples that they will do the same works that he has done and indeed even greater works. A traditio-historical consideration of Mk 11:23f par. Mt 21:21f will help us here to understand this and the next promise, this is, the prayer will be heard. Two of Jesus' logia are merged together in this synoptic text: faith that is free from all doubt has the strength to move mountains; and prayer in faith is always heard. The early Church was very preoccupied with the promise of miraculous power (see, for example, Lk 17:6 and Mt 17:20[Q]; the miracles narrated in Acts; Mk 16:17f). The fourth evangelist was also familiar with this tradition – this is clear from the connection made in the gospel between the 'works' and the hearing of prayer and the use of the verb αἰτεῖν for this asking.[73] The evangelist obviously reflected about this tradition and including it in his theology. The works that Jesus promises every believer will do are consciously placed alongside Jesus' own works in the text and this juxtaposition suggests a possible interpretation, namely that the one who is really acting in these works is Jesus himself, even after his departure to the Father (see v. 13). This also defines the works themselves and their nature more precisely. They have to be seen, in other words, in the same light as Jesus' works on earth. Jesus' works are, of course, not simply miracles, but 'signs', with the special intention of pointing either to Jesus as the giver of life or to his gift of life. They are not simply external works, but rather spiritual works which help man to achieve salvation.[74]

The 'greater works' that Jesus promises his disciples will do can now be defined rather more precisely as a result of these considerations. Although they are, according to the evangelist, even greater than his own works,[75] it is evident that they are not meant to be more astonishing miracles than those performed by Jesus himself. The healing of the man born blind and the raising of Lazarus are the absolute climax for the evangelist – as external events and even more as translucent signs showing Jesus to be light and life for the world. If indeed they have to be considered in the same perspective as 5:20 (see above), since the same expression – 'greater works' – is used in both texts, it is at first surprising that Jesus promises in the present text that the disciples will do even greater works than he, when in the earlier text it was Jesus who was to do greater works than the Father. The effect, however, is deliberately intended to stimulate further reflection. The disciples will go further than Jesus by giving his 'greater works' – raising to life and judgment – an even greater effect, since Jesus goes to the Father and continues to act through the disciples. It is not until after his glorification that he is able to reap the full fruit of his life and death (see 12:24, 32; 17:2). We may therefore conclude by saying that the interpretation of the 'greater works' that has prevailed since the patristic period is to some extent justified. These 'greater works' can, in other words, justifiably be applied to the missionary successes of the disciples.[76] If, however, we are to preserve the full meaning intended by the evangelist, we must be on our guard against a purely external view, since the 'greater' works were not for him external expansion and successes that could be counted, but the increasing flow of God's power into man's world (17:2), the gathering together of God's scattered children (11:52) and the judgment of the unbelieving world (see 16:8–11). This cannot be done until Jesus' exaltation (12:31f), his departure to the Father and the activity of his disciples.

14:13   The further promise, that prayer will be answered, is closely connected by καὶ to the previous promise. It is also related to v. 12 by its thought. The disciples will do 'greater works' again because Jesus will, with the Father (v. 12c), hear their requests and do what they ask.[77] In contrast to the synoptic statements about the hearing of prayer, in which the divine passive is used (Mt 7:7f; Lk 11:9) or God's granting of the request is made evident in another way (Mk 11:24/Mt 21:22; Mt 7:11/Lk 11:13; Mt 18:19), the ποιήσω in this verse (and in v. 14) is very striking. It is indeed all the more remarkable in view of the fact that it is, in the Johannine parallels (15:16; 16:23f, 26), the Father who grants what is requested (cf. Mt 18:19 with 15:7). The statements with ποιεῖν link the two promises together in such a way that what the disciples do (v. 12) once again reach a climax in what Jesus will do (vv. 13 and 14). The sentence in 15:5 'Apart from me you can do nothing' is entirely in accordance with the idea in the background. The disciples do the same works as Jesus and Jesus does what they ask him to do, so that their works become his works. Jesus does this 'so that the Father may be glorified in the Son', as he has glorified him on earth (17:4) by accomplishing the works that the Father gave him to do (cf. 5:36; 10:25, 32). In the last resort, then, it is the Father who 'does his works' (v. 10c) both in Jesus and in the disciples. The whole circle of thought is closed with this. The disciples are promised nothing less than a share in Jesus' activity with and for the Father after and on the basis of his departure to the Father.

Seen in this light, there can be no misunderstanding about which requests will be heard. The evangelist does not have every possible intention in mind here. He is thinking rather of the tasks and the difficulties of proclaiming the gospel (as is also probably the case in the synoptic logia of Jesus). There is no need in this context to be assured that prayer should only be 'in accordance with God's will (cf. 1 Jn 5:14). Even the additional phrase 'in my name', which occurs here and in other Johannine texts, does not have this meaning. It only occurs in connection with petitionary prayer in the gospel of John – even in Mt 18:20, the words 'in my name' (εἰς τὸ ἐμὸν ὄνομα!) do not belong to the request, but to the gathering together. A 'mystical' explanation, according to which those who pray are in such an intense state of community with Jesus that they appear before God as completely one with him,[78] is not justifiable. On the other hand, the datum based on the study of comparative religion that 'in Jesus' name' means no more than 'on the invocation of Jesus' name',[79] because, in 16:23, the Father gives what is requested 'in Jesus' name', also does not apply here. It is, on the contrary, a Johannine formulation which is most obviously connected with the OT and Jewish modes of expression used in the context of revelation and mission.[80] The person sent 'in the name of' another, in order to proclaim his word and will, may appeal to his name. The Johannine Jesus therefore appeals to his Father's name: 'I have come in my Father's name' (5:43; cf. Deut 18:18–20) and his disciples may also appeal to him, because he has sent them (cf. 4:38; 17:18; 20:21). This is, however, not an appeal that is based on a legal right. It is an appeal to Jesus based on their deep association with him. The Father also grants the disciples the requests that they make in their prayer, because he loves them himself because of their love for Jesus and their faith in him (16:26f). It is this special quality of the relationship between the disciples and Jesus and the Father that provides the reason for their being able to pray 'in Jesus' name'.[81] Their prayers will certainly be heard because Jesus sent them and remains closely associated with them, because he himself shares in their activity and wants to make it possible for them to do even 'greater works'.

14:14   The repeated promise that prayer will be heard has meant that this verse has from time to time been regarded as superfluous. In some of the traditional manuscripts it is absent, but most of the texts provide it.[82] Its omission from a number of manuscripts can easily be explained – its content is very similar to that of v. 13. It has also been disputed and omitted by many recent literary critics of the gospel.[83] If, however, the evidence of the best texts is followed (these have $\mu\acute{\epsilon}$ as the object of the asking in the subordinate clause and a stressed $\dot{\epsilon}\gamma\acute{\omega}$ in the main clause),[84] the verse will be preserved as original. In v. 13, praying in the name of Jesus is generally discussed and the unlimited assurance that whatever the disciples might ask, Jesus would do it ($\tauο\tildeυ\tauο$), in order to glorify the Father. In v. 14, however, Jesus, as the one who is asked and who carries out the request, is at the centre. This verse therefore has the purpose of making it more precise, clear and emphatic that Jesus himself continues to be active on behalf of the disciples. This, of course, is the specifically Johannine concern in the interpretation of the traditional statement about the hearing of prayer.

14:15   Many recent commentaries begin a new section at this point, entitled 'the demand made by love'. In so doing, their authors have clearly overlooked the fact that what is required here is not that the demands made by love should be met, but that Jesus' commandments (vv. 15 and 21) or his word or words (v. 23) should be kept. The love of Jesus and the Father are mentioned in the promise made in vv. 21b–c and 23b with the aim of emphasizing the *key-word* 'love' (that has not been used up to v. 14).[85] But this is hardly sufficient reason for beginning a new section, all the more especially since, from v. 18 onwards, the theme of Jesus' 'coming' and of the Father's and the Son's 'coming and making their home with' men (v. 23) is equally important. I therefore decided to make a division after v. 17 and to begin a new section with v. 18, which goes back to Jesus' announcement in v. 3 that he would come again and which in this way opens the second part of the discourse. The recapitulation in v. 28 confirms the correctness of this division.

What is the meaning of 'keeping the commandments' in John?[86] The repetition of these ἐντολαί (cf. verse 21) with λόγος or λόγοι (v. 23 and especially the concluding v. 24) ought to prevent us from thinking in this context of moral precepts and especially of the 'new commandment' of love (because of the plural form).[87] The 'word', which is not Jesus' own word, but which comes from the one who sent him (v. 24), is related to the whole of Jesus' activity in the sphere of revelation (see 8:28, 31, 43, 51; 12:48ff) and the demand τηρεῖν τὸν λόγον of Jesus refers to faith (8:51f; 15:20; cf. 17:6). The evangelist might, then, have had the disciples' constancy in faith in mind in this admonition in v. 15, together with all the demands that this makes on Christian existence. If this is so, then the statement means, in this context, that Jesus will do everything with his Father, but that he also expects his disciples to remain close to him in love and faithfulness.

14:16   Subject to this condition, Jesus makes them another promise affecting their life on earth. It is that, in answer to his prayer, the Father will give them 'another Paraclete', so that he may be with them always. This is the first of five sayings about the Paraclete made in the farewell discourse – and nowhere else (see also 14:26; 15:26; 16:7b–11, 13f). The whole problem of these sayings, which are marked by the term ὁ παράκλητος, for the Holy Spirit, will be discussed in detail in a later excursus (Excursus 16). Here, however, it is important to point out that these sayings were not interpolated into the structure of the farewell discourse, as is commonly suggested, like already polished stones. On the contrary, each of them has a special, irreplaceable function to perform in its own context. This is immediately borne out, in the case of the discourse in Chapter 14, by the second saying about the Paraclete in 14:26.[88] I shall therefore not follow any theory of interpolation. I prefer to accept a tradition of the Paraclete that the evangelist (and his school) found in existence and expressed as a statement about the Paraclete.

The κἀγώ at the beginning is in accordance with the expectation of the disciples ('And I, for my part . . .'), but it is also connected with the ἐγὼ ποιήσω of v. 14. Jesus intends to pray with his Father for the disciples ('pray' here is ἐρωτήσω) and the Father will give them the Spirit of truth. In Chapter 14, it is the Father who gives (v. 16) or sends (v. 26) the Spirit; in 15:26 and 16:7, Jesus himself is the one who sends the Spirit. There is no great material distinction here (see παρὰ τοῦ πατρός in 15:26), but the presentation in Chapter 14 would seem to be more original. The Spirit who is promised, is moreover, called 'another Paraclete' (the predicative construction: 'another than' or a 'different one from' the Paraclete is laboured[89]). This must mean that Jesus is describing himself indirectly as the Paraclete. In 1 Jn 2:1, he functions as the heavenly Paraclete; in our present text, however, he may be presupposed as being the one who has so far functioned here *on earth* as the disciples' Paraclete. The emphatic assurance that that Spirit of truth will be with the disciples 'for ever' is, after all, based on Jesus' present departure from them and his going to the Father (v. 12d). His function hitherto as the disciples' Paraclete has been based on his care for his 'own' (cf. the discourse of the shepherd and the sheep and, later, the prayer in Chapter 17). This is, however, more presupposed than expressed. For the Paraclete, the preposition μετά with the genitive points to his presence and the protection and help that it affords (cf. 3:2; 8:29; 16:32; 17:2).

14:17   The description of the Paraclete who is promised as the 'Spirit of truth' is hardly provided as a variation, because the Paraclete is known by different names. It is a more precise definition.[90] It is, moreover, the term that was preferred by the Johannine community, a definition that was quite firmly established in the community as a description of the Holy Spirit (cf. 14:26). For the Johannine community, he was the Spirit who bore witness to the truth (cf. 1 Jn 5:6), who guided the disciples into all truth (16:13) and kept them from the 'spirit of error' (see 1 Jn 4:6). As the 'Paraclete' (for the formation of this word and its significance, see Excursus 16), the Spirit has several functions. He teaches the disciples and calls to mind what Jesus has taught (14:26). He bears witness to Jesus (15:26) and he 'proves' the world 'guilty' (16:8–11). None of these functions is, however, especially mentioned here. All that is done in this first saying about the Paraclete is that attention is drawn to the fact that he is given to the disciples and that his significance for the disciples in the world is emphasized. The community left behind by Jesus has to find its way in this strange world that is unbelieving and hostile (see 8:23; 12:25, 31; 13:1). It has also to understand itself as the community of Christ. To perceive in this statement only a theme of consolation would be too narrow an interpretation, although the 'Paraclete' can be understood as the 'comforter' according to one very early interpretation that is linguistically quite possible.[91] It is clear from the development of the evangelist's ideas that it was above all a question of strengthening the faith of the disciples in their tasks in the world. Jesus, returning to the Father, gives their activity support from heaven, but the Spirit of truth fills them inwardly and is a lasting help to them (παρ' ὑμῖν) in their self-assertion over the world. He also gives them constant inner strength (ἐν ὑμῖν).

The disciples' consciousness that they had been chosen (see 15: 16, 19) is reinforced by the clear division made between the 'Spirit of truth' and the 'world' and the essential assigning of the Spirit to the disciples. The world cannot receive the Spirit or take him into itself (λαβεῖν; cf. 7:39, 20:22) and it is not able to do this because it is inwardly incapable of doing it; the reason given for this is that it 'neither sees him nor knows him'. It has no organ by means of which it can grasp or understand him.[92] The disciples, however, 'know' him because they possess him inwardly and have a direct insight into him and certainty of him. This knowledge that they have of the Spirit is a knowledge of community with God based on their possession of that Spirit. This knowledge is referred to in an almost formally catechetical way in 1 Jn 3:24; 4:13. The 'spiritual' experience of the community and its understanding of itself and its consciousness of having been chosen, which are supported by that experience, are all included in the promise of the Paraclete.

The promise that the Spirit will 'dwell with them' and 'be in them'[93] should not be separated. It should rather be seen as a single figure of speech, in the sense that help and strength, as given by the Spirit, come from his permanent presence with and in the disciples. To ask whether the Spirit is promised to the community of the disciples as such or to individual disciples is to miss the point. Jesus addresses the disciples as a group (in the plural) and that group represents the later community of believers as well. He promises that group of disciples the protection of the Paraclete ($\pi\alpha\rho$' $\acute{\upsilon}\mu\tilde{\iota}\nu$). The $\grave{\epsilon}\nu$ $\acute{\upsilon}\mu\tilde{\iota}\nu$, however, refers not only to his presence in the community, but also to his inner presence in individual believers, since it is only in this way that it is possible to understand inwardly the Spirit and his activity.

6. Jesus' Return. The Community of Life and Love with Jesus and his Father (14:18–24)

[18]'I will not leave you desolate; I will come to you. [19]Yet a little while and the world will see me no more, but you will see me; because I live, you will live also. [20]In that day you will know that I am in my Father and you in me and I in you. [21]He who has my commandments and keeps them, he it is who loves me; and he who loves me will be loved by my Father and I will love him and manifest myself to him'. [22]Judas – not (the one with the surname) Iscariot – said to him: 'Lord, how is it that you will manifest yourself to us and not to the world?' [23]Jesus answered him and said, 'If a man loves me, he will keep my word and my Father will love him and we will come to him and make our home with him. [24]He who does not love me does not keep my words; and the word which you hear is not mine, but the Father's who sent me'.

The unity of thought in this part of the discourse is made clear by the theme of 'coming'. Jesus speaks of his coming in v. 18 and of his coming together with the Father to the one who keeps his word in v. 23. Since there has been no further reference since v. 3 to Jesus' coming to the disciples (even in the saying about the Paraclete!), it is clear that the second part of the logion in v. 2f is included here and that its meaning is more fully revealed. The new beginning in v. 18 is also characterized by the image of the disciples as 'orphans' which presupposes the death of Jesus. It is also possible that the idea of 'living' in v. 19 can be explained by this. The disciples are only apparently made orphans or left desolate; in reality they are shortly to experience a new community with Jesus that is deeper and more spiritual than in the past – a community of a 'familiar' kind with him and his Father. Judas' intervening question serves, like Philip's objection, to develop the thought further, but it probably also has an additional intention – to reject any objection to experiences of Easter that are only accessible to the disciples.

In this definition, one particular problem that arises loses some of its urgency. It is this: What is the relationship between the Paraclete who is promised and Jesus, who is to come himself to the disciples after Easter? Three possible solutions have been suggested: (a) The juxtaposition is quite consistent, since the function carried out by the Spirit can be distinguished from Jesus' function. The Paraclete helps and supports the disciples, but does not do away with their loneliness and their longing for Jesus. The threefold coming of the Spirit, of Jesus and of the Father with Jesus discloses a 'triadic' structure that the evangelist intended.[94] In this saying about the Paraclete, however, the stress is placed on the Spirit's dwelling with and being in the disciples, who do not appear as orphans and desolate. There is an undeniable tension and the sequence is also remarkable. (b) Jesus himself comes in the Spirit and Jesus' resurrection has the meaning in the fourth gospel of the communication of the Spirit (see 20:22). The sequence of sayings about the Paraclete can therefore be explained in the light of this theological understanding.[95] This view, however, cannot be inferred from the text. Ought it not to have been more clearly expressed? (c) According to the third attempt to find a solution to this problem, the promise of the Paraclete should be regarded, from the point of view of literary criticism, as a later insertion in the development of the gospel. It can therefore easily be removed, especially since v. 18 follows v. 15 quite appropriately.[96] The sayings about the Paraclete, however, can hardly be regarded as previously prepared stones that were introduced later (see above, v. 16). What is more, v. 26 also forms an organic part of this text. They can all claim, according to their individual functions, to be original.

If a division is made between vv. 17 and 18, the promise of the Paraclete and the saying about Jesus' coming are not so sharply in conflict with each other. Each has its own place in the literary structure of the text, the promise of the Spirit at the end of the first part, which dealt with Jesus' departure to the Father, and v. 18 at the beginning of the new part, which has the theme of Jesus' coming. The theological question about the relationship between the Paraclete and Jesus remains, but it does not hinder the progress of the thought. Each of the various theological aspects of the problem exists in its own right, but they do not have to be confronted with each other. The evangelist is clearly convinced both by the lasting unity of the disciples with Jesus and by the presence of the Spirit. It is unlikely that he wanted to identify the Spirit with Christ; even according to 20:22, 'Holy Spirit' is a gift given by the risen Christ.

14:18   The image of the orphan left desolate is not so remote from human experience that it is necessary to seek out every possible parallel.[97] Despite 13:33, with its form of address: 'Little children', the relationship between Jesus and his disciples should probably not be seen as that between a father and his children, since the name of 'father' is reserved exclusively for the Father of Jesus himself. The image is clearly used with the imminent death of Jesus in mind. It is sketched in very briefly and in a negative way, and it prepares the way for the statement: 'I will come to you', which is introduced without any conjunction. This coming of Jesus, mentioned as early as v. 3 but formulated in ways that can be differently interpreted, is now set forth in a more profound way, in which the death of Jesus can be understood as no more than a brief and unimportant interruption in the disciples' community with him.

14:19   The phrase 'yet a little while' goes back to the previous use of the same words in 13:33, but this time it is without the oppressive element for the disciples. Only the 'world' will not see him any more and the 'seeing' of the world (cf. v. 17) is directed towards what is external and in the foreground, whereas the eyes of faith can see more, and more deeply. With a deliberate use of the same verb ($\theta\epsilon\omega\rho\epsilon\tilde{\iota}\nu$[98]) in the same tense (the present), the disciples are promised a 'seeing' of Jesus that will be given to them as a result of their community with him. Confrontation with the unbelieving world ($\kappa\acute{o}\sigma\mu o\varsigma$) runs through the discourse as an undercurrent. It can already be detected in the saying about the Paraclete in v. 17. It is particularly striking in this part (for example, in Judas' question) and can still be discerned in the statement about peace (v. 27) and in Jesus' final words (vv. 30f). The members of the community are to reflect upon these profound words about their relationship of life and love with Jesus and the Father and they have to recognize that, because of their understanding and experience of faith, they are separated from the unbelieving world. An esoteric attitude is to some extent unmistakably present in the community, but it does not lead to a complete sealing off from the world (see v. 31).

The basis of the disciples' 'seeing' is to be found in their shared possession of life with Jesus – the $\acute{o}\tau\iota$ clause, after all, also includes the statement about the disciples.[99] The parallel with the saying about the Paraclete should also not be overlooked – the disciples know the Spirit of truth because he dwells in them and will be in them and for this reason they are also able to see Jesus, because he lives and they will live. The similarity between the two texts extends as far as the tenses of the verbs ($\mu\acute{\epsilon}\nu\epsilon\iota$ - $\acute{\epsilon}\sigma\tau\alpha\iota$ and $\zeta\tilde{\omega}$ - $\zeta\acute{\eta}\sigma\epsilon\tau\epsilon$). The rather surprising mode of expression can be more easily explained if we think of the evangelist writing the promise of the Paraclete, first and then being influenced by it in the discourse about Jesus' coming again when he formulated this. Since life is promised repeatedly in the gospel as a present possession for all who believe (cf. 3:36 and Excursus 12), the use of the future tense $\zeta\acute{\eta}\sigma\epsilon\tau\epsilon$ (with the variant $\zeta\acute{\eta}\sigma\epsilon\sigma\theta\epsilon$[100]) here is surprising. There are, however, no far-reaching theological conclusions to be drawn from this. The choice of tenses is not only determined by the demands of rhetoric, but also theologically justified. As the Son of God, who originally has life in himself from the Father (see 5:26), Jesus can only speak in the present tense: I live. The disciples, on the other hand, to whom Jesus mediates life, can be addressed as believers in the present (see 5:24 and elsewhere), and as men who will only receive life from the glorified Christ (see 17:2) in the future (see 6:57). In our present text, the second aspect suggested itself, since the period following the resurrection was clearly indicated. When the disciples see Jesus (again), they will encounter him as the living one and will possess the same life as that which he possesses. It is precisely because of this that they will also be able to 'see' him. The Easter experience is the subject of reflection in this statement and the disciples' 'seeing' of the risen Lord forms part of the expression of this experience. The evangelist is apparently rather naive in his depiction of this 'seeing' of Jesus on his return: Jesus 'showed' them his hands and his side and the disciples were glad when they 'saw' the Lord (20:20). Our present text, however, provides evidence that the evangelist was aware of the special nature of this 'seeing'. The encounter between Jesus and the disciples was an experience that was made possible by Jesus and was accepted in faith by the disciples. The choice of tenses for 'living' is also suitable as a way of indicating how that life and the community with Jesus that is established because of it continues – Jesus goes on living and, in the same way, no limit is set to the continued life of the community (see 11:25f). Without any new Easter experience, the 'seeing' at Easter becomes a lasting 'knowledge' (v. 20) in a community of love (v. 21).

14:20   On 'that day', that is, the day of Easter,[101] that true knowing, into which faith grows, begins (cf. 10:38). This statement also has references at many different levels. In the first place, the expression ἐκείνη ἡ ἡμέρα must go back to early Christian terminology referring to the parousia, but here it is used in the sense of the Johannine present eschatology and related to the day of Easter itself and the time that begins with Easter, in other words, the presence of salvation (see 16:23, 26; see also Vol. 2, pp. 426ff). The γνώσεσθε also looks back to the dialogue with Philip in 14:7–9. A dialectical process can be observed in the decline leading from that dialogue to the promise made here. In the dialogue, Jesus says: 'If you have known me, you will also know the Father' and then intensifies this statement with: 'Now (already) you know him.' In our present text, there is a promise: 'You will know that I am in my Father.' In faith, the disciples ought to be able to understand this in the presence of Jesus on earth (cf. vv. 10–11), but they will not really grasp it as a reality until they are confronted with the risen Lord. The statement contains a comforting encouragement: Your insufficient faith will then become a full knowledge in faith. Finally, even those who come later to believe ought also to know what true faith is and how it is made possible.

The content of the knowledge that the disciples will have is given in the ὅτι clause. In the first part of this clause, Jesus goes back to vv. 10a and 11a, but the phrase ἐγὼ ἐν τῷ πατρί μου also includes the idea that he has gone to the Father (see v. 12): that he has withdrawn from the world and is united with the Father in his previous glory (cf. 17:5). In the second part of the clause, the disciples' community with Jesus is described with the same formula that was previously used to describe the community between Jesus and his Father: 'You in me and I in you.' This analogy, which was previously only paralleled in the formula for union in the Eucharist with Christ (6:56), points to the fact that the disciples are closely connected not only with Jesus, but also, through him, with the Father (see 6:57). The disciples, in other words, share in Jesus' living community with the Father.

14:21   The community that was disclosed to the disciples after Easter is one that is founded on love and that reveals itself in love. In this verse, then, the theme of v. 15 is resumed: love reveals itself in keeping the commandments. This theme is, however, expressed in reverse order so that it leads up to the idea of love: He who has Jesus' commandments and keeps them is the one who loves him. This, however, is only the first sentence in this verse and it leads on at once to the statement that is really intended: 'He who loves me will be loved by my Father.' The whole verse confirms that the evangelist has the post-paschal period, in other words, the existence on earth of Jesus' disciples, in mind.[102] An essential precondition for the sending of the Holy Spirit and therefore for the concrete realization of Jesus' community with God is that the disciples should keep to Jesus' words and teachings. It is hardly possible to reject the evangelist's authorship of this pragmatic ethical theme, which is even more emphatically expressed in the first epistle – despite the fact that he is powerfully inclined to speak of a 'mystical' union with God. In any case, Jesus' 'commandments' are not more precisely defined here and the evangelist is clearly satisfied with the disciples' faith in Jesus, their faithfulness to his words and their loving response to the community with God that he offers them. The disciple who lives in this way will also be loved by the Father and in this way reach the same goal as Jesus (see vv. 3 and 6). The Father's love is placed in this position because the idea of finding one's way to the Father is the end-point of the development of the theme; it is only after saying this that Jesus assures the disciple who reaches this point that he will also love him and reveal himself to him. Jesus' revelation of himself on 'that day' precedes the disciples' efforts (see v. 19: θεωρεῖτέ με), but it is clear from our present text that it is also a permanent process. Jesus will reveal himself even more powerfully – and inwardly – to the disciple who turns in faith and love to his Lord in an attempt to carry out his commandments. The verb ἐμφανίζειν is not an early or a special word used only for the Easter event (note, however, Acts 10:40; Mk 16:9), but a powerful expression for 'making visible'[103] and this is certainly what it means here. Jesus will disclose himself more and more in love to the disciple who loves him and is loved by the Father.

14:22 Judas' question, which follows closely on this ἐμφανίζειν ἑαυτόν, makes the distance between the disciples and the 'world' quite evident. Jesus has been speaking about an inward manifestation of love; Judas, on the other hand, is asking about the outward manifestation of that love to the cosmos. The question implies a misinterpretation on the part of the disciple, but this is not (as it was in the case of Philip) exposed in this verse. The disciple expresses surprise[104] at the exclusion of the world from Jesus' revelation of himself.

This Judas, who is explicitly distinguished from 'the one with the surname Iscariot' (cf. 6:71), certainly belongs to the group of twelve as far as the evangelist is concerned (6:67, 70), but he is only mentioned in this verse in the gospel. A second Judas only appears, in the other evangelists' lists of apostles, in Lk 6:16, where he is called 'Judas (the son) of James' (James is presumably the name of this Judas' father). This Judas is named immediately before 'Judas Iscariot' in Luke's gospel. The same 'Judas of James' is placed together with 'Simon the Zealot' in Acts 1:13. It is clear, then, that the evangelist displays here, in our present text, a knowledge of the synoptics and especially of the Lukan tradition. Since the time of Origen,[105] the apostle Judas has been identified with the Thaddaeus named in the list in Mk 3:18: Mt 10:3 (the variant of this name is Lebbaeus). In the Syrian tradition, Thomas has the name Judas Thomas (see 11:16 and the commentary, Vol. 2) and is regarded as a twin brother of Jesus. In Jn 14:22, the text we are considering here, sy[sin] has Thomas, while sy[cur] has Judas Thomas. It is, however, unlikely that a better historical knowledge was preserved in the Syrian tradition.[106] In the tradition of the Church, a combination with the 'Lord's brother' Judas also came about (see Mk 6:3; Mt 13:55; this is probably also intended in Jude 1). Later, there was even greater confusion in the tradition.[107] All that can be said with certainty about the name in the fourth gospel is that a distinction is made between Judas and Thomas, and that Judas is not treated as one of the Lord's brothers who, according to 7:5, did not believe in Jesus.

There may be a historical apologetical concern behind Judas' question in this Johannine text. The same objection to the restriction of the risen Lord's appearances to the disciples can also be detected in Acts 10:40ff. Further evidence of this can also be found in the critical demand made by the pagan Celsius (*ca.* AD 180),[108] which is similar to that made by a later philosopher (probably the neo-Platonist Porphyry),[109] that Christ must have appeared to his enemies, and the presentation in the *Gospel of Peter* (*ca.* AD 150), according to which the guardians at the tomb and the Jewish elders observed Jesus emerging from the tomb (*Gospel of Peter*, 38–42). It may therefore be conjectured that the contemporary Jews, with whom the gospel of John was in conflict, were expressing an objection behind this question. The secondary tendency, however, still remains and the intermediate question above all results in giving Jesus the opportunity to speak even more clearly about the Father's love that is revealed to the disciples and of his and the Father's coming.

14:23   Jesus' reply to this question does not seem to deal directly with it. He at first repeats, with a slight variation, the assurance that the one who loves him and keeps his word will experience the Father's love. He then, however, goes beyond what he said in v. 21 and declares that both the Father and he will come to that disciple and make their home with him.[110] It is clear from the choice of words that this is the climax of the passage about Jesus' 'coming' which began in v. 18. The Father will also come, with Jesus, who reveals himself inwardly to the disciples, to them and they will be included in God's community of life and love. This, however, is not all. The statement in v. 2 about the 'many dwellings in the Father's house' is now fulfilled, but with a paradoxical change of emphasis: Jesus and his Father will 'make their home' with that disciple. The same word is used here in the singular ($\mu o\nu\acute{\eta}$) that was used in the plural in v. 2. The evangelist must have chosen the expression $\mu o\nu\grave{\eta}\nu$ $\pi o\iota\varepsilon\tilde{\iota}\sigma\theta\alpha\iota$, for which there is evidence in profane sources,[111] quite deliberately (cf., for example, his use of the simple verb $\mu\acute{\varepsilon}\nu\varepsilon\iota\nu$ for 'to stay' or 'remain' in 1:38). Our present text must therefore be to some extent an elaboration of the previous image of 'dwelling'. Exegetes have often commented on this; to give only one example: 'God's dwelling with his people was expressed in cultic terms in the Old Testament (Exod 25:8; 29:45: Lev 26:11). The fulfilment of this promise was expected to take place at the end of time (Ezek 37:26f; Zech 2:14; Rev 21:3, 22f). This dwelling is here included in a spiritualized way in the presence of the community.'[112] The disciples are now 'where Jesus is' (see v. 3), in the sphere of God's love. This does, however, not mean that this promise is ultimately fulfilled in this inward and spiritual community with Jesus and God. Since John has not lost sight of physical death and even uses, in 12:25f, the same phrase

'Where I am, there shall my servant be also' in the context of a martyr's death, he also clearly expects that the final revelation and sight of glory will take place in the heavenly world (see 17:24) and that Jesus will precede the disciples in entering that world. It is then that the Father will 'honour' the disciple who has followed Jesus in service (12:26c).

The negative formula with which the statement that began in v. 23 ends: 'He who does not love me does not keep my words' is an indirect reply to Judas' question. It can hardly have been the evangelist's intention, after making this promise, to warn the disciples. It is, however, obvious that the 'world' does not heed or observe Jesus' words. It neither loves nor understands him (cf. 8:42) and therefore Jesus cannot and does not wish to reveal himself to it.

14:24   The idea that Jesus' word is not his own, but the Father's who sent him is repeated here in an almost stereotyped manner and helps to confirm that what is said in this verse, including the negative statement discussed briefly above, is directed towards the unbelieving world. This idea predominates in Jesus' controversy with the unbelieving Jews (7:16; 8:26, 28; 12:49f; cf. 3:11, 32; 15:22f) and it recurs again and again in Jesus' statements as an apology. The world cannot therefore complain if Jesus does not appear to it. Since, however, the disciples are addressed in Jesus' word ('the word which you hear'), this word may also refer to the positive promise in v. 23, which the disciples should 'remember' (see 2:22; 12:16; see also 14:26). As a whole, this verse has the effect of a cadence and forms a resounding conclusion to this main part of the entire discourse.

7. Concluding Words (14:25–31)

[25]'These things I have spoken to you, while I am still with you. [26]But the Counsellor, the Holy Spirit, whom the Father will send in my name, he will teach you all things and bring to your remembrance all that I have said to you. [27]Peace I leave with you; my peace I give to you; not as the world gives do I give to you. Let not your hearts be troubled, neither let them be afraid. [28]You heard me say to you, "I go away and I will come (again) to you". If you loved me, you would have rejoiced, because I go to the Father; for the Father is greater than I. [29]And now I have told you before it takes place, so that when it does take place, you may believe. [30]I will no longer talk much with you, for the ruler of this world is coming. He has no power over me; [31]but the world should know that I love the Father and do as the Father has commanded me. Rise, let us go hence.'

14:25   The conclusion of this discourse, at least as far as its fundamental theme is concerned, is marked by the expression ταῦτα λελάληκα ὑμῖν, which recurs frequently in the following discourses (15:11; 16:1, 4, 6, 25, 33). The comment that Jesus has spoken these things to the disciples while he was still with them also has a theological significance, because it marks the end of his internal instruction of the disciples as well as the end of his public proclamation before the world in 12:36b. Jesus himself draws attention to the importance of what he says in his physical presence and, in the following verse (26) observes that the Paraclete will call to mind what he has said.[113] What is also expressed in the present verse is that his words are limited by the ability of the disciples to understand them; they continue to be 'cryptic' (see 16:25) and their deeper meaning remains hidden from them.

14:26   It is the Paraclete who will 'teach all things' to the disciples. This second saying about the Paraclete is directly connected with the previous statement and provides an antitype ($\delta\acute{\epsilon}$) to the present situation, in which the disciples' understanding is incomplete. The saying is indeed so completely in accordance with the present text that it has to be attributed in its existing form to the evangelist himself. In such a relatively short discourse, it was not possible for Jesus to say everything and certainly not possible for him to express everything completely comprehensibly; for this reason, he leaves further instruction to the Paraclete. This 'teaching', which formed part of the authentic exposition of Scripture in Judaism and, moreover, entitled the 'teacher of righteousness' in Qumran to interpret the present and the future prophetically,[114] is, for John, an event of revelation. The revelatory activity of Jesus on earth is also described in the gospel as 'teaching' (7:16f, 28; 8:28, etc.). The Paraclete, then, simply continues Jesus' revelation, not by providing new teachings, but only by taking what Jesus himself 'taught' to a deeper level (cf. also 16:13). The second function ascribed to the Paraclete, that of calling to mind everything that Jesus has said himself, is very closely related to this first function of 'teaching' and indeed all that it really does is to make more explicit ($\varkappa\alpha\acute{\iota}$ is used in an explanatory sense) the content of his teaching. The Paraclete is also called the 'Holy Spirit' in this saying, not because the adjective[115] has an important content here, but rather because this term was simply the most usual in the practice of the early Church (cf. also 1:33; 20:22). The evangelist follows this tradition, but at the same time interprets the activity of the Holy Spirit above all as a disclosure of Jesus' proclamation to the community. This is the special understanding of the evangelist, who thus situates his gospel in the proper perspective and justifies it.

In this saying about the Paraclete, we are told of the 'sending' of the Spirit by the Father; he is sent in the same way as Jesus himself was sent from the Father. There are only two other comparable texts in the NT where such an expression occurs. The first of these is Gal 4:6, in which Paul goes on, after speaking of the sending of the Son of God (4:4), to say that God has sent ($\dot{\epsilon}\xi\alpha\pi\acute{\epsilon}\sigma\tau\epsilon\iota\lambda\epsilon\nu$) the Spirit of his Son into our hearts. The second is 1 Pet 1:12, in which it is said of those who proclaim the gospel that they brought news of God's salvation 'in the Holy Spirit sent ($\dot{\alpha}\pi\sigma\sigma\tau\alpha\lambda\acute{\epsilon}\nu\tau\iota$) from heaven'. This second text is evidence of the possibility of such language in early Christianity and, what is more, as in the case of John, in connection with the proclamation. The Pauline text is of relevance to John, because the sending of the Son of God is equated with the mission of the Spirit. In v. 24, there was reference to the 'Father who sent me' (with the same verb $\pi\acute{\epsilon}\mu\pi\epsilon\iota\nu$); in John, the sending of the Spirit is regarded to some extent as a continuation of the sending of the Son. Jesus says: The Father will send him 'in my name'. One is tempted to translate: 'in my place', because the Paraclete is in fact a kind of representative 'in the place' of Jesus (cf. v. 16), but the idea behind it is that Jesus wants to send the Paraclete to the disciples and therefore asks the Father for him (cf. again v. 16).[116]

The question that caused difficulty for later theologians, namely whether a promise was made in this statement about the Paraclete (as in 16:13) to the disciples who were present at that time (that is, the 'apostles') that they would be especially enlightened by the Holy Spirit, or whether he would be active in teaching the whole community, presents us with a false choice. In this and the following farewell discourses, the disciples who were present at that time are addressed, partly in the situation before Jesus' departure, but mainly also as representatives of the future community. In the case of this promise of the Paraclete, the second is most likely, especially as an 'anointing' (by the Holy Spirit) is attributed to all believers in 1 Jn 2:20, 27 as well, which 'teaches them about everything'. This does not mean that those who are called to proclaim the gospel are not to rejoice in the special help of the Spirit (this certainly formed part of the evangelist's self-understanding and that of his school). It does mean, however, that all believers are included within the promise of the Spirit.[117]

14:27 Instead of the usual 'go in peace', said on taking leave (see, for example, 1 Sam 1:17; 20:42; 29:7, etc.), Jesus bids farewell to his disciples with the gift of peace. This promise of peace, even in the synoptic tradition, means more than a mere wish or good wishes. 'Peace' is eschatological salvation (cf. Is 52:7; Ezek 37:26), offered and given to man with Jesus' coming (Lk 2:14; 19:38, 42; see also Acts 10:36), gained by individuals with his word (see Mk 5:34 par.; Lk 7:50) and also present in the proclamation of the disciples (see Lk 10:5f/Mt 10:13). In Luke, at least in the majority of texts,[118] the risen Christ greets the disciples with 'Peace to you!' (24:36) and this is yet another link binding this evangelist and John closely together, since in the latter the risen Lord also repeats the same greeting several times (20:19, 21, cf. 26). If, then, peace is really Jesus' gift after his resurrection, nothing else can be intended in our present text. He does not give his disciples his peace here, specially for the period following his passion, but for the whole of subsequent time during which they will externally ('in the world') continue to have 'tribulation' (16:33). The present tenses show that Jesus' peace is his lasting gift ($\delta i \delta \omega \mu \iota$) on leaving them ($\dot{\alpha} \phi i \eta \mu \iota$).

It is, moreover, 'his' peace that he leaves with them. It is also he who gives it and it is by him that the nature of this peace is determined. Cyril of Alexandria believed that this peace was the same as the Holy Spirit mentioned in the preceding verse.[119] This interpretation is wrong, but it reveals a better understanding of the text than an explanation which narrows this peace down to a purely interior and spiritual state.[120] Christ's peace surrounds the disciples and is capable of exercising many spiritual effects. It is the all-embracing sphere of his life (see v. 19), his love (vv. 21, 23), his joy (15:11; 16:22; 17:13). In Paul's letters, peace is the striving of the Spirit (Rom 8:6), the fruit of the Spirit (Gal 5:22), and, together with justice and joy, the manifestation of the kingdom of God (Rom 14:17). John attributes different functions to the Spirit, but he also recognizes that peace is a special characteristic of the time of the Spirit.

The world does not give such peace. Does it give peace at all? The negative formulation of the present text, which is reminiscent of the contrasts in vv. 17, 19 and 22, is probably intended to deny that the world can give peace. There is no indication that John was thinking here of the *pax romana* or some similar form of peace which the world might give. The cosmos was for him closed to the peace of Christ. The text also contains a restriction to the unworldly kingdom of Christ (18:36) and a rejection of all attempts to find peace or to create it in the outside world. The aim of the Johannine community is to be a centre and a sign of true peace.

The admonition: 'Let not your hearts be troubled, neither let them be afraid' is not a description of the way in which Christ's peace ought to be realized. On the contrary, it goes back to the beginning of the discourse (v. 1). After everything that Jesus has already said about the disciples' community with him and with God and about their security in his love and peace, he here repeats his initial admonition very emphatically and reinforces it with the encouragement not to be afraid. δειλιᾶν (which only occurs here in the NT) belongs to the vocabulary of fear and fear (φόβος) accompanies the disciples until they see the risen Lord (20:19). It is also an admonition to the community to overcome all fear in the presence of Christ (cf. 16:33: θαρσεῖτε).

14:28   In summing his discourse up once again under the headings 'I go away' and 'I will come to you' (cf. vv. 2f, 4–17, 18–24), Jesus clearly intends to lead on to the statement that follows in this verse; in it, he calls on his disciples to rejoice that he is going away to the Father. This joy should be born of their love for Jesus, which calls for reflection about and keeping his words (see vv. 15, 21, 23). There can be no doubt that the evangelist wants to stress not only peace – the peace that Jesus gives – but also joy as the fundamental attributes of the Christian community. The argument that the Father is greater than Jesus himself preoccupied the Fathers of the Church especially during the period of Christological controversy.

'Orthodox' exegesis of this text in the patristic period followed two courses: (a) The Trinitarian explanation is represented, among others, by Tertullian, Athanasius, Basil of Caesarea, Gregory Nazianzen and John Chrysostom.[121] According to their being and in themselves, the Father and the Son are equal, but because of the relationship between the divine persons, the Father is 'greater'. He is only predicatively greater, in so far as the Son always proceeds from the Father and the Father does not proceed from the Son. (b) The explanation based on the incarnation and the kenosis of the Son of God is represented above all by Cyril of Alexandria in his long exposition of this text. It can be briefly summarized as follows: While the Son was still in the form of a slave, he called the Father greater and as man he was subordinate to him.[122] Similarly, Augustine said: 'In the form of a servant, the Son of God is the lesser . . . the Father is the greater; after which the Word was made flesh.'[123] Even this explanation, however, is unsatisfactory, because the statement is not made sufficiently intelligible within its context. It is none the less preferable to the first explanation, in that it gives emphasis to Jesus' way to the

Father. Its disadvantage is that it is too subject to dogmatic thought and too influenced by the need to combat Arianism.

An explanation based on subordinationism, and therefore asserting that the Son is really lower than the Father (the classical Arian explanation and the position adopted by many more recent exegetes), is not relevant to the gospel of John, in which the voluntary subordination of the Son to the Father is dialectically combined with the Son's claim to equal fulness of life (5:26), the same divine being (1:1; see the commentary, Vol. 1), and the same glory (17:5) as the Father. What, then, does this statement mean in the present context? Does it perhaps mean that the Son's inferiority is now at an end? This is not what is said. According to the text, the Father is still the 'greater' and elsewhere in the gospel of John being 'greater' implies a real superiority, although on closer inspection it is a superiority in ability, in the function that is performed or in power to command (see 4:12; 8:53; 13:16; see also 1:51; 5:20; 10:29). The Father is 'greater' because everything that happens originates with him and is taken to its end by him, including the Son's mission and glorification. It is certain, then, that the glorification of the Son also lies behind 14:28 (cf. 13:32), but this does not concern only the Son – it also concerns, as the prayer in Chapter 17 shows (see the commentary below, especially under v. 2), those who are entrusted to him. The Father, who is 'greater' than the Son, will prove himself to be greater in the glorification of the Son, which at the same time fulfils everything of which Jesus has previously spoken for the disciples. What was said at the beginning, that Jesus is going only to prepare a place for the disciples (v. 2), also applies to this statement. It also contains an echo of the later idea expressed in 16:7: 'It is to your advantage that I go away.' The emphasis, of course, is different, since Jesus and his glorification are more central ('if you loved me'), but the statement is also made for the sake of the disciples, so that their joy may be fulfilled by their sharing in Jesus' glory (cf. 15:11).[124]

14:29   The admonition to believe (v. 1b) is echoed here at the end. The perfect tense εἴρηκα is in keeping with the perfect λελάληκα in v. 25 and therefore looks back at the whole discourse. The event to which Jesus refers can only be his departure. It is now no longer surrounded by fear, because Jesus has told them about it in advance – this is, of course, the same theme as that in the announcement of the betrayal in 13:19. After pointing to the future, Jesus once again turns to the present situation.

14:30   Jesus will no longer talk much[125] with the disciples, because the 'ruler of this world' is approaching. If the discourses that follow in Chapters 15–16 do not belong to the original material of the gospel, the readers can learn nothing more about a dialogue between Jesus and his disciples before his arrest. But 'no longer much' cannot refer to the long discourses in Chapters 15–16. One explanation for this surprising situation is that the evangelist, who wanted to conclude the farewell discourse with 14:31 (see v. 25 and the call to go away in v. 31b), was thinking of short dialogues on the way to the garden of Gethsemane (18:1), but said nothing about this because he had already said everything that was essential. This comment may have been a point of departure for the editor to add further discourse, although if he did so, he did not do it very adroitly.

The 'ruler of this world' is already known to readers of the gospel from 12:31 (see the commentary above), but in contrast to that triumphant statement this text is confusing, since it says that he is coming and is already on the way. The evangelist may be thinking concretely of Judas, who is already 'coming' with the band to arrest Jesus (18:3)[126] and is, for him, an instrument of Satan (cf. 13:27). As the name 'ruler of this world' shows, the formulation is Johannine, but there may objectively be a memory of the text in Mk 14:41f behind the evangelist's words: 'The hour has come . . . see, my betrayer is at hand.' The 'power of darkness' (cf. Lk 22:53) is at work.

It is, however, characteristic of John at once to resist the idea (using $\varkappa \alpha i$ in opposition) that the adversary has any power over Jesus or any claim to power. The expression $\check{\varepsilon}\chi\varepsilon\iota\nu \ \tau\iota \ \check{\varepsilon}\nu \ \tau\iota\nu\iota$ (= to have something in someone), which is reminiscent of the rabbinical way of speaking, although there is also evidence of it in profane Greek texts,[127] is also reminiscent of similar Johannine expressions (cf. 3:15; 5:39; 16:33?; 20:31). It comes closest to the meaning in Jn 19:11; 'You would have no power over me ($\varkappa\alpha\tau$' $\dot{\varepsilon}\mu o\tilde{\upsilon}$) . . .'. Jesus hands himself voluntarily over to his opponents (cf. 18:4ff) in order to carry out his Father's task (cf. 10:18).

14:31   The idea introduced by $\dot{\alpha}\lambda\lambda$' $\check{\iota}\nu\alpha$ can best be understood as an independent sentence (cf. 1:8; 9:3; 13:18; 15:25) extending as far as $\pi o\iota\tilde{\omega}$.[128] The world may know his love for the Father by the fact that Jesus allows the ruler of the world, at least outwardly, to have his way. That love is demonstrated ($\varkappa\alpha i$ used epexegetically) by Jesus' doing what the Father has commissioned him to do. This is an idea that occurs frequently in the gospel and is in accordance with Johannine Christology (see especially 8:28; 10:18; 12:49). On the other hand, it is surprising that it is the 'world' that is to know Jesus' love for the Father. This is not, however, the same, sharply dualistic concept of $\varkappa\acute{o}\sigma\mu o\varsigma$ as the one found in vv. 17, 19 and 22, but it is an idea of the world that is within the scope of Johannine thought, which is not completely in accordance with the fundamentally negative gnostic judgment about the world.[129] The basic statement expressed in 3:16 and the prospect revealed in 17:23 both provide evidence of this and the present text is also particularly close to 8:28, according to which the Jews, who stubbornly resist faith, may know Jesus' sovereignty because of his exaltation. An explanation that is similar to that which can be provided for the present text can also be given for the statement in 8:28, namely that Jesus is only doing what is in accordance with the Father's will. A conciliatory prospect is therefore revealed after the harsh statement about the world's ruler. It is clear that the world of men can still know, on the basis of the event of the cross, that Jesus is the one who was sent to save it (cf. 12:32).

The signal to go is undoubtedly meant to be taken, not metaphorically,[130] but literally. In 2:16 and 7:3, $\dot{\varepsilon}\nu\tau\varepsilon\tilde{\upsilon}\theta\varepsilon\nu$ refers to a change of place and, in 19:18, it refers to a position. It is only in 18:36 that it refers to the transcendent sphere and has no verb of movement. Here too, a memory of Mk 14:42 may play a part. The most suitable continuation of this passage is 18:1ff. The parts of the discourse that come in between the end of Chapter 14 and the beginning of Chapter 18 have now, however, to be explained from the point of view of literary criticism.

The Further Farewell Discourses (Chapters 15–16)
The Literary Problem of the Farewell Discourses in Jn 15–16 (and the Prayer in Jn 17)

If the gospel of John is only seen as a work with a fairly long genesis (see Vol. 1, pp. 44–74), then all earlier attempts to fit the lengthy discourses in Jn 15–16 into the situation of departure (14:31) have to be rejected. On the way to the garden on the other side of the Kidron valley (18:1), they are not outwardly marked in any special way as dialogues between Jesus and his disciples (it is only in 18:1 that it is stated explicitly that Jesus 'went forth' with the disciples) and they cannot be seen as such dialogues simply on the basis of their content. Even if it is assumed that they are a literary composition, however, several solutions suggest themselves.

1. Hypotheses on the Basis of Literary Criticism

The least satisfactory hypotheses are those suggesting a change in the sequence of texts in Chapters 13–17 and the restoration of an originally more meaningful arrangement of those texts. If such a hypothesis is accepted, the question still remains as to why the original order was not preserved by the final editor. J. H. Bernard assumed that certain pages had become displaced (see Vol. 1, pp. 53f) and suggested the following sequence: 13:31a; 15; 16; 13:31b–38; 14; 17.[1] This relatively simple solution, however, fails not only because the whole theory of the displacement of pages is questionable, but also on the basis of the content of the discourses themselves – the announcement of Jesus' departure (13:33) is already presupposed in Chapters 15–16 and everything essential is already said, so that the discourse in Chapter 14 would be too late. The same objection also applies to the other hypotheses.[2] R. Bultmann's attempt to reconstruct this section of the gospel[3] was based on the idea that the farewell prayer (Chapter 17) should be at the beginning. He therefore transposes the prayer with an introduction (from 13:1) to 13:30, allows 13:31–35 to follow and then joins 15–16; 13:36—14:31 to this as farewell discourses and dialogues. The prayer in Chapter 17 poses a very special problem (see below), but there is no very strong reason for placing it at the beginning, especially in view of the fact that 13:31f fits well into the present context (see the commentary *ad loc.*).

We have therefore to follow the hypothesis that Chapters 15–16 (and possibly also Chapter 17) were a later insertion. The simplest explanation, which is also followed by most recent commentators, is that this was done by the editor in Chapter 13 (see the commentary above). At the same time, however, other questions arise at once. Can the long discourses in Chapters 15–16 be seen as a single coherent composition? Is there, in other words, only one 'second' farewell discourse or do several discourses have to be distinguished?[4] If so, how ought they to be marked from each other? What smaller textual units can be distinguished? How are they related to each other? How can they be classified with regard to longer discourses?

2. Attempt at a Provisional Elucidation

There is a striking relationship between the discourse in Chapter 16 (from v. 4b or 5 onwards) and that in chapter 14.[5] This also concerns a departure (vv. 5f) and refers to the advantage to the disciples of Jesus' departure (v. 7), to the short period of separation and to the fact that they will see each other again quite soon (vv. 16–22). It also directs attention to the Paraclete and his activity (vv. 7–11, 13–15), makes certain promises to the disciples, especially that their prayer will be heard (vv. 23–28) and ends with the idea of peace (v. 33). The language is rather different and there are certain new aspects (especially with regard to the Paraclete), but the effect of this discourse is that of a variant of the farewell discourse in Chapter 14.

But what is the situation with regard to the discourse in Chapter 15? The most striking characteristic of that discourse is the change in perspective – Jesus' gaze goes beyond the period of separation directly to the future existence of the disciples in community. In this respect, it is in fact a continuation of the 'farewell discourse' of Chapter 14. It is, however, not characterized as a continuation, but begins abruptly with the figurative discourse of the vine and the branches. The question therefore arises as to whether it is a subsequent addition by the editor, using material left by the evangelist. This is certainly possible in itself (see Vol. 1, pp. 72f), but it is still necessary to examine this whole question more closely, with particular attention to the nature, language, ideas and intentions of the discourse itself. Such an examination reveals that the discourse is the work of an editor, in which certain material left by the evangelist himself is employed (see especially the figurative discourse at the beginning).[6] It is not difficult to understand the reasons for this editorial insertion. On the basis of the farewell discourse in Chapter 14, the editor or editors wanted to address, admonish and strengthen the community in its existing situation with words used by the departing Lord. This will be made clear in detail in the commentary below.

The further discourse in Chapter 16 may also have come about as the result of similar endeavours. Since, however, it goes back to the situation of departure and also refers to that departure (in a similar way to Chapter 14) as a point of departure for an address to the future community, it would appear rather to be a 're-reading' of the original farewell discourse, a reconsideration and a retelling, with the existence of the community in the world (see 16:33) especially in mind. This question will also be examined in detail in the commentary (it is not so important as the previous question), but, in the meantime, we can say with some certainty that, since the evangelist hardly ever repeats himself in this way elsewhere in the gospel, this discourse is probably the editorial work of a disciple or disciples.

The problem of the prayer in Chapter 17 is different again. If it is true that 18:1 originally followed 14:31, this prayer, which forms a complete unity in itself, can only have been inserted into the literary composition at a later stage. Its contents are certainly related to the content of the saying in 13:31 and the question therefore arises as to whether it is not connected to that saying. But in that case, how is it connected? In the prayer, Jesus asks to be glorified, whereas, in 13:31, his glorification is mentioned as a fact. Because of this, the prayer can be placed either immediately before or else after the saying. The saying could therefore have been an external reason for the idea of that prayer.

On closer inspection, however, another tendency can be discerned – that of Jesus' praying for his own glorification only with the disciples or the community that they represent in mind.[7] As a literary genre, the triumphant statement in 13:31f should be distinguished from the prayer of intercession in Chapter 17. From the editorial point of view, the ταῦτα ἐλάλησεν in 17:1 is important – the expression in the aorist is a statement concluding the discourse that immediately precedes it (cf. 8:20; 12:36). It can, if necessary, be made to follow 14:31, but then comes into conflict with ταῦτα εἰπών in 18:1. It therefore undoubtedly goes back to the editor and refers to the discourses in Chapters 15–16. It is probably even more closely related to the discourse in Chapter 16, because it powerfully reflects the situation of the community of disciples ἐν τῷ κόσμῳ. It is still possible that the editor found a prayer of this kind in the evangelist's material, but we have also to take into account the possibility that it goes back to the school of disciples. This too will be considered in the exegetical commentary.

3. Demarcation and Structure of the Discourse in Chapter 15

Most exegetes regard Jn 15:1–16, 4a as a single, connected discourse, with a decisive turning point between vv. 17 and 18. From v. 18 onwards, Jesus does not speak about his unity with the disciples or the commandment to love that he imposes on them, but about the fact that they are different from the world, which hates and persecutes them as it has him, and that they must remain separate from it. His speaking about the unbelieving world creates a link between this second half of the discourse in Chapter 15 and the section in 16:8–11. It is therefore possible to ask whether the second part of Chapter 15 does not belong more closely to the section in Chapter 16. J. Becker (and Bultmann before him) concluded from this that the sections of the discourse should be arranged in the following way: 15:1–17; 15:18—16:15; 16:16–33.[8] This conclusion can, however, be proved wrong by careful structural analysis. Both formal aspects and similarities in content between the first and the second parts of Chapter 15 point to the correctness of the generally accepted arrangement.

(a) The frequently-repeated phrase ταῦτα λελάληκα ὑμῖν constitutes, to some extent, a structural element, dividing the passage up.[9] It occurs in 14:25; 15:11; 16:1, 4, 6, 25 (with the addition of ἐν παροιμίαις), 33. The rapid succession in 16:1, 4, 6 is particularly striking. It would seem that 16:1 forms the conclusion to the whole section 15:18–27, that this conclusion is emphasized and clarified by the announcement that the disciples will be prosecuted by the synagogue (16:2–3), and that the whole section is terminated by the repetition of the same words (16:4a). 16:6a is a resumption, as it were in brackets, of the previous section and 16:6b is a transitional statement. 16:5 is clearly the beginning of a new discourse, dealing with Jesus' departure, the coming of the Paraclete, and the situation of the disciples in the world. The phrase 'I have said all this' therefore marks the end of one discourse (14:25; 16:33) or of one unit of discourse (15:11) and, with the repetition of the phrase in 16:1, 4, 6, almost certainly points to the fact that the end of one discourse is reached in Chapter 15.

(b) It is not advisable to think of 15:1–17 and 15:18–27 as two different discourses because there are lines connecting the two sections and brackets between them:

(α) The contrasting verbs 'love–hate' are very characteristic of Johannine thought; for example, in the gospel, 3:19 can be compared with 3:20, and in the first epistle with 2:9–11; 3:13–15; 4:19–21. This dualism, especially when it is presented in terms of the contrast between light and darkness, is connected in 1 Jn with the commandment to love the brethren. The same principle is stressed in 15:12, 17 as Jesus' instruction to his disciples.

(β) The same applies to the contrast between Jesus' disciples (or community) and the world. In the gospel, this contrast concerns Jesus himself and the unbelieving Jews first (8:23; cf. 12:46–48; 13:1), but, from the farewell discourse onwards, it also concerns the community of the disciples (16:8, 20, 33; 17:6, 9, 14, 16) and, in the long epistle, the community (2:15–17; 3:1b, 13f; 4:4f; 5:5, 19).

(γ) The idea that the disciples are chosen ('out of the world') forms a link between the first part of Chapter 15 (v. 16) and the second part of the same chapter (v. 19).

(δ) There are also other connective phrases, although these are not so clear: τηρεῖν τὰς ἐντολάς (v. 10) or τὸν λόγον (v. 20) and δοῦλοι (vv. 15 or 20).

(c) The two parts are also closely connected with each other, because Jesus is, in both, the inner reason for the community of the disciples or their separation from the world. The community of the disciples is brought about by their 'abiding in Christ' and 'abiding in his love', and the world hates the community because of their bond with Jesus ('because of my name', v. 21).

I therefore regard Chapter 15 as a discourse conceived as a single whole, admonishing the disciples to make their unity with Jesus fruitful and to endure the hostility of the world. The sub-division of 15:1–17 has been the subject of considerable debate. Several scholars have suggested an incision after v. 8, because the image of the vine and the branches ends here and the discourse changes to the call: 'Abide in my love!'[10] We have, however, already considered the structural element in v. 11: ταῦτα λελάληκα ὑμῖν which divides the passage. In addition, the μένειν ἐν ('abiding in') of the first verses is retained, but disappears after v. 10. Finally, the idea that the disciples' joy is to be full (v. 11) also marks a conclusion of a kind.[11]

The incision after v. 11 is confirmed by the following unit of discourse, which is marked by the commandment of Jesus to love one another. In v. 17, this commandment, mentioned at the beginning (v. 12), is once again resumed (inclusion). It is true that this short section is initiated by the mention in v. 10 of the 'commandments' of Jesus. This is the procedure, which is frequently to be observed, especially in 1 Jn, of mentioning a key-word or a theme at the end of a section that is expanded more fully in the following (association).[12] For the further development of this idea in vv. 1–11 and 12–17, see below in the commentary.

In the second part of the discourse, the world, with its quite different character and its hostility to Jesus' disciples, is contrasted with the community of Jesu. Up to v. 25, the structure is quite clear: the hatred of the world (vv. 18–19); the reason for this: the bond between the disciples and Jesus (vv. 20–21); the inexcusable sin of those who represent the 'world' and who have hated Jesus, despite his revelation in word and deed (vv. 21–25). The saying about the Paraclete that follows (vv. 26–27) appears to break the connection and has been regarded by many exegetes as an interpolation.[13] It is true to say that the theme of persecution is continued in 16:2–3, but it is also possible to view the situation differently. What, then, does this saying about the Paraclete mean, bearing above all its content in mind?

The Spirit of truth will bear witness to Jesus and so will the disciples. Those who were hostile to Jesus have not accepted his testimony that he was sent by the Father. They have accepted neither the testimony of his words, nor that of his actions. Now the Paraclete takes over the task of bearing witness and continues to do so, together with the disciples, who are to be strengthened and encouraged by the thought of the Paraclete. The statement about the exclusion of the disciples from the synagogue and their being killed because of religious convictions (16:2–3) refers to the situation at the time when the gospel was being written, when the Jewish authorities were taking harsh measures against apostates (cf. 9:22; 12:42). These verses give the impression of being additional and they may well have been written by another. In any case, the second concluding comment (16:4a) is, in contrast to 16:1, a later addition.[14] The discourse probably ended originally at 16:1.

For the structure and sub-division of Chapter 16, see the introduction to Chapter 2 below.

Chapter 1

An Admonitory Discourse: Bearing Fruit from Unity with Jesus
and Standing Firm against the World
(15:1—16:4a)

Perhaps the best way of explaining the resumption of the discourse in the gospel and its insertion at precisely this point is to compare it with the farewell discourse in Chapter 14. There are several reasons for believing that the editor or editors regarded this discourse as a suitable continuation of Jesus' farewell discourse and did so, moreover, on the basis of the ideas proposed in Chapter 14.

(a) In Jn 14:20, Jesus spoke of the inner community that would exist after Easter (cf. v. 19) between him and his disciples: ὑμεῖς ἐν ἐμοὶ κἀγὼ ἐν ὑμῖν. Jn 15:4 gives the impression of continuing this idea: μείνατε ἐν ἐμοί, κἀγὼ ἐν ὑμῖν. What Jesus promises in the farewell discourse is presupposed as fulfilled in the following discourse. At the same time, however, the consequence of this is an admonition to abide in this community and to bear fruit (see v. 5b).

(b) Following the promise, Jesus speaks in 14:21 of keeping his commandments: the man who keeps them is the one who loves him. This affirmation, which contains an admonition, is repeated in v. 23. In both texts, Jesus says that such a disciple will also be loved by his Father. This admonition to keep Jesus' commandments appears again in 15:9f. The Father is also mentioned here as the one who is glorified by the disciples' bearing much fruit (v. 8). Just as Jesus abides in his Father's love by keeping his Father's commandments, so too will the disciples abide in Jesus' love by keeping his commandments (v. 10). The Father is introduced into the figurative discourse of the vine and the branches as the vine-dresser (v. 1), whose entire concern is directed towards the bearing of abundant fruit (v. 2; cf. v. 8).

(c) The promise that prayer will be heard, which is mentioned in 14:13f (where it relates to Jesus), recurs in 15:7 and 15:16 (where it relates to the Father). In the second discourse, it is promised to the one who abides in Jesus and bears fruit.

(d) 14:23 is concerned with τηρεῖν τὸν λόγον of Jesus; here, however, we only find a variation on τὰς ἐντολάς (v. 21). The same phrase appears again in the section on the hatred of the world in Chapter 15, but extended to the disciples' word: 'If they kept my word, they will keep yours also' (15:20).

94

(e) The 'world' is mentioned as a negative factor in 14:17, 19, 22, 27 (cf. also the 'ruler of this world' in 14:30). It is as such excluded from Jesus' revelation at Easter and from the activity of the Spirit. This explains why the 'world' appears in the second half of Jn 15 as the opposing sphere and a hostile element. In 14:24, Jesus says: 'He who does not love me does not keep my words.' Jesus' disciples also participate in this experience (cf. 15:18, 20c).

(f) The sayings about the Paraclete are also to some extent related to each other in the two chapters. The disciples are promised the help and teaching of the Holy Spirit in the two sayings in Chapter 14. In the saying about the Paraclete at the end of the discourse in Chapter 15, the disciples are urged to stand firm against the world and to bear witness to Jesus. The Paraclete has a task not only within the community of disciples (Chapter 14), but also with regard to the world, to help the disciples in their activity in the world and in their persecution by the world.

The discourse in Chapter 15, then, clearly continues the farewell discourse, transfers it to the sphere of the community and applies it to that community by expressing openly the admonitions that are contained in Jesus' words of farewell. The easiest way of understanding it is to see it as having been given form, directly for the situation in which the community was placed, by editors who were disciples and shared the aim of their Master and made use of his words.

We must now look at the development of the ideas and the subdivision of the first part of the discourse (vv. 1–17). Within the units that have already been established, that is, vv. 1–11 and vv. 12–17, the thought develops in accordance with the linguistic and stylistic laws that can be studied elsewhere in Johannine discourses. The metaphor introduced by $\dot{\epsilon}\gamma\dot{\omega}$ $\epsilon\dot{\iota}\mu\iota$ in v. 1 is repeated in v. 5, but, on the basis of the exposition in v. 4, it is continued with 'you are the branches'. Attention is now drawn more emphatically to 'bearing fruit' (vv. 5b–6), which is, in any case, the most important idea. The disciple who abides in Jesus and his words is also promised that his prayer will be heard (v. 7), so that the Father will be glorified by an abundant bearing of fruit (v. 8). The expression at the end of v. 8: 'so that you may be my disciples' is the point of contact for the admonition to abide in Jesus' love by keeping his commandments (vv. 9–10). The concluding sentences continue the account, then, in an associative manner.

Only v. 3 does not come within the framework of the development of the thought directed towards 'bearing fruit' (vv. 2–4–5–8). It sounds like an incidental comment on the word $\varkappa\alpha\theta\alpha\dot{\iota}\rho\epsilon\iota$: 'You are already clean because of the word that I have spoken to you.' We have to take into account the possibility of its being an editorial gloss (cf. also 13:10b).

We can summarize the structure as follows:

The vine and the vine-dresser, vv. 1–2 (gloss, v. 3)
Admonition to abide in Jesus in order to bear fruit, v. 4
The vine and the branches, vv. 5–6, with a renewed admonition to abide in Jesus

Promise that prayer will be heard, v. 7, and glorification of the Father by
the bearing of abundant fruit, v. 8 (cf. v. 1)

Admonition to abide in Jesus' love by keeping his commandments, vv. 9–
10

Conclusion: the joy that comes to the disciples, v. 11.

In the unit consisting of vv. 12–17, the thought develops in an associative
manner. As we have seen, the idea of τὰς ἐντολάς in v. 10 is resumed in v. 12,
which expresses the commandment to love one another. We need do no more
here than name the words used in association: ἠγάπησα → v. 13 ἀγάπης; v. 13
τῶν φίλων → v. 14 φίλοι; (contrast:) v. 15 δούλους-φίλους; v. 15 ἐγνώρισα → v. 16
(thought-association) ἐξελεξάμην. In v. 16, ἔθηκα leads to recollection of the
idea of bearing fruit and the promise that prayer will be heard is once again
taken up. Finally, a repetition of Jesus' commandment in v. 17 forms the
inclusion.

1. The Figurative Discourse of the Vine and the Branches and the Closing Words (15:1.11)

[1]*I am the true vine and my Father is the vine-dresser.* [2]*Every branch of mine
that bears no fruit, he takes away and every branch that does not bear fruit he
cleans, that it may bear more fruit.* [3]*You are already made clean by the word
which I have spoken to you.* [4]*Abide in me and I in you. As the branch cannot
bear fruit by itself, unless it abides in the vine, neither can you, unless you abide
in me.* [5]*I am the vine, you are the branches. He who abides in me, and I in him,
he it is that bears much fruit, for apart from me you can do nothing.* [6]*If a man
does not abide in me, he is cast forth as a branch and withers; and the branches
are gathered, thrown into the fire and burned.* [7]*If you abide in me and my
words abide in you, ask whatever you will, and it shall be done for you.* [8]*By
this my Father is glorified, that you bear much fruit and so prove to be my
disciples.* [9]*As the Father has loved me, so have I loved you; abide in my love.*
[10]*If you keep my commandments, you will abide in my love, just as I have kept
my Father's commandments and abide in his love.* [11]*These things I have
spoken to you, that my joy may be in you and that your joy may be full.'*

15:1   The metaphorical discourse on the true vine and the branches begins
quite abruptly with the authoritative words ἐγώ εἰμι (see Excursus 8, Vol. 2,
pp. 79–89). I have chosen the very general term 'figurative' discourse to
describe this passage because it is neither a pure allegory nor what E.
Schweizer has called a 'literal discourse' (see Vol. 2, pp. 279f).[15] In contrast
to the other sayings using the ἐγώ εἰμι formula, and speaking figuratively, this
image is developed in a more powerful way (vv. 2–4–6). It would not be
difficult to make it into a coherent description similar to that of the shepherd
and the sheep in the 'cryptic' discourse in 10:1–5. The ἐγώ εἰμι sayings about
the door and the good shepherd are subsequent to this discourse and are
formally very similar to the discourse of the vine and the branches, even in the

twofold beginning of the ἐγώ εἰμι saying (15:1 and 5). There may perhaps even have been a description (provided by the evangelist himself) comparable to that in 10:1–5,[16] but a 'cryptic' discourse of the kind used by Jesus in the presence of unbelief would not be appropriate here, because this is a case of a direct revelation and admonition for the disciples. The similarity with the figurative discourse in Chapter 10, especially with regard to Jesus' unity with his own (10:14f) should be borne in mind in considering the origin and meaning of the image of the vine, but, before we do this, the figurative discourse itself has to be examined with particular reference to its content and meaning.[17]

Jesus described himself as *the* vine and does so with a precision that is similar to that of the other images. The addition of the words ἡ ἀληθινή is striking, because they are strongly emphasized by being placed after the noun. In this instruction of the disciples there is no indication of any polemics directed against outsiders. One possibility that cannot be ruled out is that this polemical tone was present in an original version and that the attribute of 'true' was retained from that original narrative. If, however, this assumption is not made, the best interpretation is that Jesus is the true vine; he merits the name of 'true vine' and the name applies fully to him. The use of ἀληθινός here is, in other words, similar to its use in 4:23 and 6:32. It is possible to detect, in these texts, a certain distance from and a transcendance of similar Jewish statements (worship in Jerusalem and the gift of manna); the same may be assumed here and we shall have to examine the discourse later for this when we consider its figurative aspect. It is difficult to say to what extent there is a difference between this adjective and ἀληθής (cf. 6:55 and 8:16; see also Vol. 2, pp. 225ff). In accordance with 6:32, the special qualitative character of the vine had to be stressed by this attribute.[18]

In the second half of the sentence, the Father of Jesus is included in the figurative discourse as the 'vine-dresser'. Although the principal idea in this discourse is that of 'abiding in Jesus' (vv. 4–7), the Father does not play a secondary part. His activity, as described in v. 2, leads to the idea of bearing fruit and this is another dominant aspect of the discourse (vv. 4–5) and its objective (v. 8). The Father is mentioned again in this latter verse, according to which he is glorified in the disciples' bearing of abundant fruit. As the vine-dresser, God carries out his work in Jesus, the vine, and this increases the importance of the activity of the disciples as well. What we have here is similar to what emerges in the prayer in Chapter 17 (and especially vv. 9f) – a theocentric view.

15:2   The vine-dresser does two things to ensure that there will be as much fruit as possible – in the winter, he cuts off the dry and withered branches and, in the spring, he removes the rank and useless growths from the branches.[19] This embellishment, which is reminiscent of a parable and yet still allows the matter itself to be perceived (in a metaphorical way), is expressed in Greek (paronomastically) by the use of two verbs that are similar in sound (αἴρει-καθαίρει). It is, moreover, fully in accordance with Semitic and eastern thought, in that it is concerned with the utilitarian value of the vine (cf. the parable of the barren fig-tree, Lk 13:6–9). The vine therefore appears here above all as a fruit-producing plant and not – or at least not primarily – as a life-bearing one.[20] Only the comparable Mandaean texts and the Johannine idea of life would induce us to think that. The bond between Jesus and his disciples that is given prominence by this image, and further emphasized by the words μένειν ἐν, is mediated by the divine life that is common to them (although the term ζωή is not used; cf. 14:19f). This idea is present, but only in the background. Because it is expressed in figurative language, 'every branch ἐν ἐμοί' means in the first place 'every branch that is found on me'; it is only when it is used in the phrase in v. 4 that it has the deeper meaning of abiding *in* Jesus. The removal of the dead branches is developed later as a theme of admonition (v. 6). There is no allusion here to the traitor Judas; those members of the community who apostasize are described in this verse as branches that do not bear fruit and their separation from the community (cf. 1 Jn 2:19) is interpreted as a cutting away by God.[21] The pruning or 'cleaning' of the branches of useless growths plays no further part in the figurative discourse and has therefore no need of an extensive interpretation. At the most, it is reminiscent of purifications and trials undergone by the disciples,[22] but καθαίρει, the use of which in this image is understandable,[23] is not used elsewhere in the New Testament in an extended sense. It is a metaphor that is introduced here for the idea of 'more fruit'.

15:3 The word καθαίρει, however, leads to an incidental comment, namely that the disciples have already been made clean by the word which Jesus has spoken to them. In its present context, this sentence can only be understood in the following sense: God, the vine-dresser, does not need to clean or purify the disciples, because they are clean already and can therefore bear abundant fruit, so long as they abide in Christ.[24] In that case, however, the use of 'clean' and 'purify' would be ambivalent. Without this verse, the figurative discourse would have a better structure, in that the matter which the one giving the discourse wanted above all to stress, namely his admonition to the disciples to abide in Jesus (vv. 4ff), would immediately follow the figurative exposition (vv. 1–2). It is probably a reflection on the word καθαίρειν, as in 13:10b. It is not, however, merely a reference back to that word.[25] If it were, the verse would have to read ὃν εἶπον ὑμῖν (cf. 2:22; 4:50; 7:36; 12:38; 15:20; 18:9). The word λελάληκα is a clear reference to Jesus' revelatory discourse as such (λόγος). That is why διά with the accusative must be interpreted, as it can be when used in the language of the time (see under 6:57), as διά with the genitive: through the discourse of Jesus, which contains life and spirit (6:63), the disciples, who have received it in faith into themselves, have been made clean. The fact that a 'purifying' force is attributed here to Jesus' word can certainly be reconciled with the 'word' theology of the gospel of John (cf. 5:24; 6:63; 8:31, 51; 14:23; 17:17), but it is still rare and striking. One suspects a connection here with the early Christian theology of baptism (cf. Eph 5:26; Heb 10:22; 1 Pet 1:23; James 1:18).[26] The disciples who have not been baptized with water have already experienced the efficacy of the word of God, which makes baptism effective, by personal association with Jesus, and that word has purified and sanctified them.

This interpretation, however, is still uncertain and it would be unwise to draw any far-reaching conclusions from this intervening comment, which was undoubtedly a later editorial addition.[27]

15:4   The figurative discourse, the meaning of which has naturally to be clear to the disciples, is now applied more directly and in an appellative manner to them (or the community). Jesus as the true vine and the disciples as the branches – this idea, which is stated explicitly in v. 5, is presupposed here and expressed as an admonition. The call: 'Abide in me' stands at the beginning and at the end of this verse, making it a small, complete unit in itself. The καθώς clause that follows the introductory 'Abide in me' must therefore be taken into account in a consideration of the whole if the intention of the verse is to be understood. The disciples are admonished so that they will bear fruit. This idea of bearing fruit connects this verse with v. 2. The assurance: 'And I (abide) in you', which follows the admonition 'Abide in me', is directed only towards this intention, but it does also make it clear to the disciples that they cannot bear fruit on their own and that it is something that results, not from their own merit, but from their 'abiding in Christ'. Nor is it a promise that is completely self-contained. The whole mode of expression is abbreviated and elliptical (the second verb is omitted) and the thought flows on quickly to the notion of bearing fruit. The disciples are not addressed 'moralistically', but are referred to the ground for fruitful activity, which is their unity with Christ, in which they must continue (cf. 8:31). This idea is developed in the next sentence, which contains the comparison with the branch that can only bear fruit if it abides on or 'in' the vine, and it is confirmed in the further exposition in vv. 5–6.

The metaphorical use of the image, which can be seen in the deeper significance of the word ἐν – the disciples' 'being in' Christ is inadequately expressed here by comparing it with the organic attachment of the branches to the vine – is made completely clear by the formula 'you in me and I in you'. This formula goes beyond the metaphor and draws attention to the disciples' special and indeed unique union with Christ in faith. We have already come across a 'reciprocal immanence formula' of this kind before, expressing the relationship between the disciples and Christ.[28] This was in the eucharistic verses of the discourse on the bread of life (see, especially, 6:56). This might be a reference to the possible eucharistic character of the present figurative discourse, but, because the formula is first used for Jesus' relationship with his Father (14:10f; cf. 17:21) and, in 14:20; 17:21, 23, 26, includes the disciples in Jesus' community with his Father, it would be wrong to apply it to such a *Sitz im Leben* (cf. also 14:20). When it is used in connection with μένειν and especially when it occurs in the imperative, this expression in Jn 15 has close links with the first epistle of John (see Joh-Br, pp. 109f). There seemed to the evangelist to be no more suitable and pressing way of strengthening the faith of the community or of making its members more conscious of their moral commitments than to remind them of the community with Christ that had been given to them and the obligation that was the result of that community.

It is from this perspective that the idea of 'bearing fruit', which is not defined more precisely in the whole section, has to be explained. The vocabulary of 'fruit' and 'bearing fruit' does not occur at all in 1 Jn and in the gospel only appears, apart from the discourse on the vine, in 4:36 and 12:24. These words were not incorporated more fully into the metaphorical language of the Johannine community.[29] The grain of wheat that bears much fruit by 'dying' (12:24) points, in the context in which it occurs, to the rich missionary yield. In 4:36, 'fruit' is connected in a different way with the images of sowing, reaping and gathering in. Here too, the clear reference is to winning over believers. Even on the basis of this previous occurrence in the gospel of the language of 'fruit' and 'fruit-bearing', however, it would be unjustifiable to restrict our present text to the idea of mission.[30] This 'bearing of fruit' in Jn 15 should, on the contrary, be given a much wider interpretation, particularly because of the proximity of the image to the admonition to the community to abide in Christ. This wider meaning is confirmed by the statement in v. 5: 'Apart from me you can do nothing.' We have therefore obviously to think here of all the fruits of a Christian life lived in close union with Christ and especially of a 'fruitful' community life which bears witness to itself in faith and love. There can be no doubt that the disciples were anxious to win over new people for Christ and, in this way, to make the dying of the 'grain of wheat' fruitful, but the emphasis here is certainly on the development of the power of Christ to save and to give life in the community, in other words, on an increasingly abundant yield of fruit and especially of love (see v. 12:17).[31]

15:5 The relationship between Jesus and the disciples is expressed in this verse with another introductory ἐγώ εἰμι statement. As far as its content is concerned, nothing new is said, but, taken together with v. 6, it makes the admonition to abide in Christ more insistent and gives it a deeper foundation. A conditional participle[32] is used here instead of the imperative μείνατε and this is followed in the negative construction (v. 6) by a conditional clause. These are linguistic variations of a kind that the gospel uses quite frequently. The antithetic mode of expression (positive in v. 5, followed by a negative statement in v. 6) is also typically Johannine. As in v. 4, the close union of life with Christ is designated only by the immanence formula and not defined more precisely. The disciples are called, not to a mystical experience, but to bear abundant fruit and they will do this thanks to the community with Christ that they have been given. The admonition to abide in Christ, then, is reinforced so that it can lead to action: apart from him they can do nothing. This is a fundamental statement for the Christian's understanding of himself and his function and activity. In the early Church, it had an important part to play in the doctrine of grace,[33] although it was perhaps too narrowly interpreted and too restricted to the question as to what man could do himself for his salvation. In the gospel, it occurs within the wide context of 'bearing fruit' and makes it clear that only the Christian who lives from his communion with Christ can produce the fruits of his Christian condition.

15:6   The antithesis is surprising because of the sombre description of what will happen to the disciple who does not abide in Christ. God the vine-dresser can be seen behind the passive voices (cf. v. 2a) and the immediate consequence for that disciple is indicated by the aorist tenses:[34] like a branch that has been severed from the vine, he is 'thrown out' and allowed to become dry. His fate is sealed. As the image goes on to say, such withered, dead branches are gathered, thrown into the fire and burnt. The whole description is, in a sense, an illustration of the judgment that the disciple who separates himself from Christ calls down on himself (cf. 3:18, in which the passive voice and the perfect tense are used). How does a disciple become separated in this way from Christ? With the community in mind, this can hardly have taken place only because of a falling away from faith. It must also have come about through a 'sin to death' (cf. 1 Jn 5:16), although we do not know what the community regarded as such a sin. The warning given to such a disciple is general in form, but quite strong and ἐβλήθη ἔξω is reminiscent of the judgment passed on the 'ruler of this world' (12:31; see the commentary, *ad loc.*). The figurative aspects, which follow closely the situation outlined in v. 2 and indeed form an appendix to it (the branches that are removed by the vine-dresser are gathered and burnt), should not be weakened, nor should they, however, be allegorized. Fire, which is frequently a symbol of judgment and punishment,[36] is here part of the whole image and does not point to hell and its fire (as in Mt 13:40–42). Such ideas of judgment do not occur again in the Johannine community. For that community, it was punishment enough to be separated from Christ and God and therefore exposed to 'withering' and death. It is possible that the members of the community are thinking here of their fellow members who have left them.

15:7   This threat is, however, followed by a promise. After having been deliberately kept in the third person in order to stress the fundamental character of the statement in vv. 5b–6, the discourse returns here to the second person plural and the disciples are addressed directly. The expression beginning with ἐὰν μείνητε follows v. 4a and assures the disciples that their prayer will be heard so long as they keep to the admonition 'Abide in me'. The movement of the language is similar to that in 14:10–13, in which the appeal to faith is also followed by promises made to those who believe, including an assurance that their prayer will be heard. The reappearance of τὰ ῥήματα (14:10 and 15:7) also gives rise to the suspicion that the passage in the previous chapter served as a model for our present text. The evangelist's pupils might have read the discourse in Chapter 14 and have wanted to continue the admonition to believe in their community as an admonition to abide in Christ and to bear fruit, in which case it is possible that they followed a serious admonition of increasing intensity with an encouraging promise, as here. The 'greater works' mentioned in 14:12 are, in accordance with their meaning, included in the 'bearing of abundant fruit', so that only the assurance that prayer will be heard has still to be expressed. The variation of the immanence formula: 'you in me and my words in you' can be seen as a reference back to 14:10, once again expressing the obligatory claim made by Christ, in union with the disciples. The man who assimilates Jesus' words into himself accepts him as the one sent by God and also at the same time commits himself to keeping his words and realizing them (cf. 12:47f; 17:8). The assurance that prayer will be heard applies particularly to him because he will, on the basis of his union with Jesus, ask for what will make Jesus' work fruitful (cf. 14:13). There is only one difference between the promise made in the present text and the same promise in Chapter 14 and it can be explained in the light of the different situation in each case: in our present text, it is clearly the Father who grants these petitions (for γενήσεται ὑμῖν, cf. Mt 18:19). This is borne out by the following verse, in which the Father is explicitly mentioned. The community is also promised in 1 Jn that its prayer will be heard (3:22; 5:14f). The certainty that prayer will be heard is a sign of the 'openness' of Christians to the Father. This assurance is, however, stated more freely and boldly in our present text than anywhere else in the gospel: 'Ask whatever you will!' As Borig has observed (p. 54), it is expressed in this way because 'it is from the situation of immanence (abiding in Christ) that the gift of prayer that is certain to be heard comes'. This idea connects our present passage closely to the long epistle to the community, in which further reflections about the hearing of prayer can be found (5:14f).

15:8 God, who hears the petitions of the disciples who are united to Jesus, is 'glorified' by their bearing fruit, in other words, he is honoured and shown to be true in his glory, because, as the 'vine-dresser', he is intent on an abundant yield of fruit (cf. v. 2). The Father's activity and that of the disciples come together in the production of fruit and Jesus, as the 'vine', is the 'place' where this is made possible. The Father does everything to obtain more fruit (v. 2b) and the disciples who are in union with Jesus produce abundant fruit (v. 5). The Father also hears their prayers, in order to guarantee and increase the yield of fruit (v. 7). The Son is only intent on the glorification of the Father (cf. 13:31f; 14:13; 17:1) and, after his return to the Father, makes use of the disciples for this purpose (cf. 17:10). This verse too, with its idea of the glorification of the Father, may, like the previous verse, have been inspired by 14:13 and adapted to the discourse on the vine. Those who are addressed here, however, at the same time show, by bearing much fruit, that they are Jesus' disciples. A reflection about discipleship can be discerned here. Apart from the texts in which the disciples are simply mentioned in the course of the narrative, this type of reflection can be found above all in 8:31; 9:27f and 13:35. True discipleship consists in abiding in Jesus' word (8:31). It is different from the pharisees' discipleship of Moses (9:27f) and it is positively expressed in the new commandment to love one another (13:35). In all these texts, there is an underlying reference to the Johannine community. For this reason, our present text also contains this reference. All believers were called disciples of Christ (see 6:60 and the commentary on that text), but what is most important is that believers should become true disciples by bearing fruit and above all by brotherly love (13:35) or to show that they are such disciples (γενήσεσθε).[38] It is only then that Jesus will accept them as his disciples (ἐμοί in the dative, *ethicus* or *commodi*)[39] who are dear to him and who really serve him (cf. 12:26).

15:9 The idea of discipleship can also be used to explain the sentence that follows: as disciples, those who are addressed in this discourse are included in Jesus' love and they ought to abide in it. The close connection with v. 8 is clear from the further reference to the Father. In his choice and acceptance of disciples (see v. 16), Jesus hands on the Father's love, which also surrounds him and furthers his work (see 17:26). It is from this, however, that the new admonition comes: Abide in my love, that is, by showing yourselves to be my disciples! This is why it would be wrong to begin a new section of the gospel here (see pp. 92–3). This verse continues and deepens the discourse on the vine with regard to the disciples' bearing of fruit. In it, the bearing of fruit is revealed at the deepest level as love. The fruit of being a disciple of Jesus grows in the soil of love, as a gift of Jesus' love, and is essentially love itself, as Jesus demonstrated it. This idea of love was also suggested by the discourse in Chapter 14, where it appears in vv. 15 and 21–23. The appeal to keep Jesus' commandments on the basis of his love, however, has now become an admonition, within the image of the vine and the branches, to abide in the love he has shown to the disciples. The aorist ἠγάπησα undoubtedly also includes Jesus' giving of himself in death (see v. 13). This is confirmed by the position, which is different from that in the farewell discourse – this discourse presupposes Jesus' death and is directed towards the post-paschal community.

15:10 As in 14:15, 21, 23, love is demonstrated in 'keeping Jesus' commandments'. Now, however, in accordance with Jesus' demand to abide in his love, the sequence is reversed – it is no longer 'if you love me . . .', but 'if you keep my commandments . . .' The basic idea, on the other hand, is the same,[40] although in Chapter 14, faith is the main consideration in the case of Jesus' 'commandments' (or 'word', v. 23), whereas, in Chapter 15, it is brotherly, mutual love (vv. 12, 17). As in 1 Jn 2:4; cf. 2:7f, the plural form 'commandments' is defined more precisely as the commandment of brotherly love (v. 12) and is used here only as a means of emphasizing the all-embracing obligation resulting from Jesus' love. As in the previous verse, Jesus' love is rooted in the Father's love and 'keeping his commandments' is at the same time a theme for the disciples. The entire unit of discourse (vv. 9–10), although very small, is complete in itself and artistically composed. Its point of departure, to which it returns, is the love of the Father and the two καθώς clauses are arranged chiastically, with the admonition to abide in Jesus' love in the middle. This appeal is the real aim of the statement and it gives depth to the admonition 'Abide in me'.

15:11 As the phrase ταῦτα λελάληκα ὑμῖν indicates (see p. 92), this verse marks the end of the discourse on the vine. The ταῦτα therefore does not simply relate to v. 10 (as Lagrange, Wikenhauser and others thought), although the promise to abide in Jesus' love is a special reason for joy. In the farewell discourse in Chapter 14, the disciples' rejoicing is only fleetingly mentioned (v. 28). Now, however, the joy resulting from community with Christ is emphatically named. It is the joy of the time after Easter and therefore of Christ's lasting presence. (In accordance with the Johannine eschatology, the OT promises were fulfilled in the present.[41]) Even John the Baptist speaks about this joy (3:29) and, in those texts which point to the community's possession of salvation, the note of joy is sounded more frequently. This happens, for example, especially in the last farewell discourse (16:21f, 24), the prayer of the departing Christ (17:13), and the Johannine epistles (1 Jn 1:4; 2 Jn 12; 3 Jn 4). This joy is entirely connected with Christ ('my joy') and it is also embedded in the disciples ('in you'). This is reminiscent of other statements in 1 Jn, according to which the truth (1:8; 2:4), the word of God (1:10; 2:14) and the love of God (3:17; 4:12), among other things, are in believers (see Joh-Br, p. 106). It is also reminiscent of the promise that the Paraclete will be in the disciples (Jn 14:17). As for Paul (see Gal 5:22; Rom 14:17), so too for John, joy is one of the fruits of the presence of Christ or the Spirit. What is very distinctive, however, and exclusive to Johannine linguistic usage, is that this joy is to be 'full' ($\pi\lambda\eta\rho o\tilde{v}\sigma\theta\alpha\iota$). The joy of Christ that is mediated to the disciples can become a full measure approaching that of the fullness of eschatological salvation. It is also a joy that cannot be taken away (16:22). The Johannine school was, however, also conscious of the goal that is not reached on earth. This is clear linguistically from the fact that, apart from in Jn 3:29, this 'being filled' with joy is almost always expressed in $\iota\nu\alpha$ clauses.[42]

The Background and the *Sitz im Leben* of the Discourse on the Vine

1. The Comparative and Historical Background

The question that arises in connection with comparative religion is which texts can best explain the figurative aspect of the Johannine discourse on the vine, and therefore which source or sources provided the editors with their point of departure for that discourse. This question has been debated for some time now, but there is still no generally accepted answer to it. As in the case of the other metaphors in the gospel, the argument is between two main sources: on the one hand, a gnostic, and in particular a Mandaean source and, on the other, the OT and Judaism. E. Schweizer is the principal protagonist of a Mandaean source, although in his later writings he has not clung so firmly to this view.[43] S. Schulz has in principle accepted this finding, that is, he agrees that there are formal similarities between the Johannine and Mandaean texts, but he has modified it in respect of its theoretical and philosophical content because of the existence of material parallels in the OT.[44] Several exegetes, on the other hand, have favoured certain OT and Judaistic parallels because of similarities in content and meaning[45] and R. Borig has provided further justifications for this view in his monograph.[46] The problem is similar to that presented by the discourse on the shepherd in Chapter 10 and the words about the door and the good shepherd that follow this discourse (see the commentary on these). Since both Schweizer and Borig have written very extensively about this matter, I shall do no more here than briefly discuss the problems that arise from them.

There are many statements about the vine (or vines), many phrases that are similar in their wording and a number of texts in which the redeemer calls himself 'the vine' ('I am') – all these point to the Mandaean documents as the main source. One typical text, for example is:

'I (Hibil) am a gentle vine; I was planted (created) from the place of glorious splendour. I was planted from the place of glorious splendour and the great (life) was my planter (creator)' (*Ginza*, 301:11–14).

According to Mandaean thought, the redeemer represents individual man or the soul, with the result that:

'We are a vine, the vine of life, a tree on which there is no lie, the tree of praise, from the odour of which each man receives life' (*Ginza*, 59:39—60:2).

The Mandaean vine is clearly presented here as the tree of life. As K. Rudolph pointed out, 'the vine (*gūfnā*) is often used in Mandaean figurative language as a symbol of the tree of life and the world of light'.[48] R. Borig has also shown that the image of a celestial vine with mythical functions and characteristics was originally present in the minds of the authors of the Ginza and that this was followed by personifications – the soul was called a vine and the one who was sent was also described as a vine.[49]

These few examples show the very different origin and meaning of the Mandaean image of the vine. It is at the same time clear that the Johannine discourse on the vine, with its figurative and partly parabolic description, can only be understood in an entirely natural and indeed earthly light. There is, for instance, no reference at all in the Johannine discourse to the 'odour' of the vine, which, moreover, only appears at the most marginally as the 'tree of life'. Its fruitfulness is by far its most prominent feature and this is an aspect that plays no part at all in the Mandaean understanding of the vine.[50]

Even fewer formal parallels can be found in the OT. There is, however, abundant material belonging to the same sphere of metaphorical or figurative language and usage. The well-known song of the vineyard in Is 5 (cf. 27:2ff) can also be compared with other texts dealing with the vine itself, as denoting the people of Israel.

Hos. 10:1: 'Israel is a luxuriant vine that yields its fruit'
Jer 2:21: 'Yet I planted you a choice vine, wholly of pure seed (LXX: ἄμπελον ἀληθινήν)'
Ezek 15 (the judgment of fire on the wood of the vine)
Ezek 19:10–14 (the planting of the vine in the desert)
Ps 80:9–12: 'Thou didst bring a vine out of Egypt; thou didst drive out the nations and plant it . . .'
Ps 80:15f: 'Have regard for this vine, the stock which thy right hand planted . . .'[51]

Again and again Israel is reproached for failing to keep and testify to the truth of itself as the noble and fruitful vine planted by God. As in Jn 15, the emphasis is on bearing fruit. God has planted the vine; the only difference is that Jesus Christ replaces Israel in the Johannine discourse. Is this transference of the earlier vine of Israel to Christ not intentional? Even in the OT itself, the image of the people is transferred to the king (Zedekiah); see especially Ezek 17:6–8. It is not, it is true, applied to the Messiah in the OT, although there is one text in the Syrian *Apocalypse of Baruch* (36, cf. the interpretation in 39:7): 'Then the rule of my Messiah is revealed: it is like the source and the vine.'

It is also clear from several rabbinical texts that post-biblical Judaism was also concerned with Israel as a vine.[52] This symbolism has also been frequently found on ceramics and coins from the time of the Maccabees onwards. According to Josephus (a XV, 395; b V, 210), there was a great golden vine on the entrance to the sanctuary of the Herodian temple. By far the most common symbol on coins, tombs, ossuaries and lamps was the vine.[53] The most obvious interpretation and one that was, in the past, suggested by many exegetes, namely that this vine pointed to Israel, has been shown by recent scholarship to be less certain.[54] In itself, however, the mere fact provides a broad basis for tracing the symbol of the vine back to Judaism, although, as a whole, a derivation from a single source or a direct connection with individual texts would not seem to be possible in the case of Jn 15. As elsewhere in the gospel, this Johannine figurative discourse also displays a distinctive creative power of its own and an ability to incorporate and fashion material from many sources. The main source and origin of the image of the vine, however, must be (as they are for the images of the shepherd in Chapter 10) the OT.

2. The Theological Background

Typological thinking, applying images and ideas derived from the OT to Jesus and regarding them as fulfilled in him is frequently encountered elsewhere in the gospel of John (examples of this are the Lamb of God, the bronze serpent, the bread from heaven, the source of living water, and the good shepherd etc.). For this reason, it may be suspected that this way of thinking also lies behind the statement that Jesus is the true vine. This view is, moreover, strengthened by the attribute ἀληθινός, which is similarly added to the bread from heaven (6:32) and, in that context too, it is the Father who gives the bread. If Jesus is the 'king of Israel' (1:49; 12:13), then the idea that he represents the true Israel is not far removed from this. The texts accusing Israel, the vine planted and tended by God or the vineyard for which God cared, must have been heard again with some urgency in the constant polemics against contemporary Judaism and its denial of its king and saviour (see, for example, 19:14f). In this respect, several points of departure were already provided by the pre-Johannine tradition (especially Mk 12:1–12 par.; Lk 13:6–9). The true Israel is a dominant theme in the theology of Matthew (see, for example, 21:43) and, in a different way, in that of Luke.[55] John gives the idea of the true Israel a Christological emphasis and concentrates on Jesus Christ himself. He interprets the logion of the temple (2:19), which is related in the synoptics (and especially in Mk 14:58) to the community, as pointing to the body of Christ (2:21). The other image in the gospel which is also connected with the same vocabulary of bearing fruit – that of the grain of wheat (12:24) – may also have contributed to this. After having already identified the vine of Israel with the Messiah, there is no need to look further. This step can be more easily explained in the light of the Johannine theology with its Christological emphasis.

There is also another connection between ideas which has to be mentioned in this context – the relationship between the discourse on the vine and wisdom. This connection seems to be rather remote from the idea of the 'true Israel', but it is provided by the OT and other texts in the gospel itself. There is a comparison in Ecclus 24:17 between personified Wisdom and a vine: 'Like a vine I caused loveliness to bud and my blossoms became glorious and abundant fruit.' The same elements as those that occur in the figurative discourse in Jn 15 also appear here – the vine, buds (branches) and abundant fruit. In addition, the first person singular is used in both texts. There is also a reference to Israel in the passage in Ecclesiasticus, when Wisdom is said to live in the midst of the people of Israel 'in the assembly of the most High' (vv. 1f, 7f, 10ff). This is, of course, only one comparison among several others (cf. vv. 13–16) and the call to come to Wisdom and eat one's fill of her fruit (v. 19) is not simply in accordance with the Johannine exhortation to the disciples to bear rich fruit. A relationship between the Johannine discourse and the Wisdom literature, then, cannot be excluded so long as it is accepted that various associations can be evoked by the figurative language (as also, for example, in the case of the 'Lamb of God') and complete agreement between the views expressed by each discourse is not required. The gospel has also been influenced in other places by the sapiential writings.[56] In the discourse on the bread of life, for example, 6:35 would seem to have been influenced by Prov 9:5 and Ecclus 24:21 (following our text!) (see Vol. 2, pp. 44f). Wisdom undoubtedly introduces a distinctive note into the exhortatory discourse addressed to the disciples and promising them a rich yield of fruit (cf. Ecclus 4:11–16, etc.: Wisdom teaching her 'sons').

3. Sitz im Leben

Should the discourse on the vine be situated within the framework of the controversy over the doctrines of salvation (gnosticism) that were in competition with the Johannine teaching or with Judaism, or should it be placed within the context of cult in the community (the Eucharist)? There are arguments in favour of each view. We have already encountered certain emphases in the exegesis that point to the need for defence. These include, for example, the attribute $\dot{\alpha}\lambda\eta\theta\iota\nu\dot{\eta}$, the idea of cutting off ($\alpha\check{\iota}\rho\epsilon\iota$) branches that do not bear fruit and the removal and burning of dry, dead branches (v. 6). On the other hand, attention has frequently been drawn to possible references to the Eucharist – the image as such, which is reminiscent of the wine of the Eucharist (although wine itself is not mentioned at all in the discourse), the immanence statements, which are most closely paralleled in 6:56, that is, within the eucharistic verses of the discourse on the bread, the relationship with the discourse on the bread from heaven (6:32, 35), the affinity with the prayer in Chapter 17, which can also be related to the Eucharist and other eucharistic texts in early Christian writings, especially Did 9:2: 'We thank you, our Father for the holy vine of David, your servant, which you have made known to us through Jesus, your servant.'[57] If we think, moreover, of the fruits of the Christian mission in connection with the disciples' bearing of fruit, we have a more powerful vision of their task in the world. All these aspects can be grouped under the heading of Christian worship and its promise to the community. We have, however, to consider the fact that the different aspects require divergent points of departure.

In the exegesis, the suspicion has been expressed that the discourse on the vine originally had an earlier, narrative form. We can now state this more precisely. Vv. 1–2 and 6 have certain narrative characteristics and it is particularly these verses with which we are concerned. The narrative presentation had a polemical and aggressive character similar to that of the 'cryptic discourse' (10:1–5). It was a Christian 'mashal'. When this mashal was used with a paraenetic emphasis to address the community (see 15:12–17) and was inserted into the context of Jesus' discourses addressed to his own, the entire stress was placed on the positive content of the narrative. It was then given a special tone for the community's celebration of the Eucharist and a new meaning (see especially vv. 4–5, 9–10). We have therefore to assume, as it were, that there are two *Sitze im Leben*. The first provides the context for the original self-revelatory discourse given by Jesus (now overlaid) and the second is the setting for the discourse that was fashioned by the editor or editors, composed especially for the community and given an appellative emphasis. This hypothesis is proposed for debate. A one-sided and purely eucharistic interpretation is unlikely. It is more likely, as R. E. Brown has suggested, that the mashal of the vine served as paraenesis in Johannine circles, stressing that the unity brought about by the Eucharist should last and bear fruit.[58]

2. The Commandment to Love One Another (15:12–17)

[12]'*This is my commandment, that you love one another as I have loved you.*
[13]*Greater love has no man than this, that a man lay down his life for his friends.*
[14]*You are my friends if you do what I command you.* [15]*No longer do I call you servants, for the servant does not know what his master is doing; but I have called you friends, for all that I have heard from my Father I have made known to you.*
[16]*You did not choose me, but I chose you and appointed you that you should go and bear fruit and that your fruit should abide; so that whatever you ask the Father in my name, he may give it to you.* [17]*This I command you, to love one another*'.

15:12 There now follows a more detailed treatment of Jesus' commandment to his disciples, so that they may abide in his love (v. 10). It is the one commandment of mutual love – this is once again stressed at the end of this unit of the discourse (v. 17). All Jesus' commandments are concentrated and proved to be true in this love, which is the sign of true discipleship (13:35). The same idea is stressed again and again in the long epistle (see 2:9–11; 3:11–18, 23; 4:7, 11f, 20f; 5:1f). In 1 Jn too, the background to this need for emphasis and the reason the disciples are so urged to love one another is made clear. It is above all a question of a defence against a non-Christian and Gnostic attitude, a sharpening of the Christian teaching and a manifestation of the Christian community in action (see the excursus in Joh-Br, pp. 117–121). The language in this text in the gospel – the use of demonstrative pronouns with an epexegetical ἵνα clause – is frequently paralleled in 1 Jn.[59] Love for one another (1 Jn 3:11, 23; 4:7, 11f; 2 Jn 5) is the same as brotherly love (1 Jn 2:10; 3:10, 14, etc.) Both expressions point to sphere of activity of this love in the community. There is, in this, an apparent narrowing down of the teaching to the circle of the brethren and this may indicate an esoteric attitude. It can, however, be explained as an expression of the desire that love should be realized in practice (cf. 3:16–18). In this text, Jesus' own love is named as the basis and the model for the disciples' love for each other. This is a continuation of the statement in v. 9 and there is also a connection with 13:34 (see the commentary above). The first letter to the community also, however, points repeatedly to the example of Jesus himself (2:6; 3:3, 7, 16).

15:13 The supreme proof of love is the giving of one's life. This is a general statement, but it is made striking by the addition of 'for his friends'. This key phrase is resumed in the following verses (14f) and Jesus' relationship with his disciples is thus seen to be one of friendship. In the context, Jesus' love is presented as a love of his friends that cannot be transcended and his giving of his life is presented as a paradigm and a call to the disciples to be ready to do the same. This idea is also expressed in 1 Jn 3:16. There are many parallels in ancient literature for this statement about the love of friends going as far as death,[60] and we are therefore bound to conclude that this gnomic pronouncement was taken from that literature, developed into a reflection about Jesus' love and used to express an obligation for his disciples.[61] The employment of a fairly widespread ethical maxim is confirmed by the fact that the idea of Jesus' friendship for his disciples is only formulated here, in this verse. The vocabulary is used in several other texts, however, and examples of this are: John the Baptist's description of himself as the 'friend of the bridegroom' (3:29), the naming of Lazarus as a friend (11:11; cf. 11:3, 36) and the reference to the disciple 'whom Jesus loved', in which the verb φιλεῖν (20:2) can be seen in the same light (cf. also 16:27 for all the disciples and 21:15ff for Simon Peter).

'Friendship' is in fact a theme that played a very important part in the Graeco-Roman world.[62] There is no corresponding word in Hebrew, but the matter is present in Hebrew literature (see, for example, the 'bond of friendship' between

David and Jonathan, 1 Sam 18:1–4). The idea of friendship, however, first appeared in a much more emphatic way in the sapiential literature (see especially Ecclus 6:5–17). In Judaism, Abraham is described as the 'friend of God' (according to Is 41:8; 2 Chr 20:7) and this description appears frequently in the non-canonical writings (Jub 19:9; Dam 3:2; *Apoc Abr* 9:6; 10:6; *Test Abr* 13:6; Philo, *Sobr* 56, etc.; see also James 2:23). Other patriarchs and even Moses, however, are also called friends of God (Moses in Exod 33:11; see also Jub 30:20; Dam 3:3f; Philo, *Mos I*, 156; *Sacr* 130, etc.). The Israelites are also given the same honorific title (see, for example, Jub 30:21; see also the rabbinical writings[63]) as are those who are concerned with the Torah (Abot VI, 1). Jn 15:13, with its special reference to dying for one's friends, cannot, however, be traced back to Judaism.[64] Jesus himself hardly ever made use of the idea of friendship. We can be quite certain, then, that, in the case of this evangelist, a Hellenistic influence was at work.[65] This is clear from the evidence available for this particular vocabulary. What is more, there is also evidence of Johannine language in Jn 15:13; see especially τιθέναι τὴν ψυχήν[66] and μείζονα . . . ἵνα, 3 Jn 4. This idea must therefore have been formulated by the Johannine school.

This statement about Jesus' love for his friends shows that Hellenistic thought was influential in Johannine Christianity. It is also evident that the more Jewish 'brotherliness' can be combined in the Johannine writings with the Greek idea of 'friendship' (see, for example, 3 Jn 15). But Jesus' 'love of friends' gave a new identity to Christian friendship (see v. 15f).

15:14 The title of 'friend' gives the disciples a reason for carrying out Jesus' commandment to love. This sentence has an appellative power: the disciples may regard themselves as Jesus' friends if they do what he commands them to do. This emphasis on moral action (cf. 13:17) points once again to the closeness between the gospel and the first epistle (see 1 Jn 2:29; 3:7, 18, 22; 4:20; 5:2f).

15:15 The statement that the disciples are Jesus' 'friends' now leads beyond the exhortation to a reflection about the nature of this friendship. It is a gift. Jesus raises the disciples from the status of servants, as they must have seen themselves with regard to God and Jesus himself, to the level of friends. This friendship gives them an intimacy with and a proximity to God of the kind mentioned in Judaism and known as 'friendship with God'.[67] Jesus, after all, disclosed and entrusted to his friends everything that he had heard from the Father and revealed to them the 'name', the very being, of his Father (17:26, with the same verb, γνωρίζειν), thus mediating to them the love of God (*ibid.*, cf. 16:27). If, then, they are no longer servants, they have become free men. Although the word 'free' does not occur in the text, the same freedom is certainly meant that was discussed in 8:32–36 (see the commentary above). The image of the servants (or slaves) and the son in the Father's house is related to this text. In the text in Chapter 8, only the son was able to 'abide' in the Father's house. In our present text, Jesus enables his disciples to participate in the intimacy and trust of the Father, by means of which they acquire that 'openness' (παρρησία) which is the privilege of a free man and a friend (see 1 Jn 3:21).

Some of Philo's texts are particularly illuminating in connection with the ideas on friendship expressed above. He had this, for example, to say about Moses: 'In this way, he reached the peak . . . of nobility, because all wise men are God's friends and they are this also in the opinion of the divine lawgiver himself. Openness (παρρησία), however, is related to friendship, for to whom other than to one's friend will one speak openly?' (*Heres* 21). In a different context, he says: 'Wisdom is more friendly than subject (δοῦλον) to God' (*Sobr* 55). Again: 'It would be simple-minded to believe that servants rather than God's friends inherit the land of virtue' (*Migr* 45). Philo regarded the wise, the good and the pious (and, in a particularly exemplary way, the therapeutes, see *Vita contempl*. 90) as God's friends, because they were close to him and could be seen by him (see *Leg all*, III, 1). This idea can also be found in the sapiential literature; see Wis 7:27: 'In every generation she (Wisdom) passes into holy souls and makes them friends and prophets'.

In the case of the introductory sentence, 'No longer do I call you servants', a parallel has often been made with 13:16, but the second statement is made in a different context and it would be wrong to think that Jesus is now saying that only the disciples are his friends. On the other hand, the tenses in v. 15b[68] and the reminder that the disciples were chosen in v. 16 are evidence to the contrary. From the time that he chose them (see 6:70), Jesus has seen them as his friends. The οὐκέτι does not have a narrow and purely temporal meaning; it is a fundamental introduction to the new relationship that Jesus has created. The freedom and friendship that the Son gives replace the old dispensation (cf. 8:33, 36). It is also possible that the idea of Abraham, to whom the Jews wrongly appealed (8:33, 37–40), is present here. God did not, after all, hide his thoughts from Abraham (Gen 18:17) and, according to the Jewish Haggadah, he showed him everything in this world and the next (see the commentary on 8:56; Vol. 2, pp. 221f). It was, however, said of Moses (Exod 33:11): 'The Lord used to speak to Moses face to face, as a man speaks to his friend.' What individual men of God were granted in the OT was extended by Jesus to all disciples.

15:16   The train of thought moves from the idea of Jesus' friendship for the disciples to the fact that they have been chosen and turns back to the wider context. 'Election' is hardly ever mentioned in the case of the OT 'friends of God' (Abraham and Moses).[69] It is, however, made explicit here with regard to Jesus' disciples, though not for the first time in the gospel – attention has already been drawn to their having been chosen by Jesus in 6:70 and 13:18. This is a distinctively Christian way of speaking (cf. Lk 6:13). It is evidence of the fact that the idea of friendship (which corresponds to that of discipleship; see v. 8) is fundamentally Christian, that is, that it has to be interpreted as pointing to the special relationship between Jesus and his disciples. A man is called to be a disciple by Jesus and for this it can be emphatically stated that 'you did not choose me, but I chose you'. The disciples are in this way made conscious of the unmerited gift of their friendship with Jesus and this at once implies an obligation on their part. What Jesus is looking for in the friendship that he gives them is that they should go out and bear fruit. The idea of mission may perhaps be found in the expression 'I appointed you (ἔθηκα) (cf. 4:38; 17:18; 20:21), but this is not necessarily the case.[70] The expression 'that you should go' ($\dot{\upsilon}\pi\acute{\alpha}\gamma\eta\tau\varepsilon$) may also indicate missionary activity, but it does not necessarily point to this.[71] The terminology in this verse hardly entitles us to tie the bearing of fruit down to missionary activity.[72] It is rather that the discourse turns back at this point to an appeal to the disciples to remain united with Jesus and to bear fruit. The idea of bearing fruit is deliberately kept very open (see v. 4) and this means that it may contain a missionary aspect which is brought into prominence by the reminder that the disciples have been chosen, but the dominant aspect is undoubtedly the fruitfulness of Christian life, especially demonstrated in brotherly love, as the following verse makes clear. The fact that the fruit should 'abide' can also be explained on the basis of the admonition that the disciples should abide in Jesus and his love (cf. v. 10). The 'fruit' of the disciples' activity is not men, but God's life and love in men (see 1 Jn 3:14f; 4:16).

In the Mandaean texts the redeemer often addresses those who are united to him as his 'friends' and as the 'elect' to whom he reveals everything. The question therefore arises as to whether Jn 15:14–16 was influenced by those texts and, if so, to what extent. There are also moral exhortatory discourses in the Mandaean literature, for example, *Ginza* 16–17; 34–42. In *Ginza* 22:9ff, we read: 'O you chosen and perfect ones! Be humble and modest, so that you may be called chosen, faithful and believing! Love one another in faithfulness and take your love to its fulfilment!' In *ibid.*, 61:9f too, we read: 'I call to you, plants that I have planted, chosen ones whom I have chosen . . .' The idea of election is combined with that of 'friends' in JB *Mand*, 92:3ff: 'I call and instruct, I instruct my friends who dwell in the world: My chosen ones! Be without fault and defect and may no lie be in your speech!' Again in *Ginza* 388:26–29: 'It is the voice of Mandā dHaijē calling and instructing all his friends. He speaks to them: My chosen ones! Make your hearts submissive . . .!' It is clear, then, that what is discussed in these texts is an esoteric 'instruction' or teaching (*gnosis*) given to the chosen gnostics, who have also to practise love, brotherliness and truthfulness within their group. The connection with 'bearing fruit' and the contrast between 'servants' and 'friends' are not, however, present in the Mandaean texts. There is a very similar attitude in the Johannine community towards being 'chosen out of the world' (Jn 15:19), but it is not necessary to regard the idea of friendship, which in fact takes its point of departure from the statement in v. 13 (which has no parallel in the Mandaean literature!), as having been derived from Mandaean thought. We may therefore conclude that it is unnecessary and only raises problems to go back to a gnostic source, as Bultmann, H. Becker and J. Heise have done, in vv. 14–16.

The promise that prayer will be heard is once again made explicit in a second (subordinate) ἵνα clause (cf. v. 7). This promise is made again as a result of the repetition of the idea of bearing fruit. It is not possible for the disciples to bear lasting fruit if their requests are not granted by the Father. From the formal point of view, it would seem as though the hearing of their prayers were dependent on their bearing fruit, but in fact, as in v. 7, what we have here is not a condition and its consequence, but a desire and a promise. Jesus wants his disciples to bear fruit that will last and he therefore promises them that their prayers will be heard. This 'asking in Jesus' name' can therefore even be seen as a part of their bearing fruit, since the promise also becomes an obligation to pray for full and lasting fruit. 'In Jesus' name' is, as it were, an addition to v. 7 made in this verse and should be understood in the same way as the similar phrases in 14:13f (see the commentary above). Abiding in Jesus and his words, however, is even more strongly presupposed in our present verse than it is there (see v. 7). It is only on the basis of a living union with him that an appeal can be made to him that one's prayer will be heard by the Father.

15:17   The passage concludes with a repetition of Jesus' commandment to love one another (cf. the inclusion in v. 12). This completes the unit of the discourse and throws light once more on the place that it occupies in the whole discourse. The object of this discourse on the vine was to point to the bearing of fruit by the disciples. This is given concrete expression and is even more powerfully motivated – by the idea of the love of friends – in the exposition in vv. 12–17. The admonition to the community, which consists of Christ's disciples and friends, culminates in this repeated commandment of mutual love.

3. The Hatred and Hostility of the World (15:18–25)

[18]'*If the world hates you, know that it has hated me before it hated you.* [19]*If you were of the world, the world would love its own; but because you are not of the world, but I chose you out of the world, therefore the world hates you.* [20]*Remember the word that I said to you, "A servant is not greater than his master". If they persecuted me, they will persecute you; if they kept my word, they will keep yours also.* [21]*But all this they will do to you because of my name, because they do not know him who sent me.* [22]*If I had not come and spoken to them, they would not have sin; but now they have no excuse for their sin.* [23]*He who hates me hates my Father also.* [24]*If I had not done among them the works which no one else did, they would not have sin; but now they have seen and hated both me and my Father.* [25]*It is to fulfil the word that is written in their law, "They hated me without a cause".'*

So far, the discourse has concentrated on the disciples' life in community with Christ and each other. Now it turns to consider their situation in the world. The love that they ought to practise among each other in accordance with the example of Christ (vv. 12–17) is sharply contrasted with the hatred that they experience on the part of the 'world' and for Christ's sake (vv. 18–25). The concept 'hate' in the first and last verses binds this new unit of the discourse together and the concept 'world' is given its most emphatic dualist emphasis in this unit. The sequence is intentionally arranged so that the community of those who love one another is confronted with a world of hatred. This is also a clear reflection of the way in which the Johannine community understood itself, a view that is summarized in 1 Jn 3:13f: 'Do not wonder, brethren, that the world hates you. We know that we have passed out of death into life, because we love the brethren'. Even the phrase 'out of the world' has been included, with the same meaning, in 1 Jn 4:5. This concept of the cosmos can be found in the gospel, especially in Jesus' controversy with his unbelieving brothers (7:7) and with the Jews who reject him (8:23). The disciples wi⁺¹ experience what Jesus himself experiences and this is announced here so that they will know how to cope with their situation.

It is possible that the evangelist himself wrote this section. The unforgivable 'sin' of the world, with which vv. 22–24 are concerned, is, like the concept 'world', reminiscent of 8:21–24. The inability of the world to grasp God's being and incorporate it into itself has also been discussed in the farewell discourse in Chapter 14: it cannot see the Paraclete (v. 17), the risen Christ does not reveal himself to it (v. 22), and it does not know the peace of Christ (v. 27). It is, however, more likely that it was composed by an editor or editors (from the circle of disciples). As in 15:1–17, it is connected with the farewell discourse; the editor consciously made this connection and extended the line of thought to the situation in which the community was placed. Similarly v. 20, in which the saying 'a servant is not greater than his master' (13:16) is included, taken from a context which we believed should be attributed to an editor (see the commentary). The 'apology' of Jesus' activity in vv. 22–24, which looks back to the whole of his active life on earth, is appropriately situated in the controversy with the surrounding world and clearly goes further than the situation of Jesus' departure from his disciples. Finally, the introduction of the scriptural quotation is remarkable (see the commentary below).

15:18   The disciples are bound to encounter the hatred of the world because they belong to Jesus. They experience it already as a fact – this is expressed linguistically by the conditional clause.[73] But why are the disciples told this in this appellative discourse? Not in the first place to comfort them by predicting that hatred and to strengthen their faith (this is done for the first time in the secondary addition in v. 16:1, 4a), but rather to encourage them to proclaim the word (see v. 20b) and to bear witness in the world (see v. 27). They have to carry out the same task and go the same way as Jesus. Even before they encountered it, he experienced the hatred of the world. A close consideration of this call to the disciples shows that the Johannine community cannot be accused of turning away from the world as the gnostic communities did. In the formal sense, the concept of the 'world' is closer in 15:18f ('chosen out of the world') to the gnostic understanding of that concept and their relationship with it than anywhere else in the gospel, but it is only possible to say with considerable reservations that 'it was the intention of the Johannine and the Gnostic communities to take men out of the world'.[75] Certainly the Johannine community was filled with a desire to be set free 'from the world by the revelation of the unworldly God', but its members saw both the 'world' and their task in it differently. For them, the 'world' was not originally evil; as the world of men, it continued to be the object of God's love (3:16, 1 Jn 4:14).[76] Men had become the 'world' that was hostile to God by their rejection of the one sent by God, who offered them the possibility of salvation and continued to keep that offer open (see 14:31). With the help of the Paraclete, the disciples therefore have the task of bearing witness to this fact (vv. 26–27), despite all the hatred and persecution, either for faith or for judgment. There is a dialectical tension in the concept of the 'world' in the gospel of John, causing it to be seen on the one hand as needing to be and capable of being saved and, on the other, as hardened, without faith and full of hatred.[77] This tension cannot be dismissed or glossed over lightly. The words of the Johannine Christ, who subjects the 'world' to judgment or calls it to faith, also apply to the Johannine community, because its members are conscious of their obligation to imitate that Jesus. They take both possibilities into account – persecution or the acceptance of their proclamation (see the commentary on v. 20). Negative experiences, of course, obscure the prospect (see 1 Jn 4:5), and the aim of this discourse is to open men's eyes (γινώσκετε) to this situation and inspire them with courage.

15:19   The world's hatred of Jesus' disciples can be explained by its nature, which is remote from God. The Johannine ἐκ of origin and belonging (cf. 3:6 and 1 Jn 2:16) is used here to the full extent of its range. Love in the sense of natural inclination (φιλεῖν) presupposes homogeneity (ἰσότης φιλότης), but Jesus' disciples do not have the same nature as the world, because Jesus has chosen them 'out of the world'. 'Choosing', which goes back to v. 16, is, when it is used in connection with the world, very close to being 'taken out of' or 'excluded from'. The 'world' and discipleship are two clearly separated spheres, pointing to the gulf between God and everything that is against God. This contrast is expressed openly in 1 Jn 4:4–6: the false prophets are 'out of the world' and the true believers are 'out of God'; but see also Jn 8:23; 18:36f. In the phrase 'the world would love its own', the cosmos is presented as a personal reality and in fact what is meant by it are also those men who persecute Jesus and his disciples (v. 20). Their alienation from God is expressed in v. 21. There can be hardly any doubt that the language and manner of presentation were influenced by dualistic (Gnostic) thought,[78] but the reference to this historical Jesus and the situation in which the disciples were placed enable this metaphorical way of speaking about the 'world' to be seen simply as a reflection about an experience which does not release the disciples from their mission to their fellow men.

15:20   The disciples are reminded of the word that was known to the Johannine community from the tradition of Jesus: 'A servant is not greater than his master.' This saying has already been quoted in a different context (13:16) and this shows what an important part the words of Jesus played in the community's understanding of itself. This memory is tied to the history of Jesus. 'Persecution' must also have been taken from the traditional sayings (cf. Mt 5:11f; Lk 21:22); this is all the more likely since the same tradition, although remote and obscure, can be detected behind the 'bearing of witness' in v. 27. In the otherwise pessimistic context, the positive statement 'if they kept my word' is surprising. It can hardly be interpreted as a merely rhetorical statement or as the kind of antithesis that is so often encountered in the Johannine style. The Johannine community took both possibilities into account: rejection and persecution on the one hand, and acceptance in faith of their proclamation on the other hand.[80] Their task was to proclaim the word of Jesus, and they did not abandon their mission despite all their sad experiences (see 4:38; 3 Jn 5–8).

15:21   It is also clear from the phrase 'because of my name' that a synoptic tradition is included in this verse.[81] These words do not occur elsewhere in John. The statement in the eschatological discourse (Mk 13:13 par.): 'You will be hated by all for my name's sake' would seem to have influenced John here. Persecution is the result of hatred and, although no details are listed here, it is said: 'All this[82] they will do to you . . .'; the individual persecutions are mentioned only later (16:2f). The graphic eschatological discourse must therefore have been known to the Johannine community, but it is clear that it was not taken over as a whole. The Johannine school simply took its essential elements and applied the idea to the situation in which the community found itself. At the same time, however, it was associated with another idea that is frequently expressed in the gospel: namely, that those who hate and persecute do not know the God who sent Jesus (7:28; 8:19; see also 8:27, 55). Their alienation from God is disclosed in their rejection of Jesus (see 5:38; 8:42f, 46f). This statement is clearly directed against the unbelieving Jews.

15:22–24 The unforgivable 'sin' of the Jews is that they rejected the one whom the Father had sent. It is unforgivable because Jesus has done everything to lead them to faith. The argument is a summary of Jesus' controversy with the unbelieving 'Jews' in the gospel of John. It is a concise apology of Johannine Christianity confronted with contemporary Judaism. Jesus' words and works are evidence of his divine origin and they provide this proof in an indissoluble relationship with each other. His works are mentioned only in the second place because they are able to make a greater impression on non-believers (cf. 10:37f). Their description as 'works which no one else did' points to a tendency towards apology and for the Johannine community the great 'signs' that are narrated in the gospel are not simply symbolic actions, but facts. The 'seeing' (which, despite the correlative $\varkappa\alpha i$ . . . $\varkappa\alpha i$ can only be related to the works[83]) was a purely external (cf. 6:36) and blind (cf. 9:39, 41) seeing, because it was obscured by hatred. In this apology, which is based on rational arguments, unbelief can only be seen as irrational, emotional and amoral, in other words, as 'sin' and indeed simply as *the* sin (see 3:19ff; 5:40–44; 8:40, 44; 9:41). It is for this reason (and because of the context) that hatred rather than unbelief is the theme here. Hatred of Jesus is also directed against his Father. In this context, this statement reinforces the accusation that this rebellion against God is a 'sin'. It cannot be regarded as an unsuitable addition.[84] The line is also extended to the Father in the argument of the 'works', thus leading to an extremely pungent and unreserved accusation. This also occurs in the Johannine presentation of the trial, but there it is only concerned with the leaders of Judaism who are responsible for having handed Jesus over and in particular with the high priest Caiaphas (19:11b). This situation is obscured by the very generalized statement in our present text, which can be explained in the light of the controversy with the unbelieving Jews of the time (see 12:42f). This terrible accusation of hating God could not have been applied generally to unbelievers.[85] What is more, anyone quoting this text against Judaism as such would be in error and would misunderstand the milder note that is also perceptible in the gospel (see, for example, 7:50f; 19:38f, etc.).

15:25   This unfounded hatred of the one sent by God is, like the lack of faith in 12:39f, brought more powerfully home to man's understanding of faith by a quotation from Scripture. Whereas a text from Isaiah is quoted in 12:40, however – a text that played a part elsewhere in the early Christian tradition – , there is no other evidence of the terse quotation in 15:25 having been used elsewhere. Even the long introductory formula – the longest in any of the Johannine quotations of Scripture – is remarkable. There are other phrases in which πληροῦσθαι is employed: 12:38; 13:18 (17:12 without any scriptural text); 19:24, 36. Generally ἡ γραφή is used. It is only in 12:38 that ὁ λογος as 'the word of the prophet Isaiah' occurs. The phrase 'written in the law', with a quotation from a psalm ('law' is therefore used here in the sense of 'holy writ'), only occurs once, in 10:34, where a similarly remarkable and isolated scriptural text is cited. These all point to the special way in which the Johannine school used Scripture.[86] This is confirmed by the reserved expression 'in their law', which corresponds to the Johannine Jesus' use of the phrase 'in your law' (8:17; 10:34; see also 7:19). The Johannine quotations are also characterized by the fact that they do not usually follow a particular text literally, but are rather an adapted rendering of one or more texts (see 6:31). The closest parallels for 15:25 are Ps 35:19; 69:5 (οἱ μισοῦντές με δωρεάν) or Ps 109:3 ('They attacked me without cause'; this is more in accordance with the meaning of the Johannine text); Ps 119:161 ('Princes persecute me without cause'). The complaint of the psalmist is transferred to Jesus, Ps 69 being used in the pre-Johannine representation of the passion (Mk 15:36; Mt 27:34).[87] The emphasis is on δωρεάν, which can only mean 'without a cause' or 'without reason' here, unlike other uses of the word elsewhere in the NT. Those who hate Jesus without any reason are, like the traitor (13:18; 17:12), the subject of scriptural prophecy.

4. The Witness borne by the Paraclete and the Disciples to Jesus (15:26–27)

[26]'But when the Counsellor comes, whom I shall send to you from the Father, the Spirit of truth, who proceeds from the Father, he will bear witness to me; [27]and you also are witnesses, because you have been with me from the beginning.'

15:26   This saying about the Paraclete has frequently been regarded as a later insertion into the text.[88] In fact, 16:1–4a would very suitably follow the section 15:18–25 and would follow v. 20 even more closely. I have, however, already shown (pp. 92–3) that the whole context can be judged quite differently. If the saying about the Paraclete is more closely connected with vv. 22–24, the Paraclete can be seen as having the same function as Jesus in his words and works on earth. He is Jesus' witness.[89] The Paraclete cannot, however, speak to the world directly, but has to make use of the disciples to do this. This means that v. 27 is indispensable, providing clarification and the context in which the disciples are addressed. The witness borne by the Paraclete and that borne by the disciples are expressed in two separate sentences placed side by side, but they come together to form a single witness. In their unity, these two verses are meaningful in the context in which they are placed and can therefore be regarded as a single, unified and carefully reflected formulation.

Another question that arises here is what led to the formulation of vv. 26f, since certain aspects of these two verses are very remarkable: (1) the statement about the origin of the Paraclete is repeated ('whom I shall send to you from the Father' and 'who proceeds from the Father'); (2) the 'Paraclete' (or 'Counsellor') and the 'Spirit of truth' appear side by side (but see also 14:16f); (3) the Paraclete's and the disciples' bearing of witness are co-ordinated (not subordinated one to the other); (4) the phrase 'from the beginning' is striking (v. 27b). It is not a satisfactory explanation to say that a previously existing saying about the Paraclete was adapted.[90] It is possible that there was already in existence a tradition of the theme of the Paraclete,[91] but in that case, it was completely in the background. The form as it exists at present can most satisfactorily be explained as a formation of the Johannine school. The 'coming' of the Paraclete and his 'sending' by Jesus is also discussed in 16:7 (cf. 13), whereas, in the two sayings about the Paraclete in Chapter 14, it was said that the Father would either give or send him. This view must have been included in the second statement about the origin of the Paraclete ('proceeding from the Father'). ἐκπορεύεσθαι is found in only one other place in the gospel of John – in the editorial text 5:29. It was customary to clarify the name 'Paraclete' in the Johannine community by the term 'Spirit of truth' (cf. 14:16f; also 16:7 with 13). ἐκεῖνος and μαρτυρεῖν περὶ are Johannine stylistic criteria.[92] ἀπ' ἀρχῆς occurs frequently in 1 John and there (2:7, 24, where it is found twice; 3:11) it means the beginning of the proclamation. On the basis of these comments, we may assume that a tradition of the 'witness borne by the Paraclete' was expressed in the Johannine school more or less as: 'The Paraclete, whom Jesus sent from the Father, bears witness to him' (cf. 1 Jn 5:6f). The editor had the sayings about the Paraclete mentioned by the evangelist in the farewell discourse (sending by the Father) in mind when inserting it in this text; and he added the witness borne by the disciples because it was important in the context (to the 'world').

The statement made in this saying about the Paraclete can be readily understood as soon as it is recognized as editorial. The coming of the Paraclete is presupposed – ὅταν looks forward, as it does in 16:13, to the whole of the time that he will be with the disciples (see 14:16). The double statement, that is, that Jesus will send him and that he proceeds from the Father, is a synonymous parallelism, expressing the same idea in variation. Most of the church Fathers and several twentieth-century Catholic exegetes[93] interpret this 'proceeding from the Father' in an internally trinitarian sense as a proceeding of the third divine Person of the Trinity from the Father (in the case of the Greek Fathers) and the Son (in the case of the Latin Fathers: filioque). Although this interpretation is in itself possible and is consistent as a dogmatic idea, it did not come within the Johannine vision (see 14:28 above). The 'Johannine Jesus' having been sent by the Father can also be expressed by the formula: 'I came forth (ἐξῆλθον) from God (or the Father)' (8:42; 13:3; 16:27f; 17:8) and we have already seen (7:29 and 8:42 above) that this does not have a different meaning, ἐκπορεύεσθαι being merely a stylistic variant of ἐξέρχεσθαι. It is, however, only in our present text that the Paraclete is said to 'bear witness'. According to the context, this bearing of witness to Jesus is directed towards the 'world'. It is clear that, according to vv. 22–24, this testimony should expose the unbelief of the 'world' and find it guilty, but this activity is not defined more precisely until 16:8–11, when the unambiguous word 'to reprove' (ἐλέγχειν) is used. When it is borne in mind that the witness that the disciples bear on the basis of their having been with Jesus 'from the beginning' is also added to this, then it is hardly possible to deny that this bearing of witness is to some extent ambivalent. There is at least the slight possibility that men will accept the word of the disciples (see v. 20c). The words are to encourage the disciples to bear witness. The choice of this term can probably be explained on the basis of the history of traditions, that is, as reminiscent of Mk 13:9, 11 par. According to the traditional synoptic logion, the disciples were to be brought to trial for Jesus' sake 'for a testimony to them' (εἰς μαρτύριον) and that should not cause them to be anxious about what they would say, since they would not be speaking, but the Holy Spirit (in Mk) or the 'Spirit of the Father' (Mt 10:20).

The text in the Markan eschatological discourse, which is included in the Matthaean discourse addressed to the disciples (Chapter 10), raises a number of questions. Mark inserted v. 10 between the announcement of legal prosecution (13:9) and the promise of help from the Holy Spirit (13:11): 'And the gospel must first be preached to all nations.' This interpolation, which was probably made by the evangelist himself, interprets 'for a testimony to them' in the missionary sense.[95] This phrase may, however, also have pointed to the testimony incriminating those who persecute the disciples or bring them to trial (see Mk 6:11). Another interpretation of this statement is provided by Luke ('It will be a time for you to bear testimony'), who also expresses the help of the Spirit in his own version (21:13–15) and explicitly in a different context (12:11f), which is more reminiscent of Mk (possibly from Q?). In any case, however, the logion of the help of the Spirit as the disciples' defending counsel when they are on trial is very early. It may also be the only saying of Jesus himself in which the Spirit was originally mentioned. It is of great importance in the tradition of the Paraclete, since the Holy Spirit is seen in it in the function of providing legal defence (in other words, as the 'Paraclete').[96]

The saying about the Paraclete can thus be seen as an integral part of the discourse. It belongs closely to the idea of the hatred of the world and the persecution that the disciples have to endure for Jesus' sake. It also points forward to 16:8–11, in which the activity of the Paraclete with regard to the world as a legal procedure is described. At the same time, however, 15:26 retains its own function and overtones.

15:27 The bearing of witness by the disciples follows that of the Spirit; it is not contrasted with it ('but also . . .'), rather, because of the καί . . . δέ,[97] closely connected with it ('and also . . .').[98] This idea of testimony is included in 1 Jn in the vocabulary of proclamation (1:2; 4:14); it occurs in connection with the 'seeing' that empowers men to bear witness (see the excursus on 1 Jn 1:1ff and my commentary on the epistles of John, pp. 52–58). Although it only goes back remotely (by means of the union and solidarity existing between the second and the first generations of those who proclaimed the message), it does in fact look back to the experience of the eye-witnesses and ear-witnesses during the life and activity of Jesus on earth. This is also the explanation of the statement which appears to provide a reason: 'because you have been with me from the beginning'. This 'beginning' does not establish a point of departure in time, but instead emphasizes the origin to which all later proclamation can be traced back. It is because the disciples are in communion with Jesus, the historical revealer who brought God's ultimate word to mankind and is in fact the 'word of life' in person (1 Jn 1:1; he is himself 'from the beginning', 2:13), that their 'witness' has a lasting and insurpassable value in the word of proclamation. The community of believers must also let what it heard 'from the beginning' abide in it (1 Jn 2:24; 3:11). This principle of the 'beginning' is evident at various levels and especially at those of the personal Logos, existing from the beginning, those who are associated with him 'from the beginning' and proclaim the message and the proclamation itself which is heard 'from the beginning' and which the community must let abide in itself. The same principle is also a criterion for every form of gnosis which is unhistorical and teaches what is unaccustomed and new. There is, on the other hand, no evidence at all in Johannine Christianity of any guarantee by means of office or official succession – in contrast to the pastoral epistles. In our present text, the disciples are not described as holding office. They are, on the contrary, seen as witnesses of the event to which they are, with the Spirit and illuminated and strengthened by that Spirit, to continue to bear witness.[99] If the promise of the Paraclete is not confined exclusively to the disciples who were immediately present with Jesus (see 14:26 above), the present text has also to be interpreted as saying that those who are addressed are 'reminded' by the Holy Spirit of everything that Jesus has said. They were with him 'from the beginning', certainly, but their testimony entered the community, which, as a whole, becomes a witness and testifies to the world, its testimony being based on that of the first witnesses and also being carried further by the Holy Spirit (see 16:13). The Holy Spirit expresses the words and actions of Jesus not only through the first men who proclaimed the event, and those who did so later and were united with those first men, but also through the existence and the activity of the whole community, thus carrying out his task to bear witness (see v. 26). It is not possible to exclude from the Johannine vision an understanding of office, according to which those who proclaim the event of Christ have a special place in the community. Indeed, such an understanding may well have been within the intention of the gospel. It is, however, an understanding that is quite removed from all institutional considerations. The whole perspective is dominated by the Spirit of truth as Christ's real witness and advocate.

5. Jewish Hostilities (16:1–4a)

[1]'I have said all this to keep you from falling away. [2]They will put you out of the

synagogues; indeed, the hour is coming when whoever kills you will think he is offering service to God. ³And they will do this because they have not known the Father, nor me. ⁴But I have said these things to you that when their hour comes you may remember my words.'

16:1   The concluding formula: 'I have said all this' could perhaps mark the end of this discourse, but the stated aim, that the disciples should not take offence, points to what follows. Since the description of concrete persecutions that follows is linked to the prediction of persecutions in v. 20f, this verse may be an addition composed by a second person or persons who wanted to clarify Jesus' prophecy of persecutions in the light of the community's immediate experiences (see above, p. 94), 'Taking offence' (or 'falling away'; σκανδαλίζεσθαι) means endangering faith (cf. 6:61). It is a word that already existed in the logia of Jesus. It was current in the language of the community and always pointed to the serious danger of loss of salvation.[100] The worst that can happen is not harsh persecution, but the fact that the disciples can be persecuted in the name of God and that their faith in Jesus as the one sent by God might be shaken by those persecutions. This part of the discourse has the aim of depriving such doubts of their power to harm.

16:2   Unlike excommunication from the synagogue, which was a corrective punishment within Judaism, exclusion from the synagogue broke the bond between the early people of God and those who were affected by this measure. The rabbinate used it from about AD 90 onwards against Christians and there can be no doubt that it was painful in its effects on the members of the Johannine community who had been Jews (see 9:22 and 12:42 above). When this break with the community was accompanied by harsh arguments against Jesus' messianic character – and there is abundant evidence of this in the gospel of John – those who had been Jews and had accepted Christian faith could easily begin to waver (see 8:31 above). The struggle seems to have become so concentrated in the Johannine community ('the hour is coming') and so urgent that fanatical Jews even wanted those who confessed Christ to be put to death (as blasphemers; see above, 10:33), in order to 'offer service to God'.

The formulae used in this verse are striking even within the framework of the gospel of John. 'The hour is coming' is certainly a Johannine phrase (4:23; 5:25; differently in 5:28; 16:25, 32), but elsewhere it refers to the eschatological presence of Jesus (4:23; 5:25). In 5:28 (which is editorial), it also refers to the future hour of raising from the dead, though not to the historical future of the community (in 16:25, the permanent presence of the exalted Christ is intended). It is here used in a similar way to the prophetic and apocalyptic expression 'the days are coming' (Is 39:6; Jer 7:32; 16:14, etc.; Zech 14:1 LXX; 2 Ez 5:1; 13:29, etc.), which was also taken over by the early Church (Mk 2:20; Lk 22:21, 6; 23:29), but is in Johannine diction here. The expression λατρεία for the cultic service of God (prayer and especially sacrifice) occurs only once in John and very rarely in the NT as a whole.[101] What is remarkable is the combination λατρείαν προσφέρειν (very rare in the NT, elsewhere meaning 'making gifts and offerings'), since λατρεία means cultic sacrificial service. These may be signs of another member of the Johannine school.

The increasingly frequent announcement of intentions to put the disciples to death for religious reasons is at first perhaps surprising, but there are indications that this desire on the part of Jewish extremists was a real possibility. In his (fictitious) disputation with the Jew Trypho, Justin Martyr observes: 'Your hands are still raised to commit crime! Even after putting Christ to death, you are not converted. You even hate and kill us, who through him believe in God, the Father of the universe, as often as you have power to do so' (*Dial* 133:6; similarly in 95:4). In the *Martyrdom of Polycarp*, 13:1, we read that it was principally Jews who were prominent in bringing brushwood and kindling for the bishop's death by burning, 'as is the custom with them'. Although Christian polemics against Jewish hostilities may be heard in these and similar pronouncements (and Christian persecutions of Jews were no less severe than the Jews' actions against Christians), it is true to say that the Jews behaved in this way because of their 'holy zeal' for God. There are many examples of this zeal.[103] What we have here, then, is not simply an imaginary announcement, nor do we have a case of putting to death as such (such killings took place, but undoubtedly as individual cases). On the contrary, this verse provides a motivation that those who persecute Christians in this way live under the illusion that they are offering service to God.

16:3   Jesus disputes that men who, in their blind zeal for God, want to put his disciples to death can have a knowledge of the Father and therefore true communion with God. The criticism that is frequently made in the gospel, namely that Jesus' unbelieving partners in dialogue do not, despite their claim to the contrary, know God (see 5: 37b–38; 7:28; 8:27, 55), is resumed here, in order to invalidate the arguments of Jews persecuting Christians at a later stage. The same idea is also expressed in 15:21b; here, however, there is added, with a retrospective glance at Jesus (the aorist οὐκ ἔγνωσαν) that neither have they known him. This shows that neither have they known the Father – and that, of course, is the fundamental position of Johannine Christianity with regard to Judaism. For this reason, this verse fits very well into the context.[104] It is, in part, a literal copy of v. 21.

16:4   The discourse is definitively concluded at this point and, what is more, by the same hand that added 16:1–3. This is clear because the expected 'hour' is the same as in v. 2. What is striking, however, is the phrase '*their* hour'. The personal pronoun, which is omitted from several manuscripts, but is undoubtedly original,[105] certainly refers to the Jewish persecutors. This places the 'hour' within the same perspective as the 'hour' in Jesus' statement on being arrested in Lk 22:53: 'This is *your* hour and the power of darkness.' It is possible that the Johannine text is reminiscent of the Lukan statement. The second αὐτῶν, which is also omitted from several manuscripts,[106] names what the disciples should remember (ταῦτα) and the ὅτι clause points to the fact that Jesus (ἐγώ) has told them this. The mode of expression is complicated, but it emphasizes the same theme that is found in 13:19 and 14:29. It is clear from the details in the formulation ('their hour' and μνημονεύειν) that this is a later addition. Indeed, the whole of this short unit of discourse (vv. 1–4a; enclosed by ταῦτα λελάληκα) is an addition resulting from the hard-pressed situation in which the Johannine community was placed. A similar situation is also reflected in Rev 2:9; 3:9, in which the Jews of Smyrna and Sardes are called a 'synagogue of Satan'. The Johannine community may therefore have settled in Asia Minor (perhaps Ephesus; see Rev 2:3).

Chapter 2

A Consolatory Discourse: The Activity of the Paraclete
Joy and Peace despite all Distress (16:4b–33)

The most remarkable aspect of the new discourse in Chapter 16 of the gospel is that it goes back to the situation of farewell (see vv. 5–7). This means that it is close to the original farewell discourse in Chapter 14, with which it has many structural and thematic affinities (dialogues with the disciples especially, although not with individual disciples; see above, p. 90). Is it perhaps no more than another draft written by the evangelist?[1] Several factors that are in contrast with Chapter 14, however, tend to disprove this theory. (1) The introduction in v. 5: 'Yet none of you asks me, "Where are you going?" ' is not in accordance with Thomas' question in 14:5 (or with Peter's in 13:36). These questions asked by the disciples are ignored because of the attempt to establish a definite point of departure for the discourse. (2) There is no reference in Chapter 14 to any activity on the part of the Paraclete with regard to the world. On the contrary, it is said in that chapter that the world cannot receive him and neither sees nor knows him (v. 17). The new discourse places great stress on the fact that the world will be exposed and proved guilty by the Paraclete (16:8–11). (3) According to 14:19, there is only one short period of time (a 'little while') until Jesus is withdrawn from the world and is once again present with the disciples. According to 16:16, on the other hand, there are two short periods (a 'little while' and 'again a little while'), the first until Jesus leaves the disciples and the second until they see each other again. The evangelist's view, that Jesus' death (his 'exaltation') and his glorification coincide, is relaxed here, even though this new discourse is dominated by the perspective of his permanent presence after Easter (see 16:22). (4) Another new aspect in this discourse is the direct relationship with the Father that is mentioned in 16:26f. In 14:13f, it is emphasized that *Jesus* will do everything for his disciples and his mediating function with the Father with regard to the community of disciples is also stressed in 14:21–23. (5) Finally, the farewell discourse in Chapter 14 was above all concerned with the need to strengthen the disciples' faith and prevent it from being shaken by the imminent passion of Jesus. In 16:30, however, the disciples declare their faith in Jesus and he calls the effectiveness of that faith into doubt (v. 31f). All this leads us to conclude that the discourse in Chapter 16 was conceived by a different author and from a different point of view; although it is to some extent modelled on Chapter 14, it has been rethought on the basis of a new intention. (It is, in other words, a re-reading or *relecture*.) It is, however, closely connected in its thought and expression to the evangelist, as the essentially identical ideas (the activity of the Paraclete, reunion with the disciples, the assurance that their prayer will be heard etc.) and concepts (the Spirit of truth, joy and peace) so clearly show.

A structural analysis of the language of this discourse will help us to understand the positive meaning of the text. The word 'sorrow' (λύπη) occurs frequently, both at the beginning (v. 6) and then very emphatically in the middle (v. 20: 'weep and lament'), where it is stressed in the parable of the woman in labour (v. 21f). Closely related to this word is the 'distress' or 'tribulation' (θλῖψις) at the end of the discourse (v. 33), which is to be experienced by the disciples, although the time of joy has already begun. This vocabulary of sadness is completely absent from Chapter 14; λύπη is confined exclusively to Chapter 16 in the gospel of John. This observation is strengthened by the occurrence of the antonym 'joy' (χαρά) four times in Chapter 16 (vv. 20, 21, 22, 24) and the verb χαίρειν twice, with a sharp contrast between the 'rejoicing' of the world (v. 20) and that of the disciples (v. 22). In 14:28, on the other hand, the reference to 'rejoicing' is made simply in passing. 'Joy' is the dominant mood of the community in Chapter 16 and the attitude which the disciples should strive to have. They should be of good cheer (θαρσεῖτε, v. 33) in their courageous encounter with the world in the knowledge of Christ's victory (νικᾶν, v. 33; cf. the statement about judgment being passed on the ruler of this world in v. 11). As the parable in v. 21 shows, joy follows sorrow and distress (θλῖψις – χαρά) and this joy already exists for the disciples and cannot be destroyed (v. 22).

The occurrence of 'world' (κόσμος) is also interesting. Word-counting alone shows that this word is found six times in Chapter 14 and eight times in Chapter 16. The emphasis given to the 'world' as a reality to be controlled in the last discourse can be seen in the weighty theme at the beginning of proving the world guilty (vv. 8–11) and in the note sounded at the end, that of victory over the world (v. 33). The confrontation between the disciples and the world is elaborated in all three discourses (see 14:17, 19, 22, 27; 15:18f; 16:20). The harsh confrontation with the world forms a stronger link between 15:18–27 and 16:8–11, 33. The existence of the disciples in the world and their struggle with the world (mentioned in 14:30f only in connection with Jesus' encounter with the 'ruler of this world') are brought to the fore in the two additional discourses.

It is therefore possible to describe the discourse in Chapter 16 as a consolatory discourse for the comfort and encouragement of the community of disciples in the world. The aim of the farewell discourse in Chapter 14 was – within the framework of the gospel as such – to indicate the way that the disciples' faith should follow in the future, despite Jesus' passion and departure; the discourse in Chapter 16, however, has the task of overcoming the sorrow and despondency of the community of disciples. It is therefore much more of a truly consolatory discourse than the farewell discourse, and for this reason the situation of farewell is used once again. It is possible to imagine the author of this chapter knowing the evangelist's farewell discourse and making use of it for his own intention. He also knew the discourse in Chapter 15 and linked his discourse particularly to the second part (with its theme of 'separation from the world'). Whereas the discourse in Chapter 15 is parenetic, that is, admonitory in its concern, that in Chapter 16 is above all 'paracletic', that is, it has the intention of consoling and encouraging. It should be noted that this only indicates a prevalent tendency and not a completely different orientation. Seen as a whole, all three discourses were written to strengthen the faith of the later community and to admonish and encourage its members.

The construction of the discourse in Chapter 16 is essentially clear enough, but it is possible to see certain details differently. After an introduction in which the situation is described (vv. 5–6), the first part deals with the coming (v. 7) and the activity of the Paraclete, especially with regard to the world (vv. 8–11) and the community of disciples (vv. 12–15). Because the sayings about the Paraclete belong together, it would be unwise to make a division after v. 11.[2] The situation at the point of departure is once again resumed at v. 16 and vv. 16–22 form a single unit under the heading of 'Jesus' painful departure and reunion in joy'. The idea of lasting joy (v. 22) then draws attention to the time that already exists and will continue to exist for the disciples, a time for which they have received the promise that their prayer will be heard (vv. 23–24). Finally, a new beginning ($\tau\alpha\tilde{\upsilon}\tau\alpha \lambda\varepsilon\lambda\acute{\alpha}\lambda\eta\kappa\alpha$, v. 25) marks the contrast between the time when Jesus' discourse still cannot be understood and the time of a direct relationship with the Father. This leads on to a concluding dialogue with the disciples that culminates in a prospect of consolation (vv. 25–33). The disciples' present lack of understanding will then be overcome and their faint-heartedness will be transformed into confidence. The later community is also exhorted to persist in its situation in the world in this address to the disciples of that time (v. 33).

1. The Coming of the Paraclete and his Activity with regard to the World (16:4b–11)

[4b]*'I did not say these things to you from the beginning, because I was with you.* [5]*But now I am going to him who sent me; yet none of you asks me, "Where are you going?"* [6]*But because I have said these things to you, sorrow has filled your hearts.* [7]*Nevertheless I tell you the truth: it is to your advantage that I go away, for if I do not go away, the Counsellor will not come to you, but if I go, I will send him to you.* [8]*And when he comes, he will prove the world guilty (and expose) what sin, righteousness and judgment are;* [9]*sin (is) that they do not believe in me;* [10]*righteousness (is) that I go to the Father and you will see me no more,* [11]*judgment (is) that the ruler of this world is judged'.*

16:4b–6 The new discourse is editorially bracketed with the previous discourse. It probably began with the announcement of Jesus' departure (ὑπάγω κτλ.) and presented the theme of sorrow. The editorial transition must have been linked to 15:27 (cf. ἐξ ἀρχῆς with 'απ' ἀρχῆς and μεθ' ὑμῶν with μετ' ἐμοῦ). There is also a linguistic similarity which has a connection with the ideas in the previous discourse – because the disciples were with Jesus from the beginning of his revelatory activity, they will bear witness to him, but Jesus has, up till now (that is, since the beginning), not told them that (ταῦτα); that is, he has not informed them about their late situation of persecution and their later task to bear witness (15:18–27), because his being with them exempted them from this concern. The text can hardly mean that he wanted to remain silent about it until this and to tell them. It must surely mean that they were secure in his community. Now, however, the editor or editors add, at a time of separation, he must inform them of this. The sorrow, which forms the point of departure for the new discourse, can therefore be provided with a more precise motivation – because Jesus now has to tell them this (for the ὅτι clause, see the beginning of 16:1), they are made so speechless by sorrow that they are unable to ask him where he is going. In the discourse as it previously existed, the disciples' 'sorrow' was undoubtedly related to the announcement of Jesus' departure, but the perfect tense (λελάληκα, v. 6) can only be related to the previous discourse.

Without the editorial transition, then, the discourse would probably have begun in the following way: 'I am going to him who sent me; yet none of you asks me, "Where are you going?" But sorrow has filled your hearts'. This enables us to see that the reproach simply provides a rhetorical basis for the situation of sorrow – they are made speechless by Jesus' announcement. Attempts to explain the discrepancy between 16:5b and the disciples' questions in 13:36 and 14:5 in other ways[3] therefore cease to be valid. There are two different approaches to the problem of throwing light on the disciples' lack of understanding and perplexity. The common point of contact, however, is Jesus' statement that he is going away (ὑπάγω). This word is exchanged for others meaning 'go away' in the following passage (ἀπέλθω, πορεύομαι, v. 7), but it recurs, with some theological relevance, in vv. 10 and 17 and points to what was important to the Johannine school. This is that Jesus' statement about his departure (ὑπάγω) was enigmatic and scandalous for the unbelieving Jews (7:33; 8:14, 21f) and, for the disciples themselves, a word of revelation which they did not at first understand (13:33; 16:5, 17), but was none the less deeply meaningful (see 14:28; 16:7, 10). It became clear to John and his pupils in their reflection about Jesus' 'departure' that he came to his own in a different way (14:28) and that the Spirit, who is with them and in them, continues his work (16:7). What took place, then, was not a separation, but the coming about of a new communion on a higher and wider plane that was necessary for the completion of Jesus' work on earth (see 14:12, 28; 15:16; 16:8–15; 17:2).

The disciples' 'sorrow' is the result of their having been left in the world and their alienation from the world, which is hostile towards them (see 16:20).[4] One of the main intentions of this discourse is to overcome this sorrow and it should therefore not be confined to the situation of those particular disciples at that time. Together with those disciples, the later community has also to overcome sorrow and fear resulting from the 'tribulation' and distress which it experiences in the world and because of the world (v. 33). This takes place when the disciples and the members of the later community reflect in faith about the joy which has been given to them since Easter and which cannot pass away (v. 22). Their sadness is no more than the dark background to the light of joy and peace that has since then been shed for all believers.

16:7 Jesus' departure should not fill the disciples with paralyzing sadness. On the contrary(ἀλλ'), it is to their advantage, because the Paraclete will come to them. The addition: 'I tell you the truth' is certainly not merely a way of strengthening the statement – it also provides the words with their revelatory character (see 8:40, 45)[5]. The disciples misunderstand their situation and Jesus (ἐγώ) tells them what the meaning of his departure really is. The fact that he does not speak again of the goal to which he is going confirms the rhetorical character of his criticism in v. 5. The emphatic way of speaking that presents his going away as the prerequisite for the Paraclete's coming to them (ἐὰν μή . . . οὐ μὴ ἔλθῃ[6]) can only be understood as a strong desire to disclose to the disciples the meaning of the event. The Paraclete is introduced as a known factor and appears here, as he does in no other saying, emphatically as the one sent by Jesus. At first, nothing is said about his function. The fact of his coming is so important for the disciples that they are able to make the best of Jesus' departure. The statement presupposes a very high appreciation of the Paraclete in the community and also leads the community to appreciate him. Its members are made conscious of the fact that it is not Jesus who says the ultimate word and gives them the ultimate gift during his earthly life, but the Spirit, who is present in the community and reveals his words to them and who discloses the lasting content of those words and opens them to the future (v. 13). The statement about Jesus' being replaced by the Paraclete, which has a mythological ring, really points to the appointment of Jesus in his full effectiveness, since all that the Spirit does is to express Jesus and set his saving power free. The earthly Jesus is present in the community in the Spirit; the community lives from his words and is active on the basis of his strength.[7] In this way, he puts an end to the situation of paralysing sadness and abandonment without consolation. Just as the disciples were called upon to be joyful in the farewell discourse in Chapter 14, because Jesus was going to the Father who was 'greater' than he (14:28), so is the same suggestion made to them here in the thought of the Paraclete. The joy that is promised to the disciples when they see Jesus again – in other words, in their encounter with the risen Lord (see v. 22) – becomes, through the Spirit, a joy that cannot be destroyed, because the Spirit preserves Jesus' presence and makes it fruitful. The statement about Jesus' departure therefore paradoxically becomes a promise of his presence, although he is present in a different way. It reveals the deep insight that the Johannine circle had into the fact that the words and deeds of Jesus during his life on earth only became spirit and life for the community in *Christus praesens* or, to express this idea in a different way, that their full effect was only developed in the Spirit.

16:8   The activity of the Paraclete with regard to the world is presented in this verse as a legal battle or a cosmic trial. This is clear not only from the term ἐλέγχειν, which summarizes the Paraclete's function, but also from the concepts 'sin, righteousness and justice' that are elucidated in the verses that follow and in the context of ideas created by them.

The verb ἐλέγχειν can have several very different meanings. In the Bible (LXX), the meaning 'to correct, reprove, chastise' is dominant, together with 'expose' and 'prove guilty'. It is not, however, used in a forensic sense, but in a moral and pedagogical sense, that is, by exposing sin and guilt, man is led to conversion.[8] According to the two comparable texts that are available, the word is, however, more narrowly defined in Johannine linguistic usage (cf. 3:20; 8:46): who commits evil actions does not come into the light, so that his works are not 'exposed' and, according to the context, in which the 'judgment' is discussed (3:18f), the term acquires forensic overtones. When Jesus, in the second comparable text, says: 'which of you convicts me of sin?', that is, 'who can reprove me concerning sin' or 'prove me sinful' (8:46), then the intention of the Jews, in the wider context (8:37, 40), to put him to death shows that condemnation is meant here and that there are also forensic overtones. In this respect, this text is also close to 16:8ff, in which ἐλέγχειν is used with περί (not as in the Septuagint) and a 'controversial object' is named which also occurs in our present text: sin, used in both texts without the article. In the rest of the NT, the conceptual use of ἐλέγχειν (also with περί) in Jude 15 comes closest to its use in our present text. A text from the *Book of Enoch* (1:9) is cited in Jude 15, dealing with God's eschatological judgment of the godless, and the author of the epistle goes on to say that God will prove them guilty of all their godless works. This text is concerned quite clearly with a forensic case of proving guilty with the aim of condemning and punishing and, in it, God appears even more clearly than in Jn 16:8ff as judge. The quotation from the *Book of Enoch* is not purely coincidental, since ideas which may throw light on the background to the Johannine text are found in that book and in related documents.

The whole passage, then, has a forensic character and, within the image of judgment, which is deeply rooted in the gospel of John, leads up to an obvious climax.[9] The Johannine Jesus is involved in a legal battle with the unbelieving world (see 3:19; 5:22, 30; 8:16, 26; 9:39 above in the commentary) and the earthly trial conducted against Jesus is, in John, a representation of this underlying battle but in a paradoxical transformation. The present saying about the Paraclete can be seen in this perspective. It also has certain points of contact with 8:46; the Paraclete will prove the world guilty of the 'sin' of which Jesus' opponents want to show him guilty, although they are not capable of doing this, by exposing what sin really is and showing that it is closely associated with the world. It is also related to 12:31: 'judgment' takes place in that the 'ruler of the world' is judged and, what is more, judged precisely at the point where he believed that he could triumph over Jesus, that is, on the cross. This does not, however, fully explain the saying about the Paraclete, whose distinctive characteristic can be found in the fact that the

Paraclete has a very special part to play in Jesus' legal battle with the world. The Paraclete can be described, according to the subject itself, as an 'advocate', a 'prosecuting counsel' or the one who argues the case, but ὁ παράκλητος is not a technical term for this office, but is rather 'friendly assistance'.[10] Why, then, is he said to be active in 'exposing' and 'proving guilty'? What views are concealed behind this term? Before I discuss this, however, I must try to elucidate the relationship between this 'exposing' and 'proving guilty' and the three concepts that are connected with it in our present text.

'Sin, righteous and judgment' are not 'points of accusation';[11] at the most, this description can only be applied to 'sin'. Nor is it simply a question of elucidating concepts or explaining what the three factors mean,[12] since judgment is at the same time passed on the world in the activity of the Paraclete. In exposing the situation concerning sin, righteousness and judgment, the Paraclete shows the world that it is guilty and includes it within the judgment that has already been passed on the 'ruler of this world'. This is an existential event in which revelation takes place at the same time both as a disclosure of reality and as the realization of revelation. One is therefore tempted to regard the ὅτι clauses that follow partly as factual statements ('that') and partly as causal clauses ('because'). Because of this existential character, they have to be seen, however, as explicitating clauses.[13] We are not told precisely how this activity that is attributed to the Paraclete takes place in the concrete, but, according to 15:26f, there can be no doubt that he makes use of the disciples or the believing community in it.[14] It is also not simply by means of the disciples' proclamation that the Paraclete gains a hearing with regard to the world – we ought rather to think at the same time of the existence and the life of faith of the community in this context. It is only in this way that the fact can be exposed that the 'ruler of this world' has been stripped of his power, that Jesus has taken possession of his power to save as the one who has returned to the Father and that the 'world', together with its lack of faith, has been shown to be in the wrong. The whole statement is supported by the community's self-understanding that its faith has conquered the world in and through Christ (see 16:33; 1 Jn 5:4).

The background to this activity of the Paraclete that exposes and proves guilty in word and deed, in other words, the possibility of the existence of such a way of speaking, is illuminated by certain Jewish views, especially, as Betz has so convincingly demonstrated,[15] in the *Books of Enoch*. Although the problem of the Paraclete is not fully solved by an examination of these texts (see Excursus 16), they do at least throw a great deal of light on the saying about the Paraclete in Jn 16:8–11.

According to the *Book of Jubilees* (4:23), Enoch, who has acquired sovereignty and honour in the garden of Eden, 'wrote down the judgment passed on the world and all the evil actions of men'. He performed this task of heavenly scribe 'in order to count all the deeds of all generations until the day of judgment' (Jub 10:17). In this function of accuser of all the godless – and indirectly also that of the counsel for the defence of the righteous (see Jub 10:3f; the prayer of Noah) – in preparation for the day of judgment at the end of time, Enoch resembles the Johannine Paraclete. The main difference is that the latter already carries out this function, in accordance with the Johannine theology, here and now: God's judgment is already passed on the world from the moment of Jesus' 'exaltation'. According to the Ethiopic *Book of Enoch* (14:1), Enoch is writing a 'book of words of righteousness and accusation that proves men guilty' and this book is intended for the eternal watchmen, that is, the disobedient angels. According to the same book (89:62f, 70), another scribe (probably Michael) has the task of writing down the transgressions and misdeeds of the seventy shepherds of the people and, according to 90:17, he reads aloud from this book at God's judgment. The same terminology at least occurs in the Qumran documents and an appeal is made to God's judgment as the ultimate authority against unjust men. It is, however, hardly possible to speak of the 'teacher of righteousness' as having a similar function to Enoch's.[16] Gnostic texts also provide no real parallels, even in the case of *Ginza*, 436:28ff, according to which Adam reports his lawsuit to the first life or when, in *Ginza*, 256: 28f, the Uthras are sent into the world to conduct the trial of the souls that they are to take back to the heavenly world.[17] Another text that is often cited in this context (*Test Jud*, 20:5) points in a different direction: 'The Spirit of truth testifies to everything and accuses everything', since this statement is concerned with man's inner life and the 'cosmic' sphere is absent.

Using the image of a cosmic trial that is conducted in the presence of God, then, the saying about the Paraclete develops the ideas that already existed in Judaism in connection with God's eschatological judgment and applies them to the present situation of the Johannine community. In the Spirit who has been given to it, the community has an advocate of God who argues Jesus' case, exposes judgment on unbelief and helps the community towards victory. The eschatological event takes place already in the present existence of the community. In mythological language, which is none the less not inaccessible to reflection in faith, the community is encouraged and consoled. Its members are told that God is on their side and that he is in their community and active through it. He is superior to all powers that are active against it (see 1 Jn 4:4).

16:9   Unbelief as sin was discussed in 8:21–24 in Jesus' dispute with the Jews (see the commentary above) and its inexcusable character was harshly pointed out in 15:22–25. The Paraclete reveals that 'sin' in the real sense of the word[18] also consists in not believing in Jesus and that lack of faith with regard to Jesus is therefore the real sin. How does he reveal this? Through the believing community! The faith of that community is, after all, a lasting testimony against the unbelieving 'world' and against its wrong refusal of faith. This constant element that is present in the community is expressed by the present tense οὐ πιστεύουσιν. The community is irritated by the lack of faith that it encounters, but it is itself a constant accusation against those who do not believe. It has reason for its faith and carries its point through to the end.

16:10   The next stage in the process of thought can be characterized thus: the correctness of faith is proved by Jesus' justification by God. 'Righteousness' is the second point which is elucidated by the Paraclete and by means of which he furthers the trial conducted against the world. The wrongness of unbelief is exposed by his positive presentation of the nature of 'righteousness'. In what sense, however, is 'righteousness' intended here? Is the Paraclete pointing to *Jesus'* righteousness? There is no genitive and, from the purely linguistic point of view, the expression may be understood as fundamentally as 'sin' and 'judgment'. Jesus' righteousness is involved objectively in that he is going to the Father and is justified in the presence of his opponents. In this forensic context, however, 'righteousness' is also related to the judgment passed on the 'world'. The world is shown to be in the wrong in that justice is done to Jesus.[19] There are two cases of 'righteousness' or 'just' judgment in the gospel of John (5:30; 7:24), so that the forensic meaning can be proved. On the other hand, Jesus Christ, who dwells with God, is described in 1 Jn 2:1 as 'righteous' and this Christological meaning can be detected here.[20] This is also suggested by the continuation of our present verse – Jesus, who is no longer seen by the disciples, dwells with the Father and is thus seen to be 'righteous'.

The idea of Jesus' 'righteousness' is given a firmer preparation in the gospel than would appear from the unique occurrence of the word δικαιοσύνη here.[21] Jesus is not looking for his own honour (δόξα), but 'there is one who seeks it and he will judge' (8:50). It is the Father who 'glorifies' Jesus (δοξάζων, 8:54). God's 'judging', which draws attention to Jesus' innocence, his separation from 'sin' (8:46) and his 'honour', takes place definitively with his 'glorification', when the Father takes him to himself. In his greatest distress, God is with him (see 8:29; 16:32) and, even while he is still on earth, he will also glorify him (see 12:28). In opposition to Jesus' enemies, Moses appears as an accuser (5:45) and scripture (5:39) and Jesus' own word (12:48) are witnesses. Jesus' antagonist, the 'ruler of this world', has no claim to him and no power over him (14:30). All these statements come within the perspective of 16:10 and a confirmation of this idea of Jesus' righteousness can be found in a little known text in the NT, the hymn of Christ in 1 Tim 3:16, in which it is said of Jesus' entry into the heavenly world that he was 'glorified in the Spirit' (ἐδικαιώθη ἐν πνεύματι). However this δικαιοῦσθαι may be interpreted,[22] it is certainly close to the Johannine conception.

The phrase that is addressed to the disciples: 'and *you* will see me no more' is surprising. One would have expected: the *world* will see me no more' (cf. 14:19; also 7:34; 8:21; 12:36b). This statement may perhaps be connected with the way of thinking which occurs in the *Books of Enoch* and which we have already discussed; as O. Betz has pointed out, 'No longer seeing a righteous man may be evidence of the fact that his ascent has taken place'.[23] The fact that this statement is addressed to the disciples, however, can be explained by the context and the intention of the discourse. The disciples are to understand the meaning of Jesus' departure and if they no longer see him (see 16:16), this should not be a cause for sorrow, but rather be a sign that God is demonstrating his 'justice' in him. The disciples are drawn into the Paraclete's trial of the world and, if they no longer see Jesus, the Paraclete is still there and proves to the world that Jesus is dwelling with the Father.[24]

16:11   The ultimate certainty which caused lack of faith to lose its case against God is the fact that the ruler of this world has already been judged. The verb, κέκριται, is in the perfect tense and is as definitive in its implication as it is in 3:18. The judgment has taken place and, as 12:31f shows clearly, at the very 'hour' when Jesus was 'exalted'. Our present verse, 16:11, is directly related to this proclamation of the taking away of power from or 'casting out' (ἐκβληθήσεται) of the 'ruler of this world' in 12:31f, which affirms, after the announcement of Jesus' exaltation, that Jesus' personified adversary and, together with him, the unbelieving world (12:31) are already judged. How, then, does the Paraclete show this? Once again by means of the community which believes and lives from faith! 1 Jn provides a commentary on this: 'You have overcome the evil one' (2:13, 14). Only the world is 'in the power of the evil one' (5:19). The children of God are withdrawn from his power because they have, through the Spirit, the strength to avoid sin (see 3:9f; 5:18) and are, in the community of the Son of God, protected from the grip of the evil one (5:18, 20).

If we look once again at the whole of this very distinctive saying about the Paraclete, we can see that its structure is quite consistent. The Paraclete exposes the sin of the lack of faith of the world and shows that unbelieving world that it is guilty by confronting it with the faith of the community. The community knows that it is in the right, because Jesus has been justified by God and the adversary has been judged. This leads to the passing of judgment on unbelief – who does not believe is already judged (3:18). This, of course, presupposes that the community believes that the Paraclete, the Spirit of truth, has been given to it. By having this faith in the gift of the Paraclete made fully conscious in the saying about the Paraclete and by being thus strengthened in that faith, the community is encouraged in its distress both the bear witness to its faith and to resist unbelief. In this way, it also shares in the function attributed here to the Paraclete.

2. The Activity of the Paraclete in the Community of the Disciples (16:12–15)

[12]'*I have yet many things to say to you, but you cannot bear them now.* [13]*When the Spirit of truth comes, he will guide you into all the truth; for he will not speak on his own (authority), but whatever he hears he will speak, and he will declare to you all the things that are to come.* [14]*He will glorify me, for he will take what is mine and declare it to you.* [15]*All that the Father has is mine; therefore I said that he will take what is mine and declare it to you*'.

16:12   The description of the activity of the Paraclete with regard to the world is followed by an account of his activity in the community. As is clear from what was contained in vv. 8–11, both passages are very closely connected. The Paraclete accuses and exposes the world and proves it guilty only by means of the community, and the community also requires faith in the Paraclete and the support of the Paraclete in order to fulfil that task. The discourse, however, sets the internal function of the Paraclete within the community off against the saying in vv. 8–11, which was presented in the image of judgment, by means of the intervening comment in v. 12, with the result that vv. 13–15 represent a distinctive saying about the Paraclete.

Jesus' present revelation to the disciples seems in this verse to be more open than it is in 14:25f, where he was looking back to his words spoken at the hour of his farewell and promised the Paraclete as the spiritual teacher who would remind the disciples of everything that he himself had said. Here, however, he states explicitly that he still has many things to tell the disciples that they cannot bear to hear now and that he will therefore not tell them at that time. The Paraclete is not only his interpreter, but also his 'successor', who will continue his revelation. This difference, which is not, on the basis of the contents of the texts, a contradiction, is connected with the intention and perspective of the new discourse. Jesus' departure and the coming of the Paraclete are presented in v. 7 figuratively as an exchange of two persons. In vv. 8–11, the Paraclete assumed a special function with regard to the world. Here, his 'independent' task with regard to the community of the disciples is also elaborated. It is, however, once again explicitly and emphatically stated that the Paraclete only receives what belongs to Jesus (vv. 14f), in other words, it is clear that Jesus' position as revealer is not obscured by the Paraclete. The fact that attention is entirely directed here towards the community led to this way of speaking.

As soon as this intention is understood, it becomes clear what Jesus cannot yet tell his disciples. The observation that the disciples cannot bear it now also provides us with a further indication. What they, in other words, cannot yet bear to be told concerns the later situation of the community, which is still beyond the grasp of the disciples who are present with Jesus, the intelligibility of Jesus' words in his disciples' present existential situation, and the constantly open future, in which revelation will have its present meaning and also a new meaning (see τὰ ἐρχόμενα ἀναγγελεῖ). The image of carrying heavy burdens underlies the term 'bearing' and this leads on to the situation of 'sorrow', which was the point of departure for the discourse. The community will have a heavy burden to bear in its confrontation with the world, but then the Paraclete will disclose to it the meaning of its existence in the world.

16:13   This (last) saying about the Paraclete brings the 'Spirit of truth', as he is once more called with the aim of elucidation (see the commentary on 14:17 above), to the attention of the disciples and tells them that he will guide them into all the truth. This function, which is quite different from the one that he carries out with regard to the world, is more in accordance with the original meaning of 'Paraclete', to stand up *for* someone, but it is not identical with that meaning, since no one who is over and against that someone is visible. The saying therefore probably deals with the activity of the Holy Spirit that is directed towards the disciples or the community, as this emerges also in 1 John (see my *Johannes-Briefe,* Excursus, pp. 209–215, especially pp. 210f). In comparison with the other functions that are attributed to the Johannine Paraclete, this activity bears the most powerful impress of Christian experience and points most clearly to the Johannine school's understanding of itself. It is possible to justify the 'pneumatic' exposition of Jesus' message on the basis of this function.

An interesting textual variant is διηγήσεται ὑμῖν τὴν ἀλήθειαν Tat[ar. it. neerl.] e aur m

The Gospel according to St John

(Speculum) Vg (*docebit*; cf. 14:26), georg Euseb Cyr of Jer, Aug. This διηγεῖσθαι, which clearly resulted, by reflection, from ὁδηγ, is reminiscent of the statement made about Jesus in Jn 1:18 (ἐξηγεῖσθαι) and characterizes the Paraclete as the 'narrator' or revealer of the whole truth. Unlike the distinctive image of guiding on the way, this variant has no claim to originality.

Wis 9:11 (ὁδηγήσει με) and 10:10 (δίκαιον ὡδήγησεν, that is, Jacob) have to be considered above all as providing a background to this saying, which displays distinctively Johannine linguistic characteristics and must have been formulated for this purpose. Wisdom, sent down from heaven by God (9:10), may have been used by the Johannine school, in which sapiential texts were also employed christologically (see, for example, the hymn to the Logos; 6:35; the discourse on the vine), as a model of the Paraclete's function with regard to Jesus' disciples. In the psalms too, God is asked to let his good Spirit lead the people on a 'level path' (Ps 142:10, LXX), to lead them himself to his truth (ἐπὶ τὴν ἀλήθειαν; 24:5) or to conduct them on his way (85:11). All these texts contain instruction for right behaviour and action that is both morally correct and productive of happiness. This illuminating and revealing function of Wisdom, or God's Spirit, is even more prominent in the work of Philo Judaeus, who says, for example: 'The human spirit (νοῦς) would not aspire to go forward with such clear-sightedness if there were not a divine Spirit (θεῖον πνεῦμα) guiding him towards the truth' (*De Vita Moysis* II: 265). For Philo, Moses was the 'teacher of divine things' who had the divine Spirit to help him and lead him on the right way (*De gig.*, 54f). The gnostic authors write most clearly of all about man's introduction to the light of knowledge, although they do this, of course, in the sense of gnosis as the soul's knowledge of itself.

In the Hermetic literature, for example, we read: 'The Noῦs rises and enters the God-fearing soul and leads (ὁδηγεῖ) it to the light of knowledge' (*C Herm*, X:21); 'Look for a guide, who will lead you to the gates of knowledge, where the bright light is!' (VII: 2); 'The Noῦs is great and, if he is led from the word to a certain point, he can go on to the truth' (IX:10). The part played by Hermes (= the Noῦs) as the guide of the soul, however, is different from that played by the Johannine Paraclete, who has the task of guiding, not the soul, but the community of the disciples into the truth. There is a stronger OT note in the *Odes of Solomon* (3:10): 'It is the Spirit of the Lord, who is without deception, who teaches men so that they know his ways', but the gnostic emphasis reappears, for example, in 36:1: 'I found peace in the Spirit of the Lord and he raised me up to the heights.' In the Coptic Gnostic texts, the Spirit gives man the power to rise up into the realm of light. In the so-called *Being of the Archons*, 144:22ff, for example, we read: 'The powers will not be able to approach them because of the Spirit of truth dwelling in them'; *ibid.*, 145:14ff: 'All the children of the light will then know the truth, their true roots, the Father of the universe and the Holy Spirit' (translation by M. Schenke). In BG 67, we also read: 'Those to whom that Pneuma comes will certainly live and forsake evil . . . If, however, this powerful, divine Pneuma comes to life, it will strengthen the power, that is, the soul, which will not go astray into evil.' In none of these examples is the Spirit seen as a true guide on the way.

The 'truth' to which the Paraclete leads the disciples or into which he accompanies them can only be understood in the same sense as in the rest of the gospel – as the revelation brought by Jesus Christ and promising life (see the Excursus in Vol. 2, pp. 225–237). It cannot be limited to moral action, nor can it be explained in the gnostic sense. It is concerned with a more profound penetration into the content of revelation and at the same time with the application of that revelation to the behaviour of the community within the world. Whether preference is given to either of the two equally strong readings makes no difference to this interpretation.

(1) ἐν τῇ ἀληθείᾳ πάσῃ (or with a different arrangement of the words) ℵ D Θ L W λ 33 565 al. b c ff² sy^s bo^pt Victorin Nonnus Cyr

(2) εἰς τὴν ἀλήθειαν πᾶσαν (or with a different arrangement of words) A B K Δ Π Ψ 054 068 φ 28 700 892 al. P a f q r¹ Tert Chrys Epiph Theod al.

The editors' views are divided. Merk and Nestlé-Aland prefer the second reading. Bover, the UBS Greek NT, on the other hand, prefer the first. The linguistic usage of the Septuagint can be cited in favour of the first: this is the image of one who is accompanied on a way or in a territory. It is certainly the *lectio difficilior* as far as the Johannine thought is concerned. The second reading is more likely as 'leading into all truth' or 'leading to the full truth'.

It is said as an explanation (γάρ) that the Paraclete 'will not speak on his own', but will speak 'whatever he hears'.[27] He will, in other words, say the same as Jesus says, as the revealer on earth, of his relationship with the Father who sent him (see 7:17f; 8:28; 14:10; see also 5:19, 30; 8:42). If this idea of mission is extended, this emphasis ought to bring the connection between the Paraclete and Jesus and the continuity of Jesus' revelation into prominence in the present saying about the Paraclete (see v. 14). The last statement in this present verse, 'he will declare to you the things that are to come', cannot therefore be seen as a completely new pronouncement extending beyond Jesus' revelation, in other words, as a new disclosure of future events. It is not an allusion to the visions of the future outlined in the Apocalypse of John, nor is it even a reference to the book itself or an announcement or justification of primitive Christian prophets.[28] All that is attributed to the Paraclete here is that he will guide the community into the future and make clear to it what is coming. The verb that is repeated twice here, in this and the following verse, ἀναγγέλλειν, is a term used in the vocabulary of revelation (cf. 4:25) and hardly differs at all from ἀπαγγέλλειν, which is employed for Jesus' open or 'plain' speaking of the Father in the future (16:25). It may even have the nuance of 'proclaiming what has been heard'.[29] The Paraclete will not, in other words, proclaim anything with a new content. All that he will do is to expound anew to the community Jesus' message in the situation in which that community finds itself and set forth what is coming to it. His guiding the community into all the truth, then, can be seen as an instruction by means of which Christ's revelation can be understood more and more perfectly in each historical context and the community's life can be more and more nourished by it. The 'truth' contains a reference here to action –

it has to be 'done' (see 3:21; 1 Jn 1:6; with περιπατεῖν, 'walking in' the truth, 2 Jn 4; 3 Jn 4).[30] In the context of the promise, the community is reminded, though not directly, of its moral behaviour, but rather of the expression of faith that is required by the future situation. The Spirit proclaims to the community what is coming as what is coming to it, so that its members will act accordingly.[31]

16:14–15   The concluding sentences have the sole purpose of stressing the revelation brought by Christ and giving it even greater emphasis by the activity of the Paraclete. In Johannine language, this is expressed as the Paraclete's 'glorifying' Jesus. Jesus' real 'glorification', that is, his being recognized and given the power to complete his work (see 13:31f; 17:1f), is brought about by the Father, but the Paraclete participates in the continuation of his saving work and therefore contributes to Jesus' 'glorification'. The mode of expression in these verses has many points of contact with the prayer in Jn 17: the Paraclete will take from Jesus' 'possession' (τὰ ἐμά), just as Jesus gave the words that the Father gave him to the disciples (17:8). The causal statement: 'All that the Father has is mine' recurs in 17:10. The Johannine school recognized the event of revelation that proceeds from God as the Son's sharing in the Father's 'possession' and the activity of the Paraclete as a drawing on Jesus' possession. The Father has placed everything at the Son's disposal for his revelation (see 3:34f) and the Paraclete draws on this fullness. Jesus is therefore confirmed by the Paraclete as the one to whom everything is entrusted. This text has given rise to trinitarian reflections,[32] but it has a clearly Christological intention and points to the fullness and absolute nature of revelation in Jesus Christ. Any later proclamation and all the exposition and interpretation of the event of Christ that takes place 'in the Spirit' is connected with this intention, however historically necessary it may be.

Are those disciples who were present and their 'successors in office' promised a special charisma to enable them to penetrate more deeply into the truth of revelation or is the whole community led by the Paraclete and kept by him in the truth? This question has to be answered as that raised by 14:26 (see the commentary above) was answered. In so far as Jesus' disciples at that time were called to proclaim the message, they were particularly concerned by this saying about the Paraclete. They were the ones who had to overcome 'sorrow' at Jesus' departure and later to interpret everything that was difficult for the communities. In addition, John and his pupils must have seen their understanding of themselves as teachers inspired by the Spirit firmly based on this saying. If, however, the whole discourse is regarded as an appeal to the community to understand and manage its own existence under the guidance of the Spirit of truth and to protect itself against the doctrines of false teachers (see 1 Jn), then the promise cannot be limited just to that group of men. Through the Paraclete, the whole Church is intimately connected with the revelation of Jesus Christ and at the same time taken beyond it in so far as new insights and decisions are required by changing historical situations. Through the help of the Paraclete, the truth of the gospel is increasingly disclosed and its message becomes a source of new strength to the Church, which can, in and from the Spirit, thus know what Jesus told, gave and promised it. However difficult that process by means of which the truth is discovered at every period of history may be, it remains valid that 'we know that he abides in us by the Spirit which he has given us' (1 Jn 3:24; cf. 4:13).

The Paraclete and the Sayings about the Paraclete

Now that I have completed my exegetical consideration of the five sayings about the Paraclete (14:16f, 26; 15:26f; 16:7b–11, 13–15) in accordance with the text and context in which they occur, I have to assess them as a whole. Even the name 'Paraclete' as such, which occurs in the NT only in these sayings and in 1 Jn 2:1, requires an explanation. This is all the more necessary in that the meaning of this word is not constant, and only with considerable effort can its usage be seen as corresponding to the normally accepted history of the term.[1] The functions ascribed to the Paraclete in the five sayings are very diverse, but they are given coherence by the fact that they are grouped under the same name. This at once gives rise to the problem of the idea underlying them. The one bearer of these functions is the Holy Spirit or the 'Spirit of truth' and the teaching of this Spirit, who is active after Jesus' departure, is important enough for us to investigate it. The statements made about the Spirit cannot, however, simply be identified with the doctrine of the Spirit in the rest of the NT. We have always to bear in mind that they are connected with the figure of the Paraclete, which is a distinctive phenomenon in the NT. This leads us on to the further question about the origin of the title 'Paraclete' and the point of departure in the history of comparative religion for the figure of the Paraclete, who appears in the gospel as a person. Finally, we have also to examine the question of the lasting significance of this Johannine teaching about the Spirit, since these sayings about the Paraclete have had a considerable influence in the history of Christianity.

The problem of the Johannine sayings about the Paraclete has been the subject of research for a long time now. I need not concern myself here with a detailed, individual survey of the various studies made, since most recent authors go back to them and take them into account.[2] Many different positions have been taken in this field, especially with regard to the 'background' to the 'figure' of the Paraclete or its origin in the sphere of comparative religion, many scholars believing that it must go back to other 'figures' or ideas. It is only fairly recently that more interest has been taken in the function of these sayings within the framework of the farewell discourses,[3] that research has been done into new critical aspects of the form and literary genre of the sayings and that the question has been raised as to whether the five sayings may not reflect stages in the development of the gospel of John.[4] This methodological procedure, the progress of which has been impeded by the emphasis on origin, ought to be given precedence. It is only when the literary level has been studied in all its aspects that questions can be asked about the history of traditions and comparative religion. First, however, I shall look briefly at the semantic problem.

1. The Formation and Meaning of the Word

J. Behm has assembled the semantic material available for the Greek word παράκλητος in a concise and comprehensive way.[5] The verbal adjective derived from παρακαλέω has a passive meaning in classical and later Greek. It means 'the one called for' and is used especially for 'defending counsel'. It is very similar to the Latin *advocatus*, although it is not an established technical term for this forensic activity. The Paraclete, then, may be an intercessor or mediator, who intervenes for someone to help him and protect him from others. This linguistic use also explains why the Greek term was taken over as a loan-word into Hebrew and Aramaic (*parqlīṭ* or *parqlīṭa*), which is related in meaning to συνήγορος (which was also taken over as the loan-word (*s'negor*), which was employed for 'lawyer' or 'defending counsel'. In this sense, there are many references in Judaism to 'intercessors' with God. The angels, the patriarchs, the prophets and certain righteous men were intercessors and the same function was performed by fulfilling the commandments and by sacrifices, penance and good works. It was by means of such intercessors that the Jews found salvation in the court of God.[6]

What is remarkable is that the concept is extended to include other factors than either human or heavenly persons and that it is also simultaneously narrowed down to apply only to intercessors with God. It is clear, then, that the term is capable of being adapted to a very great extent and that it has different functions and shades of meaning according to its context and linguistic usage. This, however, does not in any way change the basic, passive meaning of the word (the 'one called for'). A mixture with παρακλήτωρ, παρακλητικός in the active sense (= 'one who encourages, consoles, admonishes') cannot be established, at least originally. This active meaning is secondary. It occurs once only in the Greek OT (Job 16:2), where Aquila and Theodotion translate the Hebrew word for 'comforters' by παράκλητοι. The Septuagint has παρακλήτορες and, in the early Church, the Greek Fathers thought of the Johannine Paraclete as the παρακαλῶν or the παρακλήτωρ (cf. the Latin *consolator*).[7]

It is therefore questionable to trace the Johannine Paraclete back to a presupposed ὁ παρακαλῶν and to interpret it actively as the 'one who encourages, consoles, admonishes and teaches'. Recently, U. B. Müller has returned to this derivation of the word, following the tendency of earlier advocates, but basing his hypothesis on different presuppositions.[8] On the basis of criticism of the literary genres, he has compared the sayings about the

Paraclete with the farewell discourses and instructions in the apocalyptic literature and has come ·to the conclusion that the Johannine Paraclete's functions are similar to those of the 'continuers' or 'successors' mentioned in that literature. He is also convinced that ὁ παράκλητος should be explained semasiologically as ὁ παρακαλῶν.[9] I shall examine these valuable considerations based on the comparison of literary genres later in this Excursus (section 3 below), but would state now that they hardly justify Müller's semasiological conclusion. He is clearly afraid that he will be criticized on the basis of linguistic analysis – according to the material available, the basic, passive meaning of the word has in general to be retained.[10] It may, however, be possible to find quite a different explanation for the datum.

It is important, at the outset, to make a few observations that may be relevant to the linguistic side of the problem. The evangelist obviously found the name 'Paraclete' already being used for the Holy Spirit, automatically accepted it and employed it for his own purpose. This is the essence of S. Schulz' hypothesis of a 'theme tradition', which is, in the way in which Schulz raises it up to the level of a method, at least questionable.[11] The second saying about the Paraclete is particularly instructive in this respect, because the evangelist first speaks of ὁ παράκλητος and then at once clarifies this term by using the general early Christian expression, 'Holy Spirit'. This process can even be detected in the first saying about the Paraclete (14:16f). Within the context in which this saying is placed, he clearly aims to introduce the Paraclete as the counsel for the disciples' defence after Jesus' departure – this explains the unique formula: 'another Paraclete'. If he knew the discourse of the 'Paraclete' and wanted to present him here, in respect of the period following Jesus' departure, as Jesus' representative and 'successor', it is not difficult to understand that Jesus is also presented as 'Paraclete', that is, as the 'Paraclete' of the disciples up till that time, while he was still active on earth. If this is so, it provides a reason for evangelist's clarification of the promised Paraclete by means of the term 'Spirit of truth', which, we may assume, was the current term for the Holy Spirit in the Johannine community (see ad loc.). The same applies to the third saying about the Paraclete, which first looks back to 14:16 (Jesus as the one who sends) and then adds, by way of clarification, 'the Spirit of truth, who proceeds from the Father'. The situation is rather different in 16:7 or 13. In v. 7, the Paraclete is mentioned without any addition, while, in v. 13, he is called the 'Spirit of truth', this time without any inner motive, because he 'guides into all the truth'.

We may conclude from all this that the evangelist – or his circle – received the term that already existed, the 'Paraclete', and made theological statements about him that were in accordance with the Johannine teaching about the Spirit. In that case, it is not necessary to base all the functions that are ascribed to the Paraclete in the Johannine school on the term itself. Thanks to the creativity of the evangelist and his friends, the concept is given new dimensions. This is a procedure that happens quite frequently in the sphere of language. An existing term is accepted and filled with a new and richer content. In the case of the gospel of John, we have only to think, for example, of the

'Lamb of God', the 'Son of man' and the symbols of light, the bread from heaven, shepherd, door, way, vine and so on. The result of this is that a distinction must be made between the origin of the Johannine title 'Paraclete' and the content of meaning in the Johannine sayings about the Paraclete and each must be investigated separately. The second problem is easier to solve, but requires very careful examination and differentiation. We shall consider it first.

2. The Functions of the Johannine Paraclete on the basis of the Individual Sayings about the Paraclete

No definite activity of the Paraclete is mentioned in the first saying about the Paraclete (14:16f). All that it contains is a promise made to the disciples that he will come as a gift of the Father ($\delta\dot{\omega}\sigma\epsilon\iota$) after Jesus' departure (in the context). The disciples will receive the Spirit of truth; this can be deduced from the negative statement that the world is not capable of receiving him ($o\dot{\upsilon}$ $\delta\dot{\upsilon}\nu\alpha\tau\alpha\iota$ $\lambda\alpha\beta\epsilon\tilde{\iota}\nu$). For the disciples, he is a factor that they can experience – they 'know' him because he abides with them and will be in them. The real promise is to be found in the fact that the Paraclete will be with them for ever (v. 16c), in Jesus' place, since he is now leaving them. This promise is reinforced by the causal clause at the end of v. 17. In considering this question, it is important to distinguish between vv. 16 and 17. In v. 16, $\pi\alpha\rho\dot{\alpha}\kappa\lambda\eta\tau\sigma\varsigma$ is the main concept and it is said of him that he will be 'with' the disciples ($\mu\epsilon\theta$' $\dot{\upsilon}\mu\tilde{\omega}\nu$). In v. 17, on the other hand, certain statements are appended to $\tau\dot{o}$ $\pi\nu\epsilon\tilde{\upsilon}\mu\alpha$ $\tau\tilde{\eta}\varsigma$ $\dot{\alpha}\lambda\eta\theta\epsilon\dot{\iota}\alpha\varsigma$, as the neutral pronouns – also used for the promise to the disciples ($\alpha\dot{\upsilon}\tau\dot{o}$) – show. Here it is said that this Spirit will be 'with them' and 'in them'. The different pronouns used with 'Paraclete' and 'Spirit of truth' may not be without some significance. It is clear that the preposition $\mu\epsilon\tau\dot{\alpha}$, which, in this kind of context, points to the community that provides protection, fits very well into the concept 'Paraclete' that has been taken into the gospel. The Johannine Jesus says to the Jews who have rejected him: 'He who sent me is with me; he has not left me alone . . .' (8:29; see also 16:32). The reference to the inner presence of the Spirit of truth provides a better motive for the fact that the disciples will know that Spirit and the progression from $\pi\alpha\rho$' $\dot{\upsilon}\mu\tilde{\iota}\nu$ to $\dot{\epsilon}\nu$ $\dot{\upsilon}\mu\tilde{\iota}\nu$ may be intended to stress this inner presence.

The functions of the Paraclete are described in the second saying about the Paraclete at the end of the discourse in Chapter 14 as 'teaching' and as 'calling to mind' Jesus' words (14:26). It was argued in the commentary that this saying fits very well into this place and must therefore have been the work of the evangelist. We should also consider 1 Jn 2:27 in connection with this 'teaching' function of the Spirit. According to this text, the 'anointing', which is certainly a metaphor for the Holy Spirit (see ad loc.), teaches those addressed in the epistle about everything and they are able to abide in Christ precisely because of this teaching. Even if this epistle was written by someone who was not the evangelist, it none the less expresses an original Johannine view about the

Spirit, since 'teaching' as a function of the Holy Spirit is encountered elsewhere only in Lk 12:12 (for this text, see below), although there are several related statements in the rest of the NT (see 1 Cor 2:10–13; Eph 1:17; 1 Tim 4:1; 2 Tim 1:14; Heb 10:15). This function of the 'Spirit of truth' (see 16:13), which consists of a 'calling to mind' of Jesus' revelation and a commemorative deepening of that revelation (see 16:14f) and which was extremely important to the Johannine community, could not originally have depended on the concept 'Paraclete', but may have been transferred to it when the evangelist took over the term 'Paraclete' for the Holy Spirit. In 14:26, the word 'Paraclete' is obviously chosen in association with 14:16, where the Paraclete has a rightful place in the context of the farewell discourse.

The third saying about the Paraclete (15:26f) mentions a function that is different from those outlined in 14:26 – bearing witness to Jesus. Taken on its own, it could be connected with the 'calling to mind' of Jesus' words, but it is not a bearing of witness to Jesus for the sake of the disciples, but a testimony directed outside the community, for the sake of others. This is clearly shown by the continuation (v. 27), according to which the disciples also bear witness. It has been disputed whether this saying belongs to this context, but it has its place here as an encouragement to the disciples, who have to endure the hatred and persecution of the world (see the commentary above). Although there is no reference to a μαρτυρεῖν previously, it is possible to point to the 'works' of Jesus in v. 24 as fulfilling this function (see also 5:36; 10:25): 'Just as the works of the earthly Jesus have borne witness, so too will the Spirit bear witness after his departure and, what is more, he will do it in the testimony of the disciples (v. 27).'[12]

This saying presupposes the presence of the Paraclete with the disciples and his activity in them and is therefore a continuation of the first two sayings about the Paraclete, just as the whole discourse in Chapter 15 is based on the farewell discourse in Chapter 14 and extends this, as it were, into the space occupied by the community. In the period following Jesus' departure and after the coming of the Paraclete, the disciples have to establish the truth of their existence in the world and to expect the hatred and hostility of the unbelieving cosmos. Following almost immediately this saying (16:1f), concrete persecutions and sanctions are mentioned, so that it can hardly be disputed that this saying brings us very close to the legal sphere. It is not exclusively concerned with bearing witness in a lawsuit, but it is to a very great extent concerned with this. In this function, the Paraclete is acting in a way that is eminently suited to him in the semantic sense (see above, Section 1). This legal function is also known within the history of traditions from the synoptic logion in Mk 13:9, 11 par. The disciples appear in this logion, in court before their judges εἰς μαρτύριον (Mk 13:9). In that hour, what they should say, will be 'given' to them, because the Holy Spirit will speak through their mouths (13:11). The other synoptics attempt to interpret this logion. According to Matthew, it is 'the Spirit of your Father speaking through you' (10:20). According to Luke, 'I will give you the gift of speech (a mouth) and wisdom' (21:15). In an earlier text, Luke interprets this saying as follows: 'The Holy Spirit will *teach* you in that very hour what you ought to say' (12:11f). This διδάσκειν is different from the word as it appears in Jn 14:26; it is a prompting of the right words in a lawsuit. The saying about the Paraclete in Jn 15:26f resumes, in a new Johannine form, a tradition that is, because of its distinctive character, extremely important in the synoptics. This is a logion about the Holy Spirit who appears in a forensic function as a Paraclete, although the word 'Paraclete' does not appear itself in this synoptic logion. This 'point of contact' in the history of traditions deserves our attention, even though the discourse in Jn 15 goes back to an editor or editors, whose work seems, as a whole, to be closer to the common Christian way of thinking than that of the evangelist himself. For the wording of this saying, see the commentary.

From here, it is only a logical step to the fourth saying in 16:8–11, in which the function of the Paraclete is described as 'exposing' and 'proving' the unbelieving world 'guilty'. In this process, judgment is repeatedly passed on the world and this judgment is in principle and definitively followed by the victory of Jesus over the 'ruler of this world' (v. 11). Having been counsel for the disciples' defence in human lawsuits, the Paraclete now becomes the plaintiff in God's judgment against the world. This is a function that was not originally present in the concept of a Paraclete – in Judaism, the *parqlīṭ* (= *s'negor*) is simply the counterpart to the plaintiff or accuser (*kategor*). In the Johannine thinking about the 'crisis', however, this interchange between the two functions is already established and given a firm foundation. In other words, just as the accused is really the accuser in Jesus' trial, the one who is condemned is the one who is justified and the one who is defeated is in fact victorious, so too is this the case in God's 'trial' with the unbelieving world, which the trial of Jesus before Pilate represents in a hidden way and which also takes place in the encounter between Jesus' community and unbelieving and hostile men.[13] The community continues Jesus' legal contest and God's lawsuit in respect of lack of faith in its existence and in bearing witness to faith. It does not, however, do this on its own, but by means of the Spirit who is active in and through the community. Helped by the Spirit as the counsel for their defence, Jesus' disciples are no longer accused, but become accusers, and this means that the Paraclete's function also changes. He has been defending the disciples; now he is God's advocate against the world, with the task of proving that world guilty. This function of the Paraclete is therefore a further development of the idea of the Paraclete in Johannine theology.

After describing the function of the Paraclete with regard to the unbelieving world, the gospel now turns, in the fifth saying about the Paraclete (16:11–13) to the function of the Paraclete within the community. As in 14:16f, the Paraclete here replaces Jesus and continues his activity (see v. 12). The functions mentioned in 14:26 (teaching and calling to mind) are resumed and to some extent developed in this fifth saying. The Spirit of truth, as he is once again called here, has above all the task of guiding the disciples into the truth revealed by Jesus and to accompany them as one indicating the way. They still have very much to learn relating to the present and the future, but it is hardly likely that the gospel is concerned here with any special or catechetical forms of teaching.[14] The Paraclete's teaching is a kind of 'recollection' or calling to mind of Jesus' words. This is clear from the emphasis in this saying on the close relationship between the Paraclete and Jesus and the Paraclete's 'taking from his possession'. This saying, then, can best be regarded as a re-reading of 14:26, although its orientation towards the Wisdom literature (see the commentary above) gives it a new aspect. In the later books of the OT, Spirit and Wisdom are closely related factors and this means that a clearer light is thrown on the 'guidance' of the Spirit. It does not, however, mean that the Spirit's teaching function is changed, for example, from an inner to a more external form of teaching. The editor or editors, who, as we have seen in the commentary above, composed a new discourse (16:4b–33) for the community with the emphasis on sorrow and joy, distress and victory, had a view and understanding of the Paraclete that was in no way radically different from that of the evangelist. He was simply seen, in this editorial discourse and therefore in this fifth saying, as more emphatically present and active in the community and as directly at work and, what is more, at a time of great distress, when the community was perhaps troubled by false teachers.

Seeing the five sayings about the Paraclete as a whole, then, it is clear that they are not foreign bodies or units that were subsequently introduced into the discourses contained in Chapters 14–16.[15] They have a definite part to play in the place in which they are found in the gospel and were interpolated by the editors quite deliberately. They cannot, admittedly, be regarded as being all on the same level. The second saying (14:26) presupposes the first and forms, together with the first saying, the promise of the Paraclete and the evangelist's teaching about the Spirit. The third and the fourth sayings, on the other hand (15:26f; 16:8–11), are constructed on this basis and constitute an extension or an amplification, in setting forth the Paraclete's function with regard to the unbelieving world, admittedly, of course, by virtue of his presence in the disciples. The last saying (16:11–13) goes back to 14:26 and throws light on it in respect of the period in which the community is living. If, then, a distinction has to be made between the original statements made by the evangelist and the further pronouncements made by his 'school', it has at the same time to be recognized that the whole Johannine circle is in agreement in taking over the title 'Paraclete' and about the teaching of the Spirit. We still have to consider how the Johannine community arrived at the tradition of the Paraclete and how it came to use this distinctive mode of expression and to follow this way of thinking. We shall do this in the following section.

3. The Source of the Title 'Paraclete' and the Statements about the Paraclete

Scholars have been more concerned with the question of the origin of the 'figure' of the Paraclete and the 'background' to this idea than with any other in connection with the Paraclete and the sayings about him. I would like now to review briefly a number of attempts to answer this question.

(a) The 'Gnostic' origin, represented most powerfully by R. Bultmann

Bultmann believed that the Johannine Paraclete could not be described either as an 'intercessor' or as a 'comforter', but was more of a helper or defending counsel, and consequently considered carefully the Mandaean statements about the 'helper'. The Gnostic revealer is depicted mythologically as a helper, an escort and a guide of souls, especially in the figure of Yawar. It is not necessary to quote individual texts here, since the idea occurs frequently enough. Critics of Bultmann's theory have pointed out, for example, that there are many such figures in Mandaeanism and that these change, but that there are only two in John (Jesus and the Paraclete) and that these are especially related to each other. They have also shown that Gnosticism is concerned with the ascent of souls and that John does not speak of this at all. The representation or replacement of Jesus by the Paraclete in John has no parallel in Mandaeanism. This attempt to explain the origin of the figure of the Paraclete has therefore been almost universally rejected now.

(b) A development from the idea of the precursor

The relationship between Jesus and the Paraclete suggested the idea of the precursor to G. Bornkamm.[18] The same idea is found in the relationship between John the Baptist and Jesus, and in early Judaism Elijah appears as the main precursor of Moses, Moses as the precursor of the prophets of the Messiah (Deut 18:15, 18), and the Qumran 'teacher of righteousness' as the precursor of the eschatological teacher (*Dam* 6:11). There are other examples. Bornkamm looked to the expectation of the Son of man as a possible source for the figure of the Paraclete. In Jn, he points out, the myth of the Son of man is divided between the two figures of Jesus and the Paraclete. The critics of this hypothesis have put their finger on its weak points, namely that Jesus cannot be fitted into the role of a precursor, that the story of his passion is not emphasized in the sayings about the Paraclete and that there is no clear and indisputable connection with the myth of the Son of man.

(c) A connection with the theme of the Son of man.

S. Schulz also believes that there is a connection with the idea of the Son of man, since the tradition of the Paraclete and that of the Son of man have certain features in common.[20] In a later book, he claims that there were other influences, especially from the Yawar of Mandaeanism and the Jewish figures of the intercessor.[21] In his commentary, he expresses his conviction that there is a close connection with the apocalyptic tradition of the Son of man, but keeps generally to his syncretic view.[22] This ambiguous standpoint has given rise to some criticism.[23]

(d) A derivation from the Jewish idea of an intercessor

S. Mowinckel and N. Johansson are the leading protagonists of the hypothesis that the Johannine Paraclete has its source in the widespread Jewish idea of an intercessor.[24] Not only the name itself, but also the adaptability of the idea, which is capable of being applied to various functions, point, in their opinion, to this origin. This interpretation, which Johansson gives to the abundant material at his disposal, has been seriously criticized by O. Betz.[25] In addition to this, I am bound to observe that, although the idea of an intercessor is eminently applicable to 1 Jn 2:1 (Jesus Christ as the heavenly Paraclete), it can only with difficulty be adapted to all the sayings in the gospel. It fits most easily into the tradition expressed in 15:26f and least easily into the fundamental statements made in 14:26. It is, however, true that certain texts, which speak about a heavenly 'witness' and 'vouchsafing for' or 'defending' (Job 16:19f; 19:25; 33:23, 26), about the Spirit (Wis 1:7–9) and about Gabriel as an *angelus interpres* (Dan 8:16; 9:21ff; 10:21) are worth noting in this context.[26]

(e) An origin in ideas prevalent in the Qumran community

O. Betz, who recognizes the efforts made by the scholars mentioned above to establish a link between the Johannine Paraclete and Jewish ideas, is convinced that the origin of the Paraclete can be found in certain ideas that flourished in the Qumran community. Following the line indicated by the 'intercessors of the earlier period', the patriarchs and Moses as well as the interceding angels that appear in the Ethiopic *Book of Enoch* and the *Book of Jubilees*, this author draws new and concrete conclusions from their dualistic thinking that is so closely connected with judgment. This is that the Spirit of truth and the Spirit of error, Michael and Belial and the teacher of righteousness and his adversaries are opposed to each other.[27] In addition, Betz believes that all the functions that are attributed to the Johannine Paraclete can be found in these texts and that the replacement of Jesus by the Paraclete can also be explained on the basis of the same texts. What is particularly remarkable, Betz thinks, is the coming together of ideas that were originally distinct and the application of these ideas to Jesus and the Spirit sent by him. The evangelist divided the twofold function of the Paraclete (in heaven and on earth) between two figures: the intercessor officiating in heaven and the 'other Paraclete', who enlightens and teaches the pious on earth and bears witness and accuses the hostile world.[28]

Those who have criticized Betz' hypothesis of a direct derivation from Qumran have pointed first to the questionable nature of the combinations and modifications[29] and second to that of a direct connection between Qumran and the Johannine community and a real dependence on Qumran views on the part of those of the Johannine circle. It cannot be proved that there was originally an angelic being (Michael) behind the Paraclete. In addition, it cannot be established that the name given to the Paraclete – the 'Spirit of truth' – goes directly back to the Essene 'Spirit of truth'.[30] However valuable this comparative study may be, then, it has found few supporters as an attempt to solve the problem of the Johannine Paraclete.

(f) A development of early Christian ideas about the Holy Spirit in the situation in which the Johannine community was placed

English-speaking exegetes have reserved their judgment with regard to all attempts based on a study of comparative religion and have preferred to base an explanation of the Johannine Paraclete on presuppositions found in the early Christian teaching about the Spirit and to see the Paraclete as the expression of a specifically Johannine theological concern. R. E. Brown, for example, regards an indirect influence by Qumran ideas as possible, but also draws attention to two aspects of early Christian experience which led to a change of view in the gospel of John – the death of the eye-witnesses of Jesus' life and the delay in the coming of the parousia.[31] It is for this reason, Brown thinks, that the Paraclete replaces Jesus in the gospel. I doubt, however, whether the distinctive view of the Paraclete is sufficiently explained in this way. The name itself requires a concrete point of contact in the history of traditions and it is extremely doubtful whether the Paraclete should be equated with Jesus, as though Jesus comes in the Paraclete.[32] G. Johnston has suggested a different reason for the formation of the Johannine sayings about the Paraclete. This is that the evangelist identified the 'Paraclete' with the 'Spirit of truth' in an attempt to combat heretical assertions that an angelic mediator was the spiritual guide and guardian of the Christian Church.[33] This cannot, however, be established (the 'worship of angels' mentioned in Col 2:18 is a different phenomenon) and is very unlikely.

(g) An explanation based on the literary genre of farewell discourses

U. B. Müller's recent attempt to solve the problem of the Paraclete represents a new methodological departure. He has investigated the sayings about the Paraclete in accordance with the principles of form criticism as elements in the farewell discourse (or discourses). He has in this way established a connection between these sayings and the early Christian teaching about the Spirit and the epistle of the Apocalypse. He has also included in this certain other Johannine statements about the Spirit and has appealed to farewell discourses as comparative material in the Jewish (and especially the Jewish apocalyptic) literature. Müller's method is to examine the texts, with special attention to their form and function, both within the context of the farewell discourses and within the larger framework of the whole work. We can only applaud this procedure. He has also combined this with a comparative study of literary genres, with remarkable results. In fact, the same basic problems occur both in the so-called 'Testaments' (and especially the *Testaments of the Twelve Patriarchs*), and in the apocalyptic works – a situation of farewell with an outlook towards the future and an admonition of those who remain behind, as well as concern for 'succession' in the person of an important figure. Several texts (*Jub* 45:16; *Ass Mos* 10:11; *4 Esr* 14:19; *Apoc Bar* syr 77ff, etc.) throw a light on the need for correction, consolation and instruction in the case of those left behind. The Holy Spirit also plays a very important part, either through the inspiration of the books that have to be handed down (see *4 Esr* 14:42ff) or by the successor's possession of the Spirit, so that he is armed for his office.[34] According to Müller, 'the only difference is that the parallel Jewish texts present primarily the actual bearers of the Spirit, whereas Jn 14 has the "Spirit of truth" himself in mind' (p. 61). This, of course, is a very important difference.

These observations, based on a criticism of literary genres, are very valuable, because they provide a good explanation for the existence of the sayings about the Paraclete in the Johannine farewell discourses and the functions that are primarily ascribed to him in Jn 14. The author's derivation of the title ὁ παράκλητος from the literary genre of farewell discourses is, however, questionable. He sees it as meaning the same as ὁ παρακαλῶν, but that is in itself hardly certain from the semantic point of view (see above, Section 1). Why too does the verb παρακαλεῖν not appear even once in the sayings about the Paraclete, if that is in fact his all-embracing function? It would have had a particularly suitable place in the (secondary) discourse in Chapter 16, in the last saying addressed to the community (vv. 13–15). Should we not rather assume that the reverse process took place, that is, that the title that is present in John attracted to itself those functions in the farewell discourse that were in accordance with the situation and the literary genre of the farewell discourse? It is not difficult to understand that attempts were made at a later stage, when the sayings about the Paraclete were read in the gospel, to explain the title on the basis of the function of παρακαλεῖν. The only comparison with the title that can be made within the NT is 1 Jn 2:1, where the term has the unambiguous meaning of 'intercessor' or 'advocate', in accordance with classical and Jewish linguistic usage.

If a distinction is made between the question of the source of the title 'Paraclete' and the use of that title and the meaning given to it by the evangelist and other members of the Johannine circle (see above, Section 1), the search for a completely unambiguous derivation of the term has to be abandoned, although considerations based on the history of traditions and influences exerted by the environment can certainly be taken into account. My own point of departure in this problem is the assumption made by most scholars that the title 'Paraclete' already existed for the evangelist and, what is more, within the Christian tradition. The only certain point of contact in this case is the logion of the help of the Holy Spirit as the counsel for the disciples' defence when they are on trial, which we have already discussed above (Mk 13:11 par.). It is extremely probable, on the basis of Jn 15:26f, that this logion was known in the Johannine circle. Because of Lk 12:11f, it can be attributed to the source of sayings (Q). Matthew used the Markan text from the eschatological discourse in his discourse addressed to the messengers (10:20) and Luke freely adapted his original Markan version in his eschatological discourse (21:14f) with the earlier text in mind.[35] The saying, then, was certainly known in the early Palestinian community, whose members saw it as an encouragement and a comfort for their missionaries who were being persecuted and put on trial. In the same way, it was also known in the later Johannine community in its new, but similar situation. We may therefore justifiably assume that the Holy Spirit was at quite an early stage called the Paraclete with this function in mind.[36]

If the title 'Paraclete', as applied to the Holy Spirit, goes back a long way, it is fairly evident that there must have been further reflection about the Spirit precisely as the Paraclete and that further functions were ascribed to him in the community, again as the Paraclete, including especially the functions of teaching and calling to mind Jesus' words, both of which are so prominent in John. Both the theme of Jesus' prediction (see 13:19; 14:29) and the acceptance and interpretation of Jesus' words (cf. 2:19 with 22; see also 4:44; 6:42; 12:16, 25f; 13:16, 20, etc.) can be clearly observed. The evangelist (and together with him, his pupils and friends) saw himself chiefly as one who interpreted Jesus' words and actions as well as his appearance and his person, and he did not make this interpretation on the basis of his own ability and power, but because he was guided and enlightened by the Spirit. The term 'Paraclete' therefore became more firmly established in the Johannine community and at the same time the meaning of the term became extended. There is no sign that enthusiastic experiences of the Spirit took place. The Spirit was above all experienced as the community's teacher and interpreter. Many ideas (from the apocalyptic literature and from Qumran) may well have been absorbed as a result of contact and controversy with the surrounding world and transferred to the Spirit, including, for example, the idea that the 'Spirit of truth' was opposed to all error (see 1 Jn 4:6). To begin with at least, hardly any part was played by personal characteristics. The Spirit is above all the illuminating and strengthening power of God which enables the community to continue to belong to God and to possess the truth ('the Spirit is the truth', 1 Jn 5:6).

The Spirit, whose presence causes the Johannine community to rejoice, is, however, inseparably bound to Jesus Christ. It is only through him that the Spirit came to exist for the community (see Jn 7:39) and it is from him that the community received the Spirit (20:22). The Spirit also constantly refers to him in his activity. He bears 'witness' to Jesus Christ as the one who came by water and blood (1 Jn 5:6). This, then, is the idea and the experience that the community had in faith of the Spirit, whose essential functions were expressed when Jesus promised that Spirit at the time of his departure. He thus becomes Jesus' representative and in this way continues his revelation of salvation within the community and makes it effective and fruitful. The idea of a Paraclete, in this new form that is enriched with new meanings, clearly suggested itself as a linguistic instrument for this purpose, assuming personal characteristics as Jesus' 'successor'. It is also quite possible that many ideas originating in Judaism played a part in this process. Similar situations, in which the bearer of revelation departs after having made preparations for the continuation of his work, may also have contributed to the linguistic formation of the sayings about the Paraclete and to that of functions that we have been considering here. It would surely hardly be possible to discover a completely suitable and sufficient model on which the Johannine sayings about the Paraclete were based. The form and content, mode of expression and meaning of the sayings as we have them now in the gospel are ultimately the work of the evangelist or his school. They express the Johannine community's faith in the fact that Jesus Christ came once and for all as the eschatological revealer and bringer of salvation, and that community's faith in the present and lasting activity of the Spirit, who continues the work of Jesus Christ and at the same time preserves and discloses it ever again.

4. The Significance of the Sayings about the Paraclete for the Johannine Community's Understanding of Itself and the Later Church

The sayings about the Paraclete, then, that are found in the Johannine farewell discourses were formulated on the basis of the faith in Christ and the experience of the Spirit that existed in the Johannine community and in particular among its leaders and those who were responsible for preserving the community's traditions. If this is the case, it is possible to draw certain conclusions with regard to the self-understanding of that community (or of those communities) and its view of the Holy Spirit. The gospel of John was accepted by the Church as a whole during the second half of the second century AD at the latest and was soon deeply assimilated. These statements about the Spirit therefore acquired a lasting theological force that has not diminished throughout the centuries. The theological significance of these sayings has to be reconsidered at every period of history and this has also to be done in our present situation. I shall therefore conclude this excursus on the Paraclete and the Johannine sayings about the Paraclete with a few comments grouped under three headings.

(a) The Johannine community was convinced that it was filled by the Spirit and accompanied by him. His presence and his reality determined its life and thought. This can be said without reservation in the light of the long epistle, in which the community is directly addressed (see my *Johannes-Briefe*, Excursus 9). The promise, made in Jn 14:16f, that the Paraclete, the Spirit of truth, will always be with and in the disciples, was fulfilled for the community. The knowledge that they possessed the Spirit impressed itself on their consciousness of themselves, even with regard to the unbelieving world and the false teachers who had once belonged to their community, but had in the meantime left it (see 1 Jn 2:19f; 4:1–6). This possession of the Spirit nevertheless did not lead to an enthusiastic form of piety or expectation of the future; on the contrary it gave rise to a rich inner experience and to brotherliness. The Johannine community may have tended to withdraw into itself, but its members did not in any way forget the words that Jesus addressed to them about their mission in the world (see Jn 17:18; 20:21).

The question as to how the community thought of itself as being taught by the Spirit, that is, how the Paraclete carried out those functions attributed to him in 14:26, according to the community's understanding of itself, is more difficult to answer. Were those functions exercised by those who were recognized by the community as responsible for tradition and for proclaiming the truth as revealed by Jesus, calling Jesus' words to mind and mediating the Spirit's teaching to the community? Did especially gifted men, who were filled with the

Spirit, appear – prophets who re-interpreted Jesus' words or even proclaimed new words of the Lord? Or did the Spirit teach each individual believer by enlightening him inwardly and giving him inner certainty? According to 1 Jn, external proclamation by men who keep to what was proclaimed 'from the beginning' and proclaim it themselves (see 1:1–4; 2:7f, 24; 3:11) and inner instruction by the Spirit (2:20f, 27) are not in contradiction with each other, but on the contrary complement each other and are dependent on each other. The believer receives the testimony of God that is mediated to him in the proclamation, assimilates it into himself and finds that it is confirmed in his experience of the Spirit (cf. 5:9–11 with 3:24b; 4:13). Nothing is said, on the other hand, about the appearance of early Christian prophets. There may have been such prophets in the community and it is possible that a bad experience of false prophets (4:1) resulted in the silence with regard to early Christian prophets. In any case, prophets seem to have played no part in the community at the time the letter was written.

Is the gospel of John itself not a product of prophecy and a justification of prophetism? Does it not reflect the tension between office and prophecy and is it not true to say that the sayings about the Paraclete prepare the way for a prophetic and Spirit-filled interpretation? There is a wide variety of attempts to interpret the sayings about the Paraclete in this way,[37] but they have to be treated with critical reserve. I have repeatedly referred to tradition in this commentary, in connection with individual texts, and in the sayings about the Paraclete themselves the greatest emphasis is placed on the fact that the Spirit only recalls what Jesus said (14:26) and that, when he guides the disciples into all the truth, he is not speaking on his own, but only what he hears (16:13). If there were any sign of polemics in this latter text, it would not be wrong to suspect that it contained a barb against abitrary and false prophecy, but it is a positive statement addressed to the community for the encouragement and consolation of its members. This verse therefore also contains the frank statement: 'He will declare to you the things that are to come'. Seen as part of the whole statement, this cannot be a recommendation for a prophecy in which the future is interpreted. In 15:26f too, the disciples are explicitly called witnesses, because they have been with Jesus 'from the beginning'. These sayings about the Paraclete therefore obviously have in mind those men whose self-understanding can be traced back to the first epistle of John. The men who are to proclaim the truth and are to safeguard the tradition of the community and preserve a correct understanding of Christian faith, then, will do this, not in an authoritarian and official way, but in the power of the Spirit who has been given to them. I shall return to the question of the relationship between office and the Spirit when I come to deal with the problem of the disciple whom Jesus loved.

Those who proclaim the truth and are confirmed in their function by the sayings about the Paraclete as teachers who are enlightened by the Spirit are not, however, particularly emphasized, unless we regard the disciples who were present at that time and their successors who were called to be active in the same way as the only men to whom the promise that the Paraclete would come was made. In my detailed commentary on the individual sayings, however, I showed that this was too narrow a view. I also argued that the disciples at that particular time were primarily addressed, but that the fundamental promise of the coming of the Paraclete applied to the whole community, as represented by that small group of disciples who were present at the last supper. Only the unbelieving cosmos is excluded from receiving and understanding the Spirit (14:17). Behind the sayings of the Paraclete, then, we have an image of a community which is guided and instructed by the Spirit, but which in fact also receives this teaching from those who are qualified to teach and called to proclaim the message. Seen in this light, we are clearly not entitled to regard Johannine Christianity as distinct from the rest of early Christianity.

(b) It is difficult to assess the history of the effect of the sayings about the Paraclete on the Church and theology, and to investigate it would make excessive demands on the powers of any exegete. All that can be done here is to provide a few indications that may draw attention to some aspects of the question.

In the course of the Church's history, ecstatic and pneumatic movements have from time to time appeared and these based their teachings not only on Revelation, but also on the sayings about the Paraclete in the Johannine gospel. We have too little authentic material at our disposal to be able to judge the Montanist movement of the second and third centuries fairly, but it would seem that this 'new prophecy' also appealed to the Paraclete, who presumably spoke through prophetesses or prophets who were ecstatically excited,[38] and that the Johannine texts were fundamentally misunderstood and the view of the Johannine community was strikingly contradicted.

Joachim of Flora (†1202) taught a doctrine of the three periods of history which had a deep influence not only on religious thinking, but also in the social and political sphere. Although it was above all based on Revelation, it was not entirely unconnected with the Johannine Paraclete. Joachim, who was a personally blameless monk who was faithful to the Church, expected, after the first period of the Father (the OT period) and the second period of the Son (the NT), a time of the Holy Spirit and, after the 'Petrine' Church, a 'Johannine' Church.[39] It hardly needs to be stressed that these historical and theological speculations find no support at all in the Johannine doctrine of the Paraclete. Indeed, none of the movements that have been concerned with an ecstatic experience of the Spirit can justifiably appeal to the Johannine texts. At the same time, however, it has to be emphasized that, despite all the attempts made to confine the Spirit to the sphere of doctrine, the Johannine community was convinced that it was possible to experience the Spirit in the life of the community.

The sayings about the Paraclete played an important part in the dogmatic development of the teaching about the Holy Spirit and the pneumatological controversies in the early Church. They proved to be particularly suitable as a basis for the personal nature of the Holy Spirit and as a means of clarifying his relationship with God the Father and God the Son. The manuals of dogmatic theology provide information about the development of this teaching, which did not take place without difficulty and controversy (for example, in the case of the question of the *filioque*). It cannot be denied that excessive demands were made of the Johannine texts in certain cases, such as, for example, the appeal made to Jn 15:26 as evidence for the Trinitarian origin of the Holy Spirit as coming from the Father (see *ad loc.*). Any Catholic theologian who gives his assent to the Church's tradition and to the development of teaching within that tradition will understand this situation, and know that the teaching about the Spirit also required clarification in the theological process of increasing knowledge. Now, however, we are able to see more clearly than we did in the past that, in the course of this clarification, other aspects of the Johannine teaching about the Spirit – and especially his dynamic activity in the Church and his 'calling to mind' words – have been thrust into the background.

Finally, the Johannine texts have played a very important part, especially in the Roman Catholic Church, in such questions as the Church's teaching office, the special help of the Holy Spirit in decisions about doctrine, the infallibility of the Church's ordinary and extraordinary teaching office and the Church's continuing in the truth of Christ. The Churches of the Reformation appeal to the same texts as well as to others in 1 Jn (especially 2:20, 27; 5:10) in order to justify their conviction that all believers possess the Spirit and that the Holy Spirit bears witness in this way in believers. The exegete will always be on his guard against a one-sided exposition of the texts; this will mean that he will not interpret them as applying exclusively to the Church's teaching authority (see 14:26 and 16:13 in the detailed commentary) or as simply disputing all teaching authority in the Church,[40] It is, however, hardly possible to come to a decision about many of the controversial questions that have arisen in recent years simply on the basis of exegesis, if only because the questions that existed at that time were different.

(c) From the exegetical point of view, it is most desirable to see the sayings about the Paraclete in the right perspective. This means above all attempting to understand the original intention of the evangelist and his pupils. In order to do this, many previously held convictions may have to be abandoned. Within the framework of the farewell discourses, the sayings about the Paraclete have the primary function of encouraging, admonishing and consoling the community by promising the Spirit or by reminding the members of that community that they possess the Spirit. They can only carry out that function if the promise is in accordance with the community's living experience of the Spirit, in other words, if the soil is properly prepared to receive that promise. The evangelist and, together with him, the editors of the other discourses in Chapters 15 and 16 of the gospel were able to presuppose this in the case of their community. In the twentieth century, however, consciousness of the presence of the Spirit has to a very great extent disappeared, even in the believing community, and has therefore to be aroused as a prior condition. It is possible to say that the only person who will understand the words about the Spirit is one who has already experienced the presence of the Spirit.

A Christian who lets himself be 'taught' and 'reminded' of Jesus' words by the Spirit is led by that Spirit into a closer relationship with Jesus. The one who once came becomes for him, through the Spirit, the one who is present and close now. Jesus' words become for him 'spirit and life' (6:63, 68), strength, admonition and consolation. In this way, he can more easily understand the present and the future and find an answer to the questions raised by the contemporary world and his own existence. The Spirit who is present in this way is not prevented from, but is rather urged to lead man to reflect about the traditional words of Jesus and to be orientated towards Jesus' will and attitude. Admittedly this does not take the form of a mere repetition and codification. It is rather a reinterpretation that is applicable to the place and the period. Jesus' words and intentions have to be interpreted 'in the Spirit', that is, in *his* Spirit. However difficult it may be in individual cases, the Holy Spirit none the less encourages Christians and makes them capable of doing this, gives them new insights and new impulses. He is the dynamic principle that urges the Church forward.

The Johannine sayings about the Paraclete do not tell us how the Spirit teaches. We are not told whether this takes place from outside, by means of the words of those who proclaim and teach, or from within, by means of inner enlightenment and guidance. This, however, is not the most urgent question, nor is it really an alternative. In the epistle to the community, it is clear that hearing the words of those responsible for the transitional teaching and hearing the inner voice of the Spirit can be combined. This means for the contemporary Church that those bearing office and the 'simple' faithful are both guided by the Spirit and are, in the Spirit, dependent on each other. Tensions and conflicts are inevitable in human relationships, but they can be endured and overcome in the knowledge that the Holy Spirit is present and active in the Church. Only a community that bears witness in faith to the presence of the Spirit can become at the same time a witness that will prove the unbelieving world guilty.

These aspects of the Johannine sayings about the Paraclete to which I have drawn attention above may not solve all the theological problems involved, but they deserve to be taken seriously in the contemporary context.

---

3. Jesus' Painful Departure and Reunion in Joy (16:16–24)

[16]'*A little while and you will see me no more; again a little while and you will see me*'. [17](*Some) of his disciples said to one another, 'What is this that he says to us, "A little while and you will not see me and again a little while and you will see me" and "I go to the Father"?'* [18]*They said, 'What does he mean by "a little while"? We do not know what he means'.* [19]*Jesus knew that they wanted to ask him; so he said to them, 'Is this what you are asking yourselves, what I meant by saying, "A little while and you will not see me and again a little while and you will see me"?*

²⁰*Truly, truly, I say to you, you will weep and lament, but the world will rejoice; you will be sorrowful, but your sorrow will turn to joy. ²¹When a woman is in travail she has sorrow, because her hour has come; but when she is delivered of the child, she no longer remembers the anguish, for joy that a man is born into the world. ²²So you have sorrow now, but I will see you again and your hearts will rejoice and no one will take your joy from you. ²³In that day you will ask nothing (more) of me. Truly, truly, I say to you, if you ask anything of the Father, he will give it to you in my name. ²⁴Hitherto you have asked nothing in my name; ask and you will receive, that your joy may be full'.*

16:16   After the sayings about the Paraclete, the discourse recommences at Jesus' departure. In their reflection (v. 17), the disciples explicitly go back to Jesus' statement about his departure (see vv. 5, 7, 10). The presence of the sentence 'I go to the Father' in v. 17 has led to the later addition of this statement in many manuscripts to v. 16.[33] Something of the mysterious character of the cryptic repetition of the two 'little whiles' and the 'not seeing again' and the 'seeing again' is, however, lost by this inclusion, which only motivates the disciples' reflection (and that of the community). Viewed from the outside, the process is very similar to that in Chapter 14: the announcement of Jesus' return (14:18ff) follows the promise of the Paraclete and there is an incision in the discourse between the two. Despite this external similarity, however, the inner structure and intention of each discourse point to the fact that the two announcements have a different function. In the 'consolatory' discourse of Chapter 16, the situation of sorrow (see v. 6) is once again made present and, at this point in the discourse, in order to express the fact that it will be changed into joy. The idea extends as far as v. 22 and then further to v. 24.[34]

The saying 'a little while' occurs frequently in the gospel. The evangelist used the term χρόνον μικρόν for a cryptic statement made by Jesus which led to the unbelieving Jews misunderstanding him (7:33). The announcement that Jesus would be with them ἔτι μικρόν (13:33) enabled the disciples to know that he would be leaving them. In the farewell discourse (14:19), however, this ἔτι μικρόν was for them – as it was not for the world – a promise that they would once again encounter Jesus. Now this μικρόν – reduced to its shortest form – occurs again and is at the same time seen in its most oppressive and its most joyful aspect. At first, however, the disciples find it cryptic and cannot understand it. In the context of the discourse, this is intentional. Now is still the time for speaking cryptically (see v. 25) – it is only 'on that day', after Jesus' resurrection and the sending of the Spirit, that the disciples will cease to ask questions and will understand (vv. 23a, 25). In the farewell discourse, the prevalent idea was that there would be only a 'little while' until the disciples saw Jesus again. Here, however, there is a dialectical tension between the sorrow of the passion and the joy of Easter, and for this reason the two 'little whiles' are stressed. This is connected also with another linguistic refinement – a different verb for 'see' is used for each of the 'little whiles'. For the not seeing at the time of sorrow, θεωρεῖν is employed (cf. v. 10), while, for the seeing again at Easter, ὁρᾶν is used (as it is in the chapter on Easter, 20:18, 20, 25, 29). This use of two different verbs has no qualitative significance (θεωρεῖν can also point to a spiritual seeing; see 6:40, 62; 8:51, etc.). It does, however, have the function of setting the two 'little whiles' off against each other. The disciples will, unlike the 'world' (see v.. 20–22), experience a contrast, and through this experience will also learn how to overcome their present distress (see v. 33).

In considering the Johannine tradition and the linguistic significance of the twofold μικρόν in 16:16ff, there is no need to look for a more remote point of contact. Reference has been made to the prophetic discourse in the OT, in which judgment (Hos 1:4; Is 10:25; Jer 51:33; Hag 2:6) and salvation (Is 29:17) are announced 'in a little while'.[33] It is possible that a distant memory plays a part here, since the language is Semitic in character (μικρὸν καί). There is, however, no direct or intentional reference to the prophetic proclamation of salvation and perdition. The Johannine community is simply reflecting about its own situation in the light of faith in Christ.

Within the context of the discourse, it is clear that the two 'little whiles' point to the time up to Jesus' death and from there to his resurrection. John retained this time pattern from tradition (see 2:19ff; 20:1, 19). This does not, of course, mean that this view is limited to the day of Easter, since the Johannine community regarded Easter and its continuing joy as lasting (see the commentary on vv. 22 and 23), because there was certainty that the Lord was present. Augustine's interpretation, that the second 'little while' pointed to the time until the parousia,[36] departs from the original meaning, but it is in a sense right when used in a community living at a later stage. But it also applies to the Johannine community, not in the perspective of the parousia, but in its existence at that time. For that community, the promise of reunion with Jesus was already fulfilled.

16:17–18 The disciples' reaction to Jesus' words shows how perplexed and depressed they were and how they did not understand. As in vv. 5f, the fact that they do not question him is a sign of their sorrow. There is no conversation with Jesus, who in fact takes up their uncomprehending question of each other and elucidates his own cryptic saying by means of the image of the woman in labour. The detailed description of the disciples talking to each other is given in order to stress the cryptic nature of Jesus' first statement. To begin with, some[37] of his disciples repeat his words among themselves, the only change in the language itself being that οὐκέτι is a simple οὐ in the disciples' repetition. There is also an addition: a memory of the statement about Jesus' departure (καί . . . ὅτι κτλ.). This additional clause, for which there is excellent evidence in the textual tradition, cannot be regarded as a later gloss.[38] It clearly expresses the intention of the author of the discourse to show that the disciples have understood enough to know that Jesus is speaking of his departure. In this way, the material reason for the cryptic statement is disclosed. The ὅτι, however, is hardly causal; it should be seen as a ὅτι used in indirect speech.[39]

Neither as spoken by Jesus nor as a reflection on the part of the disciples is the clause meaningful as providing a reason for Jesus' departure. He has already said that he is going away (v. 5a) and the disciples remember this statement on hearing his cryptic words. The reader is in this way made conscious of the fact that his statement is connected with his departure and that it also gives it a deeper meaning. Finally, the mysterious character of Jesus' statement and the disciples' perplexity are once again elucidated in the continuation in v. 18, which contains a number of less important textual variants.[40] The other element in Jesus' pronouncement – the 'little while' – is taken up again in v. 18 and similarly presented as cryptic. The disciples' entire reflection therefore has the aim of making the reader reflect on Jesus' words.

16:19   Jesus is aware of the disciples' intention to ask him and anticipates their question with his answer. Part of the essential image of the Johannine Jesus is that he knows men's thoughts (see 1:47f; 2:24; 6:61, 64, etc.). Indeed, in the same discourse, the disciples tell him that he knows everything and 'needs none to question him' (v. 30). This gives greater certainty to Jesus' prediction, but here the primary reason is to direct attention to the parable that follows and the decoding of Jesus' cryptic statement.

16:20   This verse is introduced by the emphatic, solemn Johannine formula (which occurs again in v. 23). In it Jesus discloses what he wanted to say to the disciples in his previous statement, first without an image, then more insistently with a parable. The change, which is indicated by the twofold 'little whiles', is concerned with the disciples' situation with regard to the world and in the world. They will be sorrowful when Jesus goes away in a little while and this sorrow is expressed in an even more emphatic form than in v. 6 by the use of the words 'weep and lament'. This sorrow that the disciples will experience is contrasted with the joy of the world of unbelieving men who reject Jesus (see v. 9). The clear dualistic vision of 15:18f is therefore preserved – the community will experience in the world the icy wind of those who hate and deny Jesus. At the same time, however, the statement with its twofold 'little whiles' is, precisely for this reason, also very consoling, since the disciples' sorrow will be changed into joy. The whole emphasis is therefore on the second part of the cryptic statement – the tension is released in the promise of reunion.

16:21   The parable that follows (the article in the women giving birth is a Semiticism[41]) can be quite satisfactorily explained as a clarification of the idea contained in v. 20 and therefore it is a true parable which is only concerned with the change from sorrow to joy (in accordance with the principle of the *tertium comparationis*). 'Parabolic forms', especially those in which there is an easy transition from a parabolic to an allegorical way of speaking,[42] occur quite frequently in the gospel of John. In other such 'parables', the 'matter' itself can often be perceived with greater or lesser clarity in the images and concepts chosen; these 'symbolic elements' occur for the most part in reference to Christology (see 3:29; 8:35; 10:11b–13; 12:24). We are therefore bound to ask in this context whether the everyday image of the woman in labour, which often has a symbolic character in the Old Testament, might not also have other overtones and, what is more, intentional overtones.[43] The expressions that call for particular attention are: ἡ γυνή, ἡ ὥρα (αὐτῆς); 'a man is born into the world' and the term ἡ θλῖψις, which is used in apocalyptic literature for the distress experienced at the end of time. Many exegetes are of the opinion that the whole text may have been influenced by Is 26:17f and/or Is 66:7–10.

It would be too extreme to try to establish a connection between this parable and the story of Eve in Gen 3:16 (childbearing in pain) and 4:1 ('I have begotten a *man*'). The expression 'a man is born into the world' can be more simply explained as a Semitism (cf. the rabbinical term for a man: 'one who is to come into the world'; see 1:9 above). It is even more doubtful whether there is a connection with Mary, the mother of Jesus, who is addressed in 2:4 and 19:26 as 'woman'. Nor can the word 'hour', which is used in the image ('*her* hour'), hardly be related to Jesus' hour.[44] Such interpretations are based on the principle, which is certainly open to criticism, that an important word in an authors' work always has the same meaning, even in different contexts.

The situation is different in the case of certain possibly intentional references to other texts. In Is 26:17f, Israel is compared with a pregnant woman who 'writhes and cries out in her pangs'; the Israelites, however, give birth only to 'wind' and do not bring salvation to the earth. A contrasting image is provided in Is 66:7–10, in which Zion is said to have given birth before the writhing and everyone who has been sorrowful is urged to rejoice. It is not possible, however, to see more in these two texts than a point of contact with John in the first case (Is 26) in the image itself and, in the second, in the change from sorrow to joy (Is 66). A more impressive description can be found in a Qumran text (1 *QH* 3:9ff), which many exegetes believe refers to the birth of the Messiah by the community and others think refers to the 'birth of the community by the teacher', because the hymn in which this text occurs deals with the 'teacher of righteousness'.[45] Even if the first group of exegetes are right, however, this is not a real parallel with Jn 16:21, because the Johannine text gives the disciples an active part to play in the 'birth of the Messiah' (or the exaltation of Jesus). There is also, for the same reason, no direct connection between the Johannine text and the heavenly woman in Rev 12 and the image of her childbearing (vv. 2–5). The childbearing woman cannot be interpreted allegorically as pointing to the disciples. The only point of comparison is the transition from sorrow to joy. In addition to the woman's λύπη (D 579c also have the reading λύπης) her θλῖψις is also mentioned in the Johannine text; this clearly calls the situation of the community in the world to mind (see v. 33), but it is doubtful whether the Johannine community was concerned with the idea of 'such tribulation as has not been from the beginning of creation' (Mk 13:19 par.).[46]

Nothing points with certainty to the fact that v. 21 may be more than a parable. The image was clearly chosen because of its rich and varied use in Judaism and the hard-pressed situation in which the community was placed. It is also employed here independently, in the context of Johannine eschatology.

16:22   On the basis of the experience of the woman who is filled with joy after the birth of her child, Jesus promises the disciples (καὶ ὑμεῖς)[47] lasting joy which no one will take from them and which goes far beyond the joy of the parable when he sees them again. This forms the climax, not only of this statement, but also of the whole discourse, which had, as its point of departure, the disciples' sorrow (v. 6). Because both aspects – the time of sorrow and that of joy – are contrasted with each other, the future version λύπην ἕξετε[48] is certainly not original; αἴρει in v. 22c, for which there is more evidence than ἀρεῖ,[49] has a future meaning. 'Your heart will rejoice' is literally in agreement with Is 66:14, but this could not have been an intentional quotation. The sentence corresponds to v. 6 (cf. also 14:1, 27c) – the sorrow that now fills the disciples' hearts will then give way to joy. The change from 'You will see me again' to 'I will see you again' can be explained by the fact that Jesus brings about a transformation in the situation, by coming to them as the risen Christ and, with his peace (see 14:27; 20;19f), also brings joy. The negative formulation, 'No one will take your joy from you', of this imperishable joy helps to stress once again the opposition of the world (see v. 20). The unbelieving world is powerless against the one who has overcome it (v. 33) and who has accepted his disciples into his freedom, peace and joy (see 15:11; 17:13).

16:23 The imperishable joy of Christ's presence also does away with the disciples' perplexity, with the result that they cease to ask questions. 'That day' in this verse means primarily the day when they see Jesus again, as in 14:20, in which the same 'Easter terminology' is found (cf. 20:19f). What follows, however, also shows that not only Easter day, but also the whole of the new age that begins with it is in mind here. There is no allusion here to the parousia, and the early and more recent exegetes who have thought of the words 'that day' as relating to the parousia have misunderstood the joy of the Johannine community, which in fact anticipates the eschaton (see 14:20 above). The immediate consequence (see the καί) of the overwhelming joy caused by the certainty of Christ's presence is that the disciples cease to ask troublesome questions.

Jesus then gives the disciples not only a solemn assurance (cf. v. 20), but also a further promise that their prayer to the Father will be heard. This step in the thought process may be surprising, but it is certainly connected with the previous idea, because the disciples' joy is stressed again at the end of v. 24. Because their prayer is heard by the Father, their joy will be 'full'. There may be an external association here between the two Greek words for 'ask' in this verse, since, in John, ἐρωτᾶν can mean both 'ask' and 'request' or 'pray' (see especially 14:16; 16:26). There is undoubtedly a bridge, as it were, connecting the two ideas: the disciples do not need to 'ask' Jesus, because they can turn directly to the Father and overcome all darkness in asking him in 'prayer'. This assurance that prayer will be heard (always with αἰτεῖν) is familiar, from the farewell discourse (14:13f) and also from the following discourse (15:7 and 16). It is here more closely associated with the second of these instances (15:7, 16), because the asking or prayer is addressed to the Father in both these cases (and not, as in 14:14, to Jesus) and, in the context, the disciples are promised the same perfect joy (even including the wording) (15:11). It is worth noting that the phrase 'in my name' is transposed from the prayer of the disciples (15:16) to the giving of the Father. In many manuscripts, this change has been – quite certainly subsequently – eliminated, because the readers would have been used to 'praying in the name of Jesus'.[50] It is also said, however, in 14:26 that the Father will send the Spirit in the name of Jesus. In the better sequence in v. 16:23, the disciples are even more strongly referred to the Father as one to whom they can call without Jesus' intervention and as one who will give them what they request – things concerned with their life of faith – 'in the name of Jesus'. 'In Jesus' name' therefore means 'in view of the fact that they belong to Jesus' or even, in this context, 'in Jesus' place'.[51] Their asking is included in their prayer to the Father and, because of this, it ceases. This unquestioning attitude is the consequence of a prayer that is certain of being heard. It is also the sign and the seal of the life in joy that is here disclosed to the disciples.

16:24   In this verse, there is further reflection about this frank prayer to the Father, seen now again as requesting or asking 'in the name of Jesus' (see 14:13 above). The community must be aware of this precious gift (see also 1 Jn 3:21; 5:14f) and this is made clear to the disciples in the form of an admonition: 'Ask and you will receive'. This formula is remniscent of the synoptic logion of Mt 7:7 par., which is also echoed in 1 Jn 3:22; James 4:3. This is another indication of the fact that the Johannine school preserved and gave further consideration to many early traditional statements of Jesus (see 13:16, 20;15:20 above). In this context, it is, however, not so much an admonition as a promise: if you ask, you will receive and in that way come to full joy. This frank and open prayer to the Father that is certain of being heard is reserved for the time of Christ's spiritual presence. 'Hitherto', the disciples have not prayed in the name of Jesus. This ἄρτι once again stresses the present time, when they are oppressed and uncomprehending (see vv. 12 and 31). That time is contrasted with the time of openness and perfect joy that is to come. This concludes this section of the discourse, which has so far been dominated by the contrast between sorrow and joy and which completes what has been said about the Spirit and his activity within the framework of 'joy'.

4. A View of the Time to Come and a Concluding Dialogue with the Disciples (16:25–33)

[25]'I have said this to you in figures; the hour is coming when I shall no longer speak to you in figures, but tell you plainly of the Father. [26]In that day you will ask in my name; and I do not say to you I shall pray the Father for you; [27]for the Father himself loves you, because you have loved me and have believed that I came from the Father. [28]I came from the Father and have come into the world; again, I am leaving the world and going to the Father'. [29]His disciples

said, 'Ah now you are speaking plainly, not in any figure! [30]*Now we know that you know all things and need none to question you; by this we believe that you came from God'.* [31]*Jesus answered them, 'Do you now believe?* [32]*The hour is coming, indeed it has come, when you will be scattered, every man for himself, and will leave me alone; yet I am not alone, for the Father is with me.* [33]*I have said this to you that in me you may have peace. In the world you have tribulation; but be of good cheer, I have overcome the world'.*

16:25   As in the farewell discourse (14:25), the formula ταῦτα λελάληκα points to the fact that this consolatory discourse is approaching its end. Apart from announcing the scattering of the disciples (v. 32), these concluding words have hardly any new content. At the same time, however, this last part of the discourse does not summarize the whole, but only takes the thoughts expressed in the last section to a deeper level (vv. 16–24). The addition ἐν παροιμίαις cannot refer to the words about the Paraclete, which do not cause the disciples to ask questions. It was rather the cryptic statement in v. 16 that led to this and it is to this that our attention is first drawn, then to the statement about Jesus' departure (see v. 17c), and finally to the parable of the woman giving birth to a child. The use of the plural implies a generalization; this is confirmed by the fact that the same word is used in the singular ('not in any figure') in v. 29. We should therefore not simply think, in the case of παροιμία, of the parable in v. 21, although the employment of the same word in 10:6 might tempt us to do so.[53] The underlying Hebrew word *mašal* has a similar range of meanings (see the commentary on 10:6). Here the present discourse ἐν παροιμίαις is contrasted with Jesus' future speaking παρρησίᾳ. His present discourse is still cryptic and concealed from the unenlightened disciples and on 'that day' (see v. 23) it will give way to open and 'plain' speaking about the Father.

But how is it possible for Jesus to say that he will speak 'plainly of the Father' to the disciples in the future? According to vv. 12f, he intends to leave it to the Paraclete to guide them into all the truth. It is hardly likely that this is a reference to a 'proclamation' of the risen Christ – only Mary Magdalene 'proclaims' (ἀγγέλουσα; v. 1: ἀπαγγέλουσα) to the disciples that Jesus is ascending to his Father and her Father (20:18). The Paraclete is therefore to be the mediator of that full revelation of the Father (see ἀναγγελεῖ, vv. 13ff).[54] The fact that this function is here ascribed to Jesus himself can be explained in the light of the underlying theological idea. It is a question of the relationship between Jesus revelatory discourse on earth and the disciples' understanding of it after the Easter event.[55] It is the same Jesus who speaks to the disciples at that time as the earthly Jesus and who reveals himself to the community as the exalted Christ who is present among them, firstly to all those who proclaim the truth and then, through them, to all believers. We may assume that the latter is the case, because the verb ἀπαγγέλλειν in 1 Jn 1:2, 3 (which is singular in the gospel) refers to those who proclaim the truth (cf. also ἀγγελία, 1:5; 3:11). Jesus expresses himself in the Spirit, but the disciples, the members of the Johannine circle, see themselves (as in v. 13) as to those to whom the Spirit interprets the message of Jesus and who themselves speak of it to the community.

This understanding of the relationship between Jesus' revelation on earth and his post-paschal revelation is illuminating and also theologically important. The whole nature and configuration of the gospel of John bear witness to the fact that the Johannine community regarded a transformation of the words that Jesus spoke and the acts that he performed as necessary in the light of their paschal faith and subject to the guidance of the Spirit. This whole process that is carried out in faith is subjected to conscious reflection in the discourse in Chapter 16 and this takes place in our present text under the heading of 'concealed and open (plain) speaking'. This contains a certain dialectic tension, because the earthly Jesus has already spoken 'openly' to the world in the presentation of the gospel (see 7:26; 10:24f; 18:20), but, if examined more closely, this 'open' speaking ($\pi\alpha\rho\rho\eta\sigma\acute{\iota}\alpha$) was in another way also concealed, that is, from unbelief (see 7:3ff, 17; 8:46f; 10:25f). This shift in man's ability to receive the message continues to exist and is even intensified by Jesus' death and resurrection. The 'ascent' or 'exaltation' of the Son of man forces men even more powerfully to come to a decision regarding faith or unbelief (see 6:62; 8:28; 19:37). The dialectical tension in our present text is slightly different. All Jesus' speaking on earth is here seen to be cryptic, even for the disciples who believe, and full revelation will only come in the future. This view of the Johannine school provides a fundamental answer to our modern theological problem of the 'historical Jesus' and the 'Christ of faith'. The tension is found, even for believers, in the relationship between the Jesus who was active on earth and the exalted and present Christ.[56]

The terminology used in 16:25 is remarkable, especially if it is compared with the vocabulary in the rest of the gospel. Attention has already been drawn to the wider meanings of $\pi\alpha\rho\omega\iota\mu\acute{\iota}\alpha$. In most of the other places where it occurs (apart from 11:14), $\pi\alpha\rho\rho\eta\sigma\acute{\iota}\alpha$ has a reference to 'public', in other words, it suggests that Jesus' revelatory discourse is not a secret doctrine, but is something that takes place in the presence of the 'world'.[57] The need to emphasize this is not felt in the dialogue with the believing disciples and for the community's instruction in faith. The expression $\check{\epsilon}\rho\chi\epsilon\tau\alpha\iota$ $\check{\omega}\rho\alpha$ also does not accord with specifically Johannine usage, which is to point to the presence of salvation that has already begun with Jesus' work on earth (4:23; 5:25:$\varkappa\alpha\grave{\iota}$ $\nu\tilde{\upsilon}\nu$ $\check{\epsilon}\sigma\tau\iota\nu$). It stresses the period after Easter that is still to come and therefore has the same significance as 'that day' (vv. 23, 26). Although the terminology of the gospel is retained, a material shift of emphasis or a transposition in the perspective has taken place, with the later community in mind. If we include the rare $\grave{\alpha}\pi\alpha\gamma\gamma\epsilon\lambda\tilde{\omega}$, which we have discussed above, the obvious conclusion is that this discourse originated in the circle of the evangelist's pupils, who were pursuing a special interest that was of concern to the community. It is, however, also possible that the evangelist may have modified his language here in the light of the changed sphere of understanding – 'revelation' as something public in the world and 'revelation' for those who believe.

16:26–27 'Asking in the name of Jesus' is once more the theme (cf. vv. 23f), but this time it is not subject to the promise that such prayer will be heard, but to the idea of direct access to the Father. There is no explicit assurance that prayer will be heard. On the contrary, it is emphasized that Jesus does not need to intervene on behalf of the disciples with the Father,[58] because the Father himself loves the disciples. The Father's full revelation, which the disciples will receive on 'that day', corresponds to the Father's immediate turning to the disciples. The fact that the disciples will ask 'in the name of Jesus' is not called into question by this. The nature of this prayer is simply revealed more clearly. The disciples, who are in full communion with Jesus, are also certain of the Father's love (v. 27). They do not need to appeal to Jesus or to use his name like a magic formula. 'In the name of Jesus' simply indicates that they have a true communion with Jesus because they give their consent to his mission, as sent by God, and love him. The word for 'to love' employed here is $\phi\iota\lambda\epsilon\tilde{\iota}\nu$ and it was certainly chosen with great deliberation. In the farewell discourse, the word $\dot{\alpha}\gamma\alpha\pi\tilde{\alpha}\nu$ was used for 'to love' throughout in every case where the disciples' community with Jesus and the Father was mentioned (14:15, 21, 23f, 28). Its demanding character is not denied by this use (see also 15:9, 12, 17). Now, however, Jesus reveals to the disciples the relationship of friendship that the Father promises to them for his sake. Jesus' own friendship, which he guaranteed to the disciples in 15:15, explaining that he has made known to them everything that he has heard from the Father, is extended for them to a direct friendship of God. This idea already existed in Judaism and Hellenism[59] and here it is given an entirely Christian sense. God's friendship with Christ's disciples is a free gift of his love in respect of their love for and faithfulness to his Son. The perfect tenses in v. 27b emphasize the disciples' relationship with Jesus, which has existed for some time and is firmly established, their love, which they have already proved, and their faith in Jesus as the one sent by God, to which they have already borne witness.[60]

16:28 The last statement in the previous verse, that Jesus came from the Father, is repeated at the beginning of this verse[61] and this is followed by a double sentence which, as it were, draws a line under Jesus' discourse to the disciples and concludes it. The carefully-articulated sentence structure describes Jesus' way from the Father into the world and from the world back to the Father – a variation of the idea of the redeemer's ascent and descent (Vol. 1, pp. 392ff) and of the 'passing over' of Jesus from the world to the Father (13:1). In this context, there is particular emphasis on Jesus' going to the Father, to which the disciples were previously quite insistently referred: they are loved by the one from whom Jesus came and to whom he is returning. Despite the symmetrical structure of the clauses, the last statement is particularly stressed: Jesus' departure from the world is a way ($\pi o \rho\epsilon\dot{\upsilon}o\mu\alpha\iota$) to the Father. In this way, the discourse also returns to its point of departure (vv. 5–7). The announcement of Jesus' departure makes the disciples sorrowful, but, after everything that Jesus has told them, they ought to understand that his going away is good for them. His stay in the world, that place that is remote from God (see 3:16), was no more than transistory. His task in the world has been accomplished. Now he is going back to his real home (see 17:4f). Within the framework of the whole discourse, the community, which is in the world, is also reminded of its real home and its goal. The disciples will no longer see him, because he is going to the Father (see v. 10), and yet they will 'see him again'. They therefore have a sphere in common with Jesus and that is the realm of the Father, who turns towards them for Jesus' sake. A victorious certainty can be heard in Jesus' declaration.[62] This certainty is brought into the open (v. 33) after the dialogue with the disciples (vv. 29f).

16:29–30 Now, at the end of the discourse, the disciples express themselves, but their reaction to what Jesus has said is to some extent obscure. On the one hand, they are convinced that they have understood Jesus and they gladly declare this. On the other hand, however, they also contradict what he has said, saying that he is already speaking 'openly' and plainly and that his statements are not cryptic. This ambivalence is intentional. Their words, addressed to Jesus in affirmation of their faith, are meant well (see v. 30b), but they also reveal that they do not yet have a full understanding of faith – if they had, Jesus would not have wanted to 'correct' them (with typically Johannine irony). The readers of these verses are to recognize, together with the disciples, that Jesus 'knows all things' and they are to believe, again with the disciples, that he 'came from God', but they are also to be on their guard against a false self-confidence. This, of course, is a theme that was prominent in Simon Peter's contradiction (13:36f). There is a reference to this present text in the additional chapter and the words 'you know all things' are repeated by the 'converted' Peter (21:17). Like Peter, the disciples are unenlightened in their love for Jesus and not yet firmly established in their faith. The readers are intended to learn from this.

Apart from οἶδας πάντα, there are other indications that our present text should be seen within the same framework in 13:36ff and 21:15ff. Points of comparison are φιλεῖν for the disciples' love for Jesus in 16:27 and 21.15ff; λύπη in Chapter 16 and 21:17; the use of νῦν with ἄρτι in 13:36 and 37 and 16:29f and 31; finally Jesus' doubting question in 13:38 and 16:31. Even if these are not convincing evidence, there is a further point of comparison. In 13:38, the synoptic tradition of the announcement of Peter's denial is included, while in 16:32 there is the Johannine version of the announcement of the dispersal of the disciples. These are both predictions of Jesus that are closely connected with the synoptics (Mk 14:27–31/Mt 26:31–35; Lk does not report the flight of the disciples). We may therefore assume that the editor or editors, who reflected about Jn 13:36ff in Chapter 21, also composed 16:30–32.

It is particularly worth noticing the expression (οὐ) χρείαν ἔχειν. This forms part of the Johannine vocabulary (it occurs four times in the gospel and twice in 1 Jn), but has a special meaning here, in connection with Jesus' knowledge. As in 2:25, it emphasizes his *divine* knowledge (see the commentary above) and, again as in the same text (and in 1 Jn 2:27), it is also constructed with the following ἵνα clause. The impersonal τις also connects the two texts together. It was suspected that the section 2:23–25 was an editorial addition and that it may have come from the same editor as the discourse in Chapter 16. If 2:24f is compared with 16:30, the same fundamental idea can be recognized: Jesus' knowledge, which is expressed positively (he 'knew all men' or 'knows all things') and negatively (he 'needed no one to bear witness' or 'to question him'), is a sign of his divine origin. The sentence, which is kept general, may refer back to vv. 19 and 23a, within the context in which it occurs, and need not have a broader background.[63]

Finally, there is also the striking phrase ἐν τούτῳ. This occurs frequently in 1 Jn and may be used, as it is in 1 Jn, with γινώσκειν with the meaning: 'by this we know or believe'.[64]

16:31–32   Jesus' reaction to the disciples' words should be seen as a question expressing doubt; this is clear from a comparison with 13:38. In itself, however, the sentence can also be understood as a statement or confirmation,[65] in which case the announcement that follows, that the disciples will be scattered and leave Jesus alone, provides a contrast, namely that a wrongful denial follows their present faith. This interpretation is, however, improbable in the context of this discourse, in which the present sorrowful situation of the disciples is contrasted with the future time of joy and friendship with God. If, on the other hand, Jesus is, in this text, now questioning their faith and providing a basis for their flight in the near future by means of this doubt, then the present hour must be seen in the same perspective of weakness and lack of understanding on the part of the disciples. Their denial and their leaving Jesus is included in this 'now', since it is stressed that the hour of their dispersal has already come (ἐλήλυθεν).[66] The real change will not come until Jesus has overcome the world (v. 33). This contains the promise that the disciples will emerge from this dark hour confirmed and strengthened (see the 'example' of Peter, 21:15ff).

This announcement that the disciples will be scattered betrays an influence of the synoptic tradition[67] and also of Johannine interpretation. As in Mk 14:27/Mt 26:31 (a quotation from Zech 13:7), the image here is derived from that of God's scattered flock. There may also be a reminiscence of 10:12 in Jn 16:32: 'The wolf snatches and scatters (σκορπίζει) them (= the sheep)'. The background both to the synoptic version and the Johannine text must be the prophecy of Zechariah (see also Jn 11:52; Vol. 2, p. 295). The idea that the scattered disciples will be gathered together again ought also to be present, but our present text aims to tone down the disciples' self-confidence and therefore emphasizes their failure. The expression, that each one will be scattered εἰς τὰ ἴδια can hardly be interpreted, on a basis of the meaning of the words, as 'to his own home'. Even though seven disciples are said, in the additional chapter, to return to fishing in the lake of Gennesaret, the editor or editors know about Jesus' appearance in Jerusalem, where the disciples were gathered on the third day (see the enumeration in 21:14). The phrase can also be understood in a metaphorical sense and this is indeed how it should be interpreted in the context: every disciple is concerned with his own safety and not at all with Jesus.[68] The theme of Jesus' abandonment is parallel to that of the Son of man's way to his passion in Mk, which describes the flight of all the disciples (14:50) and reaches its climax in Jesus' abandonment by God on the cross (15:34). The Johannine school could accept the first of these incidents, but not the second, because of its distinctive theology. The Johannine Jesus is not alone. The Father does not leave him, but remains with him, even in his darkest hour. Jesus tells the disciples what he has already told the unbelieving Jews (8:29). This departure from the synoptic line is present in John because he interprets

Jesus' cross as 'exaltation' and in the sense of a 'glorification' (see the commentary on 3:14; see also Excursus 13 in Vol. 2).

16:33   The certainty that the Father is with Jesus leads on to a view of his victory and glorification – a prospect that should give the disciples courage. This is at the same time the concluding statement in the whole discourse (ταῦτα λελάληκα ὑμῖν),[69] the aim of which has been to help the disciples to go beyond their sorrow and discouragement. The idea of peace expressed in this verse is a point of contact with 14:27, but peace is not at this moment Jesus' farewell greeting and gift. It is rather a wish and promise for the disciples' existence in the world. Opposition to the 'world' was expressed in 14:27, but here it is expressed more vigorously, because of the distress or 'tribulation' that the disciples will experience in the world. They are not, however, exposed to the world without any protection. They have peace 'in Jesus'. This ἐν ἐμοί has local overtones, because of the contrast with the ἐν τῷ κόσμῳ that follows. This cannot be interpreted in a mystical sense. The prepositional phrase can best be explained on the basis of Jn 3:15 (the believer has eternal life 'in him') or 20:31 (life 'in his name'), that is, the disciples will have joy (v. 22) and peace (v. 33) in combination with Jesus or in their shared life with him. An interpretation pointing to peace is therefore insufficient (see 14:27). It is a question here of a way of life that is revealed to the disciples in Christ as something providing them with security despite all the distress that they may experience in this world. They are to share in Christ's victory over the world. The word νικᾶν, which occurs only here in the gospel, directs our attention at once to the first epistle, in which it occurs frequently (the verb occurs six times and the noun once).[70] Behind the cosmos is the 'evil one' (1 Jn 2:13f; see also 5:19), who is known in the gospel as the 'ruler of this world'. 16:33 takes 14:30 into the sphere of the community. The best commentary on how the believers share in Christ's victory is provided by 1 Jn 5:4f (see my *Johannes-Briefe, ad loc.*). Finally, the impression is once again reinforced that this whole discourse was composed by editors of the gospel for the community that was in the world and confronted by the 'world' and perhaps by the same editors who address the community in the first epistle and that is was made to follow the farewell discourse of Chapter 14 (and the further discourse in Chapter 15).

The Prayer of the Departing Redeemer.   (Chapter 17)

The three great discourses in Jn 14–16, which are usually, but not very adequately grouped together under the one title 'farewell discourses', are followed in Chapter 17 by a great, solemn prayer that Jesus addressed to the Father in the presence of (presumably) all the disciples. This new composition stands out clearly against the so-called farewell discourses as a distinctive genre of discourse and purely·externally as Jesus' prayer on his departure from the disciples. The most striking problem of all that arises in connection with this great prayer and its structure, content, literary genre and meaning is the mere fact of its inclusion at all in the gospel of John. There is nothing comparable in the synoptic gospels and, in the fourth gospel, it forms a climax, precisely at the point where Jesus has ended his discourses to the disciples (ταῦτα ἐλάλησεν, v. 1) and before setting off on the way of the passion (18:1). In·the present configuration of the gospel, there is no more suitable place for this prayer and there would also be no better place in a possible original form of the gospel. It would also be out of the question to place it in front of the farewell discourse in Chapter 14 (that is, between 13:30 and 31), because such a climax has to occur at the end of all the discourses.[1]

As I have already pointed out in the introduction to Chapter 15 (see above, p. 91), the dominant idea of Jesus' glorification connects this prayer (Chapter 17) with the statement in 13:31f. This introductory statement to the farewell discourse is now developed with the community of the disciples who remain behind in the world in mind and in the form of an intercessory prayer. The affinity between 13:31f and 17:1–5 is disclosed very clearly by the following elements: (a) the key-word δοξάζειν occurs five times in 13:31f and four times in 17:1–5; the noun δόξα occurring once; (b) the νῦν in 13:31 is repeated in 17:1 with ἐλήλυθεν ἡ ὥρα; cf. καί νῦν in 17:5; (c) in both passages, the mutual glorification of God and the Son of man – or of the Father and the Son – is expressed: God will glorify Jesus after and on the basis of God's glorification by the Son of man – or the Father's glorification by the Son. The development of the idea contained in the statement in 13:31f can be seen in the following elements: (a) God's glorification by Jesus is more clearly disclosed. In 13:31f, everything is orientated towards the hour of the glorification, that is, the event of the cross, whereas, in 17:4, the work that Jesus has accomplished on earth is also included; (b) Jesus' glorification by God, which, according to 13:32, is to take place 'at once', is more fully revealed in 17:1–5 and, what is more, this takes place in two ways: Jesus himself regains the glory that he had with the Father before the creation of the world (17:5) and he also obtains the power to give those whom the Father has given him eternal life (17:2); (c) this last idea, which did not emerge in 13:31f, becomes the leading theme of the prayer in Chapter 17. Jesus' prayer on leaving the disciples reveals the real meaning of his 'glorification'. It has the purpose of releasing those forces which bring salvation and mediate life and which he has made available to men by his death. The prayer culminates in the request that the disciples may also be where he is and that they may participate in his glory (17:24). There seems to be a particular emphasis in Jn 17 on this soteriological interpretation of the Christological text concerned with glorification and the orientation of the redeemer who is leaving the world towards his believers who remain behind in the world. This prayer, which is said aloud in the presence of the disciples of that particular time by the departing redeemer is, like the discourses that precede it in the gospel, also intended to be heard by later believers.

The suspicion therefore arises that Jn 17 was inspired by the saying about glorification in 13:31f and was the idea of the Johannine school, the members of which wanted to provide a firmer basis for the significance for the community of Jesus' passing from this world and going to the Father (13:1). It is less likely that the saying in 13:31f is a concentrated version of the long prayer in Chapter 17, as the conclusion of that saying would seem to suggest. In itself and because of its significance and its closed nature, the saying about the Son of man would seem to be more original. It is difficult to say whether the prayer was written incidentally or additionally by the evangelist and then elaborated by a final editor or editors. What is rather more probable, however, is that it was composed by the evangelist's pupils (who, we suggested, composed the discourses in Chapters 15 and 16) or that it was a carefully considered prayer composed by an outstanding member of the Johannine circle in the spirit of the evangelist himself. This question, which is in any case not so very important, can only be answered after an exegesis and a linguistic analysis of the prayer itself.

It is more important to consider the structure and thought of Jn 17. The high-priestly prayer is usually sub-divided in the following way (the term 'high-priestly prayer'[2] will be considered more fully after the detailed exegesis of the text): (1) Jesus' petition for his own glorification (vv. 1–5); (2) his intercession for his present disciples (vv. 6–19) and (3) his intercession for later believers (vv. 20–23 or 26). The uncertainty about whether the last three verses of the prayer (24–26) should be counted as part of the third section of the prayer or should be considered as a separate, fourth section (and entitled, for example, 'petition for the fulfilment of his own') points to the questionable nature of this sub-division. The unequal length of the sections is also striking. For these and other reasons, recent exegetes have tried to replace this method of articulating the prayer according to its content and ideas by one based more on external and formal aspects and to find the structural principle of the discourse. A. Laurentin, for example, has based its structure on the formula of articulation καὶ νῦν.[3] G. Malatesta has divided the chapter according to rhythmic figures,[4] and J. Becker has analyzed it in accordance with its literary genres and historical development.[5] My own structural analysis has led me to a new result. (I would refer the reader here to my preliminary investigation of Jn 17 based on its linguistic structure.)[6] The essential aspects of this new analysis are: Jesus' petition for his own glorification (vv. 1–5, with the exception of v. 3, which is an additional gloss) is only made so that he may 'give eternal life to all whom the Father has given him'. This intention is provided with a reason with regard to the disciples in vv. 6–11a. This is followed by the real intercession, which is presented in two units, which are complete in themselves, but which also complete each other and are connected with each other: the petition that the disciples would be kept . . . (τήρησον) in vv. 11b–16 and the request that they should be sanctified in the truth (ἁγίασον) in vv. 17–19. The desire expressed at the beginning of the intercession (v. 11b), 'that they may be one, even as we are one', is then developed in the third unit (vv. 22–23; vv. 20–21 are a secondary supplement). Finally, we are given (in a new and twofold address to the Father) a vision of the fulfilment (vv. 24–26), which both forms a connection with the beginning and completes the whole prayer: the disciples are to share in Jesus' δόξα.

The other questions that arise in connection with the prayer (its literary genre, a comparison with other religions, its *Sitz im Leben*, or existential context, and a possible relationship with cult, especially with the celebration of the Eucharist, and its theological content) will be considered after the detailed exegesis. If the literary genre were easy to establish, it would certainly be able to contribute to my exegesis, but, despite many possible comparisons, Jn 17 has a very distinctive character and it is therefore far safer to go into the question of the nature and literary genre of this chapter only after it has been subjected to a careful structural and exegetical analysis. The various methods cannot be completely separated from one another or arranged in order of importance, but the point of departure must be a very careful investigation of the existing units of the discourse (an examination at the synchronic level). After this, it is possible to consider the question of the pre-history of such farewell prayers (the diachronic view) or that of comparable forms of religious discourse within the circle of Johannine Christianity. This is because a reliable comparison can only be made at this second stage. Such an additional investigation can, however, help to throw light on the meaning and significance of the prayer in Jn 17.

1. Jesus' Petition for his Own Glorification to Enable him to Give Eternal Life to Men (17:1–5)

[1]*When Jesus had spoken these words, he lifted up his eyes to heaven and said, 'Father, the hour has come; glorify thy Son that the Son may glorify thee,* [2]*since thou hast given him power over all flesh, to give eternal life to all whom thou hast given him.* [3]*And this is eternal life, that they know thee, the only true God, and Jesus Christ whom thou hast sent.* [4]*I glorified thee on earth, having accomplished the work which thou gavest me to do;* [5]*and now, Father, glorify thou me in thy own presence with the glory which I had before the world was made'.*

17:1 The end of the previous discourses is marked by a phrase (ταῦτα ἐλάλησεν Ἰησοῦς καί⁷ . . .) which also appeared at the conclusion of the discourses in the first part of the gospel (12:36b). It therefore probably looks back at all the discourses in Chapters 14–16. The 'farewell discourses' addressed to the disciples – it is certain that the final editors thought of them as such – are followed by this farewell prayer for the disciples. Its importance is stressed by Jesus' gesture of prayer – he raises his eyes to heaven (see 11:41 above) and turns towards the Father. It has been suggested – wrongly – that Jesus may have prayed at the last supper (cf. 18:1) or that he said this prayer on the way there, in the open air.⁸ Such suggestions result from an attempt to situate the prayer on the basis of what is in fact a special emphasis in the text. 'Heaven' here symbolizes the transcendent space of God, to which Jesus belongs and with which he is closely connected (cf. 1:51; see also 12:28). When he uses the form of address 'Father', Jesus enters, praying, the familiar space that is close to God – the space from which he had never been released. The disciples are to hear his words, just as those gathered around the tomb of Lazarus were intended to hear his words (11:42).

The recurrence of the address throws light on the structure of the prayer. The address 'Father' is pronounced again in v. 5 and thus completes the first small unit. The more solemn address 'Holy Father' opens the intercession (v. 11b), the adjective 'holy' possibly pointing ahead to the petition for sanctification (vv. 17–19). Finally, in the concluding section (vv. 24 and 25), the address occurs again twice. In between, it is only found in v. 21, a verse that was probably added later, in the prayer for unity. There is no need for this observation to be taken particularly seriously, but, if the discourse was the result of careful reflection, the placing of these forms of address and of certain adjectives may have been intentional and may therefore provide clues for our understanding of the structure.

The 'hour' towards which Jesus' activity is moving, that is, the hour of his crucifixion and glorification (see Vol. 2, p. 401), and of his passing over to the Father (13:1), has come. It is not described in detail now, but simply mentioned, in order to provide a reason for Jesus' request to the Father. The word is heard formally as an echo of 12:23 and it is materially presupposed in 13:31f. Because the Son has glorified the Father, the Father should now also glorify the Son. But the idea goes further than this – what the Son requests for himself only takes place now so that the Father may be glorified. This is the point of departure for the whole of the following prayer, since this aim, in which attention is directed towards the future, is, as we have just seen above, a way in which the power that has been bestowed on the Son to give life to men is exercised. Jesus' prayer for his own glorification and his request to be able to give life to men cannot be separated from one another.⁹ The last sentence is like a hinge which compels Jesus' establishment in glory with the Father to mediate salvation to believers. Jesus' repetition in vv. 4f of his petition for his own glory is not counter- evidence, but rather the prerequisite for the achievement of the aim mentioned in v. 2, which forms the theme of the whole of the following discourse.

17:2 This verse, which follows the previous one very closely, provides an insight into the nature of this continuing glorification of the Father by the Son. It is that Jesus is established in his power and that he will, because of this power, give all the men whom the Father 'has given' to him, that is, all believers, eternal life. The construction – a καθώς clause with another ἵνα clause – can also be found in 13:34 in connection with the commandment to love (see the commentary above); cf. 13:15. It can best be understood as a repetition and a clarification of the first ἵνα clause with an intervening causal clause ('in accordance with the fact that').[10] This makes the all-embracing idea in the καθώς clause, which forms the basis of the argument, clear: Jesus has, by virtue of his glorification in that 'hour', obtained 'power over all flesh'.[11] The Semitism 'all flesh' for 'all men' is only found in this place in the gospel. If, on the other hand, the communication of life is limited to those whom the Father has given to Jesus, the power bestowed on him 'over all flesh' has, on the contrary, to be understood as a plenary power that is capable of deciding about life and death and of bringing about salvation or judgment. This is confirmed by simply glancing back at 5:20–27: the Father has given the Son the power to give life and to judge; he has in the first place given him the power to give life, but he has also given him power to judge those who do not hear Jesus. The same phrase as the one used in 17:2 is employed in 5:27: 'he gave him power (or authority)'. The idea of judgment remains completely in the background in Jesus' prayer for his own. The Son's all-embracing plenary power is presented as a saving power for all men who belong to him. The universality is preserved and a πᾶν is added for those who receive life. The whole phrase is then placed as a *nominativus pendens* (which is repeated *ad sensum* with αὐτοῖς) at the beginning.[12]

What is remarkable is that there is no reference here to 'believers', but only to those whom the Father has 'given' to the Son; elsewhere in the gospel, 'believe' corresponds to 'having life'. The way of speaking in Jn 17 is clearly influenced by the image of the flock that the Father has entrusted to Jesus (cf. 10:29 and the figurative discourse 10:1–18). It can also, however, be found in 6:37ff in a reflection about faith and lack of faith (where the neuter form πᾶν also occurs; see the commentary above). It was therefore included quite consciously in Jesus' prayer for his own. Although predestination is not a theme here (see Excursus 2 in Vol 2, pp. 259–274), there is a strong consciousness of election in Jn 17 (see especially vv. 9f, 14, 25), which may well have come about in such an 'esoteric' community. We should, however, be on our guard against such premature judgments (see, for example, Excursus 17 below). In praying explicitly for those whom 'the Father has given him', Jesus reminds the community of its dependence on God and the fact that it is guided by God.

The mode of expression is crucial to the structure of the discourse. After being introduced here, in this statement of aim, it is emphatically taken up again in the following section (vv. 6 and 9), in which the reason for Jesus' intercession for the disciples is given (vv. 6–11a). This is because the fact that the Father has handed them over to Jesus justifies his petition for the Father's care and protection of the disciples whom he leaves behind in the world: 'Thine they were and thou gavest them to me' (v. 6). Now, when Jesus is going away, the Father should take care of those who belong to him (v. 9). This expression does not appear in the detailed petitions, but it occurs again very emphatically (by being placed at the beginning) at the end of the discourse (v. 24), because the participation of believers in Jesus' glory is the aim of the entire prayer. The use of this expression brings the discourse back to its starting-point and confirms the intention stated in v. 2, showing that it is the really important perspective.

17:3   This verse and the next provide an insight into the meaning of the important Johannine concept of 'eternal life', which is not explicitly mentioned again in the rest of the prayer. It is replaced by the δόξα, in which this fulfilled eternal life is manifested (see v. 24). The present verse can therefore best be seen as an added gloss on ζωὴ αἰώνιος and as undoubtedly editorial. This assumption is reinforced by the following considerations:

(a) This verse is not essential in its present context and to regard it as original on the basis of its being a rhetorical figure[13] is arbitrary, since the structure (that is, the development of the petition for glorification) is satisfactory even without it.

(b) The name 'Jesus Christ' is unsuitable and contrary to the style of the prayer as a whole, as spoken by Jesus. There is only one other text in which this occurs. This is in 1:17, which is a commentary following the Logos hymn, but the name 'Jesus Christ' is meaningful in this verse, in contrast with the name 'Moses'.

(c) It is only here in the gospel that 'eternal life' has the article and the adjective placed in front of the noun. The concept, which is elucidated in this way (δέ), but not defined, is presupposed elsewhere in the gospel as something that is already known.

(d) In view of this intention, it is surprising that there should be a construction with ἵνα, expressing an aim or a purpose.[14] There is therefore an appeal or even a promise in this sentence (cf. 1 Jn 2:25).

(e) The very unusual formula 'the only true God' may perhaps be derived from missionary language (cf. 1 Thess 1:19), but the two attributes of God that are combined here are also found in confessions of faith and in cultic formulae (see 1 Tim 1:17; 6:15f; Rev 6:10, etc.).[15]

(f) 'Knowing God' has the previously established, OT meaning of 'having communion with God'.[16] In 1 Jn, it is a prominent expression, used for the communion with God which was claimed by the false Gnostic teachers, but which the author of the letter disputed that they possessed (see my *Johannes-Briefe*, Excursus 3, pp. 95–101). The exclusive claim of the orthodox community can also be heard here, in Jn 17:3, although it is not in the forefront.

(g) The text with the strongest link with Jn 17:3 is 1 Jn 5:20, although the latter verse calls Jesus Christ himself (in whom God is fully present) 'the true God and eternal life'. Eternal life is achieved through community with God and his Son Jesus Christ (see 1 Jn 1:3) or through Jesus Christ, who leads men into community with God. The sentence about eternal life in Jn 17:3 aims to say no more than this and, what is more, to say it encouragingly, as in 1 Jn 2:25. As a gloss, then, it may come from the same circle that was responsible for the first epistle.

As evidence of Johannine theology, the text is very important. Various Greek Fathers have pointed out that it contains a rejection of all forms of pagan polytheism.[17] It is also possible that it includes a shaft directed against other redeemer figures, since Jesus Christ is emphatically stated to be the one sent by God. A twofold confession – of the one God, the Father, and the one Lord Jesus Christ, as the mediator of salvation – can also be found in the pre-Pauline formula in 1 Cor 8:6. Jn 17:3 is, so to speak, the Johannine version of this text. Several Latin Fathers believed that the text referred to the beatific vision in heaven. In accordance with the Johannine view of 'eternal life', however, it is important to recognize that believers possess this life already while they are still on earth, even though it is not ultimately fulfilled until the eschatological vision of God is experienced (cf. 1 Jn 3:14f with 3:2). It is also not possible to conclude from this 'knowledge' that the beatific vision of God is essentially cognitive, although it is connected with love and leads to blessedness through both knowledge and love. This very influential interpretation, proposed by Thomas Aquinas,[18] became a bone of contention between Thomists and Scotists, who insisted on the primacy of love. Quite apart from the fact that no real definition is provided in Jn 17:3, this question is not asked in Johannine theology, which is content to present community with God as the fulfilment of man's longing for salvation, achieved in believing and loving union with Jesus Christ.

17:4 Jesus justifies his petition for glorification by saying that he has done the work that he was given to do on earth (cf. 4:34; 5:36; 14:31). This idea is found again and again in the gospel and even the same linguistic term (the 'giving of work or works'; see 5:36) is used earlier. The addition 'on earth' can be explained on the basis of the glorification with the Father ($\pi\alpha\rho\grave{\alpha}$ $\sigma\epsilon\alpha\upsilon\tau\tilde{\omega}$) that is expected in heaven (cf. Jesus' looking up to heaven in v. 1). Apart from in the statement in 13:31f ('in him God is glorified'), there has been no previous reference in the gospel to the fact that Jesus has 'glorified' the Father with his work on earth and it is on that previous text that the petition that the Father may now glorify the Son depends. The event of the cross has also to be included in this work that the Son has accomplished in obedience to and love of the Father (see 10:18; 14:31).[19] It is, however, not justifiable to conclude from this that the exalted Christ is already speaking here. This is the prayer of the departing Christ, who is certain of the fulfilment of his work (see 19:30) and of his own fulfilment.

17:5 Now, at the hour when he is to depart, Jesus expects and requests to be established in his original glory with the Father. The $\kappa\alpha\grave{\iota}$ $\nu\tilde{\upsilon}\nu$ corresponds to the 'hour' in v. 1, but it also has a consecutive meaning. On the basis of its use in the rest of the Bible, A. Laurentin has observed that this florid expression announces a new relationship between persons.[20] This also applies to the situation which Jesus has in mind: a decisive turning-point on his way, which is characterized by the 'descent' from heaven and the re-ascent (see 3:13, 31; 6:62), the 'ascent' to the Father (see 20:17). This hour is, in a sense, irrevocable[21] and, in it, the whole way of the redeemer can be seen. It is therefore hardly surprising that, according to Johannine theology, Jesus' pre-existence is also included in this perspective (see Vol. 1, Excursus 2, pp. 494–506). What is new in our present verse is the link with the idea of δόξα. The status of divine being is also attributed to the pre-existent Christ in the hymn in Phil 2:6–11. The theological perspective, however, is different. In Philippians, Jesus' establishment in his cosmic rule after his emptying of himself on earth represents a growth or exaltation above his previous status (ὑπερύψωσεν). This was the view that prevailed generally in early Christianity with regard to Christ's δόξα (see Lk 24:26; 1 Cor 2:8; 1 Tim 3:16, etc.). In John, on the other hand, Christ regains the glory which was previously his (see 6:62) and which belongs to him as the Son (see 1:14b) and does so also to enable believers to share in that glory (17:24). These, then, are different categories of thought and different kinds of statement, but they all merge together in the fundamental intention to make believers understand more intimately the greatness of the redeemer and the fruit of his work. The way was prepared for this manner of speaking about Jesus' pre-existent *doxa* by speculation in the wisdom literature (see Wis 7:25, a text that was taken over by the author of Heb 1:3 in a protological context for the 'Son'; see also Wis 9:10f). The glory that Jesus possessed 'before the world was made' characterizes not the pre-mundane, but the supra-mundane existence of the Logos, and ultimately the superiority of the divine revealer to and his transcendence over the world.[22]

2. The Reason for Jesus' Petition with Regard to the Disciples (17:6–11a)

[6]' *I have manifested thy name to the men whom thou gavest me out of the world; thine they were, and thou gavest them to me, and they have kept thy word.* [7]*Now they know that everything that thou hast given me is from thee;* [8]*for I have given them the words which thou gavest me, and they have received them and know in truth that I came from thee; and they have believed that thou didst send me.* [9]*I am praying for them; I am not praying for the world, but for those whom thou hast given me, for they are thine;* [10]*all mine are thine and thine are mine and I am glorified in them.* [11]*And now I am no more in the world, but they are in the world, and I am coming to thee'.*

17:6 Jesus, in prayer, now reiterates the idea expressed in v. 2. His gaze is directed towards those whom the Father has given him and he gives his reason for praying for them. They are the disciples who are present, who have accepted his words and who believe in him as the one sent by God. It is, however, clear from the way in which he speaks of them, characterizes them as God's possession and contrasts them with the 'world' and from the way in which he stresses their acceptance of his revelation and believes himself to be 'glorified' in them, that he also has the later community and their understanding of themselves in mind. Despite their unique function as direct recipients of Jesus' revelation here on earth, the present disciples are also representatives of all later believers. This section of the prayer contains, in a compressed form, the whole Johannine theology of revelation and the community of salvation, which is God's holy sphere in the world. It is true, of course, that the situation of departure becomes apparent at the end, just before the petition ('I am coming to thee') and that the theme of the special need that the disciples have of the Father's protection at this moment also plays a part, but Jesus' words about the disciples who belong to God are spoken so unconditionally and in such a fundamental way that they must apply not only to the disciples who were with Jesus, with their very defective understanding (see 14:9–12; 16:18f, 29–32), but also to all those who accept Jesus' revelation and show that they belong to God.[23]

The language itself also contains elements that point in this direction. The verb φανεροῦν also occurs in Jn 2:11; 9:3; see also 7:4 as a term of revelation, but it has stronger links with the language of the editors (21:1, 14, in connection with the appearances of the risen Christ) and the long epistle (five times in reference to the historical coming of Jesus and once or twice in connection with the parousia). What is new here and remarkable is the phrase 'to manifest or reveal the name of God', which is also found in a similar form (with γνωρίζειν) in 17:26 and is continued in vv. 11 and 12 ('keeping in the name of God'). The idea that Jesus reveals the Father in his words and work and in his whole person is fundamental to the gospel of John (see 8:19, 27; 10:38; 12:45; 14:9ff). The mode of expression in Jn 17, however, is quite distinctive. Does the 'name' simply point to the name of the Father?[24] The combinations of words in vv. 11, 12 and 26, however, call for an interpretation that goes further than this. The name stands for God's being and nature, his holiness, 'justice' and love, which are certainly expressed in the address to the Father and the attributes connected with the name.

Where should we look for the background to this way of speaking? As is often the case, there is a contrast here between a derivation from the OT and Judaism and a 'Gnostic' source. In Ps 21:23 (LXX), we read, for example: 'I will tell (διηγήσο-μαι) of thy name to my brethren',[25] but the continuation of this text ('In the midst of the congregation I will praise thee') shows that this verse in the psalm is concerned with naming God in praise, not with revelation. Other OT texts that speak of 'knowing' (γινώσκειν) God's name may be closer; for example, Is 52:6: 'Therefore my people shall know my name; therefore in that day they shall know that it is I (ἐγώ εἰμι) who speak.'[26] But the opposition to v. 5: 'My name is despised among the people' provides us with a different perspective, namely that God's name is again to be great and recognized. This idea is more clearly expressed, for example, in Ezek 39:7: 'And my holy name I will make known in the midst of my people Israel and I will not let my holy name be profaned any more. And the nations shall know that I am the Lord, the Holy One of Israel.' From here there is a broad way to the revelation of the name of God mentioned in Jn 17:6. All that is missing is the mediation through a bearer of revelation and acceptance by a particular circle of recipients of the revelation.

Although the relevant Gnostic texts are not completely in agreement with each other and are as a whole different in specific ways from Jn 17, they should be considered in this context. Certain Hermetic texts are linguistically close to John, but are materially different in that they declare God's name to be 'inexpressible' or claim God to be superior to every name and indeed ultimately to be 'nameless' (ἀνώνυμος).[27]

It is particularly interesting to compare the Johannine text with the prayer of thanksgiving in the Latin version of Aesculapius (Asclepius), which is preserved in a mutilated form in Greek in P. Mimaut and now exists in Coptic in the *Nag Hammadi* Codex VI:7.[28] The Latin text is: 'tua enim gratia tantum sumus cognitionis tuae lumen consecuti, nomen sanctum et honorandum, nomen unum'. The Greek has: ἄφραστον ὄνομα and the Coptic text reads: 'O name, to which we do not become a burden, which is glorious in the naming of God and which will be praised in the naming of the Father'. Although the translations are at the same time interpretations, they have this in common: to substitute the '(true) life of life', the 'name', for God. In the *Corpus Hermeticum* V, we read of the invisible (ἀφανής) God who is none the less completely revealed (φανερώτατος); the uncommon verb φανερόω occurs quite frequently in the treatise.[29] The God who is raised above every name reveals himself to the Gnostic, through gnosis, as the φανερώτατος (vv. 10 and 11). According to one papyrus, then, 'I am the one who has encountered you and you have given me as a gift τὴν τοῦ μεγίστου σου ὀνόματος γνῶσιν'.[30] The speaker also wants to preserve (τηρήσω) the same 'knowledge of your great name' on a magic papyrus and communicate it only to those who are enclosed with him.[31] This last idea is reminiscent of Jn 17:26. The speculation about the name in the *Gospel of Truth* (especially pp. 38–40) is quite different: 'The name of the Father is the Son . . . He, the Father, gave him his name, which he had. . . . For the name of the Father is not said. He is, however, revealed in a Son. In this way, the name is great. Who will then be able to pronounce a name for him, this great name, if not he himself, to whom the name belongs, and the sons of the name, in whom the name of the Father dwelt (and) they also dwelt in his name' (38:6–31).[32] The *Gospel of Philip* (*Ev Phil*, 12, p. 102) also speaks of the Father having given the name to the Son: 'A single name is not pronounced in the world: the name which the Father gave to the Son. It is more exalted than all (names). That is the name of the Father.' There are also echoes of this in the *Odes of Solomon*, where it is said of the redeemer that 'he will make the soul live in eternity through the truth of his name (*Od Sol*, 41:16); 'I place my name on their heads, for they are my free sons and they belong to me' (42:20).

The 'name' has an intense reality in these Gnostic texts, in which it is a means of expressing the gnosis that is mediated by the redeemer. Only certain men (the Gnostics) have the 'name' (the being and mystery) of God revealed to them and through that revelation they acquire a share in God's life, light and joy. There is a radical difference between this revelation and that brought by the historical Jesus in his words and work to the disciples, but it is impossible to deny that the language and mode of presentation are similar. A derivation from the OT and Judaism is, moreover, not ruled out by this, since Judaism exerted a considerable influence on Gnosticism, especially in this speculation about the name. This is particularly clear from the magic texts. A direct and exclusive derivation in the case of the statements in Jn 17, however, is not possible. The author of the great prayer in this chapter of the gospel fashioned his own language, although he was subjected to various influences, including Gnosticism.

Jesus revealed the name of God only to those whom the Father gave him 'out of the world'. This dualistic idea of standing at a distance from the 'world' or of excluding the disciples who accept his revelation and taking them 'out of the world' is not new (see for example, 15:19), but it confirms the esoteric view that leads to the exclusion of the 'world' from Jesus' intercession in v. 9. This narrowing down of Jesus' intention to the sphere of those who believe should not be overemphasized, however, since it is possible to detect an opening to the world in v. 23. The principal intention here is to provide a reason for Jesus' intercession for those who have been God's possession and whom the Father has handed over to the Son. They continue to be God's possession (see vv. 9b and 10) and Jesus recommends them to the Father, because 'they have kept his word'. Both in the gospel (8:51) and later in the farewell discourse (14:23), the exhortation to keep Jesus' word was heard. Here, Jesus reaffirms that the disciples have kept his Father's word. This is clear from the context of the prayer, but it also reveals the community's consciousness of itself (cf. 1 Jn 2:5, 14).

17:7 The following sentence also emphasizes the faith of the disciples, which has clearly reached a deeper level of knowledge.[33] The verb 'know' is preferred to 'believe' throughout the whole prayer. Knowledge appears as the final stage of faith (see v. 25). The νῦν at the beginning, which can hardly have the same importance as καὶ νῦν in v. 5,[34] draws attention to the level of maturity in faith that has now been reached, and this can hardly have been done with a conscious glance back at the disciples' lack of maturity up to this time (see 16:30f). It is more likely that those responsible for this prayer had the confrontation between the community and the 'world' that has not known Jesus (see v. 25) in mind. Materially, this knowledge refers to Jesus' relationship with the Father, but the formulation is distinctive and almost tautological. The intention of the speaker must, however, be borne in mind in any consideration of the choice of words in the phrase 'everything that thou hast given me' ('that I have revealed or manifested to them' is what we would have expected). He is anxious to lead everything in this sphere back to God. The πάντα is defined more precisely in what follows by the ῥήματα, but is consciously kept at a distance from the latter. The prayer above all creates an aura which draws attention to the Father as the one who possesses, gives and grants everything. It does this by the use of the very significant word 'give' (seventeen times), the word πάντα with its wide-ranging meaning (see v. 10) and its direction of attention to the Father by the frequent employment of personal and possessive pronouns in the second person singular.

17:8 V. 7, as we have seen, elucidates the final sentence in v. 6: 'they have kept thy word.' In the same way, v. 8 also describes how the disciples acquired the knowledge to which v. 7 referred. This way of developing and amplifying a theme belongs to the style of the prayer and makes it more impressive and effective. It would therefore be wrong to ask which words are superfluous or unnecessary.[35] In the same vocabulary of διδόναι, the sentence throws light on the fact that Jesus has 'given' the disciples the words given to him by the Father and that they have 'received' them. Because these words were from the Father, the disciples knew that Jesus came from him and believed that the Father sent him. The change from λόγος (v. 6) to ῥήματα (v. 8; in Chapter 17 occurring only once) has already taken place in the gospel (cf. 6:60 with 63; 8:43 with 47; 12:48b with a; 14:23f with 10) and the phrase 'to receive the words' (λαμβάνειν) is also to be found in 12:48. The two parallel statements at the end of the verse express, in variation, the same idea, namely that Jesus comes from God. There is also an echo of the παρὰ σοῦ first heard in v. 7 and in our present verse it is connected with ἐξῆλθον, as in 16:27,[36] thus making a change with the familiar expression: 'that thou didst send me' (cf. vv. 21, 23, 25). The corroborative ἀληθῶς is also a feature of the Johannine style. (It has so far occurred six times in the gospel.) The whole statement has the intention of throwing a clear light on the disciples' knowledge in faith and of showing them to be worthy of Jesus' intercession and the Father's care.

17:9 Jesus now says that he is praying for them; they have shown themselves to belong to God. The exclusion of the 'world' from the intercession was foreshadowed in v. 6 (ἐκ τοῦ κόσμου) and should, in the context, be seen as an emphatic recommendation of the disciples. The 'world', which has not known God in the words and work of the one sent by him (v. 25), can make no claim to Jesus' intercession. If this statement is taken out of its context, then the harshness of Jesus' refusal to include the 'world' is very striking.[37] This refusal, however, is completely in accordance with the statement about the inability of the world to receive the Paraclete (14:17). The unbelieving cosmos has in fact excluded itself from the divine sphere and to pray for it, asking God to keep it in his name (v. 11) and sanctify it in his truth (v. 17) would therefore be meaningless. All the same, this is not Jesus' last word on the subject of the cosmos. The community, made one in the divine nature, is to give it a further inducement to know the one sent by God (v. 23). This points to the community's firm consciousness of its own election and mission and its sense of being a sign of the presence of God in the world. All those who belong to it know that they are God's possession, that they have been given to Jesus by God and that they have been entrusted by Jesus to the Father. The historical situation of the Johannine community has to be taken into account in any critical consideration of this exclusive self-understanding (see Excursus 17).

17:10 Ornamental additions should cause no surprise in a prayer of praise. The logical progress of the ideas is undoubtedly impeded by the phrase 'all mine are thine and all thine are mine', but these words follow the last words in the previous verse 'they are thine' quite naturally. In the more restricted context, they can only refer to the disciples: Jesus is recommending his own to the Father, because all those who belong to him also belong to the Father. The second half of the sentence, however ('and thine are mine'), shows that it is a statement about the full 'community of possessions' between Jesus and the Father. In the wider context, then, the statement is closely connected with v. 6: the disciples belong to the Father, who gave them to Jesus and Jesus regards them as his and the Father's common possession and now gives them back to the Father. This idea accords with the Johannine Christology (see 16:15) and the image of the shepherd and his flock in Chapter 10, in which the sheep are seen as the shepherd's own (τὰ ἴδια, vv. 4, 12) and as Jesus' (τὰ ἐμά, vv. 14, 27) and yet as also in the Father's hand (v. 29). In caring for the sheep, the Father is behind Jesus and both are one (v. 30). The same theme is present in 17:10. The Father is to take care of these men, who belong both to him and to Jesus, when Jesus departs (v. 11a).

After this Christological diversion, the prayer returns to the main theme: because the disciples have received Jesus' words as God's words, Jesus is 'glorified' in them.[38] The discourse is once again dominated by the vocabulary of glorification. Jesus has glorified the Father by his work on earth and the acceptance of the believers who have been given to him by the Father forms part of this (see 6:39). These believers form the community of faith and, because this community represents his work, he is shown as the one who obediently fulfilled the divine task through it. The Father is now to glorify him at least partly because he has taken these men into his care.

17:11a   This is necessary in the situation that arises as a result of Jesus' departure: Jesus is no longer in the world, but the disciples remain in the world while he goes to the Father. These three co-ordinated statements form a unity. In isolation, the statement: 'I am no more in the world' could be easily misunderstood.[39] It sounds as though Jesus were already speaking as one who had returned to the Father. The following statement, namely that he is going to the Father, shows clearly enough, however, how the prayer should be interpreted: Jesus is still speaking in the world (v. 13), but already in the knowledge that he is leaving it and leaving the disciples behind in it. At this hour of departure, his care is for the disciples and their existence in the world without him. This implied idea would seem to be in contradiction to the discourses on the vine (15:1–10), the announcement of his new 'coming' to them (14:3, 18, 28) and his 'seeing them again' (16:16–19, 22). The view that emerges from Chapter 17, that Jesus is completely withdrawn from the disciples in the world, can, however, be explained in the light of the intention of the prayer, since Jesus has to take the disciples' situation into account if he is to provide a reason for his intercession with the Father.

3. Jesus' Petition that the Disciples should be kept in God's Being and that they should be kept from the Evil One (17:11b–16)

11b'*Holy Father, keep them in thy name, which thou hast given me, that they may be one, even as we are one.* [12]*While I was with them, I kept them in thy name, which thou hast given me; I have guarded them and none of them is lost but the son of perdition, that the scripture might be fulfilled.* [13]*But now I am coming to thee; and these things I speak in the world, that they may have my joy fulfilled in themselves.* [14]*I have given them thy word; and the world has hated them because they are not of the world, even as I am not of the world.* [15]*I do not pray that thou shouldst take them out of the world, but that thou shouldst keep them from the evil one.* [16]*They are not of the world, even as I am not of the world'*.

The intercession itself now follows. It opens with the resonant address 'Holy Father' and it ends at the conclusion of v. 23. Linguistically, it is subdivided by the two imperatives τήρησον (v. 11b) and ἁγίασον (v. 17) as well as by the final statement: 'that they may be one even as we are one' (v. 22; cf. v. 11b). Materially, however, the whole prayer forms a single unit. The petitions that the disciples should be kept and sanctified and the desire for their unity come together in the one great intention, that the community of disciples left behind by Jesus should continue in the divine sphere revealed to them by Jesus and grow, in the world and in confrontation with the world, in the divine nature which Jesus has placed in them during his time on earth by means of his revelation and his community. These are simply various aspects which emerge in the individual petitions, although they do so as the result of mature reflection and with the situation of the disciples in the world in mind. In the presence of the influence exerted by the evil one, it is important for them to preserve the divine being mediated by Jesus, to realize the sanctification brought about by him and to bear witness by means of the divine sign of unity. It is certainly possible to detect something of the concrete situation in which the Johannine community is placed here, but only very obscurely, since the believing community is conscious of its closeness to the glorified Christ in the world.

17:11b   The form of address, 'Holy Father', which is striking in the gospel of John because it occurs only here in this combination of the adjective and the noun,[40] may have been derived from liturgical usage (in the celebration of the Eucharist; see *Did*, 10:2),[41] but it certainly has a specific function in our present text. It above all provides a motive for the request that the disciples should be kept in the Father's name and the second request for 'sanctification' (v. 17). God is 'holy' in his divinity. In the OT, he is holy above all because of his nature, which arouses fear,[42] but here he is holy as the God who reveals his being (his 'name') in his Son, who communicates himself to those who believe in him and who therefore takes them out of the 'world' (that is, 'sanctifies' them). This address does not, unlike the address used in other Jewish texts (such as 'Holy art thou and fearful is thy name' in the *Shemoneh esreh* or *Eighteen Benedictions*, 3), create a distance. On the contrary, it establishes a thankful closeness, as does the second form of address provided with an attributive adjective in v. 25 (πατὴρ δίκαιε), because those who believe in Jesus have gained access to the Father through him, the Son.

The petition that the disciples should be kept in God's being has a Johannine ring because of the verb τηρεῖν. Elsewhere, however, this verb is followed by an accusative and usually has the meaning of 'keeping' the words and commandments of Jesus that is required of believers. Here the Father is to 'keep' the disciples who have 'kept' Jesus' word (see the end of v. 6) and, what is more, he is to keep them 'in his name'. This idea is connected to the statement that Jesus has revealed the Father's name to those whom the Father has given him (v. 6a). Because Jesus is now leaving them, the Father himself is to preserve and strengthen them in what Jesus has mediated to them. The striking expression ἐν τῷ ὀνοματί σου can therefore be explained in the same way as the similar view expressed in v. 6 (see the commentary above). If the speculation about the name that was outlined above is borne in mind, the idea that the Father has given his name to the Son will cause no surprise, and the best attested reading ᾧ δέδωκάς μοι will be retained.

There are, however, other readings which deviate from this:

ὃ δέδωκάς μοι	D* X 2148 Lect.
οὓς δέδωκάς μοι	D^b al. aur f q Vg Diat^{it}.

If the idea that the Father gave his name to the Son was not impossible for the author of this prayer (if it was, in other words, Johannine in the sense of 3:34f; 5:26), but gave rise to difficulties later, then the reading with ὃ must be regarded as an attempt at alleviation. It must have suggested itself because of 17:2, 24 and have fitted into the text in apposition to αὐτούς (although not very well, being placed after this word).[43] In this case, the second variant must act as a clarification of this idea. Other texts leave out everything from ᾧ onwards, no doubt for the same reason: the VL manuscripts a b c e ff^2 r^1 as well as sy^s achm^2 Hil. Chrys. Nonnus. In the UBS Greek NT, in which the textual situation is precisely accredited, a greater degree of certainty than 'C' should be given.

Although the desire 'that they may be one, even as we are one' is missing in P^{66} (unlike the other Egyptian texts), it undoubtedly belongs to this fundamental petition. This request for unity among the disciples in accordance with the unity that exists between the Father and the Son is repeated at the end of the intercessions and developed further there (v. 22; cf. v. 21). As long as Jesus stayed with the disciples, he was their bond of unity, but now, after his departure, they are to preserve this unity, because it is the sign and expression of the divine being. Preparation has also been made (in vv. 9f) for this idea.

17:12   As is often the case in the gospel of John, the ideas previously expressed in a striking statement are developed individually and impressed more firmly on the reader. The meaning of being 'kept in the Father's name' can be more powerfully brought home to the disciples by a consideration of what Jesus himself has done for them. As long as he was with them, he kept them in the Father's name. It is clear that this is more than simply care for their loyalty to faith and their way of salvation, because the words 'which thou hast given me' are once again added to 'thy name'.[44] It was indeed an inner revelation of the reality of God, an introduction into the sphere of God and a communication of the love and joy of God from which Jesus himself lived. This is something that the Greek Fathers, whose thinking was based firmly on the mystery of the Trinity and the perfect revelation of the Father in the Son (Cyril of Alexandria is particularly noteworthy in this respect), understood more fully than the Latin Fathers who grasped the meaning of 'in nomine tuo' less perfectly and also preferred the reading 'quos dedisti mihi'.[45] Thomas Aquinas explained 'in nomine tuo' as 'per virtutem nominis tui et tuae cognitionis'[46] and, in later exegesis, the tendency to emphasize almost exclusively Jesus' plea to the Father to keep the disciples in faith gained more and more ground. The Johannine image of Jesus the 'shepherd', of which the reader (despite the different terminology) will undoubtedly be reminded here, has a deeper and more all-embracing grasp of Jesus' care to preserve in faith (cf. e contra,

181

10:13): he 'knows' his own, gives his life for them, gives them eternal life (10:28a) and keeps them in God's sphere.

The continuation of this verse, with the 'son of perdition' in view, is a justification on Jesus' part with regard to the traitor, whom he himself chose from among the twelve (see 6:70; 13:18). What is striking here is the new beginning with καὶ[47] ἐφύλαξα, since this verb (which is used elsewhere in the gospel only in 12:25 and 12:47, but with a different meaning) narrows down the idea of 'keeping' to 'guarding' or 'protecting'. The only one of this protected discipleship who has been lost is the 'son of perdition', who can only be the traitor Judas.[48] The obscure fact of his betrayal and his elimination from the group of disciples chosen by Jesus, the circle of 'his own' (see 13:1, 30), is once again, as in 13:18, illuminated by the statement that 'the scripture might be fulfilled' (the same formula occurs again only in 19:24, 36). The scriptural text of Ps 41(40):10 quoted explicitly in 13:18 is clearly in mind here. No other scriptural reference to the 'son of perdition' can be found.

Other texts that have been considered here are: 2 Sam 12:5 ('a son of death'); Is 57:4 ('children of transgression'); Jub 10:3 (the same); Mt 23:15 ('a son of hell'). These are similar formations to those that occur in the Qumran documents (1 QS 9:16; 10:19; Dam 6:15; 13:14), but they are not the source of Jn 17:12, nor are they closely analogous, since the Johannine text mentions an individual person. Another text that cannot be seriously considered is Prov 24:22a (LXX).[49] There is also no direct connection with 2 Thess 2:3, in which the same expression is used for the Antichrist. In the *Gospel of Nicodemus* 20:3 (Tischendorf, *Ev. Apoc.*, p. 327) Satan himself is addressed in this way by Hades.

The term 'son of perdition' probably came about as a result of ἀπώλετο, an extremely harsh word indicating condemnation and exclusion from salvation. In the context of the gospel, there may have been some idea of the influence of Satan on Judas (see 6:70; 13:2, 27). The community is reminded here that separation from the true community of salvation means a loss of salvation, a return to the sphere of the 'world' and even a reversion to satanic power (see 1 Jn 2:18f; 4:3; 5:19b).

This consideration of the 'son of perdition' certainly seems to be superfluous in this context (v. 13 follows v. 12a quite easily). It is not in accordance with the style of the intercession and its details (the new beginning, striking words and the reference to Scripture) make it quite different from the rest. For these reasons, it may well have been introduced by a second author, possibly an editor, with a special interest in the figure of the traitor (cf. 13:2, 10b–11).[50] It would therefore be quite wrong to attribute the basic datum of v. 12 to the source and individual phrases (including the reference to Scripture) to the evangelist, as Bultmann did. On the other hand, the reasons for excluding the digression about the 'son of perdition' from the original prayer are also not completely convincing.

17:13 Jesus' petition that the disciples should be kept in God's being is given its full emphasis in his departure. This is therefore brought to the fore once again (cf. v. 11a) and contrasted with the period during which the disciples have been together with Jesus on earth (δέ). At this point of time (νῦν), Jesus expresses his petition to the Father, but still 'in the world'. He is aware of the situation to which the disciples are exposed (see v. 11a), yet they are to have his joy perfected in themselves in that situation. This desire, which is only expressed here in the prayer, is reminiscent of 15:11 and especially of 16:20–22, 24. This is a clear indication that the prayer was conceived with a knowledge of Chapters 15 and 16 and also following them. Jesus' joy, of which he speaks while still in the world, presupposes his departure, but he wants to communicate it, as he also wants to communicate his peace, to his disciples who are staying in the world, so that they will endure the hostility of the world. For this 'perfect' or 'fulfilled' joy, see also Jn 15:11.

17:14 The request that the disciples may be kept in God's being also has another aspect in the light of the 'world' – that they may be kept from the evil one. The reason for this second aspect is given in v. 14. The petition is expressed in v. 15, and – if it is original – v. 16 emphasizes the gulf between the disciples and Jesus himself and the world. As in v. 6, there is a close connection between the revelation of the divine 'name' and that of Jesus' word – Jesus has communicated God's being to the disciples through his word. This, however, caused the 'world' to hate them, because it opposes everything that comes from God. This sharp, dualistic concept of the world has already appeared in v. 9, but it was formulated most powerfully in 15:18f, which may have been directly assimilated into 17:14, our present text. What was announced there to the disciples (in the future use of the present tense) is now expressed by Jesus in our present verse as a fact (in the aorist used for making a statement). It is clear that the post-paschal situation is presupposed, as in v. 18 (ἀπέστειλα).

The use of tenses in Jn 17 can, at least in part, be confusing. The tenses are employed quite regularly when referring to the period when Jesus was active on earth; they are predominantly the aorist (see vv. 6f) and sometimes, in individual places and with good reason, the perfect (of Jesus in vv. 8 and 14a and of the disciples in v. 7, at the end) or the imperfect (ἐτήρουν in v. 12). The two aorists – referring to the world's hatred of the disciples in v. 14b and to their having been sent into the world in v. 18 – are not, however, grammatically correct. The situation of the disciples in the world, with which this present verse is concerned, had in the meantime (at the time when the prayer was composed) come about and was such an active reality that the aorist was obviously required (cf. 4:38). The poetic style of the Septuagint (for the Hebrew perfect) may perhaps have been influential, as it clearly was in the case of the Magnificat (Lk 1:51–54); see Blass-Debr § 333, 2. In any case, it would be wrong to conclude from this use of the aorist that Jesus was already speaking as the exalted Christ.

As in 15:19, the world's hatred of the disciples is caused by their union with Jesus and God and therefore by the nature of their existence. The καθώς clause is missing from certain manuscripts,[51] possibly because it has the same conclusion as the clause in v. 16, but it is certainly original since it occurs again there. It provides the reason (καθώς) for the world's hatred of the disciples as being based on their belonging to Jesus (see the development in 15:18–21).

17:15   In a statement that is of importance for the self-understanding of the Johannine community, Jesus does not ask the Father to take the disciples out of the world, but requests that he should keep them – in the world – from the evil one. The emphasis is on the second half of the sentence, but the first half shows that the community does not want to withdraw completely from the world. It is conscious of its mission in the world (v. 18), but at the same time regards that world as a sphere that is dominated by the evil one. According to the closely-related text in 1 Jn 5:18f, the 'evil one' is God's and Christ's personal adversary (see *ad loc.*). In the gospel, he also appears as the 'ruler of the (or this) world' (12:31; 14:30; 16:11). Jesus himself has already taken up a position against him (14:30), but overcame him on the cross. 'Being kept from the evil one' means, then, that the evil one is to have no power over Jesus' disciples (cf. 1 Jn 2:13f). A link is formed between the gospel and the first epistle by this term, which occurs only here in the gospel, and the defensive position with regard to the world as dominated by the evil one that is so strongly emphasized in 1 Jn (see especially 2:15ff; 3:13; 4:4f; 5:f).

   It cannot be denied that there is a great distance between our present understanding of the world, our openness to the secular reality and our sensitivity to modern, mainly non-Christian society on the one hand and the attitude of the Johannine community towards the 'world' on the other. The formula 'in the world, but not of the world' should not be regarded as the absolute expression of the Christian understanding of the world. It has its origin in a fundamentally dualistic way of thinking and in the situation in which an oppressed and inward-looking community was placed. But the evil one still threatens our world and the community which is on its guard against that evil power and prays (our Father!) to be kept from it is performing a positive and provocative task on behalf of mankind.

17:16   Once again – and with the same words as those used in v. 14, but even more strongly stressed (by the placing of the words 'of the world' at the beginning) – we are told that the disciples are not of the world, just as Jesus is not of the world. The verse is absent from several manuscripts (33 pc), but, since these also omit v. 15, this omission must have occurred inadvertently because v. 14 had the same ending (ἐκ τοῦ κόσμου). If the verse is attested from the point of view of textual criticism, there still remains the question as to whether it may not be an editorial addition to the original prayer.[52] This unit in the discourse would have been brought to a more satisfactory conclusion by τηρήσῃς in v. 15 and the transition to the positive petition in v. 17 would have been more clearly marked by ἐκ τοῦ πονηροῦ, but, since recapitulation as a means of reinforcing an idea (in this case, the idea enclosing the petition in v. 15) is not unusual in a literary style of this kind, it is possible to defend the originality of this verse.[53]

4. Jesus' Petition that the Disciples should be Sanctified in the Truth (17:17–19)

[17]'*Sanctify them in the truth; thy word is truth.* [18]*As thou didst send me into the world, so I have sent them into the world.* [19]*And for their sake I sanctify myself, that they also may be sanctified in truth'.*

17:17   This new request for 'sanctification' deepens and develops the petition to be kept in God's being. The connection between the two requests can be seen in two ways: the 'word of God' brings about a separation from the world (v. 14a) as well as sanctification in the truth (v. 17b); secondly, the phrase 'in the name of God' (v. 12) corresponds to the term 'in the truth'. This also defines the idea of 'sanctification' more precisely as being included within the sphere of God and being penetrated with God's nature and being. The only parallel provided by the gospel is to be found in 10:36: God 'sanctified' his Son for his mission in the world. The idea of santification is also connected with being sent into the world here (v. 18). The disciples have to be equipped for their activity in the world and they are in fact equipped by the 'truth', that is, by bearing within themselves the word of God mediated to them by Jesus Christ and by bearing it as reality and as power.[54] If that word of God, which is 'truth',[55] transmits his being and fills man with it, then ἐν τῇ ἀληθείᾳ can be seen as acting instrumentally,[56] but the parallel, ἐν τῷ ὀνόματί σου (v. 12) makes a local or medial interpretation more acceptable, with the meaning of 'in the sphere of the truth'. This concept of truth is in accordance with the Johannine view generally (see Excursus 10, Vol. 2, pp. 225–37).

If this makes the disciples appear as a 'community of saints', they were certainly not saints in any mysterious sense of being 'consecrated', since they were sanctified not by any dramatic or ostentatious means, but only by the word of the one sent by God, which was proclaimed to all men, but only accepted by them. There is an unmistakable closeness to Gnostic ideas here; see the Mandaean literature 165: 'You are set up and established, my chosen ones, by the discourse of the truth that has come to you'. The way by which the word of truth has come to Jesus' disciples, however, is different from this Gnostic understanding, since Jesus, as the historical revealer, disclosed that word to them in his person.

This close connection with Jesus' word also distinguishes the Johannine community from the Jewish understanding of sanctification. After the cult of the Temple, with its sacral and ritual forms of sanctification, had ended, sanctity was sought above all in the fulfilment of God's commandments. This is expressed in the frequently-repeated formula: 'Praise to Yahweh, our God, king of the world, who has sanctified us by his commandments'.[58] In this, it is in no way forgotten that all sanctification comes from God, but it is clear that God grants it through the Torah, as commandments given to Israel and to be carried out by the people.[59] John saw the Torah as superseded by Jesus' word, which took over all the healing and sanctifying functions of the Torah – giving life (5:38ff; 8:51), purifying (15:3), granting freedom (8:31f) and making love, the 'new commandment', an obligation (13:34f; 15:12, 17). Jesus' word, in which God's word is present, becomes, in the gospel of John, a frontier dividing Judaism from Christianity (see 5:38; 8:31, 37, 43; 12:48).

The emphasis that falls in v. 17b on the word of God as the bearer and mediator of 'truth' is also discernible in 1 Jn. 'The truth is not in us' (1:8) means the same as 'his word is not in us' (1:10). Because the word of God abides in the young men, they have overcome the evil one (2:14). The sanctifying and strengthening power of the word of God becomes known to the community in its resistance to sin and 'lying' (see 2:21, 27). The Spirit, as the quintessence of that power dwelling in the word of God or the words of Christ (see Jn 6:63; 1 Jn 2:20, 27 χρῖσμα; 3:9 σπέρμα) is not named, but this is no doubt because of the brevity of the petition, which is orientated towards the presence of the word of God in the community.[60] There is also no obvious reference in this prayer for 'sanctification' to the celebration of the Eucharist, unlike the petition made after the Eucharist by the community in *Did* 10:5, that it may, as a 'sanctified' community, be 'gathered' into God's kingdom. It would, however, be wrong to contrast the 'community subject to the word' with a 'cultic community', if the latter, like that in the *Didache*, aimed to follow the 'way of life' on the instructions of their Lord (Chapters 1–5) and to be 'made perfect in the love of God' (*Did* 10:5). The intercession in Jn 17:7 has no cultic *Sitz im Leben*, but it may be given one and thus give a sense of direction to a community that celebrates a liturgy.

17:18   As in the request that the disciples should be kept in God's being, attention is also directed in the petition for sanctification towards the world, in which the disciples have to continue to exist. This verse continues the idea in v. 15 and intensifies it. Jesus does not want the Father to take the disciples out of the world – on the contrary, he has himself sent them into the world. The 'unworldly' nature of the disciples and the desire for 'sanctification' are not reasons for a withdrawal from the world. They are, on the contrary, an invitation to continue Jesus' mission in the world. Just as Jesus himself was equipped, 'sanctified' (10:36) and, thus prepared, sent into the world by the Father, so too are the disciples prepared and sent out by Jesus. The aorist ʼαπέστειλα can be explained from the standpoint of the one who formulated the prayer and, as in v. 14 (see the commentary *ad. loc.*), its occurrence is also at least partly due to the preceding ʼαπέστειλας, with the intention of establishing the closest possible parallel between the sending of the disciples and the sending of Jesus.[61] The community's consciousness of having been sent is revealed in the light of Jesus' mission, as this is understood in the gospel of John. This cannot be reduced either to a mute protest against the world and its hostility to God or to an existential testimony to a desire for a liberating form of desecularization, nor can it be raised to the level of a committed involvement in missionary activity. Jesus was sent into the world 'to bear witness to the truth' (18:37) and to testify openly to the whole world to what he had 'seen and heard' with his Father (3:11, 32; 8:26). This same voice has to continue to be heard in the world through his disciples. Jesus, however, only found a hearing with those who were 'of the truth' and the disciples are to have the same experience (see 15:20). The testimony of those who were with him from the beginning (15:27) and the sign of the unity of the community will enable the world to know that God sent Jesus and has transferred his love to the community (17:23). In this sense, the community sees itself as sent into the world with the task of proclamation. This may not be such a vital missionary impulse as the one found in Paul's writings or those of others who proclaimed the gospel in the early Church, but it is certainly a fundamentally different attitude from that prevailing in gnostic and esoteric groups, since 'the sending out into the world of the chosen ones by the redeemer has no parallel in myth'.[62] The most powerful missionary force of all is found in a testimony that hands on Jesus' word in faith and makes God's love a reality in man's existence in reciprocal love and harmony.

17:19   The petition for the sanctification of the disciples was formulated in a strictly theocentric way: sanctification proceeds from God, his truth is the sphere of that sanctification and his word mediates it. The idea of mission (v. 18) led to Jesus as the one sent by God, who makes it possible for men to be sanctified and included within the divine sphere. If the disciples are to continue his work, they must themselves be sanctified. To bring this about, Jesus has a function as mediator. The progression of the thought as far as v. 19 can therefore be understood. This verse says more about Jesus: he 'sanctifies' himself for the disciples so that they may also be sanctified. Using the same vocabulary, Jesus aims to clarify what he is doing for the disciples and therefore employs the word ἁγιάζειν with the reflexive pronoun. This usage is unique in the gospel of John and very rare elsewhere. This together with the word ὑπέρ leave us in no doubt that Jesus' self-offering in death is meant here. In John, Jesus' free disposal of himself to death – in obedience to the Father – is stressed again and again (10:17f; see also 13:27b; 14:4; 18:11; 19:11, 17, 30) and the formulae with ὑπὲρ express this giving of his life done for the benefit of others (6:51; 10:11, 15; 15:13) and in their place (see 11:50–52; 18:14). Although the idea of Jesus' reconciliatory death does not emerge very prominently in the Johannine soteriology, it is retained from the common early Christian tradition (see also 1 Jn 3:16; also 2:2; 4:10). In addition, Jesus' death on the cross is also probably interpreted as a passover offering (19:36; see also 13:1; 18:28; 19:14; see also the 'Lamb of God', 1:29, 36). It is therefore hardly surprising that the vocabulary of sacrifice is used in 17:19, brought about by the context. In the Septuagint, ἁγιάζειν is used for the consecration of sacrificial animals (Exod 13:2; Deut 15:19) and it is also employed for the consecration of priests for the performance of their sacred duties (Exod 28:41; 40:13; Lev 8:30; 2 Chr 5:11). The Christian understanding of Jesus as priest and sacrificial gift is developed in Heb 9:13; 10:4–14; 13:12. These texts in the epistle to the Hebrews are close to Jn 17:19, because those who are purified by the blood of Christ are regarded as 'sanctified' (2:11; 10:10, 14, 29). All the same, it would be wrong to claim a direct connection with the theology of the epistle to the Hebrews.[63] It is more likely that already existing ideas were simply taken over. An allusion to the words of institution at the last supper (cf. Jn 6:51c) is possible, but by no means certain.[64]

It is not possible to exclude the idea of sacrifice from Jn 17:19. R. Asting traces Jesus' 'self-sanctification' back to his return to the heavenly sphere and to his self-fulfilment in that return with sanctifying powers 'for the benefit' of the disciples (ὑπὲρ αὐτῶν).[65] In this way, Asting's interpretation of 'sanctification' in vv. 17–19 is consistent, but it does not take the way in which ὑπέρ is used elsewhere into account and overlooks the change in meaning of ἁγιάζειν. Feuillet, on the other hand, treats this text as too important in seeing Jesus against the background of the liturgy of the Jewish day of atonement, so unequivocally as high priest and in basing the NT priesthood on this understanding.[66]

The disciples, then, are 'sanctified' for their mission in the world by Jesus' sacrificial death. The καί preceding αὐτοί presupposes a comparison with Jesus which can only refer to his being equipped to be sent into the world after v. 18 (see 10:36). The same idea of sanctification as in v. 17 is included in the ἵνα clause, and it is for this reason that the phrase ἐν ἀληθείᾳ without the article should not be interpreted in the sense of ἀληθῶς,[67] but in the sense in which the noun is previously used with the article. It is possible for the article to be omitted in such prepositional phrases.[68] The transition from use with the article to use without it can also be found in 8:44. The petition to the Father is reinforced by Jesus' consecration in death for the disciples and it takes place so that they may be firmly and lastingly filled with God's being and his power (perfect). In this way, this small unit in the discourse is complete in itself.

5. Jesus' Petition for the Unity of All Believers (17:20–23)

[20]'I do not pray for these only, but also for those who believe in me through their word, [21]that they may all be one; even as thou, Father art in me, and I in thee, that they may be in us, so that the world may believe that thou hast sent me. [22]The glory which thou hast given me I have given to them, that they may be one even as we are one, [23]I in them and thou in me, that they may become perfectly one, so that the world may know that thou hast sent me and hast loved them even as thou hast loved me.'

The idea of unity appears in the fundamental petition in v. 11b as a final wish or rather as the aim of the prayer to the Father. Jesus now returns to this desire again, after dealing in detail with the other petitions. The same desire is also expressed in the verses that follow in a series of ἵνα clauses, thus giving special emphasis to this idea of unity among the disciples. Even the manner in which this unity is described is extremely remarkable: it is to be a unity of the kind that exists between the Father and Jesus himself, a community with the Father and the Son and an inclusion in the unity of God and Jesus. It is only if this emphatic way of speaking is taken into consideration that the idea of unity and its meaning within the framework of this prayer can be properly understood. It is, of course, not surprising that the text should have been applied to the intentions of the contemporary ecumenical movement, but we have first of all to think of the intention underlying the Johannine statement itself. Its application to modern needs can only be secondary.[69]

The language of this verse is dense, compressed and even overcharged. The accumulation of ἵνα clauses is particularly striking and they are not easy to define in their relationship with one another. If the text is analyzed more carefully, even more problems arise. In v. 20, the disciples who were present at that time are contrasted with later believers, but in v. 22 the discourse clearly returns to those present. It is, after all, to them (αὐτοῖς) that Jesus gave the δόξα that the Father gave him, just as he gave them the Father's word (v. 14; cf. v. 8) and revealed the Father's 'name' to them (v. 6; cf. v. 12). Earlier literary critics have been struck by the abrupt transition from v. 21 to v. 22[70] and many exegetes have concluded that this, together with other considerations, means that vv. 20–21 were an addition by a second author.[71]

The reasons for this are important:

(1) In the other petitions, only the present disciples are considered. This is clear from the reason given for Jesus' petition in vv. 6–11a. This prayer of intercession may perhaps end at v. 19 and the perspective may at this point be extended to the later believers – if v. 22 did not direct it back again to those present.

(2) The work that Jesus has to carry out as the glorified one extends to 'all whom the Father has given him' (v. 2) and therefore must also apply to later believers. If, then, he is praying for the disciples who are present, they are at the same time also representative of the future community of believers, which is therefore already included in Jesus' intercession. In this case, there is no particular need to turn explicitly to 'those who believe in me through their word' (even though a request of this type is quite possible).

(3) The λόγος of the disciples is only mentioned in v. 20. Elsewhere this word is reserved for the word of God revealed by Jesus (vv. 6, 14, 17). Even in the rest of the gospel, it does not occur in this connection. For the most part, it refers to Jesus' word, which results in life and salvation or judgment (see especially 5:24; 8:31, 37, 43, 51; 12:48; 14:23f; 15:3).

(4) The formula in v. 21 is 'more colourless and stereotyped' than that in vv. 22f.[72] The phrase σὺ ἐν ἐμοὶ κἀγὼ ἐν σοί (v. 21) may have been taken from 10:38; 14:10, 11, but ἵνα ὦσιν ἓν καθὼς ἡμεῖς (v. 22) follows 17:11b literally, apart from the fact that a ἕν is added at the end. The idea of unity is further elucidated in v. 23a–b. The material presentation is similar to that in the καθώς clause in v. 21, but it is done in a way that expresses Jesus' function as mediator more powefully (ἐγὼ ἐν αὐτοῖς). The phrase ἐγὼ (κἀγὼ) ἐν αὐτοις is repeated at the end of v. 26 and the verb τελειόω forms a link back with v. 4 and the word δόξα used in v. 22 forms a similar link with v. 5. Vv. 20f would therefore seem to be secondary to vv. 22f in the formulation.

(5) If vv. 20f are placed between brackets, v. 22 follows the preceding section more naturally, since κἀγὼ κτλ. keeps our attention firmly on Jesus' activity, which was the subject-matter of v. 19. Jesus sanctifies himself for the disciples, so that they may be sanctified in truth. In the same way, he has given them the glory (δόξα), so that they may be one. V. 22 follows v. 21 much less well.

(6) The reason an early editor added vv. 20f to this passage on the model of vv. 22f is also difficult to state. He was led to do it by v. 18 (sending into the world), and wanted the later believers (who are represented in the discourse by the disciples present at the time) to be explicitly mentioned.

Even if we regard vv. 20f as an early addition by a second author, at least from the literary point of view, these two verses are, from the theological point of view, not alien to the passage as a whole and they have to be explained in the light of Jn 17.

17:20   The post-paschal situation was powerfully envisaged in vv. 14 and 18 (the use of the aorist tense) and here it is taken even more emphatically into consideration in an explicit reference to those who will believe in Jesus through the word of the disciples who are present. Jesus' word, which the disciples received (v. 14) as the word of God (see v. 17b), has to be handed on by them with their word. What is clearly presupposed here is missionary proclamation, but the petition is expressed with those who already believe in mind and extends the intercession to the believing community. Its members are also included within the proclamation of faith made by the original witnesses or by those who have the task of proclaiming and are connected with the witnesses (see 1 Jn 1:1–4). In this way, the same perspective as that revealed in the first epistle of John is also disclosed here and it is therefore possible to ask whether the latter may perhaps throw light on the background to Jn 17:20f. In the first epistle, Jesus Christ appears as the heavenly Paraclete with the Father for sins (2:1) and as the bond of unity with the Father (see 2:23f; 5:11, 20).

17:21   The petition for unity among the believers is, however, not obviously echoed in the longer epistle. The community that is faithful to Christ gives the impression of being closed in on itself and firmly united. The false teachers have never belonged, at least inwardly, to the community and now they have already separated themselves from it (2:19; cf. 4:1, 4f). What, then, was the cause of the emphatic request for unity among the future believers? Were there still false teachers in the community when the prayer was composed (or when vv. 20f were formulated)? Did these teachers of error cause confusion and divisions in the community? Or had they already formed new groups which called themselves 'Christian', with the result that other communities existed alongside the 'orthodox' community and there was prayer for their reunion with the original community? Although this view would certainly be in accordance with contemporary ecumenical intentions, it is very unlikely on the basis of the evidence in 1 Jn, since the name 'Christian' was denied to the members of the separated groups (see 2:22; 4:3). The intercession, then, certainly only applies to the true Christian community. Was its unity perhaps threatened by the existence of competing groups and agitation on the part of 'tempters' (see 1 Jn 2:26; 4:1–3; 2 Jn 8–11)? Or were there inner tensions within the community itself (see 3 Jn 9f)? We do not know the concrete background and no information is provided about a possible threat to the unity of the community by the positive formulation of the petition.

The καθώς clause that follows the request that all (later) believers may be one should not be separated from that petition,[73] since it defines that unity more precisely. It is to be a unity that corresponds to the unity existing between the Father and Jesus. The ἵνα clause that follows takes up the petition again and also includes the idea expressed in the καθώς clause: believers (καὶ αὐτοί) are also to be one as the Father and Jesus are one and they are to be one by being received into the unity of the Father and the Son (ἐν ἡμῖν).[74] This is the same construction as in 13:34 (see the commentary there). The basic thought is expressed first (in the earlier text, this is the 'new commandment' of reciprocal love; in our present text it is mutual unity). This idea is then clarified (καθώς). Finally, it is once again stressed in a co-ordinating ἵνα clause in which it is repeated.[75] This linguistic similarity between the two texts points to a closeness of ideas, namely that the unity that is desired is brought about in reciprocal love. The two belong together like the two sides of the same coin: the prayer for brotherly unity in accordance with the unity that exists between Jesus and the Father corresponds to the commandment of brotherly love in accordance with the love that is realized by Jesus. This co-ordination between unity and love not only follows a good tradition[76] – it is also confirmed in Jn 17 by the idea of love that appears in vv. 23 and 26. The culminating ἵνα clause in v. 26 includes the aim of unity in the idea of love. Love, then, is not the result of human exertion, but God's gift and the handing on of that received love to the brethren.

The unity that exists between the Father and Jesus is expressed in the same reciprocal formula σὺ ἐν ἐμοὶ καγὼ ἐν σοὶ as in 14:10f, 20, although it is, because of the prayer and the address made to the Father, in the reverse order (but see 10:38). It is not necessary to define this unity more precisely (that is, its being or activity, its essence or its desiring or loving; see the commentary on 5:19; 10:30 above), since our present text deals with the foundation of divine unity that is manifested and effective in love. Full knowledge of the unity between Jesus and his Father in love is revealed even in the farewell discourse in Chapter 14: the disciples have this knowledge by being included themselves in the community of love (vv. 20–23). The same existential process is present in the farewell prayer, which says that the disciples are to be ἐν ἡμῖν. The unity existing between Jesus and the Father is not only the fundamental model for the unity that should exist among believers – it is the basis for making it possible in their lives. Any explanation that points simply to external harmony, reunion or 'horizontal' oneness is inadequate. The unity to which this text refers is based on God himself and his love. It is a unity that penetrates believers 'from above' and also impels them to be one in brotherly love.

The unity of all believers is to lead the unbelieving world to faith in Jesus as the one sent by God. This is clear from the last ἵνα clause, which is a real final clause. In its existence in union with God and its brotherly love, the community bears witness among the world of men who are still far from God, but towards whom God's love is directed (see 3:16) and to whom Christ's work of salvation applies (see 3:17; 17:2). The tension existing between our present verse and v. 9, in which Jesus refuses to pray for the 'world', can hardly be explained away by saying that the 'world' is only seen in a situation of crisis.[77] The desire to win men over to faith and salvation is intended to be taken seriously. It is, however, different when Jesus looks at the community that has accepted his word and at the same time remembers the world that has rejected it (see also v. 25). The missionary concern of the Johannine community, which does not cease to exist despite the community's separation from the world and the dualistic conception of the 'world' (see 15:18, 20; 17:9 above), is announced in this desire to bring the world of men to faith in the one sent by God.

17:22   In this verse, somewhat surprisingly, Jesus speaks of the glory that he has given to the disciples. This statement can be grouped among a series of statements in which Jesus refers, in this discourse, to what he has done for the disciples: he has kept them in the Father's name (v. 12); he has given them the word of the Father (v. 14); he has sent them into the world (v. 18) and he has sanctified himself for them (v. 19). Our present statement is, on reflection, the culmination and the summary of what Jesus 'has given' to the disciples whom he leaves behind in the world and sends out into the world. This view is reinforced by the fact that he refers here to the δόξα that 'the Father has given to him', just as the Father gave him the words (v. 8) and his 'name' (vv. 11f). The perfect tenses of the verbs point to the lasting quality of what has been given to them. Jesus himself possesses the Father's glory and has possessed it from eternity, but he also regains it after his exaltation on the cross (see v. 5). The disciples are to have a share in this glory (see v. 24) by the glorified Christ's communication to them of divine life. This, as we have seen, was the meaning of his petition to be given once again the glory that he has always had with the Father (see v. 2). Here, then, δόξα must point to the fulness of divine life, which is directed towards 'glory', in an anticipatory language that already makes present what will only be fully realized in the heavenly or future world. The more powerfully the reality of that divine life – what W. Thüsing has called the 'splendour and power of divine love' – is present in the believers, the more fully unity is achieved among them. The language also shows that this fulfilment is intended in the text: the disciples are to become 'perfectly' one (v. 23b). This, then, is the culmination of the Johannine vision of the presence of salvation which is certain for those who believe in Christ and which will be theirs in such fulness that it can at least once (it is exceptional even in John) be designated by the highest term for fulfilment (δόξα). (In Paul, it is similar, but at the same time different; see 2 Cor 3:18.)

Other interpretations of this δόξα that Jesus gave to the disciples stress individual aspects which seem to be possible within the framework of Johannine theology, but which are at the same time remote from the context of the prayer in Jn 17 or are too narrow and specialized. Zahn and Tillmann have emphasized miraculous power, Wikenhauser interpreted it as the revelation of the word and Loisy believed that it pointed to the Eucharist. It is certain that the word, truth, grace and the idea of 'children of God' are within the same sphere of divine communication of life, but the choice of such an all-embracing term which points to fulfilment was not unintentional.[78]

The petition for unity, expressed as the goal of Jesus' gift of δόξα to the disciples, is formulated in exactly the same way as in v. 11: 'that they may be one even as we are one'. This is clearly a resumption of the basic theme of the prayer. Unity is the mark of divine being; hence the addition of 'as we are *one*', which acts as a reinforcement.

17:23   Through Jesus, who is one with the Father, the disciples are included in the unity of God and the community with him. This idea, which can easily be recognized in the gospel (10:38; 14:10f, 20, 23; 15:4f) and is expressed repeatedly in the first epistle (see especially 1:3; 2:23f; 5:11, 20), is changed in

Jesus' request on behalf of his own. It is, as it were, seen here in the reverse perspective. Divine unity is implanted in the disciples by Jesus being 'in them' and the Father being 'in Jesus'. This mutually complementary mode of expression can be represented in the following schema:

Inclusion in the Community with God:

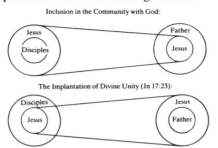

The Implantation of Divine Unity (Jn 17:23):

By Jesus being in the disciples and the Father being in Jesus, the community of disciples is entirely filled with God's being and in this way joined and kept together themselves. It becomes a perfect unity ($\varepsilon i\varsigma\ \check{\varepsilon}v$[79]) and is at the same time called to make the mystery of divine unity visible in brotherly love. It is this[80] that will enable the world to know that Jesus, who makes the Christian community the visible manifestation of the divine being, is the one sent by God. The community's unity and expression of love is ultimately a mystery of divine love. Through Jesus, God has included those who believe in his Son in his love (see 16:27) and has filled them with the power of his love. Jesus does not speak of his love for the disciples in this prayer directed towards the Father – he speaks of the Father's love for them. The other reading ($\dot{\eta}\gamma\dot{\alpha}\pi\eta\sigma\alpha$)[81] certainly came about as the result of a memory of Jn 15:9. The vocabulary of love continues until the conclusion of the prayer (vv. 24, 26).

The idea of unity that emerges in these verses serves above all, as we have seen in our exegesis, to make the Christian community conscious of its nature as founded in God, of strengthening it in that consciousness and of encouraging it to bear witness to Jesus Christ, as the one who is sent by God, in the world. This idea is also to be found in other parts of the gospel. The scattered children are, for example, to be 'gathered into one' ($\varepsilon i\varsigma\ \check{\varepsilon}v$; 11:52) and there is to be one flock and one shepherd (10:16). In this way, the positive view that is *not* brought about by separated groups is confirmed: unity is in itself a supreme good for the believing community and the sign of its election (see 11:52) and its character as the true community of God (see 10:16). These ideas have their origin in the OT (see the commentary on 10:16; 11:52 above) and there are also ideas in the Qumran literature that are analogous. The Qumran community also described itself as *yaḥad* ('union')[82] and was strongly conscious of its election. There are, however, considerable differences between the Johannine and the Qumran views. Above all, the Johannine community had no thought of being the 'holy remnant' of Israel and it aimed at community with God (in Qumran, community was sought with the angels) in quite a different way from those who belonged to Qumran. In other early Christian groups, the idea of unity also arose, as time progressed, even more powerfully. This is particularly evident in the epistle to the Ephesians (4:4–6), in which the unity of the Church consisting of members who were previously Jews and gentiles is stressed as it is in Jn 10:16 (cf. Eph 2:14–16). In the letter to the Ephesians, Paul has the unity of Christianity throughout the world in mind and 'that unity is here too made the overriding criterion for the true Church'.[83] The Johannine community, however, maintained its own view by keeping itself separate from the world. There is hardly any trace at all in its close togetherness of the juxtaposition of those who were originally Jews and gentiles. Although it withdrew more completely from the world and into itself than other early Christian communities, it did not, however, become introverted or esoteric and its 'solidarity with the heavenly reality' (Käsemann) was not the same as the Gnostics' remoteness from the world, despite the existence of a certain tendency towards Gnosticism. Finally, the Johannine idea of unity certainly points the way for contemporary ecumenical endeavours, since it presents reunion not as something that has to be sought superficially within the institutional framework, but as a deep reality that has to be aimed at in shared Christian faith, in community with God and in prayer and love.

6. Conclusion: the Fulfilment of Believers (17:24–26)

[24]*'Father, I desire that they also, whom thou hast given me, may be with me where I am, to behold my glory which thou hast given me.* [25]*O righteous Father, the world has not known thee, but I have known thee; and these know that thou has sent me.* [26]*I made known to them thy name and I will make it known, that the love with which thou hast loved me may be in them, and I in them'.*

17:24   Addressing the Father again,[84] Jesus expresses his desire and his will ($\theta\dot{\epsilon}\lambda\omega$)[85] that his own should behold his glory. The division that occurs at this point is also made clear by the fact that, after his detailed intercession (vv. 11b–23), Jesus once again speaks of those whom the Father has given to him and, what is more, speaks of them with the same emphasis as in v. 2. This emphasis is indicated by the placing of the phrase in the neuter at the beginning ($\dot{\delta}$ $\delta\dot{\epsilon}\delta\omega\varkappa\dot{\alpha}\varsigma$ $\mu o\iota$)[86] and by the repetition with the personal pronoun ($\varkappa\dot{\alpha}\varkappa\epsilon\tilde{\imath}\nu o\iota$) later. This mode of expression also appears in the section of the prayer in which the reason is given for the intercession (vv. 6 and 9), but it is not emphasized in the same way. The prayer, then, moves towards its conclusion, which itself refers back to the beginning. This is confirmed by the fact that Jesus once again speaks of his 'glory' which he possessed with the Father 'before the foundation of the world' (cf. v. 5) or which came to him at that time from the Father's love (v. 24). This new beginning at v. 24 and the conclusion marked by vv. 24–26 mean that these final verses cannot be described as a 'prayer for later believers' (v. 20),[87] although these, who are represented by the disciples who are present (see v. 25), are also intended. The concluding statements look back at the whole prayer and it is important in many ways to bear this in mind in our attempts to understand this section.

Jesus does not make any more requests (ἐρωτᾶν, vv. 9, 15), but expresses his earnest desire that his own should be fulfilled (see the ἵνα clause in v. 2). He knows that his will is also the will of the Father (cf. 5:21 with 5:30; 6:38ff). His intercession applied to the disciples in their existence on earth, in their confrontation with the world and their mission in the world. Now his will is turned towards their union with him in heaven and their fulfilment beyond this world in the vision of his glory. The δόξα that he has already given them (see v. 22) is a temporary gift, an anticipation or a foretaste of the full δόξα, consisting of a participation in his own revealed δόξα. This is why Jesus also says 'my glory'.[88] His glory is the glory of the Son (see 1:14) that is assigned to him. It is the glory that he has possessed from eternity, 'before the foundation of the world',[89] in the Father's love. He has revealed this glory even during his active existence on earth so that the disciples might behold it (ἐθεασάμεθα, 1:14), but he did this only in faith (see 2:11; 11:40). The new kind of (direct) vision to which Jesus is referring in this prayer can be recognized in the context by the statement that the disciples are to be 'with him', that is, together with him 'where he is himself'. This expression of place has already appeared in 12:26 and 14:3 and it sounds like a formula used to describe the disciples' union with Jesus in heaven. As in 14:3, there is no reference here to the parousia,[90] but it is also not possible, for the reasons that we have given, to think of a present vision of Jesus' glory that can be enjoyed here on earth. From the material point of view, the only possible conclusion is that attention is directed here to the fulfilment of believers after death (see 11:25f),[91] although this is only one conclusion. The question concerning the way in which salvation is ultimately realized is over-shadowed by the fact that the goal is ahead of them. The community lives in this hope and longing, but it does so in a serene confidence, because it has already experienced the present revelation of the Father's love (see v. 26).

This text is closely related to 1 Jn 3:1–4. The direct vision of Jesus' δόξα is reminiscent of the 'seeing καθώς ἐστιν', especially if Christ is intended in 1 Jn 3:2b in the personal pronoun. Other points of contact in the context are the prominence given to God's love for believers or the 'children of God' and the rejection of the 'world' that has not known God (cf. Jn 17:25 with 1 Jn 3:1b). Certain differences between the two texts should not, however, be overlooked. In 1 John, the idea of the parousia emerges; although it may not in 3:2 (ἐὰν φανερωθῇ), it certainly does in 2:28. Neither the ideas of 'children of God' nor of 'being like (or equal to)' God or Christ are themes in Jn 17. There is also no reference to 'hope' in the gospel text. On the other hand, however, the word δόξα is completely absent from the text in the first epistle. Neither the vision of the future nor of fulfilment is so strongly marked in the prayer in Jn 17 as it is in 1 Jn 3:1–4. These differences can be explained on the basis of different intentions, but they may also be an indication that the prayer was not the work of the same author.[92] Whoever was responsible for the prayer, however, it is certain that he occupied a central theological position between the evangelist and the author of 1 Jn.

The expectation of the fulfilment of salvation which emerges clearly here may also be in many respects close to the gnostic idea of the 'ascent of the soul',[93] but the Christian character of the Johannine text is preserved by the personal bond with Jesus, in whose glory believers are to share. Union with Christ is also the connecting link with other early Christian expectations of salvation.[94] The avoidance of apocalyptic ideas does not necessarily imply a 'spiritualization'. The Johannine view is rather a mature reflection about what is essential in Christian hope;[95] it should therefore help to show us how to understand the idea of fulfilment and consummation.

17:25 After providing this prospect of the ultimate goal, the prayer returns to the present, the situation in which the community of disciples finds itself. The Father is addressed again, this time with another adjective, and this gives the last word of the departing Christ a special and incisive force, although the word δίχαιε is not unambiguous here. Does it indicate God's 'just' rule, which hands the unbelieving world over to judgment (see 16:10f) or does it refer to his 'gracious' and good turning towards those who believe in Jesus (see 1 Jn 1:9)?[96] The second interpretation is preferable, firstly because of the analogy with the attributive address in v. 11 (πάτηρ ἅγιε) and secondly because of the continuation in v. 26, which deals with the love of God in the disciples. The mention of the cosmos that has not known God has no value in itself. The connection between the statement about the world and that about the disciples by means of καί – καί forms a contrast,[97] but, since nothing more is said about the world, but more is in fact said about the disciples, the latters' attitude of faith and acceptance of the one sent by God are clearly to be outlined more prominently so that the disciples will appear to be worthy of God's turning towards them in love (see vv. 8f). The words 'but I have known thee' are introduced into this train of thought because the disciples have come to their knowledge of God and have turned towards him through Jesus. The tenses of the verbs (aorist) show that Christ in prayer is mindful of the historical experience that he has shared with men in the world.

17:26 The way that the community has to follow on earth towards its fulfilment takes the disciples through an even deeper revelation of God's being and an even more powerful inclusion in communion with God, who discloses himself in love to them and accepts them more and more into his love. In this final statement in the prayer, the repeated καί probably forms a bracket between ἐγνώρισα and γνωρίσω, with the result that the progress from already experienced revelation of the name of God to further revelation is strongly stressed. The heavenly goal (v. 24) does not exclude an inner growth on the part of believers on earth. On the contrary, they are to grow towards that goal even now, in their existence on earth. The revelatory term γνωρίζειν was also encountered in 15:15, in which Jesus, within the context of friendship, said that he had communicated 'everything' to the disciples – 'all that he had heard from his Father'. The apparent contradiction – that he is announcing a further revelation to them now – can be explained on the basis of the dialectical tension existing in the Johannine theology between Jesus' revelation of himself on earth and the continuing revelation of the Paraclete, who 'reminds' them of Jesus' words (14:25f) and takes from Jesus' 'possession' (16:13f).

196

The Paraclete is not, of course, mentioned in the prayer in Chapter 17. Jesus declares his intention to make the Father's name known (see also 16:25). It is clear, however, that he does this through the Spirit, through whom he continues to be present in his community and close to it. The striking fact that the Spirit is not named in the language of our prayer does not imply a denial of the reality and activity of that Spirit in the community – this presence has been correctly perceived by Greek Orthodox exegetes.[98] There were various categories (or 'codes') in the Johannine school to indicate the spiritual presence of the heavenly Christ in the community. In this prayer, the two categories used are the continuing revelation of the 'name' of God (see vv. 6 and 11f) and the mediation of the love of God. Both are intimately connected with each other and closely interrelated. God's 'name' cannot be restricted simply to the name 'Father' (see the commentary on v. 6). It points rather, as we have seen, to that Father's good and holy being (see the adjectives used with the name in vv. 11 and 25). Through Jesus' revelation and its reception among believers, this divine being is implanted in the disciples, so that the love of God, with which he loves his Son, is also present in them, dwells in them and continues to have an effect in them. Love, proceeding from God as its primordial source, is the bond that unites not only the Father and the Son, but also the Father and the Son on the one hand and believers on the other. Mediaeval theologians clearly interpreted this love as pointing to the Holy Spirit.[99]

The last phrase added to the prayer, κἀγὼ ἐν αὐτοῖς, would at first seem to be superfluous in this reflection on the revelation of the Father and the communication of his love, but it contains something of importance to the whole meaning of the discourse, since, like the previous discourses, it is concerned with Jesus' abiding (as the glorified Christ) with his community. He is not only the mediator of God's love for that community and the link in the members' community with God, but also the constant presence of God in the community. The words at the end of the first epistle are important in this context: 'This (Jesus Christ) is the true God and eternal life' (5:20). Jesus fulfils his task to give those who believe in him eternal life (Jn 12:50), the task which his glorification has given him the power to perform (17:2), in the later community by abiding in it with his word, his Spirit and his love. In this way, he is able to lead it to the fulfilment previously discussed – the vision of his glory in the heavenly world.

THE LITERARY GENRE, SITZ IM LEBEN AND ORIGIN OF THE PRAYER OF JOHN 17

At the end of our exegesis and analysis of Jn 17, there are still many questions unanswered. What, for example, is the literary genre of this prayer of the departing redeemer? Do comparable discourses and prayers exist in the author's environment? What is the *Sitz im Leben* of this prayer? Is it to be found in worship or the celebration of the Eucharist? Did the evangelist compose it or was it perhaps a subsequent, editorial addition? Or should we assume that another author was responsible for it? Finally, what is the lasting significance of this prayer for Christianity? What meaning does it have for a community living in different historical circumstances and subject to different spiritual pre-conditions? These are questions which have often been asked and to answer them fully would require separate comprehensive treatment. Here, they can only be discussed very briefly.

1. Literary Genre

Since this chapter in the gospel is a prayer within the framework of farewell discourses, it is important to bear both these aspects in mind. Farewell discourses were a very widespread literary form in the ancient world,[100] but a distinction has to be made between the 'last words of famous men', which was a favourite form in pagan antiquity, and exhortatory discourses and testaments in the Bible and Judaism. The latter extend over a long period, beginning with the blessing of Jacob in Gen 49 and going as far as the many 'Testaments' of the Jewish world. It is at once obvious that the Johannine farewell discourses are in no sense a glorification of a hero and that they are in fact much closer to the Jewish literary form and tradition. Yet, even in the farewell discourses of patriarchs and in similar discourses, prayers are found relatively seldom.

The Song of Moses in Deut 32 which, because of the arrangement of the whole book, deserves very special attention as the testament of the departing Moses,[101] is a hymn of praise in honour of God's rule in the history of his people. This gives an impressive reason for the preceding commandments and instructions (see 32:43–47). Moses' prayer in *Jub* 1:19–21, on the other hand, is an intercession, made on Mount Sinai, but looking forward to the future, like Noah's prayer in *Jub* 10:3–6. Abraham's detailed admonitions to his offspring, his thanksgiving to God and his blessing of Jacob in *Jub* 20–22 are also many of the characteristics typical of testaments. Isaac also departs with 'admonitions and blessings' (36:17).

The situation is somewhat different in the apocalyptic literature. In these books, prospects of the future are provided (see especially *Methuselah Ethiopic Enoch*, 91). Because the future seemed dark and ready for the judgment, the visionary's prayers were directed towards God's mercy on his people Israel (*4 Esdr* 8:20–36, 45; *Apoc Barsyr* 48:1–24). Trust that the divine law would be observed had been lost and the patriarchs prayed even for the righteous to be spared the judgment of God (*Apoc Barsyr*, 84–85). The two great Jewish apocalyptic works (*4 Esdras* and the *Apocalypse of Baruch*) were written around the turn of the first Christian century and were therefore very close in time to the gospel of John, yet there is a great distance between them and the prayer in Jn 17. The apocalyptic literature, in which shorter or longer prayers have a purely literary function (they connect various revelations together; see, for example, *Apoc Barsyr* 21 and 34), could at the most have stimulated the formulation of a prayer. In form and function, however, these works are very remote from the prayer of intercession.

Linguistically and stylistically, some of the Hermetic writings are closer to the prayer of the departing redeemer in Jn 17. At the end of *Poimandres* (I,

31–32), in other words, at the climax of the instruction, there is a prayer consisting of a eulogy of God, the Father of all, and a petition that the Father may accept the λογικὰς θυσίας (the 'true sacrifices of reason and word') and confirm the one who prays in the gnosis that he has reached, so that he will also be able to enlighten his still unknowing brethern. There are certain verbal reminiscences: 'holy is God'; the man who belongs to God (the Gnostic) helps the Father in the work of sanctification, 'because you have given him full power' (cf. Jn 17:2). We are bound to ask whether, in Jn 17, Christ is not a true Gnostic. Despite a certain similarity, the literary genre of Jn 17 is quite different from the concluding prayer of *Poimandres*, because Christ's prayer is an authentic intercession for his disciples and the later community. At the end of the treatise on 'rebirth' in the *Corpus Hermeticum*, XIII, the one who has been initiated into the mystery turns to the Father with praise and thanksgiving (§§ 21–22) and the expressions and ideas are very similar to those found in the first treatise (*Poimandres*). It is only here that the mediation of the revealer (the 'Logos') is stressed. It is a prayer of thanksgiving offered by those who are redeemed and there is no reference to the unknowing brethren. This treatise too is, however, also different, as far as its literary genre is concerned, from the prayer of the departing redeemer for his own.[102] The same also applies to the prayer in the so-called λόγος τέλειος (P. Mimaut), in which there are also many linguistic echoes.[103]

Some of the Mandaean writings have also been mentioned in this context.[104] In the Mandaean *Book of John*, Anoš-Uthra prays to the Great Life, his father, for his disciples and their children, 'who have been thrown into great impurity', so that they may rise up to the place of light (236–239). This long text, which is full of mythical ideas, is, however, from the point of view of its literary genre, a conversation between Anoš-Uthra and the Great Life, and its intention is to provide instruction about the liberation from the lower world and the ascent to the world of light and life. In *Mand Lit*, 140, the Mandaeans themselves pray for themselves and their friends: 'Bring us your splendour! Increase your light on us!' As in the previous prayers, we have an insight here into the prayer of the community and there are certain similarities between it and Johannine ideas, but its literary genre is not the same as that of the prayer of the departing redeemer in Jn 17.

The prayer in Jn 17 is quite distinctive because of the person of Jesus Christ. In it, the 'Son' prays to his Father for his own. This means that this Johannine prayer is very close to the synoptic 'cry of rejoicing' (Mt 11:25–27/Lk 10:21f), although this is not an intercession, but a prayer of praise (see Vol. 2, pp. 178f). Lk 22:31f is a short intercession by Jesus in the upper room during the last supper for Simon Peter, but it only has a traditio-historical significance, since it forms part of a Lukan composition of farewell words and is quite different from the prayer genre. It is in fact a promise and an admonition addressed to Simon.

When all this is taken into consideration, it is still not at all easy to classify the prayer in Jn 17 in a particular literary genre. It is most closely related to the farewell words and the farewell blessing of the patriarchs in the biblical and Jewish tradition. It also, however, makes use of the idea of intercession that is

found in other texts of the same tradition (including the apocalyptic literature). There are also linguistic points of contact with gnostic texts and, in the
special type of prayer of the Son, with the synoptic 'cry of rejoicing'. It can
therefore be assumed that the author of the prayer had received ideas from
different directions, but that in the last resort he produced something quite
distinctive and unique, firmly marked by the Johannine Christology. Just
as in the two short prayers in Jn 11:41f and 12:27f, the Johannine Christ
can be clearly recognized here, in this special manner of praying. Something
that is quite incomparable has been created here by mature theological
reflection.

2. Liturgical 'Sitz im Leben'?

We have already considered the question whether the Johannine language
was influenced by the liturgy of the community several times in this study.
The many titles of Christ (especially in Jn 1), certain symbols (the 'Lamb of
God') and the solemn ἐγώ εἰμι statements might well point to liturgical use
(see Vol. 1, pp. 512–514). Whatever connection it may have with the
discourse on the bread of life,[105] the 'eucharistic' section (6:51c–58) certainly
refers to the community's celebration of the Eucharist (this is clear from the
terminology of 'flesh and blood' and the words of institution in v. 51c). The
'calendar of feasts' and in particular the observation of the passover feasts and
the significance of Jesus' death as the passover lamb might point to a cultic
concern on the part of the Christian community (which had already separated
itself from Jewish cultic practices). All these considerations apply even more
forcefully to the prayer in Jn 17, and others have to be added to them. Among
the links with the section on the Eucharist (6:51c–58) are the formula with
ὑπέρ in 17:19 (cf. 6:51c), the formulae used to indicate oneness (cf. 17:21ff
with 6:56), and the idea of handing on life (cf. 17:2 with 6:57). The style and
form of the prayer, the dominant idea of glorification and the special petition
for sanctification (vv. 17–19) give Jn 17 a certain liturgical flavour which could
hardly have occurred in any context other than the celebration of the
Eucharist in a Christian community.

Apart from this, the prayers in the *Didache* also provide us with a
comparison, since they are clearly related to the prayer in Jn 17. The
following points of contact are especially valuable: (a) the address 'holy
Father' (Did 10:2); (b) the 'making known' (γνωρίζω) of his 'holy name' (10:2)
or of 'life and knowledge' (9:3) through Jesus Christ; (c) the gift of 'eternal
life' (10:3); (d) the deliverance of the Church 'from all evil' (10:5); (e) the
perfecting of the Church or its 'fulfilment in love' (*ibid.*); (f) the 'sanctification' of the Church (*ibid.*) and (g) the idea of unity (9:4; see also 10:5).
Finally, the doxologies in the *Didache* (9:2, 3, 4; 10:2, 4, 5) have the same
language and ideas as the Johannine δοξάζειν. On the other hand, there is no
reference in Jn 17 to the eucharistic gifts and their symbolic aspects. This
absence can be compared with the frequent references in the *Didache*: the
'holy vine of David' (9:2); 'broken bread' (9:3f); 'eating and drinking of your

Eucharist' (9:6) and 'spiritual food and drink' (10:3). There is clearly some connection in the language, although it is hardly a question of direct dependence, but rather one of sharing the same place of origin (perhaps Syria?). Since the prayer in Jn 17 could not, simply for reasons of time, have had an effect on the language of the ancient prayer in the *Didache*, it is possible to ask whether the language of Jn 17 was perhaps influenced by the cultic prayer of the community. This cannot be ruled out; in which case the author would have used the language of prayer employed by the Christian community for his prayer of Christ. This assumption is, however, unlikely, because the formulae as a whole follow the theological language of the gospel very closely and, when they go beyond that language (as, for example, in the case of phrases with the 'name of the Father'), they can be explained in the light of the language of the religious environment (see *ad loc.*).

There is, however, no question of the prayer of the departing redeemer being a directly cultic prayer. Its literary genre is opposed to this (see above). For this reason, the title commonly given to this prayer ('high-priestly prayer') is only partly justified and to some extent misleading. If we take the Christology of the high priest in Hebrews as our point of departure, then Christ is the high priest in the heavenly sanctuary.[106] Our exegesis of Jn 17, however, showed clearly that Jesus was regarded for the purpose of this prayer as being still on earth, although he played the part of an intercessor for his disciples – a part which can, in the wider sense, be called 'high-priestly'. He looks forward in the prayer to his sacrifice that is to 'sanctify' his own 'in the truth' (vv. 17 and 19), but this purpose is connected with their being sent out into the world (v. 18), whereas, according to Heb 9:13f; 10:10, 14, the high priest sanctifies those who united to him in order to take them into the heavenly sanctuary and perfect them (see 10:19ff). What is more, the situation of farewell and the intercession that arises from this situation should not be overlooked. It would be equally and perhaps even more correct to say that Jesus prays for his own as a 'shepherd', whereas, in 1 Jn 2:1, the heavenly Christ intercedes for his community on earth as the 'Paraclete'. The cultic aspects of Jn 17, then, hardly allow us to conclude that the prayer is a liturgical *Sitz im Leben*.[107]

3. Origin and Meaning

The prayer undoubtedly originated in the Johannine school. This is clear both from its language and its content. What is doubtful, however, is whether it can be attributed to the evangelist himself. The most important reason against this is that Chapter 17 may not form part of the original composition of the gospel of John. We have already seen that 18:1 most suitably follows 14:31 and that, if Chapters 15 and 16 are later additions, Chapter 17 is certainly also an addition. The prayer can, if need be, be placed after the 'signal to go' (14:31), in which case it would have to be regarded as a delay until the real departure (18:1) and as taking place in the upper room of the last supper. Because of the very energetic exhortation to go, however, this is unlikely. This leaves us with the other possibility, namely that the evangelist himself later inserted the prayer.

On the other hand, if the discourses in Chapters 15–16 were composed by a different author or editor, this would also seem to apply more probably to Chapter 17 as well.

I have already pointed to a number of unusual linguistic expressions in the detailed exegesis and especially to the phrases employing the name of the Father, but I could not find any really decisive examples that went counter to the evangelist's language. Theological differences can be found more easily and J. Becker[108] has cited several. These include a different dualistic theology, the use of $\dot{\alpha}\lambda\dot{\eta}\theta\varepsilon\iota\alpha$ as the quintessence of the revelation of the word, the exclusive mission of Jesus to his own in the light of a predestinarian understanding of the Church, and a somewhat different Christological view with a change of emphasis in the idea of glorification (Jesus' pre-existent $\delta\delta\xi\alpha$) and in eschatology. All these points are rather exaggerated and they do not, as the author believes that they do, bring Jn 17 closer to 1 Jn. In my opinion, the theological links between Jn 17 and the rest of the gospel are stronger than those between the prayer and the epistles of John. The author could, after all, have been a member of the Johannine circle who was very close to the evangelist himself.

It is ultimately not so very important whether the evangelist himself or a pupil who was particularly congenial to him in speaking here. The whole prayer clearly breathes the spirit of the Johannine community, even including that tendency towards exclusiveness and introversion that prompted E. Käsemann to put forward his provocative theses.[109] My detailed exegesis has shown, however, that the Johannine community did not succumb to the danger of encapsulation and isolation from the world. The prayer bears witness to a concentration on what is essential and a reflection about what has been given to the community by God through Christ, namely life in God and in his love that is filled with inner glory. This call to the inner life, to inner recollectedness and to unity with God and within the community, is still significant even in our own age, which is so characterized by external activity. On the other hand, we also encounter in this prayer the risk and limitations of this Christian attitude and these can only be avoided by a community that is conscious of its mission to the world as a permanent task.

The Disciples, the Community and the Church in the Gospel of John

The farewell discourses and the prayer of the departing Christ draw our attention even more strongly than other parts of the gospel of John (with the exception of the concluding chapter, 21) to the Johannine community and its understanding of itself. We have no direct knowledge of the community or communities within which the evangelist and his friends and pupils lived and for which they composed the gospel. In this respect, we are in the same position as we are with regard to the synoptic gospels, since we can only conclude from the internal evidence supplied by those gospels who formed the circle of those addressed. A community's understanding of itself as a church has to be distinguished from its external situation, composition and structure, although the former is not entirely exempt from external conditions. The Pauline communities were externally connected by the activity of the great apostle to the gentiles, but they were also fashioned by their founder's view of the Church, especially as far as their consciousness of themselves as communities and the inner relationship with other early Christian communities were coincerned. We know from his letters that Paul was always attempting to bring the newly established communities into contact with those that already existed, with other communities in his missionary territory (see 1 Cor 1:2) and with the 'mother church' in Jerusalem (see the great collection, Rom 15:25–27). In his efforts, he also tried to arouse a consciousness of the Church as a whole. It cannot be doubted that a similar external and internal incorporation into the greater community consisting of all those who professed Christ also applied to the communities addressed by the synoptic gospels, however different they may have been in the understanding of faith and their Christian way of life. There are certainly signs towards the end of the first century AD of a growing consciousness of the Church as a whole, in the sense of '*one* Lord, *one* faith, *one* baptism' (Eph 4:5) or a Christian 'brotherhood' in the whole of the world of that time (see 1 Pet 5:9). This is, however, disputed in the case of 'Johannine Christianity' of the kind encountered in the gospel and the first epistle of John and the question is rather whether it was not in many respects quite remote from the rest of early Christianity.[1]

We cannot discuss both the historical situation in which the Johannine community was placed and its understanding of itself that is closely linked with that situation. To do justice to this would require a more lengthy reflection, in which the first epistle, the two shorter letters and the Johannine Apocalypse would also be taken into consideration. Each of the letters and the Apocalypse is able to throw a special light both on the external situation and on the understanding that the communities had of themselves. Of paramount concern are the ecclesial aspects discernible in the gospel of John itself and the possible conclusions that can be drawn from these for the evangelist's attitude towards the 'Church' or that of the editor or editors who worked on his gospel. An investigation of this kind is naturally made more difficult if we assume that there were also editorial additions or levels pointing to a different attitude towards the 'Church', one that was closer to the faith of the community and to church practice.

R. Bultmann believed that the work originally written by the evangelist was first made acceptable to the community and to the Church as a whole by a 'Church editing'. This conviction is to some extent also shared by more recent scholars who have attempted to distinguish several levels in the gospel pointing to the different theological positions and attitudes towards the 'Church' of the individual authors or editors. As a methodological precaution, then, I shall keep to those parts of the gospel that are beyond dispute the work of the evangelist, even though the decision has to be made in any attempt to analyse the gospel in this way whether a man who was at a distance from the faith and life of the community, in other words, an 'outsider' with regard to the Church, was supported and encouraged in this work of editing that was more firmly connected with the community. It looks very much as though the editors regarded the evangelist, despite his personal theological view, as an outstanding representative of Christian faith and even as the normative interpreter of the Christian message, with the result that they aimed above all to facilitate the expression and the effectiveness of his gospel within the community. In my investigation in this Excursus, however I shall try not to let myself be influenced by this belief, but will rather base my considerations on the text itself.

Because of the special place occupied by the fourth gospel among the New Testament documents and the problem of an early Christian 'consciousness of faith', which has already been mentioned in this context, several exegetes have considered this theme of the 'Church' in specialized monographs.[2] In most of these works, the gospel has been considered as a single theological testimony and the work has been examined for expressions, images and ideas relating to the Church, for the special Johannine nature of this understanding of the Church and for the significance of worship and the sacraments, preaching, catechesis and so on. The results of these investigations have been very varied, since many of the conclusions can only be drawn indirectly. (This applies particularly to the Johannine community's understanding of the sacraments and their function in the community; see Excursus 15.) These questions about the Johannine community's understanding of itself as a 'Church' cannot be excluded altogether, since this understanding was expressed in the life of the community, but an attempt to answer them has been postponed for as long as possible, because I would have been dependent on other conclusions and have preferred to keep to directly ecclesial concepts and references in the gospel. In a document which looks back at Jesus' activity on earth and introduces the theme of the present into this perspective, the first and most obvious datum that has to be taken into consideration is the concept of discipleship or the gospel's understanding of the group of disciples. Only secondarily should we consider what is made clear about the community's understanding of itself in Jesus' words. In this examination of the problem, I shall give special attention to one question: does the gospel provide evidence of a narrow, limited concept of community or does it have a much wider horizon, pointing to a perspective of a universal Church that goes beyond the strictly Johannine community?

1. The Circle of the Disciples and the Concept of Discipleship in the Gospel of John

The word μαθητής occurs seventy-eight times in the gospel. This is a greater frequency than in all the other gospels (Matthew: seventy-three times; Mark: forty-six times; Luke thirty-seven times). This is not simply the result of pure chance. In the evangelist's thought and his presentation of the gospel, discipleship and the circle of the disciples are very important. This is hardly surprising in view of his deep interest in Christology, as revealed in Jesus' words and signs, his revelation of himself and his confrontation with the unbelieving world. In addition to this, Jesus is also accompanied from the very beginning by disciples in the fourth gospel and the calling is the first disciples is described in that gospel in greater detail, with a more carefully planned composition and including more traditions than the synoptics.[3] These disciples at the same time share in Jesus' activity (the wedding feast at Cana, the cleansing of the temple and the baptism in Judaea). In Chapter 6, at the climax and turning point in Galilee, they are given considerable prominence and, later in the gospel, they also play an important part in the evangelist's presentation of the events on the way to Jerusalem and before the journey to Bethany, in the section dealing with the story of Lazarus, which I ascribed to the evangelist himself (11:7–16).

There is also an important interlude in the chapter on Samaria which describes a conversation between Jesus and his disciples (4:27–38). The disciples also at least make an appearance in the accounts of the second miracle of Cana (4:46–54), the healing at the pool of Bethesda (5:1–9) and the healing of the man born blind at the pool of Siloam (9:1–7; the disciples appear in this incident at the beginning, v. 2). This may perhaps be connected with the fact that these stories were taken from the *semeia*-source. In the 'great feeding', they already had certain functions in the tradition, but in the gospel of John there are some special emphases (see 6:5–9). They are essential to the account of Jesus' walking on the lake as those who are chiefly concerned. They do not appear, at least externally, in the chapters describing Jesus' conflict with his Jewish opponents and other Jewish groups. This, however, is quite understandable and the idea of discipleship nonetheless enters these chapters as it were in a concealed way (see 8:12, 31; 9:27f; see also especially the discourses on the shepherd in Chapter 10). I shall have more to say about this question later.

This brief survey of the presence of the disciples in the first main part of the gospel should make it clear that, in those passages in which the disciples figure, they are not simply mentioned in passing, as though they had been drawn into the gospel from the tradition in which they may have appeared together with Jesus. On the contrary, they are introduced into these Johannine texts quite deliberately. They participate with Jesus in the activity in question and are actively involved in the event.[4] If we consider the tradition that the evangelist took over and bear in mind its own creative form, we are also bound to recognize that sections dealing with the disciples which can only go back directly to the evangelist (4:27–38; 9:2–5; 11:7–16) have been inserted by him at certain points in the gospel. This is all the more striking in view of the fact that John otherwise keeps teaching and instruction for the disciples (Jesus' 'own') for the hour of farewell in the upper room of the last supper. (This is, of course, in contrast to the synoptics.) The only conclusion that we can draw from all this is that the circle of the disciples had a definite theological meaning in Jesus' work and activity on earth for John.

But what part do the disciples play in the Johannine presentation of Jesus' public appearance? It is not possible to come to any rigid conclusions and we should not view the matter one-sidedly or be too influenced by the synoptic vision. A line of development is visible in Mark, for example, but this does not appear in John: the call of the disciples (Mk 1:16–20); the choice and composition of the circle of the twelve (3:13–19) and the sending out of the twelve (6:7–13). In John, on the other hand, nothing is said about the formation of the circle of the twelve. The twelve are introduced quite abruptly (from a previously existing tradition) in 6:67, 70f and, apart from here and in 20:24 (the reference to Thomas as one of the 'twelve'), they are not emphasized. We are also told nothing in John about the disciples being sent out during Jesus' time on earth. A number of intentions can, however, be distinguished in the gospel of John. They can be grouped under three headings.

(a) The disciples represent those who are made believers by Jesus through his word and his signs. This is already made clear in the calling of the disciples: the first men, who are referred to Jesus by John the Baptist, remain with him for an afternoon and become convinced, as their companions do later, that he is the Messiah (1:39, 41, 45). The 'conversion' of Nathanael is described in a very impressive way: his scepticism is overcome by Jesus himself and he subsequently confesses his faith to Jesus (1:46–49). It is also the disciples who believe in him on the basis of the miracle at Cana (2:11). In the cleansing of the temple, they function as believers (although they do not understand until after his resurrection) in contrast to the unbelieving Jews (2:17–22). In the 'Galilean crisis', the twelve prove themselves to be unswerving and unshakable believers (6:66–71).

(b) The disciples also represent the later community in contrast to the unbelieving Jews. This can already be conjectured on the basis of a consideration of the cleansing of the temple and the Galilean crisis. There are also other signs that this was the evangelist's view. The man healed of blindness, for example, also appears as Jesus' 'disciple', in sharp contrast to the pharisees, who play the part of 'disciples of Moses' (9:27f) and we have seen that it is precisely this chapter of the gospel that provides a glimpse of relationships at the time. The same also applies to Joseph of Arimathaea, who is described in the gospel as a 'disciple of Jesus, but secretly, for fear of the Jews' (19:38). All these texts extend the concept of disciple itself (see below). The theme of 'fear of the Jews' is also mentioned in the account of Easter with regard to the smaller circle of disciples (19:38). When he was arrested, Jesus also stood up for his disciples (18:8). This defence of his disciples is expressed indirectly in the cross-examination before Annas (18:19f). Even more important is the contrast between Jesus' private instruction of the circle of disciples in the upper room at the last supper and his public speaking, which, as a whole, resulted in failure (12:37–40). The separation of the Christian community from Judaism, which, at the beginning of the first century AD, was led by pharisaical rabbis (see 12:42), is reflected in this arrangement. In this confrontation, the disciples have, not entirely, but at least now and then, a representative function.

(c) The disciples also represent the later believers in that they are challenged and tempted and their faith is inadequate. In several places in the gospel they are portrayed as men who are slow to understand and defective in faith. They are even presented in this way at the last supper (see especially 14:4–11). They do not represent the future community of believers ideally, but serve rather as an image for consideration, so that the later community may be aware of the dangers and wrong attitudes that stand in the way of a full and true faith. I have already discussed this question at some length in Excursus 7 on the notion of faith in the gospel (see Vol. 1, pp. 558–575). On the other hand, the gospel tells us nothing about the moral demands made of Jesus' disciples, apart from the 'new commandment' of brotherly love (13:34f; 15:12, 17). There is no hint in John of the radical moral teaching of the Sermon on the Mount or the harsh conditions imposed on those who follow Jesus. Whenever the disciples are mentioned by the evangelist, it is their faith that is the important issue. In this way, however, discipleship is given a clearly 'ecclesial' significance. It has something to tell us about the self-understanding and concerns of a community that has to assert itself and prove its value in a hostile and unbelieving environment.

The concept of discipleship conforms to the 'opening' of the group of disciples to the period of community. It is usually possible to recognize from the context when the closer companions of Jesus are meant. Individual disciples are also quite often named. This occurs more frequently in John than in the other gospels. Why certain disciples, among them several who play no part in the synoptic accounts, and not others should be named in this way is a problem in itself, possibly connected with the development of the Johannine tradition or with the bond between later communities and individual personalities (see the texts concerned). We know from the gospel that there was a smaller circle of disciples, but there are also places in which 'disciples' in a much wider sense are mentioned. The first reference is in 4:1, where the pharisees learn that 'Jesus was making and baptizing more disciples than John' (see *ad loc.*). Another reference to disciples in the wider sense is to be found in 6:60f, 66. Here we are told that 'many of his disciples' were scandalized by Jesus' words in the synagogue at Capharnaum and ceased to accompany him. These μαθηταί are explicitly distinguished from the twelve. Should they be identified with the 'multitude' (ὄχλος), which was said at the beginning of the chapter (6:2) to be following him? In the gospel of John, ὄχλος is a relatively colourless concept, however, and does not normally indicate a close relationship with Jesus.[5] The μαθηταί in 6:60f, 66 are clearly those who were following him more closely. The μαθηταί in 7:3 were probably also 'adherents' of Jesus in the same way; in this verse, Jesus' unbelieving brothers want him, supported by a large number of such adherents, to appear publicly in Judaea. Jesus in fact made 'disciples' in Jerusalem. These did not belong to the smaller circle of disciples. Among them was Joseph of Arimathaea.

There is an internal reason for the vagueness about the μαθηταί, which is that the concept has already been used, extended and applied to a new situation. This can be seen in those texts referring to discipleship in a way that concerns all those who hear. An example of this is 8:31: 'If you continue in my word, you are truly my disciples.' This statement is addressed to Jews who have become believers, but it is also basically a statement made to the Christian readers of the gospel. Its content is related to that of 8:51, according to which being a disciple of Jesus is receiving and keeping his word. Discipleship and the imitation of Christ have the same origin and belong together and for this reason the statement made in 8:12 has also to be included here: 'He who follows me will not walk in darkness, but will have the light of life.' Clearly, then, the idea of discipleship is transferred to all believers. The man healed of blindness, who, despite the attempts made by the pharisees to prevent him, comes to believe in Jesus, is the type of a disciple of Jesus (see 9:28). Together with those disciples who were present at that time in the upper room at the last supper, the later disciples, that is, all those who joined the community, were also addressed and urged to bear fruit, to show in that way that they were Jesus' disciples (15:8). The mark of discipleship, moreover, is not an external characteristic, but reciprocal love (13:35).

K. H. Rengstorff believes that there are points of contact between the Johannine use of language and certain sections of the Acts of the Apostles in which οἱ μαθηταί occurs regularly as a term for Christians (from 6:1 to 21:16).[6] This is correct in the material sense, but it has to be emphasized rather more strongly that this word was not a firmly established term in the gospel of John. It may possibly be true of the Acts of the Apostles that the title 'disciple' originated as a name which the Palestinian Christians gave themselves, but the situation is different in the case of the gospel of John, in which disciples are firstly Jesus' close companions, secondly his serious adherents and finally all later believers. This extension of the meaning of the term is based on theological reflection and an intended application of the word. This process is in accordance with the evangelist's intentions as regards the group of the disciples at the time of Jesus himself. The later believers are included among Jesus' disciples in any reference to the original disciples chosen by Jesus. This is a procedure of considerable importance in the Johannine understanding of the Church.

2. Ecclesial Expressions and Images

Quite a number of expressions and images which occur in the gospel of John and which are of importance in connection with the idea of the community of believers and the status of community can be cited and have indeed already been quoted and discussed in the books and articles that have been written about this theme. It is very valuable to assemble and examine this material, because the 'individualism' of the fourth gospel with regard to salvation has from time to time been stressed and this would seem to be in a state of tension with the ecclesial aspect of the gospel.[7] It is, of course, true that the singular form is used in the so-called 'soteriological type of discourse'; this is particularly notable in the *ego eimi* sayings (see Excursus 8, Vol. 2, pp. 79–89) and the promise to believers individually. Jesus also calls each individual to make a decision regarding faith. The impression that is given in the gospel, then, is that it presents an individual view and does not emphasize the idea of community. This is, however, a deceptive impression, since the community of faith formed by Jesus himself is never entirely absent. Johannine Christianity is no different from the rest of early Christianity in that it was convinced that Christian existence could not be realized outside or without the community. This is certainly true of the Johannine epistles (see 1 Jn 2:19f; 4:4f; the address in 2 Jn 1; see also 3 Jn 9f). Would the evangelist have thought differently?

In the commentary, I have drawn attention again and again to a fundamental conception, according to which the believer has a certain place in God's plan and in the missionary activity of the Son: in other words, a theological *locus* in which he is able to understand himself as a believer and as one who participates in God's life. The text in which this conception is most clearly revealed is 6:37–40, where the evangelist reflects about faith and the absence of faith. The Father, the Son and the believer are situated here in a frame of reference in which each is referred to the other and each is bound to the other. The Father 'gives' certain men to the Son and takes them to him. The Son rejects none of these people who 'come' to him. The man who 'sees' the Son and believes in him has eternal life, of the kind based on God's saving will. This could be seen as a description of the way of salvation made available to everyone through the revelation of Christ if he follows God's call in Jesus Christ by deciding in favour of faith. This view is in fact implied and the verses are an invitation to faith. If we interpret them in this way, however, we are not doing full justice to the content of this text. The word $\pi\tilde{\alpha}\varsigma$ occurs three times (vv. 37, 39, 40) and points to the great number of those who are called to faith and life (see also 6:45), but there is also something else behind this collaboration between the Father and the Son and the voluntary following of those who believe. This is the idea of the flock, which the Father entrusts to the Son and which the Son is to gather together and protect, carrying out the Father's will. The same ideas appear in the discourse on the shepherd in Chapter 10: the Son calls his own sheep and they follow him (10:3–5), the good shepherd knows his sheep and they know him (10:15) and no one can take them from him because the Father, who gave them to him, keeps his protective hand over them (see 10:28f). Finally, there is an emphatic clarification of this idea in the prayer of the departing Christ in Chapter 17, which again and again stresses the fact that the Father has 'given' the believers gathered around Jesus to the Son and has entrusted them to his protection and keeping. 'Thine they were, and thou gavest them to me, and they have kept thy word' (v. 6). These words are clearly spoken with the many believers in mind, that is, those who in fact remained with Jesus. The departing Christ intercedes in this prayer for them, handing them back to the safe care of the Father (see vv. 11–13). If this great farewell prayer was not in fact composed by the evangelist himself, the vision of the believing community that emerges from it would still be an echo and an adaptation of the evangelist's ideas already expressed earlier in the gospel in the image of the flock.

The image of the shepherd and the flock, which John uses to further his proclamation of Christ, has to a great extent an OT background (see Vol. 2, p. 295). It is planned with Jesus, the true and good shepherd, firmly in mind and the discourse clearly shows his intention to feed and protect the sheep entrusted to him by the Father and his readiness to lay down his life for them. The idea of Israel, the flock chosen by God and handed over to human shepherds, is, despite this orientation towards Jesus, still present in the discourse. The chapter on the shepherd and the flock in Ezekiel (Chapter 34) is particularly relevant here.[8] Because those who were appointed by God to rule over his people have failed in their task, God himself, the owner of the flock, wants to look for his sheep and take care of them (34:11). Both the negative behaviour of the bad shepherd and the good example of the good shepherd provide a model for Jn 10. According to Ezek 34:5–8, God's sheep became the prey of wild animals (cf. the wolf in Jn 10:12) and the shepherds appointed to care for God's flock cared, not for the sheep, but only for themselves (cf. the hired man in vv. 12f). What, then, does God do to save his flock? According to Ezek 34:23f, he appoints one shepherd to be in charge of it. His servant David is to feed the sheep (cf. Jn 10:3, 9) and to care for them (cf. vv. 14f): 'I, the Lord, will be their God and my servant David shall be prince among them.' Jesus is the fulfilment of this messianic promise and the messianic shepherd, in contrast to the leaders of the Jewish people, who have failed. Through Jesus, God intervenes definitively to save his people. It is certainly important in this context not to overlook the special Johannine features in this discourse. These include: Jesus as God's unique representative (ἐγώ εἰμι); his giving of his life, as the shepherd of the flock, for all those entrusted to him (but cf. Zech 13:7–9); and the dissociation of this theme from the idea of the unity of Israel as a people.[9] The Johannine discourse also goes beyond prophecy, which faith experiences with the fulfilment of the promise in question in mind and interprets with reference to other scriptural evidence. The basic structure of prophecy is not abandoned in the Johannine discourse, but it is raised to a new level. The fulfilment of the prophecy is not simply a making explicit of the original promise, but a transposition of it.

The Johannine image of the shepherd and the flock is not fixed in a one-sided way on the person of the shepherd or on the relationship between the shepherd and the individual sheep. It also includes the idea of God's flock, which is, as such, entrusted to the shepherd. Jesus, as the true and good shepherd, has the task of taking those whom God has entrusted to him and who therefore similarly belong to him to the pasture of life. Christ the shepherd cannot be imagined without his, that is, without God's flock. The leader of salvation cannot be considered without the community that is to be saved. This gives an entirely new dimension to the category 'revealer', in that the Johannine Christ mediates God's life to each of those who receives and keeps his words and also, in addition to this, includes them in the community of believers assigned and entrusted to him. The Johannine Christology is in other respects soteriologically orientated, but this new dimension acquired in the discourse on the shepherd and the flock is ecclesiological. The idea of 'predestination' in Johannine thought (see Excursus 11 in Vol. 2, pp. 259–270) is also partly connected with this ecclesiological emphasis, in that the idea of Israel's election is part of this theological view. The Jewish leaders, with whom Jesus is in conflict, do not believe because they are not among Jesus' sheep (10:26). Those who believe see themselves as a new community that belongs to the shepherd, Christ.

The hidden reference to Israel, as the old people of God, can possibly be seen more clearly in the image of the vine and the branches (15:1–8). Although many OT texts in which different images and metaphors are used (for example, those of the vineyard and the vine) have to be considered in connection with this figurative discourse, which, as we have seen, goes back to the evangelist himself, even if Chapter 15 is an editorial composition, the OT background can be regarded as certain (see above, pp. 105–6). In all the relevant texts of the OT, what is under discussion is Israel's having disappointed God's expectations and loving concern. In the Johannine discourse, Jesus is the *true* vine and the disciples are the branches. The whole discourse is orientated towards the disciples' bearing of fruit. They cannot, however, bear fruit if they do not abide in Jesus. Jesus represents Israel, but not simply in himself. He only represents Israel together with the disciples. The Father is the ground and the goal of the event that is described in vivid images in the discourse. He is the vinedresser, who plants, prunes and cleans the vine and the disciples are to bear fruit for his honour. The image of the vine together with the emphatic way of speaking about the disciples' abiding in Jesus and Jesus' abiding in the disciples point even more powerfully than the image of the shepherd to the indissoluble unity existing between Jesus and the community of the disciples. It is also quite clear that an individualistic view is out of the question. For this reason, then, this figurative discourse of the vine and the branches is often held up as demonstrating the Johannine ecclesial tendency and even as the Johannine counterpart to the Pauline doctrine of the body of Christ.[10] Even if the editor or editors placed a stronger emphasis on the community, the figurative discourse itself already contained an inner reference to the community of the disciples.

In these images, then, the close bond between the community of believers and Jesus is very characteristic of the concept of Church in the gospel. The community is not only firmly based on Jesus – it has its permanent existential centre of being in him. This is why the term 'his own' (οἱ ἴδιοι), placed purposefully at the beginning of the second main part of the gospel (13:1), is constitutive in the Johannine community's understanding of itself. This term is also linked with the image of the shepherd in the phrase 'his own sheep' (10:3; see also 10:12) and the words: 'I know my own and my own know me' (10:14). There are also powerful echoes of this idea in the prayer in Jn 17, in which the fact that those who belong to Jesus also belong to God is stressed more than once: 'Thine they were, and thou gavest them to me' (v. 6) and 'All mine are thine and thine are mine' (v. 10). The same idea also has the function of emphasizing the disciples' separation from the world. They are men whom the Father has given to the Son 'out of the world' (v. 6a). The self-understanding of the Johannine community is also expressed in the confrontation between this community and the unbelieving world, as presented in the first epistle (especially 4:4f) and Jn 15:18f. This understanding was deeply rooted in the evangelist's way of thinking and expressed in the term 'his own'. The disciples gathered around Jesus in the upper room at the last supper, that is, the group of faithful disciples who remained with Jesus after the departure of the traitor, are also sharply contrasted in the first saying about the Paraclete (14:16f) with the unbelieving cosmos.

This community of disciples is the final result of God's concern for the world of men who had become estranged from him. With this in mind, the term οἱ ἴδιοι should also be reconsidered in the context of the Logos-hymn. In sending his Son, God offers life and salvation to the whole of humanity. The Logos came 'to his own domain', but 'his own' did not accept him (1:11). The separation that points to judgment for the unbelieving world (see 3:18f; 12:46f) takes place through Jesus' appearance on earth and the proclamation of Christ by the community. Thus, the circle of disciples is narrowed down to the group of faithful disciples or the community of faith. In this process, attention is drawn in the gospel particularly to the representatives of unbelieving Judaism at the time of Jesus or at the time of the evangelist. The fundamental dividing line, however, is between the believing community and the unbelieving 'world'.

K. Haacker has pointed to the ecclesiological significance of the phrase 'children of God'.[11] He regards this term as a traditional concept for the Church that is given a polemical sharpness in the gospel of John. It is traditional in his opinion because it was applied to Israel in the OT (Deut 14:1; Hos 2:1) and was a disputed term between the Church and Israel in the NT (see Rom 9:4, 8; Gal 3:26—4:7). This dispute reaches a climax in John, where the Jews, who call themselves 'children of God', are said to be sons of the devil (8:41–44). Haacker maintains that 'John means that a new community came about, after Israel's failure as the community of God, as the result of an act of acceptance in faith of Jesus and that this new community was given the right to call itself the children of God'.[12] Haacker also thinks that the disputed image of the bridegroom used by John the Baptist (Jn 3:29) probably refers to the

Church. According to him, the image of the bride and the bridegroom, which cannot be proved to have been a metaphor in Judaism for the Messiah and the messianic community, but which was certainly used in the NT, where it is applied in various texts to Christ and the community (2 Cor 11:2; Eph 5:22–33; Rev 19:7, 9, etc.), is based at least to some extent on 2 Sam 17:3 (LXX), in which Ahithophel uses a similar image.[13] Even without Haacker's observations, I was of the opinion that the evangelist was, in this text, referring to the messianic community in the image of the bride (see Vol. 1, pp. 416f).

These reflections about expressions and images in the gospel of John only confirm the fundamentally ecclesial tendency of Johannine thinking, which is clearly revealed especially in the important image of the shepherd and the flock (and in that of the vine). The idea of the establishment of a new community of God by Jesus is in fact more firmly present in the gospel than it would be at first sight seem to be. We have now to turn to the question of the understanding that the Johannine community had of the idea of a universal Church and the development of that idea during the last decades of the first century AD, and at the same time we have to try to define this idea of a community of Christ or Church more precisely.

3. The Johannine Community and the Universal Church

The opinion has often been expressed that the evangelist had a Church of the 'elect' or the 'children of God' in mind, consisting of members who had to be gathered 'out of the world'. Ernst Käsemann insisted that 'according to John, the Christian mission does not in fact apply to the world as such, but to those who are given to Christ in the world by the Father, that is, the elect and those called to faith . . . The world, then, is only the object of that mission in so far as it is a question of gathering the elect.'[14] In Käsemann's view, then, the Johannine community was an inward-turning, esoteric group that was withdrawn from the world of unbelievers. It was, in other words, a 'Christian mystery-community'.[15] In my exegesis of Jn 17, we saw that there is some reason to support this notion in the statements relating to the community, but that it does not do full justice to the text of the chapter. It is not possible to pursue here the question of the dangerous and even distorted attitudes and teachings that might result from a Christianity that so radically deflected from the world. I have to confine myself to the fundamental question as to whether the Johannine idea of the Church was open to the notion of universality, and whether Johannine Christianity could be integrated into the greater Church that was coming into being.

Jn 10:16 provides us with a good point of departure for a Church consisting of Jews and gentiles: 'I have other sheep, that are not of this fold; I must bring them also, and they will heed my voice. So there will be one flock, one shepherd.' This text has, it is true, been frequently disputed from the point of view of literary criticism, mainly because it breaks the connection between vv. 15 and 17, but, as we have seen in the commentary on this text (see *ad loc.*), it is quite possible to extend the horizon to those called from among the gentiles in this particular text in the discourse on the shepherd and the flock. The contents of this statement are also supported by 11:52, a text for which there is no reason to doubt that it originated with the evangelist, since it is his commentary on the 'prophecy' of the high priest. The idea of gathering the scattered ones is supported by a very firm prophetic tradition, which employed it to announce the restoration and reunion of the twelve tribes of the people of God at the time of salvation (see *ad loc.*). In Is 43:6, for example, the children of Israel, gathered together from far and wide, that is, from the Jewish diaspora, are also called God's 'sons and daughters'. It is clear, then, that the 'children of God' in Jn 11:52 is not an entirely new conception; it is simply a concept transferred to the new level of Christian understanding. K. Haacker has even suggested that 'the "children of God" are related to the previously mentioned Jewish people as they are in 1:12 to the ἴδιοι in 1:11. Here, however, in 11:52, the missionary communities are meant by the addition διεσκορπισμένα and these have to be distinguished from the Palestinian Church.'[16] It would be wrong to interpret the general concept of 'children of God' in the sense of the 'elect' here. The evangelist is thinking in this context of the gentiles, who form the Church of God that was established at the death of Christ together with the believing Jews.

It is clear from the negative evidence that the word for 'choose' is only encountered in the gospel with a very restricted meaning that it is quite wrong to attribute an exclusive and spiritual significance to the community of the 'chosen' ones in Jn 11:52. The word is almost entirely confined to the choosing or election of the twelve by Jesus and in this it obviously follows the synoptic tradition (6:70; 13:18); see also 15:16). It is only in 15:19 that the word is used in the sense of choosing 'out of the world', but even then it is still applied to Jesus as the one who chooses (see Vol. 2, p. 260). It is not possible to find anywhere in the gospel of John a divine predestination and election of certain men to a circle of perfect, enlightened beings in the gnostic sense, that is, men who come to themselves, rise up and are saved by gnosis. It would be much more correct to say that this election takes place 'in the history of the life of the disciples and God's only means of choosing is through Jesus'.[17] This, then, is the negative evidence. It is also possible to provide positive evidence of the Johannine understanding of the 'scattered children of God'.

The chapter on Jesus' revelation of himself in Samaria gives us, at least to some extent, a model for the acceptance of men and women into the community of Christ. Apart from the dialogue with the Samaritan woman, which has a distinctive content because of the themes discussed in it, there is also the passage on the addition of the inhabitants of Sychar, in other words, of a Samaritan community (4:49–42). It must continue to be an open question whether there are historical reminiscences and interests that play a part in this chapter (the Church in Samaria). What we know with relative certainty is that it was a missionary example for John. The theme of 'mission' is deliberately discussed in the intervening conversation with the disciples (vv. 31–38) and the idea of universality is expressed in the Samaritans' final confession: 'This is indeed the Saviour of the world' (v. 42). The statement about the gathering together of the scattered children of God (11:52) should also be situated within this context.[18]

Just as the Samaritans are included within the new people of God, so too are the Greeks. The 'misunderstanding' among the people of Jerusalem that Jesus intends to go 'to the dispersion among the Greeks and teach the Greeks' (7:35) was for the evangelist and his knowledgeable readers a hidden prophecy similar to that made by Caiaphas. It meant that Jesus would enter the Greek territory of the diaspora by means of those proclaiming the Christian faith and gain Greeks, gentile Hellenists and others for his teaching and message (see *ad loc.*). The evangelist raises this ominous preview of the mission to the Greeks to the level of certainty for his Christian readers in a later episode. Greek pilgrims also come to the final passover feast reported by the evangelist and state their desire to see Jesus (12:20ff). These pilgrims are a sign of hope for the Christian mission to the Greeks. The meaning of this scene is similar to that of the chapter set in Samaria. The historical event, the circumstances and the number of those who come to see Jesus are not important in themselves. The encounter with the Greeks is not even completed as a narrative. The datum, which is rooted in Jesus' life on earth, is as such a pointer to the later period of the early Christian mission.

The evangelist proceeded carefully, thoughtfully and with a great deal of literary skill in his presentation because it was not at all easy for him to include these scenes in his gospel. He has in fact extended an episode on a journey to make it a theological lesson (chapter 4) and a timid desire expressed by some Greek pilgrims to the feast is used as a 'peg' for an extremely important theological prospect (12:23f). This fading of the idea of mission into Jesus' activity on earth is all the more remarkable when it is borne in mind that the evangelist bases that mission and its success for the first time on Jesus' death. The statement about the gathering of the scattered children of God follows the prophecy of Jesus' death and that gathering is only possible because his death has a universal power to save. This is yet another argument against the idea of election that is found in Gnosticism and in the Jewish apocalyptic writings. Jesus' death and the Christian proclamation of that death lead directly to the formation of the community of salvation. Anyone who wishes to belong to that community has to make a decision in faith. This idea is developed very clearly in 12:23f, 32f, that is, in the last section of the first main part, which prepares the way for the passion of Jesus and its significance in the Johannine view. With the Greeks who were looking for him in mind, Jesus speaks about the grain of corn that must fall into the earth and 'die' if it is to bear abundant fruit. (v. 24). The hour of his death – his 'exaltation' on the cross, is to be the hour of his glorification (cf. 12:23 with 32). This can be seen in that he will draw all men to himself as the 'exalted' Christ (v. 32). It is not necessary to examine this section in detail here (for this, see the commentary *ad loc.*), since, even without this, it should be clear that the universal mission is behind this idea.

It should also be evident that the evangelist does not place the community in a sharply delineated space. On the contrary, it is situated in the missionary field of early Christianity, which has no boundaries. There can be little doubt that the Johannine community owed its existence to the activity of early Christian missionaries. At the same time, however, it was not closed itself to the idea of mission. It may not be possible to know to what extent it was able to develop a missionary activity of its own, but its attitude can hardly be interpreted as a mere readiness to accept the children of God who came to it. Such a view would be drawing wrong conclusions from the evangelist's Christological interpretation, namely that all missionary success is the result of the death of Jesus. After all, this does not in any way mean that Jesus did not send out his disciples to harvest the fruit of the mission (see 4:38). The evangelist's authorship cannot be rejected in the case of every text that contains the idea of mission (see, for example, 17:18; 20:21), nor can these texts be differently interpreted in the case of the evangelist from the way that they were understood by the editor or editors (see 17:20). His Christological interest means that the emphasis was different. It does not mean that the idea of mission was completely absent.

It is not possible to learn from the gospel itself what contacts the Johannine community may have had with other communities. The sphere of the Church is, however, extended a little if we take the additional editorial chapter into consideration as well. I accept, together with many other exegetes, that chapter 21 has an 'ecclesial' character and refers to the community. (For details of this aspect, see the commentary below.) The acceptance of the tradition of Peter (his being appointed to the pastoral office and his death as a martyr) shows that the Johannine community recognized the authority of this leading disciple who had, at least in certain spheres, exercised a normative influence and who continued to have power beyond the time of his death and possibly even more power after his death as the Lord's delegate.[19] In connection with our particular problem, this is a clear indication that the Johannine community wanted to remain in contact with other early Christian circles. Whatever its geographical location may have been, it certainly did not lead an isolated existence, but rather had an orientation towards the greater Church, in spite of its special traditions and its connection with the 'disciple whom Jesus loved'. The same chapter 21, as we shall see in the detailed exegesis below, also contains other indications of its links with early Christian life and thought elsewhere. The net with the one hundred and fifty-three great fish that did not break (21:11) is a symbol for the many believers and at the same time a symbol of their unity. If we accept the symbolic value of this datum, then it is surely one of the most striking images and most attractive examples of the Church as a reality that is constantly expanding, but at the same time keeps together. What is more, this symbol of the unbroken net with the great catch is one given to us by the Johannine community, which was on the 'fringe' of Christianity at that time and later. The eucharistic aspect of the meal scene (21:12f) also reveals a self-understanding on the part of the Johannine community that it shared with other communities in early Christianity of the period that are known to us. The eucharistic meal is the centre of its inner life, a lasting encounter with its Lord, the sign of fellowship, an exhortation to love the brethren and a source of strength in its existence in the world.

There are many possible reasons why these ideas in the gospel of John are not immediately visible, but continue to be hidden. One is that it is essential to bear in mind the evangelist's primarily Christological view and his intention to provide the community with a deep vision of Christ as well as his aim to strengthen its members in their struggle for faith and their attempt to preserve their own faith. The editors of the gospel were more concerned with the inner life of the community and its needs and problems. At the same time, they were also very anxious to make the community closely acquainted with the profound ideas of the evangelist himself. In all these intentions, the community's life and understanding of itself were presupposed. Finally, the gospel of John was not primarily a missionary or propaganda document, but a work written for the community itself and concerned with its faith in Christ (see the commentary on 20:30f). It should therefore not be difficult to understand that the Church did not constitute the dominant theme of the gospel, even though it was one of its constant perspectives.

The Arrest of Jesus and his Trial before the Jews
(Chapter 18:1–27)

INTRODUCTION TO THE JOHANNINE PASSION NARRATIVE

The depiction in John of Jesus' passion as following his last meeting with his disciples in the setting of a meal (13:2), shows, unmistakably, the individuality of John's theology and his dramatic skill. Theologically, it is nothing other than the carrying through of the idea of the 'lifting up' or exaltation of Jesus (3:14; 8:28; 12:32f). His majesty or, more precisely, his royal and divine dignity, is brought out in precisely that event which was regarded by the earlier evangelists and other theologians as the nadir of his humiliation. From the time of the earliest Church, there was a concern to lighten the sombre suffering of Jesus, to give a deeper meaning to his ignominious death. With the Old Testament as source, various starting-points were found (the suffering of the righteous, the atoning servant of God, God's hidden wisdom in the foolishness of the cross, and so on), in order to come to terms theologically with this cruel and incomprehensible happening. For believers it was continually, in some way or other, illumined by what came after: God's justification of Jesus; the raising of the crucified One; the certainty of his coming in glory; his enthronement in the power of God. But no theologian had yet undertaken to let Jesus' glory shine directly through the degrading case brought against him, his road of suffering and his death on the cross. This paradoxical viewpoint was left to the fourth evangelist who was inspired by and equipped for it through his theological approach of framing everything in the presence of his Christ. This basic element in his thinking sets an indelible seal on his description of the passion.

Of course, other special themes come to the fore in John's account of the passion, such as the weight of polemic against the leading Jews, Jesus' confrontation of Pilate as the representative of the Gentiles and a way of thought limited by the 'world', the paschal typology, and others; but all this is part of and subordinate to the main concern – the opening of spiritual eyes to the mysterious enthronement of Jesus on the cross, his consequent 'exaltation' there, and his hidden conquest of the power of evil. The cross is Jesus' throne (19:14, 19), his last breath, the completion of his work (19:30). The main reason John's portrayal of the passion of Jesus is distinctively his own, is Christological. In the *literary structure,* the evangelist's skill can once more be observed in the composition of single short scenes (in the trial before Pilate no fewer than seven) which, together, form an intensified dramatic whole (cf., similarly, in Chapters 4, 7, 9). The passage of events moves the story forward to its undoubted main objective, the trial before Pilate, which reaches a climax whenever Jesus speaks. Even in the preordained course of Jesus' 'hour', even, so to speak, in the sign-language of the events, the voice of the one who reveals becomes the all-explanatory and enlightening mediator of a deeper meaning (cf. 18:5ff; 20, 36f; 19:11, 30). The omission of traditional material which could hardly have been unknown to the evangelist also demands our attention. As far as the Jewish proceedings against Jesus are concerned, the evangelist confines himself to the hearing before Annas (18:19–23), with only a brief mention of despatch to the high priest Caiaphas (18:24), and has Jesus immediately handed over to the Roman judges (18:28). The omission of the 'official' Jewish proceedings is best explained as an intentional literary construction. Because this omission is compensated for by the extended theatre with rapid scene-changes which takes place in front of and inside the Roman praetorium (18:28—19:16), and it is there that the official representatives of Judaism ('the Jews') are given chance enough to speak. They utter their thoughts, say why they condemn Jesus and demand his death, before the Roman judges, before the forum of world public opinion. The secret Jewish investigation is left out intentionally in order to make the enemies of Jesus appear all together on a single stage, and ultimately to arraign them before God's tribunal. Similar intentional abbreviations, so that something else more important for the evangelist should be discussed, are to be supposed in the case of the comparatively short account of the walk to the cross and Jesus' sufferings on it (19:17–30).

If, to this extent, the whole Johannine passion narrative from the taking prisoner to the death of Jesus shows the indelible characteristics of the evangelist's hand, it can, nevertheless, not be denied that here John rehandled traditions used in an account of the passion which he probably had in front of him. This older and not infrequently stated supposition has won greater support through more recent, precise investigation,[1] even though we have to remain aware of the difficulties and limitations of the methods used, such as comparison of the synoptics, literary and stylistic criticism, classification according to the history of tradition, and so on.[2] John's tendencies can certainly be made even clearer by sifting out a *pre-Johannine passion narrative*; however, its extent and word-order can only be reconstructed approximately and with gaps, since many fragments were possibly suppressed by the evangelist and many sentences substituted by his own statements. His language forms such a thick layer over everything, that even careful stylistic research as well as comparisons with both non-Johannine and Johannine material often make no certain conclusions possible. Methods come up against border-line cases in which lack of clarity in matters of language and style prevents further progress. With individual sections of the text, we shall have to look on each occassion both at what the evangelist possibly had in front of him and at his own composition; but we can only form a complete judgment at the end; this is also true of the beginning and extent of the 'source' (to the death of Jesus? to the laying in the tomb? to the reports concerning the tomb and the appearances?). However, our highest aim remains a deeper understanding of the text before us from the viewpoint of the evangelist.

The *division* of the Johannine passion narrative both as a whole and within its shorter units, is totally clear:

1. The arrest of Jesus, 18:1–11.
   (a) The arrival of the arrest troop under the leadership of Judas in the garden beyond the Kidron, 18:1–3.
   (b) Jesus's behaviour before the soldiers, 18:4–9.
   (c) Peter's sword-stroke and Jesus' answer, 18:10–11.

2. The examination by Annas and Peter's denial, 18:12–27.
   (a) The bringing of Jesus before Annas, 18:12–14.
   (b) Peter's entry into the court of the high priest and his first denial of Jesus, 18:15–18.
   (c) Annas's hearing and the sending of Jesus to Caiaphas, 18:19–24.
   (d) The second and third denials of Jesus by Peter, 18:25–27.

3. The trial before Pilate, 18:28—19:16a.
   (a) The handing over of Jesus to Pilate, 18:28–32.
   (b) First examination of Jesus by Pilate in the praetorium, 18:33–38a.
   (c) Pronouncement of Jesus' innocence by Pilate and offer to release him instead of Barabbas, 18:38b–40.
   (d) Scourging and mocking of Jesus in the praetorium, 19:1–3.
   (e) Presentation of Jesus as mock-king. Further declarations of his innocence by Pilate and demands by the Jews he be crucified, 19:4–7.
   (f) Pilate's second examination of Jesus, his attempt to release him, and the objection of the Jews, 19:8–12.
   (g) The condemnation of Jesus to death on the cross, 19:13–16a.

4. Crucifixion and death of Jesus, 19:16b–30.
   (a) Crucifixion on Golgotha, 19:16b–18.
   (b) The title on the cross and the dispute about it, 19:19–22.
   (c) The sharing out of Jesus' clothes and the casting of lots for his tunic, 19:23–24.
   (d) The women at the cross, the words of Jesus to his mother, and to the beloved disciple, 19:25–27.
   (e) The drinking of the vinegar and the death of Jesus, 19:28–30.

5. The piercing of Jesus' side and his laying in the tomb, 19:31–42.
   (a) The piercing of Jesus' side, 19:31–37.
   (b) The preparation of Jesus' corpse and the burial, 19:38–42.

Since the first two textual units belong more closely together and the trial of Jesus before Pilate is set off in sharper relief, they will form only two sections of the commentary. Similarly, the last two sections (crucifixion and burial) can be dealt with together. In this way the long passages of the text, as befits the importance of the space they occupy, should stand out even more clearly, even though they are connected and share certain notions throughout.

1. The Arrest of Jesus (18:1–11)

[1]When Jesus had spoken these words, he went forth with his disciples to the other side of the Kidron brook, where there was a garden, which he and his disciples entered. [2]Now Judas, who betrayed him, also knew the place; for Jesus often met there with his disciples. [3]Judas came there with the troop of soldiers and servants from the chief priests and pharisees, with torches and lanterns and weapons. [4]Then Jesus, knowing all that was to befall him, went out and said to them, 'Whom do you seek?' [5]They answered him, 'Jesus of Nazareth'. Jesus said to them, 'I am he'. [6]When he said to them, 'I am he', they drew back and fell to the ground. [7]Again he asked them, 'Whom do you seek?' And they said, 'Jesus of Nazareth'. [8]Jesus answered, 'If you seek me, let these men go'. [9]This was to fulfil the word which he had spoken, 'Of those whom thou gavest me I lost not one'. [10]Then Simon Peter, having a sword, drew it and struck the high priest's slave and cut off his right ear. The slave's name was Malchus. [11]Jesus said to Peter, 'Put your sword into its sheath; shall I not drink the cup which the Father has given me?'

John's account of the passion begins straightaway with the arrest of Jesus. Thus, he leaves out the prayer-struggle and Jesus' horror of death in Gethsemane described by all the synoptics. As is plain from 12:27f (see *ad loc.*) such an account was not unknown to the fourth evangelist. However, he has purposely taken it out of the passion narrative, using it earlier in an altered form, because anguish of the soul in the case of Jesus does not fit his idea of the 'passion' of Jesus. The arrest-scene, which, for the synoptics, shows Jesus' composure and greatness, his conscious acceptance of suffering (cf. Mk 14:42, 48f), is intensified by John as a revelation of Jesus' power and majesty (cf. vv. 4–8). It is true that the traditional elements in the story (time and place, the betrayer, the sword-thrust of a disciple), are used in the account, but they are subordinated to this main purpose.[3]

18:1   After the link ταῦτα εἰπών which is typical of the evangelist's style (cf. 7:9; 9:6; 11:43; 13:21; with τοῦτο 18:38; 20:20, 22 – but 17:1 is different) and probably originally joined it to 14:31, he describes Jesus' departure with his disciples for the place of the arrest. The Mount of Olives, at the foot of which it was to be found, is nowhere named in John's gospel (save in the non-Johannine pericope 8:1). Against this, John adds two facts to the synoptics which show him to have a good knowledge of the area: The group, taking a walk at night, cross the brook called *Kidron*[4] and arrive in a *garden*. This defining of the place fits in well with the 'piece of land' or 'estate' ($\chi\omega\rho\acute{\iota}o\nu$), which Mk/Mt mention and for which they hand down the name 'Gethsemane' ('oil-press').[5] John's specific expressions originate, for certain, from the pre-Johannine account. It is important for the evangelist that the disciples accompany and enter the garden with Jesus,[6] because in the arrest-scene Jesus shows particular concern for them (vv. 8b–9).

18:2   Likewise, the remark about Judas, who is always otherwise (except in 13:29 where 13:26 is briefly echoed) called the 'Iscariot' or son of 'Simon Iscariot', was probably already in the source. This explains why the traitor could find Jesus. Analogous to the comment that Jesus often met there with his disciples[7] is Lk 22:39 ('as was his custom') which perhaps allows the conclusion that the pre-Johannine account was connected with Luke's special source used by the latter for the scene on the Mount of Olives (cf. also the angel, Lk 22:43 with Jn 12:29b).

18:3   The arrest troop which Judas brings consists of two groups, the 'cohort' or 'detachment' ($\sigma\pi\epsilon\tilde{\iota}\rho\alpha$) and servants from the chief priests and pharisees ($\dot{\epsilon}\varkappa$). The main discussion is about the first group: is it the Roman cohort (about 600 strong) stationed in the Antonia fortress (or a maniple of about 200), or is it the Jewish temple police composed of Levites?

The article indicates a known and definite size. The $\sigma\pi\epsilon\tilde{\iota}\rho\alpha$ is commanded by a $\chi\iota\lambda\acute{\iota}\alpha\rho\chi o\varsigma$ (v. 12). Given normal NT usage, the Roman occupiers under a military tribune must be intended. In the LXX these Roman terms are also used with the non-Roman military ($\sigma\pi\epsilon\tilde{\iota}\rho\alpha$ Jud 14:11; 2 Macc 8:23;12:20, 22. $\chi\iota\lambda\acute{\iota}\alpha\rho\chi o\varsigma$ occurs twenty-nine times for civil or military officials). It is the same in Josephus (*Ant.*, XVII, 215; *Bellum*, II, 11).[8] Thus the evangelist or his source could have used these expressions for the military-style temple police.[9]

There is agreement that the Romans' taking part in the arrest of Jesus is as good as impossible. The Johannine narrative itself speaks against it. The Roman commander could hardly have brought Jesus to the former high priest Annas who had been deposed by the Romans; besides, it is most unlikely that such a powerful military force would have been used to arrest a single person. However, there are difficulties in the way of the idea, at least as far as the Johannine narrative is concerned, that the Jewish temple police are referred to: they would have had to have been sent out just as the servants by the 'chief priests' (to whose number the captain of the temple also belonged); further, in v. 12, the soldiers with their commander are expressly distinguished from the servants 'of the Jews', so the evangelist certainly regarded this $\sigma\pi\epsilon\tilde{\iota}\rho\alpha$ as Roman. Whether Pilate knew anything of the move is not absolutely clear from 18:29ff. However, it may be supposed that the underlying source had in mind the Jewish police.[10] The second group, that of 'servants', probably refers to court officials who worked for the Sanhedrin (cf. to 7:32), and also servants in the houe of the high priest (cf. 18:10, 26). Only the expression 'chief priests and pharisees', to describe the highest Jewish judicial authority, is a Johannine formula (cf. 7:32, 45; 11:47, 57). There is no historical objection against this being the composition of the group making the arrest, in which case it cannot have been all that big. Furthermore, the equipment of torches, lanterns and weapons (expressions other than those used by the synoptics) is appropriate for night-time. The source, then, would have described the affair not unconvincingly.

But why did the evangelist insinuate the participation of the Romans and, on top of that, in such great numbers? Just as at Jesus' trial he gathers together on one stage the Jewish leaders and the Roman judges, and just as he burdens the Jews more heavily (cf. 19:11b), so he gives a share to the representative of the gentiles, of the faithless world opposed to God (cf. 18:37f; 19:9ff): in the same way, even at the time of the arrest, he would have Jesus confront the whole unbelieving cosmos. His 'report' becomes a theological representation.[11] What happens in the foreground reveals a deep insight of faith for which historical exactitude is unimportant. At the same time, the reverse holds for the scene of the arrest in the case of the crucifixion, where the unprejudiced reader at first gains the impression that the Jews were the executioner's assistants (cf. 19:16 in context). With such a type of story-telling, a verdict such as 'mistake' or 'deception' is quite out of place.

18:4   Jesus is not surprised by the action taken against him. He had pressed Judas to do his deed (13:27) and he now goes out of the garden to meet the crowd brought by Judas – the synoptics say that Judas hurries forward to Jesus while he is still speaking to the disciples who are there (Mk 14:43 par.). It is clear that in John the initiative passes to Jesus, which is why Judas' kiss is left out. The evangelist's hand becomes altogether visible in the remark: 'Since Jesus knew everything,[11a] that had to befall him'; for with this the evangelist picks up the fundamental phrase in 13:1 about Jesus' knowledge concerning the 'hour' determined for him by the Father. From the very beginning, Jesus' suprahuman knowledge (cf. 1:47f; 2:24f) is so much part of John's picture of him (cf. also 6:61, 64), including concrete events (cf. 4:17f; 6:6; 11:11; 12:27), that even his knowing beforehand 'everything of that which had to befall him' is not surprising. To Jesus' knowledge of the future at the beginning of the passion, there corresponds πάντα τετέλεσται (19:28) at its close. When Jesus there, in addition, takes the drink of vinegar 'to fulfil the scripture', he shows his intention of actively accepting all the sufferings pre-ordained for him. The 'which was to befall him',[12] is no perverse destiny, but the suffering revealed to him beforehand by the Father (cf. 19:11b) down to the details. The comparison with 19:28ff also shows that John's account does not spring from an apologetic tendency (against the objections of the Jews),[13] rather, at least in the main thrust, it is Christologically inclined towards a positive delineation of the figure of Christ.

Jesus' question, 'Whom do you seek?' could, in itself, have belonged to the pre-Johannine account. However, it introduces the following scene containing Jesus' sovereign response, hence, it will have been constructed *ad hoc* by the evangelist.

18:5   The armed men answer briefly: 'Jesus the Nazarene.' Here the much discussed term Ναζωραῖος[14] can only describe origin. The same form of the word in the inscription 19:19 allows one to conclude that it also appears in the pre-Johannine document. But it does not yet allow the assumption that the evangelist found the short exchange in his source. Jesus' question and his answer in v. 5b are so closely related to the mention of the name, that the scene has certainly been wholly put together by the evangelist (in place of relying on the traitor's evidence). Nevertheless, the use of the name could have appeared in a part of the source text which has been omitted.[15]

Jesus answered only with ἐγώ εἰμι, which is appropriate stylistically in the situation, so as to identify himself as the one for whom they were looking; but for the readers of the gospel he answered in accordance with the wholly god-like majesty bound up with this formula (cf. Excursus 8, Vol. 2, pp. 79–89). That this was the evangelist's intention is confirmed by the effect, in v. 6, of Jesus' self-revelation. The saying's central position in the story marks the climax: Jesus is not handed over powerless, but he is the one who surrenders himself and thereby proves his power. The accusing and explanatory words of Jesus in the synoptics (Mk 14:48f par.) are omitted; in their place comes a dramatic event which directly uncovers the deeper meaning.

Superficially, the statement that the traitor Judas was also standing with the armed men seems odd – it was he that had brought them (v. 3). Is this an editorial addition made in order to draw attention to him once again? But the evangelist is fond of using ἕστηκα,[16] and for him too the reference can have a meaning. Has Judas to be marked out more clearly as one who does not belong to those whom the Father has given to Jesus (cf. v. 9), but who stands on the side of the adversary? As it follows Jesus' sovereign statement, another explanation is nearer at hand: the moment has now arrived when Jesus' prophecy in the supper room is fulfilled, that the one eating his bread lifts his heel against him (13:18); the disciples are to believe, when it happens, that Jesus rightly says: ἐγώ εἰμι (13:19).

18:6   The effect of Jesus' majestic words is the drawing back and falling to the ground of the armed men. This dramatic moment can be explained neither in a psychologically rationalistic way, as if they were falling over each other in dismay; nor can it be considered as an amazing miracle which might have happened thus. Rather, it is a means of presentation used by the evangelist in accordance with already existing ideas and his Christological viewpoint.

The theme is widely found in biblical and post-biblical thought, though in different connections. A falling down as 'before the epiphany of Deity' (Bultmann) might be suggested by the revelation formula ἐγώ εἰμι. But here only the enemies of Jesus fall to the ground, so that it is not quite the same as the behaviour of those receiving a revelation, cf. Ezek 1:28; 44:4; Dan 10:9; Rev 1:17; 19:10; 22:8; also Paul according to Acts 9:4; 22:7; 26:14. The *mysterium tremendum* alone, which overpowers those involved with it, binds all these texts together. In addition, there is another theme: the powerlessness of the enemies when confronted with the might of God, and the power of those who belong to God. We may compare it with the story of Elijah in 2 Kg 1:9–14, according to which the soldiers who were dispatched are destroyed. Closer still is the description in *Gen Rabbah* 91:6: seventy Egyptians are to arrest Simeon; as soon as they hear his voice, they fall on their faces while gnashing their teeth.[17] Finally, the power given to the Messiah comes to mind. Thus, it says in Is 11:4: 'He shall smite the impudent with the rod of his mouth, and with the breath of his lips he shall slay the wicked.'[18] And in the Apocrypha further colour is added (cf. *2 Esd* 13:3f; *Hebrew Book of Elijah* 6:1f). The evangelist will have been inspired less by eschatological-apocalyptic descriptions than by OT-biblical ideas. For the words used, cf. Ps 27 (26):2: 'My adversaries and foes, they shall stumble and fall (ἔπεσαν)'; Ps 35 (34):4: 'Let them be turned back and confounded (ἀποστραφήτωσαν εἰς τὰ ὀπίσω) who devise evil against me!'[18a]

In point of fact, the same theme is found in 7:46 when the officers sent out by the council do not carry out the order for the arrest (7:32), because the way in which Jesus spoke made an extraordinary impression on them. Just as earlier attempts to lay hands on Jesus went wrong because 'his hour had not yet come' (7:30; 8:20; cf. 7:44), so now that it has arrived, and Jesus gives himself up to the envoys, his greatness, which they cannot touch, is again to be demonstrated.

18:7-8 Only Jesus himself can allow the soldiers and slaves to take him. For that reason, he once again asks: 'Whom do you seek?' and then hands himself over to them, at the same time asking them to let his disciples go. There is great narrative skill in this *indirect* encouragement of his own arrest.[19] Not for a second does Jesus lose his spiritual superiority, just as, later on, he surrenders neither to physical force (cf. 18:23) nor to threats by the authorities (cf. 19:10f). Even at this hour he shows himself the shepherd of those who belong to him, who cares that nothing evil happens to his disciples. The disciples' behaviour which the synoptics, at least, also take into consideration (Mk/Mt: flight; Lk: readiness to defend [22:49] no flight), is no longer debatable in John. Even the sword-stroke taken over from the tradition serves only to allow Jesus to speak the words about the destiny pre-ordained for him by the Father (v. 11). The request by Jesus for the release of his disciples is explained with difficulty, or at best, only in part, by the evangelist's apologetic intention.[20] The foreknowledge of his destiny and the failure of the disciples are stressed rather in an attempt to strengthen the faith of the Church. In the same way, the intervention of Jesus on behalf of his disciples is primarily intended to deepen the picture of Christ.

18:9 The intention to show Jesus in the rôle of the good shepherd who, voluntarily, chooses death (cf. 10:18) so as to save the life of his sheep (cf. 10:11, 15, 28), becomes obvious with the comment in v. 9. The passage which contains Jesus' words cannot be established with certainty: 'Of those whom thou gavest me,[21] I lost not one.'

Three passages may be considered in this connection: 6:39, where the same thought appears to be a duty of Jesus' but where the fact that none is lost by him is not stated; 10:28, where the concern of the shepherd, Jesus, is mentioned as a fact, though without the emphatic 'not one of them'; 17:12, where this last point is underlined, but in the passive ('none of them is lost') and with the addition 'but the son of perdition'. Should the last passage be intended, then v. 9 would be simply an editorial addition.[22] However, the quotations which refer to the words of Jesus, are often imprecise (cf. 6:35, 65; 10:25, 36; 11:40); thus, 10:28 considered together with 6:39, could come into question. In 18:32 there is, likewise, a summary in the form of a reference back to something earlier (cf. 12:33 with 3:14). It is not necessary to attribute such remarks other than to the evangelist (cf. also 2:22; 11:13, 51; 12:16, and others). Jesus' words are already handled like quotations from the OT, with the introductory formula ἵνα πληρωθῇ (cf. 12:38; 13:18; 15:25; 19:24, 36).

There is a problem in that, in the image of the shepherd, the sheep are guarded from eternal perdition, whereas here the concern is to save the disciples from the threatened loss of their physical life. Speculations that the disciples, by being arrested and killed, could also stray from their belief in Jesus, are far-fetched (cf. against this 12:25f!). But, similarly, the thought that physical salvation is to be a 'symbolic anticipation' of eternal salvation (B. Lindars) is not indicated. The combination of ideas is best explained by the Christological tendency to emphasize the concern of the shepherd, Jesus, which affects every aspect. In 10:28f too, the sentence, 'no one shall snatch them out of my hand (or) out of the Father's hand', has something of a double meaning: No one can tear the believers away from Jesus, that is, can separate them from his Church, and Jesus gives them eternal life (cf. *ad loc.*).

18:10   After the 'release' of the disciples effected by Jesus, the intrusion of Simon-Peter and his ready use of the sword are disturbing, and affect the flow of the story as well. In Mk/Mt the servants lay hands on Jesus, at which 'one of those who stood by' draws a sword (in Lk 22:49 those who are with Jesus want to use their swords when they notice 'what would follow'). That is a logical description of the events. When John brings in the scene at this point, he thereby on the one hand shows his dependence on a tradition, and, on the other hand, he indicates a different narrative intention. He does not bring in the episode of the sword-stroke out of interest in the disciples' resistance, but only for the sake of the subsequent saying of Jesus. His narration goes beyond that of the synoptics in two ways: the man using the sword is identified as Simon-Peter, and the high priest's slave is named Malchus.[23] Already, Luke mentions that this man's *right* ear is cut off (22:50); but then again, John does not say that Jesus healed it again, as reported by Luke (22:51).

What can be determined from this about the tradition which John was using? The independence of what he hands down is deduced from the name of the servant, who is referred to again in 18:26. The source was obviously close to Lk without being directly dependent on this gospel. The addition suggests a development to a relatively late stage.[24] One question is whether the evangelist already found the name of Simon-Peter determined by his source, or whether he himself was responsible. The use of both names is characteristic for him; on the other hand, there is no special reason why he was interested at this point in Peter, unless in his rôle as spokesman for the group of disciples (6:68f), or his assurance in 13:37. But both belong to the tradition, so that Peter's identification with the one who took the sword can, similarly, already be made there. If the servant who was struck was named there, it is very likely that the one who struck him should be mentioned by name.[25]

18:11 Jesus' reply to Peter, which completes John's account of the arrest scene, again has a theological emphasis. Jesus accepts, willingly and knowingly, the journey to his death ordained for him by his Father. For this, John again uses traditional material which, in this case, is most akin to Mt. The order to put the sword back in its sheath is found only in the Matthaean pericope of the arrest (26:52) where, however, it proceeds differently.[26] The metaphor cup (of death)[27] with roots in the OT, which occurs in the synoptics again in another passage, namely, Jesus' answer to the sons of Zebedee (Mk 10:38f; Mt 20:22f), has its origin in the prayer-struggle of Jesus in Gethsemane (Mk 14:36 par.). John's version is nearer to Mt to the extent that Mt 26:42 is a repetition which explicitly speaks of *drinking* the cup. But John formulates the saying in his own way ('the cup which the Father has given me'), and it sounds more determined in his version: Jesus not only surrenders to the Father's will, but takes it over with total conviction.

John also probably found the saying about the cup in the context of the prayer-struggle of Jesus at the Mount of Olives which he, however, reproduces in a shortened and altered version at an earlier point (12:27f). John found the traditional saying of Jesus addressing God as Father to be appropriate as Jesus' answer to Peter.

The disciple lays about him violently, whereupon Jesus, who possesses divine power and nevertheless gives himself up to his enemies, teaches Peter the lesson that God's will is supreme. Peter, the leading man among the disciples, just as in the synoptic scene at Caesarea Philippi (Mk 8:33 par.) is made to represent human understanding which does not grasp God's plan. Peter's opposition, which there is suppressed by John (cf. 6:70), breaks out here at the time of the arrest of Jesus and is rejected by him. This pregnant question closes (similarly also in 18:23, 38) John's brilliantly-constructed scene of Jesus' arrest.[28]

2. The Examination by Annas and Peter's Denial (18:12–27)

[12]*So the band of soldiers and their captain and the servants of the Jews seized Jesus and bound him.* [13]*First they led him to Annas; for he was the father-in-law of Caiaphas, who was high priest that year.* [14]*It was Caiaphas who had given counsel to the Jews that it was expedient that one man should die for the people.* [15]*Simon Peter followed Jesus, and so did another disciple. As this disciple was known to the high priest, he entered the court-yard of the high priest along with Jesus,* [16]*while Peter stood outside at the door. So the other disciple who was known to the high priest, went out and spoke to the maid who kept the door, and brought Peter in.* [17]*The maid who kept the door said to Peter, 'Are you not also one of this man's disciples?' He said, 'I am not.'* [18]*Now the servants and officers*

had made a coal fire, because it was cold, and they were standing and warming themselves; Peter also was with them, standing and warming himself. [19]*The high priest then questioned Jesus about his disciples and his teaching.* [20]*Jesus answered him, 'I have spoken openly to the world; I have always taught in synagogues and in the temple, where all Jews come together; I have said nothing secretly.* [21]*Why do you ask me? Ask those who have heard me, what I said to them; they know what I said.'* [22]*When he had said this, one of the officers standing by struck Jesus with his hand, saying, 'Is that how you answer the high priest?'* [23]*Jesus answered him, 'If I have spoken wrongly, bear witness to the wrong; but if I have spoken rightly, why do you strike me?'* [24]*Annas then sent him bound to Caiaphas the high priest.* [25]*Now Simon Peter was standing and warming himself. They said to him, 'Are you not also one of his disciples?' He denied it and said, 'I am not.'* [26]*One of the servants of the high priest, a kinsman of the man whose ear Peter had cut off, asked, 'Did I not see you in the garden with him?'* [27]*Peter again denied it; and at once the cock crowed.*

THE GENERAL PROBLEM OF THE SECTION (JN 18:12–27)

The Johannine description of the Jewish trial to which Jesus was subjected, and of Peter's denial, introduces difficult questions, not only when it is compared to the synoptic reports, but it also presents, in itself, various contradictions and breaks in the text. We must begin from the text as we have it before us, since the evangelist could have drawn on a special source which he re-worked. It is worthwhile to make a comparison with the synoptics, because, in addition, this sharpens our insight into the peculiarity and the problems of the Johannine presentation. The suggested solutions include rearrangement of the text, changes in his source made by the evangelist, uncertainties in the source itself, and editorial additions.[29] But first, the difficulties of the text as we have it must be taken on their merits and clarified by comparison with the synoptics.

1. The Internal Problem of Jn 18:12–27

The thoughtful reader comes up against the following stumbling-blocks:

(a) First of all, Jesus is led to Annas who is introduced as the son-in-law of Caiaphas 'who was high priest that year' (v. 13). We are not told why this happens. Also, Annas himself is not, at first, called 'high priest'; however, in v. 19, it simply says: 'The high priest then questioned Jesus.' Who is this, Annas or the officiating high priest Caiaphas? In v. 24, once again only Caiaphas is called 'the high priest'.

(b) Peter's three denials are forced apart by the trial (vv. 17–18, 25–27). Since v. 18 already prepares the position in v. 25 where the last words of v. 18 are taken up again ('Now Simon Peter was standing and warming himself'), we have to do here with an intentional literary creation which, clearly, has as its purpose a 'synchronization' of Jesus' trial with Peter's denial. But in the meantime, there is a change of venue: Annas sends Jesus bound, to the high priest Caiaphas (v. 24). How is the reader to relate to the questions of place? The favourite answer, that Annas and his son-in-law occupied different wings of the same building, is not confirmed by anything in the text. Does not v. 24 ruin the intended synchronization?

(c) Even without knowledge of the synoptic accounts, it is amazing that the text before us tells only of the interrogation of Jesus by Annas, without saying anything about a trial by the officiating high priest or proceedings before the Sanhedrin. After all, in v. 12, 'the servants of the Jews' are mentioned, and they, according to v. 3, came from the 'chief priests and pharisees' – which is a Johannine expression for the highest Jewish authorities (cf. 11:47). Further, 18:14 expressly recalls the advice of Caiaphas during the meeting at which Jesus' death was agreed (11:49–53). The total silence about what happened before Caiaphas after Jesus was taken to him, is very striking.

(d) There are some further details in this section which are puzzling. There is the 'other disciple' who arranges Peter's entry into the palace courtyard; a disciple of Jesus, 'an acquaintance of the high priest'? Also, it is not usual that a female door-keeper should watch the entrance into the courtyard during the night. She is next described as the maid (v. 17a) to whom Peter makes his first denial that he belongs to Jesus' disciples. Was this denial scene intended to support the appearance of a woman door-keeper? Lastly, we notice that Malchus's relative only recognizes Peter at the end (v. 26); however, this may be due to the internal consistency of the story.

2. Additional Problems due to the Comparison with the synoptics

Without going into all divergences (especially those to do with Peter's denial), some points of tension will be mentioned here which are of great importance to the Johannine presentation:

(a) The synoptics know nothing of Jesus' being brought before Annas. They know only of a meeting of the Sanhedrin during the night (Mk/Mt), alternatively a morning session (Lk), presided over by the high priest whom Mt 26:57 calls 'Caiaphas'. According to all three synoptics, Peter's denial takes place in the courtyard of the high priest. As a result, the examination by Annas which John synchronizes with this scene, becomes even more doubtful.

(b) The questioning of Jesus by the high priest is known to the synoptics only within the context of the proceedings of the Sanhedrin; but for them it has another object: the high priest calls upon Jesus to speak out concerning himself (the Messiah question), whereas Annas in Jn 18:19 seeks information about his disciples and teaching. Were there, then, two examinations of Jesus, a 'preliminary hearing' before Annas and an 'official' proceeding in the Sanhedrin? But, since the fourth evangelist passes over this latter in silence, the presumption arises (strengthened by the considerations in (a)) that John simply deals in another way with the one Jewish proceeding against Jesus.

(c) The synoptics tell of Jesus' abuse and ill-treatment by the Jews: In Mk/Mt, following Jesus' condemnation by the Sanhedrin (Mk 14:65 and par.); in Lk, by the men guarding him during the night (22:63ff). John knows of a blow to Jesus' face given him by one of the servants who was standing by (18:22f). Some verbal similarities between the presentations stand out (ὑπηρέται, ῥάπισμα, δέρειν), so that it is probable that we are dealing with the same event as far as the history of tradition is concerned, only it is related differently. Consequently, we have to ask once more whether it was not originally meant to be the same trial which occasioned this.

(d) In the synoptics, also, there is a tendency to synchronize Peter's denial with the proceedings against Jesus. Mk/Mt mention Peter's entering the courtyard of the high-priest as before the proceedings of the Sanhedrin (Mk 14:54 par.) and bring in Peter's denial immediately after them (Mk 14:66–72 par.). Lk, who tells of it before the session (in the morning) comments, after the denial: 'The Lord turned and looked at Peter' (22:61), without clarifying the situation; there then follows, in his case, the mocking by the Jewish guard. So the tradition seems throughout to have confronted Peter, who denies his Lord three times, with Jesus who, resolutely, holds his ground and puts up with abuse and ill-treatment. This too does not leave the impression that there were two trials. I am not here concerned with the historical question as to what happened in the night,[30] but solely with the divergences between the reports and, in particular, the tension which exists between the synoptic presentations and the Johannine examination by Annas.

3. Attempted Solutions

(a) Rearrangement hypotheses

Early copyists sought to improve the Johannine presentation by rearrangements of the text. The particular textual sequences in question are to be found in the following manuscripts:

vv.: 12, 13, 24, 14, 15, 19–23, 16–18, 25b–27   sy[s]
vv.: 13a, 24, 13b–27   min. 225
vv.: 13, 24, 14–23, 24, 25–27   min. 1195 sy[pal (pt)] Cyr. v. A.

If the text of Syr. sin. is read, then there are two recognizable trends:

1. By bringing forward v. 24, to identify the interrogating high priest with Caiaphas;
2. to take Peter's three denials together.

Obviously, this arrangement is founded on reflection; but it opens up new difficulties. Why is the handing over to Annas mentioned at all, if he immediately sends Jesus on to the high priest, Caiaphas? Also, the position of v. 24 in the mass of manuscripts (in P[60] and P[66] as well) cannot be made plausible. Only the different objective of the trial in John could have influenced other copyists in attributing the interrogation to Annas – but all others? The placing of this scene, framed within Peter's denials, is clearly intentional. Thus, the order of the text in Syr. sin. is certainly interesting as an early attempt at literary criticism, but it is not tenable as the original text.[31]

Min. 225 is content to rearrange v. 24 between vv. 13a and 13b – even less convincing. The third reading uses a repetition of v. 24, thereby betraying the copyist's dilemma. Therefore the rearrangement hypothesis has only a few supporters left.[32]

(b) Other suggestions of literary criticism.

Older literary criticism wished to make the text smoother and more understandable by positing interpolations. But whether v. 24 is struck out (Wellhausen), or all details about Caiaphas are removed (Spitta, Hirsch), difficulties enough remain, above all the position of Peter's denials. More recent literary criticism prefers to base itself on a source re-worked by the evangelist.

Bultmann[33] attributes practically everything to a source, except for vv. 13 (from πρῶτον)–14 and v. 24. He thinks that the source wrongly regarded Annas as the officiating high priest and the evangelist, from his own knowledge (cf. 11:49) corrected this. Bultmann admits that the source related much more about the proceedings, but the evangelist left this out because he had already moved this discussion back to the time of Jesus' ministry.

R. T. Fortna[34] reconstructs a text from the source which, in the main, consists of the following verses in this order:

vv.: 13, 24, 15, 16a, 19–21 (in part doubtful), 22–23, 16b, 17–18, 25b–27, 28.

Thus, for Fortna, the examining high priest in the source is again Caiaphas. But his reconstruction is weakened by the stated objections to the reconstruction hypothesis.

(c) History of tradition and the evangelist's own version

Here, we must first of all mention those scholars who give the Johannine tradition an intrinsic value, and who regard a 'preliminary hearing' before Annas as possible. Questions arise due to considerations of history. Somebody who does not consider the existing literary composition as causing problems, can see in the Johannine report, an old, historically acceptable tradition.[35] Furthermore, he can even picture to himself the course of the formation of the tradition, as follows:

Originally, only the preliminary hearing before Annas was set down as being in the night (Jn); against that, the main proceedings in the Sanhedrin under Caiaphas were assigned to the morning (Lk); then, in the course of the oral tradition, this last was put back to the night in place of the preliminary hearing (Mk/Mt).[36] But, in this reconstruction too, problems remain (cf. the reliability of Lk's information).

But whoever finds that the text before us leaves much to be desired (see above 1), will seek an explanation as to how this came about. For this purpose, if literary-critical methods are eschewed, an explanation from the history of tradition can be offered which not only distinguishes between a source and the evangelist's additions (cf. Bultmann), but goes still deeper into the tradition of the source and the alteration by the evangelist. There are two recent attempts of this sort, by F. Hahn and A. Dauer.

Hahn supposes a source which was competing with the synoptics, 'a parallel tradition to Mk 14:55–65' (but with Annas as high priest), but which was greatly re-worked by the evangelist. The course of the trial (18:19–23) is, just as Pilate's proceedings, extremely freely reconstructed by the evangelist, in accordance with his theological intentions.[37] If, in this way, F. Hahn gives a decisive share to the activity of the evangelist, including the introduction of Caiaphas, A. Dauer gives more weight to the source. Indeed, in his meticulous (independent) research, he agrees with F. Hahn that the content of the trial is, in the main, put together by the evangelist. But he attributes the introduction of Caiaphas in addition to Annas to the pre-Johannine source; already in that source, there was mention of two trials. His main reasons for this are the following: were this not so, the evangelist could have simply replaced Annas, who is named in the source, with Caiaphas, and he would also have had no reason to postulate a second trial before Caiaphas (v. 24, cf. 28). Admittedly, the pre-Johannine source is itself already the product of a mixing process. To the original tradition, which tells of the trial before Annas and Peter's denial, Caiaphas has been added, 'due to the influence of synoptic material', especially from Mt. The (unsuccessful) fusion process took place at this stage of the tradition.[38]

4. Conclusion

The solution must be sought in the direction indicated by the latest research. It is true that disclosure of the source used by the evangelist remains difficult because he himself intervened quite inventively, especially in regard to the trial before the high priest. This last can only be doubted to have been Annas in the source if rearrangement of the text is undertaken (namely, if v. 24 is put before the trial); but these efforts are unconvincing. One problem remains, that of how Caiaphas came into the text. Was he already represented in the source, or was he brought in for the first time by the evangelist? Dauer's argument that the evangelist could have substituted him for Annas had he not found him already in the source, loses its force if one may invest the evangelist (as has often happened in this commentary) with a knowledge of synoptic material which is not that of the synoptic gospels known to us. For, in this case, it could have mattered to him that the details of his source should be made to accord with the synoptic reports of the proceedings of the Sanhedrin (cf. the Lukan morning session). If he does not mention this, we cannot assume ignorance; the sending of Jesus to Caiaphas (v. 24) and his handing over to Pilate (v. 28) betray the opposite. But John intentionally omitted the entire Sanhedrin proceedings (on which point, nowadays, most exegetes agree), because he had described Jesus' controversy with the leading Jews already, in the course of his public ministry (chapters 5–12). Besides this, he is ruled by his intention to cover the disagreement with Judaism in the course of the Roman trial, in order, by this means, to present the one great 'case' of Jesus against the unbelieving world.

That is why the evangelist formulated the hearing before Annas differently (probably, as against his source) after mature reflection. This then fits into his picture of Jesus' ministry – that of the one who reveals.

The idea of the 'preliminary hearing' by Annas and of the Sanhedrin's proceedings under Caiaphas takes its inspiration from the fourth evangelist's presentation, and it is possible that he himself saw things in this way. But one can hardly draw historical conclusions from his *presentation*. If his source meant the same proceedings as the session of the Sanhedrin described by the synoptics, with, admittedly, marked differences (Annas!), the most that can be concluded is that the synoptic reports of the Jewish proceedings are to be accepted with care, and perhaps need correction. Then, the Jewish proceedings hardly bore the character of a trial. But I cannot pursue these questions further.

For the purpose of exegesis, it is advisable, following this preliminary probing, to pay special attention to the theological objectives of the evangelist. For even if he used a source, we still have to reckon with his strong and individualistic shaping of the material.

Exegesis

18:12   Jesus, who has given himself up to the arrest troop, is now seized and led away bound. Though bonds were normal for prisoners, it is still remarkable that both here and in v. 24 this is stressed. The old accounts of the passion saw in this, as also in the contrast with Barabbas (cf. 18:40 par.), and the crucifixion between two other convicts (19:18; cf. Lk 23:33), the disgrace of Jesus being treated like a common criminal. Thus, the reference certainly originates from the pre-Johannine account, as does the mention of the σπεῖρα and the 'servants' (cf. with v. 3). The χιλίαρχος (peculiar to John) too, will have been mentioned in it, perhaps, with reference to the captain of the temple.[39] But τῶν Ἰουδαίων might have been added by John to the 'servants', because this expression for the Jewish authorities is typical for him (cf. 1:19; 2:18; 5:16, 18 and more often). He sees, in Jesus' being led off in disgrace, the tragic triumph of these enemies of Jesus who have already been seeking his death for some time past (cf. 5:16, 18; 7:1, 19, 25; etc.). The 'powerlessness' of Jesus in his bonds is soon (v. 23) to show itself as the strength of an unbroken spirit.[40]

18:13–14   Jesus is 'first' brought to Annas. As this former high priest,[41] who is also mentioned in Lk 3:2 and Acts 4:6, was certainly named in the evangelist's source, the only question is whether the pre-Johannine account also made mention with him of the officiating high priest, Caiaphas. When, in what follows, this man is introduced, the expression 'high priest that year' stands out, which is, likewise, already found in 11:49, 51, and is discussed because of the curious mode of expression (q.v.). The evangelist's interest in Caiaphas is betrayed by his comment in 11:51 that Caiaphas, as high priest that year, involuntarily prophesied. His 'counsel' in the Sanhedrin to let Jesus die for the people is cited once again in 18:14. It reminds the reader what he should think of this man, but also what an instrument of God he became through his involuntary prophecy. Therefore, it is likely that these remarks about Caiaphas are to be attributed to the evangelist. He could have known from general acquaintance with contemporary history that he was Annas's son-in-law, because the high priests under the Roman occupation were the dominant political leaders of Judaism.[42] Probably the source spoke only of the high priest Annas, and the evangelist made the connection with the officiating high priest, Caiaphas, by means of the comment in 13b. If, according to what the evangelist knew, a council meeting of the 'chief priests and pharisees' with Caiaphas had taken place, at which Jesus' death was decided (11:47–53), he probably thought of two proceedings against Jesus, namely, one hearing before Annas, and a session of the Sanhedrin under Caiaphas which, admittedly, he only hints at (v. 24, cf. 28). In that case v. 24 also originates with John. There is doubt about $\pi\rho\tilde{\omega}\tau\sigma\nu$. By it, the evangelist could be anticipating v. 24; but it can just as well have been found in the source, which thereby took into consideration the second leading away ($\check{\alpha}\gamma\sigma\upsilon\sigma\iota\nu$ v. 28) to Pilate.

The source spoke only of *one* high priest. As, doubtless, Jesus' interrogation by the high priest and Peter's denial were already connected with one another there, the source could hardly have spoken otherwise in the Peter narrative about the 'courtyard of the high *priest*' (v. 15), and the 'servants of the high *priest*' (v. 26). If the 'other disciple' already belongs to the source, this also covers his description as 'an acquaintance of the high *priest*' (v. 16, cf. v. 15). The difficulty resulting from this that in vv. 13b–14 both the former high priest, Annas, and the officiating high priest Caiaphas, are named, and in what follows, there is mention only of 'the high *priest*', is best solved if vv. 13–14 as well as 24 are reckoned as coming from the evangelist, who, apart from this, in the Peter narrative and in the course of the trial, takes 'the high priest' from the source.[43]

The evangelist is not interested in portraying Annas, who was 'one of the most remarkable personalities in the priestly aristocracy of that time' (Blinzler), maintained himself in the office of high priest for ten years (AD 6–15) and even afterwards, exercised a decisive influence (five of his sons later attained the rank of high priest). Therefore, all psychological interpretations of his investigation of Jesus are misdirected. The high priest Caiaphas also gains the attention of the evangelist not so much because of his character as because of his 'prophetic' utterance. When he recalls that advice of Caiaphas, he also wants to bring to mind Jesus' death 'for the people'. The Jewish leadership (cf. $\tau\sigma\tilde{\iota}\varsigma$ $\text{'}Iou\delta\alpha\acute{\iota}\sigma\iota\varsigma$ v. 14), in its blindness, in fact only furthers God's plan of salvation by its deadly hatred of Jesus.[44]

18:15–16   The reader is not surprised (as is not the case with Mk/Mt) that the subject of Simon Peter comes up again in the course of the Johannine narrative (cf. v. 10f). The disciple wants to discover what is to be Jesus' future destiny, and follows him. The second disciple who follows Jesus at the same time remains unnamed – unusual in John's gospel, which tends, rather, to give the names of individual disciples. It simply says 'another disciple'; the article which not a few manuscripts contain,[45] is secondary from a text-critical point of view, and is evidence of the early trend to identify him with the 'disciple, whom Jesus loved' (13:23). Since he is once more mentioned beneath the cross (19:26), and then, in connection with the visit to the tomb (20:2), here again at Peter's side and introduced with the words, 'the other disciple, the one whom Jesus loved (ἐφίλει), this identification suggested itself especially when he was seen as John, the son of Zebedee. This opinion has continued right up to our time;[46] but weighty objections are raised against it:

1. The lack of the article forbids our supposing a reference back to 13:23;

2. there is no reason why the anonymous one who was already introduced as 'the disciple, whom Jesus loved' should not be described in the same way here;

3. his acquaintance with the high priest not only rules out, with some certainty, his identification with John, the fisherman's son from the lake of Gennesaret,[47] but would also be astonishing for a close intimate of Jesus. This last, is, admittedly, no serious argument against the disciple whom Jesus loved, because John's gospel knows of still more 'disciples' of Jesus in Judaea (7:3), describes Joseph of Arimathaea as a 'secret disciple' (19:38), and reports much else about Jesus' connections with Judaea-Jerusalem (cf. Nicodemus, Bethany and Ephraim [11:54]).[48]

But it remains quite incomprehensible why the evangelist did not speak here also of 'the disciple, whom Jesus loved' *if* he was that 'other disciple'. So the supposition suggests itself that this disciple who was 'known to the high priest'[49] already appeared in the source so as to explain Peter's entry into the courtyard of the high priest.[50] For that reason the evangelist does not identify him with the beloved disciple. His appearance next to Peter, his mediating rôle on Peter's behalf, has another significance from that in 20:2–8 or 21:7; he simply leads him into the high priest's court-yard.

18:17–18   Peter's first denial to 'the maid, the female doorkeeper' follows immediately. The ἡ θυρωρός added so as to clarify that the maid is identical with the doorkeeper[51] makes a secondary impression and, indeed, breaks up the story. If Peter has already entered the courtyard (v. 16), the doorkeeper, who has to stay at her post, will not have followed him; otherwise, she would have had to stop him at the entrance. The later identification of the 'maid' with the doorkeeper must be due to the evangelist.

The source was immediately able to pass on, without difficulty, to the trial by the high priest (v. 19a), and *following* the chastisement of Jesus (v. 22) tells of Peter's three denials *in a continuous narrative*. Additional evidence in favour of this is that the denials are unnaturally split up. In v. 25a, the last sentence of v. 18 is repeated except that, instead of 'Peter', use is made of the Johannine dual appellation 'Simon Peter'. Who the speakers are, who are not more closely defined in v. 25b, is also known to the reader merely from v. 18. Vv. 17–18 put together with vv. 25–27 form a narrative progression (a maid, servants and officers in general, the relative of Malchus). Besides this, an effective contrast results between Jesus who has been beaten, and Peter who denies him three times. Finally, this arrangement corresponds to the synoptic report in Mk/Mt. The evangelist's supposed rearrangement, is easy to explain: he wanted to frame Jesus' trial before the high priest within Peter's denials, and so syncrhonize both events even more closely. For it was obvious for him to identify the 'maid' who is mentioned at the beginning of the account of the denial, with the 'female doorkeeper' whom he found in the source (or was it originally a male doorkeeper?). He had to repeat the end of v. 18 (except $\mu\epsilon\tau$' $\alpha\dot{\upsilon}\tau\tilde{\omega}\nu$) in v. 25, on account of the splitting up of the denial story.

The three separate scenes of the denial are variously given by all evangelists: that belongs to the way things were related in those days, which was intended to be fresh and lively rather than a record. Nevertheless, all gospels agree that the first questioner is a maid, and then (second or third in the order) the servants, warming themselves by the fire, press the disciple further. The negative answer which Peter gives to the maid ($o\dot{\upsilon}\kappa$ $\epsilon\dot{\iota}\mu\dot{\iota}$), is found in this form, only in Lk (22:58) whose way of telling the story John most resembles in other respects also (neither invocation of curses against himself nor oaths). Peter comes off best in John; he does not speak a word directly against Jesus (synoptics: 'I do not know him'). One often reads that Peter's denial, $o\dot{\upsilon}\kappa$ $\epsilon\dot{\iota}\mu\dot{\iota}$, contrasts with Jesus' witness to himself, $\dot{\epsilon}\gamma\dot{\omega}$ $\epsilon\dot{\iota}\mu\iota$ (18:5, 6, 8). But the evangelist could hardly have intended that; he found Peter's manner of speech in his source. Rather, he is guided by the thought that Jesus intervened on behalf of his disciples (v. 8, cf. vv. 19f), but the leading disciple does not wish to be numbered among them. The location around the fire, convincingly described in view of the cold spring nights, is found in all the evangelists; however, the expression $\dot{\alpha}\nu\theta\rho\alpha\kappa\iota\dot{\alpha}$ (coal-fire),[52] betrays the independence of the Johannine source.

18:19–20   The examination by the high priest (Annas, see above on v. 13) and Jesus' answer, can only be understood as a unit intentionally constructed by the evangelist according to content. Question and answer relate to each other so as to bring out an important aspect of Jesus' ministry of revelation, although it may also be to ward off later Jewish attacks and to proclaim the Christian faith as a teaching accessible to all. If the interrogation carried out by the high priest is seen as a historical record of the Jewish proceedings against Jesus, the hearing becomes unlikely.

Jewish court procedure, consisted, in the main, in hearing witnesses (cf. the story of Susanna, Mishnah-tractate Sanhedrin, also Mk 14:55–59 par. Mt). The questioning of the accused was not normal; he could, it is true, himself raise an objection, in which case, he had to be heard (Sanh 4c, cf. with 7:50f). Thus, Jesus' interrogation by the former high priest, Annas, could not have been in any way official;[53] but what would Annas have wanted to gain by it? Psychological explanations such as, that the shrewd politician wanted to trick Jesus into a confession that his 'messianic' efforts were directed towards a liberation struggle, are not convincing. If there were such a suspicion, the disciples would not have been allowed to go free; besides, the inquiry about Jesus' 'teaching' does not fit this. As to the source, one can only suppose that it presented the trial by the high priest differently, perhaps, in a similar way to the synoptic reports of the proceedings in the Sanhedrin. The evangelist, who also betrays himself by his language (especially in v. 20), has not followed his source here, but has offered something of his own.

It looks different when we are dealing with a literary-theological construction of the evangelist. The essential meaning of the high priest's dual question about Jesus' disciples and teaching, becomes clear when Jesus' answer in v. 20 is added: Jesus proclaimed his revelation (=his teaching) openly, quite 'plainly', before and confronted by the 'world'. In this, the evangelist reminds us of Jesus' ministry of revelation and his controversy with Judaism, as he has presented it in the first main section. From that point of view, the words chosen here become comprehensible: λαλεῖν as revelatory speech (cf. 3:11, 34; 6:63; 7:17f; 8:12 and more often), παρρησίᾳ λαλεῖν (7:26; cf. 10:24f), λαλεῖν εἰς τὸν κόσμον (8:26; cf. 19:37). Jesus' 'teaching' in a synagogue (6:59) and in the Temple (7:14, 28; 8:20), where 'all Jews come together' (cf. 6:41, 52; 7:11, 15, 35, etc.), can, likewise, be accurately supported. Of particular importance is the scene in 10:24–26: at the feast of the dedication of the Temple, 'the Jews' gather round Jesus in the portico of Solomon, and ask: 'If you are the Messiah, tell us plainly (παρρησίᾳ)', and Jesus answers: 'I told you, and you do not believe.' This passage can be connected, from the viewpoint of the history of tradition, with the proceedings before the Sanhedrin according to Lk 22:68 (cf. Vol 2, p. 306). John already moved the question of Jesus' messiahship (and sonship of God), which, according to the synoptics, is dealt with during the Jewish proceedings, forward into his gospel account, and now, in the investigation by Annas, only wants to refer back to it. To that belongs also the dialectic of Jesus' speaking 'openly' and quite 'plainly', which, for unbelieving ears because of unbelief, is hidden, so that for such people Jesus appears to work 'in secret' (cf. 7:4; 10:24). Accordingly, Hahn has quite rightly recognized, that in the case of the hearing before Annas also, according to the evangelist's intention, the ultimate concern is with the question of Jesus' self-revelation. But the time of revelation before the world is past (cf. 12:36b), and Jesus does not answer the high priest any more, because everything has already been said and explained. Thus, the content of this trial would be neither something fundamentally different from the proceedings of the Sanhedrin, according to the synoptics, nor would it be of a wholly 'unofficial' character. But it would simply be an intentionally novel offering based on the evangelist's premises.[54] In any case, Jesus' answer is framed in such a way that he refers back to controversies with unbelieving Judaism.

The opinion is often expressed, that, looked at from the history of tradition, the evangelist picks up Jesus' answer to the arrest troop (Mk 14:49 par.), and uses it in his own way.[55] The correspondence is limited to the words: 'Day after day (Jn: Always) I taught . . . in the Temple', which, moreover, according to Lk 22:52, were directed to 'the chief priests and captains of the temple and elders' present. Perhaps there is an obscure reminder of the synoptic tradition; but in it, Jesus protests (Mk 14:48 par.: 'As against a robber . . .') against his arrest, and the words quoted have a different intent (they could have captured him). The Johannine intention and linguistic character, as demonstrated, demand no such recourse; rather, they permit the postulation of a free invention of the evangelist.[56].

But (as was already the case with Jesus' messiahship), it is also necessary to remember that the scene throws light upon the confrontation of the evangelist and his community with contemporary Judaism. For that, the high priest's question about Jesus' disciples can have a significance. The term μαθητής, in John's gospel, covers all believers in Christ (cf. on 6:60; 8:12; 8:31), and these disciples of Christ stand in marked contrast to the 'disciples of Moses' (9:27f), a proud self-designation of the later Jews who were led by pharisaism. With Jesus' refusal to speak about his 'disciples', he prevents unbelieving Judaism from judging those who believe in him, because, on account of its unbelief, it is simply unable to understand them. It is similar in the case of his 'teaching': Only he who does the will of God who sent him (that means, believes in him), will know, concerning his teaching, whether it is from God (7:17; cf. 9:31ff). So, with his answer to the high-priest, Jesus also becomes a defender of his followers against the attacks of Judaism. Less important is the question whether the statement that Jesus 'said nothing secretly' is also meant to defuse the accusation that the Christian faith is a secret teaching practised by an obscure sect,[57] or whether it contains a barb against the Gnostics who did in fact claim secret doctrines.[58] Probably, the answer is No.

18:21 The following defiantly audacious saying of Jesus, which leads to his being beaten by one of the officers standing by, also has, as well as its obvious meaning, a theological significance for the evangelist. When the high priest is referred to the hearers of Jesus' preaching, a call goes out with this to the later Jews to turn to the Christian teachers, who 'have heard' what Jesus spoke (cf. 1 Jn 1:1, 3), and who 'know' what his words mean (cf. 1 Jn 5:20). Jesus' message in the world, which, for the moment, is silenced (cf. 12:36b), continues to find fulfilment in the proclamation of those who are associated with him 'from the beginning', and only becomes fully understandable through their witness (cf. 15:27; 1 Jn 1:2).

18:22 The reaction of the officer who strikes Jesus in the face does fit the situation, but looks entirely like the adoption of a motif which, in the synoptics, is found in another connection, namely, the Jewish guards' mocking and ill-treatment. The verbal echoes (ῥάπισμα, δέρειν) are scarcely there by chance. In Mk 14:65, Mt par., the scene takes place after the judgment on Jesus, in Lk 22:63ff, during the night before the proceedings. The Johannine source, which probably recorded the Jewish night session (see above), followed Mk/Mt in this. In distinction from the synoptic reports, however, John relates nothing of a mocking of Jesus which, in Mk/Mt, belongs together with Jesus' condemnation: the servants demand of Jesus (whose eyes have been bound) that he prophesy who had struck him. Obviously, Jesus' witness to himself was a prerequisite and the servants make fun of Jesus as a false prophet (cf. Lk: 'And they spoke many other words against him, reviling him'). That can be a further indication of the fact that, for the Johannine source as well, the Messiah-question was an element in the trial. But, as John omits this, he could not reproduce the mockery. If this opinion is correct, the evangelist has made considerable alterations; still, that is to be expected of him.[59]

18:23   Whereas, in the synoptics, Jesus puts up in silence with mocking and ill-treatment, in John, he gives the servant a sovereign answer. This corresponds to the rest of the behaviour of the Johannine Jesus during the trial. Once, the silence motif is briefly suggested (19:9). To the Roman's question: 'Where are you from?' Jesus gives no answer (with complete justification, see *ad loc.*); shortly afterwards the discussion continues (cf. 19:11). For John, Jesus remains, even in his passion, the self-authenticating vessel of revelation, who, at the same time, puts his opponents in the wrong. It is from this point of view also, that Jesus' answer to the servant who strikes him, is formulated. The man who accuses him of injustice against the high priest, has to be told that justice is on Jesus' side. This is so in the Roman trial as well: the Jewish accusers have to hear three times from Pilate, that he finds no guilt in Jesus, and the Roman judge is condemned on account of his unjust judgment based on human failure. Jesus speaks from his consciousness that he has been sent into the world as witness to the truth (cf. 18:37). Therefore, it is also beside the point to play off Jesus' words and behaviour to Annas, against the advice of the sermon on the mount in Mt 5:39, par. Lk 6:29a, or to treat it as a correction of this metaphor in another situation. What is said to the servant is only overtly the rejection of an unjust molestation, but its real meaning is that, in the drama of the trial, Jesus is, at the same time, the innocent and triumphant one. Augustine rightly replies to those who question that Jesus does not answer angrily, but that 'he is ready, with a quiet soul, to take upon himself the heavier burden';[60] but the theological scope of the saying escapes him.

18:24   For John, everything has been said about the hearing before Annas which he wants to say about it. The presentation of Jesus' arrest, similarly put together out of short narrative elements, also ended with a question on Jesus' part (v. 11). When the evangelist now reports Jesus' transfer to Caiaphas in a single sentence, he wants at least to hint at the trial before Caiaphas known from the synoptics. That he knows more about it, is clear from the indefinite 'they' in v. 28. This can only refer to 'the Jews', which means here the official representatives of Judaism (cf. on v. 12). V. 24 should come from the evangelist, if the interpretation so far is correct; that Caiaphas is again described as high priest, also fits this (cf. v. 13b). Annas sends Jesus 'in bonds'. Is it possible to conclude from this that, during the hearing, he had Jesus' bonds removed?[61]

Such attempts at historical questions, ignore the narrative intention of the evangelist. He probably means by this that Annas regards Jesus as guilty, as a criminal (cf. v. 12). Similarly fruitless is the question as to where Caiaphas is, whether in his palace or the meeting-place of the Sanhedrin;[62] that does not interest John.

18:25   The evangelist again follows the source in the case of Peter's last two denials, without bothering about the change of place. As a link, he says that, Simon Peter (still) stood at the fire and warmed himself (cf. v. 18b). The servants and officers ask him the same question as the maid, whether he does not also belong to Jesus' disciples. These questions introduced in the Greek with μή express only a suspicion.[63] The only intensification as compared with the first denial (v. 17), is the addition of 'he denied'. The Johannine source dispensed with a heightening by means of oaths.

18:26–27 Peter's third denial follows immediately. Here, the 'pre-Johannine' report reaches a climax by means of a special tradition: a relation of Malchus, whose ear Peter had cut off (v. 10), who is also one of the servants of the high priest, claims to identify Peter. Now the question is put more incisively (with οὐ), roughly in the sense of: I myself (ἐγώ) did see you in the garden with him? (Yes, certainly!).[64] But Peter refutes that also. After this follows the comment that immediately a cock crowed. Whether, like the synoptics, the source said something more about Peter's reaction, that he remembered Jesus' words and wept (bitterly), is no longer to be determined. It is indicative of John that such a comment has no importance for him; it is enough for him that the reader recognizes Jesus' saying in the supper-room (13:38) has been precisely fulfilled. Jesus knew everything beforehand. The cock-crow also belongs to Jesus' prophecy; it was far from his thoughts to consider it further (as the exegetes like to do from a historical concern[65]). It is only the editors in the supplementary chapter who reflect about Peter, his miserable failure despite his love for Jesus, his grief when Jesus reminds him of it (21:17 ἐλυπήθη). In the Johannine account of the passion, Peter, because of his unconsidered impetuosity (18:10), and his miserable failure (denial), serves to thrust Jesus, with his readiness to fulfill the divine will (18:11), and his persistence on this road, into an even more radiant light.

As all the synoptics as well as the Johannine source which is related to them, tell this story which taints the chief disciple, there is no reason to doubt the historicity of the event (however it happened in detail). In John, at least, we cannot detect a projection of the judgments of early Christian circles about Peter.[66] The whole section, Jn 18:12–27, is informative about the evangelist's relationship to the tradition. It takes it over, reflects it and uses it in a sovereign way so as to draw his picture of Christ. He is not concerned with exact historical reproduction, but with theological interpretation; but neither does he speculate freely; rather, he holds to what supports his tradition, because for him the Christ of faith is none other than the historical Jesus (cf. 20:20, 27).

The Trial Before Pilate (18:28—19:16a)

This section, because of its length alone, stands out from the Johannine report of the passion; it is the heart of the entire account. Even without the synoptic texts with which it is comparable, through Jesus' words which are consistently directed to Pilate, it is seen to be as a consciously-intended creation of the evangelist. These words taken together are, so to speak, Jesus' last revelatory pronouncement,[1] which he makes before the representative of the Roman state and of the Gentiles, while his words to the Jews are silenced (cf. 12:36b; 18:20f). It is Jesus' witness and self-confession as the hidden king, in another sense than the accusation intends, and yet in a real deep sense (18:37). From this basic idea the entire trial is clear. For what Jesus says inside the praetorium (18:36f; 19:11), is simultaneously revealed in what takes place actually: the 'King of the Jews', who is handed over to the possessor of worldly power and who is condemned by him under pressure from the Jewish leaders, is, in reality, the king whose kingdom is not of this world. Even as one mocked and humiliated, he bears the marks of sovereignty and divinity (cf. 19:5-7), and emerges from the trial the guiltless and justified one as even his judge has to agree with his thrice repeated declaration of innocence.

If notice is taken of the thoroughly *theological shaping* of the events of the trial[2] (which will be worked out in detail in the exegesis), the *historical question* will be allowed to recede. A more exact picture can scarcely be obtained from the Johannine presentation, as to how negotiations went between Pilate and 'the Jews' on the one hand, and on the other, between Pilate and Jesus; the alternation of the setting in front of and inside the praetorium, is only a device of literary style. Also, it is hardly possible to argue from John, that the scourging and the crowning with thorns occurred at a different place from that reported by the synoptics. It is not a matter of vital importance what the relationship is between John's presentation and the synoptic accounts. Admittedly, it is of historical interest whether, in those days, the Sanhedrin had the authority to carry out death sentences (18:31), or whether the Johannine information concerning the day and hour of the trial (18:28; 19:14) deserves to be given more credit than the synoptic details.

Such questions only become more justifiable, if, for this section of John's account of the passion too, we may suppose that the evangelist had a *source* available, presumably the same as the one which was already recognizable behind the arrest and the Jewish proceedings. But the scholars who have occupied themselves with this problem of literary criticism and history of tradition,[3] agree that this section is the one most influenced by the evangelist's literary-theological shaping. They differ only in their judgment as to whether and how far the source used by John can be recognized beneath his editorial hand. This problem is of lesser importance for a commentary which has to clarify the text as it is. It is true that the literary means and theological motifs used by the evangelist can come more strongly to the fore from consideration of his source.

The *structure* of section 18:28—19:16a has already been described as a series of seven individual scenes (see above, p. 220).

A discussion as to whether a different arrangement recommends itself[4] hardly seems necessary; for in this case, the scene-changes themselves are a means of presentation constructed by the evangelist. According to whether the scene takes place inside or outside the praetorium, a particular setting results which, for the evangelist, is not only an outward direction, but is also a symbolic, inwardly significant 'place', included in which is the Roman's continual to-ing and fro-ing between these two areas:[5]

Exposition: Jesus led into the praetorium, the Jews outside (18:28).
1st scene: Outside: Pilate and the Jews (18:29–31 [32])
2nd scene: Inside: Pilate and Jesus (18:33–38a)
3rd scene: Outside: Pilate and the Jews (Release of Barabbas) (18:38b–40)
4th scene: Inside: Scourging and crowning with thorns (19:1–3)
5th scene: Outside: Pilate's presentation of Jesus (19:4–7)
6th scene: Inside: Pilate and Jesus (second discussion) (19:8–12)
7th scene: Outside: Condemnation of Jesus by Pilate to the accompaniment of the Jews' shouts (19:13–16a)

The two settings are not totally unconnected. Towards the end of the presentation, both the personages and the places move nearer to each other. In the fifth scene all those taking part are on the stage, and Pilate, because of what the Jews say (19:7), is practically driven back inside (cf. v. 8). In the sixth scene which takes place inside the praetorium, Pilate is once more made to act by the shouts of the Jews who are standing outside, and then he appears with Jesus for the final scene in which, this time surrounding the judgment-seat, all those taking part are gathered together. The whole episode is a well-considered and dramatically-developed play.

1. Jesus' Handing-over to Pilate (18:28–32)

[28] *Then they led Jesus from Caiaphas to the praetorium. It was early. They themselves did not enter the praetorium, so that they might not be defiled, but might eat the passover.* [29] *So Pilate went out to them and said, 'What accusation do you bring against this man?'* [30] *They answered him, 'If this man were not an*

evil-doer, we would not have handed him over.' [31] *Pilate said to them, 'Take him yourselves and judge him by your own law.' The Jews said to him, 'It is not lawful for us to put any man to death.'* [32] *This was to fulfil the word which Jesus had spoken to show by what death he was to die.*

18:28   The leading of Jesus to Pilate is described without circumlocution. The evangelist wants to present a vivid scene, as is shown by the historic present.[6] But who are those doing the leading? In 18:13 where the same verb (in the aorist) is found, it could be thought to be the guard who had also arrested Jesus; but because of the following καὶ αὐτοί it must be the Jews, and indeed, the leaders (members of the Sanhedrin), those who then deal with Pilate. If the earlier observations are correct that the source reported only *one* Jewish trial (before Annas), and that the evangelist brought in Jesus' transfer to the high priest, Caiaphas (see above on 18:13f), the following explanation suggests itself: in the report in the source, it was the same people that brought Jesus to begin with to Annas; but the evangelist connects the term with 'the Jews' because for him, the proceedings before the high counsel under Caiaphas were a prerequisite. Hence the comment 'from Caiaphas' will have its origin with the evangelist who had also added v. 24 (q.v.). For him, as for the synoptics, Jesus' handing over to Pilate is an official transfer to the Roman court (cf. v. 30). On this account, to begin with, not the holder of the office, but the place, the 'praetorium', where it is exercised, is named. The word borrowed from the Latin means (in the civil context), the residence of the provincial governor, where he also gave judgment in legal matters on the *sella curulis* (cf. 19:13 βῆμα).

The evangelist will have taken over the term from his source. Mt 27:27 also used it, and in Mk 15:16 it is made equivalent to αὐλή (=palace, residence), (cf. BauerWb col. 241 and col. 1383). There is disagreement up to the present time as to where Pilate's praetorium is to be sought: in Herod's old palace near the Jaffa gate because the Roman governors in general, and also in the particular instance of Jerusalem (according to the information in Josephus and Philo, *Legatio*) set up their residence in the palaces of the previous rulers; or, in the fortress of Antonia which was north of the Temple square and permitted the supervision of this dangerous district. The latter view is favoured in more modern times[7] because of the excavation of an old floor paved with flagstones in that place (cf. Jn 19:13), but it continues to be contested by other scholars, above all because of the historical details in Josephus and Philo.[8] There is a good summary of the learned debate in J. Blinzler, who himself, together with other exceptional experts, decides for Herod's palace.[9]

Also, the detail 'it was early', which refers to the beginning of the day (about six o'clock), (cf. 20:1), will already have been found in the source if it only knew of a single trial during the night. The evangelist scarcely calculated how long the investigations of Jesus lasted, and he does not need to have known anything of a morning session of the Sanhedrin (cf. Lk 22:66). The early morning was the time when the Roman civil servants took up their office duties.[10] The indication gave the evangelist sufficient freedom for the rather long agitated dealings of the procurator with the Jews and with Jesus, as he presents them; for, according to Jn 19:14, the judgment is pronounced at the sixth hour (twelve o'clock). It is possible that for him, these details of time also acquire a symbolic meaning.[10a]

Another fact is more important for the evangelist, namely, that the accusing Jews do not enter the official building so as 'not to defile' themselves before the passover meal. For, with this he provides the basis for the following scenes in which the Jews negotiate with Pilate outside the praetorium. They exclude themselves from Jesus' words of revelation, which he speaks inside the praetorium to the Roman. Also, the motif of not becoming unclean in a levitical sense, can be explained as a concern of the evangelist. He distances himself from the Jewish cleanliness laws, scarcely, indeed, from an antinomian standpoint, but because of an inward distancing from the Torah religion which had been overtaken by the faith in Christ (cf. 1:17; 2:6–9; 2:13–22 and more often). Yet this is not the real reason for this comment; rather, the Jews, anxiously concerned for their cleanliness, 'so that they can eat the passover (lamb)',[11] miss the way to the true passover lamb, Christ. Because of this small-mindedness they drive Jesus to a death which becomes a fulfilment of their passover feast. Perhaps the Christian community celebrating Easter is indicating its distance from the Jewish community which keeps to its old passover, strictly and ritualistically.[12]

Why are the Jews afraid that, because of levitical uncleanness, they cannot eat the passover lamb? Contact with the gentiles, as such, did not make one unclean; but the opinion is demonstrable from early times, that entering a gentile house makes one unclean because it is to be supposed that premature children were buried in it (uncleanness through dead bodies). Nor, in this instance, could the contamination be removed by immersion in the evening; it lasted seven days. This explanation given by Billerbeck[13] might still be tenable despite occasional criticism.[14] It may be supposed, that the evangelist who, elsewhere also, betrays knowledge of rabbinic viewpoints, was aware of this attitude through contact with Jews around him.

18:29 Pilate who, as a well-known personality, is not introduced further, comes out to the accusing Jews, by whom is meant the chief priests and other members of the council – the first scene outside the praetorium. It is not clear whether the Roman judge is already aware of Jesus' arrest. Perhaps the evangelist imagines the situation to be, that he has already been informed by the commander of the detachment of soldiers, and expects also that the chief priests have established the guilt of the one arrested; but this is not certain. The procurator could hear of it for the first time now (as the synoptics suggest), and be dealing with the case. After the prisoner is brought in, he officially asks the purely factual question what accusation the chief priests bring 'against this man'. For him, Jesus is an ordinary man, a case like many others.

Pontius Pilate was procurator, or, as he is described in an inscription discovered in

Caesarea in 1961, prefect of Judea, AD 26–36. Being from the Roman nobility but not a member of the senate, he was unable to be a legatus; but for the less important Roman provinces, such men sufficed and exercised the Roman ruling rights administratively and militarily, in the Roman provinces with limited autonomy. According to the secular sources (Philo, *Legatio ad Caium* 38; Josephus, *Ant.*, XVIII, 35, 55–62, etc.; Tacitus, *Ann.*, 15, 44) Pontius Pilate is described as a mercilessly hard man who despised the Jews and who, because of his brutal action against the Samaritans, was deposed by Vitellius the legate of Syria and sent to Rome to render account of himself (Josephus, *Ant.*, XVIII, 88f). The picture in the gospels which differ from this, showing Pilate as a weak and compliant man, has often been disputed. It is certainly partly explained by the evangelist's descriptive tendencies, but partly too, it is not quite unbelievable (despising of the Jews, political calculation).[15]

18:30   The petulant answer of the Jews is less to illustrate the tension between the representatives of the Jewish authorities and the Roman procurator,[16] than to show up their inability to bring a water-tight charge against Jesus. There is no doubt about the fact that they accused him as a political agitator (as 'kingly' pretender). That is John's premise when the subsequent trial by Pilate refers to this point. But the evangelist is not concerned with an exact formulation of the charge (different, Lk 23:2), rather with a characterisation of the accusers, who describe Jesus, in their hatred, as an 'evil-doer',[17] that is, generally as a criminal. This is all the weightier when, in the course of events, they themselves see Jesus' 'crime' in the fact that he has made himself out to be 'Son of God' (19:7). In the eyes of the evangelist, their unbelief drives them to regard the Son of God as a common criminal.

18:31   Pilate's answer to the Jews' defiant declaration can be variously interpreted. It is, as such, objectively consistent: since they do not define and justify their charge, he refers them to their own jurisdiction; they themselves must take over the responsibility. For disputes of a civil nature, and especially in religious affairs, the Sanhedrin had its own authority.[18] But if the following assertion of the Jews that they may not carry out a death sentence is taken with this, in the mind of the evangelist, the exchange must certainly be a humiliation of the Jewish leaders. He presupposes that Pilate knows or sees through the intention of the high priests. So the Roman's answer acquires an ironical, if not sarcastic tone. When the Jews have to speak out, the evangelist achieves a multiple purpose: the members of the council are forced to speak out now for themselves (cf. also 19:7), their intention to kill, known for a long time to the readers (cf. 5:18; 7:1, 19, 25, etc.), on which they had finally decided in a secret session (11:50, 53). At the same time their pride (cf. 8:33) is humbled, and they are exposed, despite all theocratic claims, as ignominious collaborators of the gentile world-power (cf. 11:48). The evangelist wants to say: this is how far unbelief and hatred drive the blinded Jewish leaders (cf. 19:15). Finally, the apologetic tendency comes in even here, to relieve the Roman judge and burdening the Jewish hierarchs with the greater guilt (cf. 19:11b).

There is disagreement to the present day whether the Jews of those times really did not have the ability to carry out death sentences. It is adduced in refutation, above all, that there are enough proved instances from this period of executions for which the Jews were responsible, Thus: Stephen's stoning (Acts 7); the execution (Josephus, *Ant.*, XX, 200, likewise stoning) of the 'Lord's brother', James, in AD 62; and, the burning of a priest's daughter who had acted immorally.[19] But the question is whether we are dealing with legal executions, or lynch-law (Stephen), or the exceeding of authority (James at a period between two procurators). In general, in the provinces subjected to them, the Romans' practice was to reserve the *ius gladii* for themselves. There were certainly exceptions; to these belongs the prohibition placed on non-Jews (including Romans) entering the inner part of the Jewish temple, on pain of death, as inscriptions which have been discovered on the balustrades of the outer Court of the Gentiles, prove.[20] A significant, if not uncontested witness in favour of the highest Jewish court of that era not having any power to carry out death sentences, is a Baraita in the Palestinian (or Jerusalem) Talmud that 'forty years before the destruction of the Temple' the 'judgments concerning life and death' were taken away from the Sanhedrin.[21] The attempts made by J. Juster (1914), H. Lietzmann (1931) and others right up to the present time (P. Winter, 1964), to prove the opposite, ought to be regarded as wrong.[22] John's information, wherever he found it, is, looked at historically, credible; only, he is concerned with more than an historical judgment.

18:32   An aside reminds the reader of Jesus' words with which he hinted at the manner of his death; it clearly takes up 12:33. In that position, the short commentary to 12:32 which was a deeply symbolical saying, admittedly had a greater justification. On that account it can be considered an editorial gloss.[23] Yet a reference back by the evangelist that a saying of Jesus should be fulfilled, as in 18:9, is not to be ruled out.[24] So he would be concerned here not so much with the sign-nature of Jesus' crucifixion as 'lifting up', but with the fact that the Jewish leaders are responsible for the shameful death of Jesus on the cross. They are the ones who raise the son of man on the cross (cf. 8:28); their repeated cry that Jesus be crucified (19:6, 15) confirms this.

2. Jesus' First Examination by Pilate.
The question of Jesus' kingship (18:33–38a)

[33]*Pilate entered the praetorium again and called Jesus, and said to him, 'Are you the King of the Jews?'* [34]*Jesus answered, 'Do you say this of your own accord, or did others say it to you about me?'* [35]*Pilate answered, 'Am I a Jew? Your own nation and the chief priests have handed you over to me; what have you done?'* [36]*Jesus answered, 'My kingship is not of this world; if my kingship were of this world, my servants would fight that I might not be handed over to the Jews; but my kingship is not from the world'.* [37]*Pilate said to him, 'So you are a king?'* *Jesus answered, 'You say that I am a king. For this I was born, and for this I have come into the world, to bear witness to the truth. Every one who is of the truth hears my voice.'* [38a]*Pilate said to him, 'What is truth?'*

Jesus' first examination by Pilate which, following the tradition, begins with the question whether he is 'the king of the Jews' ends with Jesus' self-confession of his kingship, which is 'not from this world', and with the Roman's sceptical question. Jesus interprets his kingship: he bears witness 'to the truth' and calls those to himself who are 'of the truth'. His judge is doubtful: 'What is truth?' and with this closes himself to the challenge and call of Jesus. Because Jesus' purpose in the world is to reveal the truth of salvation, he is unable to keep silent before the representative of the Gentiles either. In answering the Roman judge and explaining his kingship, he, at the same time, exercises the function of the one who reveals, who makes all men, even one possessed of worldly power, take a decision. But since this latter cannot decide positively, the outcome of the trial is already becoming apparent. John's interest in the trial is not for what takes place in the foreground, but, because of the yawning abyss indicated by 'Jesus' hour', everything takes its consequent course from this – from the preference given to a real criminal as against Jesus, the king (18:38b–40), the mocking of his kingship (19:1–3), and his public discrediting (19:4–6), right up to his condemnation to death on the cross (19:14–16). But the triumph of Jesus' enemies is an illusion; for, through the trial, Jesus is confirmed in his kingship and is enthroned as King, precisely, on the cross (19:19).

In this way, the theme of Jesus' kingship, which John takes up from the tradition and interprets in his own way, becomes the leading aspect of the presentation. Jesus' self-revelation in this first discussion with Pilate, which is deepened in the second discussion by the question of his origin (19:8–12), is the basis of all that follows during the trial and is the key to the evangelist's theological understanding. The significance of this theme is recognized in the more recent exegesis; but both in the general interpretation and in details, there are still various differences.[25]

18:33   In the order of the outward presentation, after the declaration of the accusers that the concern here is with a capital matter within his competence, Pilate must subject the accused to an examination. Roman court procedure (in contrast to the Jewish examination of witnesses) provided for a detailed examination of the accused, for Roman citizens according to the rules of legal procedure (*accusatio*), for non-Romans especially in the provinces, in a simplified procedure of *cognitio*.[26] The judicial proceedings were public and gave the accused enough opportunity to defend himself against the accusation, as indeed, the synoptics presuppose. When Pilate goes back inside the official building, calls Jesus, and apparently opens the examination without the public, it is not, indeed, considering the circumstances and a provincial governor's extent of power, historically impossible,[27] but for John it is only a means of presentation (see above, introduction). The 'world-changing' encounter of the Roman with Jesus takes place for him on a theological level. The question handed down by the synoptics in the same words: 'Are you the king of the Jews?',[28] which the fourth evangelist probably found in his source, betrays the Jewish accusation: it spoke of political rebellion, and presupposes that the chief priests accused Jesus of wrongly giving himself out to be the Messiah (in the sense of a national liberator, of the 'Son of David').

The expression 'King of the Jews' is, admittedly, formulated from the point of view of a non-Jew. In the synoptic gospels, it only occurs in the mouths of non-Jews; the Jews themselves speak of 'King of Israel' (Mk 15:32/Mt 27:42).[29] John takes up this honorary title of the Messiah in a positive sense, cf. on 1:49; 12:13. To be distinguished from this, is the designation βασιλεύς without qualification, which has a political sound in the mouth of the Jews (cf. 6:15; 19:12, 15), but, by Jesus, following Pilate's question, it is interpreted of his kingship. The opinion of W. A. Meeks that behind Jesus' witness to himself lies the thought of the prophet-king belonging to the Moses-typology[30] is doubtful (cf. on v. 37).

18:34–35   In the synoptics Jesus answers Pilate's question immediately: 'You have said so' (however this expression is interpreted). Since this answer likewise occurs in Jn v. 37, it can be supposed that in John's source too there was also nothing more. What is found in between is thus the evangelist's interpretation. Jesus' rejoinder whether Pilate asks of his own accord[31] aims at the Roman judge's answer. It was intended to make clear that the accusation is from the Jewish authorities who are more clearly identified in Pilate's answer. Pilate distances himself: 'Am I a Jew?' In these words his historically attested scorn of the Jews can, but need not be heard. He shifts the responsibility for the proceedings which have been set in motion against Jesus on to the Jews, more exactly: on to Jesus' 'nation and the chief priests'. By 'nation' – Pilate used the neutral term ἔθνος[32] – he cannot mean the whole Jewish nation which had not, after all, handed Jesus over to Pilate; rather, it refers to its representatives in the Sanhedrin, probably the elders (from the ranks of the lay nobility, οἱ πρεσβύτεροι),[33] who are nowhere mentioned in John. These Sadducees, influential because of birth and riches, are for him part of the past.

The chief priests are expressly mentioned again at the time of Jesus' presentation (19:6, together with 'officers') and at the end before the pronouncement of judgment (19:15). That is no accident; for John they have already come to represent those people who pursue Jesus' death (cf. 7:32, 45; 11:47, 49ff, 57; 12:10), and are, then, directly responsible for Jesus' arrest and handing over to Pilate. The Pharisees are more often mentioned second in the order; this is explained by the contemporary situation in which they are the adversaries as far as the Johannine community is concerned. But after 18:3 they are not named any more, and that too is no accident. The proceedings against Jesus were mainly brought about by the chief priests, who fought them through to their desired end. Thus, the fourth evangelist certainly comes near to the historical truth.[34]

Like Lk, John, in the whole course of the trial, nowhere speaks of a crowd (ὄχλος), much less, as in Mt 27:25, of 'all the people' (πᾶς ὁ λαός). When he does not single out the chief priests, he says, οἱ Ἰουδαῖοι, in whose number (as in other places) the leading men of contemporary Judaism are to be understood; thus, at the trial the chief priests supported by other members of the counsel, namely, the Sadducean elders.[35]

For the Roman judge only what Jesus has done is decisive. The objective question gives Jesus the chance to defend himself against the accusation of the high counsel.

18:36 Jesus' saying about his kingship is constructed in negative-positive form, as is often the case in John. Also typical of his thought is that he determines the nature according to the origin (ἐκ) (cf. on 3:6, 31; 8:23; 15:19, etc.). Jesus' βασιλεία does not here signify his 'kingdom' but, in accordance with Pilate's question it is a designation of function ('kingship'). Thus, *Jesus' βασιλεία* is not the heavenly realm like the *βασιλεία τοῦ θεοῦ* in 3:3, 5. While in the conversation with Nicodemus the synoptic expression is taken up and transformed into the Johannine understanding of it (see *ad loc.*), it is not at all permissible to forge a link between the answer to Pilate and Jesus' Kingdom of God preaching. At most, John could be referring back to the early Christian way of speaking about the lordship of Christ.[36] He is concerned with Jesus' royal rank and his sphere of operation which is in the world due to his proclamation of salvation. The field covered by the words 'king, kingship' is only transcribed, as it were, in terms of the Johannine kerygma. This explanation is important so that Jesus' *βασιλεία* is not interpreted wrongly. It has an unworldly nature but it is not shut off from the world; rather it manifests itself just there in the world wherever his voice is heard. The expression 'this world' need not sound completely negative (as in 'ruler of this world' 12:31; 16:11; cf. also 8:23b); sometimes it also only sets off the sphere of earthly existence from the transcendent world, cf. 12:25; 13:1. This meaning is confirmed here by the following words of Jesus. Jesus wants to make clear to the Roman who is used to thinking in terms of power politics, that he is not planning a rebellion which would be achieved by 'worldly' means, with weapons. Otherwise, he argues, his 'servants' – the same word in Greek as that used for the officers sent out against him (18:3, 12) – would have fought to prevent his being handed over to the Jews, obviously a reference to the arrest scene. The evangelist presupposes that Pilate is informed concerning this, but he does not mention the Roman military detachment. Again he means to put the blame on the Jews. Thus, Jesus' kingship is not 'from here', that is of a worldly kind.[37] The question of the origin is only suggested here; it is taken up by Pilate later on (19:9), after the chief priests' assertion that Jesus made himself Son of God. The representative of the Roman state is increasingly confronted by a truth which he does not understand, but he suspects and, in its inconceivability, fears it (19:9, it *μᾶλλον ἐφοβήθη*).

18:37 But since Jesus does speak about his *βασιλεία* Pilate follows up with the question: 'So you are a king?' and, in this way, gives Jesus the opportunity to describe his kingship positively. Now Jesus speaks the words with which we are acquainted from the synoptics: 'You say so', here, doubtless, in an affirmative sense, strengthened by the affirmation, 'that I am a king'.[38] But immediately Jesus explains further in what sense he understands himself to be a king. What he asserts about himself puts into the strongest relief the fact that he originates from another world, and has no other purpose in this world than to bear witness to that other world and its reality. Hence the pleonasm, that he 'was born for this' and has 'come into the world for this' to bear witness to the truth. Pre-existence and incarnation are the precondition for, but not the point of this way of speaking. Rather, Jesus knows himself to be the only competent envoy from God's realm who reveals the truth of salvation. That is the Johannine kerygma, as propounded in its most concentrated and clearest form in Jn 3:31–36. There too there is mention of 'witness', and the theme of truth is heard in the sentence, 'He who receives his testimony sets his seal to this, that God is true (ἀληθής)' (3:33).

The sentence is wholly moulded by the Johannine use of words, and can only be understood in that light. To begin with, the idea of testimony does not have here any earthly forensic sense but means the heavenly witness who speaks those things in the world which he 'has seen and heard with the Father' (cf. 3:32; 8:26)[39] and who reveals this knowledge to mankind as the 'truth' which brings salvation (cf. 8:32 and Excursus 10). All his ministry is bearing witness to God, who turns himself in love towards the world and desires man's salvation (cf. 3:16f). But, before the Roman judge, this testimony is also forensic in character; accused, the witness for God and his truth once again gains a hearing.[40]

The statement, 'every one who is of the truth hears [(German verb is 'listens to' – *translator*)] my voice' recalls the controversy with the Jews in Chapter 8, and later on, the shepherd-saying of Chapter 10. Jesus holds against the unbelieving Jews that he has proclaimed the truth to them (8:40, 45f) and they reject him, because they are not 'of God' (8:47). Now Jesus appeals to Pilate to listen to his voice if he wants to be 'of the truth' (='of God'). In positive contrast to those Jews stand the believers who listen to the voice of their shepherd (10:3, 16, 27).[41] Pilate is challenged as to whether he would belong to this or the other group.

Jesus' kingship, with which the representative of earthly power is confronted, has repeatedly tempted people to define more closely the relationship between the two realms of 'authority' represented by Jesus and Pilate. The range extends from the spiritualization of the 'kingdom' of Christ to a 'political' claim which is supposed to be implicit in this. Against the first opinion, which restricts Christ's kingship to the heavenly sphere or the eschatological future,[42] speak the clear statements concerning Jesus as present king, and also the reference to those men who listen to his voice and thus subject themselves to his kingship on earth. The second view, which, on account of this earthly dimension of Christ's 'rule', is formed in terms of a 'politically relevant nature for Jesus' kingdom',[43] can, at the least, be misunderstood, because Jesus rejected an earthly political activity for himself. Only in the broad sense that all human action, including that of those believing in Jesus, has a social consequence, is it possible to speak of 'political' relevance. But since Christ's disciples are constrained by their Lord's word and example, following Jesus is much more persecution on his account (cf. 15:20f) – this also, admittedly, a necessary testimony to the world which rejected the witness to God's truth.

W. A. Meeks wants to prove a special connection in our passage with the Moses-like prophet and king who was expected in certain Jewish and Samaritan circles.[44] 'Listening' to Jesus' voice is said to recall Deut 18:15 (αὐτοῦ ἀκούσεσθε), and in support of the 'king' is to be the picture of the shepherd in Jn 10. Now we too have established the connection with that metaphor (ἀκούειν τῆς φωνῆς); but it is very questionable whether the shepherd in

Jn 10 is understood as a royal personage. The Moses traditions which had such an influence, can hardly have affected our passage directly; the notion of kingship is due to the traditional question by Pilate.

18:38a   Pilate's famous question, 'What is truth?', is meant to express, as a reaction to Jesus' saying concerning the truth to which he bears witness, neither philosophical scepticism nor cold irony, and certainly not a serious search for truth; for the evangelist it is an avoidance and so a rejection of Jesus' witness.[45] Jesus offers Pilate God's truth, indeed, he stands before him as the voice of the truth; but Pilate does not hear it, does not understand it, else he could not ask concerning some 'truth' or other. The same phenomenon is demonstrated in his case as, in Chapter 8, in that of the Jews who do not understand what Jesus says (8:43). He too does not belong to those who are 'of the truth'. With that, the Roman judge has already decided against Jesus; this is only confirmed by what follows. All these episodic and dramatic tableaux of the evangelist, whether they are concerned in Chapter 8 with the unbelieving Jews, or here, during the trial, with the Gentile Pilate, lay bare the conviction that the revelation of God which is found in Jesus compels a decision, causes a crisis (cf. 3:18f).

3. Attempt to set Jesus Free; Barabbas instead of Jesus (18:38b–40)

[38b]*After he had said this, he went out to the Jews again, and told them, 'I find no crime in him. [39]But you have a custom that I should release one (prisoner) for you at the passover; will you have me release for you the King of the Jews?' [40]They cried out again, 'Not this man, but Barabbas!' Now Barabbas was a robber.*

18:38b   After Pilate's question which, for the time being, draws a line under the conversation with Jesus, the scene changes. The Roman goes out again to the Jews and informs them that he finds no guilt in Jesus. This (first) pronouncement of innocence cannot be connected psychologically with the examination as though Jesus' words had actually had an effect on Pilate. The account picks up again after vv. 29–31; and there the meaning of the scene for the evangelist becomes clear: the Jews have charged Jesus as a common criminal, the Roman Judge acquits him of this, and attempts to set Jesus free. But the Jews refuse and show preference for a real criminal.

Here again, we have an interpretation by the evangelist of a previously existing tradition. He used it only to the extent that it seemed useful for his purpose. So it is scarcely possible to say, whether the source was not more detailed and related something else.[46] In its wording 'the proclamation of innocence' is closely paralleled by Lk 23:4; only John confronts the members of the counsel with Pilate in a more pronounced form by putting ἐγώ at the beginning. For this scene, as other observations (on vv. 39f) confirm, John's source will have been close to Lk.[47]

18:39   The most noticeable peculiarity of John's account is Pilate's initiative. All by himself, he reminds the Jews of the passover amnesty and makes them the suggestion that he release Jesus on account of this custom. This is not only historically unlikely, but also distinguishes John from the account of the synoptics. According to Mk 15:8 (cf. Mt 27:15, 17) there is a demand from a crowd. In Lk this is not expressly said but obviously presupposed (cf. 23:18). At best, John's source (like Lk) will have told of Pilate's effort to release Jesus; the Roman's *offer* is certainly a move introduced by the evangelist.[48]

If we pay attention to the words, then the intention of the narrator is recognized somewhat more clearly. 'There is a custom to your advantage'; ὑμῖν is very close here to being a *dativus commodi*.[49] Pilate, who accommodates himself to the custom-clause (Johannine style), builds, as it were, a bridge for the accusers, so that, without 'loss of face' they can draw back from their demand that Jesus be killed (v. 31). When they reject Pilate's spirit of compromise, their spite becomes even more blatant. On the other hand, the Roman appears in a better light (apologetic tendency).

The historical likelihood of the passover amnesty has been often questioned, because the Jewish sources seemingly know nothing of it (it is never mentioned in Josephus). According to Roman law an amnesty was possible, before the judgment (*abolitio*), or after (*indulgentia*). Such a case is recorded on an Egyptian papyrus from the year AD 85: The governor frees a wrongdoer, in accordance with the people's wish ('I want to give you up to the mob').[50] But that was an exception; in Jesus' trial, we have to do with a regular custom at the time of the passover feast. Now C. B. Chavel has shown on the basis of a Mishnah text that, apparently, such a custom really did exist. In *Pes* VIII, 6a, five groups of people are listed on whose behalf also the passover lamb may be slaughtered. Among these there is mention also of one whose release from prison had been promised. This must refer to Roman arrest, because Jewish prisoners in Jerusalem could have a piece of the passover lamb brought to them in prison. But since, according to the text, the lamb may not be slaughtered for that person by friends, this concerns a promise still in doubt because the procurator's permission is necessary. Chavel can also make out a credible case as to how, possibly, the custom arose.[51] If that is right, the Johannine chronology of the passion is confirmed; the release would have had to take place before the eve of the passover.

18:40   But the Jews do not fall in with Pilate's offer but cry out: 'Not this man but Barabbas.' The wording is close to the Lukan text: ἐκραύγασαν corresponds to Lk 23:18 ἀνέκραγον; in both cases, Jesus' execution is demanded first, and then Barabbas' release; following that it is explained who Barabbas was. Thus, in the main, John will have taken his text from his source. He has added the historic οὖν, and perhaps also the noticeable πάλιν.[52] The shouting of the Jews is a motif from the tradition, which John has taken over and extended. There is no previous mention of κραυγάζειν, but there are another three later occurrences (19:6, 12, 15). It is possible that John already considers the words of the accusation in vv. 30 and 31c to be a 'cry'.[53]

Barabbas, whom the Jews want freed instead of Jesus, is characterized by John as λῃστής. He probably found the expression in his source; in Mk 15:27/

Mt 27:38 the two men crucified with Jesus, about whom John also knows (19:18), are called λῃσταί, and there is much in favour of this referring to Barabbas' accomplices; for, according to Mk 15:7 (cf. Lk 23:19) he was captured together with other rebels. Then, the source probably understood λῃστής to mean a 'freedom' fighter, a (zealot) gang-leader, a usage supported with many examples in Josephus.[54] But John is not interested in this background. The two men crucified with Jesus are not described by him as λῃσταί, and in those other places where he again uses the word, namely, in 10:1, 8, the reference to (zealot) 'freedom' fighters is remote, if not excluded by the connection with 'thieves' (cf. Vol. 2, pp. 281f together with n. 1). So the evangelist probably intends the term in the source to be understood in our passage probably as 'robber'. The Jews, who dismiss Jesus as an evildoer (v. 30), even prefer a highwayman to him! The Barabbas scene too was given a new aspect in the course of the Johannine presentation.[55]

4. Scourging and Crowning with Thorns (19:1–3)

[1]*Then Pilate took Jesus and scourged him.* [2]*And the soldiers plaited a crown of thorns, and put it on his head, and arrayed him in a purple robe;* [3]*they came up to him, saying, 'Hail, King of the Jews!' and struck him with their hands.'*

The new scene, that of Jesus' scourging and crowning with thorns taken from the tradition, becomes for John an interlude between the offer of the passover amnesty and Jesus' presentation to the Jews. Since, in both these instances, Pilate 'goes out' to the Jews (18:38; 19:4), it is thought of as taking place in the praetorium, although that is not especially noted. In spite of his pronouncing Jesus innocent, Pilate allows himself to be carried away so far as to have Jesus scourged. From this act of giving in follow weighty consequences, leading as it does to the Jews' demand that Jesus be crucified (19:6), and, as matters proceed, leaving the Roman no other choice than to pronounce the death sentence (19:15f). This presentation is intended by the evangelist: Pilate, who closes himself to the call of God's messenger (18:37f), is entangled more and more, for all his power, in the schemes of men. The interlude which directly combines the scourging with the crowning with thorns, is narrated only briefly so as to lead on to the Ecce-homo-scene. Thus, for the most part, are explained the differences from the synoptics, even if John might have followed a special source.

19:1 The scourging of Jesus, which, in the synoptics too, is only briefly mentioned – not as a punishment on its own account but as one connected with the crucifixion[56] – is introduced by John with the remark: Pilate 'took' Jesus. This seemingly superfluous ἔλαβεν thrusts the responsibility on to the Roman: it is an unjustifiable measure. In 18:31, Pilate seeks to thrust the accused on to the accusers (18:31: λάβετε αὐτὸν ὑμεῖς), and after Jesus' presentation and the shouts of the Jews, he tries once more in the same words (19:6). But it does not help him at all: his indecision forces him to join in their machinations. Finally, he 'hands over' Jesus 'to them' (the Jews?) to be crucified, and they 'take' him (19:16). The parts are assigned, each carries his share of responsibility, the greater responsibility, admittedly, is the Jews' who handed Jesus over to the Roman (cf. 19:11f).

Jesus' scourging is described briefly as in the synoptics. But in John it is not the prologue to the penalty of the cross, but a punishment in its own right which occurred independently of and before it. What we have here is the Roman *verberatio*,[57] which, as a primary punishment, was mostly only given to slaves or soldiers requiring to be punished, and in court proceedings also served as a torture to obtain a confession (cf. Acts 22:24). Nothing iin the text suggests the latter and it is out of the question for John, because Jesus had already confessed himself to be 'king'. The separation from the punishment of the cross is due to the Johannine presentation in which scourging and crowning with thorns are brought together. For the evangelist it (the scourging) is a humiliation of Jesus, which, together with the crowning with thorns, makes possible his presentation as a flayed and derided man, as a mock-king. The different choice of words as compared with the synoptics, $\mu\alpha\sigma\tau\iota\gamma\acute{o}\omega$ (Mk/Mt: $\phi\rho\alpha\gamma\epsilon\lambda\lambda\acute{o}\omega$) allows us to suppose an independent source, which was, perhaps, influenced by Is 50:6 ($\mu\acute{\alpha}\sigma\tau\iota\gamma\epsilon\varsigma$, $\dot{\rho}\alpha\pi\acute{\iota}\sigma\mu\alpha\tau\alpha$).[58]

19:2–3 The mocking of Jesus as king of the Jews is confined, by John, to the crown of thorns, the purple robe, the mocking salutation and the dishonouring blows on the cheek. Then (19:5), Jesus is presented to the Jews with the crown of thorns and purple robe. In contrast to the broader synoptic picture in Mk/Mt, the reed which the soldiers put in his hand as a sceptre and with which they then strike him on the head, the spitting, and the kneeling in homage, are missing. We cannot determine whether the Johannine source narrated these things equally briefly. If John leaves out other matters, he does so either because he wanted to protect the hidden (divine) majesty of Jesus, or because he wanted to concentrate his attention on the presentation with the two mock insignia.

The source probably contained nothing about the reed as a staff of office. The description of the crowning with thorns agrees almost word for word with Mt 27:29; Mk/Mt describe the salutation similarly. In the choice of words for the purple robe (which Mt interprets as a soldier's red cloak) John is more akin to Mk. Differing from both, John speaks of the blows on the cheek ($\dot{\rho}\alpha\pi\acute{\iota}\sigma\mu\alpha\tau\alpha$) presumably according to his source. This detail is dispensable for the presentation; whether it is meant to recall 18:22 is doubtful. A comparison with Lk is not possible, since this evangelist omitted the scene altogether. So the observations made previously are confirmed, that John is indeed following a source which is similar to the synoptics, without himself being directly dependent on these gospels.

Taken together, scourging and crowning with thorns in John demand an evaluation other than in the synoptics. Whereas in the latter, the crowning with thorns belongs to the scenes of mockery which reveal Jesus' suffering on its deeper level, and show clearly the destiny of the persecuted righteous one (Mk 15:29–31 par.) and of the messiah-son-of-man rejected by the Jews and handed over to the Gentiles (Mk 8:31; 9:31; 10:33; cf. 14:65), the Johannine scene has a different function: it prepares for the presentation of Jesus before the Jews which represents a new high-point in the confrontation with the chief priests. Because of that, the crowning with thorns comes to be found prior to the judgment. Looked at historically, its place is certainly after the pronouncement of the judgment, say, during the interlude in which preparations were made for the execution (cf. Mk), because the Roman soldiers could only then do what they wanted with the prisoner.[59] John has arranged the facts in such a way, that the succession of the scenes progressively builds up to the pronouncement of judgment, and Jesus' hidden kingship comes ever more clearly to the fore in the contradiction of his enemies.

5. Pilate's Presentation of Jesus (19:4–7)

[4]*Pilate went out again, and said to them, 'Behold, I am bringing him out to you, that you may know that I find no crime in him.'* [5]*So Jesus came out, wearing the crown of thorns and the purple robe. Pilate said to them, 'Here is the man!'* [6]*When the chief priests and the officers saw him, they cried out, 'Crucify him, crucify him!' Pilate said to them, 'Take him yourselves and crucify him, for I find no crime in him.'* [7]*The Jews answered him, 'We have a law, and by that law he ought to die, because he has made himself the Son of God.'*

The scene, which has no parallel in the synoptics, is clearly put together by John. The specifically Lukan narrative according to which Herod with his soldiers mocked Jesus and then sent him back to Pilate dressed in a magnificent robe (Lk 23:6–12), shows only few similarities: the derision, clothing in gorgeous apparel, afterwards the calling together of 'the chief priests and the rulers and the people' by Pilate, and his declaration of Jesus' innocence (Lk 23:13f). But the conditions are quite different and the presentation of Jesus does not happen in the same way as in John. It cannot be determined whether the Johannine source described something similar; John may equally have freely fashioned the scene.[60] Only the call for crucifixion is traditional; but the presentation by Pilate ('Ecce, homo') gives it a new resonance. The meaning of Jesus' presentation as ὁ ἄνθρωπος has puzzled many people; we have to pay particular attention to it within the framework of the Johannine account.

19:4   For the third time it says that Pilate goes out to the Jews. The first time, it was to hear their charge against 'this man' (18:29). The second time, after the examination inside the praetorium, to declare to them that he finds no guilt in Jesus (18:38b). Now – and in this is to be found the progression – he leads Jesus out to them and once more states that he regards him as innocent. It is a dramatic appearance designed for effect, so that they themselves recognize that their accusation that Jesus has claimed to be 'King of the Jews', seems to him, the Roman, void.

19:5   Jesus comes out flayed and wretched, the caricature of a king. He is crowned with a crown of thorns[61] and wears a purple robe, presumably a shabby soldier's cloak, as a robe of office. What does Pilate want to say with this? Jesus shows nothing of royal rank and authority in his person, for him, he is no political rebel. Since this presentation is linked with the declaration of innocence (v. 4) the meaning cannot lie in the fact that the alleged 'King of the Jews' has now *become* a figure to be mocked, but that, according to Pilate's investigations, he is not at all a disturber of the peace with political ambitions. Certainly, this is also a challenge to the Jews, but not, in the first place, to show them, scornfully, in the figure of Jesus, how powerless they are; rather, so as to make clear to them their false accusation in the case of Jesus.[62] The seriously intended declaration of innocence underlined by the repetition at the end of v. 6, so that the presentation is framed by the two pronouncements, cannot be left out of consideration if the scene as a whole is to be understood.

Pilate's brief pronouncement, the famous 'Ecce, homo', is probably meant once more to draw attention to Jesus in his appearance as mock-king.[63] Pilate has announced Jesus' presentation (v. 4: ἴε κτλ.), and now, as Jesus, wretched and decked out as a figure of scorn with the insignia of a king, has come out of the praetorium, he points to him. ἰδού is a demonstrative particle corresponding to the Hebrew הִנֵּה (cf. LXX), but is also found in secular Greek.[64] The article (missing in Vaticanus), which entices many exegetes to the supposition of a titular use of ὁ ἄνθρωπος, is not peculiar in this context. Already in 18: 29 Pilate had spoken of Jesus no differently ('this man'). In 18:39 he had, admittedly, called him 'the King of the Jews', in the expectation that the Jews would ask for his release on the grounds of the passover amnesty. Now he shows them their 'king', whom he himself only regards as a figure of fun. So he says, certainly with an undertone of scorn: 'Here is the man!', the man whom you have accused as claimant to the throne.[65] If Pilate does not say (as in 19:14) 'Here is your king!', then that is because he does not want to anger the Jews but to convince them of Jesus' innocence. His dramatic build-up is meant to demonstrate his decision about Jesus.

When Pilate's words are allowed, in the context of the Johannine presentation of the trial, this obvious and 'simple' meaning, various other interpretations which look for an obscure meaning in them, are to be rejected:

1. An allusion to the *anthropos*-myth which some scholars suppose to be behind the Johannine christology, especially behind the descent and ascent of the son of man;[66] but cf. together with that Excursus 6 (Vol. 1, pp. 543–557).

2. ὁ ἄνθρωπος is made equivalent to ὁ υἱός τοῦ ἀνθρώπου. This currently not infrequently represented opinion[67] claims support particularly from Jn 8:28, where Jesus says to the Jews: 'When you have lifted up the Son of man, then you will know . . .'. This saying, which attributes to the Jews an active interest in Jesus' 'lifting up' (= crucifixion), is supposed to find its fulfilment now, as they shout their demand for crucifixion before the Roman tribunal (19:6). Pilate could say 'the Son of man'; but the readers who were familiar with the evangelist's thoughts could and should understand that. Without going into all the problems connected with it[68] the following brief remarks apply. The passage in 8:28 does not necessarily have to refer directly to this scene but generally

The Trial Before Pilate

thrusts the responsibility for Jesus' crucifixion on to the Jews; 19:5 would be the only place in John's gospel where ὁ ἄνθρωπος stands for ὁ υἱὸς τοῦ ἀνθρώπον; also the rule that the title only otherwise occurs spoken by Jesus (or in answer to him, 9:35; 12:34) would be broken; the title 'the Son of man' would represent a summit beyond which one could not go, and yet everything leads towards the parallel constructed saying in 19:14 ('Here is your king!')

3. The connection with a Messiah-expectation in the Judaeo-Hellenistic sphere where the bringer of salvation is called ἄνθρωπος (Num 24:17 LXX; Philo, *Testament of the Twelve Patriarchs*);[69] but the basis for this seems too weak, and, it would certainly be expecting too much that the readers understood this.

Thus, if Pilate's exclamation means nothing more than 'the man', perhaps 'this pathetic man', and no meaning is to be sought behind the expression itself, the other point is not affected by this, that, for the evangelist, the whole trial, has a meaning beyond what happens superficially, which is revealed to the eye of faith. The *entire* scene throughout which Pilate scornfully makes clear that Jesus is no real king for him, and in which the Jews nevertheless demand his crucifixion, is to be seen in this perspective. Is the trial as such meant to represent the 'epiphany of the king' Jesus, and with it the mockery scene meant to be the enthronement and investiture, and after that the presentation by Pilate, the epiphany to and acclamation of the people?[70] That also is already an over-interpretation because just here it is not the 'people' (as in Lk 23:13) who are present, and the real 'enthronement' only takes place at the cross (Jn 19:19–22). But it is true, as the readers are meant to grasp, that the mock-king presented by Pilate is, nevertheless, even in this travesty, the king who bears testimony to the truth as Jesus previously affirmed (18:37). Despite his pitiable appearance, he has a dignity which, shortly afterwards, is referred to by the chief priests in, 'Son of God' (19:7).[71] The evangelist will not want to recall, in this connection, the logos becoming flesh,[72] but presumably the hidden divinity of the earthly Jesus and the paradox that the one who is apparently humiliated on the cross is in reality the exalted and glorified one (cf. Excursus 13 vol. 2, pp. 398–410).

19:6   The reaction to the spectacle organized by Pilate is the Jews' demand for crucifixion. This shout is found in the synoptic accounts in the Barabbas scene (Mk 15:13f par.), twice indeed, with a crescendo effect. Although the Johannine account comes into contact with this in the crucifixion demand – most clearly with Mk, who has the same form (σταύρωσον) – it differs considerably as to the circumstances. In the Johannine Barabbas scene, this cry is not yet audible, but only, for the first time, when Pilate presents Jesus. Again, in Mk/Mt a scene like that in Jn 19:4ff cannot be accommodated, because the soldiers, after mocking Jesus, reclothe the convicted one in his own clothes (Mk 15:20 par.). John (or his source?) took up the motif of the crucifixion demand and transferred it to the presentation – a progressing dramatisation. A second difference concerns the actors: in John it is 'the chief priests and the officers' who raise the double cry,[73] 'Crucify him, crucify him!' In Mk it is the mob goaded by the chief priests (15:11), in Mt it is 'all' (27:22), and according to Lk also they shout 'all together' (23:18). In Jn, the information could come from his source, because the 'officers' (ὑπηρέται) of the chief priests already play a part at Jesus' arrest and at the Jewish trial (18:3, 12, 18, 22) and the evangelist elsewhere prefers to speak of 'the Jews'.[74] Apart from the dramatization of the scene a historically worthwhile reminder perhaps breaks through here, that those connected with the chief priests were solely responsible for the pressure put on Pilate (cf. also on 11:49ff and 18:3). This realization could have prevented much injustice against the Jewish people. Pilate does not give in to the shout of the chief priests, at least, not immediately – that is a third difference as against the presentation of Mk/Mt. Rather, he tries once more (cf. 18:31a) to shift the proceedings against Jesus on to the Jewish authorities. In the evangelist's view, here deliberately delineated, Pilate's attempt to rid himself of the accused ('Take him yourselves'), is seriously meant (cf. 19:12a), but his answer to the chief priests is phrased sarcastically and as a provocation. For, Pilate knows, of course, that they are not allowed to crucify Jesus (cf. 18:31b), and his challenge to do so can only provoke and humilate them. The following (third) pronouncement, that he himself finds no guilt in Jesus belongs inseparably to this, and gives his answer, at last, the desired colour: *You* do with the prisoner what you will, *I* want to have nothing to do with him!

At this point, the Johannine account is close to Lk 23:13–16. After Herod has sent Jesus back to Pilate, Pilate gathers the chief priests, the leaders and the people and tells the assembled crowd that neither he nor Herod have found anything against Jesus deserving of the death penalty. In Lk this is the second pronouncement of innocence (after 23:4); Pilate's intention to release Jesus (after 'chastisement'), is likewise seriously meant, but it then comes to nothing because of the stubbornness of the crowd which demands Jesus' death (Barabbas scene). But the differences also cannot be overlooked: the different situation, the wider circle of participants, the fact that the demand for the crucifixion does not come until the Barabbas scene. The pronouncement of innocence is a stylistic device which Lk uses in the same way as Jn, likewise three times, but in different places. A direct influence on Jn or his source by Lk is pretty well excluded; at most one can suppose that that stylistic device goes back to a common tradition. The most important Johannine motif: 'Take him yourselves!' is lacking in Lk.[75]

19:7 Driven into a corner by the Roman judge's rebuff, 'the Jews', that is the chief priests, now bring a new argument forward. They call upon their law according to which Jesus has to die, because he has made himself 'the Son of God'. What is meant is the blaspheming of God's name according to Lev 24:16, but for which the penalty was stoning. It is the same accusation already known to the readers from Jn 5:18; 10:33; cf. 8:59 (see on these passages). From a legal point of view this would have given the whole trial a different direction because the accusation would have moved from a civil to a religious offence. The Roman prefect was only responsible for it because the Jews were not entitled to carry out a death sentence (see on 18:31). From a historical viewpoint this account would completely contradict the synoptic narratives which base the Roman trial exclusively on the charge of political rebellion. However, nor does Jn want to regard the chief priests' move as being, in any way, a turning-point in the trial.[76] For him too, the trial before the Roman tribunal ends with Jesus' condemnation as the 'King of the Jews' (19:15), and the inscription on the cross confirms this (19:19). The new intervention by the Jews, clearly formulated by the evangelist himself, only has validity and meaning at the level of Jn's theological presentation. Here, admittedly it is of an eminent significance and that from several points of view:

(1) The chief priests are exposed in that their charge that Jesus is a political rebel was only put forward as a pretext; now they have to say openly, that they are pressing for Jesus' death (cf. 18:30f) on other grounds.

(2) Their deadly hatred of Jesus has its deepest roots in their unbelief concerning Jesus who claims to be God's messenger, the Son of God. This Jewish unbelief, the sin above all others for John, which in Jesus' collisions with the Jews during his public ministry has already been demonstrated sufficiently, is now to be uncovered before the Roman tribunal and so established before world public opinion, so to speak, with the force of law.

(3) Jesus' kingship, with which this trial is concerned, is revealed in its true character, correctly interpreted by the Jewish leaders themselves. For when Pilate rules out an earthly political kingship of Jesus, demonstrates that to be ridiculous, makes it into an absurdity and, nevertheless, condemns Jesus as the 'King of the Jews' on the grounds of the new Jewish accusation, then Jesus' kingship can only be of that sort which finds expression in the words of the chief priests, but which is indeed most decisively rejected by them. It is the confirmation of the interpretation of his kingship given by Jesus himself (18:37).

(4) Pilate does not reject the new charge, rather, he is greatly impressed by it. When he heard these words, 'he was the more afraid' (v. 8). His unresisting acceptance of the objection is the confession that he does not want to be rid of Jesus merely because he does not regard him as a rebel, but also because he senses Jesus' inner majesty and superiority. In this way, the humiliating mockery-scene becomes a secret triumph for Jesus. The 'Man' scornfully presented by Pilate, shows himself, precisely in the Jews' opposition, as the 'Son of God'.

6. Jesus' Second Examination by Pilate. Attempt to release Him, and the Jews' Objection (19:8–12)

[8]*When Pilate heard these words, he was the more afraid;* [9]*he entered the praetorium again and said to Jesus, 'Where are you from?' But Jesus gave no answer.* [10]*Pilate therefore said to him, 'You will not speak to me? Do you not know that I have power to release you and power to crucify you?'* [11]*Jesus answered him, 'You would have no power over me unless it had been given you from above; therefore he who delivered me to you has the greater sin'.* [12]*Upon this Pilate sought to release him, but the Jews cried out, 'If you release this man, you are not Caesar's friend; everyone who makes himself a king sets himself against Caesar.'*

Jesus' second examination by Pilate has an unmistakable connection with the first (18:33–37). The questions concerning Jesus' origin and the nature of his 'authority' are taken further. If Jesus' kingship was only restricted in a negative way in 18:36 ('not of this world', 'not from here'), so now, after Pilate's significant question: 'Where are you from?' we hear the (for John) so expressive ἄνωθεν (v. 11). The external details too: the 'increased' fear of the Roman, Jesus' silence, Pilate's determined attempt to release him, only become fully understandable with the background of the first encounter. It is the climax (not from the point of view of the political history of the world, but in respect of the majesty of Jesus and his witness to the truth) of the meeting between Jesus and the representative of the Roman civil power.

19:8 Pilate's reaction to the chief priest's words, in which there was a suggestion of Jesus' claim to be the Son of God, is 'increased fear'. It is not, say, outward fear of the Jews (until now, nothing of that was to be seen in the Roman's demeanour); rather, it is the numinous terror before the divine, which falls upon this representative of earthly power.[77] If such fear has not been mentioned before, the comparative[78] nevertheless shows that the evangelist presupposes a similar reaction by Pilate already in the case of the first conversation, only he covers it up with the question: 'What is truth?' (18:38a). Such fear by the judge of the accused, who appears to him as a higher being, is also related in the *Vita Apollonii*.[79] John inserts this narrative motif so as to demonstrate the 'reversed roles' of the judge Pilate, and Jesus the accused; for in what follows, Jesus shows himself the superior party, the one making the sovereign decisions, in fact, as the judge (v. 12).

19:9 The question 'where' Jesus is 'from', was heard repeatedly during Jesus' confrontation with the unbelieving Jews (7:27f; 8:14; 9:29f); the heavenly origin of Jesus is a cornerstone of his witness to himself. In Pilate's mouth the question, full of misgivings, refers to the same; but after the sceptically unbelieving question of 18:38a, it is not any indication of an honest searching or incipient faith, but only the expression of uncertainty and fear. Because Jesus knows of Pilate'a unbelieving stance, he keeps silent. What more should he say to him, since Pilate does not listen to his voice (18:37d)? With this, the evangelist picks up the traditional motif of Jesus' silence which, in the synoptics, already plays a part in the Jewish proceedings (Mk 14:61/Mt 26:63), then again in the trial before Pilate (Mk 15:5/Mt 27:14), and in Lk 23:9 during the questioning by Herod. In John, its function is limited (after it, Jesus does speak again) and its theological evaluation is different (certainly not reference to Is 53:7). He who reveals does not give any answer to the one trapped in earthly thought processes, because he cannot grasp it anyway (cf. 8:25).

19:10 Because of this, Pilate's uncertainty grows, and he withdraws into the false certainty of a man who is aware of his power. Looked at superficially, the attempt to make an accused person say something in a Roman court hearing is justified, and the threat of the extensive administrative power (imperium) possessed by the provincial governor[80] is understandable. But for the evangelist, it is the ineffectual attempt of one protecting himself so as to get away from God's challenge. The power with which Pilate vaunts himself (ἐμοί emphatically at the beginning) would be an illusion if he were to use it arbitrarily. The accused, seemingly powerless man standing before him, represents another power in the presence of which Pilate is secretly afraid.

19:11   Jesus does not break his silence because he gives into the threat, but because he has something to say to the Roman prefect on the subject of ἐξουσία (power or force).[81] Jesus' answer has to be examined precisely in respect of its formulation. The first part of the sentence is an unfulfilled condition[82] so that, factually, Jesus confirms Pilate's administrative power over him; but the second part restricts this power. In the latter case, ἐξουσία is no longer the subject, but a Johannine mode of expression is used which points to God's freely-disposing activity (see on 3:27; 6:65). On account of this meaning, 'Unless it had been given you from above, to release me or to crucify me' would have to be added. Then: Jesus' answer relates to the concrete situation and is not a specific statement concerning the state power exercised by Pilate. As soon as one (wrongly) translates: 'You would have no power over me unless *it* [(the power–*translator*)] had been given you from above', one is led towards an interpretation according to Rom 13:1. Our passage has, in fact, often been interpreted as a theological statement on the power of the state as such, and Jesus' encounter with Pilate has been thrust on to the level of political discussion.[83] But Jesus' words are applied to the situation of his day, they apply to *Jesus*' destiny (κατ' ἐμοῦ!) and it is held before Pilate that his administrative power is not solely dependent on him. In the present case, he can, indeed, proceed with Jesus as he wills, but only because God lets him have his own way.[84] With ἄνωθεν John describes the heavenly divine realm (cf. 3:27, 31c ἐκ τοῦ οὐρανοῦ), whence Jesus himself originates and by which he is conditioned in his being and in his will (3:31; cf. 8:23). This origin gives him a superiority over all who are 'of the earth', 'from below' (3:31 ἐπάνω πάντων ἐστίν). Jesus acknowledges himself to be one with him who lets Pilate have his way (cf. 10:17f; 14:31). With these words, Pilate, who subjects Jesus to his supposed power, becomes the one subjected, and Jesus, the seemingly powerless one, shows himself to be the one who is free and possesses power.

With the freedom of the one who holds firm to God alone, and judges everything as God does, Jesus immediately pronounces his judgment also, concerning those who sit in judgment on him. Now they are placed before God's tribunal, and the one accused by them becomes their judge. Because Pilate is only the extension of God's arm (διὰ τοῦτο referring back), among the human participants more one directed than directing, he bears a lesser guilt. He is, it is true, in no way released from his responsibility; but compared with him, those who handed Jesus over to him bear the greater guilt. The formulation in the singular (παραδούς[85]) expresses a general meaning: All those who have done it.[86] Caiaphas of whom one could think, on account of 11:49, does not appear at the trial before Pilate, and Judas, who is generally identified by means of the same verb (6:64, 71; 12:4 and frequently), is, it is true, at the

261

arrest (18:2, 5), but not at the handing over to Pilate (18:30). The sentence also exhibits an apologetic tendency as is more and more noticeable in early Christianity (especially clearly in Lk): the blame is taken from the Roman at the cost of the Jews, he is almost 'excused'. But John does not go so far as to clear him of guilt, and he also knows (from his source), that the main culprits are not all the Jews ('all the people' Mt 27:25), but the chief priests (see on 19:6).

19:12   After Jesus has spoken, Pilate shows himself determined to release Jesus. The reference back, ἐκ τούτου, intended rather in a causal than a temporal sense,[87] is hardly referring only to the last sentence, which puts the lesser guilt on Pilate, rather, to the whole of Jesus' words which show that he belongs to another world. The evangelist wants to underline the impression which Jesus makes on his judge, the majesty which he radiates; also, indeed, Pilate's growing embarrassment and fear (cf. v. 8). When he now expressly points out the desire to set free (imperfect: a serious and repeated attempt), this could be an echo of a sentence from his source; Luke speaks of it in a similar way (23:16, 20, 22).[88] But immediately, the Roman is hit by the scarcely veiled threat of the Jews to report him to Caesar. The more precise details – that Pilate goes out again, and announces his wish to release Jesus, and so comes up against the opposition of the Jews – are not mentioned. The evangelist wants to depict the inner drama: Pilate has lost the initiative after his earlier indecision and compliance, his inattention to Jesus forces him to listen to the unbelieving opponents of Jesus.

The trump-card which the chief priests have so far held back but now play, is the threat that, in that case, Pilate is not 'Caesar's friend'. Possibly, this does not only refer in general to the emperor's favour, but in particular to the title 'amicus Caesaris', which belonged to all senators ex officio, but was also granted to other exceptional men.

Pilate was only an equestrian, but he was a favourite of Sejanus who had attained the greatest influence with Tiberius; so Pilate too can have come to enjoy this distinction.[89] On the 18th of October, AD 31, Sejanus was overthrown, and many of his creatures suffered from his fall. Whether, indeed, it already occurred before Jesus' trial is doubtful on account of the uncertain date of Jesus' death (in the year 30 or 33?). But it sufficed, that the chief priests cleverly exploited the Roman prefect's situation vis-à-vis the suspicious Tiberius, to put Pilate under massive political pressure. It is known from Roman sources that the emperor reacted in an offended and extremely brutal fashion to every indication of high treason.[90]

If this question does not allow of a historically certain answer, then that is also less important for the Johannine account. The synoptics know nothing of this threat by the chief priests, and we cannot say whether there was anything about it in the Johannine source. The evangelist can also have deduced the Jewish accusers' means of pressure, from a general knowledge of the contemporary political situation. His intention lies along theological lines: the same Pilate, who just a moment ago still prided himself on his power (v. 10), had to suffer being told by the Jews how vacillating and brittle it is. He cannot release, as he wants to, the innocent prisoner of whom he is secretly afraid, but he is the helpless victim of the wishes of the Jews. These return to their earlier charge, which has been proved by the Roman judge to be untenable. With this they confirm Jesus' words. They bear the greater guilt.

7. Jesus' Condemnation to Death on the Cross (19:13–16a)

[13]*When Pilate heard these words, he brought Jesus out and sat down on the judgment-seat at a place called The Pavement, and in Hebrew, Gabbatha.* [14]*Now it was the day of Preparation of the Passover; it was about the sixth hour. He said to the Jews, 'Here is your King!'* [15]*They cried out, 'Away with him, away with him, crucify him!' Pilate said to them, 'Shall I crucify your King?' The chief priests answered, 'We have no king but Caesar.'* [16a]*Then he handed him over to them to be crucified.*

Pilate's resistance is broken. The tragedy of the trial which had already reached its dénouement with the Roman's rejection of Jesus (18:38a), and which made possible already before for us to surmise his total failure when confronted by the insistent accusers of Jesus, a tragedy only sustained by fruitless attempts to be rid of the innocent and puzzling accused, is coming to an end. The theological line of the account is strictly followed through: the aim of the Jews, openly proclaimed at the beginning, to have Jesus put to death, and indeed, as the evangelist makes clear, to death on the cross (18:31f), is now attained. Jesus is condemned as 'King of the Jews', about which charge the official representatives of Judaism wish to know nothing. But he is their king in a much deeper sense than they think, precisely in the form of the one subjected to the cross. The gentile Roman for whom his majesty and greatness do not remain hidden, seeks to save him right up to the last minute and then still condemns him against his better judgment. The unbelieving world judges the one sent by God – and at the same moment is itself judged.

19:13 There follows the last scene: Pilate again leads Jesus out without saying anything. The scene corresponds to the first presentation of Jesus (19:4–7), of which it is the climax and fulfilment. The difference lies in the fact that Pilate now seats himself upon the judgment-seat, a sign that he is willing to pronounce the judgment. Or does he seat Jesus on the judgment-seat, as some exegetes wish to understand the text?[91]

The verb καθίζειν can have both a transitive and a intransitive meaning.[92] The possible objection that with the transitive meaning the accusative object would have to be repeated (here: αὐτόν), has been weakened by I. de la Potterie by careful examination of Johannine usage (seventeen examples).[93] Besides, he draws attention to the lack of the article in ἐπὶ βήματος, which, according to him, speaks rather for the transitive meaning (op. cit., 226–233). On the other hand, however, it cannot be denied that the obvious meaning according to the historical situation, that Pilate sat himself on the judgment-seat, remains philologically just as possible. The only place where $\varkappa\alpha\theta\dot{\imath}\zeta\varepsilon\iota\nu$ again appears in John's gospel (apart from the non-Johannine text 8:2), namely, 12:14, supports this use of the verb: Jesus found a young ass $\varkappa\alpha\dot{\imath}\ \dot{\varepsilon}\varkappa\dot{\alpha}\theta\iota\sigma\varepsilon\nu\ \dot{\varepsilon}\pi'\ \alpha\dot{\upsilon}\tau\dot{o}$.

Conclusive for one or other of the interpretations is thus the decision as to the evangelist's intention. For his implicit theological line of thought Jesus sitting on the $\beta\tilde{\eta}\mu\alpha$ (the *sella curulis*) seems to be the high point: Jesus is not only the king of the Jews, but also their judge, accentuated by the circumstances: on the Gabbatha, which probably means 'the raised place', at the sixth hour of the 14th Nisan, as the passover of the Jews was beginning. Now is the hour of their judgment, but for those who believe the hour of salvation, since the true passover lamb is sacrificed (cf. de la Potterie pp. 236–246). Impressive as this interpretation is, weighty objections remain: first of all, the question whether the evangelist wants to depart so far from history and encroach on pure symbolism; for there is no middle, no 'double-meaning', because the reader has to decide whether he wishes to see Pilate *or* Jesus on the judgment-seat.

Further: it is just the use without the article which can underline the juristic nature of the act: 'To seat oneself for judgment' (but not 'set somebody up as judge').

Finally: the high-point is not the seating on the judgment-seat, but the call 'Here is your King!', which, for John, is then only fulfilled on the cross (19:19). Only there does Jesus' glorification take place, which becomes also the judgment of the unbelieving world. Therefore, with many other exegetes, I am not able to follow this interpretation of the text.[94] The text makes good sense also, without affecting the theological thought of the evangelist, on the assumption, that for John, Pilate ascends the judgment-seat.

Jesus is to be 'lifted up' on the cross in the sight of all (cf. 3:14; 12:32; 19:37), and to that belongs also his public, legally enforceable condemnation by the appropriate authority. If, in what follows, the judgment is not formally pronounced, then the handing over of the accused for crucifixion (v. 16a) is recogizable as an official act, in that Pilate seated himself on the judgment-seat. Before this judgment-seat, the chief priests take the burden of guilt on themselves of Jesus' being sent to the cross as King of the Jews (v. 15). The official character is also underlined with the details of the place on which the judgment-seat stands.[95] It is the broad platform in front of the praetorium, which, on account of the flagstones with which it was paved, was called Lithostrotos (on the subject of its position, cf. on 18:28). The Aramaic name which the evangelist (from his source?) adds (cf. 5:2; 19:17), is no translation of the Greek term, but means, perhaps, 'elevation' or 'bald brow', presumably according to its position or form.[96] John seems not to have seen a symbolic meaning in it, otherwise, he would presumably have translated the term (9:7).

19:14 The evangelist will have taken over the indication of time also, in the same way as that of place, from the source. It sounds as if left on record: day and hour are mentioned, so as to specify the moment of the judgment. Before any attempts at symbolic interpretation, this simple meaning which the information in the source could have had, should be kept in view. In this way, the difficulties raised in the comparison with the synoptic reports, are best explained: the 'day of preparation for the passover', which can scarcely be understood otherwise than the day prior to the passover eve (14th Nisan),[97] is, according to John, throughout the day on which the trial before Pilate took place (18:28) and on which Jesus finally died on the cross (Good Friday, cf. 19:31) – contrary to the synoptic chronology, according to which Jesus was only condemned and executed on the day after the passover meal (Friday, 15th Nisan). The sixth hour (the reading ἕκτη is certainly the original[98]) also fits badly the synoptic account according to which Jesus was already hanging on the cross at mid-day (cf. Mk 15:33 par.), even if the special detail in Mk 15:25, that Jesus was crucified at the third hour, is credited to the Markan time-scale or regarded as an interpolation. The most likely interpretation is then, that the Johannine source differed from the Synoptics on this matter, however that is to be evaluated. If the evangelist already found the details,[99] he will have at first likewise have treated them as a fixing of that significant hour at which the death sentence on the 'King of the Jews' was officially pronounced. On top of that, he admittedly can have found in this, in his meditative way, a deeper meaning also. This particularly applies with the reference to the passover feast. For him, Jesus is undoubtedly the NT passover lamb, of whom 'not a bone' was 'broken' (19:36; cf. on 18:38). He could likewise have connected the 'sixth hour' with this. It was the hour at which, in those days, preparation was made for the slaughtering of the passover lambs in the Temple. Other interpretations are less probable, as for instance, a reference to Amos 8:9,[100] a passage which fits better to the eclipse of the sun, which, according to the synoptics, lasted from the sixth to the ninth hour when Jesus was suffering on the cross (Mk 15:33 par.); or the opposite, it is a reference to the highest point which the sun reaches, which is meant to be an image of Jesus' lifting up and glorification.[101] We should be as sparing as possible with symbolic interpretations (cf. v. 13).

Pilate sitting on the judgment-seat once more points to Jesus: 'Here is your King!' It is a last effort to dissuade the Jews from their unjustified accusation that Jesus makes himself out to be the king (v. 12d), and from their demand that Pilate should have him crucified (v. 6). The scene which now takes place is constructed like the first presentation of Jesus (vv. 5f): A statement by Pilate – the shouts of the Jews demanding the crucifixion – Pilate's answer – a new reaction of the chief priests. There is a progression: Pilate no longer says, 'Here is the man!' but, 'Here is your King!' and the shout of the accusers is even more vehement ('Away with him, away with him, crucify him!'). But there is also an important difference: in the first scene, Pilate appears mocking and scornful, now, he is totally serious, yet he fails miserably.[102]

19:15   The renewed wild shouts of the Jews – as dramatic as in the synoptic Barabbas scene, with the cry, 'away with him, away with him' similar to Lk 23:18 – leads to a last 'discussion' between Pilate and the chief priests. The theme is, once more, Jesus' kingship, which, as a controversy with Judaism, is now concluded. In spite of the shouting, Pilate still hesitates and asks, rather helplessly: 'Shall I crucify your King?' The question is an instrument of the evangelist's style, which provokes the chief priests' answer: 'We have no king . . .' The contrast is intentional: The gentile is reluctant to crucify this 'king', the representatives of Judaism disavow him and proclaim instead their loyalty to the Roman colonial power which is otherwise hateful to them precisely on religious grounds. It is to be noted that the chief priests are again expressly mentioned in this passage (cf. 18:35; 19:6). For the sake of their prestige, their authority, they betray their conviction of faith (cf. 11:48, 50).

The utterance, 'We have no king but Caesar' sounds shocking on the lips of Jews. How can they, who regard God as their true and only king, speak like this? They actually pray to God in the eleventh benediction of the ancient *Eighteen Benedictions*, May you be our King, you alone!' In the context, admittedly, the saying is not intended as a direct denial of God's kingship over Israel, but as a denial of the expected anointed one of God, the Messiah who is to set up God's righteous rule. In refusing to accept Jesus as the Messiah, the 'King of Israel' (cf. 12:13), and declaring themselves loyal to the Roman Caesar alone, the chief priests throw away their messianic hope.[103] From a historic point of view, the Jews continued to pray for the coming of 'David's Son',[104] as, for example, those benedictions of the *Eighteen Benedictions*, which date from after AD 70, show. But the pronouncement of the chief priests is formulated from the viewpoint of the evangelist, who knows only one Messiah: Jesus, the Son of God (20:31). Behind the dreadful words of the chief priests is to be found the Christian accusation contained in the contemporary controversy with Judaism: when you reject Jesus to whom the scriptures bear witness (5:39), about whom Moses wrote (5:46), at whose day Abraham was glad (8:56), then your hope is at an end (5:45). It is hardly possible to put this presentation by the fourth evangelist on one level with that of the first evangelist according to whom 'all the people' say, 'His blood be on us and on our children!' (Mt 27:25); for in John's gospel there is, with all the polemic against the leaders of Judaism, no condemnation of the entire Jewish nation, rather, a continuing appeal to Jewish people to believe in Jesus the Messiah and Son of God. But John too draws a clear line of distinction: that Judaism which rejects its true king of salvation is, for him, lost to the salvific rule of God.

19:16a The reminder of the emperor is enough to break down the last resistance of Pilate; he cannot and will not risk the threatened report to his chief superior (cf. v. 12). He too sacrifices his conviction, the knowledge of the accused's innocence, to his personal ambition, to his concern for rank and well-being. So he hands Jesus over 'to them' for crucifixion. The verb παραδιδόναι has a judicial meaning here[105] and presupposes the pronouncement of judgment. An uncertainty arises because of the personal pronoun αὐτοῖς. In the context, in which mention was made only of the chief priests, it would have to refer to the Jewish accusers. The 'handing over' corresponds in v. 16b to the 'taking over' of the condemned, who began his journey to the cross. Thus, we expect 'to the soldiers' who are then also mentioned in connection with the crucifixion (v. 23). But why does the evangelist not say this plainly? Does he want to awaken the impression in the readers that the Jews carried out the crucifixion? That would be an unhistorical, even for the readers an unrealistic, attitude. The correct answer to this problem was probably given by A. Dauer: 'Here, the evangelist takes over sentences from his source which, after Jesus'

scourging, reported his condemnation, the mocking and the execution.'
Actually, the (Roman) soldiers are mentioned for the last time in 19:2, and
when the mockery scene originally stood at the end of the trial, the personal
pronoun was sufficient.[106] But it is possible that John intentionally allowed the
uncertainty to remain, so as to insinuate the 'taking over' by the Jews. They
have achieved their purpose and receive, in triumph, the one condemned to the
cross.[107] The trial is finished, the 'King of the Jews' condemned, the judgment
of men on the Son of God set in motion – yet, the unbelieving world together
with its ruler is to be judged by him (cf. 12:31; 14:30; 16:11).

SECTION VI

The Passion: Journey to the Cross,
Crucifixion and Laying in the Tomb (19:16b–42)

John logically places the actual events of the passion within the theological perspective which he has followed throughout the whole gospel. The theme of Jesus' kingship which dominated the trial before Pilate, is now brought to a close. Jesus ascends his 'kingly throne' on the cross, between two other condemned persons: utter degradation in the eyes of men, 'lifting up' on the part of God. His kingship is proclaimed through the inscription on the cross before the whole world (in three languages), contradictory for the 'chief priests of the Jews', confirmed by Pilate, its meaning recognized by the believing church (cf. 12:16).

With that, the King-theme is concluded (v. 22); but John picks up some further material from the tradition, which is significant for him in his theological reflection: the people at the cross, and, in contrast, the soldiers, and the women, among them Jesus' mother; further, the drinking of the vinegar; and the last words of Jesus. Both in the selection as in the shaping of it in his own way, in part differing from the tradition, his theological objective is demonstrated with great power. If we consider other traditional elements which are lacking in John, above all the blasphemies beneath the cross, and the signs prior to and following Jesus' death (eclipse of the sun, rending of the curtain, etc.), then we will have to see in this limitation, certain intentions, a leaving out of unnecessary and 'distracting' elements, and a concentration on what is important for him. The line of thought concerned with majesty is carried through to Jesus' last word and right up to the accusation that he 'gave up his spirit'.

The evangelist pursues his own tendencies in the scene with the disciple whom Jesus loved, and in the piercing of Jesus' side – two narrative units which are peculiar to him. Against that, he again takes over traditional material for the the burial of Jesus by Joseph of Arimathaea, but also brings in Nicodemus (v. 39). On the whole, his procedure of taking up the tradition and enriching or interpreting it with his own statements, is confirmed. Therefore, for this section too, it is sensible and advisable to try to separate tradition and redaction,

268

although the extent and nature of the source remain doubtful. The two quotations from scripture during the events on the cross (v. 24 and v. 28) are connected with the synoptic tradition, the other two after the opening of Jesus' side (v. 36 and v. 37) on the contrary are not. All John's own fragments and statements are especially difficult to interpret (and disputed), because in them are supposed to be found special (also symbolic?) ideas, but they cannot be stated with certainty. The following units commend themselves for the division of the text:[1]

1. The crucifixion on Golgotha and the inscription on the cross (19:16b–22);
2. distribution of the clothes and casting of lots for the tunic by the soldiers (19:23–24b);
3. the women beneath the cross and the words to Mary and the disciple (19:24c–27);
4. the drinking of the vinegar and Jesus' last words (19:28–30);
5. the request that the legs be broken and the piercing of Jesus' side (19:31–37);
6. The dignified burial of Jesus (19:38–42).

But since the whole hangs together and is a well thought-through narrative unit, the connections of the smaller sections to each other and the consistent lines of thought, as it were, the evangelist's theological concept, will also be kept in view: the picture of Christ, the persons involved (Pilate, the soldiers – the Jews and the chief priests respectively – those "standing by" Jesus, the women and disciples), the importance for salvation of Jesus' death.

1. The Crucifixion on Golgotha and the Inscription on the Cross (19:16b–22)

[16b]*So they took Jesus,* [17]*and he went out, bearing his own cross, to the place called the place of a skull, which is called in Hebrew Golgotha.* [18]*There they crucified him, and with him two others, one on either side, and Jesus between them.* [19]*Pilate also wrote a title and put it on the cross; it read, 'Jesus of Nazareth, the King of the Jews'.* [20]*Many of the Jews read this title, for the place where Jesus was crucified was near the city; and it was written in Hebrew, in Latin, and in Greek.* [21]*The chief priests of the Jews then said to Pilate, 'Do not write, "The King of the Jews", but, "This man said, I am King of the Jews"'.* [22]*Pilate answered, 'What I have written I have written'.*

19:16b–17   The judgment is immediately followed by its execution, which John relates in a similarly brief way to the synoptics. The 'taking over' by the soldiers which corresponds to the 'handing over' by Pilate (cf. on 19:16a), introduces the execution. In the source used by the evangelist, which is here close to Mt[1a], there probably followed first Jesus' mocking as the King of the Jews, which, however, John has put earlier. The journey to the cross (which is set against this background[2]) is compressed into the one sentence: 'And he went out, bearing his own cross, . . .' This stands out in comparison with all three synoptics because they lay emphasis on the cross being carried by Simon of Cyrene. In Lk the thought of imitation by carrying the cross ('behind Jesus') is expressed (23:26) and it is further associated with Jesus' conversation with the lamenting women from Jerusalem (23:27–31). If we consider that John also uses a different verb for 'to bare' ($\beta\alpha\sigma\tau\acute{\alpha}\zeta\epsilon\iota\nu^3$) and underlines Jesus' action with the dative ἑαυτῷ, then it is scarcely possible to doubt that the evangelist made an intentional alteration: Jesus actively takes the cross upon himself, just as, when he was taken prisoner he went in a self-possessed way to meet the troop making the arrest (18:4–8), and, in dying also, of his own free will, 'he gives up his spirit' (19:30). The Christological interest (cf. 10:18) is stronger, for John, than is the parenetic which is still evident in the saying concerned with serving and following (12:26), and also stronger than the historical interest as to how he carried the cross to the place of execution.[4] An allusion to Isaac upon whom Abraham laid the wood for the sacrifice (Gen 22:6) and which then, both in the Jewish Haggadah[5] and also in Christian typology,[6] played a large part,[7] is improbable in the case of John, because such a comparison does not clearly occur elsewhere in John's gospel.[8]

The evangelist certainly found the name of the place where Jesus was crucified, just as he previously found the designation of the place of judgment (19:13), in his source. He agrees with Mk 15:22/Mt 27:33, save that the 'Hebrew' (=Aramaic) name is only mentioned after the Greek designation. That is an indication that John here follows his source, because otherwise he does the opposite (cf. 1:38, 41, 42; 4:25; 9:7). Accordingly, a symbolic meaning (as in 9:7) need not be sought behind it. 'Golgotha' means 'skull', probably because of the shape of the piece of ground recalling the top of a skull, and the Greek expression does not mean anything else.[9] Interpretations pointing beyond this to the skull of Adam allegedly buried there or the skulls of those executed,[10] are thus out of the question.

When the evangelist carefully notes this information about the place, this accords with an intention of the presentation which was already noticeable in 19:13. The event of the cross is clearly fixed within the scope of history, place and time are fixed and determinable, demonstrable before world public opinion. That last fact is confirmed to be an objective of the evangelist by the inscription on the cross in three languages, his concern with place by the more exact information, as compared with the synoptics, about Jesus' tomb (19:41f.). For John, the cross of Jesus is an immovable sign for man's evident guilt and for the hidden intention of God to 'lift up' the crucified one. He becomes the source of salvation for all who raise their eyes to him and believe.

19:18 The crucifixion of Jesus is described as briefly as in the synoptics. This grim occurrence was known to the people of those days, and the Christians avoided a description of this martyrdom of their Lord due to delicacy of feeling. John, like Lk, omits the pain-killing draught (Mk 15:23/Mt 27:34); it is questionable whether his source spoke of it. Nor does John fail to mention the crucifixion of 'two other' men with Jesus. His main intention is recognized in that, over and above the synoptics, he emphasizes 'and Jesus between them'. Jesus has a place of honour and even in the midst of this macabre scenery he is the king, as the inscription confirms. John, presumably intentionally, avoids a description of those crucified with Jesus. In Mk/Mt they are λῃσταί, an expression which could also be applied to zealot rebels (cf. on 18:40); Lk says κακοῦργοί, so as to underline the shameful fact that Jesus 'was reckoned with transgressors' (cf. 22:37 after Is 53:12). It can be asked whether John wanted to avoid the politically-loaded term λῃσταί, on apologetic grounds;[11] but more immediate is the fact that he even omitted a word for 'criminal' (he was driven by another intention in the Barabbas scene, q.v. 18:40,), because for him, Jesus, the King, ought not to be defamed further. For that reason also, he leaves out all the mocking and blasphemous words which are so prominent in the synoptics. He knows how to lay the emphasis in such a way that, despite the undeniable degradation by man, Jesus appears as the one full of majesty, 'lifted up' according to God's plan.

19:19 John calls the inscription on the cross, likewise attested by the three synoptics, by the word (taken from the Latin) τίτλος; with him, it is particularly important for his theological position. According to Roman custom, such a board was carried in front of the condemned or put around his neck;[12] thereafter, it could also be attached to the cross. Thus, there is no reason to doubt the fact of the inscription.[13] But the evangelists differ somewhat from each other, admittedly, in reporting the contents. They agree in their report that 'the King of the Jews' was written on the board; Mt precedes this with 'This is Jesus' (27:37); Lk adds οὗτος (23:38); John (presumably following his source) also combines the description of origin, Ναζωραῖος (see on 18:5), with the name. There is nothing suspicious in this either: this Jesus of Nazareth is worthy of death, because he set himself up as 'King of the Jews' against the Roman rule. The inscription serves, at the same time, as a warning and to frighten others off.

John, in attributing the inscription to Pilate's initiative (the verbs are causal as in 19:1, 6, 10, 15), wants to prepare for the exchange between the chief priests and the Roman. With the reference to Pilate, the evangelist wants to say perhaps: Pilate takes his revenge by means of the inscription which humiliates the Jews, for the fact that they forced him to have the disputed 'King of the Jews' crucified (cf. vv. 14b–15). With that, Pilate becomes a witness to Jesus' kingship, the inscription an honorific title.[14]

19:20 The comment that many Jews read the inscription, is also connected with the following complaint of the chief priests (cf. οὖν vv. 20 and 21). They present themselves before Pilate because, for them, this manifestation of Jesus' kingship, the resultant publicity and the possible discussions arising from this, are undesirable. The situation of the place of crucifixion close by the city and yet outside the walls, was generally known and gave the Christians later on an opportunity for theological reflection (cf. Heb 13:12f). The verse, which in the shaping of its language also demonstrates Johannine style (separation of words which belong together), will have been constructed by the evangelist. The inscription in the three languages, that is in the vernacular (Aramaic), the language of government (Latin), the language of trade and commerce (Greek), is, indeed, entirely possible, since similar examples of tomb inscriptions and edicts are known;[15] but it is a remote possibility that a Roman should make so much fuss with someone being crucified. The theological tendency of the evangelist is clear: the three languages are to announce Jesus' kingship officially to the world.

19:21–22   Again, the chief priests are emphatically mentioned (cf. 18;35; 19:6, 15), this time again with the addition 'of the Jews'. The official representatives of Judaism take exception to the inscription 'the King of the Jews', which compromises them. They demand an alteration which is to express Jesus' alleged claim to this title. But the Roman sticks to what he has written,[16] and in this way once again defies the Jews. Yet is that the only thing that the evangelist wants to show? Implicitly he intends more: despite the objection of the Jews, Jesus remains their King, the Messiah (cf. on 19:15). The messianic question which, in the evangelist's time, is becoming a point of dispute between Judaism and Christianity, is in no way settled by Jesus' crucifixion, rather it is properly raised.[17] The inscription, its validity strengthened by Pilate, proves this: Jesus is the King who rules from the cross.[18]

2. Distribution of the Clothes and Casting of Lots for the Tunic by the Soldiers (19:23–24b)

[23]*When the soldiers had crucified Jesus they took his garments and made four parts, one for each soldier. Likewise (they took) the tunic; but the tunic was without seam, woven from top to bottom;* [24]*so they said to one another, 'Let us not tear it, but cast lots for it to see whose it shall be.' This was to fulfil the scripture, 'They parted my garments among them, and for my clothing they cast lots'.*

The new scene which John shares with the synoptics (Mk 15:24 par.), but which he narrates in much greater detail and concludes with an express scripture quotation, is a continuation of v. 18. The lengthy attention to the inscription made it necessary that that statement be taken up again (v. 23a), an indication that at least vv. 20–22 have been inserted by the evangelist. Why does John pay such attention to the sharing of the garments? It is very possible that his source gave so detailed an account of it. In the history of tradition the development can be pictured as follows: the indirect citation by the synoptics was later reproduced in full, and, indeed, precisely after Ps 22:19, Ps 21:19 LXX, and, in accordance with the *parallelismus membrorum* in the psalm verse, the sharing of the garments (ἱμάτια plural) was distinguished from the drawing of lots for the tunic (ἱματισμός singular). Such a kind of more extensive reflection based on the word of scripture, would be well-suited to a source which is to be dated later than the synoptics. Further, prior to the scriptural quotation, the account does not show any signs of John's style.[19] Yet even if the evangelist has to thank his source for the scene as a whole, this does not explain why he takes it up, and, on top of that, does so in this detailed form.

A deeper purpose can rightly be supposed for John's theologically considered account. Not a few exegetes discover it in the seamless tunic, which the evangelist is supposed to have understood symbolically; but he himself gives no kind of indication, and the attempts at interpretation do not really satisfy (see below). A better starting-point for discovering his intention might be found in v. 24c where he has composed a linking sentence that contrasts the soldiers concerned (v. 25) with the women standing by the cross (δέ). The scene of the sharing of the garments is, in this way, a kind of contrast to the following scene with the women and Jesus' words to his mother and the disciple whom he loved. That does not rule out the evangelist's seeing something more deeply significant in the action of the soldiers, in the same way as, after the death of Jesus, in the piercing of Jesus' side (vv. 32–34); but, perhaps, with this observation, we are getting nearer to his intention.

19:23 The soldiers in the execution squad were entitled to what the victim wore on his body (right to the spoils).[20] That here were four men (under a captain, cf. Mk 15:39 par.) is credible (cf. τετράδιον Acts 12:4). For this report (of the Johannine source) we certainly may not count how many pieces of clothing Jesus wore. The account is made to correspond to the scriptural saying, which must, therefore, already have belonged to the source. The information at the end, καὶ τὸν χιτῶνα, which refers back to the separated ἔλαβον, sounds as if it is tagged on. But we may not conclude from it that it was an addition, possibly, of the evangelist. Rather, it is a simple, somewhat clumsy style of narration. Something special is to be said about this χιτών, and that is then told in main clauses. The subject is the long under-garment worn next to the body.[21] It is described further in what follows: without seam, woven from top (ἐκ ἄν. unusual in John) to bottom (δι' ὅλου unique in the NT). This mode of manufacture has also been identified elsewhere in the Palestine of that time, and need not indicate anything unusual or especially costly.[22] The description is there to give a reason in the context why the soldiers did not tear the tunic so that the words of scripture were fulfilled. On the symbolic interpretation, see below.

19:24 The soldiers' thoughts are reported in direct speech which corresponds to the narrative style of those days. There is nothing remarkable about that, even though we find λαγχάειν περί instead of the more usual βάλλειν κλῆρον.[23] At most, it can come as a surprise that the phrase is not brought into harmony with the following scripture quotation. But such pedantry was far from the minds of the old story-tellers, cf. eg. ὀνάριον 12:14 with πῶλον ὄνου in the quotation belonging to it 12:15. Admittedly, the formula introducing the scriptural quotation is Johannine (cf. 13:18; 17:12; 19:36); it could have been altered by the evangelist. There are no grounds for supposing on its account that the comment of the evangelist begins with ἵνα;[24] for the preceding description simply demands such a scripture reference if it is not to be pointless, and makes itself recognizable as a development of the synoptic tradition (see above). This kind of historicising use which takes its direction from the content of the wording, has a parallel in Mt 21:2–7 (ass and foal), but it does not correspond to the normal procedure of the fourth evangelist.

If the evangelist has taken over this scripturally based account from his source he can, by means of it, pursue his own new objectives. The *symbolic interpretations* which are suggested, tend in two directions:

1. One preference is the idea that John wants, by means of the seamless tunic woven from top to bottom, to depict Jesus as *high priest*.[25] Particular attention is drawn to the description of the high-priestly robe in Josephus, *Ant.*, III, 161, where it says: 'This tunic (χιτών) consists not of two parts so that it would be sewn (ῥαπτός) around the shoulders and at the side, but it is woven (ὑφασμένον) from a single length of thread'. The description is, indeed, quite similar; but he is speaking of the long flowing *outer* robe of the high priest, which was fastened with a gold-embroidered belt (cf. Rev 1:13). Besides, it is extremely doubtful whether a high-priest Christology plays any part in John's gospel.[26]

2. Jesus' seamless tunic which is not to be torn, is thought of as a symbol of the *unity of the Church*,[27] sometimes – reference being made to Philo's logos – speculation – in connection with the high-priestly office of Jesus.[28] Now, the gathering and unity of the faithful is certainly a Johannine objective (cf. 10:16; 11:52; 17:21ff), and the net which did not tear filled with one hundred and fifty-three fish (21:11) could be a similar symbol. But this passage in the appendix, betrays a symbolic character with much more likelihood however uncertain the interpretation remains (see *ad loc.*), and the other passages in no way require that in 19:23f. the idea of the unity of the believers is found. The objection against both symbolical interpretations is the fact that Jesus is *deprived* of this tunic. So they will have to be ignored, all the more since the evangelist does not at least indicate as elsewhere, his figurative meaning.

If we keep to the context, a sensible explanation presents itself more readily: apart from the fulfilment of scripture, which is important for the evangelist particularly in this section (cf. 19:28f, 36f), he can see in the scene Jesus' 'unclothing', the rendering up of his earthly possessions and his person (as Jesus himself 'laid aside his garments' at the washing of the feet, 13:4), utter degradation from the side of mankind,[29] and yet still an indication of God's protection, because his tunic is not destroyed. A similar narrative tendency is to be seen with the piercing of Jesus' side (see on 19:33–37). With such a Christological viewpoint, the following scene too is more understandable; it leads our attention away from the soldiers to those 'standing near' Jesus, and it places before our eyes Jesus' last disposition and concern for those belonging to him. Of course, this interpretation also remains uncertain, but offers a possible reason for the evangelists's taking over material from his source.[30]

3. The Women Beneath the Cross
and the Words to Mary and to the Disciple
(19:24c–27)

[24c]*So the soldiers did this.* [25]*But standing by the cross of Jesus were his mother, and his mother's sister, Mary the wife of Clopas, and Mary Magdalene.* [26]*When*

Jesus saw his mother, and the disciple whom he loved standing near, he said to his mother, 'Woman, behold, your son!' [27]*Then he said to the disciple, 'Behold, your mother!' And from that hour the disciple took her to his own home.*

The following scene with the women beneath the cross and Jesus' words to his mother and to the disciple whom he loved, belongs to the passages in John's gospel which have not only been subjected to the greatest attention but also the most varied interpretation. It is not possible, within the framework of a commentary, to pursue the changing history of the exegesis; yet many works are available about it (though not any complete monograph).[31] It is best if we try to understand and expound the scene within the framework of the Johannine passion account, in the more immediate context of the events directly prior to Jesus' death (cf. v. 28a, which looks back to vv. 25–27), but also in the framework of the whole gospel and the Johannine theology. Only afterwards is it worthwhile to cast a glance at other attempts at interpretation and to give the reasons why we cannot follow them. The problem of the disciple whom Jesus loved is a complication for the exposition. He is expressly mentioned here for the second time (after 13:23), and it is clear that our passage is not less significant than the first, perhaps, indeed, the most significant for the whole range of the problem. But it too does not solve all the questions, least of all as to whether it concerns a symbolic or historical figure or whether both these views are to be connected with each other.[32] For this reason we wish to postpone this question to the final excursus.

But, as for the whole of the Johannine passion narrative the questions of literary criticism and history of tradition are unavoidable. Does the scene beneath the cross belong to the original content of the gospel? Does it already originate (at least in part) from the Johannine source, or did the evangelist compose it? If he did, did he use the tradition in this, or was it a free invention on his part? By a comparison with the synoptic gospels a definite if partial answer can be given: the tradition knew of women at the cross. In the synoptics they are first referred to after Jesus' death, not, so far as names are mentioned, in total agreement, but with one accord with the remark that they observed 'from afar' (Mk 15:40 par.). Again, John, in part, gives other names and says that the women were standing 'by the cross of Jesus', and that Jesus turned to his mother and to the disciple whom he loved, with words full of meaning. Despite these differences, a connection certainly exists with that tradition; the concrete details about the women are hardly free invention. On the other hand, the shaping hand of the evangelist is clearly recognizable: those looking 'from afar' have become those 'standing near', not only in a local sense but also, in the words to Mary and the disciple, in a figurative sense. That is underlined by means of the fact that this group of persons is set over against the soldiers. This intentional shaping then makes possible a further observation: the whole scene cannot have been added later, say, by editors, but it is planned by the evangelist. It is on this point that literary-critical attempts fail in bracketing vv. 25–27, or vv. 26f, or yet other fragments, as secondary.[33] The text as it stands can be understood very well as an offering of the evangelist based on the tradition of women at the cross. Apart from the question of what he found in his source – a not so important question – the only other question remaining is what he wanted to say theologically through Jesus' words to his mother and to the disciple, his 'testament' from the cross.

19:24c–25   The evangelist has composed the link between the scene with the soldiers and the new scene; for the short sentence in v. 24c could be left out, rather destroying the conclusion with the quotation from scripture. It is also not at all thought up as a conclusion for the preceding scene, because it points towards the women beneath the cross with μεν, followed by δέ.

The clumsy link[34] in itself could originate in the source; but there are indications of the evangelist's hand. He likes to contrast individuals and groups in 7:12; cf. 10:41; 19:32f with μέν – δέ. A comparison with 12:16 is interesting: the pericope of the entry into Jerusalem closes with the scriptural quotation to which the evangelist adds a comment in v. 16, in which he says in a similar way ταῦτα ἐποίησαν (αὐτῷ). On μὲν οὖν δέ cf. 20:30f (μὲν οὖν often in Acts though mostly without following δέ, cf. Blass-Debr §451, 1).

The supposition is appealing that the evangelist found the reference to the women in another place in his source, perhaps, as in the synoptics, only after Jesus' death.[35] If so, he would have intentionally made mention of them earlier (cf. the same procedure in the case of the crowning with thorns), and that for two reasons: so as to contrast the women with the soldiers and so as to be able to add Jesus' words to his mother and to the disciple. The women 'were standing' by the cross. In Lk 23:49 it likewise says εἱστήκεισαν δέ; against that, in Mk/Mt ἦσαν . . . θεωροῦσαι. But for the rest, Lk too differs from Jn. Lk might have followed Ps 37:12 LXX (ἀπὸ μακρόθεν ἔστησαν). In Jn, the phrase comes, perhaps, from his source. That he uses it arises from the fact of the persons whom he mentions; for among them occur also 'his (Jesus') mother's sister', and 'Mary the (wife?) of Clopas' who otherwise play no part.

In the enumeration of the women, it is disputed how many people come in question. The sentence structure allows of two, three, or four women; all these possibilities were already represented.[36] But the supposition that there were only two women (the names apply to those first described as bearing a degree of relationship) is rejected on factual grounds; Mary of Magdala would then be Jesus' mother's sister! According to the second view (three persons) 'Mary the wife of Clopas' would be identical with Jesus' mother's sister (apposition of the name). Since Jesus' mother is also called Mary, the two sisters would have the same name. Admittedly, 'sister' could also indicate a more distant degree of relationship. It is best to understand the enumeration (with most of the newer exegetes) in pairs: The first two women without names, followed by two with names. The first mentioned are Jesus' near relatives, then follow two other women with the name Mary distinguished by additional information. The list of women in John only agrees for certain with the synoptics in the case of Mary Magdalene. This woman described according to her place of origin (Magdala on the west shore of the lake of Gennesaret[37]) is also closely associated with the tradition of the visit to the tomb (see on 20:1). For the rest, John's list goes its own way. That is why it is risky to make 'Mary the wife of Clopas' mentioned third, equivalent to the 'other' Mary of the synoptic list (Mk 15:40, 'the mother of James the younger and of Joses'; Mt 27:56, 'the mother of James and Joseph'; Lk 24:10, 'the mother of James'). It is first of all questionable what complement is to be placed before the genitive: the wife, the mother, the daughter, or even the sister; all these are possible.[38] Mostly, 'wife' is supposed. Then the testimony of Hegesippus (in Eusebius, *Hist. eccles.*, III, 11) is noteworthy, that Clopas was a brother of Joseph the husband of the mother of Jesus, and that his son Simeon was the second bishop of Jerusalem (*op. cit.* IV, 22, 4). This 'cousin' of the Lord can be identified with the Simon named in Mk 6:3. But our passage, Jn 19:25, on account of the uncertainty mentioned, does not lend itself to the question of the Lord's brothers.[39]

Similarly, and importantly for the 'Johannine question', it is risky to suppose that the sister of Jesus' mother is none other than the mother of the sons of Zebedee who is mentioned third in Mt 27:56, the same position in which Mk 15:40 names Salome. If the mother of the sons of Zebedee, James and John, was called Salome, as is mostly supposed in this account, is she then unable to be the sister of Jesus' mother referred to in Jn 19:25? The John belonging to the Twelve would then, likewise, be a cousin of Jesus, and if he was the disciple whom Jesus loved, there would be an apparently plausible explanation for 19:26f: Jesus entrusts this disciple whom he loved to his mother because he was at the same time his cousin. This hypothesis, under consideration until recently,[40] has, however, weighty objections against it. As for a relationship between Jesus and the sons of Zebedee, we never hear anything elsewhere in the NT. Above all, the combination of the synoptic lists of women with Jn 19:25, is extremely problematical.[41] The reference to the mother of Jesus already shows that here we have another tradition, and the other women (apart from Mary Magdalene) could be persons not mentioned at all by the synoptics. Similarly, we may not prejudge the problem of Jn 19:26f, *viz.*, what Jesus' words to his mother and to the disciple mean, with such a hypothesis.

If we suppose there are four women, only two are known to us with certainty: Mary the mother of Jesus who is mentioned also in 2:1–5 (similarly unnamed), and Mary Magdalene, who according to 20:14–18 experienced an appearance of Jesus, the risen one. The other two women, namely, the sister of Jesus' mother, and the (wife?) of Clopas,[42] who play no further part in John's gospel, would also be included by the evangelist because they were mentioned in his source. Perhaps it is part of his intention to contrast the four women with the four soldiers. They are standing 'by the cross', apparently near Jesus. Whether this is historically probable, since the guard would scarcely allow the spectators to approach so close does not worry the evangelist; he is concerned with the deeper meaning of the scene.

19:26–27   Jesus' mother stands out from the group of women; Jesus turns to her in a special way. But suddenly, the disciple whom Jesus loved is also mentioned as one of those standing by the cross. He was definitely not yet mentioned in the evangelist's source, and therefore, the following scene in which Jesus' mother and the disciple are entrusted and bound to each other, is produced entirely by his hand. The earlier mention in the gospel of both persons has to be kept in mind for the purposes of interpretation: Mary at the wedding in Cana (2:1–5), and the disciple at the last supper (13:23–25). Further, the phrase in v. 28 referring to the scene is significant, 'knowing that all was now finished'. Jesus' words to his mother and to the disciple which are a single whole, have something to do with the completion of his work (cf. v. 30). But what is their meaning?

Because of the context, the saying addressed to the two people has the effect of a testamentary disposition (cf. also 'from that hour'). Whether it is meant to be a kind of adoption formula is disputed; Ps 2:7 is referred to and Tobit 7:12 LXX (at the engagement of the young Tobit to Sarah: 'From now on you are her brother, behold she is your sister'), as also are extra-biblical examples.[43] Without insisting on 'adoption' (in a legal sense), so much is certain, that we have here an expression of will by means of a formula. On this account also, 'revelation formula' does not fully render the meaning;[44] mostly, ἴδε in John's gospel has only a demonstrative function. True, the scene is meant to reveal something important for the coming time, as the statement pointing beyond 'that hour' (v. 27b) shows. The true meaning of Jesus' disposition must be connected with the two persons entrusted to each other.

Mary, to whom Jesus first turns, is once again addressed as 'woman', as in 2:4. A reference back by the evangelist to this passage, the only passage in which Jesus' mother appeared up till now, is scarcely to be doubted. Only Mary's part in the wedding at Cana is likewise disputed (see ad loc.); but perhaps a new light is also shed by 19:26 on 2:4. H. Schürmann might have indicated the way to the right understanding: Mary with her confident behaviour at the wedding represents those who expect salvation from Jesus. She stands for those begging for Jesus' gift.[45] If her plea at that time was fulfilled in such a way that the gift of the wine pointed symbolically into the future, then at this moment, she is granted lasting fulfilment. She is to receive the disciple whom Jesus loved in place of her son, and remain with him. He will obtain for her what she longs for, unfold that which Jesus leaves behind.

Moreover, it may be considered whether Jesus' mother may not represent, in a special way, that part of Israel which is receptive to messianic salvation. Before the wedding at Cana, attention was repeatedly drawn to Israel expectant of the Messiah (cf. 1:31, 41, 45, 49), and the notion of an Israel expecting its Messiah-King recurs once more with Jesus' entry into Jerusalem (12:13). As against the representatives of unbelieving Judaism (cf. 19:21) Jesus' mother represents the section of the population which was open to the 'King of Israel'. In the scene at the cross, it is not to be overlooked that not only is Jesus' mother handed over to the disciple, but also that the disciple is entrusted to Mary as his mother. The intention behind this can be to remind the Christian community of the mother from whom both Jesus and the Church originated. Despite all polemic against unbelieving Judaism, there is also an unmistakable striving in John's gospel after that part of the ancient people of God which is receptive in its belief. In this way the basic tendency to refer (in the person of Mary) all those people who expect the messianic salvation to the beloved disciple and to the Christian community, is not weakened, but rather confirmed and clarified for the 'true Israelites'.

This interpretation which understands Mary as the representative of all those who seek true salvation, is supported and strengthened by the part played by the disciple whom Jesus loved. He is Jesus' confidant to whom Jesus opens up inner thoughts (cf. 13:23–26), the one who believes (20:8) and in his belief understands (cf. 21:7), and who, as a result, is also called to be an interpreter of Jesus' revelation. The various interpretations of the figure of this disciple largely agree in that, for the Johannine Church, he is the mediator and interpreter of Jesus' message, his revelation of himself, and his revelation of salvation for mankind.

If he is to take responsibility for Jesus' mother, then that means for the understanding of Mary's rôle as just described, that he is to take care of and adopt into his circle the one seeking salvation. In this connection, the saying in the appendix is also noteworthy, that this disciple is 'to remain' until the Lord comes (21:22f). It demonstrates an understanding of the Church which certainly concurs with that of the evangelist. Finally, it also becomes clear from this interpretation, how Jesus, with this last disposition, completes his work on earth. He ensures that his revelation is passed on and made to bear fruit. The disciple who takes Mary to himself, and with her all those who seek out salvation, is the human guarantor of the fact that Jesus' earthly revelation perpetuates itself in the future, that his words are not lost, that his 'signs' are rightly interpreted and understood. Probably also, 'that hour' in v. 27 again has that deeper undertone which cannot be ignored in other passages. It is the hour, since Jesus is leaving this world to go to the Father (13:1), of the 'lifting up' and glorification (cf. 12:23, 27, 32). The usage εἰς τὰ ἴδια does not here signify 'home' in a literal sense, but, as I. de la Potterie has shown,[46] 'goods and chattels' in a spiritual sense, the spiritual area, as it were, into which the disciple receives Jesus' mother.

That, admittedly, is also an interpretation, or an explanation, which places the text in a broader context. But with John's way of thinking, as he presents and interprets tradition, as he reflects on and goes beyond it, with his drawing out of theological perspectives (which, for him, are already present with Jesus' historical appearance and ministry if only it can be seen in the light of the resurrection and the ministry of the Spirit), it is necessary to make a serious attempt at it. The interpretation just presented is appropriate to the importance which the passage in 19:26f doubtless has for John's gospel. It is the hour when Jesus 'brings to an end' his earthly task and at the same time wants to continue it through others who are led by his spirit. When the evangelist picks out for this the disciple whom Jesus loved that certainly corresponds to his and his Church's judgment: Jesus' intention is best preserved and cared for by this disciple. In this way, the testament from the cross is at the same time a confirmatory document of the gospel which this disciple guarantees. Our attempt at interpretation which, from many points of view, especially in regard to Mary, will be unsatisfactory to many readers, is now to be compared with and clarified by other interpretations.

On other interpretations:

1. A historicizing interpretation sees in the scene nothing more than Jesus' childlike concern for his mother. It was already held by Church Fathers who, in part, wanted by this means to prove apologetically that Jesus' 'brothers and

sisters' were not related in the flesh but distant relatives.[47] Against this there is (as in the rest of the passion narrative) as an unmistakable theological interest of the evangelist, and in a negative way, also the observation that up to now there was no question of Jesus' human concern for his mother. Further, most of those holding this view presuppose that the beloved disciple is the apostle John, who receives Mary into his home after Jesus' death (cf. *panhagia kapulu*, i.e., 'the house of the most sacred', a site shown to the public nowadays, south of ancient Ephesus).

2. A typological-symbolic exegesis understands Mary as a model of the Church, a view which, since the twelfth century, is found in many variations throughout the Church's exegesis.[48] Reference is made to the designation 'mother' and the form of address 'woman' reminding us of the much-liked OT picture of Israel or of Zion as woman and mother; with 'woman' a connection is made to Eve (there was already an Eve-Mary typology found throughout the Fathers); confirmation of the allusion is seen in John in 16:21 because the parable has a point of contact with prophecies concerning the barren having large numbers of children (=Zion-Jerusalem) (Is 49:20–22; 54:1; 66:7–11); and support is sought from the fact that this picture representing the Church already appeared early on in the primitive Church and is demonstrable in various passages of the NT (cf. Gal 4:26f; 2 Cor 11:2; Eph 5:25ff; Rev 19:7f; 21:2, 9). But it has to be asked whether this was also in the mind of the fourth evangelist. The other NT passages place the Church as bride or wife in bright or hopeful light up to the eschatological fulfilment (parousia, wedding of the lamb). A connection with Mary, the mother of the Messiah, can be derived at most from Rev 12:1–6 – in the event that this vision of the heavenly woman were expounded in this way; but this is thought extremely doubtful by the more modern exegesis. The picture drawn of Jesus' mother at the wedding at Cana does not provide any justification for such speculations, the parable of the woman in labour-pains does not all have to be expounded in a symbolico-typological manner (see on 16:21). Finally, the scene beneath the cross is also unable to carry the burden of proof; for the main point remains that Mary is entrusted to the disciple and he receives here as his own. Thus, Mary has rather to be regarded as the type of the ancient, and the disciple as the representative of the new people of God.[49] But with that, the figure of the disciple is made to carry too much; he is to bring into being the Church and lead it in the Spirit, but he does not symbolize it.

3. The Mariological exegesis in a narrower sense, that is, the installation of Mary in a personal rôle which has a theological relevance or one for salvation history, is also found to any degree only since the twelfth century. In more recent times attempts have been made to find support for it in John's gospel itself: at the wedding at Cana, Mary is excluded from Jesus' earthly-messianic work; but beneath the cross she is installed by Jesus as mother of the believers (represented by the disciple).[50] There are then various interpretations concerned with the manner in which she operates within and on behalf of the Church. But the difficulty which such speculations come up against consists in the fact that nothing is said by the text about any motherly concern, a right to

intercession, nor about any other mediatorial activity. The disciple accepts Mary into his own circle: that is what the evangelist intends, that is the point of what he is saying. The Mariological interpretations can only be justified as a theological foundation and development of Marian piety with a certain support from Church tradition, but not as a Johannine concept.[51]

4. Out of other symbolic interpretations are to be picked out:

Bultmann thinks that only Jewish Christianity can be understood from the mother who, keeping a vigil at the cross, confesses herself as belonging to the crucified one; and the favourite disciple accordingly represents Gentile Christianity.[52] But the interpretation of Mary as referring to Jewish Christianity is by no means compelling, and the conclusion drawn that the disciple represents Gentile Christianity, comes up against the objection that he was also regarded as a member of the group of disciples contemporary with Jesus. Also, Bultmann can support his view only by making Peter who is in competition with disciple, a further alleged representative of Jewish Christianity. According to the tradition, Peter could not be standing beneath the cross. That is also a reason for A. Kragerud to maintain his thesis about 19:26f that the favourite disciple represents the prophetic moment of the primitive Church, and that Peter represents the ecclesiastical office. The scene contrasting with that, is supposed to be the handing over of the office of shepherd to Peter in 21:15ff. The favourite disciple is said to be, already prior to Peter, 'ordained as *successor Christi.*'[53]

These and other symbolic interpretations are due to the general understanding of the figure of this disciple and are not based on the text. If, in the case of the Catholic Mariological interpretations attention is drawn too exclusively to the mother of Jesus, then not a few protestant scholars are guilty of not giving an answer as to why the evangelist also casts an eye on Mary.

The *historicity of the scene* is defended by all exegetes, who, in the disciple whom Jesus loved, see the apostle John; on the contrary, it is attacked by those scholars who regard the events as a purely symbolic account. In the history of tradition, there is support for the presence of Jesus' mother at the cross, if v. 25 (as we may suppose, on good grounds) was already found in the evangelist's source. True, with this, nothing is decided as to historicity, all the more since the synoptics are silent on the point; but a strong reason for doubting the information of the Johannine source does not exist. Less advantageous is the starting-point for the scene composed by the evangelist vv. 26–27, because here we are thrown back entirely on his knowledge and intention. The problem as to whether he wants to set down a historical reminiscence, say, including Jesus' provision for his mother even before the passion,[54] or whether he wants to concentrate a, for him, important thought in a symbolic scene, is bound up with the other question, whether the beloved disciple is a historical person. He who answers the former affirmatively, still has arguments for answering the other problem: if it was a disciple who had shared or experienced something of Jesus' earthly ministry, perhaps someone from Jerusalem,[55] then an historical essence is not ruled out. Yet even a symbolic account, the intention of which is, by means of the scene, to bring to the fore its meaning for the Church, is, in the evangelist's view of history, not to be rejected out of hand. In any case, the largely theological concern of the evangelist in the shaping of this scene cannot be denied.

4. The Drinking of the Vinegar and Jesus' Last Words (19:28–30)

[28]*After this Jesus, knowing that all was now finished, said (to fulfil the scripture), 'I thirst'.* [29]*A bowl full of vinegar stood there; so they put a sponge full of the vinegar on hyssop and held it to his mouth.* [30]*When Jesus had received the vinegar, he said, 'It is finished'; and he bowed his head and gave up his spirit.*

The giving of a drink of 'vinegar' to Jesus and – closely connected with this (Mk/Mt) – a last saying of Jesus, are also found in the synoptic tradition, though with characteristic differences. There are good grounds for supposing that John read something concerning this in his source. Then the question demands to be answered, why he still pays so much attention to the relatively unimportant drinking of the vinegar after Jesus' final enactment (vv. 26f). Normally the answer is given that he was interested to the last in the fulfilment of scripture to which his source bore witness. Yet this cannot be the only reason, because the source for which, admittedly, this was important (cf. on v. 24), presumably contained other scripture quotations (cf. the words of mockery), which are ignored by John. If the account of Mk/Mt[56] is compared, then it is noticeable that the emphasis is on the words concerning Jesus' forsakenness (Ps 22:1), which is followed by the drinking of the vinegar. It is very likely that the Johannine source told it similarly; but that saying did not fit into the theological concept of our evangelist, and for that reason he shaped this tradition differently. He places the drinking of the vinegar 'to fulfil the scripture' earlier, and formulates Jesus' last words according to his theological viewpoint. He did not take up the motif of the fulfilment of scripture in isolation, but he subordinated it to the idea of the completion of Jesus' work. That is to be noted also in the case of his understanding of the drinking of the vinegar. Jesus' saying, 'I thirst' and his acceptance of the drink, are intimately connected with Jesus' last words: 'It is finished'.

19:28 By means of μετὰ τοῦτο which, perhaps, makes a closer link with the previous scene than μετὰ ταῦτα (see on 6:1), even more through εἰδὼς κτλ., the evangelist wants to avoid the impression that anything important happened after Jesus' last enactment. The climax is already reached, John indicates it by means of Jesus' knowledge: everything is finished and completed. With that he already points to the saying in v. 30, and everything which is to be found in between, is contained within these 'brackets'. Jesus' inner knowledge and foreknowledge, which belong to the Johannine picture of Christ (cf. 1:47f; 2:25; 6:61, 64, etc.), is accentuated by the evangelist precisely for the events of the passion. Similar formulations with εἰδὼς are enlightening in this respect: 13:1, at the beginning of the second main section, Jesus knows that the hour has come to leave this world and go to the father (cf. also 13:3 which, however, is probably a redaction); and 18:4, at the arrest, he knows 'all that was to befall him'. Our passage appears to correspond directly to this remark at the beginning of the passion: 'All' is already finished; Jesus' knowledge mentioned there has been fulfilled. Perhaps even the choice of the word τελέω='bring to an end, complete', is to be explained by looking back to 13:1: Jesus loved his own 'to the end' (εἰς τέλος). In any case, the verb which is found in John only in 19:28, 30, is excellently suited to the intimation of the completion, that is, of the task which Jesus has assumed in the world.[57] The use of ἤδη once again confirms that John gives the greatest significance to Jesus' words to his mother and the beloved disciple (see above on 19:26f), which is not to be diminished by the drinking of the vinegar.

Nevertheless, when Jesus says, 'I thirst', that happens 'to fulfil the scripture'. The ἵνα-clause is hard to connect with Jesus' knowledge concerning the completion,[58] but introduces Jesus' exclamation originating from the scripture.[59] It is noteworthy that for the 'fulfilling' of the scripture, we have here, not, as elsewhere in John, ἵνα πληρωθῇ (cf. 12:38; 13:18; 15:25; 17:12; 19:24, 36), but τελειωζῇ. Perhaps John already found the word in the source; if so, then it should be understood to mean that the scripture was to find complete and final fulfilment.[60] In John, Jesus himself speaks: 'I thirst'; in the synoptics, a bystander (Mk/Mt) gives him the sponge filled with vinegar, alternatively, the mocking soldiers offer it to him (Lk 23:36). The personal manner of expression in John deserves to be noticed.

The short saying is most probably meant to recall Ps 69:21 (68:22), since only here are ὄξος and δίψα found together: εἰς τὴν δίψαν μου ἐπότισάν με ὄξος. In Ps 22:15 (21:16) in which the thirst of the suffering righteous one is described, the verbal echoes are missing. The quotations in Jn 2:17 and 15:25 also come from Ps 69. διψῶ is no reason to doubt this,[61] rather it is intentional Johannine adaptation, yet not merely for purposes of identification,[62] but certainly also as a result of deeper reflection as to what this 'I thirst' means on Jesus' lips.

The physical thirst of Jesus – while hanging on the cross a terrible torment – certainly has a still deeper meaning for the evangelist. If this saying of Jesus is connected with his last words, 'it is finished', then two other passages indicate the way in which to comprehend the evangelist's intention. In 4:34, Jesus says to the disciples who want to give him something to eat: 'My food is to do the will of him who sent me, and to *accomplish* his *work*', and at the time of the arrest he answers Peter: 'Shall I not *drink* the cup which the Father has given me?' Hunger and thirst become images for Jesus' desire to fulfil the Father's will to the end. The evangelist may particularly have in mind the saying about the cup: Jesus intends to drink the cup of suffering and death to the last dregs. Therefore, he also 'takes' the drink presented to him.

19:29   The 'vinegar' (ὄξος) which is already in a container, is 'the inferior popular drink', sour wine or with a higher acid content, 'vinegar', watered down, a favourite refreshment (*posca*).[63] It is not clearly determinable in the synoptic tradition whether the offer of the drink is meant to be a compassionate act or, whether in the light of Ps 69:21, is to be understood as an act of humiliation or mockery (as Lk 23:36). In John, the reference to the Psalm passage is clearer, the bitter drink which Jesus takes is an image for the knowingly accepted pain of death. Departing from the synoptics according to which Jesus was presented with the sponge on a reed, in John this is done by means of a 'hyssop (stem)'. That was a small bushy plant used particularly as a sprinkling-brush; it is doubtful whether, among the various sorts, there was one with a strong enough stem that a sponge could be fixed on to it.[64] The old suggestion (Camerarius †1574) of reading, instead of ὑσσώπῳ, ὑσσῷ (=javelin, pilum), also witnessed to alone by the miniscule 476 (eleventh century), is based on scholarly reflection.[65] Other exegetes suppose it to have a symbolic meaning: since, according to Ex 12:22, the blood of the Passover lambs should be smeared on the lintel and door-posts with a sprig of hyssop, it is said to be an allusion to Jesus, the Passover lamb. But this seems far-fetched and not to correspond to the course of events.[66] This question may not be answered with certainty; it also has no great importance for the events as such.

19:30   Soon after drinking, Jesus speaks his last words: 'It is finished.' There is no doubt that John himself formulated them, so as to announce the completion of Jesus' earthly work (cf. on v. 28). Probably, he wanted to replace the synoptic saying about Jesus having been forsaken by God, in this way; Lk had already altered the last words or the exclamation at death into the supplication (cf. Ps 30:6 LXX): 'Father, into thy hands I commit my spirit!' (Lk 23:46). Thus, the last words of the crucified one has greatly occupied the primitive Church and led to differing theological interpretations among the evangelists; a historical reconstruction (or a combination) is not possible.[67] There too, in the interpretation of what he took over from tradition and in his own theological emphasis, John remains consistent. For him, Jesus dies as the one who completes his earthly work, who carries out the Father's commission obediently to the end (cf. 14:31; 17:4). To the last, Jesus is the one taking the initiative (cf. ποιεῖν in the passages mentioned): in the exhortation to the beloved disciple, in the request for the final drink – and in the 'rendering up' of his spirit. For, the statement concerning Jesus' death (in the active) follows directly on the saying concerning completion: He bowed his head and gave up his spirit.

Behind the original description of Jesus' death may lie the thought in Jn 10:18: 'No one takes it (my life) from me, but I lay it down of my own accord.' True, the bowing of the head, for which no parallels have been found, can also be understood as a simple gesture of one dying peacefully: After the completion of the work, a peaceful departure to the Father. But παρέδωκεν gives it a particular emphasis; it says more than the Matthaean ἀφῆκεν τὸ πνεῦμα (27:50) which this evangelist uses for ἐξέπνευσεν in Mk 15:37 (likewise, Lk 23:46). It is in this that the giving up of the spirit (=the breath of life) to the Father, is, after all, contained; the evangelist probably uses τὸ πνεῦμα (for the human 'spirit' of Jesus, also John 11:33; 13:21), because he found it in his source. Whether the latter also used παρέδωκεν, is doubtful.[68] The evangelist's context and manner of thought, suggest, in any case, that he also understood the death of Jesus as a conscious act, an acceptance of the fact that he was destined by the Father to die, and as a self-offering to the Father.

There has been much discussion concerning the passage and its peculiar manner of expression. Besides a simple explanation which sees in it only a perhaps poetically tinged description of Jesus' death,[69] there are considered interpretations which suppose there to be far-reaching theological concepts. According to Hoskyns-Davey (532), the dying Jesus nods his head toward Mary and the beloved disciple and gives to them, as representatives of the believers, the (holy) Spirit, in fulfilment of Jn 7:37–39. This view was extended yet further by G. Bampfylde who went back to Ezek 47 and Zech 14:8.[70] But such an interpretation (cf. R. E. Brown 931) already fails on the point alone that here τὸ πνεῦμα cannot mean the divine Spirit; Jn 7:39 finds fulfilment in 20:22. The scene in 19:34 is set off against 19:30 and points to the future (cf. v. 37). Also, many interpretations of τετέλεσται go beyond what can be ascertained from the text and the scope of the evangelist's thinking.[71]

Jesus' death as John describes it, is the climax of his *Christological understanding*, the hidden triumph of the Son who is going to the Father, after he has completed his earthly work. It is a counterpoint to the synoptic description of Jesus forsaken by God, the confirmation of the Johannine saying: The Father who has sent me 'has not left me alone, for I always to what is pleasing to him' (8:29; cf. 16:32). The two ways of looking at things are close together, equally justified and not untenable; both meet in the mysterium of Jesus' person, and both reveal something to us of the secret of our own death. The Johannine passion narrative does not end with this death-scene, but there follows another which takes us directly from the Christological to the *soteriological understanding*. Out of the open side of Jesus who has been killed, flows the stream of life and salvation.

5. The Request that the Legs be broken and the Piercing of Jesus' Side (19:31–37)

[31]*Since it was the day of Preparation, in order to prevent the bodies from remaining on the cross on the sabbath (for that sabbath was a high day), the Jews asked Pilate that their legs might be broken, and that they might be taken away.* [32]*So the soldiers came and broke the legs of the first, and of the other who had been crucified with him;* [33]*but when they came to Jesus and saw that he was already dead, they did not break his legs.* [34]*But one of the soldiers pierced his side with a spear, and at once there came out blood and water.* [35]*He who saw it has borne witness – his testimony is true, and he knows that he tells the truth – that you also may believe.* [36]*For these things took place that the scripture might be fulfilled, 'Not a bone of him shall be broken.'* [37]*And again another scripture says, 'They shall look on him whom they have pierced.'*

The scene after Jesus' death which is described by John alone, the thrusting of the spear into Jesus' side and the issue of blood and water, as well as the added scriptural quotations, are similarly disputed as is the other scene which only he gives, that of 19:26f. Both the historicity of the events and the evangelist's intended meaning are controversial. The interpretations extend from the view that the scene is meant to point simply to the fact of Jesus' death perhaps as a defence against a Docetist heresy, to theological interpretations claiming that out of Jesus' side came the Church, the stream of life, or the sacraments of baptism and eucharist. The two scripture quotations also, which could give a clearer indication concerning the evangelist's understanding, are variously evaluated.

In order to come to a decision, we cannot avoid questions of literary-criticism and of history of tradition. Had the evangelist already found the scene as a whole or in part in his source? Are there, perhaps, Johannine interpretations or redactional additions? The presumption in the case of this tangible and specifically described course of events speaks for an account which has been taken over, with a certain uneasy relationship to the removal of Jesus' corpse by Joseph of Arimathaea (v. 38). That has led the literary critics to various suggested solutions.[72] Hence, to begin with, a short *analysis of the text and of the language* of 19:31–37 is to be attempted.

The introductory clause in v. 31 appears overloaded, the explanatory remark 'for that sabbath was a high day' seems to be a parenthesis. Since the unusual mode of expression recalls 7:37, it ought to be an insertion by the evangelist. The rather clumsy narrative style (for καὶ ἀρθῶσιν, contrary to the text as it stands, τὰ σώματα must be taken as the subject) can be due to the source. Particular Johannine stylistic criteria are not found; only οἱ Ἰουδαῖοι can, but need not, point to the evangelist. Without reporting Pilate's agreement, the action of the soldiers is straight away (v. 37) described, again not very ably ('who had been crucified with him' refers to both those condemned with Jesus). For a thoughtful reader it is noticeable that the soldiers do not proceed in order, else, after they broke the legs of the first criminal, they would have to come to Jesus who is hanging in the middle (19:18). But the narrator does not concern himself with this; the accentuation of 'Jesus between them', seemed to us to come from the evangelist. In accordance with the inner logic of the account, the special thing which happened to Jesus is related at the end (vv. 33f). Mostly, the evangelist uses πρός with ἔρχομαι; ἐπί is, according to the situation (they come 'to Jesus') certainly, for him also, not impossible, but is rather to be attributed to the source. The placing at the beginning of ἤδη (altered in many mss.) does indeed correspond to Johannine narrative style, but is also normal elsewhere. In v. 34, εἰς τῶν στρ. is a negative criterion in favour of the evangelist's hand, since he regularly renders the partitive genitive following εἰς with ἐκ (1:41; 6:8, 70, 71; 7:50; 11:49; 12:2; 13:21, 23; 18:26; 20:24). The only exceptions are 12:4 (though with text variants) and 18:22; but these passages might likewise be taken over from a source. Since, elsewhere too, the description does not exhibit any Johannine stylistic criteria (the peculiar words can be explained by the subject matter), a likely conclusion is that the evangelist follows his source rather closely.

At most, it can be asked whether 19:34b, the issue of blood and water, is not an addition. According to Bultmann (666f and 677f) vv. 24b–35 come from the redaction by the Church which wished, in this way, to bring in its sacramental interest (interpretation in the sense of baptism and Lord's supper). But that is greatly to be doubted; apart from the fact that the interpretation of 'blood and water' (note the order!) as being to the two sacraments is not certain, without v. 34b, something would be missing from the report about the spear-thrust. The reader expects something to be said about the effect of the piercing. Admittedly, the author of v. 35 obviously sees in it a very deeply significant event; but this does not have to be the same with the account of the source (see exegesis). V. 35 is probably an addition of the editors. The verse is missing in the Old Latin ms. e (Afr.) and in the Vg ms. Fuldensis, but it is not to be doubted as the original text. All the same, the omission in these mss. shows that the text can be dispensed with. Without this reference to 'he who saw it', the connection of the events described in vv. 33–34 with v. 36 is, indeed, even better. V. 35 gives the impression of being added for a particular reason which can be detected in the content in vv. 21–24.

The first scriptural quotation (v. 36) belongs to the description of vv. 31–34 as its conclusion, in a similar way that the quotation in v. 24 belongs to the distribution of the garments, and therefore, certainly does come from the source. With the second scripture quotation, one is uncertain whether or not it has been added by the evangelist. In favour is πάλιν, much liked by John, the mode of expression 'the scripture says' (cf. 7:38, 42), and the use of γραφή for a single passage. Against this is ἑτέρα which is only found here in John (otherwise always ἄλλος). Perhaps the source already offered a second scripture passage as a proof for the spear-thrust; that is not quite certain. Thus, the report of the source can be quite clearly crystallized out: v. 31 (without ἦν γάρ . . . σαββάτου), 32–34, 36, 37 (?).

Thus, we shall have to distinguish, in accordance with the analysis of the text, the layer belonging to the source, the evangelist's interpretation (especially for the scripture quotations), and the additional concern of the editors (v. 35). Within the framework of the Johannine passion narrative, the two units subsequent to Jesus' death, the soldiers' action (vv. 31–37), and the show of respect by the two men who were close to Jesus (38–42), contrast with each other in a similar way to those, prior to Jesus' death, the distribution of the clothes and the scene with the women and the disciple whom Jesus loved. There is also a certain correspondence between the facts that in v. 21 the 'chief priests of the Jews' demand something of Pilate, and in v. 31 'the Jews' demand that the legs of the crucified be broken. In regard to the *dramatis personae*, the evangelist puts together, certainly intentionally, though now more pronouncedly following his source, a symmetrical picture. The hostile demand of the Jews leads, according to God's plan, using Pilate and his soldiers who are nothing else than means of carrying it out, to a quite different result, to a highly significant revelatory scene. That is what the evangelist wants to uncover in his theologically thought-through presentation.

Exegesis

19:31   The request of the 'Jews' – the leaders are again meant – that the bodies of those crucified be taken down,[72a] is in the source, only a means by which the following scene is made comprehensible. Jesus is saved from the cruel breaking of the legs. For the evangelist it is certainly a hostile action; the Jews press for the completion of the execution, Jesus is to disappear from the cross and no longer to be proclaimed as 'King of the Jews' (cf. 19:20f). But God directs it differently: they are to look upon him whom they have pierced (v. 37).

The details in the source are somewhat puzzling. The 'day of Preparation' (without more) could refer back to the 'day of preparation of the passover' in 19:14 (cf. also 18:28); but the following ἵνα-clause which reminds about the sabbath, does not leave any room for doubt that the day of preparation for the sabbath (that is Friday) is intended – the normal Jewish usage.[73] It is surprising that the source accentuates the sabbath, since, according to the Jewish point of view (Deut 21:22f) one hanged upon the tree should be removed before nightfall. Perhaps the reference to the sabbath is made because the sabbath rest would have postponed the removal for a further day; whether one may conclude from the information that the synoptic chronology (according to which, the day of the passover feast was already on the Friday[74]) still breaks through here, is to be doubted. If the following remark comes from the evangelist, then he intended to underline the coincidence of the day of the passover feast and the sabbath. The designation 'high',[75] not supported in the rabbinic sources, was also used by him for the last day of the feast of Tabernacles, remarkable for its special rites (q.v. 7:37); so it can easily be supposed that he added these few words.

Generally, the Romans let the remains of those whom they crucified hang as long as possible, as a deterrent; however, Philo, *In Flaccum*, § 83, testifies that they sometimes acted differently. So the Jews' request is understandable, and the continuation shows that the Roman prefect granted it. The breaking of the legs (*crurifragium*) with iron clubs was a cruel practice which at once brought about the death of those crucified, who often remained alive for a rather long time. It was also presumably the soldiers' duty to take down the corpses. When, in the case of Jesus, this was done by Joseph of Arimathaea with Pilate's concurrence, two different traditions are recognizable.

The Johannine report clashes with the account of Mk 15:44f according to which Pilate learns from the captain that Jesus has already died, and on that grants Jesus' body to Joseph of Arimathaea. This tradition is also behind Jn 19:38; but already Mt and Lk have a shorter version and the tension between Jn 19:31 and 38 does not appear so clearly. Nothing is said about the soldiers taking the bodies from the cross, and Joseph of Arimathaea appears at the right moment to bury Jesus' remains. It is very possible that the Johannine source already combined both these events in this way and described them one after the other.[76]

19:32–33   At first, it seems as if other soldiers than those belonging to the execution squad 'came' to carry out Pilate's order. But ἦλθον can also be taken in such a way that the soldiers who were there approached to break the legs of those crucified (cf. ἐλθόντες in v. 33). As already mentioned, the soldiers do not proceed in order; the stylistic law of progression demands that what happened to Jesus is told of last. The account assumes the detail of 19:18 that there were two others crucified with Jesus. 'The soldiers' were last mentioned at the sharing out of the garments (19:23, 25); in the synoptics, they are expressly referred to only in the mockery scene in the praetorium (Mk 15:16/Mt 27:27) or beneath the cross (Lk 23:36). Their more prominent appearance in John is perhaps a pointer to the narrative style of his source. Taking account of the content, its object is to describe special features connected with the person of Jesus. If, in the case of the sharing of the garments, it was Jesus' seamless tunic which the soldiers did not want to tear, so now it is that he is already dead, which keeps them from breaking his legs. They determine it according to appearance (εἶδον), but in addition they want to make sure.

19:34   A soldier plunges a spear into Jesus' side.[77] The Greek verb which virtually means 'to thrust in, plunge in' is variously rendered in the Latin versions: *pupugit* (*b*), *inseruit* (*e*) or *percussit* (a ff² n q), *perfodit* (*c*); finally we meet with *aperuit* (aur f r¹ Vg). This rendering of 'opened', witnessed to by the Peshita as well, and which might go back to a confusion in the Greek,[78] gave some Latin church Fathers deeper cause for speculation. Augustine – basing himself wrongly upon it, to the effect that it does not say 'he pierced his side', or 'he wounded' or something similar, but, 'he opened' – expounds it in classic form as follows: 'With that, as it were, the door of life is opened at the place from which the Church's sacraments flow forth (those sacraments) without which we cannot enter into the life which is the true life.' After that, he also recalls the opening in Noah's ark and Eve's origin from the side of the sleeping Adam, a prefiguration of the Church's origin from Christ, the second Adam.[79] Such a symbolic interpretation, in many variations, dominated the age of the Fathers and the middle ages. It was strengthened by the 'issuing of blood and water', and the following verse which seems to indicate a deeper meaning of the scene. But, to begin with, v. 35 must be put on one side, because it may be an editorial addition (see above).

The soldier who sticks the spear into Jesus' side obviously aims at the heart, so as to be sure of Jesus' death.[80] The following words, 'and at once there came out blood and water'[80a] describe the effect, but there is much debate as to their meaning. Are they to be understood as referring to a natural occurrence, or do they mean that there was a miracle? Do they, right from the first, have a symbolic significance?

If this last is supposed, then the phrase is suspect as an addition (by the evangelist or the editors). But if we attribute the scene to the source, we have to probe whether these words also cannot belong to it. The spear-thrust was to confirm that Jesus was 'already dead' (v. 33); so a corresponding statement is to be expected. Can the issue of blood and water have this meaning? Present-day experts in medicine discuss the possibility that from a person who has been dead a short time 'blood and water' flow out; they see no serious difficulty as to the 'blood' but they cannot accommodate 'water'.[81] The error of such considerations lies in holding the sentence to be an objective description of the occurrence; rather it must be asked whether, according to the *understanding of the time*, it can state that death has definitely occurred.

According to ancient witnesses,[82] it was said that a great deal of colourless watery blood flows from wounds, usually called ἰχώρ but occasionally ὕδωρ. It was believed that man consisted of blood and water; that is also testified to in a Jewish midrash.[83] So v. 34b may simply have the meaning in the source: Death has claimed Jesus. The announcement of a miracle[84] is excluded because the source did not apparently relate any miracle in the passion narrative, or at any rate, the evangelist does not hand down any other. Also, the comment need not show an anti-Gnostic tendency if it was already found in the source; an explanation from 1 Jn 5:6 is not compellingly necessary.[85] Another question is whether perhaps the author of v. 35 understood the comment in another sense (see *ad loc.*), and once more it has to be asked afresh after v. 37, what significance the occurrence gained for the evangelist. Then, we can form an opinion as to the various symbolic interpretations as well.

19:35　The testimony of the one 'who saw' is added to the scene and, as a result, lends special weight to it. If the description itself is taken over from the source, the verse can only originate with the evangelist or the editors. To answer this question, we must also investigate language and style. For the field covered by 'see – witness to – believe' there are enough texts to compare in the gospel and in the 'great' letter.

In the gospel, the testimony of John the Baptist in particular, is comparable; according to 1:34 he says: κἀγὼ ἑώρακα καὶ μεμαρτύρηκα. That refers to a visible occurrence (cf. v. 32) which has a deeper meaning for faith. The Baptist's testimony (μαρτυρία) is also brought out in other places (1:7, 19; cf. 5:33f, 36a). Against that, Jesus' and the Father's testimony, is on a different level. In 1 Jn, the passage 1:2 (καὶ ἑωράκαμεν καὶ μαρτυροῦμεν) comes nearest to Jn 19:35, because there 'seeing' is likewise adopted for a statement about faith; cf. also 4:14. With ὁ ἑωρακώς (19:35) our attention is drawn to the closing remark of the editors (21:24) where the disciple whom Jesus loved is specified as a witness (cf. 21:20–23). In fact, in 19:35 also, no other can be intended (cf. 19:26f). Admittedly, there are some verbal differences: in 19:35 an absolute μαρτυρεῖν, in 21:24 μ. περί (but this is explained by the respective contexts); further, ἀληθινή against ἀληθής as predicate of μαρτυρία. Apparently, both words in the two passages have the same meaning, that is, they are used synonymously. The use of both adjectives by the evangelist is disputed; but, in general, he seems to make a distinction (cf. Vol. 2, pp. 229–231). An indication against 19: 35 and 21:24 having the same origin cannot really be deduced from this. Linguistically, the two passages also approximate to one another because of the following sentence containing 'to know' although the sentences do not exactly correspond to each other. Thus, there are certain, even if not irrefutable indications in favour of 19:35 and 21:24 belonging together.

The relationship between 19:35 and 21:24 is clearer if notice is taken of the contents. In both the concern is with the disciple whom Jesus loved; in both he is adduced in his function as witness; in both his testimony is underlined as reliable. The only difference is in those who vouch for his testimony: in 21:24 it is the circle of those connected with him (the 'we' in οἴδαμεν); in 19:35 ἐκεῖνος. Who is meant by this? Jesus, with whom the scene just ended is concerned? or God who stands surety for the testimony of a man (cf. remotely 3:33; 5:32; 8:26)? or that eye-witness himself whose knowledge concerning the truth of his statement (ἀληθῆ λέγει, cf. 4:18; 10:41) is once more accentuated in support of his testimony? All these views have been represented;[86] but simplest is the reference back to the ἑωρακώς. Such a use of ἐκεῖνος is also established elsewhere.[87] Understood in this way, the passage places an extraordinary weight on the testimony of him 'who saw': he has borne testimony – is reliable – he knows that he speaks the truth. It is the same tendency as in 21:24, to support what is related in the gospel on the authority of that disciple. Since, apart from that, the evangelist normally introduces his comments differently (cf. 2:22; 12:16; or 6:64, 71; 12:6; or 12:33; 18:9, 32), we treat the verse as an addition of the editors. But what interest are the editors pursuing by means of the addition? The object of the seeing and witnessing then also of the believing[88] is not detailed. Since the preservation of Jesus from having his legs broken is sufficiently emphasized by the quotation in v. 36, the concern is obviously centred on the issuing of blood and water from Jesus' side. Why is this so important for the editors? Two explanations are offered: Defence against a Docetic opinion, or, a deeper symbolic consideration. Here – at an editorial level – the connection with 1 Jn 5:6 has to be considered. The anti-Docetic interest cannot be overlooked in this passage, even if the more immediate meaning is disputed (cf. also 4:2). The differing order of 'blood' and 'water' can be explained from the context.[89] Thus, just these elements, signs of Jesus' true manhood, could have suited the editors' purpose in a position taken up directly against those denying that Jesus had a body. But when we also bring in 1 Jn 5:7, the verse following, where mention is made of the three witnesses (water, blood and Spirit), a purely apologetic purpose again becomes doubtful. (The three witnesses are mentioned together in the RSV in 1 Jn 5:8 and only in the Greek in 1 Jn 5:7, 8a. – *Translator*). It seems that the one who put together 1 Jn here goes over to a symbolic interpretation in the sense of the sacraments), at the least to a far-reaching significance of the events within the Church (cf. *ad loc.*). So this possibility may not be ruled out for Jn 19:35 as well; it is, indeed, even somewhat probable in the case of the absolute use of $\pi\iota\sigma\tau\epsilon\acute{u}\epsilon\iota\nu$. Faith sees more than the external event, recognizes something deeper than Jesus' bodily nature.[90] Final certainty cannot be attained as to the intention which lead to the insertion of v. 35.

19:36   A scriptural quotation is connected to the linking passage, 'these things took place that' (on account of the insertion of v. 35 perhaps invented by the editors, perhaps even already original), in order to show that Jesus' preservation from having his legs broken is according to the scriptures. The normal Johannine formula introducing quotations $\mathring{\iota}\nu\alpha$ $\varkappa\tau\lambda$. (see on v. 24), is no sure indication as to whether the quotation was still part of the account in the source or only added on by the evangelist. Yet it would already have been found in the source which attached great value to such fulfilment of scripture (cf. also v. 28). To find the source of our text some passages concerning the passover lamb or Ps 34:20 (33:21) in an individual's song of praise, come into question. Many exegetes refer to Ex 12:10 (LXX only); 12:46 or Num 9:12; other scholars[91] prefer Ps 34:20 (33:21) where God's protection of the righteous is spoken of.

   The verbal content of 19:36 does not coincide with any of these passages. Ex 12:10 (LXX); 12:46 have two differences when compared with Jn: The verb is $\sigma\upsilon\nu\tau\rho\acute{\iota}\psi\epsilon\tau\epsilon$, and instead of $\alpha\mathring{\upsilon}\tau\sigma\tilde{\upsilon}$ it says $\mathring{\alpha}\pi$' $\alpha\mathring{\upsilon}\tau\sigma\tilde{\upsilon}$. Num 9:12 has the third person plural; if we go back to the Masoretic Text the passive Greek rendering is, perhaps, more akin to this passage than to the Exodus passages.[92] Those who maintain the derivation from Ps 34:20 can draw support from the fact that there is complete agreement as to the verb, συντριβήσεται; but the rest of the text differs, 'he keeps all his bones (τὰ ὀστᾶ αὐτῶν); not one of them is broken'. Thus, no certain decision can be made from the verbal content.

The preference for one passage as against another is, for most scholars, dependent on what conception they see behind the passage: passover lamb typology, or, protection for the suffering righteous. Reasons can be adduced for both. John certainly pays attention to the paschal character of Jesus' hour of death (cf. 18:28; 19:14), even if he does not say directly that Jesus died at that hour when the passover lambs were slaughtered in the temple. On the other hand, we already met with two quotations taken from a 'suffering servant' song (19:24 from Ps 22:18; 19:28 from Ps 69:21), from two psalms which play a part in the primitive Church's tradition concerning the suffering of Christ. That is, admittedly, not demonstrable otherwise for Ps 34 (33). In this unclear situation, a further explanation presents itself: perhaps the Johannine source referred to Ps 34:20 (33:21); would it not otherwise have again pointed to the 'day of preparation for the passover' in v. 31? But the evangelist understands the scripture quotation about the passover lamb, in a way corresponding to his inclination to passover-lamb typology (cf. also 1:29, 36). But this explanation too cannot be proved; however, such a multi-layered understanding of the scripture may be reckoned with.[93]

19:37   The second quotation from scripture relates to the piercing of Jesus' side and refers to Zech 12:10; however, it also presents some problems.[94] To begin with, it is uncertain whether the evangelist found it or added it himself. The linguistic observations, which give no clear picture, were mentioned above. If the quotation was already found in the source, as is mostly supposed on account of its occurrence in other NT writings also (see below),[95] it was probably in it solely to give scriptural reasons for the fact of the 'piercing' of Jesus' side. But for the evangelist, the 'looking on' the one who was pierced was important, as may be assumed from other passages in his gospel and from his whole way of thinking. So, here too, it is worthwhile (as with the first quotation) to distinguish the levels of understanding.

Zech 12:10–14 deals with a great lament of Israel concerning a man who was killed, certainly not without guilt on the people's part, for the rest, however, he remains shrouded in obscurity (as the 'Servant' of God in Is 53). The lament becomes an expression of conversion and brings the inhabitants of Jerusalem to a state of blessedness; God pours out a 'Spirit of compassion and supplication' over them. For the words, 'They look on him whom they have pierced', John has probably taken into consideration the OT context.

In the Masoretic Text, the passage reads, translated literally, 'they will look upon *me* whom they have pierced'. That ought to refer to God. Not a few commentaries suppose a corruption of the text and change the yod to a vau ('on him'), others defend the Masoretic Text. The LXX gives a text here which is different in the second part ('because they have danced'). Theodotion stays closest to the Masoretic Text: καὶ ἐπιβλέψονται πρός με ὃν ἐξεκέντησαν; but the Johannine text scarcely follows him either. We shall have to assume, as with other quotations in John's gospel (especially 12:40), an intentional alteration to fit the text Christologically.[96]

The Zechariah passage was also echoed in other NT writings, namely, in Mt 24:30 and Rev 1:7. It is brought in both times for the apocalyptic description of the events of the parousia. Israel's lament has become a wailing of all the nations on earth who then come to see the Son of Man–judge (Mt); every eye shall see him, even those 'who pierced him' (Rev). Thus, the scripture passage occupied the primitive Church and John too will have taken it up from the tradition. But the evangelist does not have to give it the same meaning. The future ὄψονται does not refer in his case to the future-eschatological events and, therefore, also, does not need to be fixed on judgment and disaster (see below).

What does the evangelist want to say with the words of scripture in this passage? Who the people are looking on the one who has been pierced, remains indefinite. They do not need to be the same as those who have pierced him; the plural can, indeed, be understood impersonally ('one'). It is hardly the soldiers who are thought of; only one of them has made the spear-thrust. Is one to regard the Jews as the subject of ὄψονται (v. 31)? That is not to be ruled out with the evangelist's thinking; he makes them answerable for the fact that Jesus was 'lifted up', that is, crucified (cf. 8:28). But also in general, the thought can be of those guilty of Jesus' death, or of all those whose glance is now fixed on the crucified one.

The decisive question is the meaning of 'looking on the one who has been pierced'. Is it a prophecy of salvation or disaster? Often, the saying is given a doom-laden character,[97] taking into account also Rev 1:7; but this passage ought not to prejudice the interpretation (see above). In the OT context, as we saw, the prophetic word opens up a prospect of salvation (conversation and compassion). But, within the framework of John's gospel also, the salvation aspect is more to the fore when we consider the following:

1. With 'seeing' the evangelist is not only thinking generally of the 'one who has been pierced', but also of the blood and water flowing from Jesus' side. However, he understood this in detail, it was for him, undoubtedly, a stream of blessing and salvation.

2. The 'seeing' connects with another significant passage, namely, 3:14 where the 'lifting up' of the brazen serpent in the wilderness, is made the type of the Son of Man's lifting up. Certainly, here, the expression 'to look on' is not found; but this looking on is the precondition in Num 21:8 for remaining alive, and in Jn 3:15, faith replaces this, in order that we may have eternal life 'in him' who is lifted up. Now, this 'lifting up' of the Son of Man has taken place.

3. The passage in 8:28 is also related: after the Jews have 'lifted up' the Son of Man, they will recognize Jesus' true being and his significance (ἐγώ εἰμι). It is, indeed, disputed whether here the aspect of judgment or of salvation is to the fore (see *ad loc.*); but the possibility of a recognition leading to conversion and rescue cannot be ruled out.

4. Particularly important is the passage 12:32, standing in closer proximity to the passion of Jesus: 'And I, when I am lifted up from the earth, will draw all men to myself.' Then, the dying grain of wheat will be fruitful (12:24).

5. If, in addition, we take 'blood and water' from Jesus' side there is certainly, for the evangelist, a connection with the saying about the 'rivers of living water' in 7:38. This promise now finds its fulfilment: Out of Jesus' body ($\varkappa o\iota\lambda\acute{\iota}\alpha$!) flow blood and water, a life-giving river.[98] In his comment (7:39) the evangelist points to the Spirit whom those who believe in Jesus are to receive after his glorification. So it seems that, in the first place, 'those looking on' are thought to be the believers. The Jews are not excluded, even if they are not meant by themselves. As is continually the case, the affirmation of salvation is transformed into the threat of judgment, when, instead of faith, man's answer is unbelief; but that is not the first and dominating thought. The one lifted up, out of whose side blood and water flow, is not to be overlooked by mankind. They will and must look to him whom they have pierced, for their salvation or destruction.

If this interpretation conveys correctly the evangelist's ideas, we can, also, in retrospect, make even clearer his understanding of 'blood and water' and draw demarcation lines to the many symbolic interpretations. If he had already found the expression in the source, he was apparently not interested in an interpretation differentiating between the two elements. It is, for him, a single river of life that comes from Jesus' dead body. According to 7:39, it is the Spirit which the glorified one sets free for the believers. In case both the elements are, nevertheless, supposed to have a significance for the evangelist, then the blood is, presumably, a sign of Jesus' saving death (cf. 1 Jn 1:7) and the water is symbolic of Spirit and life (cf. Jn 4:14; 7:38), but both are most intimately connected. The reference to the sacraments of baptism and Eucharist is less immediate. The order (blood–water) does not speak in favour, and $\alpha\tilde{\iota}\mu\alpha$ alone as a reference to the Eucharist is also a remote probability (in 6:53ff always $\sigma\acute{\alpha}\rho\xi$ and $\alpha\tilde{\iota}\mu\alpha$).[99] Finally, as for the Church having its beginning from Christ's side, an interpretation which became popular in patristic and medieval exegesis, has no direct support in John's gospel. Certainly, this thought is reconcilable with Johannine theology in so far as the Spirit makes possible the building up of the Church and is at work in the Church; but an ecclesiastical typology is not intended in Jn 19:34–37.

The *historicity* of the scene with the spear-thrust, on account of the other, to some extent competing tradition that Joseph of Arimathaea took away Jesus' body, presents a problem. But the supposition that the scene is developed from the scripture quotation Zech 12:10,[100] is premature. This quotation only follows the other, and both together seem more like a later reflection upon a previously given tradition. Certainly, we have to do with a tradition about which the synoptics knew nothing (cf. also Lk 24:39), and reasons can be adduced for its being of late origin.[100a] Once more, the testimony of v. 35 also cannot be pushed aside. The editors put their trust in the testimony of their guarantor who, obviously, confirmed that tradition. So it resolves itself into the question, how far their source for the tradition still had access to historical facts (cf. with this, Excursus 18).

6. *The Dignified Burial of Jesus (19:38–42)*

[38]*After this Joseph of Arimathaea, who was a disciple of Jesus, but secretly, for fear of the Jews, asked Pilate that he might take away the body of Jesus; and Pilate gave him leave. So he came and took away his body.* [39]*Nicodemus also, who had at first come to him by night, came bringing a mixture of myrrh and aloes, about a hundred pounds' weight.* [40]*They took the body of Jesus, and bound it in linen cloths with the spices, as is the burial custom of the Jews.* [41]*Now in the place where he was crucified there was a garden, and in the garden a new tomb where no one had ever been laid.* [42]*So because of the Jewish day of Preparation, as the tomb was close at hand, they laid Jesus there.*

The Johannine description of the laying of Jesus in the tomb, has the unmistakable intention of revealing clearly the honour shown to the crucified one, the glorification which already begins with his 'lifting up'. It is the logical continuation of the line of thought maintained at the trial, during the crucifixion and directly after the death, that of showing the greatness and glory lying behind the dark events. The excessive quantity of the sweet-smelling spices which Nicodemus brings, the wrapping of the corpse, according to custom, in linen cloths, and the burial in a new tomb in which no other had been laid, are indications of this. But perhaps that, taken by itself, is not even the most important thing for the evangelist; it matters just as much to him that, because of the circumstances, God has arranged things in this way. Because of the Jews' day of Preparation, it is necessary to hurry. Now, the two men who, otherwise, followed Jesus only in secret, step forward resolutely. In clear contrast to the Jews (v. 31, cf. v. 38) they represent the fellowship of Jesus which shows great honour to its Lord.

What the evangelist has taken over from the tradition (that is, presumably, the same source as up till now), and what he himself has added, can be relatively easily distinguished, if we proceed as before. Joseph of Arimathaea's going with his request to Pilate and the taking away of the corpse by this man (who in John is not identified as a member of the council), was certainly already found by the evangelist in his source;[101] only that he was a disciple of Jesus in secret for fear of the Jews is made clear, as the language shows. He himself will have introduced Nicodemus although he certainly did not invent[101a] this man who appears on the scene three times in John's gospel. It is questionable whether the source already said anything about the mixture of myrrh and aloes. The ἀρώματα already play a part in the synoptic reports, admittedly, in connection with the women (Mk 16:1; Lk 23:56; 24:1). These and other details such as the linen cloths or the garden where the tomb was, can be discussed in the exegesis.

Important are the links between the burial story and the subsequent accounts of the visit to the tomb by the two disciples and the appearance of Jesus to Mary of Magdala. The linen cloths, and the napkin (not so far mentioned in the burial account), are important for the 'inspection' of the tomb by the two disciples

(20:6f), and the garden for what is told about Mary of Magdala (20:15). The events on the Friday evening and the Sunday morning are bracketed together by these features. It can be concluded from this, that the evangelist already found them in the burial account of his source. The noticeable discrepancies with the synoptic reports especially as to the mode of Jesus' burial (linen cloths or σινδών, with or without sweet-smelling spices), could already have been present in the source. Perhaps, an apologetic tendency is noticeable in it too. A more pronounced theological interest is characteristic for the evangelist. The historical question, how the burial actually proceeded on the evening of the day that Jesus died, is hard to answer on account of the various traditions and the respective tendencies in the presentations.[102]

19:38 An indefinite μετὰ ταῦτα which often introduces a new section in John's gospel (cf. 3:22; 5:1; 6:1, 14; 7:1), here, however, through δέ linking more closely to what goes before, connects the request (ἐρωτᾶν as in v. 31) of Joseph of Arimathaea with the last scene. A total harmonization of the two traditions is scarcely possible;[103] yet the tension seems hardly to be felt. The scene with the spear-thrust decribed on account of the fulfilment of scripture, is not intended to describe Jesus' burial; for this, the narrator goes back to another tradition which was already available to Mark:[104] the taking away and burial of Jesus' body by Joseph of Arimathaea. This man, identified by his place of origin, but who has obviously resided in Jerusalem for quite a while,[105] is, according to Mk 15:43, a 'respected member of the council'. The further points of characterization in the three synoptics (each with their respective emphases) are to make his courageous act understandable to the Christian readers. According to the wording, John (ὢν μαθητής) stands closest to Mt 27:57 (ἐμαθητεύθη); but this is hardly dependence. The entire detailed description of the man (ὢν . . . Ἰουδαίων) sounds Johannine: the evangelist often uses the participle of εἶναι; he has a more extended understanding of μαθητής (cf. on 6:60, 66; especially 7:3); also κρύφω, ἐν κρυπτῷ is often found (8:59; 12:36; – 7:4, 10); above all, 'for fear of the Jews' is a typical Johannine theme (7:13; 20:19; cf. 9:22).[106] With it, perhaps, the evangelist replaced another characterization of the source ('member of the council'?). The following brief remarks concerning Pilate's permission (ἐπιτρέπειν only here in John's gospel), and the carrying out of the intention (οὖν does not have to be a criterion in favour of John), will again have come from the source.[107]

19:39 Nicodemus who also comes, plays a part only in John's gospel (3:1–12; 7:50f). By itself, that would not be any reason to attribute his coming forward at Jesus burial, to the evangelist;[108] but the mode of introduction (ἦλθεν δὲ καί takes up the ἦλθεν from v. 38) does speak for it. The reminder of his first coming to Jesus at night (3:2) comes, with certainty, from the evangelist, who, in this way, names another man who secretly supported Jesus and now does not hesitate to perform, out of love, the act of burying the dead. Taking into account the line from 3:1ff – 7:50 – 19:39, as well as the fact that the evangelist does not recall the scene in the Sanhedrin (7:50f) but his first seeking out of

Jesus 'by night', the impression is forced upon us that Nicodemus too in a similar way to Joseph of Arimathaea, is pictured as a man for whom Jesus' death leads to a breakthrough of a more decisive attitude in his faith. The disciple whom Jesus loved is not mentioned; but he has another function for the evangelist (see on 19:26f). The women also (in contrast to the synoptics) are not referred to. John places no value on spectators or witnesses; Jesus' burial as later also his tomb are to reveal Jesus' glory, which is mirrored in the action of those two men. They are not identified as councillors, perhaps intentionally not, because in this way they better represent the future believers. Nicodemus brings with him a mixture[109] of myrrh and aloes. Myrrh is a pleasant-smelling resin which, among other things, was mixed with olive-oil; aloes were a kind of scented wood. Here, both scented substances must be thought of in crushed or powdered form; nothing is said about oil, the mixture is strewn between the linen cloths.

This is important because, with that, there can be no question of an anointing with oil or embalming. The anointing in Bethany (12:3) is thus another procedure which, for Jn, does not compete with the act of Nicodemus. Obviously, he has taken up two different traditions and interpreted each in his own way. The anointing of Jesus' feet by Mary is, for him, a proleptic anointing of the dead (cf. on 12:7), and the quantity of the scented spices strewn between the linen cloths, to guard against the stench of the corpse, is, according to the Jewish viewpoint, a great honour shown to the dead. An embalming of the corpse (as in Egypt) was not normal for the Jews.[110]

This way of caring for Jesus' remains is so singular, that it was probably already in the source. Remarkable is the large amount, one hundred pounds, that is in our weight 65·45 pounds (cf. 12:2); but a similarly large amount is given with the anointing in Bethany, and it is possible that already the source so described it. If the introduction of Nicodemus is an addition of the evangelist, the source can nevertheless have already made mention of it in another way, say, that Joseph of Arimathaea brought these gifts with him, or, generally, that one ('they', cf. the plural of the reading at the end of v. 38) attended to this. In any case, it is to be an extraordinary manifestation of respect. More often than not a 'royal' burial comes to mind;[111] but the special king-motif (cf. 19:19) is missing, and even without this, the scene retains its great and eloquent strength.

19:40 After the taking away of Jesus' body, v. 38, 'they' take – in the Johannine connection, Joseph of Arimathaea and Nicodemus – Jesus' body and bind it in linen cloths. The word used, ὀθόνια, is only found in Jn 19:40; 20:5, 6, 7, also in Lk 24:12 (a disputed passage for text-critical reasons, cf. on Jn 20:5).[112] He speaks here of a number of cloths which were tightly placed round the rump and the limbs as is also made clear by the use of 'bind'. The same way of dressing the dead is presupposed in the Lazarus-pericope (11:44); only there, another word (χειρίαι) is used. So it can be supposed with some certainty, that ὀθόνια comes from the source.

With this, the Johannine description comes into conflict with the synoptic information, that Joseph of Arimathaea bought a σινδών and wrapped Jesus' body in it (Mk 15:46 par.).

σινδών can describe both the material (linen cloth) and a single piece of cloth (an article of clothing, cf. Mk 14:52). The question whether, in Jesus' case, there was one large linen cloth or several pieces of linen has an enormous significance for the animated discusssion as to the genuineness of the Turin shroud. There is no shortage of attempts either to interpret the synoptic σινδών (as a description of the material) in accordance with the Johannine ὀθόνια (Blinzler), or to interpret the plural in John, as a linen cloth in agreement with the synoptics (Brown).[113] The verbs used in each case (Jn: δέω; Mk: ἐνειλέω; Mt/ Lk: ἐντυλίσσω) are scarcely of more help; they all mean a more or less tight binding, wrapping, enveloping. Even if the one or the other of the interpretations in itself is *possible*, still, for John, the idea that the body of Jesus was wrapped in several cloths or bandages by analogy with Jn 11:44 and 20:6f should be indisputable. On the other hand, for the synoptics, the notion of a single large linen cloth is obvious. In the heated discussion, too little attention may have been paid to the possibility that we have here two different traditions; for the primitive Church, this was obviously not yet such a problem. The Jewish burial customs of those days to which John refers (see below), are also not absolutely to be determined. Since often burial-shrouds were a great luxury, and the costs were burdensome for the relatives, people were grateful to Rabban Gamliel II (about AD 90), that he introduced the custom of burying the dead in a simple linen robe (*sadin*).[114] The Johannine point of view, that several linen cloths were used, is, however, also supported.[115] The apparently divergent details in the synoptics and John, do not allow of any certain conclusion as to what really happened to Jesus' remains.

The spices (ἀρώματα) which were used with the linen cloths, mean the mixture of myrrh and aloes, as shown by the article (which refers back). The comment about the Jewish manner of burial will be from the evangelist; he several times gives information to his readers about Jewish customs (cf. 2:6; 4:9; 11:55; 18:28). Yet, not all questions are answered as to how the Jews buried their dead in those days. Mk 16:1 speaks of the women's intention to 'anoint' Jesus' body;[116] but John (in accordance with his source) thinks only of the binding in linen cloths and the addition of aromatic substances. He is also less concerned to distinguish the Jewish custom from other forms of burial (cremation in the case of the Romans, embalming in Egypt), than to emphasize the orderly, even exceedingly dignified burial given to Jesus. Should the comment have already been found in the source, it could there have been intended apologetically. The washing of the body, the most important service rendered to a dead person, is, extraordinarily, not mentioned by any evangelist.

19:41 The burial in a tomb close at hand, situated in a garden, certainly still belongs to the report in the source. The details, which partly agree with the synoptics, but partly also differ from them, again show the source's self-sufficiency. There is no reference to the tomb being cut out of a rock; new, on the other hand, is the situation in a garden. The same information was given about the place of the arrest (18:1). Is that to indicate that Jesus' passion is coming to an end, to its peaceful conclusion? But that is uncertain, and there is still less justification for deeper symbolic ideas (a reminder of paradise).[117] Matthew alone says that it was Joseph's tomb. John too agrees with him about the fact that it was 'new',[118] and with Luke he adds (though in different words) that no one had yet been laid in it. The reflection of early Christian tradition on Jesus' tomb is recognizable. The specific details are important for our evangelist because they accord with his picture of Christ and confirm Jesus' glorification as willed by God.

Perhaps again, an apologetic interest was also present in the source: this tomb was easy to identify; Jesus was not taken to the far distant place for those who were executed.[119] But for John, not only the proximity but also the newness and the fact that the tomb had not been used is significant: in this way it accords with Jesus' rank and holiness. This is unmistakably a cultic reference, and it can be concluded from this detail which is already prominent in Matthew and Luke, that Jesus' tomb, early on, was held in high honour by the Christians. Looked at archaeologically and historically, there is no serious doubt that the Holy Sepulchre shown nowadays can be Jesus' tomb.[120] This is, admittedly, on the assumption that, despite all the attendant trends, historical trustworthiness is granted to the burial accounts of the gospels as to the tomb itself.

19:42 It is said with a certain emphasis that there Jesus was buried. Since before, only the tomb and the place were described, such a sentence must already have been found in the source. It appears overloaded because of the dual justification of the Jews' day of Preparation and the proximity of the tomb. Because of v. 31 the reader still remembers the haste necessitated by the day of Preparation. The reference to the tomb being nearby is rendered superfluous by the exact description in v. 41. Perhaps no such literary criteria may be used with a simple account (cf. on vv. 31f); but it is also possible that the evangelist added something to it. Most likely in this respect, is the remark about the 'Jewish day of Preparation'; for, $\tau\tilde{\omega}\nu$ $'Iou\delta\alpha\iota\omega\nu$[121] reveals the hand of the evangelist (cf. 19:31; further, 2:13; 5:1; 6:4; 7:2; 11:55). His motive for the addition is easy to recognize: it is his objective once again to bring to the fore the divine dispensation that Jesus was buried in this way in the nearby new tomb. The Jews justified their wicked demand that the legs of those crucified be broken, with the day of Preparation; but precisely this leads to the fact that Jesus finds this holy resting place. It is the only place where he was buried; hypotheses about two burials of Jesus are beside the point.[122] The succeeding stories about the tomb also presuppose that; Mary Magdalene's worries in 20:2b, 13, 15, are due to other causes. As for the rest, the evangelist restricts himself to what is important for him. He does not mention the stone sealing the tomb, though he knows of it (cf. 20:1). For him, the story of the burial represents the conclusion of Jesus' passion, a finale in peace and rest; Easter morning brings something new, which yet necessarily derives from this passion with its hidden glory.[123]

Easter: Open Tomb and Appearances.
Conclusion of Jesus' Revelation before the Disciples (Chapter 20)

The last section of the (original) gospel presents the Easter tradition according to the view and interpretation of the fourth evangelist. Probably, the passion story was never told without the Easter event in the earliest period. At least, the kerygma of the raising of the crucified one was heard (cf. Mk 16:6); yet according to 1 Cor 15:5, the appearance of the risen one was early on connected with this. It was obvious for the accounts of the gospels to describe such appearances (or whatever these phenomena are to be called) in more detail, and through them to open up from a narrative point of view, the meaning of Jesus' being raised from the dead. That is no longer apparent in Mk on account of its secondary conclusion; but Mt and Lk provide examples of this, each in his own way. If the stories about the women's visit to the tomb are still relatively compatible, then the accounts of Jesus' appearing in Mt and Lk show major differences in the conception and construction.[1]

The fourth evangelist also stands in the tradition of such stories and certainly uses traditional material – whether a source of his own as well, is still to be determined. According to his mode of presentation, as lately established in the report of the passion, a strongly individual composition is, however, from the first to be reckoned with. This does not only concern single Johannine motifs and interests (eg. the disciple whom Jesus loved, 20:2–8; or the fear of the Jews, 20:19), but also the evangelist's basic view about the resurrection of Jesus, the question as to how he understood it within the framework of his whole theological concept. For, as the programmatic sentence at the beginning of the second main section shows, he is concerned with Jesus' 'departure' to the Father (13:1) and his 'glorification' by the Father (13:31f; cf. 17:1f) respectively. How does Jesus' resurrection fit into his concept of the 'way' of the pre-existent one through incarnation and cross back into the heavenly glory, or, under another aspect, into that of the descent and ascent of the Son of Man (cf. 3:13; 6:62), so as to lead those believing in him to the same goal (cf. 14:3, 6)? Jesus' 'lifting up' on the cross leads to a direct glorification and the possibility 'to draw all men to himself' (12:32). There is a certain tension between this lifting up – glorification – Christology and the statement of Jesus' dying and rising, and this tension becomes very obvious in the words of the risen one to Mary Magdalene: 'I have not yet ascended to the Father' (20:17). Jesus' appearance on *earth* during an *interlude* between his death and his (final) dwelling with the Father, obviously makes for difficulties with the idea of a glorification in heaven beginning simultaneously with his death. Nevertheless, the evangelist took up the stories of the tomb and of the appearances, and presented them, having thought them through theologically. That is with an eye to the disciples and the later Church; for John, the Easter event is also still part of the perfection of the love with which Jesus loved his own (13:1). The stories in Chapter 20 contain important statements for future believers and serve that purpose in the evangelist's presentation which he set himself for the whole gospel (20:31). They are a part of that which happened 'in the presence of the disciples' (cf. 20:30) and is entrusted to them to be proclaimed and witnessed to. That is meant to be indicated in the heading, 'conclusion of Jesus' revelation before the disciples'.

In order to obtain a firmer grasp of the evangelist's intention in the stories of the tomb and of Easter, a discussion of the material available to him and the literary growth of the texts before us cannot be avoided. For the section 20:1–18 a literary-critical analysis is also unavoidable because the presentation contains contradictions and duplications. In the second part, the Thomas-pericope is disputed as to its authenticity. For the whole chapter, the question once more arises concerning tradition, shaping by the evangelist and possible subsequent editing. The problem of history of tradition for which the synoptic traditions and texts for comparison are helpful, may not be ignored under any circumstances. The efforts of literary-criticism, especially with Jn 20:1–18, have led to widely differing results; with the difficulty of the text before us, no certain conclusion satisfactory in all respects may be expected. The main purpose remains for us a more exact definition of the intention behind the evangelist's statement.

The division of the Johannine Easter chapter in its present form, is simple and clear; even a well-considered, well-proportioned, well-balanced structure is recognizable.[2] In general, the development is emphasized in that vv. 1–18 tell of occurrences on the *morning* of the first day of the week (=Easter Sunday), and against that, vv. 19–23 describe Jesus' appearing to the disciples during the *evening* of the same day. The Thomas narrative (vv. 24–29) follows this appearance, and is transferred to the Sunday after. Vv. 30–31 form the conclusion of the whole gospel. The events on the morning of the Easter Sunday are held together as one whole through Mary Magdalene; yet after v. 10 we find a break. The visit of the two disciples to the tomb (vv. 2–10) is set off by Mary's experience at the tomb (vv. 11–18). So we have the following units:

1. Mary Magdalene's report about the empty tomb and the visit to the tomb of the two disciples (20:1–10);
2. Mary at the tomb and her encounter with Jesus (20:11–18);
3. Jesus' appearance to the disciples in the evening (20:19–23);

4. Thomas's conversion to the Easter faith because of a further appearance of Jesus (20:24–29);

5. Conclusion of the gospel (20:30–31).

Before we proceed to the exegesis of the first two sub-sections, a literary-critical consideration of 20:1–18 commends itself, into which also questions of the history of tradition can be brought.

Literary-critical Analysis of Jn 20:1–18

1. Remarks on the texts

If we look more precisely at the two narratives brought together in this section, the visit to the tomb of the two disciples and the appearance to Mary Magdalene at the tomb, then many difficulties become apparent, to begin with, in the relationship of the two narratives to each other:

(*a*) In v. 2 Mary brings the disciples the news of the empty tomb and in v. 11 she stands weeping at the tomb – where was she in between times?

(*b*) The two disciples, on inspecting the tomb, see the grave clothes (Peter sees the napkin as well), inside the tomb; however, nothing besides (vv. 5–7). Mary sees two angels, but apparently does not notice the grave clothes (v. 12). How is that to be explained?

(*c*) The faith of the beloved disciple (v. 8) has no influence on the development of the Easter stories.

Next, there are tensions within the two narratives units:

(*a*) In v. 1 Mary Magdalene visits the tomb alone; but in v. 2 she says to the disciples: '*We* do not know where they have laid him (the Lord).'

(*b*) The description as to how the two disciples run to the tomb is remarkable: In v. 3 ἐξῆλθεν (singular) . . . ἤρχοντο εἰς; yet there then follows the 'run' in v. 4, which becomes a sort of race.

(*c*) It is emphatically stated concerning the beloved disciple in v. 8, that he 'saw and believed'; the causal clause in v. 9 conflicts with that in saying about *both* disciples that they did not know the scripture.

There are similar contradictions in the following story concerning Mary;

(*a*) The function of the angels in the tomb is altogether unclear. They announce nothing and they do not answer Mary in her complaint; they seem to be superfluous.

(*b*) The duplication of the question stands out: 'Woman, why are you weeping?' It is asked by the angels and then by Jesus.

(*c*) Likewise, it is twice stated that Mary turned round, cf. v. 14 and v. 16.

(*d*) Jesus' remark, μή μου ἅπτου (v. 17), appears groundless, since nothing is said of such a move by Mary.

(*e*) In v. 18, the last part of the sentence, καὶ ταῦτα εἶπεν αὐτῇ, 'tags' behind and, besides, goes into indirect speech (v. 1, direct speech)

2. Points of view from the history of tradition

Usually, in order to cast light on the confused narrative complex, critical attitudes are taken up as to tradition, and the Johannine account is compared with the synoptic narratives over the tomb and other traditions.[3] Now this method of procedure is, it is true, questionable because it would also first be necessary to study the text before us critically in terms of its form and its style. But in order to obtain a model for the genesis of the text, critical examination of tradition could be helpful. It is easy to recognize that in Jn 20:1–18, various traditions are worked together: the women's visit to the tomb; the disciples' inspection of the tomb; appearance of angels; Jesus' appearance to Mary Magdalene; the instruction given to the women or Mary Magdalene to carry a message to the disciples. From the standpoint of history of tradition, there is conflict, above all, between the visit to the tomb (with the discovery of the open or empty tomb) and the appearances; and here again, between the appearance of the angels and the appearance of Jesus. These problems of tradition can only here be hinted at; but they sharpen our perception of the literary-critical problem which concerns us: How did the literary composition before us come about? Did the evangelist himself put it together on the basis of the individual traditions? Did he use and work over a written source, perhaps combine it with oral traditions or expound it, alter, extend it, in his own way? Before we attempt our own analysis, we may cast a glance at the solutions attempted up till now.

3. Attempted solutions

Earlier literary criticism tried to discover the simpler basic form of the narrative complex 20:1–18, which was then extended either by the evangelist (on the supposition of a source) or by an editor (assuming a basic sketch of the gospel). Worth considering is the suggestion, which, in a modified form, retained support from Wellhausen to Bultmann, of singling out an original story in which Mary Magdalene alone plays a part: she comes to the tomb, finds the stone rolled away, looks into the tomb and searches in vain for Jesus' body. The end of the story is, it is true, variously assessed. Wellhausen eliminates the angels and has the scene end with the appearance of Jesus; Hirsch retains as part of his basic gospel both the appearance of the angels and that of Jesus; Bultmann thinks that the evangelist has broken off the conclusion of the 'Mary-narrative' belonging to the synoptic type (with the appearance of the angels) replacing it with the appearance of Jesus.[4] Common to these attempts is the elimination of the story about the disciples' expedition to the tomb.

In more modern works, Peter's visit to the tomb is, however, held to be a pre-Johannine tradition, or a part of that used by the evangelist. A. R. C. Leaney would find the reason for the similarities between Lk 24:12–53 and Jn 20, in both evangelists' use of the same tradition.[5] According to B. Lindars, the episode can be a construction based on a tradition similar to that of Lk 24:24.[6] P. Benoit recognizes in the visit to the tomb of the two disciples, a tradition which also survives in Lk 24:12: simpler story in which Peter alone looks into the tomb. A new independent narrative is found in Jn 20:11a, 14b–18: an appearance of Jesus to Mary Magdalene. In the end, the tradition which is close to the synoptics, concerning the appearance of the angels in the tomb

(vv. 11b–14a), was combined with this.[7] G. Hartmann proceeds in a similar direction, emphasizing the intimate connection between the story of the disciples with that about Mary and concluding that there was a source telling of Peter and Mary going together to the tomb and which, after Peter's return, v. 10, continued with the appearance of Jesus to Mary. Vv. 11b–14a are said to be added on later, not by the evangelist.[8] A source (namely, his 'sign-gospel') is also supposed by R. T. Fortna. It encompasses, in the main, the same verses or parts of verses as in the case of Hartmann; only the combining with the appearance of the angels is already attributed to the source by Fortna.[9] It is otherwise with R. Mahoney's dissertation on Jn 20:1–10: he is sceptical about the reconstruction of a source, as also about an extra-Johannine tradition concerning a visit to the tomb by Peter (he regards Lk 24:12 as not original from the viewpoint of textual criticism). He thinks that the Johannine account can best be explained as a further development (in the oral tradition) of Lk 24:1–11.[10]

If we survey these efforts of literary criticism and history of tradition, then some progress can be seen towards a consensus among scholars. There is agreement that the figure of the beloved disciple was introduced by the fourth evangelist (or by editors?). It is also broadly agreed that John used traditions which were already circulating before his time, less so that he also used a written source. Yet where it is thought impossible to do without a source, opinion inclines towards one containing not merely a story about Mary Magdalene, but also combined with it, a visit by Peter to the tomb. In the more detailed assessment of the limits of the source there are differences, especially in relation to the appearance of the angels (vv. 11b–14a). As to v. 17, at least a strong share in its construction is attributed to the evangelist. So our analysis can refer to the studies mentioned and use their, in part, valuable individual observations. Although the assumption of a source can only be a working hypothesis, it commends itself as such, for the reason also that it proved its worth for the passion account. Was the source for the passion supposed to have finished with the burial, or was the evangelist supposed to have abandoned it and instead to have taken up a separate narrative? That is not very probable; but let us turn to the analysis!

4. Attempted analysis of the text

The sentence with which the narrative begins (v. 1), exhibits remarkable similarities with the synoptic narratives about the women's visit to the tomb. The designation of the day of the week, the very early hour, Mary Magdalene, the stone sealing the tomb and removed from it: all that is in full accord with them factually and, in part, literally. A more precise comparison[11] results in a special closeness to Luke, yet also affinities with Mark. Specific to John are only σκοτίας ἔτι οὔσης and the verb for the removal of the stone (ἠρμένον). Since σκοτία is a Johannine criterion of style (Ruckstuhl, No. 22), this detail of time will have come from John; αἴρω is also used at the opening of Lazarus's tomb, however, already in the source (11:39, 41). If thus v. 1 may well be from a source akin to the synoptics, then the failure to mention the other women is noticeable. Was John following a source which only mentioned Mary Magdalene (cf. Bultmann)? But οἴδαμεν in v. 2 speaks rather for the supposition that, at least, at the beginning other women were mentioned together with her.[12] If so, the evangelist would have carried through this concentration on Mary Magdalene which is wholly understandable because of his preference for bringing single persons (disciples) to the fore. Nothing is said about the purpose of the visit to the tomb; since all three synoptics speak about it (Mt, on account of the story of the guard, with a weaker emphasis: θεωρῆσαι), the evangelist has perhaps also tightened up the story as to this point. Yet, if we are supposed to have here the same source as for the burial, the ἀρώματα (different from Mk/Lk) could not be mentioned any more. The remark concerning the stone used for sealing the tomb which was not mentioned at the time of the laying in the tomb, does not speak against the same source; it is not otherwise in Luke.

V. 2 points the way for the visit to the tomb by the two disciples. Mary's words are noteworthy: 'They have taken the Lord out of the tomb.' From now on, ὁ κύριος occurs as a designation of Jesus in the course of the narratives as well (until now only in side comments, probably editorial, see on 4:1; 6:23; 11:2). That can be the wording of the sources, admittedly also the evangelist's expression for the risen one (following the source?) More important, is that the motif of the removal from the tomb is constant; it occurs twice more, in v. 13 in the same words, then, related more extensively because of the circumstances, in v. 15. In v. 13, it is true, there remains the suspicion of a later addition (see below). The interest which manifests itself there seems to be apologetic (cf. the suggestion in v. 15 that the gardener has taken away the body), and a similar intention is seen behind the exact description of what Peter found in the tomb (vv. 6f). Since the evangelist was interested rather in leading his readers to an understanding in faith of the risen one himself (cf. the line through vv. 8–17–21f–28), a differently directed basic tendency than in the tradition used by John becomes apparent here. Naturally, the apologetic motif could have suited the evangelist too; but he is more interested in the significance of the risen one for the Church. Predominance of that motif and its concrete formulation (especially in v. 15) point more strongly to a source rather than only oral tradition. If this is correct, the view of the more recent scholarship is confirmed that Peter's investigation of the tomb was already combined in the source with the Mary-narrative.

Not many words are necessary to show that the figure of the disciple whom Jesus loved was first introduced by the evangelist into the story which he found. In v. 2 he was easily added to Peter, likewise in v. 3. In the source the two persons who set out for the tomb were Peter and Mary Magdalene. The description of the 'race' between the disciples, comes from the evangelist; what he purposed with it must be made clear in the exegesis. The source resumes with v. 6b, the inspection of the tomb by Peter. In his case the line can easily be followed: ἐξῆλθεν (v. 3a) – ἤρχοντο εἰς τὸ μνημεῖον (v. 3b) – εἰσῆλθεν (v. 6). The ὀθόνια in vv. 6f recall the same expression at the burial (19:40), so that this special word is a noteworthy link between the two narratives, presumably an indication in favour of the same source. V. 8 (also considering the style) again comes wholly from the evangelist for whom the statement is important, that the beloved disciple 'saw and believed'. This sentence will have pushed aside the reaction of Peter (and of Mary) in the source; perhaps it contained something similar to Lk 24:12: 'He wondered to himself' (cf. Fortna). Then, v. 9 fittingly follows, giving the reason why Peter and Mary were not yet thinking of Jesus' resurrection from the dead. In v. 10 in the source was mentioned only Peter's return.

In this reconstruction of the source, the difficulty that v. 11 says about Mary '(she) stood outside the tomb' is explained. She remained while Peter went home. The scene with the angels is difficult to make a judgment about. The suggestion of passing from v. 11a straight to v. 14b clears up the textual problem in a straightforward way. The duplication of the words spoken disappears; also, Mary only turns once to Jesus (v. 16). So this could be a case of a later addition (by editors); but with this, admittedly, the question cannot be satisfactorily answered what should have caused an editor to insert this scene. Did he want to bring in the traditional motif of the angels (most likely according to Lk 24:4), or did he once more want to give a hearing to Mary's complaint? The evangelist certainly had no interest in the angels. In this section of the narrative, terms belonging to the context are used; on παρέκυψεν cf. v. 5 (here stylistically correct for the behaviour of the second disciple), on the question of the angels cf. v. 15, with Mary's answer v. 2. The angel's position at the head and the foot of the place where Jesus' body had lain is, in another way than in vv. 6f, a sign that Jesus is no longer there, he is risen. Perhaps beside the 'natural' evidence of vv. 6f this is meant as heavenly evidence. In any case, this solution ought to be preferred over Fortna's supposition that this scene too belongs to the source; to this end, he has to strike out something from Mary's encounter with Jesus, which ought to be original.[13] In v. 11 ὡς οὖν ἔκλαιεν can still be reckoned as part of the source, which then, in v. 14b continued: θεωρεῖ τὸν Ἰησοῦν κτλ. The remark in v. 15 that Mary thought Jesus to be the gardener, is again in line with the burial story which – alone in the NT – mentions that the tomb was in a garden (19:41).

Vv. 14b–16 will reproduce the text of the source rather exactly, a lively representation of the scene. Only with v. 17 is it necessary to suppose stronger interventions by the evangelist. The prohibition μή μου ἅπτου which at this moment is unprovoked certainly belongs to the reaction of the woman described in the source in somewhat more detail as is made obvious by a comparison of Mt 28:9 with the history of tradition. In the source will have followed Jesus' commission that his 'brethren' be brought a message (cf. Mt 28:10), that is πορεύου . . . to εἰπὲ αὐτοῖς. The content of the message was perhaps only 'I have seen the Lord' (cf. v. 18). The two sentences which speak of Jesus' ἀναβαίνειν are Johannine interpretations, for that is not only a dominant theme of the Johannine theology, but also an attempt to harmonize the resurrection kerygma with the 'ascent' and return of Jesus to the Father. V. 18, as far as ἑώρακα τὸν κύριον, concludes the narrative in the source in accordance with its style. The very short sentence in indirect speech which is tagged on, must have been added by the evangelist as a reminder of the sentences inserted by him. Mary conveys not only the fact of the appearance, but also the interpretation given by the risen one himself.

5. Result

My analysis has led to no important new result (cf. especially G. Hartmann) but it has given a more distinct profile to the nature and tendency of the source (vivid description, apologetic tendency) as also to its re-working by the evangelist with his interest being somewhat differently directed. When, above all, the introduction of the beloved disciple and Jesus' words to Mary are attributed to John, and he takes over the remaining description, it is a good starting-point for the exegesis which must examine individual points still more closely. It is important to recognize that the same source which we supposed for the passion and burial can and probably also does form the basis of this section too. Although the distinction between the source and Johannine reworking remains uncertain in some instances, and the origin of the scene with the angels cannot be cleared up beyond doubt, the analysis offers a point of departure for a better understanding of the Johannine Easter account. The evangelist's procedure as observed up to this point is confirmed.

Exegesis
1. Mary Magdalene's Report about the Empty Tomb and the
visit to the Tomb of the Two Disciples (20:1–10)

[1]*Now on the first day of the week Mary Magdalene came to the tomb early, while it was still dark, and saw that the stone had been taken away from the tomb.* [2]*So she ran, and went to Simon Peter and the other disciple, the one whom Jesus loved, and said to them, 'They have taken the Lord out of the tomb, and we do not know where they have laid him.'* [3]*Peter then came out with the other disciple, and they went toward the tomb.* [4]*They both ran, but the other disciple outran Peter and reached the tomb first;* [5]*and stooping to look in, he saw the linen cloths lying there, but he did not go in.* [6]*Then Simon Peter came, following him, and went into the tomb; he saw the linen cloths lying,* [7]*and the napkin, which had been on his head, not lying with the linen cloths but rolled up in a place by itself.* [8]*Then the other disciple, who reached the tomb first, also went in, and he saw and believed;* [9]*for as yet they did not know the scripture, that he must rise from the dead.* [10]*Then the disciples went back to their homes.*

20:1   The discovery of the open or empty tomb respectively by women on the morning of the Sunday following the Good Friday, is related by all evangelists. However the historical value of these accounts, which, as to their type are certainly not 'historical reports', may be judged,[14] nevertheless, some details are noteworthy. Above all, in all four narratives, the occasion is not designated by the kerygmatic formula 'after three days' or 'on the third day', which John also appears to know (cf. 2:19), but by the day of the week;[15] further, all agree in referring to the early morning, admittedly with very great differences. The

Johannine πρωΐ[16] is also found in Mk 16:2; yet John, in the more detailed description 'while it was still dark', formally contradicts Mk 16:2 which says, 'when the sun had risen'. The tradition knew only of a very early hour; the 'darkness' (σκοτία, Johannine criterion of style) is an interpretation of the evangelist, who, perhaps, combines with it a symbolic meaning (cf. 8:12; 12:35, 46). A visit to the tomb when it really was dark, is improbable. Wherein, then, lies the symbolism? Not with Jesus who is already risen, rather with the people in whom faith in his resurrection is not yet awakened (cf. v. 9). The open tomb still causes shock and sadness as Mary's immediate reaction in v. 2 and her later weeping by the tomb (vv. 11, 13, 15) show.

Since John takes up a part of the tradition (cf. the analysis) which possibly knew of several women (οὐκ οἴδαμεν, v. 2), the mention of Mary Magdalene alone is attributable to him. Her 'surname' (after the place Magdala, see on 19:25) was important on account of the mention of another Mary in the synoptic narratives about the tomb; Mary Magdalene is the only woman in all reports named in the same way. John achieves a more pronounced dramatic effect by leaving out other persons, since the same woman who, utterly shocked, rushes away from the open tomb, is then overwhelmed by the call and revelation of the risen one (vv. 16f). The choice of Mary as messenger of the risen one is found neither in the synoptic tradition, nor is it the creation of the fourth evangelist but taken over from his source. The supposition that, originally, Mary meant the mother of Jesus, goes back to the beginnings of Marian piety, testified to in the Syrian church by Ephrem's commentary on the *Diatessaron* of Tatian; but it lacks any basis.[17]

Noteworthy, in the tradition taken over by John, are Mary's two journeys to the tomb; for, we find her, in v. 11, again at the tomb. The synoptics know only of *one* visit by the women to the tomb; according to Mt 28:9f, Jesus meets the women returning from the tomb, and this tradition also stands, to conclude from verbal similarities, behind Jn 20:17f (q.v.). As a whole, Jn 20:1–18 is thus concerned with the further development of an Easter narrative. Because our evangelist is interested, above all, in the visit to the tomb of the two disciples, it is hard to say whether the source told still more about the discovery of the empty tomb by the women. If it said something about the purpose of the early visit to the tomb, then that is unimportant for John. For him it is enough that Mary sees (βλέπει)[18] the stone that sealed the tomb has been removed, 'taken away'. This verb (αἴρειω) will already have been chosen by the source (all the synoptics have 'to roll away'), because it corresponds verbally to Mary's shocked message: 'They have taken the Lord away out of the tomb' (v. 2). Differently from Lazarus' tomb which was a cave (cf. on 11:38), the stone lay not on top, but in front of the tomb entrance.

20:2 Mary, apparently, does not look at all into the tomb (she first stooped on the second visit, v. 11), but quickly runs away and comes to Simon Peter. The open tomb suffices for her conclusion that somebody (impersonal third person plural) has taken the Lord away out of the tomb. If psychologizing is to be avoided, this conclusion is premature. The impulsive and repeated (vv. 13, 15) assertion about the Lord's removal gives the impression that the narrator knows of and takes account of the legend about the theft of the body, which, according to the testimony of Mt 28:13–15, was current among the Jews at that time (AD 80–90). John's source, then, offered another version of this legend: instead of the Jewish accusation that the disciples had stolen the body (so Mt), the mere assumption that somebody (say, the gardener, cf. v. 15) removed the body. When Mary turns to Peter (whom John names by the, for him, usual double name, cf. on 1:42), the source presupposes that this disciple is staying in Jerusalem (cf. 18:15–18, 25ff) and is the leading man in the group of disciples. From the viewpoint of the history of tradition the following account receives more weight, if Lk 24:12 or Lk 24:24 testify also to a similar tradition.

As to Lk 24:12, it is disputed from textual criticism whether the verse is original. Whereas earlier it was mostly held to be an interpolation, which came into the text on the basis of Jn 20:3–10, and was absent only in 'western' textual witnesses,[19] there is now a growing number of voices which hold that these and other 'western non-interpolations' are original.[20] The problem of Lk 24:12 is complicated and cannot be considered here in more detail. There are remarkable agreements with Jn 20:3–10 in the vocabulary, and their occurrence only once in Luke does speak for dependence on John (or his source), especially, παρακύπτειν, ὀθόνια (instead of σινδών, Lk 23:53), further, the construction ἀπελθεῖν πρός and the non-Lukan present historic βλέπει; but besides, there are also found some Lukan peculiarities of style: ἀναστάς, θαυμάζειν with accusative, and τὸ γεγονός, which occurs seven times in Luke and Acts. In the context, the verse fits badly. On account of this uncertainty, it is better not to rely on this verse from the viewpoint of the history of tradition.[21] But Lk 24:24, where there is likewise talk of a visit to the tomb by some disciples, testifies, at least, to a slight trace of that tradition of which Luke somehow obtained knowledge.

Apart from Simon Peter, 'the other disciple, the one whom Jesus loved' is mentioned. This is the third passage in which he is directly spoken of (cf. 13:23; 19:26). Since he plays a decisive role for John's gospel, and for it alone (cf. 21:20–23, 24), we regard it as certain that he was first introduced into the inspection of the tomb by the evangelist. The repetition of πρός can be an indication of this too. In our passage there are two remarkable linguistic features: ἄλλον and ἐφίλει (instead of ἠγάπα); are any conclusions to be drawn from this?

The designation ὁ ἄλλος most likely refers back to a scene in which Peter and this disciple were already once mentioned together, and that is 13:23f; yet the article can also refer back to 19:26 (cf. 19:35). There is also no reason to conclude that there was a special layer in which the designation 'the other disciple' is prominent. The addition 'the one whom Jesus loved' need be just as little due to the editors as in 13:23 (q.v.).[22] At worst, ἐφίλει could appear strange; but the alternation between the two verbs can be examined in a similar way as in the case of Lazarus (cf. 11:3 with 5); it is obvious in 21:15–17. But if Chapter 21 seems editorial it is also noteworthy that it designates that disciple in 21:7, 20, as ὃν ἠγάπα ὁ 'I.; why should they speak differently in our passage? The matter is most easily explained if the evangelist wanted to refer first to the already mentioned disciple as ὁ ἄλλος μαθ., and then wanted to describe him more precisely. In any case, the introduction of the second disciple cannot be originally attributed to the editors.

The evangelist wants to have Jesus' beloved disciple present at the inspection of the tomb in order to emphasize his exemplary faith (v. 8), that is, he is led by a theological concern, the historical question must recede into the background. It seems as if the disciple was with Peter; but the evangelist actually brings him together with Peter just for his purpose. Mary's news with its sequel, 'we[22a] do not know where they have laid him', is formulated in such a way, that the two disciples feel bound to investigate further, indeed, are challenged to inspect the tomb.

20:3   Peter falls in with Mary's expectation and goes out; perhaps the verb indicates that he had hidden himself. The singular refers in the present context to the 'other disciple' also, a not exceptional construction (cf. 2:2; 4:36; 18:15), and when we have the plural afterwards, that is according to the rule.[23] Thus, it cannot be concluded from this sentence alone that the other disciple was added and that originally Peter and Mary were meant; that only follows from v. 9 and v. 11. Just as much in accordance with the style, the second verb is in the imperfect so as to describe the course of events. Peter's entering the tomb (say, with a participle, εἰσελθὼν δὲ . . . θεωρεῖ) could have immediately followed on (in the source); but the present continuation also, in v. 4, results in an un-objectionable connection.

20:4–5   The journey to the tomb, as is naturally understandable from the circumstances, is undertaken in great haste; Mary too hurries, 'ran' (v. 2). The comment that both disciples run together, only prepares for what follows. What is really noteworthy is the behaviour of the other disciple: he runs ahead, faster than Peter, but then waits at the entrance to the tomb and lets Peter go first. If we look for the point of this narrative, then we have to read it to the end: the disciple who arrives at the tomb first (v. 4), is, at the end, the one who 'saw and believed' (v. 8). Peter, who follows him, and is the first to enter the tomb, determines the external situation more precisely; however, no more is said about him. In the present context v. 9 is an explanation which puts the other disciple's faith in a still clearer light. V. 10 is only an outward closing remark; the real conclusion, the point of the narrative, was already reached in v. 8. The precedence of the other disciple comes to the fore 'phonetically' with προέδραμεν and πρῶτος (vv. 4 and 8), and all the more through the narrative development. Peter, however, is not drawn as a negatively contrasting figure; there is no word about his lack of faith, also no criticism of his staying behind. When the other disciple lets him have precedence, it rather seems to be a gesture of respect; but perhaps this conclusion goes too far. Only one thing is clear: Peter determines the situation in the tomb which, for the question of the resurrection – in the narrator's eyes and from the viewpoint of contemporary thinking – is extremely important: Indications which permit the conclusion that Jesus is risen (vv. 6–7).

So the 'functions' of the two disciples are assigned; but the disciple whom Jesus loved plays the more important part.[24] The relationship of the two disciples can only be judged later. In v. 5 the following is also to be noted: the disciple stooped into the open tomb; that corresponds to the situation if he does not yet want to enter the tomb itself. Nothing can be concluded from the expression ($\pi\alpha\rho\alpha\kappa\acute{u}\psi\alpha\varsigma$), which is then taken up for Mary v. 11 in (Lk 24:12 it refers to Peter), as to the origin being from the evangelist or from a source. The main statement is that the disciple sees the linen cloths lying there ($\beta\lambda\acute{\epsilon}\pi\epsilon\iota$). From a narrative point of view, the progression is intended: Mary sees that the stone is removed from the tomb (v. 1b), the other disciple already sees the linen cloths in the tomb, finally Peter examines ($\theta\epsilon\omega\rho\epsilon\tilde{\iota}$) the linen cloths and the rolled-up napkin lying separately (vv. 6–7). The reader is progressively acquainted with the significant facts. The account in vv. 4–5, comes, however, from the evangelist; $\mu\grave{\epsilon}\nu\tau o\iota$, a criterion of John's style (Ruckstuhl, No. 26), also supports this.

20:6–7   Peter, who followed the other disciple ($\dot{\alpha}\kappa o\lambda ou\theta\epsilon\tilde{\iota}\nu$, here meaning outward following, cf. 18:15), enters the tomb and carefully looks at everything. He too sees the linen cloths, but in addition the napkin which had lain on Jesus' head. This description is certainly not based on any reflection as to how the risen one left the cloths enveloping and restricting him.[25] He has left behind these wrappings used for the body, because he has risen and lives, because he has obtained for ever a new, unearthly-heavenly existence. But the nature and arrangement of the discovery betrays a particular intention of the narrator. Why is the napkin rolled up and lying in a particular place? For that is how the somewhat peculiar and not totally clear mode of expression is to be understood.[26] John Chrysostom already recognized that with this the idea of the body being stolen or any other removal of the body is being guarded against. Would not robbers or others have carried away the dead man together with the linen cloths?[27] This reflection can further be supported by an observation from the context of the narrative. It is an answer to the suspicion voiced by Mary: the Lord has been taken out of the tomb (v. 2b). That is ruled out by this discovery – but neither Peter nor Mary draws this conclusion, the idea of Jesus' resurrection remains remote for them.

It is obvious to compare the story of the raising of Lazarus with this. In the description of Lazarus coming out of the tomb, the napkin with which 'his face was wrapped', is also mentioned (11:44). The somewhat divergent description in Jn 20:7 (the napkin 'had been on his head') as well as the other word for the linen cloths ($\dot{o}\theta\acute{o}\nu\iota\alpha$ instead of $\kappa\epsilon\iota\rho\acute{\iota}\alpha\iota$), make it improbable that the discovery in Jesus' tomb was conceived according to the model of Jn 11:44. Nothing stands in the way of the supposition of the same source as for 19:40. It is true that the napkin is not mentioned at the time of the burial, but, for the Jewish custom, is certainly naturally assumed.[28] From a factual point of view, a comparison admittedly suggests itself to the reader: Lazarus raised to earthly life has to be freed from the bandages, Jesus who is rising in a real sense frees himself from them and leaves them behind as a sign of his resurrection.

The fact that the narrative is so concerned about this careful inspection of the tomb by Peter, confirms its apologetic intention.[29] The 'empty tomb' which cannot be any direct evidence for Jesus' resurrection, but is open to the suspicion that the body was somehow removed, now does become a convincing piece of evidence in view of the discovery of the cloths in which Jesus' body had been wrapped.

20:8 Now, the other disciple also enters the tomb and it is said of him: 'he saw and believed'. From a narrative viewpoint, the short sentence is incomparably full of meaning. Admittedly, ἰδεῖν hardly means a special kind of seeing, a seeing combined with believing, so that there would be a progression from βλέπειν vv. 1 and 5, and θεωρεῖν v. 6, to this ἰδεῖν.[30] The verbs of seeing in John's gospel have no recognizable semantic value of their own, but are used alternately and synonymously.[31] But the change from present historic to aorist and the rapid succession of the two verbs without any kind of object, produce in the situation the meaning: This disciple understood the situation, so to say at a glance, and immediately came to believe (ἐπίστευσεν ingressive aorist). To what kind of belief? According to the context, undoubtedly, to the full faith in the resurrection of Jesus; any kind of diminution, with a view to v. 9, is ruled out. The point of the story lies in the clear and strong faith of the beloved disciple.[32] That is also confirmed by 21:7 where the same disciple, because of the plentiful catch of fish, says to Peter: 'It is the Lord.' He can, so to say, read the tracks and signs of his Lord; therein, he is the ideal disciple with an exemplary faith. May we, therefore, deny to him flesh and blood? Even if the story of the inspection of the tomb by disciples is unverifiable and that disciple's faith on Easter morning is improbable (why does he not testify to it before the other disciples?), this disciple at Peter's side may not be dissolved too quickly into a phantom or reduced into a symbol, or a merely literary figure made of him. It is possible for disciples and friends of someone to whom they owe many traditions and deep insights, to idealize him and to illustrate his truly deep faith with such stories (cf. Excursus 18).

The sentence, 'he saw and believed' may also not be set off against the words to Thomas: 'Blessed are those who have not seen and yet believe' (20:29). Both sayings have their specific place and scope in the context. Because Jesus' resurrection was not yet within the range of the disciples' expectation, the openness to and readiness for faith which that disciple manifests, is the more noteworthy. Thomas, who remains sceptical of his fellow-disciples' testimony, has to accept a criticism, which, at the same time, becomes an appeal to the later believers. The two stories come together again in the apologetic tendency against doubt about the resurrection of Jesus. 'Empty tomb' and 'appearances' of Jesus are wholly valid witnesses. Yet, the evangelist makes it clearly enough understood, as with the witnesses to Jesus' earthly ministry, that all witnesses without faith remain silent.

20:9 The explanatory detail that they did not yet know the Scripture, presupposes rather a reaction of unbelief or or bafflement (Lk 24:12). In the present order of the text, the comment is intended certainly to emphasize the faith of the other disciple, perhaps indirectly also that of Peter;[33] but the plural remains difficult.[34] The supposition of an editorial gloss represents no solution.[35] The confusion is only really resolved if v. 9 is reckoned to be a sentence from the source, which the evangelist took over, without wholly getting rid of the contradiction in his presentation which arises because of it. If previously the concern was with Peter and Mary who, through the inspection of the tomb, did not attain faith in Jesus' resurrection, then v. 9 fits excellently in that connection.

The supposition that v. 9 comes from a source akin to the synoptics,[35a] is strengthened by a linguistic and motif-critical observation. The singular γραφή for the whole of Holy Scripture is, admittedly, also found in other places in John's gospel (10:35; cf. 2:22) or is possible (7:38, 42; 17:12); but the formula δεῖ . . . ἀναστῆναι is not found elsewhere in Jn (cf. against it 2:22), but certainly in the kerygmatic announcement in Mk 8:31; cf. 9:31; 10:34. Luke also takes over the formula in the angels' message at the tomb (24:7) and in the instruction of the disciples by the risen one himself (24:46), just as, indeed, he is much concerned with the point that suffering, death and resurrection of the Messiah are foretold in the Scriptures (cf. further 24:25ff). It is a motif which appears early on in the tradition of primitive Christianity, already in the formulation of faith handed down by Paul, 1 Cor 15:4. Here, there is the plural 'in accordance with the scriptures', so that in Jn 20:9 also, no special scripture passage ought to be alluded to. We need not pursue the problem as to which passage or passages the primitive Church based its scriptural proof on for the resurrection of Jesus;[36] the old formulae content themselves with the general reference. So, too, with John, who almost always adduces concrete citations (although not word for word); (on 2:22 and 17:12 cf. the commentary). Thus, v. 9 will have been taken over by him from the source which here too is close to Luke.

20:10   The quiet return of the two disciples, which belongs to the conclusion of the narrative, confirms the impression already given in v. 9 that, originally, nothing was said about faith. Could this visit to the tomb, then, have remained without effect and echo? Must not the news of it have spread like wildfire to the other disciples? The disciple who comes to believe on account of the tomb, is foreign to the original story, and therefore, in this verse also, he could not have been meant. The conclusion is unavoidable that in the source Peter alone was mentioned, and Mary remained at the tomb.

It can, admittedly, be considered whether it was not first the editors who brought the disciple whom Jesus loved into the story, so that the evangelist told only of Peter and Mary. That is, in itself, very conceivable; the chapter would have presented an effective account with an intended progression: Mary's news – inspection of the tomb, which does not yet lead to faith – the scene at the tomb, in which only the risen one himself by means of the appearance to Mary beings certainty – the commission to bring this message to the disciples – the appearance of Jesus to the disciples as climax. However, the question must be seen and considered together with the other passages in which that disciple plays a part. For 13:23–26, it proved difficult to break out of the gospel's structure the scene with the uncovering of the traitor. Likewise, the striking out of 19:26f is not convincing; how the editors actually worked can be recognized in 19:35. Although the question needs further thought (cf. Excursus 18), it has to be said: if we grant the evangelist himself an interest in that disciple, his introduction into the visit to the tomb, that is, the reworking of the narrative already there by the evangelist, becomes completely understandable.

In summarizing the relationship of the two disciples, it must first be stated that this is not the theme or main motif of the narrative. John, too, is concerned with the fact and proof of Jesus' resurrection. For this purpose, it is not the disciple whom Jesus loved as such that is significant, but his exemplary faith. Peter, who came to the fore often enough in the gospel, and in 6:69 as spokesman of the twelve made an exalted, in no way diminished, confession of Jesus, becomes through the inspection of the tomb, an important witness to the Easter event, as it was defended by the early Church against doubt and suspicions. He appears in this narrative as leader of the group of disciples, so to say as a recognized authority. The beloved disciple's precedence over him is certainly intentional, but not in every respect, only with reference to his illuminated faith. Therefore, 'rivalry' is hardly the correct term for the relationship of the two disciples.[37] As the exegesis showed, in no place is Peter criticized or devalued. Perhaps, the 'other disciple' is meant, in a certain sense, to be 'up-valued' even, by way of Peter's authority.[38] But these questions converge in the complex problem of that disciple figure which once more comes to the fore in Chapter 21 and there actually does betray an urgent interest of the editors.

2. Mary at the Tomb and her Encounter with Jesus (20:11–18)

[11]*But Mary stood weeping outside the tomb, and as she wept she stooped to look into the tomb;* [12]*and she saw two angels in white sitting where the body of Jesus had lain, one at the head and one at the feet.* [13]*They said to her, 'Woman, why are you weeping?' She said to them, 'Because they have taken away my Lord, and I do not know where they have laid him.'* [14]*Saying this, she turned round and saw Jesus standing, but she did not know that it was Jesus.* [15]*Jesus said to her, 'Woman, why are you weeping? Whom do you seek?' Supposing him to be the gardener, she said to him, 'Sir, if you have carried him away, tell me where you have laid him, and I will take him away.'* [16]*Jesus said to her, 'Mary.' She turned and said to him in Hebrew, 'Rabboni!' (which means Teacher).* [17]*Jesus said to her, 'Do not hold me, for I have not yet ascended to the Father; but go to my brethren and say to them, I am ascending to my Father and your Father, to my God and your God.'* [18]*Mary Magdalene went and said to the disciples, 'I have seen the Lord'; and she told them that he had said these things to her.*

The scene at the tomb includes Mary Magdalene's meeting with the angels and with Jesus. The transition is marked by Mary's turning round (v. 14); with this, the scene with the angels is broken short and remains without significance for what follows. Narratively, a progression may be intended through Mary's redoubled complaint: the dramatic effect of Jesus' mode of address and the effect on Mary are strengthened. But the precise description of where the angels are sitting, without point for the narrative progression, allows us to suppose another interest in the scene with the angels: the angels too testify to the empty tomb and permit the conclusion that Jesus is risen. That is a motif competing with Peter's inspection of the tomb in that both together are not very possible; from another point of view, however, it is a further argument from the 'empty' tomb for the resurrection of Jesus. That the evangelist put together this arrangement of the story is not, indeed, excluded, but improbable. Taken together with other observations (cf. the analysis), the scene with the angels is therefore subject to the suspicion of only being an editorial addition. Undoubtedly, Mary's encounter with the risen one represents for the evangelist the climax, which, according to his Christological thought, he emphasizes strongly (v. 17).

20:11 In the present context abruptly, but in the source presumably rather more smoothly, we are told of Mary, how she stands at the tomb and weeps. 'Outside', left out by some manuscripts and versions,[39] rightly describes the situation ('in the tomb' is the reading of Sinaiticus alone), because Mary afterwards stoops into the chamber of the tomb. Her 'weeping' is not the lament for the dead (cf. on 11:31, Vol. 2, p. 334), but is an expression of her personal pain and her sadness, that she does not find her dead Lord. As she weeps for a longer while (imperfect), it is by chance that she stoops (aorist) and notices the two angels inside the tomb. In contrast to the beloved disciple, who stoops because he does not yet want to enter the tomb (v. 5), the same behaviour by Mary appears contrived. It is noticeable that another tradition is taken up and is combined with the story of how Jesus appears to Mary Magdalene. It is also noteworthy that Mary does not go into the tomb as is narrated in Mk 16:5 and Lk 24:3; but then the scene with Jesus would not follow so easily.

20:12 The *two* angels, as heavenly messengers dressed in white robes, recall the description in Lk 24:4, without, however, there being any verbal echoes. There are also some points of contact with Mk: besides the word for the white robe ($\lambda\varepsilon\nu\varkappa\acute{o}\varsigma$), the young Man (Mk) and the two angels (Jn) respectively, are *sitting* in a specific place (Mk: on the right side). In Jn, the two angels have the function to indicate the precise place where Jesus' body had lain: head and feet. The description has a similar meaning to Peter's inspection of the tomb: the precise details allow the conclusion that Jesus is risen. For the people of that period, angelic appearances were no less real than what we call 'evidence'. Both descriptions are introduced with $\theta\varepsilon\omega\rho\varepsilon\tilde{\iota}$ and mention details of which the synoptics know nothing. We are dealing here with an advanced tradition (angels in the tomb) and a rather high degree of reflection (from an apologetic viewpoint). Apocryphal writings above all, then, show the tendency for imaginative description, cf. *Gospel of Pet* 35–49 and 50–57.[40] It is noticeable that the motif of fear is missing in John, which otherwise, as a rule, is associated with the appearance of heavenly forms. This too is an indication that the writer is not interested in an angelophany as such, but in the witness which the two figures bear concerning the secret of the tomb, by their presence in the tomb and their position at that specific place.

20:13   The angels' question fits the situation; it occurs once again, word for word, on Jesus' lips, there continuing: 'Whom do you seek?' This second question betrays the background of history of tradition:. The scene with the angels in the synoptic narratives about the tomb. Although it is related differently in the individual synoptics, the motif of searching is constantly maintained. Luke, like John, has the question form (24:5: τί ζητεῖτε); with Mark/Matthew, John shares the indication of the place (τόπος) where Jesus had been laid (Mk 16:6: ὅπου ἔθηκαν αὐτόν). So we may suppose that in John there is a reminder of the synoptic account, and that mainly in the case of Mary's conversation with Jesus (searching motif). The further development or alteration of the tradition can be pictured something like this: the Johannine source, instead of an angelic manifestation, immediately told of Jesus' encounter with Mary Magdalene. With this it combined traditional motifs, but transferred the revelation of the Easter mystery to the risen one himself.[41] The evangelist took over this account, only giving to it stronger Christological accents. An editor again brought in the angels which originally proclaimed the Easter message to the women, but in John are not allowed to retain this function. Mary's answer, already known to the readers from v. 2 (now with the singular οἶδα),[42] is, admittedly, also presupposed in the scene with Jesus; the editor may have moved it forward from there.

20:14   The comment that she turned round, apparently fits very well Mary's complaining that she does not know where Jesus' body has been laid: She turns round and notices Jesus. But the 'turning round' (εἰς τὰ ὀπίσω[43]) betrays the artificial insertion of the scene with the angels which ends with this. Why should Mary who expects information from the angels, turn away from them? But since she stoops into the tomb (v. 11) such a remark was unavoidable, so as to join on the scene with Jesus. So once again, the scene with the angels is confirmed as a secondary accretion.

The source told, probably immediately, how the woman weeping at the tomb saw Jesus. Mary does not recognize him, just as the disciples in the story of the catch of fish which was told in the Johannine circles, do not recognize Jesus standing on the shore (21:4 with the same wording). Jesus' appearance to Mary Magdalene is thus presented in the form of a recognition scene. Since the Lukan Emmaus narrative also belongs to the same type[44] and in the story in Jn 21 this motif at least plays a part (cf. 21:7, 12), we come up against a form of story-telling which was widely current in the primitive Church for the appearances of the risen one.

20:15   As in the other appearance-stories of this type, Jesus himself initiates the conversation. The form of address 'woman' is quite natural and need not recall 2:4 and 19:26 (speaking to Jesus' mother). The second question: 'Whom do you seek?' which we already noticed in connection with the history of tradition, also has its function in this type of story-telling. It concentrates the conversation on the person of the one who then makes himself known. To that, Mary ought to answer at first similarly as in v. 13b. This is omitted here and the motif of the confused identities introduced, which increases the tension. The 'gardener' will come from the source, which knows of the position of the tomb in a garden (19:41). Mary addresses him courteously with 'Sir', and supposes that he has taken the body, without bad intent, to another place.[45] The motif, used here as a narrative technique, was later further worked out apparently in the Jewish polemic against Christianity: the gardener was concerned that visitors to the tomb could tread down his salad plants.[46] It is possible that already in the Johannine source, there was an apologetic intention behind it.[47] Mary's ardour with which she seeks her Lord is described graphically: she wants to bring the body back again although that is hardly practicable for a woman by herself. Pain and ardour make her blind to the one who stands before her – a dramatic means of heightening the effect of the surprise in the recognition scene. Questions as to whether and how the 'gardener' was dressed, are beside the point; the risen one assumes a form and a dress appropriate for those to whom he wants to reveal himself.

20:16   The recognition takes place as Jesus calls Mary by her name. $Μαριάμ$ as against $Μαριά$ may here be the original.[48] The form of address and the tone of voice lead to recognition; it could be like that in an everyday scene. But there is more involved in this encounter: the risen one reveals himself to one who seeks and believes. Jesus knows those who belong to him and calls them by their name; they know his voice and follow him (cf. 10:3f). The risen one is no other than the earthly Jesus; he now encounters Mary in a new way. She turns to him – an outward gesture, which at the same time expresses an opening up of her inner self and a believing openness to the risen Lord.[49] Mary too only answers with an exclamation, a form of address which, in the same way, applied to the earthly Jesus. For rabboni (Aramaic 'my master') is nothing other than the normal rabbi, only stronger, so to say, more personally expressed, and it is no differently translated into Greek by the evangelist (cf. 1:38).[50] In the simple 'narrative' structure of this recognition scene a whole theology is embedded: what faith in Jesus' resurrection and believing encounter with the risen one means.

20:17   The recognition of Jesus the risen one still needs to be deepened, and this is granted to Mary in a revelatory saying. In its extraordinary form and with the following commission that she should go to Jesus' brethren, this saying is only comprehensible from the background of a tradition, which is still preserved in Mt 28:9f. Here, on their way home from the tomb, already informed about the resurrection by the angel, the women meet Jesus himself. As he greets them, they come up to him and take hold of his feet and worship him on their knees ($προσκυνεῖν$). The Johannine source will have told similarly that Mary fell down before Jesus and embraced or wanted to embrace his feet. Some manuscripts do in fact incorporate such a sentence; it is secondary from a text-critical viewpoint, but justified by the situation.[51] John has a different verb for touching Jesus (ἄπτεσθαι) from Matthew (χρατεῖν), presumably an indication that the scene is not directly borrowed from Matthew.[52] The verb ἄπτεσθαι does not otherwise occur in John's gospel, only again in 1 Jn 5:18. It means 'touch, get hold of'; but when the act of touching has already begun, the negative present imperative can also mean, Do not hold on to me any longer, let me go![53] This sense results here because of what follows, but also retains the connection with Mt 28:9 where the women take hold of Jesus' feet. For John there is no hesitation about touching the body of the risen one (cf. 20:25, 27). That various points of view or literary strata can be behind the scene with Mary Magdalene, the appearance to the disciples (20:20: 'show, see'), and the one to Thomas, are considerations which are out of place. Jesus' exhortation to Mary not to hold him any longer, can, in the Johannine source, have been the reason given in the commission to go to the brethren and bring them the news of Jesus' resurrection, perhaps also the announcement that they would see Jesus again. John interprets differently: Mary is not to hold on to Jesus because he has not yet ascended to the Father.

The peculiarly Johannine interpretation of the as yet unachieved 'ascent' of Jesus to the Father (cf. 3:13; 6:62)[53a] is not easy to understand, as all kinds of speculation show. From the 'not yet' it may hardly be concluded that, for later on, a real or full 'contact' with the risen one, an unrestricted fellowship with him, is promised.[54] Also the information which some wanted to give in connection with the question about the 'ascension' of Jesus, that Jesus' 'ascent' takes place between vv. 18 and 19, because Jesus then already comes to the disciples from the Father (bestowing the Spirit, granting authority),[55] cannot satisfy. Does not Jesus stand before Mary Magdalene as the glorified one? Can resurrection, 'ascent', and glorification be separated from one another? Is there a peculiar in-between state between coming out of the tomb and return to the Father? All these questions are wrongly posed. We must rather probe what intention the evangelist is pursuing with these forms of expression, and seek to understand the text according to this intention, not according to wording and superficial logic.

The evangelist's intention may be read more clearly from the second, more detailed statement about Jesus' ascent, which follows the commission to go to Jesus' brethren: 'I am ascending to my Father and your Father, to my God and your God.' The remarkable formulation which sounds ceremonially solemn, must have its reason. If Mary is supposed to bring this message, word for word, to the disciples, it is easy to suppose that the disciples are meant to be reminded of other sayings of Jesus. If we look back in the gospel, the other passage that particularly comes to mind in this respect is 14:1–3, the beginning of the farewell discourse. Here alone is found the striking: 'Believe in *God*!', and then follows the saying about the rooms in the Father's house. Jesus is going there to prepare a place for the disciples – a saying which lays the basis for the interpretation of Jesus' departure. To the word-complex of ὑπάγειν, πορεύεσθαι, μεταβαίνειν (13:1) also belongs ἀναβαίνειν. What emerges in the farewell discourse with the verbs of departing as the basic concern, namely, to show the importance of Jesus' departure for the disciples, is taken up in the saying of the risen one to Mary, and interpreted by John as the content of what Mary is to tell to the disciples. The risen one keeps the promise which he gave to the disciples in the form of a prophecy as he was departing. Now is the hour of Jesus' ascent to the Father, and that means for his 'brethren' that he is preparing a place for them also with the Father, that he mediates that fellowship with God for them, which he had foretold them to be the fruit of his departure (cf. 14:21, 23, 28). That may be the main reason why the evangelist added to his source those two interpretative sayings about Jesus' 'ascent' (v. 17a and c). With that, the Easter event is brought into the theological line of the gospel and, on the other side, the announcements of the farewell discourse find their Easter confirmation and realization.

So too, it is easier to understand the tension which seems to exist between, 'I have not yet ascended' (v. 17a), and, 'I am ascending' (v. 17c). The risen Jesus still has a task to fulfil for the disciples: to mediate for them, as the one who has returned home to the Father, the full fellowship with the Father. To that belong the sending of the Spirit, (cf. 14:16f), the hearing of prayer (14:13), the achievement of greater works (14:12), the experiencing of God's love (14:23), in short, everything which is the fruit of Jesus' completed work. Jesus is, as the risen one, already 'in the course of ascending': for ἀναβαίνω may hardly be held to be a present used in a future sense, but must be understood as an already begun and continuing process.[56] The time category is only a means of expression for theologically relevant aspects, which result from Jesus' resurrection and his return to the Father.

It is true that the way of speaking about Jesus' ascent, which the evangelist incorporates in Jesus' appearance to Mary Magdalene, also uncovers a tension between the theology of John and the traditional view of the primitive Church as to Jesus' resurrection and lifting up respectively. Elsewhere, John only keeps in view Jesus' origin from the Father and his return to the Father, that is the starting-point and goal of his way (summarized in 16:28). For him, the crucifixion is already 'lifting up' and leads directly to his 'glorification'. For him, everything is compressed into Jesus' 'hour', therefore, it is not really possible to dissect the event into death, resurrection, lifting up, and installation in heavenly glory. John overcomes this way of looking at things, which can veil the transition from the historical world of space and time to God's transcendental realm. Admittedly, John too uses a 'mythological' way of speaking, when he talks of the Saviour's 'ascent', which, in his case, differently from the Lukan 'ascension',[57] corresponds to the 'descent' from heaven. But since it is a single event, which is not described in detail and retains its transcendental character, John's way of speaking makes more strongly apparent that the appearances of the risen one, with every outwardly naive description, are self-revelations of the heavenly and lifted up Lord, who already no longer belongs to this world.[58] The appearances are related to provide the Church with points of understanding basic for its faith, and instructions as to its way of life.

Finally, the designation 'brethren' which occurs in John's gospel here on the lips of Jesus for the only time, requires attention. It certainly comes from the

Johannine source, which agrees in this with Mt 28:10. But in Matthew, the women receive a different commission from the risen one, to tell Jesus' 'brethren' that they are to go to Galilee where they will see him. This commission is lacking in John, who (with Luke) transfers Jesus' appearance to the disciples to the room in Jerusalem (vv. 19–23). *Instead of* that commission, John has the words: 'I am ascending to my Father and your Father . . .', therefore, v. 17 can scarcely be attributed to a Jewish-Christian source document which has Mary Magdalene going to Jesus' *natural* brethren, so as to make known to them Jesus' messiahship by analogy with Moses being received into heaven.[59] Rather, the commission to Mary found in John, has grown out of the reflection by the evangelist on the term 'my brethren', which he had before him. When Jesus calls the disciples to whom he sends Mary his 'brethren', then (so the evangelist reflects) he also wants to place them in a new and special relationship to his Father. As we saw, this corresponds to Jesus' promises to his disciples at the time of his leave-taking. This explains the unique mode of expression; otherwise, it would remain unexplained why the evangelist took over this way of speaking in his gospel.

20:18   The conclusion of this Christophany at the tomb is formed by Mary's going to the disciples to tell them of her experience, and Jesus' words. It is also the conclusion of the longer narrative section about the visit to the tomb by Mary Magdalene, as is confirmed by her naming in full – presumably intentionally, at the beginning (v. 1) and end (v. 18). Now, differently from v. 2, Mary has something to 'tell'[60] to the disciples, and she puts it into words which, beyond John (cf. 20:25), are demonstrable as a short formula for the Easter experience (1 Cor 9:1). The phrase, 'I have seen the Lord' corresponds to the other one in the passive which occurs more frequently, 'he appeared (to me)'.[61] So we have the language of the source before us; against that, the short sentence following, in indirect speech, will be from the evangelist who, with this, wanted to take account of his interpretations of the 'ascent' of Jesus. The change from direct to indirect speech which was ironed out by not a few copyists,[62] is, indeed, possible (cf. 13:29), but it is rare in the NT and improbable for the source with its lively kind of narration.[63] For the evangelist, precisely those words of Jesus are the most important.

If, looking back, we inquire into the antiquity and reliability of this story adopted by the evangelist, it is at first necessary to state the relatively late stage of the tradition. Even if the angel-scene is left out as an addition of the editors, there remain traces of later composition (motif of the removal of the body, confusion with the gardener). The only clue of a more widely distributed tradition is the scene in Mt 28:9f; for the mention in the canonical conclusion of Mark (16:9–11) already presupposes the Johannine account.[64] A connection certainly exists, from the viewpoint of the history of tradition, with the special Matthaean scene. Direct dependence on Matthew by the fourth evangelist is not to be supposed; in the main, he owes the story to his source which could hardly have derived it from Matthew. In the present context in Matthew (after the appearance of the angel, repetition of the commission to the women by

Jesus himself), 28:9f gives the impression of being secondary; however, that does not have to mean that everything has been invented by Matthew.[65] Thus, a common tradition for Matthew and the Johannine source may be assumed. All the same, this tradition cannot be pronounced ancient and reliable.[66] The reference to the oldest list of appearances in 1 Cor 15:5–8, in which such a Christophany to Mary Magdalene or still more women is lacking, is, admittedly, no serious counter-argument, because the primitive Church obviously did not place any value on the testimony of women; but Luke's silence carries weight, because he does assign a certain rôle to the women, but does not know of an appearance by Jesus to them (cf. 24:22–24). For John, the value of the story which he found is not on a historical but a theological level. In Mary's encounter with Jesus the meaning of Jesus' resurrection for the fellowship of the disciples finds expression; it forms a prelude to Jesus' appearance before the disciples to whom the risen Lord gives the Spirit and grants authority. All the same, John's interest in the women who stood beneath the cross, can also not be ignored. Among them, Jesus' mother and Mary Magdalene are singled out, each in their own way.

3. Jesus' Appearance to the Disciples (20:19–23)

[19]*On the evening of that day, the first day of the week, the doors being shut where the disciples were, for fear of the Jews, Jesus came and stood among them and said to them, 'Peace be with you.'* [20]*When he had said this, he showed them his hands and his side. Then the disciples were glad when they saw the Lord.* [21]*Jesus said to them again, 'Peace be with you. As the Father has sent me, even so I send you.'* [22]*And when he had said this, he breathed on them, and said to them, 'Receive the Holy Spirit.* [23]*If you forgive the sins of any, they are forgiven; if you retain the sins of any, they are retained.'*

After Mary Magdalene's personal encounter with the risen one follows Jesus' appearance to the disciples on the evening of the same day. It is the appearance which is of decisive importance for the Easter faith, for the life and future of the Church. It has been found noteworthy that Mary's message is in no way mentioned in the course of it; but this was also unnecessary in the narrative context of the source. A certain parallelism can be determined for the empty tomb and for the appearance of the risen one: Mary first notices the empty tomb (v. 2), and then Peter confirms it (with the other disciple) by careful inspection; again, the risen one first encounters the woman and then reveals himself to the disciples in the entirety of the significance of his resurrection. The two appearances are bound together by the reference to the 'seeing of the Lord'. The experience which Mary reports to the disciples: 'I have seen the Lord' (v. 18), is also shared by the disciples, on the same day: 'and they were glad when they saw the Lord' (v. 20b). The climax comes with the bestowal of the Spirit on the disciples with the authoritative saying concerning the forgiveness of sins.

Because, in the present form of John's gospel, the Thomas pericope is still to come (vv. 24–29), it is true that the impression is given of a somewhat different structure: the two appearances before the disciples which belong closely together, have the effect of a block following the narrative complex 'stories about the tomb'; for this last is linked by the figure of Mary Magdalene, forming a unit. Through Thomas's confession (v. 28) a new climax is attained, and through the final saying of Jesus (v. 29) the episode ends with an appeal for faith, in accordance with the importance given it by the evangelist. Much is in favour of the Thomas pericope coming wholly from the evangelist, who, with it, gives to his gospel a final Christological accent. But this question is only to be discussed in connection with 20:24–29. Thus, in 20:19–23, the evangelist will be mainly following his source. That is recognizable both in certain linguistic peculiarities (style and vocabulary)[67] and also in theological features. Bestowal of the Spirit by breathing on the disciples, and forgiveness of sins, are unusual expressions in John's gospel, even if they can be fitted into the theological concept of the evangelist. The evangelist has certainly added the theme of the fear of the Jews (vv. 19 and 21). Likewise, the duplication of the eirenic greeting permits the supposition of an alteration. Yet which verse most likely comes into question in this respect: v. 20 or v. 21? When the risen one shows his hands and his side to the disciples (v. 20a), that is not without motive – he causes his recognition by Mary by calling her by name and by his voice – besides, it is a traditional motif (cf. Lk 24:39: hands and feet). Further, v. 20b seemed to us to belong to the narrative context of the source.[68] V. 21, on the contrary, contains the typically Johannine thought and can well be brought in by the evangelist. The source, after the eirenic greeting and the self-identification of the risen one, could have immediately told of his action: bestowal of the Spirit and granting of authority. A breaking off of the narrative with v. 20[69] is extremely improbable, since with it, the characteristic feature for this type of Easter story (appearance to the disciples), that the disciples receive the commission and authority, would fall out.[70] John expressed the sending out commission, which was, perhaps, differently formulated in the source, in his own way (v. 21), and so incorporated it into his theological viewpoint.

20:19 With mention of the time of day – in a form not normally used by the evangelist[71] – and with the emphatic reference to that first day of the week on which Mary Magdalene discovered the empty tomb (cf. 20:1), the succeeding narrative is closely tied to the one just told. The events of the morning continue in the evening and now reach their climax. The details of place, kept indefinite,[72] are given a particular accent by the remark that the doors were shut. In the source, the ability of the risen one to overcome such barriers (cf. the sealed tomb), can, by this means, be suggested: despite the closed doors, 'Jesus came and stood among them'. The evangelist who brings in the theme of the fear of the Jews (cf. 7:13; 9:22; 19:38), interprets differently. The anxious disciples are freed from fear and sorrow by Jesus' appearance in their midst. Jesus' eirenic greeting and the certainty that it is he, the crucified and pierced one, allows fear to give way to joy. There is no mention of an initial doubt or state of unbelief as in Lk 24:38, 41 (cf. also Mt 28:17 and especially Mk 16:11, 13, 14). There was possibly something about it in the source; but John avoids it and keeps this feature for the Thomas pericope. There is also nothing said about Jesus' bodily appearance. 'He came' just as he had promised his 'coming' to the disciples at the time of his farewell (cf. 14:18, 28). The eirenic greeting, the normal Jewish salutation, to begin with serves the same purpose as the way in which Mary was addressed (v. 16), but it receives particular emphasis for the evangelist for the overcoming of fear and confusion (cf. 14:27). It becomes an Easter greeting in a special sense, as the repetition in v. 21 suggests.[73]

20:20   The showing of wounds in hands and side occurs as identification, and the comparison with the scene in vv. 14–16 (Mary Magdalene) shows, that already the source was interested in the identity of the risen one with the earthly Jesus. As shown there, this is a widely current theme of the Easter stories. The recognition of Jesus is, for the primitive Church, a means of expressing the deeply significant fact that the same Jesus encounters the disciples as the one with whom they lived before his passion. The Church thus wanted to establish the reality of his resurrection (cf. Lk 24:41–43) as the continuing fellowship with him, admittedly raised to a new level. An anti-Gnostic tendency (against the putting on of a pseudo-body) is not necessarily to be connected with this, but can soon arise.[74] John is first of all interested to establish the crucified one as risen; the intention to refute Docetic interpretations ought to be more strongly emphasized. Jesus only *shows* the disciples his hands and his side; nothing is said about a touching and handling by the disciples (cf. against this 1 Jn 1:1). If 19:34 (the spear-thrust) comes from the Johannine source (see *ad loc.*), v. 20a can likewise be taken over from it unaltered. The same is true for v. 20b: 'To see the Lord' is its way of speaking of the encounter with the risen one (v. 18), and 'to be glad' the understandable reaction to it (cf. also Mt 28:8; Lk 24:41, 52).[75] Over and above that for John, 'seeing' is the keeping of the promise which Jesus gave to the disciples in the supper-room (14:19; cf. also 16:16ff). 'Joy' is, in the discourse of Chapter 16, what is promised after all sorrow and affliction, an unending and complete joy (16:20, 22, 24).

20:21   By means of the new beginning with the same greeting, there results a narrative pause which leaves room for the joy of the encounter. With it are contrasted the sending out and the granting of the Spirit as the most important events of this hour. Looked at from the viewpoint of Jesus who comes across as the only one with an active rôle, his action, pointing to the future, follows his presentation as the risen one. Nevertheless, the new beginning may not have stood in the source, but have been the work only of the evangelist. Why should the greeting, which, from its meaning, belongs at the beginning, be spoken once again? The evangelist's interest is recognized when we compare 14:27; Jesus grants the disciples his peace as a gift for the whole of the future during which he no longer is with them in the flesh. He says that to them already before the passion but effectively grants them the gift of peace only as the risen one – together with the gift of the Spirit. Therefore, from now on, 'peace' is more than a mere greeting or blessing; it is a thing of the Spirit, an inner gift, which is also to manifest itself outwardly. Certainly, the modern idea of a peace-movement, a conscious effort toward peace between men and nations, may not yet be introduced into the thought of John; but this can further the active will for peace and make it fruitful. The peace which the risen Lord brings the disciples from God is to go with them as they are sent out and to testify to the world what true peace is (cf. similarly, concerning the idea of oneness, 17:21ff).

With the second eirenic greeting the sending out of the disciples is fittingly introduced. Frequent as the idea is in John's gospel that the Father has sent Jesus, so rarely is the sending of the disciples by Jesus spoken of. That is not surprising because it concerns the time after his departure. Jesus only speaks about it once during his earthly ministry, namely, in 4:38, a passage which anticipates and brings into focus their later activity (see *ad loc.*). The sending of the disciples is indirectly spoken of in 13:16, 20, where 'synoptic' sayings are taken up. Finally, the same idea as in 20:21 is already found in the prayer of Christ as he takes his leave in 17:18, only with the addition 'into the world'. By its form, the logion in 20:21 turns out to be primary; it is more concise, less smooth because of the change from ἀποστέλλειν to πέμπειν, and marked as a present action by the present πέμπω. Now is the actual hour of the sending which the risen Lord undertakes with the authority granted him, for John, with the authority of the Son (cf. 17:2). For his sending by the Father still continues (perfect, ἀπέσταλκεν),[76] he only gives the disciples a share in it for the earthly continuation of his work (cf. 14:12) with the assistance of the Paraclete (14:16f, 26; 15:26f). So the commissioning saying is exactly in its appropriate place; it also corresponds to the other appearance accounts (Mt 28:19f; Lk 24:47; Mk 16:15). Jesus' appearance to his disciples is continually combined with commissioning and empowering, however differently it may be expressed.[77] Somehow or another, already the Johannine source too ought to have expressed the sending.

The use of πέμπειν need not point to the source, but may also be a variation of the evangelist. But admittedly, he uses the verb more predominantly, almost formally, in the participle ὁ πέμψας με, when Jesus speaks of his Father (over twenty times). Yet the same verb is used for the sending of the Paraclete too (14:26; 15:26; 16:7), further, generally, in the sayings with a synoptic tone (13:16, 20). If K. H. Rengstorf is right that 'the formula ὁ πέμψας με (πατήρ)' is used 'to affirm the participation of God in His (Jesus') work in the action of His sending',[78] then this idea can also be found analogously in Jesus' πέμπειν with reference to the disciples.

The sending is not defined more closely. The missionary accent in a narrower sense (the winning of men for the gospel) seems to be missing. Also the sending 'into the world' with the undertones which are apparent in the context of 17:18 (the world distant from and antagonistic to God), is not mentioned, although the qualification fits the sense. John is concerned with the supreme passing on of Jesus' authority and commission; the fellowship of the disciples is to make him present in the world and to continue his ministry of salvation. Any restriction to the disciples who are present is not apparent and scarcely intended; John nowhere calls them 'apostles' in the specific sense. They represent for him the entire community of believers.

20:22   After the sending follows the bestowal of the Spirit. The external sign of it is 'breathing on' (literally 'blowing in', ἐμφυσάω), in conjunction with the words: 'Receive the Holy Spirit!' – in the NT a once-only mode of presentation. Probably, the evangelist took it over from his source; for, besides the singular expression ἐμφυσάω (only here in NT, yet more often in LXX[79]), πνεῦμα ἅγιον is also unusual for John. Most times, he puts in the article, and the attribute ἅγιον only occurs again in 1:33 and 14:26, in both places, apparently, in connection with traditional primitive Christian language. From that can also be explained the lack of a connection to the Paraclete or 'Spirit of truth', without our having to resolve the disputed relationship between the promise of the Spirit in the farewell discourses and this Easter bestowal of the Spirit.

The symbol of 'blowing in' means, according to its OT references (Gen 2:7; 1 Kings 17:21; Ezek 37:9; Wis 15:11), conferring of life, and so here, the bestowal of a share in the life of the risen one who himself possesses the Spirit and now transfers it to his disciples. But with the eschatological outpouring of the Spirit is also connected the idea of the cleansing from sins (cf. Ezek 36:25–27; 1 QS, 4:20f); the attribute 'holy' can point to this. The Qumran community was convinced that the one entering into their fellowship with a pure heart already experiences such an effect in the present: 'For it is through the Holy Spirit of true counsel (which is given to the community that all his sins shall be expiated . . .' (1 QS, 3:7f).[80] For the primitive Church, baptism was the place for the bestowal of the Spirit, and among the varied ideas of baptism, forgiveness of sins and new creation likewise appear (cf. 1 Cor 6:11; Acts 2:38; Tit 3:5; 1 Pet 1:23; 2:1f; Jn 3:5). If the source presented such thoughts, the evangelist could appropriate them all the easier as, for him also Jesus is, already from the first, the βαπτίζων ἐν πνεύματι ἁγίῳ (1:33). The disciples now receive this baptism 'with the Holy Spirit'[81] as well as the authority to forgive sins. Vv. 22 and 23 have to be seen as closely connected, without restricting the bestowal of the Spirit to that authority. It is scarcely to be taken as a 'rite of ordination',[82] because the disciples are not addressed as office-holders. The Spirit has, for John, a far-reaching significance: it forms the bond between Jesus and the disciples and the Church respectively. Now the promise at the time of the farewell is fulfilled: 'You will see me; because I live, you will live also' (14:19).

Can this passage be described as the 'Johannine Pentecost'? The expression is puzzling because it is taken from that particular prominent event dramatically described in Acts 2. But for the bestowal of the Spirit which, for the whole of primitive Christianity is a certainty, the 'Lukan Pentecost' ought to be regarded not as a norm but as an exception, namely, as a special manifestation of the Spirit, which assisted the primitive Church in Jerusalem to make a break-through.[83] If by 'Johannine Pentecost' is meant the definitive bestowal of the Spirit on all believers as against only a preliminary or specific granting of the Spirit to the 'apostles',[84] then, indeed, this expression may and must be chosen. For nothing points to the fact that, for John, after the Easter bestowal of the Spirit, there follows another one (on all believers), and that the disciples present are recipients of the Spirit in an exclusive sense (as against other believers). Jn 20:22 is the fulfilment of Jn 7:39 where the believers as such are mentioned as recipients of the Spirit.[85] We must differentiate between the Paraclete sayings: to the extent that they promise the Spirit as a permanent gift for the disciples, their prophecy is fulfilled; for a new or other coming of the Paraclete cannot be detected. But the functions which the Paraclete is to take over after Jesus' departure (reminding and teaching the disciples, witness to others and conviction of the world), do not yet come into view in 20:22. The perspective is a different one; in our passage, only the fact of the receiving of the Spirit which is the foundation of the life of the Church, is mentioned, but the effect of the Spirit in the sense of the Paraclete is not yet focused upon. An express indication that those promises are now beginning to be fulfilled, seemed to the evangelist and his friends rather unnecessary because they lived in the certainty of his leading.

20:23 The granting of authority to forgive sins, which now follows, forms a strong connecting link with the synoptic tradition. John did not himself fashion the saying of the risen one expressed in this way; never, elsewhere in his gospel, does he speak about 'forgiveness of sins', that is kept for the 'main' letter (1:9; 2:12). The plural ἁμαρτίαι only occurs twice in the gospel, with reference to the Jews (8:24, alternating with the singular 8:21), or, on the lips of the Jews (9:34), frequently, on the contrary, in 1 Jn (1:9; 2:2, 12; 3:5; 4:10; cf. 1:7; 3:9; 5:16f in the plural sense). Particularly noteworthy is the double possibility of 'forgiving' and 'retaining'.[86] This double-sided formulation which sheds light on the power conferred, recalls the saying of 'binding and loosing' (Mt 18:18; cf. 16:19) and must be connected with it in the history of tradition. Through Jn 20:23 it turns out to be an authoritative saying of the risen one.[87] Thus, the evangelist will have taken it over from his source; yet here too, we must ask how he incorporated it into his theology.

The Church's exegesis later introduced many questions into this text, which are remote from it, and which, therefore, it does not or only inadequately answers.

(1) Is it concerned with redemption for sins through baptism or forgiveness of sins after baptism? In the first three centuries, exegesis concerning baptism predominated. Cyprian, indeed, concludes from the passage 'that only the leaders of the Church have been empowered to baptize and grant the forgiveness of sins' (*Ep.* 73:7; *CSEL* III, 783). Later theologians assert, taking the sacrament of penance into account, that sins committed after baptism are intended. The alternatives are wrongly set out because the primitive Church was interested in the power of salvation as such, which the risen Lord had granted it. Mt 28:19 and Mk 16:16 mention baptism, Lk 24:47 forgiveness of sins; but Mt 28:20 additionally demands the observing of Christ's commands, and with that directs the attention towards the time after baptism (cf. also Mt 18:15–17; further, 26:28). Jn 20:23 will embrace baptism *and* later forgiveness of sins.

(2) Is this the institution of the sacrament of penance? The Council of Trent claims support of Jn 20:22f in order to prove its institution by Jesus Christ (*Denz.* 807 and 894). It is understandable from the development of the Church's teaching and from the theological situation of the time; but the Council's formulation does not imply that this is the first and only meaning of the passage. It is well known concerning the sacrament of penance, that it has a long history behind it, in which the sacramental understanding as well, matured only gradually. Against the reformers, the Council excluded the view that in Jn 20:22f only the authority to proclaim the gospel is being spoken of (*Denz.* 913); on this exegesis, see below.

(3) Is it a special authority granted to the disciples as office-holders which is passed on to their successors, or an empowering of the whole Church? This too is a restrictive

choice, because the historical development of the understanding of office must be kept in mind.

In the evangelist's sense, a limitation to the 'eleven apostles' is not tenable; but if the sending out commission and the saving authority (also according to Mt 28:18ff) applies to the fellowship of the disciples as such, then certain functions and powers can be retained for the office-holders in accordance with an emerging understanding of office, as is similarly observable in the case of the one presiding at the celebration of the Eucharist. The controversy in this connection between the denominations involves further problems: What is the position with growing knowledge in the Church, with tradition hardening? What of ecclesiastical office in its permanent or changing structures? and so on. Such questions go beyond the competence of an exegete. In the following we only try to submit to the thought of the evangelist.

If the scene represents the 'Spirit baptism' of the disciples, then, via the saying of John about baptism with the Spirit (1:33) a memory of the other saying is awakened, concerning the Lamb of God, 'who takes away the sin of the world' (1:29). The universal atonement effected by Jesus (cf. also 1 Jn 3:5 with 2:2; 4:10, 14), is, as forgiveness of sins, to benefit all who believe in him and strive after cleansing from their sins (cf. 1 Jn 1:7, 9). In the gospel, the idea of purity is heard of only rarely (13:10; 15:3), and is presumably, only secondarily introduced by the editors (q.v.); but the evangelist also knows of the freedom from sin which the Son brings (8:34ff). Now the Lamb of God is slain on the cross and the stream of salvation released for all (cf. 19:34, 37f). Finally, for John too, the bestowal of the Spirit will be connected with the cleansing from sin (cf. above on v. 22). So the forgiving of sins by the disciples must be understood as the bestowing of salvation provided by Jesus. The forms in the perfect ($\dot{\alpha}\phi\dot{\epsilon}\omega\nu\tau\alpha\iota$,[88] $\varkappa\epsilon\chi\rho\dot{\alpha}\tau\eta\nu\tau\alpha\iota$), in the source certainly intended as second future (cf. Mt 16:19; 18:18), should have the meaning for John: some are granted forgiveness of sins through the once-for-all atonement achieved by Jesus, for others, this source of salvation remains closed. When the forgiveness – differently from the logion about binding and loosing – is mentioned first, this can be an indication that the evangelist here too wants to preserve the primacy of salvation (cf. 3:17; 12:47).[89]

However it was thought in the Johannine community that forgiveness of sins was mediated (through baptism, confession of sins, supplication, intercession, cf. on 1 Jn 1:9), it happens through the blood of Jesus (1 Jn 1:7) in the bosom of the Church. The authoritative saying of the risen one which the evangelist found is for him the fundamental and axiomatic promise, that forgiveness of sins occurs and will continue to occur within the Church. A limitation to the authority to the disciples present or to later office-holders, is far from the evangelist's mind; as up till now the disciples represent the Church, and in 1 Jn office-holders are not mentioned in connection with ecclesiastical practice. But it may also not be concluded from the silence, that the Johannine Church *basically* rejected teaching and leadership functions. It can just as little be proved that for John the forgiveness of sins is 'the natural function and consequence' for all believers 'of the sermon' of the preachers sent by the Son.[90] The consciousness of having received from the risen Lord commission and authority to forgive and not to forgive sins, possesses the Johannine church too. It has to decide who belongs to it and who separates himself from it by his behaviour. Like Jesus himself (cf. 8:21; 9:41) it can and must determine that certain people are gripped by sin (cf. 1 Jn 5:16). The establishment of a practice of penance in the Church belongs only to a later time; but the striving towards freedom from sin and the maintenance of the Church's purity, is there from the beginning . For John, the taking away of sins is the gift and commission of the risen Lord.

4. Thomas's Conversion to the Easter Faith because of a further Appearance of Jesus [20:24-29]

[24]*Now Thomas, one of the twelve, called the Twin, was not with them when Jesus came.* [25]*So the other disciples told him, 'We have seen the Lord.' But he said to them, 'Unless I see in his hands the print of the nails, and place my finger in the mark of the nails, and place my hand in his side, I will not believe.'* [26]*Eight days later, his disciples were again in the house, and Thomas was with them. The doors were shut, but Jesus came and stood among them, and said, 'Peace be with you.'* [27]*Then he said to Thomas, 'Put your finger here, and see my hands; and put out your hand, and place it in my side; do not be faithless, but believing.'* [28]*Thomas answered him, 'My Lord and my God!'* [29]*Jesus said to him, 'Because you have seen me, you believe. Blessed are those who have not seen and yet believe.'*

The Thomas pericope which gives emphasis to the Easter experience of the disciples, and points the way and direction for the faith of later believers, probably goes back to the evangelist. The following observations speak in favour of his having added to them on his own initiative:

1. At the appearance before the disciples, vv. 19–23, the presence of all the disciples is presupposed, because the bestowal of the Spirit and granting of authority to forgive sins applies to them as a whole. The source which the evangelist may be using for vv. 22–23 scarcely foresaw the absence of a disciple.

2. The scene with Thomas is developed from the preceding scene with the disciples. The testimony of the other disciples: 'We have seen the Lord' looks back to v. 20b, Thomas's answer to v. 20a. It is enough for the other disciples that Jesus showed them his hands and his side; Thomas demands a closer examination. Jesus' coming is related in accordance with v. 19 (closed doors, coming into their midst, eirenic greeting), and the encounter with Thomas is then developed logically.

3. The style too partly betrays the hand of the evangelist, and, for the rest also, suggests no other hand.

So, εἷς ἐκ is characteristic for John; δώδεκα is already previously taken over from the tradition (cf. 6:71 with 6:67). The οὖν historicum in v. 25 is a criterion of John's style. Also, ἐὰν μή is often found (eighteen times), with οὐ μή following (4:48; 16:7). On εἶτα, cf.

13:5 and 19:27; on γίνου in the sense of 'to be', 'to turn out to be', cf. 15:8. ἄπιστος and πιστός are, indeed, found only here in John's gospel, but contrasted with each other like this (with ἀλλά, frequently used in John) they suggest themselves in connection with faith. If the special character of the scene is noted, the form of the confession in v. 28 and the beatitude of v. 29c may also not be played off against the evangelist's style.[91] There are again good possibilities of comparison for v. 29a with its two perfects: on ἑώρακα cf. 1:34; 9:37; 14:7; on πεπίστευκα 6:69; 8:31; 11:27; 16:27. 'Believe' without an object used for faith in the resurrection, links the passage with 20:8b.

4. The evangelist's intention in adding the pericope can be explained by the interest in Christology (confession) and in the community of the readers (belief without seeing). Yet the theological scope of the scene must be examined still more closely in the exegesis. The secondary character of the Thomas pericope as against the appearance to the disciples has long been recognized.[92] Lately, G. Richter wants to attribute the story to editors supposed by him, who, by means of additions of an anti-Docetic kind wanted to prevent a misinterpretation of the original gospel and to take account of a situation newly arisen in the Church.[93] This hypothesis presupposes that the narrator is interested above all to establish Jesus' real bodily nature; but that is highly questionable. We do not even discover whether Thomas really placed his finger in Jesus' wounds and his hand in the wound in Jesus' side. The concluding words which normally reveal the real intention, point in another direction: The concern is with faith without seeing, since the later believers will, in contrast to the first disciples, experience no more appearances of the risen one, and are to believe nevertheless. Yet on that, only the interpretation of the text can bring greater clarity.

20:24   Thomas has already been given prominence twice in the gospel: in the walk to Bethany (11:16) and in the supper room (14:5), both times in fragments which undoubtedly originate with the evangelist. Also, the drawing of his character in these passages fits the picture which results of him in the following scene. Slow in the up-take, he yet remains true to Jesus (cf. on 11:16); only he does not understand his Lord's way (14:5). The prospect of Jesus' destiny, death, hinders his believing in Jesus' resurrection; so he is not a type of the unbeliever as such but of one blind to faith and of one with a weak faith to whom belief in its wholeness will be granted as a gift only by Jesus himself, and that, after the resurrection. In this respect, he represents the entire pre-Easter group of disciples as, perhaps, the addition 'one of the twelve' is meant to suggest. Otherwise, only Judas the traitor is indicated with this expression (6:71; cf. 12:4; 13:21), yet the evangelist also singles out Andrew (6:8) and the disciple at Jesus' side (13:23) to be 'one of his disciples'. Even in the most intimate circle of disciples, the 'twelve' (cf. 6:67), there was hesitation and doubt with respect to the risen one: this is what the evangelist wants to express (with the support of the tradition, cf. Lk 24:38ff; Mt 28:17; further, Mk 16:11–14), but, in contrast to Lk/Mt, only after the event, because for him, the appearance to the disciples has a different purpose (see above).[93a] The further designation as 'twin' is already found in 11:16 (q.v.). No reason is given why

Thomas was not present when Jesus[94] appeared on the evening on the first day of the week, although it certainly is remarkable – another sign of a secondary stage in the narrative.

20:25   The coming together of Thomas with the other[95] disciples, which is not described further, only serves to prepare for the scene with Jesus. Therefore, the disciples only say:[96] 'We have seen the Lord' – the short formula for the experience of an appearance (see on v. 18) – and pass over everything that Jesus had said to them. All the emphasis falls on Thomas's demand for stronger evidence of the reality and identity of the risen one. It is described thoroughly and in detail so as to underline his rejection of faith without such 'tangible' evidence. The progression from 'seeing' the prints caused by the nails, to 'placing' his finger in them and, over and above that, placing his hand in the wound in Jesus' side,[97] is clear. With οὐ μή Thomas expresses his position forcefully. The double negative particle is, in John's gospel, where it occurs seventeen times, almost always a mark of assurance (confirmation of an assurance), only in 13:8 (Peter's refusal to allow his feet to be washed) has it a voluntative undertone.[98] The connection with a conditional clause is also found in 8:51f and 16:7, however, formally, and from its content, its closest parallel is 4:48. Since this sentence, 'unless you see signs and wonders you will not believe', betrays an interest of the evangelist (see Vol. 1, pp. 466 and 468), there is a strong probability in favour of his pursuing a similar interest in the faith of his readers with the Thomas pericope (cf. v. 29).[99] Faith which maintains itself by outward sight remains inadequate, but, admittedly, does not become simply devalued when it leads to recognition of Jesus, to Christological faith (differently than in 6:26, 36); but faith in Jesus' word alone is superior (cf. 10:38; 14:11). Both the stories retain their special character; the one concerning the man in royal service does not belie the tensions arising for the evangelist from the tradition he has taken over. But both stories converge in the evangelist's intention to lead beyond the stage of a faith dependent on seeing. With Thomas, the point is the special faith in the resurrection of Jesus, which is fundamental for the age to come. The intransitive πιστεύειν means nothing else here than in 20:8. The apparent contradiction that the disciple whom Jesus loved is praised because 'he saw and believed', while Thomas is criticized: 'Because you have seen me, you believe' is explained by the respective situations. At the empty tomb, without news of Jesus' resurrection and without knowledge of the scriptures (20:9), the spontaneous faith of that disciple (cf. the aorists) was exemplary; for Thomas, to whom his fellow disciples witness concerning the Lord's resurrection, his stubbornness and reliance on seeing signifies remaining in the past and failure. The theme of 'seeing and believing' is, despite the demand to touch the body, dominant, as is shown by the taking up of 'see' alone at the end. The evangelist does not use the verb ψηλαφᾶν like Lk 24:39 and 1 Jn 1:1; 'placing in' of the finger and hand describes that kind of sensual contact which then is censured in terms of the inferior motif of 'seeing'.[100] That does not support a primary anti-Docetic intention in the pericope.

20:26   After Thomas's declaration which already prepares the reader for the
following scene, without more ado, Jesus' appearance is related. καί as in 1:19;
2:1, 13 and frequently, leads on to a new event which the reader is already
expecting. The detail of time, 'eight days later', on account of the chronology of
the Easter events, has gained much attention and instigated many hypotheses.
How is it reconcileable with the commission to the disciples to go to Galilee so
as to see the Lord there (Mk 16:7), and with the appearance or appearances
respectively in Galilee (cf. Mt 28:16–20; Jn 21)? Why did the disciples stay in
Jerusalem? But all speculations about this miss the intention of the statement
as to the detail of time. The evangelist is concerned to postpone the second
appearance at which Thomas is present to the following Sunday; for, according
to the old method of reckoning which includes the beginning and end of a
period,[101] the eight days culminate at this point. Yet, why is the evangelist
interested in this? Obviously, because in his day, the Christian Sunday has
already established itself, probably for the celebration of the Lord's supper (cf.
Acts 20:7; *Did* 14:1). It counts as the 'Lord's day' (cf. Rev 1:10), and that in
remembrance of the Lord's resurrection as Ignatius to the *Magnesians* 9:1 and
Barnabas 15:9 witness to in emphatic contrast to the Jewish Sabbath.[102]
Therefore, the choice of eight days is due certainly to liturgical practice,
admittedly, not out of a special cultic interest of the evangelist, but with a view
to the Church which, at its celebrations, is to remind itself of that appearance to
Thomas.

As to the disciples' situation, the evangelist contents himself with the
information: 'They were again in the house' namely, in the meeting-room
hinted at in v. 19. Their fear of the Jews is not mentioned again; it no longer fits
to the joy of Easter with which they are filled (cf. v. 20b). The detail that the
doors were closed is retained, but it is connected with Jesus' coming and so is
given a different role: that must make an impression on the sceptical Thomas.
Generally, everything is concentrated on surprising the boastful disciple. The
description of how Jesus appears begins, in lively fashion, with the present
historic; Jesus comes into the midst of the disciples, as on the first occasion, and
greets them with the eirenic greeting. But then, he immediately turns to
Thomas.

20:27   The infrequent εἶτα is found in John in 13:5 and 19:27 as well, and
indicates in both places a directly following act. Jesus' words which repeat what
Thomas said to his fellow disciples, must have struck home to the doubter. The
expressions are, indeed, somewhat altered (that belongs to a good narrative
style), but, factually, Jesus acts exactly in accordance with the disciple's
demand. So he perceives himself to have been seen through and is put to shame
by the goodness of Jesus who fulfills his challenging wish. Jesus' knowledge of
secrets and understanding of the heart accompanied his earthly ministry from
the outset, and very similar in conception and structure to the scene in which this
feature comes to the fore for the first time, namely the encounter with Nathanael
(1:47–50), is the scene with Thomas: a derogatory, sceptical remark of his as
Philip testifies to him that Jesus is the Messiah (1:45f) – a saying of Jesus which

shows Nathanael how well he knows him – a joyful and high-minded confession of the man as a reaction to this – a concluding word of Jesus which points to the future. This structural similarity is certainly not accidental; it reveals the same narrator despite differences due to the situation. Jesus' last words to Nathanael point to the time of Jesus' earthly ministry, the concluding saying of the risen one to Thomas, to the future of the Church.

The following warning, 'do not be[103] faithless. but believing' relates to Thomas's reluctance in v. 25, '. . . I will not believe'. With that also, Jesus shows him that he knows his impetuous utterance precisely. But the warning also has a narrative function for what follows: it prepares Thomas's confession and builds a bridge to the closing words in v. 29. So we have: v. 25 passionate striving against belief – v. 27d call not to be faithless but believing – v. 29c blessing of the believers. Yet the concern is not simply with faith in Jesus' resurrection but with seeing as the motive for this faith. Hence, the connection with this of the other line: v. 25 Thomas's demand to see and prove – v. 27b–c Jesus' offer to fall in with his demand – v. 29b criticism of this manner of attaining to faith. The warning with the contrast, 'faithless-believing',[104] signals the dénouement of the story.

20:28   To Jesus' challenge, Thomas reacts with an unconditional high-minded confession of Jesus. Because of it, the reader remains uncertain whether the disciple really placed his finger in the wounds and his hand in Jesus' side. The dispute among the exegetes as to whether he did it or refrained from it, misses the point of the account. It can be adduced in favour of contact: with Jesus' words were probably connected the appropriate gestures of the disciple, the criticism would surely presuppose that.[105] Against that, it can be said that: in v. 29, Jesus confronts Thomas only with faith based on *seeing*, and the silence as to physical contact speaks rather for Thomas having done without this verification. After the overpowering impression made on Thomas by Jesus' appearance with the doors closed, the knowledge concerning his demand, and the words of Jesus directed to him personally, the disciple can only just utter this confession which testifies to personal emotion ('my' twice).[105a] The second viewpoint seems to me better founded, but the first is not impossible. In any case, the narrator shows no interest in specifically stating the physical touching of the risen one. Rather, he is interested – similarly as with Nathanael – in the turnabout which occurs through the appearance and words of Jesus, in Thomas's attitude in that instantaneous and total change from 'unbelief' to 'faith' which is heard in Jesus' warning. Jesus has won the doubting disciple for himself.

The confession itself is tailored to the situation and, at the same time, goes beyond it. The personal tone due to the twice occurring μου is not to be ignored: Thomas has found *his* Lord and *his* God in the risen one, whom he recognises as the crucified and to him well-known earthly Jesus, and yet as another whom he understands to belong wholly to God. However, the two predicates can hardly be shared between Jesus' earthly and post-Easter modes of being, so that κύριος would have to signify the master in the circle of the disciples and θεός the one lifted up.[106] Both uses are a confession similar to the two predicates in Nathanael's confession (1:49), and the two predications form a single whole. During the time on earth, the disciples used κύριε only as a form of address (6:68; 11:12; 13:6, 9, 36f and frequently), similarly to others, although 13:13f accentuates the special master-disciple-position (cf. also 'rabbi' in 4:31; 9:2; 11:8). Now κύριος becomes a confession which applies to the risen one as the usage in Chapter 20, especially vv. 18, 20, 25 suggests. With his personal confession – by its form, either an abbreviated confession (without σὺ εἶ) or an exclamation (vocative)[107] – Thomas confirms in his own person that now he also, like the other disciples (cf. v. 25a), believes in the resurrection of the Lord. But he adds the divine predicate so as to leave no doubt as to the greatness of his faith. Just for him, the doubting one, the final consequence of Jesus' resurrection was laid bare in the encounter with the risen one: Jesus is of divine essence, in him God himself comes to him, he is for him God in his majesty, power and love.

It is necessary, in this confession of Jesus' divinity on the lips of Thomas, to guard against both a watering down and a dogmatic fixation. The addition μου gives the confession a personal note, but takes nothing from its effectiveness as a statement. As often observed, this confession stands, for the evangelist, at the end of his gospel, certainly corresponding to the statement at the beginning of the prologue: θεὸς ἦν ὁ λόγος. Attention may not be called to the lack of the article in 1:1c for which there is a good reason there (see *ad loc.*), so as to contradict the correspondence.[108] Nor does Thomas say σὺ εἶ ὁ θεός, but calls out to Jesus only in confession: ὁ θεός μου. In the evangelist's sense, Thomas' confession makes clear that the faith expected of the Church in Jesus the Son of God (cf. 20:31) implies Jesus' Godhead. He is the only true Son of God, one with the Father not only in what he does, but also in being (cf. Excursus 9 in Vol. 2). Because the evangelist is not yet thinking from the point of view of the teaching of the two natures, he combines the Godhead of Jesus with the revelatory and saving function of the Son: he is the *Messiah,* the Son of God, that is, he is the Messiah to the extent that he is the Son of God, and the Son of God in his messianic ministry. This functional understanding[109] can be found expressed likewise in the personal confession formula: '*My* Lord and *my* God.'

The combination, 'Lord and God', allows us to think of the OT form of expression;[110] but here, it originates, rather, in the evangelist's reflection. It is possible that there is also a reminder of the primitive Christian liturgy (cf. Excursus 3 in Vol. 1). A barb against the emperor cult where the same attributes, 'Lord and God' appear, is scarcely to be supposed.[111] Thomas's confession which takes its place in a whole series of confessions in John's gospel (1:49; 4:42; 6:69; 9:37f; 11:27; 16:30; 20:16) and forms their conclusion and climax, clearly shows the pen of the evangelist. With it, he achieves once more, a leading statement of a Christological kind in the light of the Easter confession.

20:29 Jesus accepts Thomas' confession, but does not spare him from the accusation that he came to believe only after an assurance through 'seeing'.

Is the sentence to be taken as a question, as not a few editions of the text and commentaries favour?[112] Then, a certain reserve would resonate with the confession, even if the emphasis is put on the first part of the sentence: '*Only* because you have seen me, do you believe?' The comparable cases, 1:50 and 16:31 where Jesus' answer is certainly meant to be a question (see *ad loc.*), seem to suggest that; but the particular context is different. The following reasons speak for a statement (in an accusing tone):

1. The high-minded confession of the disciple who (distinct from Nathanael) is already a long-time follower of Jesus, does not, as such, permit of any doubt;

2. in this situation after Jesus' resurrection, the evangelist scarcely still casts doubt on the faith of the disciple (the situation in 16:31 is different);

3. the perfect of πιστεύειν signifies a firm faith (cf. 6:69; 11:27) – the two other passages have the present tense;

4. the connection to what follows is also better: the statement is followed by the blessing of those who, without seeing, summon up this faith.

Everything which Thomas experienced in the encounter with the risen one is summed up in 'seeing'. The perfect occurs here similarly as in 6:36; 9:37; 14:7, 9. The emphasis rests on the sensual perception, yet without stressing touching. Thomas is the exponent of that experience by a disciple, of Jesus' 'appearances', which is denied to later believers.

The criticism of Thomas is constructed with a view to the subsequent blessing. The beatitude, a stylistic form used often but differently from OT to NT,[113] is special in John's gospel; the only other passage in which a beatitude again occurs (13:17), is presumably due to the editors (see *ad loc.*). The warning-character links the two beatitudes; but in form and content, they differ not a little. While the disciples are warned in 13:17 (in the second person) in respect of the humble service according to Jesus' example, so the beatitude in 20:29 (in the third person) applies to those who attain to a high degree of faith. Since this one thing is the continuing interest throughout the whole gospel, there is no reason to deny the sentence to the evangelist.

It is remarkable that the beatitude form of style is used not a little (seven times) in Rev,[114] both for eschatological promise (14:13; 19:9; 20:6; 22:14) and for warning (1:3; 16:15; 22:7). If Rev is connected with the 'Johannine circle', the use of such a mode of expression in the mouth of the evangelist cannot surprise us. C. H. Dodd considers the connection in the history of tradition of Jn 20:29b with the logion Lk 10:23; Mt 13:16.[115] But there is no need for such a basis for the beatitude in our passage which is constructed wholly in the Johannine spirit and specially connected with faith in Jesus' resurrection.

The participle forms in the aorist (instead of in the present) are noticeable but not inexplicable. The attention is turned to the future when Christians, without having seen the risen Lord, attain to faith in him. The sense of the Greek puts him vividly in the future and then looks back on events which have already taken place; comparable to the aorist in 4:38; 15:8; 17:14, 18 (q.v.). Also a need for stylistic variation can have had an effect; cf. the alternation between perfect and aorist in 1 Jn 1:1. In any case, the beatitude is no general concluding sentence, but was consciously and concretely expressed into the historical situation at the time of the evangelist, an appeal to the later believers without the 'seeing' granted Thomas, to come to the same firm faith and high-minded confession as he did. How that can happen is not expressly said: but the preaching of the word and the testimony of the first disciples is presupposed (cf. 15:27; also 19:35; 21:24 on an editorial level), or the written testimony which the evangelist provides with his gospel (cf. 20:30f).

After this exegetical investigation of the text, the Thomas pericope can be understood entirely in the light of the main objective of the evangelist, to lead his readers to a deepened faith in Christ. A special tendency (apology for Jesus' resurrection, defence against Docetic misinterpretation) is, at most, a secondary association with it. However the evangelist came to narrate this encounter of Thomas with the risen one, perhaps because of the interest which his Church had in the person of this disciple, it had for him an eminently theological and pastoral significance. As with the other Easter stories taken up by him, he is concerned to lead the believers to the risen one himself who, for him, is a permanent living reality. Presumably on this account, he does not have a farewell scene; he can do without it all the more because, in his case, the earthly Jesus had already spoken in the supper-room about his departure, his return and his constant fellowship with those who belong to him.

5. Conclusion of the Gospel (20:30–31)

[30]*Now Jesus did many other signs in the presence of the disciples, which are not written in this book;* [31]*but these are written that you may believe that Jesus is the Christ, the Son of God, and that believing you may have life in his name.*

With an eye to the coming generation of Christians, who, without appearances of the risen one, are to believe in the testimony of the first disciples, the evangelist has found a fitting conclusion to the Easter stories. Now he explicitly adds a final word with which he places his entire book in the hands of the readers. So there remains no doubt that this is the original end of the work and Chapter 21 is a postscript from whoever its content might come.[116] Such a formal conclusion is something new in gospel literature. Admittedly, the statement that we have here only a selection, is found frequently in those days;[117] but the conclusion in Jn 20:30f is intended, above all, to point out clearly the purpose of the writing. On the whole, it fits in well with the special nature of this gospel which, in historical retrospect, seeks to work out the continuous and insurpassable significance of Jesus Christ, in that it consciously selects and interprets the traditions wholly related to the scope of the readers' understanding.

Because, at the end, the evangelist himself states the object of his work, this concluding statement represents something of a key for the basic understanding of his unique gospel; so the interpretation up to this point has to prove its worth in relation to it. But this epilogue too, like the whole of John's gospel, still presents a number of interpretative problems, specifically, the following:

1. What is meant by the σημεῖα which Jesus did 'in the presence of the disciples'? Are the 'signs' in the first part (Chapters 2–12), the resurrection

appearances, the two together, or all acts and sayings of Jesus generally, intended to be included?

2. Can a σημεῖα-source be determined upon, ending with these words? If so, how did the conclusion of it run?

3. What can be learnt from v. 31 about those addressed? Are these primarily already believing Christians, or does the work wish to turn first of all to outsiders, Jews or Gentiles, so as to win them for the faith in Christ?

4. What significance does the confession formula in v. 31 have, possibly for the source, but above all for the evangelist? Does ὁ χριστός mean to emphasize the Messiah expected by the Jews (yet in what sense?), or, is the title already wholly christianized, meaning the same as the following title ὁ υἱὸς τοῦ θεοῦ? What weight does the confessional formula have for the special situation of the Church? These questions cannot be decided without a reference back to the gospel as a whole, as, again, the detailed exegesis already often enough had to orientate itself according to 20:30f (the hermeneutic circle) and now, once more, has to allow itself to be questioned in the light of this passage. The origin of the passage with the evangelist despite some echoes of Lukan style,[118] is not to be doubted; the pecularities can, perhaps, be explained in other ways.

20:30   It is noticeable that the evangelist speaks of σημεῖα, although this expression is otherwise kept for the time of Jesus' public ministry (Chapters 2–12). On 12:37 the suggestion was made (see Vol. 2, p. 411), that our verse originally formed the conclusion of the σημεῖα-source. Thence can also be explained the (for John) unusual expressions: μὲν οὖν – δέ only occurs again with him in 19:24f, ἐνώπιον nowhere else. The entire expression echoes Lk 3:18 (yet καὶ ἕτερα instead of καὶ ἄλλα), but can also have stood in the source. Whether originally, the personal pronoun αὐτοῦ after οἱ μαθηταί was lacking, is hard to decide;[119] it would not be a criterion of the style.[120] Noteworthy is ἐνώπιον instead of ἔμπροσθεν in 12:37. While, through this preposition, the public character of Jesus' signs is underlined, ἐνώπιον presumably only means to say (weaker) 'in the presence of', and the evangelist will have that in mind so the disciples became witnesses of the σημεῖα. Since the σημεῖα-source according to the miracle-stories pointed out in this commentary shows no particular interest in the disciples (cf. especially the second Cana miracle, the healing of the sick man at the pool of Bethzatha and the awakening of the dead), but the evangelist certainly does (cf. 6:6, 8; 9:3–5; 11:7–16), the possibility must be reckoned with (in spite of ἐνώπιον), that the evangelist has added the expression 'in the presence of the disciples'. There then results a, certainly intended, correspondence between 12:37 and 20:30. Just as the evangelist closed the first main section (Jesus' ministry before the world) in the light of 'so great signs', which, nevertheless, aroused no faith among men, so he now speaks of the many signs which Jesus did 'in the presence of the disciples' in order to lead his readers to faith. For him, the term 'sign' has a dual aspect: a negative one in connection with unbelief, and a positive one to the extent that, from the rightly understood σημεῖα, true and total faith can grow (cf. Excursus 4 in Vol. 1).

Yet, what does the evangelist mean here by σημεῖα? They can hardly be restricted to the appearance of the risen one, because the concern is with a look back over the *whole* book, and the expression '*many* other' for further appearances sounds exaggerated especially after the blessing of those who believe without seeing. When the disciples as witnesses of Jesus' ministry appear, it is possible that the evangelist consciously harks back to the 'book of signs' (Chapters 2–12) and with σημεῖα concentrates attention on the events reported there.[121] But the fact that he makes the statement *in this place*, after the appearances of the risen one, indeed, in the event that it was originally the concluding remark in the σημεῖα-source, that he *transfers* it to this place, certainly requires a more far-reaching explanation. Has he not here included Jesus' appearances among the σημεῖα? Extraordinary features (closed doors, the visible and tangible body) are not lacking, and it can be argued that for John the miraculous belongs to a 'sign'.[122] However, certainly in contrast to the source, he does not place the emphasis on this, but on the deeper meaning of the sign, so to say, its revelatory quality. But such belongs to the appearances in an eminent sense: they reveal Jesus as the exalted one, belonging to God's world, or, as Thomas says, as 'Lord and God', precisely in his glorified physical being. Then, admittedly, the term σημεῖον, which, until now, was firmly tied to the earthly (miracle-) deeds of Jesus, is broadened; yet it can be said with W. Nicol: 'The concept sēmeion is widened to include the appearances . . . [it] has acquired striking elasticity.'[123]

If this view is adopted (different in Vol. 1, pp. 515 and 520), the following must be said for the sake of clarity: the inclusion of the appearances among the σημεῖα is a last stage in the evangelist's concept and should not mislead us to define his understanding of the idea of σημεῖον too broadly. It remains true that the σημεῖα are (miraculous) revelatory deeds of Jesus, tied to his earthly ministry, only now extended to the appearances before the disciples. Jesus' cross is in no way a 'sign' in the Johannine sense (Vol. 1, p. 520 n. 7), death and resurrection are not the 'supreme σημεῖον' (Barrett, 65). The resurrection itself is, as R. E. Brown rightly emphasizes, not a sign; Jesus 'has passed from the realm of sign to that of truth in his passion, death, resurrection, and ascension' (1059). Finally, the σημεῖα of 20:30 cannot be extended to 'all that the Gospel of John preaches about Jesus, both the works and the words' (Nicol, 115). Such an exposition destroys what is peculiar to the Johannine viewpoint.

The evangelist's closing remark draws attention to the selection of the σημεῖα. He already found such a one in his source, and it seems that he in his turn made a further selection from it out of the 'signs' reported there. He selected few but 'eloquent' signs, which disclose the revelation of Christ, because, with them, he pursues a specific purpose in his presentation, which he states in v. 31. With his method of choice, he is distinguished from the compiler of the similar sounding (perhaps based on 20:30) closing remark in 21:25, which, significantly, no longer speaks of σημεῖα.

20:31 Due to the combination with δέ corresponding to μέν in v. 30, the verse which follows also goes back to the source. Less certain is whether it also already presented the same confessional formula.[124] Martha pronounced the same confession as her firm conviction (πεπίστευκα, with her further addition, 'who is coming into the world' (11:27). With it she become the example for all men, especially those belonging to Judaism, who are ready to believe. The confession of the Samaritans, representatives of the non-Jews, runs differently: 'This is indeed the Saviour of the world' (4:42), but it coincides with that of the Jews in the thought that Jesus is the bringer of salvation. The universal perspective is also brought in by the evangelist elsewhere (cf. 7:35; 10:16; 11:52; 12:20–24, 32; 18:37). Therefore, it can be asked does the evangelist want to turn rather to people of Jewish or non-Jewish origin? And further: Does he rather want to win non-believers for the faith in Christ, or to strengthen believers in their faith? The thesis that John's gospel is a missionary writing, was repeatedly proposed in reference to the gentiles (W. Oehler) or by some people to the Samaritans (E. D. Freed), but by many more to the Jews (K. Bornhäser), especially to Hellenistic diaspora Jews who are to be led to faith in Jesus' messiahship (W. C. van Unnik, J. A. T. Robinson).[125] But it is very questionable whether the missionary idea is at all a controlling one; the reading πιστεύσητε in the sense of an ingressive aorist ('in order that you come to believe') can scarcely be called upon.

This reading is offered by the mass of mss, among them important ones as regards age and origin (A C D λ ∮ 33. 565), (more precise evidence in UBS Greek NT); on the other side P66 (probably) ℵ* B Θ 0250 892 read πιστεύητε. The editors of the text are divided. Von Soden, B. Weiss, Vogels, UBS Greek NT opt for the reading in the aorist; the remainder prefer the present reading. A similar text-critical uncertainty prevails in Jn 13:19; 17:21; 19:35; 1 Jn 3:23. The aorist of πιστεύειν in John certainly often has an ingressive character, but not necessarily nor always (cf. 4:50; 7:39; 11:15, 40; 12:42; 14:29; 20:29). The passages 11:15 and 14:29 are noteworthy, where, in a similar ἵνα-clause, the certainly not unbelieving disciples are being addressed; they are to receive a new impulse in their faith. Further, see 11:40, where Martha, who has already proclaimed her faith, is reminded of her faith with ἐὰν πιστεύσῃς. So the aorist does not have to indicate the commencement of faith or conversion to faith. The tense used is no worthwhile argument in this matter.

The disputed question must be decided on another basis. Noteworthy are the observations of H. Riesenfeld on the Johannine ἵνα-clauses.[126] He points to the Johannine epistles, in which, by means of ἵνα-clauses, very frequently, the letter-writer's concern in respect to those to whom he is writing, in this case, clearly, members of the Church, is formulated (1 Jn 1:3, 4; 3:11, 23; 5:13; 2 Jn 5, 6), and he believes that such clauses have their *Sitz im Leben* in congregational instruction. Also, more recent researches into the nature of Johannine language confirm that the evangelist turns, to begin with and above all, to the believing congregation.[127] So, with the majority of exegetes, it is to be maintained that 20:31 is formulated for those who already believe.

But why does John underline Jesus' messiahship so strongly? If ὁ χριστός (with the article) were found only here and on Martha's lips (11:27) in John's gospel, then it could be thought that it is nothing other than a reverberation of the primitive Christian confession, following the synoptic tradition (cf.

especially, Mk 8:29 par.; 14:61f par.). But the messianic question plays a significant, indeed amazing part, in John's gospel,[128] and if ὁ χριστός in the other passages (on the lips of the Jews) has to be rendered by 'the Messiah', then certainly here also. The reason for this *new* interest in the messianic question lies, as was clear in the passages concerned (especially in Chapter 7), in the controversy of the Johannine Church with contemporary Judaism, possibly, indeed, with Jews in the immediate neighbourhood (cf. the commentary on Chapter 9). The evangelist wants to equip his Christian readers, among whom were not a few Jewish Christians, for defence against Jewish objections, and to strengthen them positively in their faith in Jesus the Messiah.[129]

The addition of the title 'Son of God' is explained by the Christian interpretation of the Jewish messianic expectation. Although this Christological title might have a different root from Jesus' leading self-designation in John's gospel, the absolute 'the Son' (cf. Excursus 9 in Vol. 2), the confession of Jesus the 'Son of God' is, for John, the recognition of that self-revelation of Jesus. That follows irrefutably from the Johannine kerygma (3:17f), from 5:25 with its context, and from the scriptural proof adduced in 10:34–36; cf. also, 11:4; 19:7. If the title 'Son of God' already stood in the σημεῖα source, it was possibly in the sense of the royal Messiah (cf. 1:49), not in the sense of the Hellenistic θεῖος ἀνήρ.[130] But for the evangelist, it has become the most exalted expression of his Christology and has taken up into itself the full significance of the 'Son'-revelation. Thomas' confession of Jesus' Godhead is still ringing in the readers' ears, and in the following ἵνα-clause, the usage 'in his name', which fixes the attention on Jesus in his just-described significance as Messiah and Son of God, shows that the only (μονογενής) true Son of God, who alone mediates eternal life, is meant (cf. 3:16, 18).

The final clause, which, over and above faith, names divine life for the believers as the goal of the writing (v. 31c), undoubtedly comes from the evangelist who, with it, takes up his basic statement: he who believes in the Son, has eternal life (3:15, 16, 36 and frequently). 'In his name' is as much as to say, on and in his person (cf. 3:18; 1 Jn 3:23; 5:13); the usage is here similarly related to 'to have life' as in 3:15. ἐν is scarcely to be understood mystically, but proclaims the close fellowship which is created by means of the union of faith in the one who reveals and bringer of salvation (cf. on 3:15). The addition of this short clause shows, once again, that for John, there is no Christology in isolation from soteriology (cf. Vol. 2, pp. 88f); his gospel is primarily intended to be a message of salvation. The bringer of revelation, come in the flesh, the Son of God, is the bringer of life for mankind who has succumbed to death, and he is, in this sense, the Messiah. The single requirement for attaining this eternal-divine life, on man's side, is faith, as is emphasised by πιστεύοντες which stands in the middle, and indicates the means. In order to make possible, to awaken, to strengthen and to deepen this faith, the evangelist has written his gospel (on faith, cf. Excursus 7 in Vol. 1).

If this analysis and exegesis of 20:30f apply, then the evangelist has used the end of the σημεῖα-source in his own way, in order, in conclusion, to tell his readers clearly once again of his intention. He is, perhaps, responsible for the remark, 'in the presence of the disciples', and certainly, the last brief clause ($\varkappa\alpha\grave{\iota}$ $\H{\iota}\nu\alpha$ . . .); he understood the 'signs' and 'the Son of God' differently, more profoundly, than his source.

Introduction: The problems thrown up by Jn 21

1. The Literary Distinctiveness of Jn 21

The many problems with which this chapter – looked at by itself, or in relation to Jn 1–20, or in connection with the 'Johannine question' – confronts us, are discussed in introductory works, commentaries and individual studies,[1] and have led to numerous theses and hypotheses. Within the compass of a commentary which requires limitation, the problems need to be dealt with by keeping as close as possible to the text. From a literary aspect, John 21:1–23 presents a rather large unit featuring a connected narrative complex with various individual elements, which, however, are peculiarly interconnected. Vv. 24 and 25 no longer directly belong to it, but are concluding remarks, which join the narrative complex to, or incorporate it into John's gospel. These verses require, each for itself, its own investigation. It is true, they accentuate the problem as to what is the relationship between the longer section vv. 1–23 and the remainder of the gospel, which has its first conclusion at 20:30f.

When 21:1–23 is looked at in the literary form in which it is found, then, to begin with, the comment in v. 14 is noteworthy, designating everything related up to this point (cf. v. 1) as Jesus' third appearance to the disciples after his resurrection. It presupposes knowledge of the two appearances before the disciples on the evening of Easter day and a week later (20:19–23, 26–29), perhaps (on account of ἤδη τρίτον) also 20:30 (πολλὰ . . . καὶ ἄλλα σημεῖα). But it does not fit at this point, to the extent that what follows also still belongs to this appearance. There is, however, no support for repositioning the comment after v. 23 (where it would, in itself, fit). So editors are here indicated, who, by means of the comments in vv. 1 and 14 which form a framework, wanted to connect the narrative vv. 2–13 with chapter 20, and, at the same time, to set off vv. 15–23 against this appearance to the disciples. If v. 14 is put in parenthesis, a connected complex results which is relatively closed as such, but allows us to recognize differing, partly interwoven fragments: an appearance of Jesus by the Sea of Tiberias, a miracle-story (a plentiful catch of fish), a scene about a meal (vv. 12–13), Peter's commissioning for pastoral duty (vv. 15–17), a prophecy of death concerning this disciple (vv. 18, 19) and a confrontation of his destiny with the one of the disciple whom Jesus loved (vv. 20–23). Considered from the literary-critical viewpoint of varied fragments are thus collected here. Yet they are all brought together into an overlapping narrative connection: the situation of time and place (Sea of Tiberias, after Jesus' death and resurrection) is maintained; those taking part (actantes) remain the same, even when the list of persons in v. 2 is subordinate; the succession of the scenes to each other makes sense although it is not without difficulties (catch of fish and meal, Peter's behaviour and that of the other disciples). From this the conclusion follows: a purposeful hand is at work; but it does not have very compliant material on which to work. The available traditions have to be made to fit the desired effect.

Already in the course of this consideration, the impression has become inescapable that the style is not that of the evangelist, who has his traditions better under control, presents them more clearly and utilizes them more ably. It is only necessary to compare the great miracle-stories which the evangelist interprets as christological σημεῖα with the miracle of the catch of fish in Jn 21, in order to realize this. This miracle remains almost a subsidiary theme in the account of the appearance, which is not thoroughly integrated with the revelation of the risen one, perhaps indicating an allegorical-symbolic feature (the 153 large fish due to which, nevertheless, the net does not tear), but it states nothing central concerning the person of Jesus. The meal-scene is strangely isolated on one side and could survive without the miraculous catch of fish (cf. v. 9); the fishing story is only bound up with it in an external and clumsy way (cf. v. 10). But there are still further threads in the story which have been woven into the first section (vv. 2–13), and then come to the fore, singled out, in the second part (vv. 15–23): the juxtaposition of Simon Peter and the beloved disciple (v. 7a), which is thematized at the end (vv. 20–22); further, Peter in his relation to Jesus. His jumping into the water (v. 7b) and his conversation with Jesus on the shore (vv. 15–17), are not directly connected with each other narratively, however they are so thematically. This note-worthy interweaving of different threads in the story, is not otherwise the evangelist's way. The question whether Chapter 21 goes back to the evangelist has still to be probed by other methods; but the different mode of narration which, for the most part, is scarcely paid attention to, should not be overlooked for this purpose.

2. The relationship of Jn 21 to Jn 20
Meaning and tendencies of the addition

The conclusion reached from vv. 1 and 14 that Jn 21 presupposes the resurrection chapter (20), can be further substantiated. In the list of names (v. 2), Simon Peter and Thomas (again with 'called the Twin' added) are named at the top. According to 20:3–10, Peter inspected the open tomb and so, as first disciple, got an idea of the extraordinary happening; Thomas, at first unbelieving, was enabled finally (20:26–29) to be convinced of the reality of Jesus' resurrection in the personal encounter with the risen one. With the naming of these two disciples, the reader is reminded of those stories. Other disciples are, indeed, added in order to prove that a new appearance is vouchsafed 'the disciples' (the circle of disciples) (cf. also 20:30, 'in the presence of the disciples'). After Chapter 20, the reader does not expect that at all; but he is also not surprised (cf. v. 30, 'many other signs') and must perceive the new appearance as a confirmation. Since this third appearance occurs in another place (in Galilee) and in different circumstances (Jesus stands at a distance on the shore), the disciples' 'not knowing' (v. 4), according to the narrator's intention may not be overrated, as if they had to be prepared and receptive for it: indeed, their 'knowing' suggests itself in the meal-scene (v. 12b). However, 21:2–13 can hardly be understood as the intended continuation by the same author who wrote Chapter 20.[1a]

The figure of Peter, who in 20:3–10 is given a not unimportant role but not any particularly personal profile, is very prominent in Chapter 21. His character is spotlighted (v. 7b) and he is invested with office (vv. 15–17); finally, the way in which he is destined to die in imitation of Jesus is disclosed and interpreted (vv. 18–19). Thus, the interest in him is resumed and taken further, and that, over and above the position at Easter, into the sphere of the Church. The case is similar with the disciple whom Jesus loved. Once again, his quick believing recognition shines out (v. 7b), and, at the end, attention is paid to him in a very special way (vv. 20–23) because of the words spoken concerning him by the risen one, and which circulated and were discussed in the Church. When attention is paid to the juxtaposition of the two disciples in 20:3–10, scarcely a doubt remains that Chapter 21 refers to it.

Finally, the meal-scene in Chapter 21, which has nothing corresponding to it, nor any point of contact in Chapter 20, needs to be considered. The motif of eating and a meal was, despite his closeness to the Lukan tradition otherwise, not important for the evangelist in his presentation of Easter; it is brought in now, if not so urgently and accentuated as in Luke (cf. Lk 24:41–43; further, 24:30f, 35). Apart from reasons from the history of tradition (see below), for the narrator of Jn 21:2–13 there will also be an intention behind it. The description in 21:13 shows, in its narrative structure, a pronounced reference to (the great feeding, cf. 6:11 and) the celebration of the Eucharist.

From these observations, these conclusions may be drawn:

1. The evangelist did not need or intend any such continuation as is found in Chapter 21, not even as 'Postscript'. After the words to Thomas (20:29) and the concluding words in 20:30f, the new appearance before the disciples has the effect of being rather unsuited and disturbing for his presentation.

2. The editors who added on 21:1–23, not only presuppose Jn 20, but consciously refer to it. They want to bring a further example of an appearance of Jesus before the disciples (vv. 1 and 14); however, they combine with it still other interests.

3. Themes of importance to the editors which they weave into the appearance in a narrative way or alternatively join on to the appearance, are: (*a*) The person, function in the Church and destiny of Peter; (*b* the person and significance of the disciple whom Jesus loved, in his relation to Peter as well; (*c*) Jesus' enduring fellowship respectively with the disciples and the Church, his presence in the Church through the eucharistic meal; (*d*) his effect on and in the Church through the pastoral office (Peter), yet likewise through that ministry

which is represented by the disciple loved by Jesus (cf. vv. 22–23); (*e*) possibly also, mission and unity of the Church (cf. the net with the 153 fish). The last three points (*c-e*) require, it is true, still be verified by the exegesis. They are mentioned here together with the others, in order to make the last and most important consequence clear:

4. The entire added chapter has been written from a pronouncedly 'ecclesiastical' point of view, from the viewpoint of the Church at the time when it was compiled. The evangelist shows, right up to his closing comment, that his concern is with the self-revelation of Jesus, in the resurrection chapter, with the crowning self-revelation of the risen one (which only takes place 'in the presence of the disciples'), as well as with the answer of faith and the gaining of salvation made possible by it (Christological-soteriological interest). The editors presuppose that and direct the evangelist's message to the Church (ecclesiastical and pastoral interest).

If that is correct, then it has to be asked how this editorial chapter is to be characterized in relation to Jn 20 and to the entire gospel: is it a 'postscript', an 'appendix', or an 'epilogue'?[2] None of these designations fully applies. It is not a postscript because there is really nothing more to be said; 'appendix' is to see it too much from an external point of view not corresponding to the inner importance given to this chapter by the editors; 'epilogue' sounds (at least in German) again too inconsiderable to be just in respect of the function intended for it. It is an ultimate editorial chapter having an explanatory function for the readers in the Church of those days. For us, it also has a certain key-position for the better understanding of the evangelist's work in its historical circum-stances;[3] for by means of it, it is recognizable that, and in what way, it is shared by a rather large circle of disciples and friends and received by the Church. If the explanation proposed in this commentary of the secondary 'farewell addresses' in Chapters 15–16 (and possibly of the prayer in Chapter 17) is correct, that namely, they are continuations and applications of the farewell address in Chapter 14 for the life of the Church(es), the analogy for the relationship of Chapter 21 to Chapter 20 forces itself upon us: in a similar way and with a similar intention the editors have worked here as there. But that does not have to mean that we are dealing with the same compilers; for, for the rest, the differences remain considerable between the shape of those addresses and the narrative material in Chapter 21.

3. Tradition- and Redaction-criticism

After the survey and characterization of the material in Jn 21:1–23 (above under 1), it is clear that within it many kinds of tradition have been taken up and re-worked. In order to recognize the traditions found by the editors and to distinguish their own work from them, an effort must be made to separate the individual layers from each other. The editors may, indeed, have proceeded in various ways: they may have taken over or partly taken over tradition (above all written) which was already laid down, and given it their own shape; or, finally, on the basis of specific traditions, shaped everything with their own hand. Correspondingly then, there are various layers to be distinguished. The attempt to do this is no waste of time, because through it, the circumstances of this chapter's (and of the entire gospel's) coming into being, can be clarified, and the age of the traditions reliably checked as well.

The top editorial layer shows itself clearly in vv. 1 and 14: the story found in between, vv. 2–13, is treated by the editors, who added on this material, as an appearance-report. But the question is whether they found the entire story as it is, or editorially re-worked a story usable by them, or perhaps combined two stories, or, finally, shaped various traditions and themes into the entity before us. The separation between tradition and what is editorial in Jn 21:2–13 is especially difficult and has not yet led to a satisfactory solution. The succeeding narrative units (vv. 15–17, 18–19, 20–23) are easier to assess, because they are not so full of internal complications. Here too, traditions are taken up which partly, for certain, go beyond the Johannine circle (vv. 15–17), partly concern the interests within it (vv. 20–23). There is scarcely any doubt as to the 'Johannine' manner of narration and the closeness to Johannine style of 21:15–23. Indeed, that is not to say that the evangelist is the narrator; it can just as well be somebody from the Johannine circle of disciples and friends. A closer ascertainment of what in the entire narrative complex is tradition and editorial, can only be undertaken in the exegesis, paying attention to the stylistic and narrative singularities. Here, only an introduction to the problem and a preliminary assessment are offered.

a. Jn 21: 1–14

R. Pesch has concerned himself in a monograph with the critical question of tradition and redaction in this section, together with Lk 5:1–11, and in this has also given a survey of research up to the present.[4] He works out a 'fishing' tradition, which he recovers in vv. 2, 3, 4a, 6, 11 (with some omissions); further, an appearance tradition for which he claims vv. 4b, 7, 8, 9, 12, 13; he regards vv. 1, 5, 10, 14 as editorial. The two traditions are woven together by the editor, not entirely successfully. The editor has incorporated the fishing miracle, which, originally, was not an Easter story, into the report of the appearance which, above all, is to be interpreted ecclesiologically. On the question why he did this, Pesch offers only a few considerations: he wanted to hand down one of the 'many other signs' of Jesus, which were not written down in the gospel (20:30). This sign suggested itself, because its exposition could be easily blended with that of the report of the appearance which was played out on the Sea of Tiberias. If the sign stood, say, in the σημεῖα-source, the editor would have wanted still to bring it into the gospel in the postscript.[5] Now, it is interesting that, independently of Pesch, R. T. Fortna too wants to crystallize out a story of a fishing miracle which he attributes to his σημεῖα-source, and wants to move it in that to an earlier position (after the healing of the official's son, 4:46–54, as 'the third sign').[6] Fortna defines the extent of the story as found, admittedly, somewhat differently. According to him, it covered vv. 2, 3, 4a, (5?), 6, 7b (in part), 8b, 10, 11, (12?), 14 ('Jesus did this as the third sign').

According to him, the main uncertainty lies in the question whether a meal was included in it (vv. 5, 10, 12a).[7]

The result of these studies is a good working basis. If we think that the story of the miraculous catch of fish looks extremely unwieldy in the present text, that vv. 1–14 wants, above all, to report an appearance of Jesus to the disciples, then the taking up and incorporation of a miracle-story which was already to hand, is, in fact, extremely plausible.

The reconstruction of the fishing story, because of the divergences between Pesch and Fortna, must, admittedly, be re-examined once again. Here, the following may be briefly said concerning the two attempts: Pesch reduces the list of persons in v. 2 to Simon Peter and the sons of Zebedee; Fortna retains all seven disciples (because the other 'Johannine' names are also otherwise found in his σημεῖα-source). According to Pesch, the editor wants to attain the number 7, which symbolizes the entire fellowship of the disciples, the Church (148). The observations he brings (90f) speak for his supposition. He may also be right about v. 5 that it is a comment of the editors connecting the two traditions (95). Peter's action in v. 7b, which Fortna wants to attribute to the source, also fits the story of the catch of fish. If the disciples were not far from the land and could not lift the net, it is understandable that Peter swims to the near shore and drags the net from there on to the land. So, with Fortna, v. 7b (without ἀκούσας ὅτι . . .) and the detail of distance in v. 8 can be reckoned to the miracle report. Pesch again assigns v. 10 to be an 'editorial link' (99). Fortna would retain the verse, bearing in mind 2: 8 (a similar exhortation) (93). The reason does not stand up due to the different situation in Cana. V. 11 originally tells how Peter comes on land and draws up the net with 153 fishes. V. 12a, the invitation to the meal, which Fortna wants to assign possibly to the fishing story, is highly questionable for the source. The theme of the meal belongs to the report of the appearance. Also beside the point is Fortna's opinion that in v. 14 one more remnant of the source is preserved (the 'third' sign); the verse clearly looks back to v 1 and is entirely editorial.

Now, what is the position with the tradition of an appearance-report, which, indeed, for the editors, is in the foreground? The exposition will have more or less coincided with the text found in vv. 2–3: some disciples have gone fishing on the Sea of Tiberias. The list of names remains uncertain; the comment that they caught nothing that night, drops out because that is the reason for the fishing miracle. When Jesus comes to the shore, the disciples do not recognize him (v. 4). Probably, the story also told that he addressed them. The saying which, in the text as we have it, clashes with v. 9, could have run differently in the report of the appearance, for instance, the invitation to come ashore and eat with him. Admittedly, that remains a suggestion, which, however, draws support from the invitation in v. 12. The meal together on the lake shore, certainly belongs to the report of the appearance (vv. 9, 12, 13), as R. Pesch also states. But against this, differently from what Pesch thinks, the scene with the disciple whom Jesus loved (v. 7), will probably only have been introduced by the Johannine editors. It contains a decidedly and exclusively Johannine concern and is important for the editors of Jn 21, also on account of vv. 15–17 (Peter) and vv. 20–23 (the disciple whom Jesus loved). Naturally, Jesus' appearance at the lake may already have been related together with that scene, early on, in Johannine circles; but the tradition of that appearance will be older. Looked at form-critically it represents a type which is similar to the Emmaus pericope: Jesus in an inconspicuous form is not recognized by the disciples at first; but, during the meal together, at which Jesus takes the lead with significant gestures, they become certain that it is their Lord.[8] In this way, too, the original story of the appearance which the Johannine circle possessed, could have ended; on account of the scene with the disciple whom Jesus loved, the editor had to change the conclusion somewhat.

This inferred appearance-story remains, admittedly, hypothetical, but explains well the tension which is set up in the text before us, between the large catch of fish and the meal prepared by Jesus (cf. vv. 9, 12f). A reason for blending the two traditions (more precisely: a story about the catch of fish taken over from the σημεῖα-source, and a, perhaps, only orally recounted appearance-story) ought to have been, as Pesch rightly saw, the similarity of the situation and individual features. But we can go still further: the narrator was primarily interested in an appearance of Jesus; by means of the large landing of fish he succeeded in showing the fullness of the risen one's power yet more emphatically. Further, it can be asked more decisively than Pesch does, whether for the narrator the large amount of fish and the net not tearing were not symbolic of the missionary ministry of the disciples[9] and of the Church's unity, exactly on the lines of the 'ecclesiological' tendency of Jn 21, which was also established by him. The editors then further brought into this the scene with the disciple loved by Jesus, because of their special intent. Perhaps, Peter's rôle too, in the Lukan story of the catch of fish (Lk 5:1–11), contributed to the inclusion; but, since according to our reconstruction of the Johannine story of the catch of fish, Peter is not here so strongly to the fore, we have to pay attention still more closely in what follows.

b. Jn 21:15–17

For this fragment, scholarship is rather agreed that some kind of connection will exist with other sayings of the Lord which grant Peter a leading position, as with the 'primacy saying' Mt 16:18f and with Lk 22:31f.[10] In Mt 16:18 the connection is the notion of the special importance of Peter for the Church (Matthew: ἡ ἐκκλησία μου; John: 'My sheep', picture of the flock); in Lk 22:31f, the care entrusted to Peter (despite his denial of Jesus) of his fellow-disciples and the Church respectively. A direct connection in the history of tradition cannot, however, be established and is, on account of the individual character in each case of these sayings directed to Peter, improbable. Rather, a common historical recollection must be supposed, which led to diverse formulations in the respective tradition.

In the perspective of history, the event which may be the origin of such Peter-traditions, can even be detailed: the first appearance (protophany) of the risen one, which the (already during Jesus' life on earth) outstanding disciple shared in. It is witnessed to in the ancient formulation of faith 1 Cor 15:3–5 (more exactly v. 5), and besides, (as if by the way), in Lk 24:34. The more recent research supposes, with good reason, as to Mt 16:18f as well, that this saying inserted by Matthew into the Caesarea Philippi scene, belongs originally to the situation at Easter.[11] But in its present place also, it is a sign of the fact that in the Matthaean Church, such a tradition led to the high estimation of Peter as the foundation of the Church and possessor of special authority. That is harder to say concerning the Simon-saying in Lk 22:31f, and we cannot here go into the problems of this logion. However, a similar proceeding can be imagined for Jn 21:15–17 as for Mt 16:18f, this time directly connected with an appearance of the risen one. The encounter with his Lord is, for Peter, bound with an important commission, which factually points in the same direction as Mt 16:18f. If the tradition reproduced in Jn 21:15–17 is so based on the protophany experienced by Peter, nevertheless, the shaping of the scene is wholly Johannine. It goes back to the triple denial and uses the picture of the flock, which was familiar and important to the evangelist (see especially Chapter 10). Whether the linguistic formulation points to the evangelist is still to be determined; but in any case, we have before us a self-sufficient tradition within the Johannine circle.

If, in accordance with these considerations, Peter's encounter with the risen one is actually the *first* appearance shared by one belonging to the circle of disciples, then this fact is obscured by the present position of the pericope. Why the evangelist keeps silent about this in Jn 20, we do not need to inquire; it may be connected with the source which the evangelist will probably have used (in part) in his resurrection chapter (q.v.). Matthew is also silent about this appearance to Peter. The editors of Jn 21 then additionally brought in the tradition, obviously because of their interest in the contrast between Simon Peter and the disciple whom Jesus loved. But in what relation does Jn 21:15–17 stand to the appearance in the presence of the disciples described in vv. 1–14? The two fragments were only combined with each other by the editors. Admittedly, they presuppose that which was related previously (cf. v. 15, πλέον τούτων); but in vv. 15–17 (and further in vv. 18–19) they present a tradition which was not originally connected with it. Hence too is explained the editorial comment in v. 14, which signifies a break. This discovery is important because then, the protophany to Peter may not be confused with the appearance in the presence of the disciples at the lake. The story, 21:2–13, comes from another tradition and does not necessarily have to have the first appearance in mind.[12] The addition of the Peter-scene in vv. 15–17 was made easier for the editors by Peter's rôle while fishing. Other disciples apart from Peter and the disciple whom Jesus loved, do not appear at all any more from v. 15.

c. Jn 21:18–19

The prophecy concerning Peter's death is nowhere echoed in the rest of the NT, but, in John's gospel, it is already prepared for by 13:36 ('you shall follow afterwards'). Admittedly, the reader does not necessarily expect an exact definition of the veiled pronouncement in the supper-room; it is offered here, obviously in the knowledge of the martyr's death which occurred in the meantime, which Peter was to suffer in 'imitation' of his Lord (cf. v. 19). This concerns a (for the Johannine circle) important matter which will also have contributed to the high estimation of Peter, although, in the Johannine church, the other disciple whom Jesus loved, is the main authority. Again, it is to be investigated in the exegesis, whether the passage comes from the evangelist or from the editors. It is also possible that the editors rely on an oral tradition of the evangelist.

d. Jn 21:20–23

Here, the special interest of the Johannine circle or Church can be grasped. V. 23 certainly presupposes the death of the disciple whom Jesus loved. We are thus being taken into the time of the Johannine Church; the saying in question of the risen one to that disciple (v. 22), which led to confusion in the Church, does not have to go back to a communication or utterance of the disciple himself, but may also have been spread in another way. In any case, this has to do with a tradition within the Johannine circle. The problem of this section is closely connected with v. 24 and must be discussed there as well as in the Excursus concerning the disciple whom Jesus loved.

4. The Origin of Jn 21

The tackling of this problem was intentionally held back to the last. It is not rare to start from an investigation of language and style; there are good works on this,[13] but they do not lead to an unequivocal result. The methodologically well conceived and careful work of M.-É. Boismard which investigates the expressions preferred by John and those which are exclusively Johannine, then hapax legomena (which he rightly distinguishes as neutral ones – dependent on the object, then those having a middle value, very unusual ones, and those of great weight), comes to the conclusion that Chapter 21, in its linguistic aspect, cannot come from the evangelist. He thinks that a disciple added it on according to the wish of his master, an anonymous editor, who was partly inspired by the evangelist's style.[14] E. Ruckstuhl disagrees with him; he points to the fact that 30 Johannine peculiarities with 13 different numbers are to be found, and seeks to refute the observations which speak against the Johannine style.[15] He has recently been followed by R. Mahoney with further word-statistical material.[16] Methodologically, all these studies criticizing the style can also be criticized. With Boismard, it is noticeable that most of his 'un-Johannine' words and usages are found in those verses which we wanted to attribute to the story of the catch of fish from the σημεῖα-source; then, they lose their power as evidence. On the other hand, the defenders of the 'Johannine style' pay too little attention to the references back to Jn 1–20 which then, naturally, contain the style of the evangelist. For Jn 21:1–14, R. Pesch has again investigated the style carefully and on the basis of this attributed specific verses to the editor (see above under 3a). Important as the criticism of style is, it alone is a too 'uncertain criterion' (R. E. Brown, 1080) for determining the origin. Yet we shall have to pay attention to it in the exegesis.

The decision about whether Chapter 21 comes from the evangelist or from somebody else, must, alongside style-criticism, also take note of many kinds of arguments as to the facts. Besides, it is necessary to differentiate: If, perhaps, not the entire narrative complex 21:1–23 originates from the evangelist, and, as such, was added on by the editors (cf. 21:24), the compiler could yet have used some material which was accessible to him through the evangelist (in writing or orally). According to our investigation up to the present, there should be no doubt: 1. A continuation is not intended by the evangelist after his account in Chapter 20 and the closing comment in 20:30f; 2. the addition of Chapter 21 goes back, in the main, to an editor; 3. the mode of presentation in 21:2–13 does not correspond to the evangelist's method elsewhere (see above under 1); 4. Chapter 21 appears, at least in vv. 1–14, to presuppose Jn 20 (see above under 2). The supposition that the evangelist *later* wanted to add Chapter 21 for whatever reason, and put together vv. 1–17 for this new purpose,[17] comes up against the objection as to why he allowed the conclusion in 20:30f to stand.

But could not the material laid out in Chapter 21 originate from the evangelist and have been added by an editor? R. Mahoney who, after observations concerning language and style does not want to recognize any other hand than that of the evangelist for Chapter 21, regards it as probable that the editors did not want to allow *older* material of the evangelist which he left aside for his gospel, to disappear, and therefore added it to the gospel.[18] This opinion seems to me difficult to maintain for the appearance at the lake, which is bound up with the large catch of fish, because the traces of the reworking, that is, the editorial 'seams' do not point to the evangelist's hand. At most, it can be considered whether the inferred report of the appearance, which bears marks of John's style, was related by him (orally) and so came to the knowledge of the editors. But that remains problematic, because it actually competes to a certain extent with Jesus' appearance before the disciples in the room (20:19–23). Such an explanation is more acceptable for the following scene with Simon Peter (vv. 15–17), which, in the way it is put together, fits in well with earlier Peter-fragments in the gospel (13:6–9, 36–38; 18:15–18, 25–27). A 'rehabilitation' of this disciple after his denial and emphasis of his 'ecclesiastical' function according to a widely current tradition (see above under 3b), can also have been in the mind of the evangelist. The same applies to the prophecy of death, vv. 18–19, which, besides, with the invitation, 'Follow me!' relates still more closely to 13:36b. From whom else should the editors have obtained this tradition? If the evangelist is not identified with the disciple whom Jesus loved, he could also spring to mind. The final fragment (21:20–23) is wrapped up still more decidedly within the problem of this disciple; increasing the difficulty, there comes to it that, with the saying handed down (v. 22a), is bound up the thought of the parousia which is foreign to the evangelist. Here, surely, everything rather speaks for the origin being from the editors.

Looked at on the whole, the origin of 21:1–23 as being from the evangelist, cannot be defended. At most, the editors who are here at work, could have received some traditions from him (and then, presumably orally). The putting together and adding on of this chapter is the more to be attributed to them, as a positive reason can be recognized for their procedure. Their interest was directed to the Church, its inner life, its situation, its questions; a Church which is influenced by the special 'Johannine' tradition and yet does not live wholly removed from the rest of Christianity.

Exegesis
1. Jesus' Appearance by the Sea of Tiberias (21:1–14)

[1]*After this Jesus revealed himself again to the disciples by the Sea of Tiberias; and he revealed himself in this way.* [2]*Simon Peter, Thomas called the Twin, Nathanael of Cana in Galilee, the sons of Zebedee, and two others of his disciples were together.* [3]*Simon Peter said to them, 'I am going fishing.' They said to him, 'We will go with you'. They went out and got into the boat; but that night they caught nothing.* [4]*Just as day was breaking, Jesus stood on the beach; yet the disciples did not know that it was Jesus.* [5]*Jesus said to them, 'Children, have you any fish?' They answered him, 'No'.* [6]*He said to them, 'Cast the net on the right side of the boat, and you will find some.' So they cast it, and now they were not able to haul it in, for the quantity of fish.* [7]*That disciple whom Jesus loved said to Peter, 'It is the Lord!' When Simon Peter heard that it was the Lord, he put on his clothes, for he was stripped for work, and sprange into the sea.* [8]*But the other disciples came in the boat (for they were not far from the land, but about a hundred yards off), dragging the net full of fish.* [9]*When they got out on land, they saw a charcoal fire there, with fish lying on it, and bread.* [10]*Jesus said to them, 'Bring some of the fish that you have just caught.'* [11]*So Simon Peter went aboard and hauled the net ashore, full of large fish, 153 of them; and although there were so many, the net was not torn.* [12]*Jesus said to them, 'Come and have breakfast.' Now none of the disciples dared ask him, 'Who are you?' They knew it was the Lord.* [13]*Jesus came and took the bread and gave it to them, and so with the fish.* [14]*This was now the third time that Jesus was revealed to the disciples after he was raised from the dead.*

21:1 With the general, in John frequent, formula μετὰ ταῦτα (cf. on 6:1), the writer of this section draws attention to a new (πάλιν) appearance of Jesus to the disciples. He designates it as a 'self-revelation' of Jesus, certainly an expression fitting John's thought (and the theological reflection nowadays concerning Jesus' resurrection). Only it is to be asked whether the reflective φανεροῦν indicates the hand of the evangelist or that of an editor. The word is relatively frequent with John (Jn: 9 times; 1 Jn: 9 times; in the rest of the NT: 31 times, of which 22 times in the Pauline writings), yet it is not used otherwise for the resurrection of Jesus (cf. against this 14:22, ἐμφανίζειν). The repetition in v. 1b and v. 14 points rather to a linguistic usage of the editors.[19] Other observations of style also do not contradict this, neither 'Jesus' without the article[20] (cf. on 20:24), nor πάλιν which is put here not only as a link. The designation of the Lake of Galilee as the 'Sea of Tiberias' is even an indication for the language of the editors, if the observations on 6:1 are correct (see Vol. 2, p. 13). Also the short sentence in v. 1b with the *forward-pointing* οὕτως does not sound like the style of the evangelist, who always immediately (possibly after determination of time and place) begins with the narrative. The whole verse makes the effect of an announcement of a theme, and this impression is strengthened by the corresponding closing comment in v. 14. The concern is with a new appearance of Jesus; the miraculous catch of fish connected with this is not what is most important. The detail 'by the Sea of Tiberias', is also necessary for the report of the appearance, because Jesus then stands on the shore, unknown.

21:2 Only now the story begins, stylistically correct, with the introduction of the persons taking part (cf. 3:1; 5:5; 11:1; 12:20). ὁμοῦ is used here as in Acts 2:1 signifying place, different from Jn 4:36; 20:4. Partitive ἐκ, characteristic for John, but with numerical terms also not unusual elsewhere,[21] does not necessarily require the hand of the evangelist. The list of persons' names, apart from Simon Peter (the normal double name in John), gives two who only appear in John's gospel: Thomas called 'the Twin' (as 11:16; 20:24), and Nathanael (1:45–49), but only here with the indication of origin, 'of Cana in Galilee';[22] then, curiously 'the (sons) of Zebedee', who are not otherwise mentioned in John's gospel; and two more unnamed disciples. This list has led to some speculation.

Above all, it was sought to identify the 'disciple whom Jesus loved' (v. 7) with one of the disciples. Can he be made to coincide with John the son of Zebedee, on the basis of this passage? But why then is he not introduced with the Johannine description? Or is he meant to be hidden behind one of the unnamed disciples? But why then is he accommodated so insignificantly at the end? Such attempts start from false presuppositions. The list of persons has another purpose and hardly reflects on the identity of that disciple. A taking over of the whole list from the source (cf. Fortna) is improbable, because typically Johannine identifications of persons are combined with non-Johannine ones. So Pesch ought to be right, that the narrator supplemented details from his source. He considers that Peter and the sons of Zebedee were in the source; the editors would have brought in Thomas, Nathanael and the two other disciples (they are editorial on account of αὐτοῦ which refers to v. 1) (op. cit., 91). That is plausible even if not strictly provable. We can wonder that with (or instead of) Nathanael, Andrew is not named (cf. 1:40; 6:8; 12:22) and/or Philip (cf. 1:44ff; 6:5, 7; 12:21f; 14:8f). But, perhaps the editor wanted least to leave a place open for the disciple whom Jesus loved, with the 'two others of his disciples'.

If we follow the notion that an editor from Johannine circles made additions, the reason for Thomas is easy to find: he wanted, in this way, to make a connection to the Thomas-story (20:24–29). With Nathanael, it can be surmised that he wanted to remind the reader of his confession (1:49), which stands at the beginning of the gospel as Thomas's does at the end. The list is not without ulterior motive; it has, at this point, a narrative function for the reader: it brings into his view the earthly circle of disciples, and shows him its continuing significance after Easter, on the basis of an appearance of the risen one. Therefore, the number 7 (the number of fullness in Semitic thought), can have a symbolic value: this group of disciples represents the future community, the Church (cf. also the seven churches in Rev 2–3).

21:3   Peter's decision to go fishing and the other disciples' willingness to join him, give rise to the impression, in this post-Easter situation, that these men are returning to their accustomed trade, because they know nothing of Jesus' resurrection and the commission of preaching and mission. It is true that the editor who, indeed, looks back to the appearances of Jesus in Jn 20 (cf. v. 14), did not understand it in this way; for him it is only the introduction to the subsequently reported event. But in the light of historical criticism compared with the presentation of the other evangelists (to the closing scene in Mt 28:16–20 on the mountain in Galilee, and, especially, to Luke according to whom the disciples stayed in Jerusalem), this Johannine appearance report scarcely fits into a plausible sequence of the events. Some suppose that parts of it contain ancient, indeed, the most ancient tradition which is only obscured by editorial reworking and arrangement.[23] We cannot here enter into the difficult problems as to how the disciples behaved after Jesus' death, whether they stayed in Jerusalem or returned to Galilee, etc.[24] Staying with the text, it is to be said about v. 3 that, to begin with, it is the introduction to the miracle of the catch of fish, as the closing sentence, which cannot be detached, shows: 'But that night they caught nothing.' The expectation aroused in the reader that he will hear something of their catch, by Peter's declaration, 'I am going fishing', the concurrence of the other disciples' 'we will go with you', and by the boarding of the boat, is fulfilled by the closing sentence which, admittedly, also arouses new tension: What now? The beginning of the appearance report did not need to tell (or not so 'dramatically') about the *setting off* to fish, but could have been satisfied with the situation that the disciples were fishing, a little distant from the land, when they saw Jesus on the shore. But the introduction to the appearance-report is, obviously on account of the miracle-story which has been taken over, broken off. That is also confirmed by the fact that in v. 3 no special Johannine peculiarities of style are to be found.

The double name 'Simon Peter' is only to be expected with a narrator from Johannine circles. πλοῖον and πλοιάριον also alternate in Lk 5 and Jn 6 (cf. Vol. 2, p. 33). Instead of σύν (12:2; 18:1) the evangelist very much prefers μετὰ with the genitive. The historic οὖν is lacking (it has been introduced in some mss. after ἐξῆλθον). πιάζω is indeed a favourite Johannine word (outside Chapter 21, 6 times, but always in reference to Jesus); but it is attested for catching animals, especially fish (P. London II, p. 328, 76 in BauerWb sv). In contrast to this passage, John usually uses the double negative οὐκ . . . οὐδὲν (cf. 3:27; 5:19, 30; 6:63; 9:33; 11:49; 12:19; 14:30; 15:5; 16:23f).

21:4   Since the story of the unsuccessful fishing during that night arouses tension (see above), what follows is fittingly joined on with δέ. In the morning (πρωΐα only found again in Mt 27:1) Jesus came to the shore (αἰγιαλὸς only here in John). The sentence is indispensable for the story of the catch of fish, more precisely, for Jesus' exhortation to cast the net on the right side, but will have also introduced either in this way or similarly, the appearance report. The comment in v. 4b only makes sense in respect of this. It corresponds, except for the numerus, with the comment in 20:14 at Mary Magdalene's encounter with Jesus. Besides, μέντοι is a criterion of John's style (Ruckstuhl, No. 26), although we do not necessarily, on this account, have to conclude to the hand of the evangelist.

An author's linguistic traits can also be transferred to those around him. That is as much true of this adversative particle as also of the historic οὖν which occurs in vv. 5, 6, 7 (twice), 9, 11 (v. 1.). An 'inimitable' linguistic singularity fo the evangelist is not found in vv. 1–14, so far as we are not concerned with things taken up from the text of the gospel (e.g.: 'The disciple whom Jesus loved').

The situation in the early morning[25] may be presupposed for both stories. R. Pesch thinks, in fact, that, for the report of the appearance, the evening is originally to be postulated;[26] but, although otherwise the appearances of the risen one, which are associated with a meal, take place in the evening, this does not have to be the case also with this special encounter with the disciples at the lake. The appearance to Mary Magdalene which is related by means of the recognition of the, at first, unknown one, likewise, occurs in the morning. At most, the evening is suggested because of the implication of the eucharistic meal (cf. v. 13).

21:5 Jesus' words establish contact with the disciples on the lake. Noteworthy is the form of address παιδία, which, otherwise, only occurs in 1 Jn (2:13, 18; 3:7 v.l.), a familiar form of address which belongs to the 'special vocabulary' of the Johannine community. It is intended to attract the disciples' attention; but only the disciple whom Jesus loved recognizes him: 'It is the Lord' (v. 7). The appearance story could have been told in this way in the Johannine circles. The adopted tradition reported, perhaps, the disciples' slowness in recognizing the 'stranger' (cf. the Emmaus story). Because of the intermingling of the story of the catch of fish, the link between v. 5a and v. 7 is broken, indeed, the impression (originally, scarcely intended) is given that the disciple beloved by Jesus recognizes the Lord only on the basis of the miracle.

Jesus' question, 'Have you any fish?' expects a negative answer,[27] thus leading to the disciples' reply. Only here in NT is found προσφάγιον, actually 'trimmings', but which (with 'bread') can also mean simply 'fish'.[28] It looks as if the man on the shore wants fish trimmings for the meal which he is preparing; but according to v. 9, 'fish' (ὀψάριον) is already lying on the fire. This inconsistency is most easily explained by supposing that the editor wants to connect the story of the catch of fish and the report of the appearance (to which the meal belongs).[29] For the account of the appearance, another saying of Jesus would be more appropriate, something like an invitation to come ashore and to have a meal with him (cf. the Introduction). Only a distant echo can be heard in the present choice of words of Lk 24:41 ('have you anything here to eat?').

21:6 The following description of how the disciples cast the net on the right side, according to Jesus' words, and are then no longer able, because of the quantity of fish, to pull it in, is taken wholly from the story of the catch of fish. This is clearly to be seen both from the language and narratively too. Instead of λέγει οὖν (vv. 5, 7) we now have ὁ δὲ εἶπεν (but cf. 4:32; 20:25); ἰσχύειν (for δύνασθαι) and ἀπό in the sense of 'on account of, as a result of' instead of διά with the accusative, are non-Johannine; πλῆθος is only found again in 5:3 (σημεῖα - source). The narrative style fits well to the miracle-story: words of the miracle-worker – execution – effect from which the miracle is established, briefly and understandably described. The cast on the right side (the side of good fortune), the quantity of the fish caught in the net (cf. v. 11: 153 large fish), the impossibility of hauling it in (ἑλκύειν[30]) in order, that is, to throw them out into the boat: all presupposes a rather large net.[31]

For the rest, the account does not coincide with Lk 5. There, several nets are spoken of which then threaten to break (vv. 5f). Besides, Peter and his companions have gone far out on to the lake (εἰς τὸ βάθος v. 4), and those fishing with him rush in another boat to help Peter. Both boats are filled with the fish so that they float deep in the water (v. 7). Thus, in the miracle story taken up in Jn 21 we are dealing with a variant: the disciples are not far from the shore, catch with a single net which, however, they cannot haul aboard. They drag it behind them (σύροντες v. 8), and Peter then hauls it on land from the shore. Since he is in a position with a firm footing, this is no contradiction to the diciples' inability to lift the net into the rocking boat. The miraculously large catch of fish is demonstrated differently.[32]

21:7   The interlude with the disciple whom Jesus loved and with Simon Peter, fits well neither into the miracle story (cf. on v. 5) nor in the appearance report. That disciple's recognition has affected the description in v. 12. During the scene with the meal, the disciples obviously want to ask: 'Who are you?', but they dare not because they know: 'It is the Lord' – the same sentence as in v. 7. Why the peculiarly restrained manner of expression in v. 12? Were the disciples not so sure after all, that it was the Lord? We have to presume that, originally, the appearance story showed how the disciples became certain during the meal that it is the Lord. But that was no longer possible after the scene in v. 7; the disciple's recognition changed the course of the narrative. That also applies to the story of the catch of fish; for in it, it was certainly told concerning Peter that out of consideration for his Lord standing on the shore, he swam to the shore clothed and, from there, hauled the full net on land (vv. 7b, 8b, 11). Because of the inserted scene regarding the disciple whom Jesus loved, his behaviour receives a different accent: he jumps into the water to be with the Lord as quickly as possible. The other disciples follow with the boat and drag the net with the fish (v. 8a, c). A consequence of this changed motivation as of vv. 9 and 10 (slipped in for other reasons), is an obscuring of the meaning of v. 11: what does ἀνέβη mean after the disciples have already touched land? (see ad loc.). So we cannot avoid the conclusion that the editors themselves brought in the scene with the disciple whom Jesus loved.

The editors' interest is easily recognized: as with the inspection of the tomb (20:8), that disciple (ἐκεῖνος points to one already mentioned[33]) is meant to be brought to the forefront as the one immediately recognizing Jesus. In this respect he surpasses Peter, and that is important for the compiler of Chapter 21, in his further presentation also, that is, in the contrasting of the two

disciples in vv. 20–22, and for the special rôle which falls to that disciple
(vv. 22–23: he is 'to remain'). But Simon Peter too is not drawn unsympa-
thetically: as soon as he hears that it is the Lord, he throws himself into the lake
so as still to reach him before the disciples. This intention of the editor can be
determined from the following features: the behaviour of the other disciples
who follow in the boat (v. 8a) set off in relief against that of Peter; they concern
themselves with the net (8c) – the narrator seems to indicate with this that Peter
has better things in mind. Also, the putting on of the outer garment which he
wore around his naked body[34] – in itself an understandable feature for the
fishing story too[35] – is given a new accent by it: he feels he must reach his Lord
standing on the shore, quickly. Finally, this interpretation is confirmed by
Jesus' question in v. 15: 'Do you love me *more* than these?' Through the new
motivation that Peter, on the basis of that disciple's assertion, immediately
(ἀκούσας temporal and causal) jumps into the water, this disciple too is given a
special profile which is important to the narrator for vv. 15–17.

21:8   With that, the direction is indicated for the explanation of this more
external description. The comment about the other disciples (v. 8a) will come
from the editor who also supplemented the list in v. 2, and, syntactically, the
last part of the verse (σύροντες κτλ.), best follows it. The middle section can only
be regarded as a parenthesis in the present word-order; but it can be added on
to the end of v. 7 without difficulty. Objectively it gives the reason (γάρ) in the
fishing story why Peter jumps into the water: it is no longer far from the shore
only still about a hundred yards.[36] The plural need to disturb us as it was
already previously present in the source (v. 6b). For the dragging of the net
which the men could not haul in (ἑλκύειν), the editor uses the verb σύρειν which is
well-suited to express their exhausting effort.[37] Noteworthy is the addition τῶν
ἰχθύων, which is possibly meant to remind of the quantity of fish (v. 6), but,
according to the above interpretation, also indicates that the other disciples are
only busying themselves with the fish.

21:9–10   The following scene is prematurely 'faded in' to the story of the catch
of fish; for in it, the men in the boat certainly do not go before Peter to the land.
The editor was interested to connect the plentiful catch with the meal which
was described in the appearance report. Some of the fish just caught were to
form part of the meal (v. 10). The appropriate invitation by Jesus clashes with
the description of the meal already prepared on the charcoal fire; for over the
fire 'fish' (ὀψάριον) is already being grilled. The singular without the article
possibly originally had a generic meaning (as also ἄρτον). Probably, when
adding v. 10, the editor understood it numerically: *one* fish, so that several
more fish from the present haul of fish, are required for the meal (there are,
after all, seven men). With that, the editor has attained a certain balance,
which, however, covers his editorial 'seam' in v. 10 only with difficulty.
  Some linguistic considerations support this judgement of the two verses. The
composite ἀπέβησαν expressly says that the men 'got out'. It is hard to imagine,
with the story of the catch, that they leave the boat without bothering about the

net (Peter only afterwards hauls it on to land, v. 11). However, with the report of the appearance, the description fits excellently in v. 9: until now, the occupants of the boat have not seen the charcoal fire on the shore at all; only when they get out do they notice it. The, at first, strange expression that they saw a charcoal fire 'lying there' ($\varkappa\varepsilon\iota\mu\acute{\varepsilon}\nu\eta\nu^{38}$), becomes clear from the situation: the glowing charcoal (cf. on 18:18) lies on the ground, on it fish and beside it bread. In the boat, that was still hidden from their view. Apart from the historic οὖν, Johannine style does not obtrude; if ἀνθρακιά only occurs again in NT in Jn 18:18, that scarcely means anything. V. 10 begins with the usual Johannine expression λέγει αὐτοῖς ὁ Ἰ. (the article is lacking in many mss.), but then surprises with the rare perfect imperative ἐνέγκατε and the partitive ἀπό. On the imperative of φέρω cf. 2:8 (φέρετε); 20:27 (twice φέρε); for partitive 'from' John regularly says ἐκ. On this account a text from the source does not have to be supposed (cf. Fortna 93), but the evangelist is indeed to be ruled out as the author. The editor who followed the appearance in v. 9, and himself put together v. 10 is recognizable.

21:11　Peter's action belongs to the story of the fishing; in it ἀνέβη means that he got out on to the shore (see above), whereas in the present context it is unclear.[39] The information that there were 153 large fish in the net and the net, nevertheless, did not tear, was thus certainly already found in the miracle account. In it, it was the confirmation of the great miracle, similarly as, with the great feeding, the statement that the disciples filled twelve baskets with the fragments remaining over (6:13). With the editor of Jn 21, however, the question is inescapable whether he combined with it a special, symbolic meaning; the number 153 has already aroused interest from the earliest times, but received differing interpretations.

Here I can only summarize the most important opinions. Two interpretations have become famous from ancient times:

1. Jerome, in his commentary on Ezek 47:6–12, refers to Greek zoologists who, allegedly, reckon there to be 153 different kind of fish; thus, it would be the number of fullness.[40]

2. Augustine gives a mathematical-symbolic explanation: if the numbers 1 to 17 are added together, the resulting sum is 153. In this sequence he also perceives a deeper meaning ('millia sanctorum ad gratiam Spiritus pertinentium').[41]

3. Together with this, Augustine already goes on to allegorical interpretation (3 times 50, plus 3 as symbol of the trinity), which was popular with other Church Fathers and in the middle ages. Cyril of Alexandria, for example, interprets 100 as the total of the Gentiles, 50 as the remnant of Israel, 3 as the Trinity.[42]

4. In modern times, gematria has been brought into play, that is, the replacement of a name by the corresponding numerical values of the letters (both in Hebrew and in Greek). Some scholars refer to Ezek 47:10 (a similar situation: fishermen will stand beside the sea; from Engedi to Eneglaim it will be a place for the spreading of nets'),[43] others calculate a mysterious expression like 'Church of love'.[44] All these attempts can be criticized. Jerome's assertion assumes that this was a widely held zoological viewpoint, and that does not apply, at least in Judaism. The mathematical-symbolic explanations appear arbitrary, and this is true, to a still greater degree, of the allegorical

interpretations. Likewise, gematria suffers from great uncertainty, although the procedure itself was widespread in ancient times (cf. the famous mysterious number in Rev 13:18).

5. Unbiased exegetes surmise an exact information, sometimes referring to an eye-witness.[45] That may be correct to the extent that this number was mentioned in the source; however, for the editor it can also have taken on a symbolic meaning.

In any case, the quantity of fish is justification for the supposition that the editors saw in it a symbol of universality. That lies within the 'ecclesiastical' perspective of the whole chapter, but also finds enough support in Jn 1–20. The picture of the flock in 21:15–17 directs our attention back to 10:16, where, likewise, mission and church unity are thought of together (see *ad loc.*). Some exegetes even treat 10:16 as an editorial addition to the shepherd saying; then, the same concern of the editors would break through. Passages like 7:35; 11:52; 12:20–24 have a similar point of view. The net in which the fish are *gathered* can even illustrate well the idea of 11:52 (gathering of God's scattered children). The missionary tendency which Luke connects with the large catch of fish (5:10: 'Henceforth you will be catching men'). is, it is true, not recognizable in the story of the catch of fish in Jn 21. The Johannine editor does not have in mind, like Luke, the missionary ministry of Peter (and the other disciples); for him the net becomes a symbol of the universal Church which has come about as the fruit of Jesus' ministry (cf. 12:24, 32). The unity of the believers is one of the great objects of Christ's prayer in Jn 17; we regarded the contemplation of the later believers (vv. 20f) as an editorial addition. All that gives the suggested symbolism in 21:11 a broader basis.

21:12   With an invitation, introduced in the same terms as vv. 5 and 10, the meal scene follows, taken over by the editor from the appearance report. The story of the catch of fish reached a fitting conclusion with v. 11; only the editorial v. 10 wrongly leads to the assumption that it too ended in a meal. For the appearance report, however, only the meal brings the climax.

The *style* partly corresponds to that of the evangelist: the unusual separation of words οὐδεὶς . . . τῶν μαθητῶν is, according to Ruckstuhl, a Johannine criterion of style;[46] he points to the analogous case 7:44. Also, σὺ τίς εἶ has a Johannine ring; cf. 1:19; 8:25; further σύ frequently placed first. Against can be adduced: after οὐδεὶς the partitive ἐκ follows in the gospel (7:19; 16:5; 17:12); alternatively, very similar to our passage, 13:28; however, this passage is presumably editorial. τολμᾶν and ἐξετάζειν (for which ἐρωτᾶν is available, cf. especially 5:12; 9:15 and frequently; 16:5, 19, 23, 30) are found only here in John's gospel. The last term after εἰδότες decides nothing, because it takes up v. 7 again. We shall best do justice to this finding of stylistic criticism if an editor from the Johannine circle is supposed.

Jesus invites the disciples to a meal. δεῦτε is similarly found in 4:29; ἀριστήσατε does not have to refer to an early meal (cf. Lk 11:37),[47] that results here from the situation. Whether originally, the appearance report mentioned a morning or an evening meal, cannot be definitely stated (see above). While up till now, the disciples appeared as the active ones, attention is now drawn to Jesus' activity. The following comment also, that none dared 'to ask' him because they knew it to be the Lord, guides the attention narratively towards what Jesus does in v. 12. The peculiar tension which is found between the disciples wanting-to-ask and their knowledge, is due to the editor who had to keep in mind the statement of the disciple whom Jesus loved (see above on v. 7). In this way, once again, the words ring out: 'It is the Lord', which, at the same time, is a signal to the reader that he should grasp what follows in its deeper meaning. It can also be said v. 13 is the Lord's answer to the questions which his disciples did not dare to put in v. 12.[48]

21:13   The events of the meal are told in simple words. Three verbs describe Jesus' actions: He goes – takes the bread – gives bread and fish. There is no mention of a conversation, not even of the disciples' eating. It is clear: Jesus, the host, is absolutely central; his gestures speak for themselves, and the disciples know: It is the Lord. But the brief 'narrative' structure is thought-provoking: what Jesus does has a special meaning at this time after he is risen. The Lord's taking an Easter meal with the disciples is also witnessed to in another tradition (Lk 24:30; cf. Acts 10:41). The reader of John's gospel must have preserved a recollection of 6:11: At the great feeding of the people Jesus' action is described very similarly, admittedly, the prayer of blessing is also mentioned ($\varepsilon\dot{\nu}\chi\alpha\rho\iota\sigma\tau\acute{\eta}\sigma\alpha\varsigma$). Since it is not mentioned in 21:13, that could be an indication against the eucharistic understanding. In fact, one may not immediately, and as the most important thing, read it into the passage. It is first to be said that the fellowship of the earthly Jesus with his disciples is continued after Easter, in a similar and yet in a new way. That is what the underlying appearance report probably intends, and that also corresponds to the Johannine theology (14:18–23).

If the whole added Chapter 21 is slanted towards the later Church in its situation, an allusion to the celebration of the Eucharist is probable.[48a] We do not know much directly, about the early gatherings for the meal, of primitive Christian fellowships, specifically those of Johannine Christians. When we think of the strong eucharistic interest in Ignatius of Antioch and Justin then the conclusion suggests itself that the Johannine community too, which is to be located not far from the Syrian area, celebrated Eucharist. In John's gospel itself the 'eucharistic' section (6:53–58) is a witness which cannot be overlooked, and a further notable piece of evidence results if the term in 6:23 $\varepsilon\dot{\nu}\chi\alpha\rho\iota\sigma\tau\acute{\eta}\sigma\alpha\nu\tau\sigma\varsigma$ $\tau\sigma\tilde{\nu}$ $\varkappa\nu\rho\acute{\iota}\sigma\nu$ is an editorial addition or an early gloss based on an eucharistic interpretation of the great feeding (cf. Vol. 2, pp. 10ff and 33ff).

Through the connection with the story of the catch of fish, the Lord's 'giving' is again underlined and deepened in its meaning. The Lord's gifts come out of the fulness of his power and love; not bread and fish, that which is necessary for earthly life, satisfaction of appetite (cf. 6:26), are the most important in what the Lord has to give, but the fellowship with him resulting through it, and the divine life which he grants. In this connection, he always reveals himself to his faithful fellowship anew.

21:14   Hence the editors close this ambiguous and thoughtful report of the appearance of Jesus by the Sea of Tiberias, and set it within the gospel before us as the third self-revelation of the risen one. 'Raised *from the dead*' the evangelist already said (cf. 2:22; 12:9, 17; 20:9). But the appearance to the disciples of that day becomes, still more than the two previously related, a revelation to the whole later fellowship of disciples.

2.   The Risen One and Simon Peter (21:15–19)

¹⁵*When they had finished breakfast, Jesus said to Simon Peter, 'Simon, (son) of John, do you love me more than these?' He said to him, 'Yes, Lord; you know that I love you.' He said to him, 'Feed my lambs.'* ¹⁶*A second time he said to him, 'Simon, (son) of John, do you love me?' He said to him, 'Yes, Lord; you know that I love you'. He said to him, 'Tend my sheep.'* ¹⁷*He said to him the third time, 'Simon, (son) of John, do you love me?' Peter was grieved because he said to him the third time, 'Do you love me? And he said to him, 'Lord, you know everything; you know that I love you.' Jesus said to him, 'Feed my sheep.* ¹⁸*Truly, truly I say to you, when you were young, you girded yourself and walked where you would; but when you are old, you will stretch out your hands, and another will gird you and carry you where you do not wish to go.'* ¹⁹ *(This he said to show by what death he was to glorify God.) And after this he said to him, 'Follow me.'*

Following Jesus' appearance to the disciples, a significant conversation of the risen one with Peter is now narrated. The fragment is only loosely connected with that appearance report and appeared to us independent of it from the viewpoint of the history of tradition (see the introduction to Jn 21). R. E. Brown's specific connection with Lk 5:8 ('I am a sinful man') and 5:10 ('henceforth you will be catching men')[49] is extremely questionable; for it is by no means certain that Peter's exclamation in view of the enormous catch of fish has anything to do with his failure, the thrice-repeated denial of Jesus,[50] and the call to missionary activity is, again, not recognizable in Jn 21. The exhortation 'follow me' (v. 19) is in another context (following in death) which is explained by Jn 13:36f. We therefore do not seek help in interpretation from the Lukan story of the catch of fish (calling of the disciples, call to mission) but instead will try to understand the Johannine scene from the internal conditions of the Johannine school. That, admittedly, does not rule out that a widely current tradition of a (first) appearance of Jesus to Peter and of him being granted primacy, was taken up and reworked; rather this is the more to be supposed as the Johannine circles are mainly interested in that other disciple whom Jesus loved. Hence, the taking over of the Peter tradition in Jn 21 requires an explanation. It is most noteworthy, therefore, that Jesus' conversation with Peter in vv. 20–22 goes further and directs itself to that disciple. That is an unmistakable interest of the Johannine editors and so the preceding words to Peter may not be separated from the writer's understanding of it. However, a separate discussion is justified because vv. 15–19 also form a self-

sufficient narrative unit and a new editorial starting-point is identifiable with
ἐπιστραφείς (v. 20).

The description is, in its narrative mode, choice of words and style, wholly
Johannine in character. Where else is the *love* of the disciples or a disciple
respectively, for Jesus, spoken of in this emphatic way? Where else by symbolic
allusions (the thrice-repeated question which recalls the triple denial; the
'girding' by another as an indication of the kind of death) is a deeper meaning
suggested? The reader, who is meant to recognize it, receives for this purpose –
also typically Johannine – some aids to comprehension: Peter's 'grief' at Jesus'
third time of asking (v. 17) strengthens the reference to the denial from a
narrative viewpoint, and the metaphor in v. 18 is made apparent to the reader
by an explanation in v. 19. That is a Johannine mode of presentation; to this
come verbal points of contact which are peculiar to John: to love – feeding of
the sheep – Jesus' knowledge. But for the interpretation, the assessment of the
style also carries weight: do the alternating words for 'to love', 'to feed', 'sheep'
have a significance as to content, do they draw attention to fine but not
unimportant differences, or do they only serve as stylistic variation? According
to my observations to the present, the second is more likely from the beginning;
for vv. 15–17 there is the additional fact that the narrator intentionally wants to
present in a 'stereotyped' way a threefold question and answer because that
brings about the deep connection with the triple denial by Peter, and yet,
probably, through the choice of words, he wants to bring in variety and colour.
This suggestion, must admittedly be tested by means of an examination of the
vocabulary chosen.

Finally, the reference back to the existing gospel is to be noted throughout.
That applies to the person of Simon Peter including his being addressed as
'Simon son of John', to the picture of the flock ('*my* sheep'), to Jesus'
knowledge and the idea of following Jesus even to death. Such reference back
is possible and close at hand, as for the evangelist, as for Johannine editors. If
21:1–14 comes from an editor, there is a presumption that he also put together vv. 15–19.

21:15   The narrator goes back to v. 12 via v. 14. οὖν serves for the taking up
again of the thread of the narrative as in 4:44; 6:24; 11:3; 13:30, where, after
editorial digression, it fulfils a similar function. A further link between the two
sections is πλέον τούτων; the μαθηταί who are mentioned six times (in the plural)
in vv. 1–14 and who again make their appearance in τούτων,[51] are not found at
all any more in what follows. In a narrative sense, they contrast with Simon
Peter; it may be said: vv. 1–14 were a disciple-pericope, vv. 15–19 are a Peter-
fragment. The question itself, looked at on its own, seems odd because, in the
synoptics, Jesus does not tolerate any rivalry between the disciples (cf. Mk
9:34f; 10:42ff par.) and in John this special love is for the nameless disciple who
lay at his breast. Strictly speaking, he should be included under τούτων. Yet
such reflections not only misunderstand the literary function of the
formulation,[52] but also the viewpoint of the narrator who had already

contrasted in vv. 7b–8 Peter's rushing to Jesus with the behaviour of the 'other disciples' (q.v.). The question as to 'more' ($\pi\lambda\acute{e}ov$[53]) love probably connects up with the declared readiness of Peter to lay down his life for Jesus (13:37). Jesus had doubted this in the supper-room and foretold Peter the triple denial (13:38). When the risen one now asks again, asks, in total, three times, Peter must have felt himself reminded of that saying of Jesus and the prophecy of his denial, as his grief at the third time of asking confirms. In the Johannine passion story there was no mention of such a 'reminder' of Peter, in contrast to the synoptics (Mk 14:72 par.). Perhaps that is an indication that the evangelist had originally planned on Peter's post-Easter encounter with Jesus; for only in this way is the story with Peter really told to an end. Admittedly, this was not necessary for the evangelist; but it is understandable that the Johannine circle (perhaps following the oral tradition of the evangelist?) wanted to do this. Now Jesus accepts Peter's readiness and challenges him: 'Follow me.'

So the tendency to 'rehabilitate' Peter, after his triple denial, in the encounter with the risen one, is hardly to be doubted. But this notion accepted by most exegetes is still in need of precision. It is not only a matter of exhibiting the pardon granted Peter by Jesus; over and above that, the scene expresses two important data of the Peter-story: his entrusting with the pastoral ministry and his death as a follower of Jesus. Out of sheer generosity and the power of disposition the risen one assigns an extraordinary duty to the disciple who has humanly failed. He repeats his prophecy of death (13:36) yet now, as a distinction: the disciple who has surrendered all pride and self-will is permitted, and is to follow him. The risen one not only 'rehabilitates' Peter but also makes him into another man whom he instals as an official and personal follower. So the Peter-scene of Jn 21 opens up the new horizon brought about by Easter.

Hence the dialogue between Jesus and Simon Peter must be understood and interpreted, in the individual questions also, debated by exegetes. Why does the risen one address Simon Peter, who at first is introduced with this double name usual with John, as 'Simon (son) of John'? The adoption of an older tradition is to be ruled out because the father's name 'John'[54] is restricted to our gospel (and the *Gospel to the Heb* 9). The same address, only with the express addition 'the son', is found again only in 1:42, where Jesus announces to the disciple his descriptive nickname Cephas ('the rock'). An attentive reader must have felt himself reminded of this and this may have been intended: at the beginning of the gospel the disciple's exalted role is indicated by the nickname, and at the end it is made clear by the words of the risen one, admittedly, without reference back to the symbolism contained in 'Cephas'. Thus, a cool attitude of Jesus cannot be read out from the form of address.[55] Likewise, all explanations which have their starting-point in the different significance of $\dot{a}\gamma a\pi\tilde{a}v$ and $\phi\iota\lambda\epsilon\tilde{\iota}v$,[56] cannot convince. Why does Jesus use $\dot{a}\gamma a\pi\tilde{a}v$ on the first two occasions when he puts the question, and on the third $\phi\iota\lambda\epsilon\tilde{\iota}v$? Is Peter grieved because Jesus asks: $\phi\iota\lambda\epsilon\tilde{\iota}\varsigma\mu\epsilon$ on the third occasion, or because he asks *for* the third time (v. 17) concerning his love? Peter always answers: $\phi\iota\lambda\tilde{\omega}$ $\sigma\epsilon$, and each time he is commissioned to feed Jesus' lambs or sheep respectively. Certainly, $\phi\iota\lambda\epsilon\tilde{\iota}v$ is used in Jn 11:3, 36 for Jesus' love, as a friend, for Lazarus; and that φιλεῖν is more appropriate in the mouth of Peter (emotional love),[57] *can* be due to the feeling for language; but it is artificial to read a distinction into Jesus' questions. The two verbs are also used elsewhere in John's gospel synonymously.[58]

Jesus' answer, the commission to feed his lambs, also poses questions because of the choice of words. Are we to make a distinction between βόσκειν and ποιμαίνειν? Philo's distinction according to which the first verb signifies provision of food ('feed'), the second sovereign leading ('tending')[59] is based on linguistic usage, but does not have to be accentuated in all texts. Why does Jesus come back to βόσκειν on the third occasion after he had said ποιμαίνειν on the second occasion? There too the intention is rather variation. In fact, the shepherd Jesus in Chapter 10 combines both functions: he leads his sheep (vv. 3ff) and enables them to find pasture (vv. 9–10), he gives them eternal life and protects them (v. 28). The two verbs which only occur here in John's gospel are meant to indicate in their alternation the all-inclusive care of a shepherd with which Jesus invests Peter. The same applies to the expressions which indicate, in the picture of the shepherd, those persons entrusted to Peter. Admittedly, the variation has led to confusing variants in the mss. Three words enter into consideration: ἀρνία, προβάτια and πρόβατα. For v. 15 τὰ ἀρνία μου may be regarded as certain.[60] Greater uncertainty prevails with the readings in vv. 16 and 17 (q.v.); but a climax involving a progression in the meaning: lambs – little sheep – sheep is hardly to be established. All three expressions indicate the persons entrusted to Jesus by the Father, and the risen one who retains his proprietary right in the 'sheep' ('*my* sheep'), now hands them over to the safe-keeping of Simon Peter. He is to lead the 'lambs' to the pasture of life, and guard them in union with Jesus.

The evangelist would hardly have said ἀρνία but most likely πρόβατα which is used throughout Jn 10 (15 times). Besides, the evangelist does not there use the personal pronoun μου but the possessive pronoun τὰ ἐμά (10:26f; cf. also 10:14). The word ἀρνία found only once in John's gospel is found very frequently in Revelation in the singular as a designation of Christ. For Christ, there is the similar symbolism of ὁ ἀμνὸς τοῦ θεοῦ in Jn 1:29, 36. Thus, the choice of words leads away from the evangelist and rather points to an editor from Johannine circles.

21:16   The second round of dialogue is narrated in almost the same words as the first. An advance in the narrative is only achieved by the third time of asking with Peter's special reaction. That corresponds to the 'triple formula'[61] which is observable in the parables; the threefold repetition is chosen here for yet another reason, but subjected to the same manner of narration. The pleonastic sounding πάλιν δεύτερον which is also to be found elsewhere, cannot be regarded as a Johannine style criterion;[62] the evangelist would rather say ἐκ δευτέρου (9:24). Peter answers again, as on the first occasion: 'Yes, Lord; you know that I love you.' This '*you* know' is heightened on the third occasion to '*you* know *everything* . . .' The accent contained within it shows that Peter has given up all self-confidence and entrusted himself humbly to his Lord. Jesus' answer points away from the first by means of ποιμαίνειν and its object. This verb too is not otherwise found in John's gospel; in Revelation it is found several times, always in OT quotations, for the lamb's reign in blessing (7:17) and victory (12:5; 19:15), in which the steadfast Christians are also to share (cf. 2:27). But it is not these texts which throw light on the content of the meaning of the verb in our passage but others which are directed to the pastors of the Church, namely, Acts 20:28; 1 Pet 5:2, at a time when the substantive ποιμήν also is already used of leaders of the Church (Eph 4:11). Christ is still always regarded as the 'first (or) chief shepherd' (ἀρχιποιμήν 1 Pet 5:4), and his function as a shepherd is also made clear with the term ἐπίσκοπος in 1 Pet 2:25: it is caring for the sheep and in this sense tending and leading. The overseeing and watching is not a main point and an authoritarian reigning and ruling is forbidden the congregation's pastor (1 Pet 5:3). With this, the function of ποιμαίνειν, within the primitive Christian context,[63] is added to that of βόσκειν (see on v. 15). Peter is to protect and lead caringly the sheep which belong to Christ, in order to keep them on the pasture of life (cf. 10:9).

For 'sheep' most mss. read τά πρόβατα in v. 16.

τά προβάτια B C 22 1582 b.

In v. 17 the text-critical situation is somewhat different:

τά πρόβατα ℵ Δ Θ 𝔓 pl.

τά προβάτια B C A 22 1582 Ambr

τά ἀρνία Λ 945 1188.

It is understandable that most editors, in accordance with the external textual witness, take up τά πρόβατα in the text for both verses (UBS Greek NT also); Tischendorf, Westcott-Hort, Nestlé-Aland decide both times for προβάτια. Finally, individual scholars (Zahn, Brown) prefer πρόβατα in v. 16 and τά προβάτια in v. 17 as the original readings, from which assimilations for the one side or the other are explained. The wider range in v. 17 and the weight of Codex Alexandrinus are noteworthy arguments in favour. In fact, the variants are of little significance, since προβάτιον the diminutive of πρόβατον, often does not indicate any difference (Bauer Wb 1394). But stylistically, the use of three different terms in the three verses would confirm the intention for the variation.

21:17 Jesus' third demand, has, despite the change to φιλεῖς, the same meaning as the first two; τό τρίτον means 'for the third time'.[64] Peter's grief is (differently from that of the disciples in 16:6, 20ff, who are depressed by Jesus' departure) shame and sadness on account of his own failure and Jesus' doubt which speaks through his repeated question. Peter can only appeal to Jesus' knowledge of the heart, he knows everything – the same term as in 16:30; γινώσκεις is the application to the particular situation of Peter. The twice repeated σύ underlines his turning to Jesus pleadingly. Jesus then repeats his commission for the third time; on the reading προβάτια see above on v. 16. With this, Jesus has finally pardoned the disciple's triple failure; prophecy of death and call to follow him in suffering complete the disciple's reinstatement.

Does the threefold repetition of Jesus' commissioning of Peter, apart from the connection with the denial story, have a still further significance? P. Gaechter wants to find in it, according to the oriental pattern, a formula on which law is based;[65] but circumstances and context speak against such an intepretation. Witnesses of the alleged legal act are more inferred (cf. v. 15) than really presupposed by the narrator; the picture of the shepherd does not point to transfer of power but taking over of a caring duty; the one entrusted with this duty is asked concerning his love and called to follow in suffering and death which, in connection with his commission, appears also as an example of steadfastness. In such a context 'law' would strike the wrong note. G. Staehlin thinks, on account of the artistic and strict construction in three three-membered parallels, that this is a set liturgical form; according to him, it could 'echo an ordination interrogatory'.[66] But that also is improbable; who would have put the questions at an ordination, which, here, are directed by the risen one to Peter? No, it is a unique conversation of the risen one personally associated with Peter and temporally with Easter, which is only brought in a deliberate form from the point of view of narration and style. Threefold stylistic forms are also found in 1 Jn, cf. 2:12–13, 14, 16; 5:7f; 5:18–20 (οἴδαμεν three times). The only thing that can positively be said concerning the threefold repetition of the words of commission is that it contains a confirmation.

But what is the meaning of this commission given to Peter alone, to feed Jesus' sheep? And what does it mean within the framework of John's gospel? Unfitting as a strictly legal interpretation is, yet an authoritative commission of the risen one and, accordingly, a sharing by Peter in the work given by the Father to Jesus, that of protecting and leading those 'given' to him and belonging to his believing flock (cf. 6:37–40; 10:27–30; 17:6, 12), cannot be overlooked. If a connection exists with the picture of the believing flock in the body of the gospel – the expression '*my* sheep' does not leave this in doubt – then the line is clear: the Father entrusted the sheep to Jesus his Son so that they belong to the son exactly as to the Father (cf. 10:3f, 14; 17:9f), and without giving up his proprietary right, the risen one entrusts them on returning to the Father, to Peter for safe-keeping. Precisely in order to protect these persons as belonging to him, Jesus imposes a pastoral duty upon Peter. On account of this commission which ultimately comes from the Father, and the authorization included within it, Peter's ministry can be designated also as an office and, in relation to Jesus, as an earthly representation, so long as the special character of this spiritual pastoral office which differs from human offices with their legal structures, is not left out of consideration.

The transfer of the pastoral office to Peter, has also to be seen in the perspective of the primitive Christian understanding of office. It is no accident that the picture of the shepherd also occurs in other writings like Eph 4:11; Acts 20:28; 1 Pet 5:2–4: the Church leaders are regarded as 'shepherds', who exercise their office in the 'Church of the Lord' (Acts 20:28), the 'flock of God' (1 Pet 5:2), answerable to the 'chief shepherd' Jesus Christ, who continues to lead and protect his Church with their help. In these writings too, the entirety of the faithful is in view, the Church as a whole, in and for which the office-holders in the individual congregations carry out their ministry. It is unique that in Jn 21:15–17 Peter is given the pastoral office over all Jesus' 'lambs' or 'sheep'; in this connection, he has a prominent position which is also confirmed by Mt 16:18f. Since this passage is a special tradition which comes from the Matthaean Church and points to the Syrian area, it is highly significant that the

Johannine church also, independently of it, witnesses to a similar tradition. It is not easy to say whether geographical proximity plays a part in this. The question as to what this Peter-tradition means to the Johannine Church is only to be discussed in the context of the contrast with the disciple whom Jesus loved (vv. 20–22).

The far-reaching problem of Peter's primacy, and of a contiuing 'office of Peter' (in the papacy), weighed down as it is by history, and which is nowadays raised afresh in ecumenical conversation, cannot be entered into by us here.[67] The contribution of exegesis can consist in defending against one-sided conclusions from Jn 21:15–17. The interpretation represented by the exegesis of the Fathers and later of Catholic theologians, that in this passage, not only all believers, but, especially, the other disciples are subordinated to Peter,[68] is not to be read into the text (for instance, by means of the distinction between 'lambs' and 'sheep'). On the other hand, more recent Protestant exegetes recognized that a genuine transfer of authority is expressed.[69] A missionary commission for Peter is, contrary to the opinion of Protestant and Catholic exegetes,[70] barely to be recognized; Peter is installed into the pastoral minstry to the already existing flock of Christ.·

21:18   The proclamation of the violent death which Peter has to expect later, follows the empowering for the pastoral ministry, without a fresh start, but with the Johannine formula of affirmation ('truly, truly . . .'). So the editor presumably sees a close connection between the two sayings; the concluding invitation 'follow me' (v. 19) can also confirm this. Just as Peter shared in the caring for Jesus' flock, so also in his destiny of death. In *both* is contained a distinction, in following to the death for the reason that Jesus now accepts the disciple's readiness to give up his life for him (13:37f). Perhaps the reader is meant to be reminded that the good shepherd lays down his life for the sheep (cf. 10:11) and that no one has a greater love than he who gives up his life for his friends (15:13). Such a way of imitating Jesus (13:15–17) is, admittedly, not explicit, Peter's following to the death is not designated as a ministry to the flock; but it is possible that the Church understood it so (cf. 1 Jn 3:16; further, 1 Pet 2:21).[71]

The prophecy of death itself is dressed up in a peculiar metaphor which well illustrates the change in the situation and in Peter's behaviour. As a young man,[72] Peter girded himself, that is, bound his cloak about him so as to go his ways according to his own will;[73] in old age, another will 'gird' him and lead him there where he does not want to go. A reference to v. 7 (Peter puts on his cloak in the boat) is hardly to be found here. Perhaps originally it was a proverb;[74] then, the stretching out of the hands could be explained more easily as the helplessness of the old man (Bernard, Bultmann). But is it that what the picture is saying here? After all, the point of the contrast lies in the fact that Peter must submit himself to another will, indeed, has to face a violent death coming to him (cf. v. 19). With John's preference for expressions with a double meaning a figurative meaning of 'gird'=put in bonds, can be surmised. Then, the stretching out of the hands need mean nothing else than that Peter has to stretch his hands before him to allow the bonds to be put on (cf. Wellhausen, Hoskyns-Davey). σημαίνων in v. 19, also points to such a metaphorical sense; the same verb drew attention to the understdanding of 'lift up'=crucify in 12:33. But that does not have to mean that Jesus here also prophesies death on the cross for Peter. It is true, some exegetes suppose that on account of the stretching out of the hands, which fits this manner of death. W. Bauer explains the sequence of verbs which is detrimental to his interpretation, with the fact that the delinquent had to carry the cross-beam with his hands stretched out on and his arms bound to it, out to the place of execution.[75] Then Peter's following to the death would make him even more like his Lord; but complete certainty is scarcely attainable on account of the not unequivocal character of the picture. The apostle's martyr's death is also testified to by 1 *Clem* 5:4; mention is made of his crucifixion only relatively late, namely, by Tertullian.[76]

21:19   The added comment corresponds to the evangelist's manner but also the editors' (cf. vv. 14 and 20); the Semitizing usage 'to glorify God' which is frequently found in the synoptic gospels, especially in Luke, has no exact parallel in the body of the gospel (cf. however, 13:31f; 15:8; 17:4). The editor may have been following 12:33 in the formulation of the sentence, perhaps intentionally, so as to make clearer in what way Peter was to follow. The in itself dispensable invitation 'Follow me', is certainly meant to remind the reader of 13:37f. What Jesus refused the disciple at that time, he now challenges him with. The (in John's gospel) variously used ἀκολουθεῖν (see on 1:37 and 8:12) is further supported (apart from that passage) by 12:26. The notion that to follow in such a way leads through death into glory (there where Jesus is), is not explicit here; however, it may be latent as a promise as in 13:36ff.[77] Jesus' prophecy of death and its interpretation presuppose the author's knowledge of the end of Peter's life.

3. Peter and the Disciple whom Jesus loved (21:20–23)

[20]*Peter turned and saw following them the disciple whom Jesus loved, who had lain close to his breast at the supper and had said, 'Lord, who is it that is going to betray you?'* [21]*When Peter saw him, he said to Jesus, 'Lord, what about this man?'* [22]*Jesus said to him, 'If it is my will that he remain until I come, what is that to you? Follow me!'* [23]*The saying spread abroad among the brethren that this disciple was not to die; yet Jesus did not say to him that he was not to die, but, 'If it is my will that he remain until I come, what is that to you?'*

A discussion about the disciple whom Jesus loved forms the conclusion of the encounter between the risen one and Peter. The editors who join this discussion, rather clumsily, to the preceding scene are obviously very interested in it. But what intentions they pursue with it is less clear and is an open question in exegesis. Is the contrast concerned only with the differing ways in which the lives of the two disciples ended, or is it basic in character? Is it simply that a saying is to be explained which circulated in the Johannine Church and caused confusion, or is there more behind it? Is that disciple's death the immediate occasion for taking up the saying or is there another explanation for it? These questions demand that the text be carefully listened to. The disciple around whom the discussion turns does not himself appear; but he is, for the editors, as already in 21:7, a historical figure. These verses are extremely significant for the literary and historical problem connected with this.

21:20   With editorial sleight of hand, the disciple whom Jesus loved comes into view. When Peter 'turns' that is not justified by anything in this situation; where are the other disciples and where is the disciple who is mentioned 'following'? There are comparable sentences in the gospel, but they fit better in the situation (1:38; 20:16); only 20:14 makes a similarly artificial impression. The compositum ἐπιστ., which is only found here, perhaps indicates another hand since the evangelist uses the simplex. Peter 'sees' (βλέπει) the disciple whom Jesus loved, and so brings him to the readers attention. The predicatively added ἀκολοθοῦντα, left out by some mss.,[78] has probably only a scenic significance or is put in so as to join on the second relative clause better (Bultmann). The interpretation which one often reads, that this disciple is one who is already 'following' as distinct from Peter who has first to be exhorted to do so (vv. 19 and 22),[79] cannot be maintained. The exhortation to Peter concerns especially his following to the death which is just what does not apply to the other disciple, and the editors certainly do not want to deny to Peter that he is following as a disciple (cf. 6:66–69).

Noteworthy is the reminder of the scene at the supper. If the editors only wanted to introduce that disciple they would already have had to do so in 21:7. They are interested, just now, to raise up once more the scene as it was before the inner eye of the reader. There, the disciple whom Jesus loved was introduced as the one trusted by Jesus, the one close to his heart. By means of the flash-back,[80] attention is concentrated on him (different from 21:7), and Peter's question which is conected with it: 'Lord, what about this man?' (v. 21) increases the expectation: There is something special about him. The reader also recalls the relationship of Peter to that disciple: Peter waved to the disciple at Jesus' side and withdrew into the background. Thus, the comment in v. 20b serves the narrative purpose of indicating the preferential position of the disciple whom Jesus loved; besides, it is also clear enough in 20:2–10 and 21:7. Only it is not immediately permissible to interpret the 'competition' between the two disciples as rivalry. Why then would the editors have reported the transfer of the pastoral office to Peter? They do not polemicise against Peter but they want to ensure his special place for the disciple whom Jesus loved, just after Peter has been honoured.

Because of this, an interpretation which wants to restrict the discussion concerning the disciple loved by Jesus to the theme of his manner of death,[81] becomes questionable. It is true, vv. 20–23 no longer refer directly to the passing on of the pastoral ministry to Peter, but Jesus' words of authorization and his prophecy of death seemed to us to form, for the editors, a singe whole, and therefore vv. 15–17 have not yet disappeared from the horizon. Outwardly, the discussion refers to the prophecy of death; but basically, the two disciples who are distinguished by their rôles and their ways, are compared as such with each other. If the intention is to protect the beloved disciple from a devaluation (let us say) by 'Petrine' circles, because he does not die the martyr's death like Peter – a possible, but not inevitable interpretation – then those circles play this trump-card surely only so as to underline Peter's primacy as such. During the further course of events it will be shown that the beloved disciple is also assigned a positive rôle. The removal of the misunderstanding in the Church is not the first and only purpose of the verses.

21:21   The narrator takes up the thread again, after the digression, with οὖν (lacking in many mss.); ἰδών once more shows his tendency to variation of style. Peter's question, formulated succinctly in dialogue style (γίνεται can be supplied)[82], does not stand any psychological consideration whether he wants to distract the attention or is jealous, and the like,[82a] but it serves to make possible Jesus' words to which the criticism of Peter also belongs.

21:22   Jesus' answer contains a tradition about the disciple whom Jesus loved: the Lord wishes that this disciple should remain until he comes. It is noteworthy that the pronouncement is not handed down as a saying of Jesus to the beloved disciple himself, different from the prophecy of death for Peter. As v. 23 shows it was a saying, circulating in the Johannine Church, the origin of which was probably unknown to it. It was apparently not traced back to a personal witness of the disciple. The narrator wants to clear up the origin and meaning of the saying, and uses for that purpose Peter's conversation with the risen one. When the editorial shaping is taken into account, the intention to contrast the two disciples appears yet more acute. Peter is told that the Lord has something special in mind for that disciple, and he is to respect it. It is unnecessary to suppose any polemic controversy between Peter's supporters and Johannine circles. What the risen one previously said to Peter, words of authorization and prophecy of death, remains in effect and is recognized by the circle of Johannine disciples; but this group is now concerned to assert also the duty and way of the disciple whom Jesus loved as the Lord's will. The concern is, if anything, a positive one: those who adhere to Peter and emphasize his authority are also to show understanding for that disciple and his Church. Without belittling Peter's authority, the Johannine circles want to enhance the reputation of their founder and master, precisely through Peter who receives Jesus' answer.[83]

The words about the disciple whom Jesus loved are remarkable in several respects. Above all they witness to a living parousia expectation; for 'until I come' cannot refer to anything else than Jesus' coming at the parousia. For the evangelist, this expectation is subordinate to the experience of present salvation, the fellowship of Christ already attained (cf. Excursus 14 in Vol. 2). Nor can 14:3 be called upon because there, the evangelist, at most indirectly, takes account of the hope of the parousia (see *ad loc.*). Against this, it is suggested several times in 1 Jn (2:28; 3:2), but formulated differently ('parousia', 'he appears') yet scarcely as a burning immediate expectation, as it will probably originally lie behind the saying in Jn 21:22. The greatest immediacy exists in the Revelation to John, for here, the immediate expectation is still vivid (cf. 1:3, 19; 6:11 and *passim*), and the parousia is not only announced with the traditional picture of 'coming with the clouds' (1:7), but also proclaimed by the heavenly Lord: '(behold,) I am coming soon' (3:11; 22:7, 12, 20). At the end of the book it occurs in quick succession, interrupted by warnings by the seer, taken up in the Church's cry of longing (22:20). The way in which the coming of the Lord is spoken about is old. Paul witnesses to it (1 Cor 4:5; 11:26), and the primitive Christian communities will have adhered to it in general. But Revelation which, at the turn of the first century, is still vividly gripped by this notion and, in the same words, expresses it (in the 'I'-form), takes us closer to the presumed *Sitz im Leben* of the Lord's saying as it has been handed down. Despite all differences of the apocalyptic work from the Johannine writings in the narrower sense, certain points of contact are apparent, which are possibly due to contacts between the compilers or Churches respectively. The saying circulating in the Johannine Church recalls Mk 9:1 par.: some of Jesus' contemporaries will still experience the coming of the kingdom in power. In the Johannine Church such a tradition was applied to the disciple whom Jesus loved.[84] So the saying permits us to obtain an insight into an earlier stage when the Johannine Church was still filled with a burning immediate expectation. At the time that Jn 21 was compiled this need no longer have been the case; but the parousia was questioned as little as in 1 Jn. The eschatological hope in Jn 21:22f fits well with that of the main letter.

Further, μένειν is noteworthy, a favourite word of John (in 1 Jn also) which occurs in many kinds of connection and with various meaning.[85] Here, it is the key word on which the 'misunderstanding' of the Church hangs and at which the editorial correction probably begins. In the context of the prophecy of Peter's death and this disciple's question, it can only mean 'remain alive'; only subsequently, in the course of rejection of the misunderstanding which arose in the Church, can another meaning be insinuated by the editors. Therefore, the new exposition can be judged in no other way than as an intentional correction of an older tradition.

The concluding renewed exhortation of Peter: 'Follow me!' confirms that the editors are concerned in this scene to contrast the two disciples. Linguistically, αὐτόν – σύ, further μένειν – ἀκολουθεῖν form a contrast. In the narrative context Peter is told he is to let that which the Lord has determined for that disciple take its course, but he himself is to go his way following Jesus to the death. At a time when Peter was already dead this also contains a warning for all circles owing allegiance to Peter in the primitive Church.

21:23 The editors' comment on the saying about that disciple concerns an internal problem of the Johannine Church, thus changing the perspective which was opened up, according to the above exegesis (contrast between the two disciples). However, it can scarcely be concluded from v. 23 that this problem forms the actual scope of the scene in vv. 20–23. It is an appendix due to current circumstance. In a similar way, special comments are annexed to traditional sayings in the gospel (cf. 2:21f with 19f; 11:51 with 49f; 12:6 with 5), without exhausting the meaning contained in the account. Here the concern is with the interpretation of the saying about the beloved disciple which, later (cf.

ἐξῆλθεν), arose among the 'brethren', that means the members of the Church.[86] On the basis of that tradition (οὖν) the saying spread: that disciple is not to die.[87] The conclusion is at hand that that disciple has died in the meantime; precisely his death caused unrest and occasioned the correction of the editors. The view that the disciple was still alive at the time of writing cannot be supported either by the present οὐκ ἀποθνήσκει, which has a future meaning, nor by the consideration: after the occurrence of his death the misunderstanding settles itself.[88] For with it, everything was by no means settled but a major problem arose: the parousia which was still expected during the disciple's lifetime, had not happened. If it was a saying of the Lord, it could not be allowed simply to be dropped. So an explanatory saying had to be found and it is just that for which the editors strive. The explanations which take their starting-point from the fact that the beloved disciple himself – still in good health or feeling his death to be drawing near – volunteered these explanatory words as a precaution (and, if possible, wrote them down), pay too little attention to the 'reporting' style: 'The saying spread abroad . . . ' The disciple concerned would have addressed himself directly to the misunderstanding ('That does not mean: that disciple is not going to die' or the like). The one who put the comment together has a specific reason for putting right an incorrect exposition, and, according to the formulation 'he is not going to die', that can presumably be only the death of that disciple.

The writer contrasts the incorrect view with the exact words.[89] But in what is the correction to be found which eliminates the misunderstanding, that that disciple will not die? Since no further explanation follows the reader must come upon it himself. The answer was sought from two points of view: Jesus had only pronounced a conditional statement, not made any actual prophecy;[90] or: Jesus had not meant that disciple was going to remain alive, but he was going to 'remain' in some other way.[91] Both opinions have their difficulties; but the second deserves preference. If the editors had wanted to excuse themselves by the conditional formulation, that would not merely be rather sophistic, but would also have had the consequence: after the disciple's death it becomes obvious that Jesus did *not* want it (alternatively, prior to the disciple's death: it remains completely open, the saying has no kind of weight). Since ἐάν with the subjunctive can replace the classical 'indicative' εἰ,[92] it is also possible to place the emphasis on μένειν: Jesus desires that this disciple 'remains', yet not in an outward sense of 'remaining alive' but in another, figurative way. That can then be understood as the continuing effect in the circle of his disciples and his Church, or as the continuance of his words, his Spirit-borne proclamation (as it is found in the gospel).[93] Perhaps the writer who only wanted to defend against the false interpretation, did not want to commit himself precisely. But this spiritual 'remaining' and continuing effect of the disciple, is in line with what is also recognizable in v. 24.

4. Closing editorial words (21:24–25)

²⁴This is the disciple who is bearing witness to these things, and who has written these things; and we know that his testimony is true. ²⁵But there are also many other things which Jesus did; were every one of them to be written, I suppose that the world itself could not contain the books that would be written.

A closing remark by the editors who added 21:1–23 to the gospel, is as good as indispensable. V. 23 with the question at the end would be a wholly unsatisfactory conclusion; but also, having regard to the evangelist's closing words in 20:30f the editors had to compose an epilogue which integrated the additional section, to some extent meaningfully, into the work as a whole. It is true the two verses pose many kinds of question if we want to evaluate them in relation to the compiling and editing of John's gospel (cf. the introductory works). The many hypotheses developed to this end cannot be discussed here. Attempts to transpose the first conclusion (20:30f) to here, from its position,[94] and to attribute 21:24f to a later stage, come to grief on the good textual witness and improbability that editors would have made new difficulties for themselves by a rearrangement. But also exclusion of v. 25 as a later gloss is not justified by the textual tradition (it was only lacking to begin with in Codex Sinaiticus).[95] Admittedly, the text as we have it, demands that an explanation be found for the existence and order of the two vv. 24 and 25 which are very different in style and content. Perhaps by this means, some light also falls on the final editing of the entire work.

21:24 With 'this disciple' no other can be meant than the previously mentioned disciple whom Jesus loved. The formerly much discussed question whether v. 24 is from another hand than the section 21:1–23, is, according to our analysis of the narrative complex, decided in the negative. If the account in 21:1–23 comes from the editors then v. 24 forms the natural continuation.[96] The further comment about the disciple whom Jesus loved fits the trend of the last part. The disciple who has been brought to the fore by the contrast with Peter is now presented in his real significance: it is he who 'is bearing witness to these things'. The present participle which can be noticed on account of the following aorist (ὁ γράψας), does not at all require the consequence that he is still alive. He lives on in his testimony, indeed, through it, the words concerning his 'remaining care fulfilled, if we have rightly interpreted v. 23. μαρτυρεῖν περί is Johannine linguistic usage even if mostly with a personal object (but cf. 18:23).[97] This disciple also functions in 19:35 as a witness and the perfect used there (μεμαρτύρηκεν) likewise indicates his persistent testimony. The investigation of that passage (q.v.) showed that it was very close to 21:24 so that both passages may be attributed to the same editors. If that disciple witnesses the events at the piercing of Jesus' side which are important for faith, the nature of his testimony also, as understood by the editors, becomes clearer: he guarantees what has been seen and handed down, and, at the same time, interprets it from the viewpoint of faith.

But what is meant by τούτων? A restriction to the previously reported saying of the Lord (v. 22)[98] is certainly incorrect; also, a limitation to the narrative complex 21:1–23[99] does not recommend itself. For the following ταῦτα hardly has any other sense; however, it is defined more closely by γράψας. Why should the editors emphasize that precisely Chapter 21 was written by that disciple (apart from the fact that this is improbable)? Thus, the two demonstratives, as most exegetes suppose, will refer to the entire gospel. This broadening of the field of vision can be understood from the intention, after the addition of the narrative material in Chapter 21, to close the whole book and give to it the authority of that disciple. To bring him into view for that reason was certainly one of the objectives of the editors as they extended the already concluded gospel.

But what of the information that that disciple has written 'these things', namely, the whole gospel? Apart from the scholars who hold it to be possible (at least in substance) that the nameless disciple who is then identified with the apostle John, really wrote it down, on account of the difficulty of this supposition (cf. Vol. 1, pp. 75–104), a weaker significance is sought for γράψας. Either, it is said, the verb is to be understood here as in 19:22 causally,[100] or it is thought that an indirect authorship fits the expression equally well, somewhat in the sense that the traditions and essential thoughts come from that disciple, but another (quite on his own) has written the work down. That best corresponds to the internal evidence of our gospel; the evangelist certainly relies on tradition and yet is an independent thinker and originator of his material. With the causal intepretation, the disciple whom Jesus loved would have to be granted enormously more direct influence (cf. Pilate in 19:22). The minimal sounding interpretation that, with γράψας, that disciple is to be called upon only as a guarantor of the content of the written work, ought to be justified by the context. The remark is not there on its own account, but is added to the main statement that he is bearing witness to these things.[101] If ματυρων at first refers to his oral witness, it is to be understood that the editors want to draw upon his authority for the written work as well, into which his oral tradition and testimonies have been put. The supposition of any mistake or misleading interpretation in order to give credibility to the gospel and make it acceptable above all within the sphere of the Church,[102] is deduced from unproved premises.

The editors' main concern is once more visible when they add: 'And we know that his testimony is true.' They are talking about the μαρτυρία of that disciple; the written form mentioned in between is important but not what they really have in mind. More important is that the testimony of that disciple is reliable. The sentence recalls what Jesus said about himself in the gospel, that his (revelation-) testimony is reliable (8:14) or that he has the Father's reliable testimony on his side (5:32; cf. 8:18). In this connection, Jesus also refers to his knowledge: 'I know that the testimony which he bears to me is true' (5:32). Similarly, in 19:35 is added: 'And he knows that he tells the truth.' Thus, the form of expression corresponds to Johannine thought; the statement of the witness is supported either by his own knowledge (8:14; possibly also 19:35), or the knowledge of others concerning the reliability of his testimony (5:32; 21:24). To whom does οἴδαμεν refer, to the editors, that is, to a rather narrow circle, or to the entire Church?[103] Both are possible; the frequent οἴδαμεν in 1 Jn (3:2, 14; 5:15, 18, 19, 20) makes the interpretation of the Church preferable. If, however, the proem to the main letter is compared (1:1–4), where a qualified circle bears witness to those addressed (1:2; cf. also 4:14), the circle of those issuing the letter may also be thought of. The question has a point, at most, at v. 25 where an individual is the speaker (οἶμαι). He would then have added v. 25 by himself; this is also to be supposed on other grounds (see below). It is not possible to make a case against the same editorial origin as that of 19:35 (where ἀληθινή is found), from the adjective ἀληθής which, up to 19:35, always indicates the truth and reliability of the testimony (see on 5:31). The two adjectives are certainly used synonymously in accordance with the already repeatedly determined tendency of the editors to vary the language.[104]

21:25   The last verse of our gospel betrays, in any case, a different hand from v. 24. Stylistically remarkable are: καθ᾽ ἕν (only εἰς καθ᾽ εἰς in the non-Johannine pericope about the adulteress, 8:9, is comparable); the interlocking construction of the minor clauses with the major clause;[105] χωρήσειν (in many manuscripts altered into χωρῆσαι),[106] a rare future infinitive to indicate the relative tense; αὐτόν . . . τόν κόσμον and οἶμαι (only here in John's gospel). What stands out even more is the rhetorical exaggeration that then the world could not contain the books. It is true that there are further examples of this from that period.[107] The hyperbole serves to glorify Jesus' deeds in a literary manner, certainly not in the sense of the evangelist who is interested in the deeper significance of Jesus' works. The affected sentence gives the impression that an ambitious writer still wanted to add a spirited conclusion. But he will have been inspired to do so also by a look back at the conclusion of the evangelist (20:30f). After the editorial closing comment (21:24) he might have been missing an indication that (despite the further material in Chapter 21) it was still a long way from everything being written down that there was to relate concerning Jesus. For he had apparently formulated the beginning of the sentence in imitation of 20:30 (πολλὰ καὶ ἄλλα, only in a different order); he leaves out σημεῖα because the meaning of the 'signs' is scarcely understood by him. He also does not take any notice of the theological intent which the evangelist manifests in 20:31. If this writer likewise belonged to the editorial circle, he was not its most capable person. Or is the verse an indication of the fact that the book passed through several hands before it was finally brought out? In any case, if we are looking for the most dignified conclusion of the 'spiritual' gospel, we are referred back to the closing sentences of the evangelist in 20:30f.

The Disciple whom Jesus Loved

The extraordinary figure of the disciple who is singled out with the honorific designation, 'the disciple whom Jesus loved' (hereinafter referred to as 'the beloved disciple'[1]), but who otherwise remains anonymous, has already repeatedly occupied us: in the Introduction (see Vol. 1, pp. 97–100); then, in those passages where he is expressly mentioned (13:23–26; 19:26f; 20:3–10; 21:7, 20–23, 24); finally, in two other places where he is surmised to be hidden (1;40, the second disciple; 18:15, the 'other disciple'). The comment in 19:35 about the witness beneath the cross, which we have attributed to the editors, can only refer back to 19:26f and likewise concerns the beloved disciple. That is the material which we have at our disposal from John's gospel. The later witnesses in the Church who identify the beloved disciple with John the apostle, the son of Zebedee and brother of James (cf. Vol. 1, pp. 77–86), we leave aside on methodological grounds because they (except for the problematical testimony of Irenaeus concerning the information of the presbyters in Asia Minor) finally rest on conclusions from John's gospel. So we want to investigate once again the internal evidence of the Johannine passages. The years that have passed since the appearance of the first volume, make this all the more required since, in the meantime, scholarship has been occupied further with this problem; also my own contribution from the year 1970[2] should not be the last word. The remaining scholarly contributions from the period in between[3] require concentration on specific questions to which an answer has to be found in this excursus. In no way does it make the claim to be a 'final answer' to this problem, which remains complex and difficult because of the available texts and the many implicit questions including those concerned with method.

Yet the reader may expect a clear point of view: information concerning what now appears to me as relatively the best sustainable scientific answer. Since the problem of the beloved disciple is bound up most closely with the questions of the composition of John's gospel, there is an opportunity at the end of this commentary to review once more the positions which were taken up ten years ago in the 'Introduction', namely, the relation of the evangelist to the beloved disciple and that of the editors to the evangelist. The method which commends itself is to start from the closing editorial chapter, because the beloved disciple is characterized there most clearly from a historical viewpoint. At least in the editors' opinion, he appears as an historical person, because, apparently, his death is presupposed in v. 23. Were they mistaken in this opinion or did they intentionally mislead the readers of the gospel? Was the beloved disciple originally (in the evangelist's sense) an unhistorical symbolic figure or a literary fiction? The answer to these questions provides a signpost for further consideration of the problem. Because, even if only the editors regarded that figure as a historical person, we are also not dispensed from reflecting on the relationship of the editors to the evangelist (as happens not infrequently). But if there are strong grounds in favour of the evangelist already having a historical person in view, a further investigation is all the more required as to who could be behind the anonymous disciple and why he remains anonymous.

1. The Beloved Disciple in Jn 21 in relation to the earlier Passages

If, for a start, Jn 21 is assumed not to be from the hand of the evangelist, it may be possible to distinguish the figure of the beloved disciple as seen by the editors, from the picture in the earlier chapters. Admittedly, the editors themselves make connections by means of the reference back to the scene at the supper in 21:20. Thus, they *want* to identify the one of whom they are speaking with the figure mentioned in the gospel; but it can naturally be doubted whether they are right in this. Before we examine pro and contra some notable opinions may be presented which illustrate the range of the possible answers.

a. For Bultmann the beloved disciple in the gospel (especially in 19:26f) is representative of Gentile Christianity, thus, a symbolic figure; in Chapter 21, on the contrary, a specific historical person.[4] He thinks that the compiler of Chapter 21 makes use of a handed-down saying of the Lord (v. 22), in order to identify the disciple (who, according to this saying, was to reach a surprisingly great age), with the figure of the beloved disciple which was found in the gospel he was editing. 'By this means he had gained a person who was acknowledged to be a witness from the earliest time as a guarantor for the worth of the Gospel, and indeed as its author'.[5]

b. A. Kragerud opposes this view. Above all he brings against it, that the postscript is very close to the gospel and Chapter 21 undoubtedly comes from the same circles as the gospel. 'If anywhere, then here, an understanding and not a misunderstanding of the riddle is to be supposed from the first.'[6] Kragerud himself wants to interpret all seven apposite passages (including 1:40 and 18:15) in the same way, and that in the sense of a symbolic figure of primitive Christian prophetism. In accordance with this he also interprets the explanation in 21:20–23 and 24 which follows the handed-down words of the Lord: whoever wrote these verses (according to K. probably the evangelist, cf. pp. 15–19), he did not see in the beloved disciple any single person.[7]

c. Kragerud's hypothesis has often been criticized particularly on account of his wilful interpretation of 21:20–24. Can the supposition of a historical person be argued away from this section which is to be attributed to editors by most scholars? So there is a growing number of scholars who start from 21:20–23 or 24, and postulate a historical figure for the passages in the body of the gospel as well. In this, the more recent studies put off the question of an identification.[8] The contribution of J. Roloff who, for comparison, draws upon the 'teacher of righteousness' in Qumran, throws light upon the compatibility of anonymity and historicity of a leading personality in a group.[9]

d. Another picture results if with H. Thyen (on the authority of H.-P. Otto) it is supposed that all passages referring to the beloved disciple in the gospel have been interpolated by the editor who wrote Chapter 21. This opinion was also represented by earlier literary critics.[9a] Then, in the original gospel there was no mention at all of the beloved disciple; only the editor was interested to introduce this figure: 'He wants in this way, on the one hand to set up a memorial to the honoured "disciple" of his circle, and on the other hand grant to his gospel the authority of the beloved eye-witness'.[10]

e. Mahoney is of the opinion in his dissertation on the two disciples at the tomb (Jn 20:1–10), that the beloved disciple is introduced only for presentational reasons in those passages where he plays a part, thus, he is a sort of literary fiction which serves the specific intentions of the evangelist.[11] In order to support this thesis which is developed out of the function of the two disciples in Jn 20:1–10, the writer also considers Jn 21. Here he claims to recognize various layers of tradition; he presumes that the saying taken up in v. 22 about the long-lived disciple originally did not refer to the beloved disciple, and that the identification is due to the editors. Only v. 24 would then elevate this disciple to the author of the gospel – 'almost certainly wrong' information.[12] Apart from the 'functional' interpretation of the beloved disciple, Mahoney differs from earlier hypotheses which do not grant the beloved disciple any historicity in the body of the gospel, in that he wants to demonstrate stages in the history of tradition as to how the statements in Chapter 21 came about. To judge these divergent views, it is appropriate to consider the respective methodological point of departure as well. For Bultmann, the main passage is Jn 19:26f from which he deduces his interpretation of the beloved disciple as representative of Gentile Christianity (in contrast to Jesus' mother as the representative of Jewish Christianity).[13] For the two other passages in the gospel (at the supper and at the tomb) he has then already to interpret further: '. . . the authentic Christendom which has achieved its own true self-understanding' (370). If, thus, the basis from which he starts is rather narrow, then Kragerud provides himself with a broad base by a comparative treatment of all the passages which come in question; but he carries out the comparison more phenomenologically (with 'types' and 'motifs') than exegetically, and in this way he obtains a uniform way of looking at things. H. Thyen's point of departure is orientated towards literary criticism and could lead to a smooth solution if the interpolation thesis could be verified in all passages. But, in my opinion, it fails just at that passage where Thyen claims to demonstrate it, namely, 13:21–26. Mahoney's opinion that the beloved disciple exercises a specific literary function is noteworthy in its textual-linguistic aspect, but is risky if this is supposed to be the only function of the beloved disciple; it fails, in my opinion, particularly with 19:26f.[14] Further, his theory as to how Chapter 21 came about is difficult, because we have to work with too many hypotheses.

We must ask whether the editors of Jn 21 really misinterpreted the beloved disciple as an historical person, thus missing the evangelist's intention (the passages in Chapters 13; 19; 20 originate with him). What can be adduced in favour of the view mentioned under c? Are there decisive arguments to the contrary? In the pro and contra, the following arguments are noteworthy:

a. To begin with it must be said that a figure drawn as a type or symbol can nevertheless be a historical person. A 'typical' significance has also been supposed for other persons in John's gospel (cf. Nicodemus, the Samaritan woman, Thomas, etc.),[15] and although this cannot be proved throughout, there may be something right in the theory. In the case of the beloved disciple, the personality setting the trend for the Johannine circle would then have become the type of an ideal disciple, the exemplary believer, the Spirit-filled interpreter, or however one wishes to define the picture of him.

b. The frequently observed though variously assessed 'competition' between Simon Peter and the beloved disciple, strengthens the supposition that this latter is a historical person as well as also an idealized figure. Since Peter is drawn with his individual features in John's gospel in accordance with the synoptic tradition, there is no abstract Peter-image. It can only be imagined with difficulty that a purely symbolic figure is placed by his side.[16] It is much more to be supposed that historical background elements as well led to the contrasting of the two persons; but I do not want to pursue such suppositions here.[16a]

c. A principal objection against the historicity of the beloved disciple arises out of the final editorial comment in 21:24: 'This is the disciple who is bearing witness to these things, and who has written these things.' From that it is concluded that he is put here as an eye-witness of Jesus' earthly ministry; however, it would be impossible for John's gospel to be the work of an eye-witness.[17] But it is necessary to make appropriate distinctions in the case of the two statements about witness and writing down which may, indeed, refer to the gospel. The testimony to these things need not mean at all that he experienced everything as an eye-witness. It is much more likely that he makes himself the guarantor of the things reported and represented in the gospel. Light is thrown on the form of his witness by 19:35, a passage which scarcely means somebody other than the beloved disciple and which might have come from the same editors. He testifies to the event that from Jesus' pierced side blood and water issued (v. 34), but obviously in such a way that he combines a deeper meaning with it. Admittedly, 'seeing' has to retain its natural meaning, thus, physical seeing; but a deeper meaning is indicated through the emphasis (see *ad loc.*). That does not rule out that the compiler relies for other things reported in the gospel, on sources whose statements he takes up and himself interprets. That the beloved disciple himself saw and directly experienced everything is not said, nor need it be concluded from 'bearing witness' (cf. the witness of the 'we' in 1 Jn 1:2; 4:14).

In this connection, the observation that the beloved disciple is only expressly mentioned at the last supper, is also not unimportant. Thus, it is quite thinkable that he is regarded as an *eye-witness* only for the passion of Jesus (*perhaps* also disguised beneath the 'other disciple' in 18:15), and for the following events. Admittedly, from an historical viewpoint, doubt likewise arises in this case (visit to the tomb, appearance at the sea); but with the editors' peculiar viewpoint it could already be enough that they knew of his presence beneath the cross. The other scenes could have been put together from a theological point of view. But even if we do not want to go so far, the comment in 21:24 does not give any justification for making the beloved disciple as understood by the editors the eye-witness for the entire gospel.

More difficult, it is true, is the second remark that 'he has written these things'; but in the commentary on the passage it was shown that a literal understanding is not necessarily required and was scarcely in the mind of the editors. Here, a certain intention is not to be denied that the editors wish to give that disciple's authority to the gospel. If we consider how in those days writings were attributed to well-known persons (cf. the pseudonymous deutero-Paulines), all possibilities remain open as to whether or not he took part in the writing down. The main statement is the 'witness' of that disciple; this remains true even if the actual compiler of the gospel (the evangelist) relies on the tradition and interpretation of the beloved disciple.

d. The relation of the editors to the evangelist is an important factor in these considerations. The fact is that the compiler of Jn 21 is close to the evangelist in style and thought, even if enough differences can be recognized.[18] Such closeness in thought and manner of expression is not gained through a passing knowledge of, or merely literary interest in the work. So the editor can hardly be denied a rather close contact with the evangelist. With that, a *mistake* concerning his identity is eliminated with considerable certainty; an intentional *deception* of the readers would have to be supposed. But that presupposes, by the same token, that those who were being addressed were little informed about the very aged disciple concerning whom that saying of the Lord was circulating. But apparently he was known to the Church – could there otherwise have been a need for a 'correction' so as to get rid of the uneasiness that had arisen? So the question is whether a deception, that that disciple is the witness behind John's gospel, would have been easily possible, quite apart from the further question, what purpose the editors were pursuing with such a deceit. The answer to this given by the proponents of the hypothesis that the editors made an historical person out of a symbolic figure, is unsatisfactory. Certainly, a 'witness from the earliest time'; but why were the editors interested in circulating this gospel within the Church, if the evangelist was an insignificant, perhaps, from the Church's point of view, suspect person? At the same time, indeed, certain deviations from his views are to be seen (no future eschatology, no sacramental teaching), so that the editors reintroduced the general primitive Christian viewpoint. Why then are they interested at all in John's gospel?

These difficulties can be solved much more easily on the supposition that the editors of Chapter 21 were informed about the beloved disciple and rightly declared him to be the guarantor of the gospel. If the gospel was already circulating within the Church, as the determinative written document of the oral proclamation of Christ as presented by a circle of teachers, then it was desired to *safeguard* – precisely after the death of that very aged disciple of the Lord – his authority, so to say, as the testament of that honoured disciple. A 'deception' of the Church could then, at most, be contained in the fact that that disciple's *share* in putting together the gospel is not precisely specified, perhaps, is exaggerated in that it was said: 'He has written.' If the real writer was another whose clearly portrayed theological views could also be misunderstood, although the editors knew and valued him as one of their own, everything becomes easier to understand. They knew that the evangelist, like all others sharing the work of the 'Johannine circle', relied on the traditions and interpretations of that extraordinary disciple of the Lord, and had written down the gospel in his spirit. So the editors did not only cover him by means of their declaration of solidarity, but also by means of the assurance that the beloved disciple bears witness to the things described in the gospel. B. Lindars has drawn attention to the significance of the plural form οἴδαμεν in 21:24. 'The *we* takes the sentence outside the structure of the gospel, so that it represents the *imprimatur* of the Church in which it originated.'[19]

e. This observation gains force from the 'ecclesiastical' character of the ultimate editorial chapter. The orthodox belief and commitment to the Church of those who are answerable for the addition of this chapter to the original gospel can by no means be doubted. Both the appearance by the sea with the net full of fish which says so much, and the meal-scene, as also the commissioning of Peter with the pastoral ministry, shows an ecclesiastical inclination which extends beyond the borders of the Johannine congregation (cf. Excursus 17). When the scene with the beloved disciple is connected with this, then the authority of this disciple (although he did not die as a martyr) is given support. The most obvious consequence is that he was the decisive personality for the Johannine congregation and his death now led to disquiet. He was not introduced in order to *find* a person of authority for the gospel, but in order to endorse his already *existing* authority in the congregation, to maintain it after his death and to commend the written gospel as his everlasting testimony.

Admittedly, with these considerations, the hypothesis that the passages in the body of the gospel in which the beloved disciple appears have only been inserted by the editors, may also be consonant. But it is scarcely verifiable, at least not for the main passage, 13:23–26. But also 19:26f and 20:2–10 can be more easily explained if it is assumed that the evangelist used an account of the passion and Easter and himself brought in the scenes with the beloved disciple (cf. the commentary). Then, it is true, the evangelist cannot be identified with the beloved disciple. After the investigation of the relation of Jn 21 to the earlier passages in the gospel has given us sufficient certainty to regard the beloved disciple as a historical person, for the same one as the editors, we want to concern ourselves a little further with the relation of the evangelist to this disciple.

2. The Relation of the Evangelist to the Beloved Disciple

In the Introduction (Vol. 1, pp. 100–104) the view was propounded that the beloved disciple has to be distinguished from the evangelist, since the latter, on account of the peculiar style and the developed theology in John's gospel, cannot be only assigned the role of a secretary. Admittedly, I had suggested at that time – having regard to the tradition – that the beloved disciple, the repository of the tradition behind the gospel, was to be regarded as the apostle John (similarly, F.-M. Braun and R. E. Brown). After further considering this figure, I then abandoned this opinion in my essay of 1970; according to the internal evidence of the gospel, according to the passages in which the beloved disciple appears, I developed the hypothesis that it is an apostle who still reaches back to the time of Jesus' life on earth, but did not belong to the group of the twelve and so also did not share the experience of Jesus' entire ministry, but was possibly a witness of the last events, perhaps a Jerusalem disciple of Jesus. On account of the close connection between tradition and interpretation, I was, admittedly, unwilling to separate him from the 'evangelist' who wrote down the gospel; thus, in essence, attributing the gospel to him.[20] I must now revise this cautiously expressed opinion, in accordance with the considerations set out above (under 1): it is true, the beloved disciple is the chief repository of the tradition, the authority who stands behind the gospel; but the gospel itself comes from another connected with him, possibly an educated Hellenist of Jewish origin, an exceptional theologian, who took up the tradition of the beloved disciple while also using other sources, interpreted them theologically, and put them together into a gospel which was to serve the Johannine Church and, over and above it, persons of that period who were seeking. In 1970, I also still laid great weight on the expression ὁ γράψας ταῦτα in 21:24; but, in the meantime, this weight has declined for me (see ad loc.). The distinction between the beloved disciple as the final authority standing behind John's gospel, and the evangelist as the answerable compiler of the concrete form of the work (apart from the editorial additions), is further underlined by the following considerations:

a. It is hardly imaginable that the beloved disciple would introduce himself with this pretentious designation. Assuming that those passages in which it is used are an integral part of the gospel, the only remaining consequence is that this designation comes from the evangelist who with it wanted to express his high esteem for the disciple to whom he owes most. But the designation seems to have been normal in general among the circle of disciples belonging to this apostle, as can be concluded from its inclusion as a matter of course in the editorial Chapter 21 (especially v. 7).

b. If it is asked what the evangelist really knew about the beloved disciple and his witness to the story of Jesus, then the answer is complicated by the fact that the evangelist apparently is combining theological intentions with the introduction of the disciple: he is the one who lies 'close to the breast of Jesus' and to whom Jesus opens himself in a special way (13:23–26). The mother of Jesus is directed to him and entrusted to him (19:26f) – according to

H. Schuermann's exegesis which I have followed,[21] an expression of the fact that all who expect salvation from the one lifted up and who would receive his word, are referred to the beloved disciple as the one handing down and interpreting Jesus' message. He is the first to attain faith in Jesus' resurrection (20:8) and so becomes the prototype of the believer. Thus, for the evangelist, the beloved disciple is already more than an 'historical' witness; he is for him already an ideal figure. So it is already necessary to reckon with ideal and symbolic features in the presentation of those scenes. But that does not rule out that the beloved disciple is still numbered by the evangelist with the 'original witnesses' who had contact with the other well-known disciples (especially Peter) and with Mary the mother of Jesus. Here, the argument used on behalf of the editors is to be repeated, that Peter with whom the evangelist associates (13:24) and also confronts (cf. 20:2–10) the beloved disciple, and Mary the mother of Jesus, are historical persons beside whom a purely symbolic or fictitious figure does not sensibly find a place. Thus, the evangelist will have known of such contacts of the beloved disciple, possibly heard of them through him personally. According to the position of the passages, we are to think particularly of Jesus' last days and the time after Easter, respectively.

c. It can be observed with the evangelist that he picks up many kinds of traditions and then actualizes them for the situation of the Church of his day. That particularly applies to the controversies with contemporary Judaism or its outstanding representatives, the pharisaic teachers, who also exercise a certain external authority. The account in Chapters 5; 7; 9 is particularly instructive for this. Following the healing of the man who had been ill for many years, in the Pool of Bethzatha (5:1–9) comes a long controversy with the 'Jews' who accuse Jesus of offending against the Sabbath and claiming equality with God (v. 18). Thus, the evangelist refers to the handed-down Sabbath-conflicts of the historical Jesus, also adding the accusation, moreover, that he gives to himself a position of equality with God and claims rights reserved to God (raising from the dead and judgment, cf. vv. 21–23), accusations which played a rôle at the beginning of the second century in the dispute between Judaism and Christianity. We noticed something similar in the messianic question, where it is of central significance in Chapter 7 (see on vv. 27f, 41f, 52). The 'chief priests and pharisees' suppress the faith which is beginning to grow among the people (vv. 32, 45), and in this, the pharisees are the acute observers (v. 32a) and spokesmen (vv. 47f). In this can be seen the pharisee-led Judaism at the time of the evangelist. The account becomes especially concrete following the healing of the blind man in Chapter 9. Here too, the transition is achieved by the comment that the healing occurred on the sabbath (v. 14). During the Pharisees' interrogation of the man who was healed, it becomes completely clear that Jesus' time was at an end and that the attention is on measures of the Jewish authorities at the time of the evangelist (exclusion from the synagogue). This lucidity of presentation recognizable throughout the account is rather to be supposed of a man who is in the middle of the later controversies, than of one handing on the tradition looking back to Jesus and his arguments with the Jewish leaders of his time which, surely, were differently slanted.

d. Finally, once again, the question of the eye-witness is to be addressed. With the majority of scholars, John's gospel as a whole can hardly be regarded as the account of a man who shared in everything or experienced it 'at first hand'. The use of sources also speaks against this; at least a source for reports of miracles ($\sigma\eta\mu\varepsilon\tilde{\iota}\alpha$-source) and a pre-Johannine passion- and Easter-account, became increasingly certain in the course of the commentary. Both sources in the form I want to accept them (without great precision), without investigating their possible connection and without excluding, on principle, other source-theories, solely on the basis of textual analysis, cannot be dated very early. Is it thinkable that an apostle of Jesus' day made use of such late sources? It can be thought rather that he confirmed much that was contained in them, or gave his approval to them as a whole. But an account built on that is, however, to be attributed rather to another man who did not already have any direct access, who no longer had any real recollections of the time of Jesus. It can also be imagined that the evangelist produced his gospel in contact with the beloved disciple, or obtained his approval; but a direct composition of the gospel by the beloved disciple who must already have attained a tremendous age, is improbable. The beloved disciple may still be regarded as guarantor of its contents even in the event of an independent composition of the gospel by the evangelist.

3. The Identity of the Disciple whom Jesus loved

The question as to who the beloved disciple was, has continued to be asked to the present day – and is without a solution. Since 1965, more authors have defended the traditional view that it is John the son of Zebedee, on the Catholic side especially J. Colson[22] and B. de Solages,[23] but certainly still more whose publications have eluded me; on the Protestant side, L. Morris (although he notices a growing reluctance to attribute authorship to the apostle John among English and American scholars[24]). The whole discussion cannot be taken up here once again; anyhow, few new points of view have surfaced. On the supposition that the beloved disciple only hands on the tradition and is the final authority behind John's gospel, which for the rest, was written by an independent theologian, his identity with the apostle John cannot, it is true, be declared as impossible in itself;[24a] but it is another question whether this is probable. Here, I-wish to mention briefly the main reasons which have made me doubt this supposition (contrary to Vol. 1, pp. 101ff).

a. The eye-witness of the fisherman's son from the Sea of Gennesaret should be more obvious. Each narrator telling of his own experiences will refer to it already when choosing his material. Now, it is true that we can point to some concrete details about the baptismal activity of John the Baptist and about the disciples who went over from him to Jesus, but whether they originate from an eye-witness or were obtained in another way, is by no means certain. Otherwise, we learn little, especially from Jesus' Galilean activity (Chapter 6). The main stress of the account is on the journeys to Jerusalem and the events in Jerusalem. Should not the authority behind the evangelist rather be sought there?

b. The anonymity of the beloved disciple can only be explained with difficulty, if the apostle John is concealed behind it. It could be understandable that he did not want to name himself; but why should the evangelist keep silent about the name of somebody who was sufficiently known to the primitive Christian Churches? The analogous case of the 'teacher of righteousness' in Qumran fails due to the fact that with the apostle John we are not dealing with a man who had significance only within the congregation, but a personality known and highly valued in primitive Christianity, as appears from the synoptic gospels and the Acts of the Apostles (here especially, 3:1–11; 4:13–22; 8:4–17; 12:2). Surely, the evangelist does not otherwise have any hesitation in mentioning by name other disciples from the circle of the twelve.

c. The editors refer to the 'sons of Zebedee' in the group of seven disciples in Jn 21:2, and yet two more besides without names. The beloved disciple who, according to 21:7, recognized Jesus on the shore, thus belongs to this group; it can naturally be conjectured that he is one of the sons of Zebedee, but just as well that he is concealed behind one of the two unnamed disciples. The latter seems more likely; for when the sons of Zebedee who were known by name in the churches, are mentioned, why is the beloved disciple not introduced here at least as John? In any case, the principle of anonymity would be half way to being breached here by v. 2.[25]

d. The anonymity of the beloved disciple becomes immediately understandable if he really was a relatively unknown man in primitive Christianity. If the Johannine Church honoured him as the bearer of its tradition and the excellent interpreter of the message of Jesus, then it must have been interested in achieving additional recognition for his authority so as to justify its own self-regard. That was the starting-point of my hypothesis in 1970 and its positive justification seems to me to be the strongest argument for the apostle John not to be identified with the beloved disciple. He only came into the discussion later with the same considerations which, to the present day, make it possible to plead for the identity of the beloved disciple with the apostle John: a man from the inner circle of the disciples, with a special connection with Peter, never mentioned by name in John's gospel yet certainly among those accompanying Jesus, an eye-witness, and so on. The Johannine circle did not want in any way to insinuate this falsely; but since scarcely anything specific was known concerning the beloved disciple in the universal Church in the second century, and people were dependent on general considerations, the apostle John was identified.

So a tradition, which is traceable since about AD 180, arose and became increasingly established within the Church. Whether the Valentinians were the first who saw the apostle John as the compiler, on account of their (Gnostic) interest in John's gospel,[26] remains to be seen. When the opinion gained predominance in the main body of the Church, that is neither a victory for Gnosticism – John's gospel could be interpreted in a fully orthodox way and even obtained a growing significance for Christology and the teaching about the Trinity – nor a fatal error, considering that the validity of John's gospel as a testimony to apostolic tradition does not depend on this authorship. The origin of our gospel of Matthew from the *apostle* Matthew is no less doubtful, and the gospels of Mark and Luke also lose nothing of their significance for us, if we cannot take them back to the *disciples* of the apostles whose names they bear. However, the question is not unimportant whether John's gospel is an anonymous, obscure work of doubtful origin, or whether it does have a connection with that original generation of witnesses from the time of Jesus, which the later Church called upon for its 'apostolic tradition'. The relatively early canonical recognition of John's gospel (cf. Vol. 1, pp. 192–202) was certainly furthered by the supposition that it came from the apostle John; but in the end, its reception and high regard is surely due to the fact that the Church recognized in it a clear and mature testimony of its faith in Christ, and adopted it as its own.

So my hypothesis of 1970 has once more to be briefly explained, further analyzed and delineated. The anonymous figure introduced by the evangelist and the editors as the 'disciple whom Jesus loved' and brought in at the last supper, is an historical person, an apostle, who, however, did not belong to the circle of the twelve, and was most likely to have been a man from Jerusalem. This surmise is not new but has been repeatedly propounded and in many variations. In the search for a specific person we come up, above all, against Lazarus and John Mark. Lazarus, for whom J. N. Sanders has lately expressed support,[27] owes his candidacy mainly to the comments in Jn 11:5 that Jesus loved Martha, her sister and Lazarus (ἠγάπα), in Jn 11:36: 'See how he loved him (ἐφίλει)', and the rumour that the beloved disciple was not going to die (21:22). But those are not convincing reasons; why is he not mentioned later any more by name, as he was again after being raised in 12:2 and 12:9? John Mark attains the same honour[28] on account of the name John (cf. Acts 12:12, 25; 15:37), and on account of the opinion that the supper-room is identical with the house where the Jerusalem Christians gathered, which belonged to his mother Mary (Acts 12:12; cf. 1:13). If Mark was the son of the house in which Jesus' last meal with his disciples took place, it is easily explained that he took part in it and – perhaps as the youngest – lay at Jesus' side. Now the tradition concerning the supper-room is quite uncertain[29] and the name of John is interesting at most in connection with a later confusion; only this much may be certain, that Mark came from Jerusalem and was still a young man at the time (but was not necessarily the one mentioned in Mk 14:51f). It is improbable that Mark, the later companion of Paul, should be not only the source of information for John's gospel but the authority for the Johannine Church. So this hypothesis too must be rejected as a supposition with too little basis, indeed, all identifications with a well-known personality in primitive Christianity must be regarded as questionable.

However, within the Mark-hypothesis, there is contained a not unimportant observation: we do not know exactly who took part in the farewell meal; only in the editorial link Mk 14:17 (par. Mt 26:20; Lk 22:14: 'the apostles') does it say that Jesus came in the evening 'with the twelve', then again, in the saying of Jesus concerning the traitor, 'one of the twelve' (only in Mk 14:20). Does the fourth evangelist know something more about the participation of the beloved disciple in the last supper? In 1970, I propounded the view that Jn 13:23–26 concerns an ideal scene so as to bring in the disciple and introduce him in his rôle as a confidant of Jesus. Now, his presence seems to me no longer wholly ruled out, although the account gives cause for doubt (cf., *ad loc.*). Historical reminiscences and theological intentions can also not easily be separated elsewhere in John's gospel. The same problem comes up again with 19:26f and 20:2–10. But that is no reason to doubt the beloved disciple's historicity and his connection with the inner circle of disciples at the time of Jesus' passion and afterwards.

If the possibility that the beloved disciple was someone from Jerusalem is pursued, it is not ruled out, although it cannot be proved, that the disciple mentioned in 18:15 who made possible Peter's entry into the court of the high priest, is supposed to be identical with him.[29a] The (correct) reading without an article 'another disciple' (see *ad loc.*) can, admittedly, also point to an otherwise unknown man. Since the evangelist elsewhere expressly mentions the beloved disciple (19:26) or refers back to him (20:2, 'the other disciple, the one whom Jesus loved'), this is even more probable. All the same, we thus get to know another man from Jerusalem, an acquaintance of the high priest, who has to belong to the followers of Jesus. With him and Nicodemus, Joseph of Arimathaea, the summarily mentioned disciples in Judea-Jerusalem (7:3), Lazarus and his sisters in Bethany, there thus results a not inconsiderable circle of people who come within the scope of followers of Jesus in and near the capital. Even looked at critically, the thesis that the authority standing behind the evangelist had special connections with Jerusalem, is not to be rejected.

For the rôle of apostles in the first half of the second century, the much-discussed citation of Papias in Eusebius, *Hist. eccles.*, III, 39:3f has some weight. Apart from the controversy as to who is meant by the 'presbyter John' (cf. Vol. 1, pp. 80f), Papias testifies to the existence of apostles outside the circle of the twelve (irrefutable 'Aristion'), who played a part in the transmission of apostolic tradition. At this period, when the general designation 'disciples' for believers had already fallen into disuse, the term becomes a name honouring those who themselves have seen the Lord.[30] The beloved disciple can be regarded as one such honourable witness who, for the Churches which were already distant from the first generation, was an important carrier of the tradition. It is better to refrain from attempting an identification by name. Aristion, named by Papias, of whom we know, according to Eusebius' testimony, that Papias mentioned him frequently, ascribing to him 'traditions' and 'stories about the Lord's sayings' (*Hist. eccles.*, III, 39:7 and 14), is sufficient proof that there were such apostles. Whether the 'presbyter John' mentioned with him (q.v.) is to be brought into any kind of connection with the beloved disciple of the Johannine Church, is scarcely to be determined. It remains possible that he was confused with the apostle John at an early period;

but that is, in principle, of less importance. Our concern was that the historically supported view which agrees with the internal evidence of John's gospel, that the beloved disciple whom the editors identify with a long-lived apostle, may have been one such honourable witness, still from the time of Jesus, whom the Johannine Church honoured as their authority, bearer of the tradition and interpreter of Jesus' deeds and words.

With that, the riddle of the disciple whom Jesus loved is, admittedly, not solved, but, perhaps, somewhat illuminated. His anonymity, his honorific designation, his receding into the background of the gospel account which does not come from him personally but from a man connected with him, out of the Johannine circle, his idealization – all this then becomes more easily understandable.

4. An Overview of the Historical Origin of the Fourth Gospel

The hermeneutic circle whereby it is necessary to approach the texts with a certain blueprint or preconception, and then yet again to test and, when necessary, correct the initial concept according to the individual texts, was also inevitable in this commentary. In the Introduction (Vol. 1) I assumed, on the grounds of the consistent vocabulary and the special theology influencing the whole of John's gospel, that this work, in its essence, originated from the hand of a single man who conceived the layout as well as the presentation. It is true that even in those days I was led by observations of individual fragments, certain dislocations in the construction, gaps in the account, complicated passages in the text (e.g., 6:22–24), etc., above all the closing editorial chapter, to the conviction that the original, perhaps not yet completed gospel was still subjected to editing. Admittedly, it appeared to me that this was done extremely cautiously and, apart from Chapter 21, with only rather small additions and no intention to alter the concept as a whole. I would want to maintain this last after completion of the commentary; but with the farewell discourses and perhaps with the prayer of the departing Christ, more precise study has taught me that Chapters 15–16 and 17 respectively are, however, rather to be ascribed to other members of the Johannine circle than the evangelist. In the same way, considerable arguments spoke in favour of the same editors having brought in the second interpretation of the washing of the feet (13:12–17) and lesser additions in Chapter 13, possibly also the 'new commandment' (13:34f). That is worthy of note for the original account of the evangelist because then his intention in putting together his gospel becomes more clearly apparent and his design gives an impression of being tauter and more directed towards a goal. But the editors did not give the work a wholly new direction, but only extended it and adapted it more to the needs of the Church. The hour of departure with the farewell discourse of Jesus to his disciples was especially suitable for this; in this way, within the circle of those belonging to him, still more points of interest for the later Church are discussed. If the editors thought themselves to have an inward affinity with the evangelist, their procedure was legitimate and they acted in the spirit of the evangelist.

The question of the sources used in John's gospel was and continues to be difficult. The supposition of a σημεῖα-source for which I had already decided in Vol. 1, became a greater certainty, partly as a result of research which has appeared in the meantime. Admittedly, agreement concerning its extent is still not reached. The literary-critical work which has again come more into the foreground has brought new hypotheses, among them the point of view that the evangelist used, besides the σημεῖα-source, a 'fourth synoptic gospel' (G. Reim). While the σημεῖα-source gained in significance especially for Vol 2 concerning Jn 5–12, the question of a pre-Johannine gospel account of a synoptic kind, is a weighty one, especially with regard to the Johannine report of the passion and of Easter. Dauer's work has provided a good basis for this; other studies also have come to similar results. Thus, we can suppose that John used an account of the passion which, on the one hand, reveals points of contact with the synoptics, and on the other hand, on specific points (chronology, the Jewish examination during the night) parts company with them. That is something I began to recognize only when working on the present volume. Admittedly, many questions still remain open. Where did that pre-Johannine account begin, or alternatively, from where did the evangelist use it? Possibly, the death-sentence of the high council already belongs to it (11:47–54 with Johannine additions); then, the anointing in Bethany, entry into Jerusalem, the last supper with the washing of the feet, and so on, could have followed. In Vol. 2, I had as yet paid little attention to this question. It seems certain to me that John found a simple account of the washing of the feet, likewise, a passion account; that is set out in more detail in the commentary. But there should also have been a source used by John behind the Easter stories (apart from the Thomas-narrative). It is difficult to postulate several sources; the more sources we try to reconstruct, the more we are involved in the area of hypotheses. Besides, the question of sources was not the most important to me; a commentary has first of all to explain the existing text and need only enter into questions of sources in so far as this serves the understanding of tradition and the evangelist's theological interpretation. So, in this respect, further researches can be left to special studies.

The basic view shared by many scholars has not changed: our last canonical gospel came into being over a rather long period in the course of which traditions of varying origin were taken up. The evangelist who incorporated and interpreted them wanted to create a gospel with his own stamp. Finally, editors of like mind with the evangelist issued his work with some insertions and additions. Still more important for me is the recognition that John's gospel finally rests upon the authority of an apostle who, admittedly, did not take a direct share in the process of the work's coming into being, but remains more in the background as the one handing down the tradition and as 'witness'. The main purpose of this Excursus was to clarify a little more this question, which is significant for the reception of John's gospel by the Church.

On the Significance of John's Gospel Today

At the close of this commentary, which has searched for the most exact possible explanation of the text, and the intention behind what the evangelist and editors respectively said, and their theological points of view, not a few present-day readers will ask themselves what lasting value John's gospel possesses for theology and the Church, and especially how it fits within the bounds of our present questioning and understanding. Now and then brief glimpses into the future were given especially with regard to the Christological, eschatological and ecclesiological view of the evangelist. He nowhere denies that his mode of presentation is directed towards time and environment, the Church he is addressing and the conditions under which it is living. But, in accordance with his faith in the final revelation of salvation brought by Jesus Christ, in his work he really wants to offer more than a robe for the Christian message which is tailored to the questions and needs of a specific Christian congregation. He has at heart the absolute nature of Christ's revelation, and expresses it throughout in the language of his Christ. The history of the effect of John's gospel in the early Church and throughout all the Christian centuries is a sufficient indication that he was eminently successful in this. But our time, with its alert and critical awareness of the historicity of all events, the relation of thoughts and modes of expression to their time, and the suitability of language for a particular epoch, hardly hesitates to call into question the competence of such a work.

1. A not insubstantial hurdle, an obstacle not easy to overcome, is presented by the *relation of the fourth evangelist to history*, since people today have a burning interest to learn how everything was and took its course. Here, our evangelist, in accordance with his way of looking at things, which is dominated by faith and little interested in individual historical questions, largely lets them down, even more than the synoptics. Although John basically pays attention to the tradition and himself wants to present it, he has a different relationship to it to a historian, because he immediately reflects it in his faith in Christ and then interprets it for the believers; attention has been repeatedly drawn to his 'free' way with the tradition. Behind his particular way of looking at things stands a theological decision, which may seem to us at first foreign and incomprehensible and which can yet have a beneficially provocative effect.

With all that we know about the 'historical Jesus' we would still be far from an understanding of the person of Jesus in its uniqueness, remarkableness and unsurpassable significance. It is the problem known since the Enlightenment

389

with regard to the strivings after a 'life of Jesus' which, after the failure of such attempts in the nineteenth century, led to new reflections about the relationship between the 'historical Jesus and the Christ of faith' in our own century. John's gospel focuses on this problem, which is propounded no less by the synoptic gospels, with extreme clarity and sharpness of emphasis. For the whole of primitive Christianity the point is not the historical aspect as such; that, taken by itself, is to a considerable extent not only unattainable but in principle remains insufficient for faith, because it still does not open up any inward approach to the person of Jesus. John's answer can be inferred from the opposition of the unbelievers in his gospel, that of the 'Jews', those first and foremost called to understand Jesus and best equipped for it: true understanding is only opened up in belief, and that requires a deep insight which bathes Jesus' words and deeds, his passion and his entire person, in a new light. Just such a deep insight is what John wants to convey. Its truth, admittedly, is such that only someone treating Jesus' entire ministry as a unified whole, subjecting it to the idea of the revelation of God, and allowing himself to be spoken to and challenged by this revelation, can be convinced of. A standpoint in regard to this Johannine Jesus can only be taken up existentially, in a personal decision; an encounter with him can only be total, or there can be none at all. For the individual he either becomes light and life, door and way, or he remains wholly incomprehensible – a stumbling-block, and an abomination. This Jesus, in whom God manifests himself to believers on the highest level, becomes for unbelief the barrier and abyss which denies access to God.

2. For the synoptics, the 'historical Jesus' is already the *earthly Jesus* as he presents himself in relation to the *exalted Christ* who is with God. Jesus of Nazareth is only fully understood in the profession of the crucified and raised Christ. The picture of Jesus in the synoptic gospels remains incomplete and incomprehensible when it is observed coldly from a distance; it is opened up in its terseness and depth of meaning only when we succeed in looking at it in believing association with the primitive Church. All the same, the synoptic Jesus speaks the language of his own time, indeed, his own believable and comprehensible language, and he goes his way even to death on the cross in a human and humanly understandable way. It is true to say that the mystery of Jesus is only revealed to the one who, with the believing community and the evangelists, is prepared to follow the way of Jesus up to his resurrection. The fourth evangelist drew the final consequence from this access to the person of Jesus which is only possible to believers: already in the earthly Jesus we encounter the exalted Christ in his function of challenging us and placing us before a decision. Therefore he speaks a language which only the believer understands, gives signs whose meaning is only disclosed to the eye of the believer, and moves among men like one who belongs to another world; he completes his earthly life in a death which is a victory over this world and a promise of eternal life.

This seemingly unhistorical Jesus becomes the greatest provocation for a way of thinking which is restricted *only* to the historically understandable, to that which is accessible to the senses and superficial. But it would be a very great misunderstanding to impute to the fourth evangelist a move away from the historical Jesus in favour of a supra-historical idea or an imaginary figure. Rather, he wants to throw light especially on the earthly Jesus by means of the Christ of faith, because for him the one who came into history unavoidably raised the question whether he is the Christ, that is, God's final revelation for the salvation of mankind. The Johannine Jesus is no God walking over the earth but the very man in whom God in his love and challenge directly encounters mankind.

Moreover, the earthly Jesus is not the Christ who is already exalted with God; this the evangelist knows very well and expresses it clearly in Jesus' anticipation of his 'hour'. But this highly-significant 'hour' of the 'lifting up' on the cross shows that his way leads via the cross into God's glory. Because, for the believing Church, Jesus lives with God, that is, is already the one lifted up, at the same time being present and near to it, the Church should hear the words of the earthly Jesus as the voice of its exalted Lord, of the Christ who is present. And so the evangelist formulates them in majestic language which is very distant from the speech of the synoptic Jesus. A look back to Jesus' earthly ministry and a lifting up of the eyes to the Christ blend with one another; history and present time are joined together in the person of Jesus Christ. Under this aspect, there is, for John, no diastasis of history and faith.

3. Not only the Johannine Jesus' language but the *language of John's gospel* in general faces us moderns with problems. Indeed, we are still or again able to hear and to consider metaphorical and symbolic language addressed to our human existence and intended to enlighten our understanding of existence – such as talk of walking in light and darkness (cf. 12:35f); but even the sharp contrast between the world 'below' and that 'above' no longer corresponds to our feeling about the world, and we are wholly reduced to aporias, where, apparently, the language of myth rules. The controversy about 'demythologizing' lies, it is true, in the past, and, meanwhile, we have again won a better understanding of myths as well as the right to speak mythologically. But we find it disquieting when the whole idea of the descent and ascent of the Son of Man, of pre-existence, the earthly life, and of the return of God's messenger into the heavenly glory is supposed to rest on a myth which John, allegedly, took over and transferred to Jesus Christ. This commentary has dealt with this opinion critically and rejected it in its radical form (see Excursus 6 in Vol. 1); but a certain influence of this kind on the evangelist's language and way of looking at things cannot be denied, and we come up against this language in John's gospel on every page. It is a barrier for modern man who is used to rational and scientific thought and is not easily able to recognize the 'truth' clothed in such language. Yet its very strangeness perhaps affords a necessary jolt, to force us out of accustomed tracks of thought and direct us to deeper consideration of the meaning and goal of our life.

All religious language finally leads to the *question of God*. Yet just this has become a problem today: how to speak of God so as to reach mankind and enable him to experience this reality as something concerning him? The language of the Johannine Jesus about God, his Father, and about himself as 'the Son', and the notion of the divine messenger are, for many today, not easily acceptable. But again, such language expresses with extreme pungency the notion that God is not directly experienced and accessible, but he is indeed in Jesus Christ, who is himself directly united with God and yet is wholly devoted to mankind. The Johannine Jesus wants to bring near to men the distant and strange, unfamiliar and misunderstood God. He who is not trapped by the 'mythological' mode of expression and the outrageous 'self-pretension' of the Johannine Jesus, but keeps listening to what this Jesus says to and assures mankind of, will understand the meaning of such a mode of expression. All *ego-eimi* sayings lead to the affirmation and promise of true, unending life for mankind. All this language intends its hearers only to become certain of the presence of the loving, life-giving, saving God.

Admittedly, for modern man, and for the Christian reader, the Johannine language has its limits. The extremely hard, unforgiving words of the Johannine Jesus concerning the unbelieving Jews, their designation as 'children of the devil' (8:44), the judgment concerning the pharisees as blind because of their guilt (9:39–41), the concealed accusation against the leaders as 'thieves and robbers' (cf. 10:1, 8) and so on, are indeed strange. We also learn from the synoptic gospels of Jesus' criticism of false piety and about his opposition to the leading circles of contemporary Judaism; but in John's gospel these emphases appear to be immeasurably increased, so that the merciful herald of God's love is scarcely recognizable any more (unless in the non-Johannine pericope of the adulterous woman). This unvarnished language can no longer be entirely explained by the Johannine kerygma of the one who reveals and calls to decision, but it must also, in part, be accounted for by the contemporary controversy with hostile Judaism. This black-and-white representation which seems to permit of no mean between faith and unbelief, good and evil, fellowship with God and falling away to Satan, can no longer be maintained in our time. But we need not take over such a viewpoint concerning certain men and groups. Rather we can learn from John's gospel as a whole to transfer the Christian message to a particular historical horizon. That gives us the right to strip off what in his account is conditioned by a certain time; it challenges us to take up some veiled and buried ideas and statements of Jesus, to bring them anew into our circumstances and make them bear fruit. When we thoroughly consider the way in which the fourth evangelist used the tradition, we are encouraged to read his gospel critically, in so far as it is an interpretation and adaptation for the Church of his day. Admittedly, we shall consider everything with a believing mind, in the same way as the Johannine circle of disciples, trusting in the guidance of the Spirit, and bearing in mind the words that point the direction for us: the Spirit of truth will guide you into all the truth, and he will declare to you the things that are to come (16:13).

4. The great strength of the Johannine gospel is the *existential way of looking at things*, the addressing of man in his human existence. That does not mean his individual and present conditions of life, but his essential nature as a man, his understanding of himself as being in the world, which is irrevocably a being for death. It is no accident that our gospel attained a special evidential strength for

a Christian existentialism in Bultmann's existential theological interpretation. The question of 'where from?' and 'where to?' is raised, it is true, not directly for every man but in regard to Jesus Christ (cf. 7:27–36; 8:14), and in him the believer receives the answer: to follow Christ means not to walk in the darkness but to have the light of life (8:12). The bounds of death are accepted but overcome in faith; he who believes in Jesus Christ who is the resurrection and the life, will live also when he has died (11:25). In general, the picture of the way which is to the fore in Christology, is appropriate to mankind as it finds itself continually under way, and provides an answer to its unrest and uncertainty as to where its path is leading. Jesus Christ becomes the way for every man because he is the truth and the life (14:6), not only showing the way but escorting us on it. In contrast to all gnosis, he mediates not only liberating knowledge but *gives* us the life which lasts beyond physical death and overcomes it. He already gives this life (with everything which distinguishes it) to the believer now. True freedom, peace, joy . . . I do not need to develop this theology of salvation further, which is based on faith in the present living Christ. I would only stress the unconquerable strength that can proceed from it, for modern man as well.

Where there is much light there is also no lack of shadow. The great theologian whom we call John stressed some things unmistakably, and obscured other things which are important for us today. Many will miss in him the social commitment which is close to our hearts in the modern world situation. In this respect, the synoptic Jesus, who more faithfully retains the voice and behaviour of the historical Jesus, offers stronger incentives. The lack of openness to society and its problems is certainly connected with the external situation and the inner self-understanding of the Johannine community. In this regard it cannot be the example for the Church of our day. But, just as John's gospel was not intended in any way to 'displace' or 'replace' the synoptic gospels, so (in this respect) we referred to the synoptics and their picture of Jesus, in accordance with the providential gift of the four gospels.

5. Another prominent feature of Johannine theology has to be discussed in regard to its modern significance – the *eschatology* which is *brought into the present*. This feature and the problems which it raises were presented in Excursus 14 at the end of Vol. 2. But how is this way in which the evangelist looks at things to be judged in the context of our time? Many people nowadays are enthusiastically occupied with the question of the future, and modern theology has rightly taken up this question, in part with firm demands for Christian proclamation and action by the Church (e.g., theology of hope, 'political' theology and theology of liberation) in the present hour, in view of the global problems of mankind and of rapid development and urgent necessity. If Christianity wants to be the 'salt of the earth' and 'light of the world', it cannot withdraw into a protected area of silent contemplation and a quiet life full of inner joy and believing certainty. John's gospel appears to introduce nothing else for the perspective of the future – yet that would be a superficial view. Its avoidance of apocalyptic thinking, its tendency to demythologizing images of the future, is not to be underestimated. But over

and above that, Johannine theology does mankind (which has to withstand the threatening future) an invaluable service. For it turns our gaze on man's inner powers, providing him with something to cling on to – a foothold in the darkness and turmoil of the world; it does not allow him to be overcome by and to drown in the seeming senselessness of existence. Man, in his decisions and actions, continues to be the decisive factor for future development; the future is determined not only by science and technology, economics and politics, but by the behaviour and responsible action of men, as futurologists too also see. In Jesus Christ the believer who understands the message of John's gospel gains a firm hold on the present and the future, and is directed to brotherly love as the decisive norm of his action.

In this commentary I have repeatedly mentioned the danger of withdrawal from the world in which the Johannine Church stands, but this is not necessarily connected with the Johannine theology. Contrary to other interpretations, I maintain that John's gospel proclaims the universal will of God to save the world (3:16f; 4:42; 12:32, 46f); the sending of the Church into the world (17:18; 20:21); and brotherly love, not in a restricted but in an exemplary sense (13:34f; cf. 1 Jn 3:14f), and hence as a comprehensive love for man (cf. 1 Jn 4:11, 19ff). Also the change of perspective to the present does not mean being closed to the future. Rather, the future is, indeed, finally decided by Christ's victory on the cross (cf. 12:31; 16:11, 33), but is still presented to the Church as the goal of its efforts. This is expressed in the final clauses of the prayer in Jn 17: 'So that the world may believe [or 'know'] that thou hast sent me' (vv. 21, 23). The Johannine Church certainly wants to win the world for God more through its existence and manner of belonging to God than through propaganda and activity; but in the experienced diastasis from the world it does not forget, however, its obligation to mankind – which the exalted One would draw to himself. In the perspective of our own times, such an attitude is not sufficient; but we have also been entrusted with a goal-oriented way of thinking. The assurance vouchsafed by Christ's victory on the cross compels us so much the more to act responsibly in the world, and the future opened up to us from God in Christ compels us to human effort in the present, in the hour of history assigned to us.

Throughout, the greatness and the limitations of the last canonical gospel are apparent. It is *one* voice in the choir of NT witnesses and interpreters of the Christian message, but an important and enduring one, if we know how to hear it aright and to translate it within the scope of our own understanding.

NOTES

INTRODUCTION TO CHAPTERS 13–20: Pages 1–5

1. For the view expressed by W. Wilkens, in *Die Entstehungsgeschichte des vierten Evangeliums* (Zollikon & Zürich, 1958), that the evangelist refashioned his work at a later stage into a 'gospel of the passion', see Vol. 1, pp. 68f. For the evangelist's intention to refashion his work in this way in the last phase of the public work of Jesus (11:55—12:36), see Vol. 2, pp. 362ff.

2. Very many different assessments have been made of the structure of the gospel of Mark. (See the recent commentaries.) The radical division at 8:27 or 8:31 is, however, recognized by most exegetes as valid, and the further division by means of the three prophecies of the passion (8:31; 9:31; 9:31; 10:32ff) in the first section of Jesus' 'way of death' is also hardly ever questioned. See, for example, my own commentary, *Das Evangelium nach Markus,* Part II (Düsseldorf, 1971).

3. See G. Richter, 'Die Deutung des Kreuzestodes Jesu in der Leidensgeschichte des Johannesevangeliums (Jo 13–19)', *BuL,* 9 (1968), pp. 21–36; R. E. Brown, *The Gospel According to John,* Vol. II, pp. 581–604; J. Becker, 'Die Abschiedsreden Jesu im Johannesevangelium', *ZNW* 61 (1970), pp 215–246; H. Thyen, 'Johannes 13 und die "Kirchliche Redaktion" des vierten Evangeliums', *Tradition und Glaube. Festgabe für K. G. Kuhn* (Göttingen, 1971), pp. 343–356.

4. See G. Richter, *Die Fusswaschung im Johannesevangelium* (Regensburg, 1967), pp. 301–320. See also the books and articles listed in the preceding note. See also the section 'Literary Criticism', notes 6–25 below.

5. See J. Blank, 'Die Verhandlung vor Pilatus Joh 18,28—19,16 im Lichte johanneischer Theologie', *BZ,* NS 3 (1959), pp. 60–81; I. de la Potterie, 'Jésus, roi et juge d'après Jn 19, 13', *Bib* 41 (1960), pp. 217–247; M. Weise, 'Passionswoche und Epiphaniewoche im Johannesevangelium', *KeDog* 12 (1966), pp. 48–62; G. Richter, 'Die Deutung des Kreuzestodes', *op. cit.;* F. Hahn, *Der Prozess Jesu nach dem Johannesevangelium* (*EEK* 2, Zürich and Neukirchen, 1970), pp. 23–96; A. Dauer, *Die Passionsgeschichte im Johannesevangelium* (Munich, 1972).

SECTION I: CHAPTER 1: Pages 6–32

6. A further question is whether the first or the second interpretation is the earlier one. Any attempt to answer this question must distinguish the traditio-historical from the literary level. Many exegetes regard the 'moralizing' interpretation as the original one and the Christological and soteriological one as later. From the literary-critical viewpoint, the process may have taken place in the opposite direction. (See the analysis.)

7. *Das Evangelium Johannis*, pp. 58–61.

8. *Das Johannesevangelium als Quelle der Geschichte Jesu*, pp. 285–296.

9. *Studien zum vierten Evangelium*, pp. 99–102.

10. *Das Evangelium des Johannes*, pp. 351f.
11. *The Gospel of Signs*, pp. 155–158.
12. '*Le lavement des pieds* (Jn XIII, 1–17)', *RB* 71 (1964), pp. 5–24.
13. *The Gospel according to John*, pp. 560f.
14. *Die Fusswaschung*, pp. 301–313.
15. 'Johannes 13 und die "Kirchliche Redaktion"', see above.
16. See, for example, E. Güttgemanns, *Studia linguistica neotestamentica* (Munich, 1971); R. Barthes, *et al.*, *Exégèse et Herméneutique* (Paris, 1971); W. Richter, *Exegese als Literaturwissenschaft* (Göttingen, 1971); R. Kieffer, *Essais de méthodologie néotestamentaire* (Lund, 1972); M. van Esbroeck, *Hermeneutik, Strukturalismus und Exegese* (Munich, 1972); W. Dressler, *Einführung in die Textlinguistik* (Tübingen, 1972); A. Stock, *Umgang mit theologischen Texten* (Einsiedeln, 1974).
17. See A. Weiser, 'Joh 13, 12–20 – Zufügung eines späteren Herausgebers?', *BZ*, new series 12 (1968), pp. 252–257.
18. Many commentators make a division between 13:1–20 and 13:21–30; these include R. Bultmann, R. E. Brown, B. Lindars, and literary critics of Scripture such as J. Wellhausen, F. Spitta and E. Hirsch; see also M.-E. Boismard.
19. See especially 12:40; 19:37. Both of these contain quotations that deviate considerably from the Septuagint; see E. D. Freed, *Old Testament Quotations in the Gospel of John* (Leiden, 1965), pp. 89–93. It is not at all necessary to conclude from τρώγειν that the same editor was at work here as in the case of 6:54, 56, 57, 58.
20. H. Thyen, *op. cit.*, p. 355, believes that verse 20 should be understood in the light of the following scene with the disciple whom Jesus loved and even more so on the basis of the controversy with Diotrephes, who 'refused to accept those who rightly appealed to the "disciple whom Jesus loved" and to give them hospitality'. Quite apart from the improbability of this hypothesis, the verb ἐπιδέχεσθαι is used in 3 Jn 9f.
21. *Op. cit.*, p. 352.
22. *Op. cit.*, p. 353. There is no reference to a 'morsel' in the synoptic accounts, only to the fact that the traitor was eating with Jesus and 'dipped his bread in the same dish' as Jesus (Mk 14:18, 20).
23. J. Jeremias, *The Eucharistic Words of Jesus* (London, 1966), pp. 41f, (to whom H. Thyen appeals) did not use the 'morsel' as proof that the last supper was a passover meal, nor did he mention this morsel anywhere among his fourteen observations. See also the commentary under 13:36.
24. For lying or reclining at meals, see Billerbeck, IV, p. 618; J. Jeremias, *op. cit.*, pp. 48f. If the evangelist accepted the synoptic tradition in vv. 21f, the ἀνακεῖσθαι of the disciple close to Jesus' breast would be understandable. This is an idea that he may himself have taken from that tradition.
25. See Wellhausen, *op. cit.*, p. 61: 'Verses 28 and 29 are meaningless and probably interpolated.' See also Hirsch, *Studien, op. cit.*, p. 102.
26. See N. Füglister, *Die Heilsbedeutung des Pascha* (Munich, 1963), pp. 21–23; J. K. Howard, 'Passover and Eucharist in the Fourth Gospel', *Scott JTh* 20 (1967), pp. 329–337. A recognition of this theological intention on the part of the fourth evangelist may and indeed must lead to the historical question about the relationship between the last supper and the Jewish feast of the passover as celebrated at that time receding into the background. R. Feneberg, *Christliche Passafeier und Abendmahl* (Munich, 1971), tried to explain the accounts of the last supper in the light of the history of the feast of Easter in the early Church; see N. Walker's review in *ThLZ* 97 (1972), pp. 844–847.
27. This was observed by John Chrysostom, Cyril of Alexandria and Ammonius Saccas (Fragment 441, Reuss, p. 307). It has also been seen more recently by W. Bauer, R. Bultmann (p. 352) and W. Grossouw, 'A Note on John XIII 1–3', *NT* 8 (1966), pp. 124–131, especially p. 128.
28. See 9:4; 11:9; 12:7, 23f, 27, 32f, 35. This direct 'knowledge' that Jesus has continues throughout the passion, from his arrest (18:4) until the last moment on the

cross (19:28). For this knowledge, which is characteristic of the Johannine Jesus, see I. de la Potterie, *Bib* 40 (1959), pp. 716f.

29. Augustine, *In Ev. Jo. tract. LV* 1 (CC, p. 464), made a connection between the 'transition' in the Latin translation (*ut transeat*) and the word *'Pascha': 'Ecce Pascha, ecce transitus'*. The Greek Fathers were aware of the difference between μετάβασις and διάβασις, but the interpretation first made by Augustine was the one that persisted in the fifth-century Latin sermons. See W. Huber, *Passa und Ostern, Untersuchungen zur Osterfeier der alten Kirche* (Berlin, 1969), pp. 126–129.

30. It does not necessarily express a relative period of time, in other words, 'after he had loved'. It may also point to an attitude that still exists. See Blass-Debr. § 339. In this verse, then, the participle clearly has an establishing function.

31. See Blass-Debr. § 318, 1.

32. C. Spicq wrote well about this special characteristic in *RB* 65 (1958), pp. 360–362: 'It is a decisive, unchallengeable and definitive proof.'

33. See the evidence in Bauer, *Wörterbuch*, pp. 1606f; for the connection between the two meanings, see also p. 453, under the word εἰς; see also C. Spicq, *op. cit.* (note 32), pp. 361f in the notes.

34. See John Chrysostom, *Photius* (fragment 77, Reuss, p. 394), P. Schanz, J. H. Bernhard and others; W. Grossouw, *op. cit.*, p. 128. In later commentaries, the emphasis is more on the death of Jesus, as in Augustine, *In Ev. Jo. Tract.*, 2; Thomas Aquinas, *In Jo. Lect.* 1 (Cajetan No. 1738).

35. According to the external evidence, the present participle takes precedence over the aorist participle (see the more recent editions), but the aorist is found in P[66] (γεναμένου) and also in D θ V L (apart from d) 33 λ ⌀ al. and persisted later (see the apparatus in the UBS Greek New Testament). It is questionable whether the aorist is the more difficult reading, because the washing of the feet would then be assumed to be at the end of the meal.

36. See Bauer, *Wörterbuch*, p. 261, under the word βάλλω, 2, b.

37. See W. Bauer, *ad loc.* The manuscripts in which the name of Judas (in various forms) follows the words τὴν καρδίαν (A D θ e λ ⌀ P pl) clearly aim to make the text easier. Bultmann, *op. cit.*, p. 353, 4, and Thyen, *op. cit.*, p. 351, think differently. This text, in their view, is the original text of the editor, which was changed by B ℵ L, to restore the balance with v. 27. (But how is this done?) For the different way of writing the name of the traitor, see the apparatus in the UBS Greek New Testament. It is worth noting that Ἰσκαριώτης (P[66] ℵ B Orig), here as in 12:4 (see 14:22; 'Judas'), does not belong to the patronymic 'Simon', as in 6:71; 13:26. Does this betray the hand of the editor? See also 6:71 in Vol. 2, p. 78.

38. Ammonius Saccas, writing on Jn 13:27 (Fragment 457, Reuss, p. 310), made a distinction between the 'prompting' (ἐμβαλεῖν) of Satan and his 'driving in', which was like an external blow with the hand, the thrusting in of a sword. According to Luke, Satan entered Judas at the beginning of the meal (22:3). There is a probable traditio-historical connection with Jn 13:27 (σατανᾶς!), but no direct dependence on Luke in the case of the fourth gospel.

39. See Bultmann, p. 353, who regarded the first εἰδώς clause together with other parts of v. 1 as the original introduction to Chapter 17 (p. 351). See also Thyen, *op. cit.*, pp. 346f.

40. τὰ ἱμάτια in the plural can also mean the outer garment; see Bauer, Wb, p. 744, under that word, 3.

41. It was not simply the duty of a slave. It was also one of the duties that a wife had to perform for her husband and sons and daughters for their father. See Billerbeck, II p. 557.

42. Origen, *Comm. in Jo.* XXXII 4 (GCS IV, 431): 'See in this how the great and glorified Word makes himself small by becoming flesh in order to wash his disciples' feet!' (trans., R. Gögler). Origen interprets the bowl as Scripture, which contains the cleansing Word (water). This symbolic interpretation was of importance to the great

biblical theologians' understanding of Scripture: the Logos in the form of a servant as it were continued in Scripture. A similar exegesis of Jn 1:27 is found in his Fragment XVIII. He explains the 'thong of the sandal' as the Word of God carrying out what he plans for men, not through his naked divinity, but by 'assuming the form of a servant' (Gögler, pp. 187f).

43. Cf. 4:31–34; 6:7–9, 67–70; 9:2–5; 11:8–10; 14:5–10.

44. ἄρτι occurs frequently in the fourth gospel (twelve times; see also 1 Jn 2:9; cf. only seven times in Mt and not at all in Mk and Lk). νῦν often has a theological meaning in the fourth gospel: it refers to the eschatological hour in 4:23; 5:25, and to Jesus' hour in 12:27, 31; 13:31; 16:5; 17:5. The neutral term ἄρτι only draws attention to the temporal difference between now and later. See Bauer, *Wörterbuch,* p. 218, under 3.

45. Many of those who have examined this text, both early and more recent scholars (Cyril of Alexandria, Thomas Aquinas, Calmes, Schanz, Lagrange and W. Bauer, for example), thought this, but this view is not in accordance with the consistent pointing in vv. 6–10 of the washing of the feet to the death of Jesus. Very few scholars suggest it now.

46. See Bauer, *Wörterbuch,* p. 1001, under 2; Bultmann, p. 357, 3, who believed that, following the OT model, the phrase meant 'having a share in a definite third party' and this can be narrowed down to the community of fate or shared fate. This is, of course, right, but Jesus' disciples' 'share' also includes community with the glorified Christ. G. Richter, *Fusswaschung,* p. 291, believes that it points to a share in Jesus' sonship, basing this conviction on Jn 20:17. For the meaning of the phrase, see M.-E. Boismard, *RB* 71 (1964), pp. 8f (having an inheritance in the OT is related, in John, to the 'eschatological world').

47. The interpretations referring to baptism (see G. Richter, *Fusswaschung,* pp. 216f) for the most part begin at verse 10a. Boismard, RB 71 (1964), pp. 16ff, however, drew a parallel between Jn 3:3 and 13:8 and saw baptism prefigured by the washing of the feet in the whole text. W. Thüsing included the moral interpretation in the symbolic and soteriological interpretation in vv. 6–11: 'Whoever refuses the service of love (the washing of the feet and the offering of life in the death on the cross that is symbolized by the washing) at the same time rejects the consequence of that service, which is to keep the commandment of love. Therefore he cannot have community with Jesus' (*Erhöhung und Verherrlichung*, p. 134). See also the works of J. A. T. Robinson and J. D. G. Dunn below.

48. H. Leroy, *Rätsel und Missverständnis,* is too exclusively preoccupied with misunderstandings whose *Sitz im Leben* is in controversy between the community of believers and unbelievers. The phenomenon of misunderstanding also affected Jesus' disciples in other ways. Leroy therefore wrongly excludes this text and others from his investigation (see pp.7f).

49. For the history of biblical exegesis from the church Fathers until the present (1967), see G. Richter, *Fusswaschung.* This book contains a useful survey of modern approaches (pp. 247–284). See also W. Lohse, *Die Fusswaschung (Joh 13, 1–20). Eine Geschichte ihrer Deutung* (unpublished dissertation, Erlangen, 1967). Among the countless books and articles published on this subject, the following are particularly worth consulting: P.-H. Menoud, *L'Evangile de Jean d'après les recherches récentes* (Neuchâtel & Paris, [2]1947), pp. 54–56; this book contains a discussion of earlier works; F. Mussner, 'Die Fusswaschung (Joh 13, 1–17). Versuch einer Deutung', *Geist und Leben* 31 (1958), pp. 25–30; J. Michl, 'Der Sinn der Fusswaschung', *Bib* 40 (1959), pp. 697–708; J. A. T. Robinson, 'The Significance of the Foot-Washing', *Neotestamentica et Patristica* (Freundesgabe für O. Cullmann) (Leiden, 1962), pp. 144–147; P. Grelot, 'L'interprétation pénitentielle du lavement des pieds', *L'homme devant Dieu* (Mélanges H. de Lubac) (Paris, 1963), I, pp. 75–91; M.-E. Boismard, 'Le lavement des pieds (Jn 13, 1–17)', *RB* 71 (1964), pp. 5–24; H. Klos, *Die Sakramente im Johannesevangelium* (Stuttgart, 1970), pp. 85–93; J. D. G. Dunn, 'The Washing of the Disciples' Feet' in John 13, 1–20', *ZNW* 61 (1970), pp. 247–252.

50. See the apparatus in the UBS Greek New Testament (which is not very comprehensive). It is worth noting that a reinforcing μόνον soon appeared behind the εἰ μὴ τοὺς πόδας: p⁶⁶ Θ sy^{s.p} bo ^{ms}; an even longer extension in D. Boismard, RB 71 (1964), p. 12, points to the unnatural position of this addition in most manuscripts (apart from D d a). It should normally follow νίψασθαι.

51. As Lagrange has pointed out, p. 354, special attention should be paid to Origen, who quoted the short text four times, but used the long text in his exegesis. For the earlier Latin Fathers, see N. M. Haring, 'Historical Notes on the Interpretation of John 13, 10', *CBQ* 13 (1951), pp. 355–380. Boismard, *RB* 60 (1953), pp. 354f, mentioned other evidence in favour of the short text: 579 (a minuscule of Alexandrian provenance, thirteenth century) and other Fathers (including Jerome). He himself accepts the shortest text, that is, the Minuscule 579, in which even the νίψασθαι is absent. This absence may, however, have been a mistake on the part of the scribe. See also P. Grelot, *op. cit.*, p. 84.

52. J. A. T. Robinson, *op. cit.*, p. 146, note 3; Sanders and Mastin, p. 308 and L. Morris, pp. 618, are in favour of the long text. J. D. G. Dunn, *op. cit.*, pp. 250f; H. Thyen, *op. cit.*, p. 348; B. Lindars, pp. 415f are in favour of the short text. See also the confrontation in Dunn, p. 250, note 15.

53. J. Jeremias, *The Eucharistic Words,* pp. 49, 81f, concluded from Jn 13:10 that the disciples took a bath in order to eat the passover meal 'in a state of levitical purity'.

54. See Trench, *Synonyma*, pp. 93–95; F. Hauck, *ThWb* IV, pp. 945f. The distinction in meaning between these two verbs is not always preserved; see especially P. Oxy, p. 840. It does, however, usually apply; see Lagrange, p. 355.

55. Attention has also been drawn to the image of baptism for death in Mk 10:38. J. A. T. Robinson, *op. cit.*, p. 145, regards Jn 13:6–10 as the Johannine equivalent of Mk 10:32–45, but the exegesis that he provides is unconvincing. Dunn, *op. cit.*, p. 249, follows him.

56. See, for example, 1 Cor 6:11; Acts 22:16; Eph 5:26; Heb 10:22; Tit 3:5; (Apk 1:5, verse 1). See also R. Schnackenburg, *Baptism in the Thought of St Paul* (Oxford, 1964), pp. 3–17.

57. The point of departure of exegetes who find a connection here with baptism is not consistent. Several of these scholars have come to this view on the basis of their acceptance of the long text, insisting that 'being bathed' here refers to baptism and the washing of the feet refers to the Eucharist (or to penance); see, for example, G. Richter, *Fusswaschung*, pp. 254–256. Other exgetes prefer the shorter text, but also interpret this as pointing to baptism; see G. Richter, pp. 256f. H. von Campenhausen, 'Zur Auslegung von Joh 13, 6–10', *ZNW* 33 (1934), pp. 259–271, held a different opinion. He accepted the long text and regarded it as an argument in favour of baptism by sprinkling (in which the candidate stood with his feet in the water). H.-P. Menoud, *op. cit.*, pp. 55f, was critical of this view. For the question involved above, that is, whether there may be an allusion to baptism apart from any reference to the event of the cross, see, among others: C. H. Dodd, *Interpretation*, pp. 401f; A. Corell, *Consummatum est*, pp. 71ff; C. K. Barrett, p. 368. Even R. E. Brown, pp. 566f, does not exclude this possibility. Among those who have opposed this view are R. Bultmann; G. Richter (see also his list of opponents of the sacramental interpretation, p. 259); H. Klos, *op. cit.*, pp. 91f; J. D. G. Dunn, *op. cit.*, pp. 251f.

58. In accordance with the relevant texts in the passage on the marriage in Cana (see Vol. 1, pp. 339f) and that on the cleansing of the Temple (see Vol. 1, p. 353), an undercurrent of polemics against the Jewish practice of purification cannot be entirely ruled out. This opinion is held by W. Bauer, p. 172; E. Lohmeyer, 'Die Fusswaschung', *ZNW* 38 (1939), pp. 74–94; F. Hauck, *ThWB* IV, p. 946. It is also possible to assume, on the basis of the polemics against the (later) disciples of John, an opposition to baptismal practices (in the Jewish baptist sects). I have myself put this idea forward as a possibility in 'Die Sakramente im Johannesevangelium', *Sacra Pagina* II (Paris & Gembloux, 1959), pp. 235–254, see especially p. 250. I am now more sceptical about the veracity of this view.

59. See especially O. Cullmann, *Urchristentum und Gottesdienst* (Zürich, ²1950), pp. 102–110; W. Wilkens, *Entstehungsgeschichte*, p. 151; L. Bouyer, p. 190; B. Vawter, *ThSt* 17 (1956), p. 158; W. Grundmann, *Zeugnis und Gestalt*, pp. 66f. For others who were in favour of this view, See G. Richter, *Fusswaschung*, pp. 254–256.

60. This is an old and very influential view, which was revived especially by P. Grelot, 'L'interprétation pénitentielle', who also thought that it was possible even if the shorter text was accepted (see p. 85). See also G. Richter, *Fusswaschung*, pp. 252f and 257.

61. See R. Bultmann, pp. 360f, who attributed vv. 10b–11 to the evangelist. R. E. Brown, pp. 561 and 568, left the possibility of an editorial addition open.

62. Bultmann, who believed that 'cleanness' came about through the 'word' (in the sense of revelation and proclamation), was only with some difficulty able to harmonize the washing of the feet with this view: 'It (the washing) represents the service that Jesus performed for his own through the word and as the word' (p. 360). For this interpretation of the washing of the feet, see G. Richter, *Fusswaschung*, pp. 262 and 266.

63. Most exegetes believe that the 'moralizing' interpretation is the earlier and more original one. The traditio-historical relationship with Lk 22:27 (see also Lk 12:37) is a strong reason in favour of this view. All that is disputed is, according to each model of the history of the gospel's emergence, how the two interpretations came to exist side by side. The three main explanations are that the Christological and soteriological interpretation of the evangelist himself was inserted into a source (see Bultmann, pp. 351f), that two independent strata came together (see Boismard, *RB*, 1964, pp. 20–24) and that an editor augmented the work created originally by the evangelist. I believe that the third explanation is correct.

64. The nominatives provided with articles ought clearly to be regarded as vocatives, as in 20:28; see Blass-Debr § 147, 3. They may, however, be 'onomastic' nominatives; see *ibid.*, § 143. If so, they would have the same value as accusatives; see W. Bauer, *ad loc.*, who refers to 1 Sam (=1 Kings in the Septuagint) 9:9.

65. The conditional clause (εἰ with the indicative of reality) is very close to a causal clause and introduces a conclusion; see Blass-Debr § 372. The version +πόσῳ μᾶλλον before καὶ ὑμεῖς (D Θ VL^{pt}sy) makes the final rabbinical procedure *a minori ad maius*. The expression occurs only once in John and probably indicates the tendency of the 'Western' text to expand.

66. See Liddell/Scott, *Lexicon*, p. 1878; Bauer, *Wörterbuch*, p. 1669; H. Schlier, *ThWb* II, pp. 32f. The Atticist Phrynichus (second century) rejected ὑπόδειγμα as less correct; see Wettstein, I, p. 930.

67. See 1 Cor 11:1; Rom 15:7; Eph 5:2; Heb 12:2f; especially 1 Pet 2:18–25; 3:17. For the difference between the two ideas, see A. Schulz, *Nachfolgen und Nachahmen* (Munich, 1962), pp. 298–302. According to Schulz, the idea of ethical imitation is found above all in Greek philosophy and Hellenistic Judaism. The difference between following and moral imitation becomes even clearer if 'following' in this sense is seen in the context of prophetic and charismatic leadership; see M. Hengel, *Nachfolge und Charisma* (Berlin, 1968). On the other hand, the idea of imitation is not completely ethicized anywhere in the NT, but is always subordinated to that of following Jesus. This also applies to the gospel of John, despite the concept of 'example' or 'model'; see Jn 12:26;13:36f. Moreover, καθώς in 13:34 also has both a comparative and a justifying meaning.

68. See Augustine, *In Jo. tr., LVIII*, 4 (CC 474).

69. For Ambrose, see G. Richter, *Die Fusswaschung*, pp. 29f. See also T. Schäfer, *LThK*, ²IV, p. 476, who believes that the washing of feet was an important part of the baptismal rite from the baptismal act of the fourth century onwards, although this was not the case in Rome or the Christian East. The idea of the washing of feet as a 'sacrament' has also been suggested in modern times by Protestant exegetes; see Richter, *op. cit.*, p. 258.

70. B. Noack argues in favour of the origin of this logion in the oral tradition in his *Zur johanneischen Tradition*, pp. 96f, in which he provides a synoptic table. C. H. Dodd has dealt with this question in detail in his *Historical Tradition*, pp. 335–338. Bultmann, p. 364, favours the idea of a (non-synoptic) source. R. T. Fortna, *The Gospel of Signs*, p. 156, believes that vv. 12–15 appeared in some form in the source and that the logia in vv. 16, 17 and 20 were collected by the evangelist, as the introductory formula with the double ἀμήν shows. This 'Johannine' introduction can, however, certainly also be attributed to an editor.

71. See the material in Billerbeck, I, p. 590; II, p. 558; III, pp. 2–4. For the juridical (and sacrally legal) character of the text, see K. H. Rengstorf, *ThWb* I, pp. 415f.

72. See H. Braun, *ThWb*, VI, p. 481.

73. The word first occurs in Hesiod, *Opera et dies*, 826f: εὐδαίμων καὶ ὄλβιος, ὅς τάδε πάντα εἰδὼς ἐργάζηται. Wettstein noted this, *op. cit.* See also Musonius, in Stobaeus, *Anthol.*, III, 29, 78 (see W. Bauer, *op.cit.*); Seneca, Ep. 75, 7: Non est beatus, qui scit illa, sed qui facit; see A. Beltrami, *L. Annaei Senecae ad Lucilium epistulae morales* (Rome, ²1949), I, p. 308.

74. The form of a macarism with an address in the second person plural is much rarer than the predicate, but it is not entirely unknown; see J. Dupont, *Les Béatitudes*, ²I (Bruges and Louvain, 1958), pp. 274–282. Since Hellenistic macarisms usually have forms of the kind mentioned in the quotations in the previous note, there must have been a biblical and early Christian influence here; see especially Mt 5:11 and Lk 6:22; 1 Pet 3:14; 4:14; see also Lk 6:20f (regarded by Dupont as original). For the blessing of those concerned with 'works', see also Rev 14:13. For the distinctive nature of biblical macarisms, see F. Hauck and G. Bertram, *ThWb* IV, pp. 365–373; E. Lipinski, 'Macarismes et psaumes de congratulation', *RB* 75 (1968), pp. 321–367.

75. μετ' ἐμοῦ P⁶⁶ ℵ A D Θ Ρ λ φ VL (apart from q) pl. For the preference for μου (with a 'D' grade of certainty) in UBS Greek NT, see B. M. Metzger, *A Textual Commentary*, *op. cit.*

76 E. D. Freed, *Old Testament Quotations*, p. 92; G. Reim, *Studien*, pp. 39–42.

77. Although Bauer, *Wörterbuch*, p. 218, under 3, gives only the meaning 'from now on' for ἀπ' ἄρτι, the words should be translated in Jn 13:19 and 14:7, according to the context, as 'now' or 'already'. This may be connected with another sense when indicating time; see, for example, 2 Kg (LXX) 24:8: ἀπὸ τέλους ἐννέα μηνῶν=at the end of nine months; see Liddell and Scott, *Lexicon*, p. 192, under ἀπό II, with other examples. The compressed form that occurs in many places – ἀπαρτί=exactly (see Blass-Debr § 12) cannot be seriously considered in this context because of the temporal πρό that follows in the sentence.

78. The manuscripts vary here, as in other places, between the aorist and present subjunctive (testified here by BC). The aorist might indicate a new impulse in faith and the present the continuation of faith; see Kühner and Gerth, *Ausführliche Grammatik* II/1, pp. 185f. In 14:29, πιστεύσητε is certainly testified and most editors accepted this also for 13:19. The present subjunctive is preferred by Westcott and Hort, Lagrange and Nestlé–Aland.

79. See above, 13:16 (p. 25, and note 71). See also P. Borgen, 'God's Agent in the Fourth Gospel', *Religions in Antiquity* (In memory of R. E. Goodenough) (Leiden, 1968), pp. 137–148.

80. See Bultmann, p. 364.

81. H. Thyen, *op. cit.*, pp. 354f, who was reminded in this context of Diotrephes' refusal of hospitality; in 3 Jn 9f, however, the word ἐπιδέχεσθαι appears.

82. ὁ Ἰησοῦς P⁶⁶ C D Θ Ρ pl] Ἰησοῦς ℵ B L. The version with the article is accepted by von Soden, Merk, Bover and the UBS Greek New Testament; the version without the article by Tischendorf, Westcott and Hort, Lagrange and Nestlé–Aland. Because of the importance of the main witnesses ℵ B, in which no tendency is indicated, I believe that the version without the article is to be preferred.

83. This version is to be found with slight variants in P^{66} A D Θ P λ ϕ sy sa pl. The Sinaiticus has this version and, after it, the other version. See the precise textual evidence in the UBS Greek NT, whose editors also include it in the text.

84. See A. Loisy, *Le quatrième évangile*, pp. 395f, where he describes him as the type of the true disciple; Bultmann, pp. 369f: the disciple (according to 19:26f) as the representative of gentile Christianity; E. Käsemann, *ZThK* 48 (1951), p. 304: the ideal bearer of the apostolic witness; A. Kragerud (see the following note): the symbol of the early Christian prophetic spirit, the prophet being in a dynamic relationship with the office-bearer, as represented by Peter. See also Vol. 1, pp. 92f.

85. *Der Lieblingsjünger im Johannesevangelium* (Oslo, 1959), pp. 21–25.

86. See Blass and Debr. § 473: 'A word such as this, taken out of its natural context, is stressed when it is at the end of the sentence'.

87. See R. Schnackenburg, 'Der Jünger, den Jesus liebte', *EKK* 2 (1970), pp. 97–117.

88. οὕτως (om. ℵ D Θ al.) may have more or less the same meaning here as in 4:6, that is, 'as he was, without further ado'; see Bauer, *Wörterbuch*, p. 1185, under 4. W. Bauer translates it in his commentary as 'accordingly'.

89. In v. 26b, P^{66} has: βάψας τὸ ψωμίον ἐπιδώσω αὐτῷ, which indicates that an attempt to improve style was being made even in this early manuscript. Several manuscripts have the reading ἐπιδώσω, but composite words are generally avoided in John.

90. See Billerbeck, IV/1, pp. 621 and 623 under q. For the dipping of green and bitter herbs into the fruit purée (without bread, it should be noted) – a practice that usually only took place at the introductory course preceding the main passover meal – see Pes. X, 3 and the commentary by G. Beer, *Perachim* (Giessen, 1912), pp., 191f.

91. ψωμίον without an article is only to be found in B. Most editions therefore have the article, although Nestlé–Aland place it between square brackets. From the text-critical viewpoint, then, the place of the article is guaranteed. Certain manuscripts – P^{66} A al. – have καὶ ἐμβάψας for βάψας οὖν.

92. P^{66} ℵ * D Θ P λ ϕ pl; enclosed within square brackets in the UBS Greek New Testament. According to B. M. Metzger, *Textual Commentary*, *op. cit.*, this question is extremely difficult to resolve.

93. Billerbeck, II, p. 559, quotes a statement by Resh Laqish (*ca.* 250: 'Man does not commit sin unless the spirit of infatuation has entered him' (Sota 3a). There is, however, no reference to Satan in the quotation. See also W. Foerster, *ThWb* VII, 163 (Jn 6:70 and 13:27): 'Both these statements are without parallel in late Judaism, according to which it was not the devil or Belial, but only one of his spirits who entered man'. This author quotes *Test As* 1, 9 as the closest parallel, but the preceding verse is more important: 'If the senses (τὸ διαβούλιον) incline to evil, all work is bad. Man thrusts aside good, clings to evil and is dominated by Beliar.' Similar ideas can be found in Mandaean texts; see, for example, *Mand. Lit.* 221: 'No, it was the evil one, the son of the evil one, who entered into his body and made him stumble.' See also, on the other hand, 1 Jn 5:18: 'The evil one does not touch him (that is, the one born of God).'

94. For points of contact with the Lukan tradition, see Vol. I, pp. 30ff; for the link between Lk 22:3 and Jn 13:27, see J. A. Bailey, *Traditions*, pp. 29–31 (who believes that John took his text from Luke). The closer relationship between the two can only be discovered in the context of the Johannine passion and its relationship with that of Luke, see A. Dauer, *Passionsgeschichte* (who does not discuss our text).

95. The 'morsel' should not, however, be seen as a magical means, through which Satan entered Judas (see W. Bauer, *ad loc.*, who refers here to 1 Cor 11:27, 29); after all, the text does not have '*through* the morsel', but '*after* the morsel' and the time is even more exactly determined by the added word τότε. The church Fathers were not in favour of a magical interpretation of this kind. (Not even Severus of Antioch, quoted by Bauer, believed this). Theodore of Heraclea (Fragment 235; Reuss, p. 127) wrote, on the other hand, that the handing over of the bread revealed Judas' lack of faith in God, but was not the cause of his falling away – Satan only entered him because he persisted in his evil.

Notes

Ammonius Saccas (Fragment 458; Reuss, p. 311) attributed the initiative to God, whereas Satan intervened because of his boundless lack of shame. Photius of Constantinople (Fragment 80; Reuss, p. 395) similarly described Judas' 'hardness of heart' and said that Satan only entered the vessel that belonged to him.

96. Compare the stylistically striking combination of words οὐδεὶς ἔγνω τῶν ἀνακειμένων (without ἐκ, it should be noticed) with the construction in 21:12.

97. See J. Jeremias, *The Eucharistic Words*, pp. 53f, whose aim was to establish that the last supper was a passover meal. His argument that 'such purchasing at night would be completely incomprehensible if the incident occurred on the evening before Nisan 14, because the whole of the next day, Nisan 14, would be available for this purpose' is not, however, convincing. The ταχίον is contained in Jesus' invitation (v. 27) and does not need to apply to the statement in v. 29.

98. See M. Meinertz, 'Die "Nacht" im Johannesevangelium', *ThQ* 133 (1953), pp. 400–407; G. Delling, *ThWb*, p. 1119.

EXCURSUS 15: Pages 33–47

1. J. Jeremias, *The Eucharistic Words*, pp. 20–26, provides sound information about this.

2. A. Jaubert, *La date de la Cène. Calendrier biblique et liturgie chrétienne* (Paris, 1957); see also E. Vogt, *Bib* 36 (1955), pp. 403–413. Jaubert's hypothesis was broadly speaking accepted by many scholars; see, for example, B. P. W. Skehan, *CBQ* 20 (1958), pp. 192–199; B. Schwank, *Bible und Kirche* (1958), pp. 34–44; J. A. Walther, *JBL* 77 (1958), pp. 116–122; especially E. Ruckstuhl, *Die Chronologie des Letzten Mahles und des Leidens Jesu* (Einsiedeln, 1963). It was also accepted, but with critical reservations, by M. Black, 'The Arrest and Trial of Jesus and the Date of the Last Supper', *New Testament Essays* (*Studies in Memory of T. W. Manson*, ed. by A. J. B. Higgins [Manchester, 1959]), pp. 19–33. Many other scholars, however, rejected it, among whom were J. Blinzler, *ZNW* 49 (1958), pp. 238–251; G. Ogg, *NT* 3 (1959), pp. 149–160; K. G. Kuhn, *ThLZ* 85 (1960) pp. 654–658, and *ZNW* 52 (1961), pp. 65–73; J. Jeremias, *The Eucharistic Words*, pp. 25f. The question was also discussed further by J. Carmignac, 'Comment Jésus et ses contemporains pouvaient-ils célébrer la Pâque à une date non officielle?', *RQum* 5 (1964/65), pp. 59–79 (this author accepts that it was possible; see his bibliography, pp. 77–79).

3. See especially J. Jeremias, *The Eucharistic Words*, pp. 41–62 (with his fourteen observations).

4. See H. Schürmann's works. Of fundamental importance is his research into the Lukan account of the passover meal: *Der Paschamahlbericht* Lk 22, (7–14) 15–18 (Münster, 1953), especially pp. 1–74. See also various articles in the symposium *Ursprung und Gestalt* (Düsseldorf, 1970), especially 'Die Anfänge christlicher Osterfeier', pp. 199–206. R. Feneberg has tried to find a hermeneutical explanation in his *Christliche Passafeier und Abendmahl* (Munich, 1971), especially pp. 17–41 and 113–139.

5. *The Eucharistic Words*, pp. 218–237. See also *idem., Neutestamentliche Theologie* I (Gütersloh, 1971), pp. 274–277.

6. See A. Jaubert, *La date de la Cène*, pp. 126f; E. Ruckstuhl, *Chronologie*, pp. 50–55.

7. Ruckstuhl, *Chronologie*, p. 52: 'One also has the impression that the evangelist presupposes, in 18:33–35, that the Jews had complained to Pilate on the previous day and had arranged with him to hold the trial on the following day.' This argument, however, misrepresents the literary character of the Johannine presentation of the trial. See the commentary.

8. The hypothesis that Jesus followed the Essene calendar of feasts implies that he was close to Essenism. (See Ruckstuhl, *op. cit.*, pp. 107–112). This idea led, among

other things, to J. Lehmann's grotesque distortion of the historical Jesus in his *Jesus-Report* (1970). See for this K. Müller, 'Die Geburt des Rabbi J. aus dem Geiste von Qumran', *Rabbi J.* (Würzburg, 1970), pp. 25–60, and especially pp. 42–50 for the problem of the calendar.

9. *Ev. Joh.*, p. 60. F. Spitta, *Joh-Ev*, p. 295, on the other hand, is opposed to this. Even Bultmann, pp. 366f, regarded 13:21–30 as traditional material, but did not conclude, because of this, that it was a passover meal. J. Jeremias, p. 81, says: 'Some of the remarks made by John presuppose that this was a passover meal', but does not mention the theme of the morsel in this context.

10. *Johannes 13* (Kuhn Festschrift), p. 353.

11. *The Eucharistic Words*, pp. 53f.

12. See E. Schweizer, 'Abendmahl', *RGG*, 3rd. edn., I (1957), pp. 17f, who has brought together in this article all the arguments for and against the last supper as a passover meal.

13. See, for example, R. Bultmann, *Geschichte der synoptischen Tradition*, p. 49; H. Windisch, *Johannes und die Synoptiker* (Leipzig, 1126), p. 51; C. K. Barrett, p. 363.

14. See H. Schürmann, *Jesu Abschiedsrede Lk 22, 21–38* (Münster, 1957), pp. 79–92, who believed that Lk 22:27 was a Lukan editing of a pre-Lukan non-Marcan tradition; see also J. Roloff, 'Anfänge der soteriologischen Deutung des Todes Jesu (Mk. X. 45 und Lk. XXII. 27)', *NTSt* 19 (1972/73), pp. 38–64, more especially pp. 55ff.

15. *Ibid.*, p. 58.

16. *Ibid.*, p. 60.

17. See J. A. Bailey, *Traditions Common*, pp. 34–37; R. E. Brown, p. 368; B. Lindars, p. 447.

18. *Ev. des Joh.*, pp. 370f; cf. p. 360.

19. See H. Windisch, *Joh und die Syn*, pp. 70–79, who believe that, according to John, Jesus 'instituted' not the Eucharist, but the washing of the feet at the last supper (p. 73); that the only conclusion that can be drawn from John is that the Eucharist came about at some time or in some place in the community (p. 75); and finally that the institution of the Lord's supper goes back to an earlier passover, the miraculous meal (p. 78). According to A. Schweitzer, *Die Mystik des Apostels Paulus* (Tübingen, 1930), p. 355, the account of the last supper is absent from John because Jesus could not have instituted the Eucharist at the last supper in the light of John's theory of the sacraments; for John, the Eucharist could only have been made possible by the Spirit. In the opinion of C. K. Barrett, pp. 42 and 71, 'because he (John) was concerned to root the sacrament . . . in the total sacramental fact of the incarnation he was unwilling to attach it to a particular moment and a particular action' (p. 42).

20. See W. F. Howard, *Christianity according to St John* (London, 1943), p. 149: 'The teaching about the Lord's Supper is removed from the sacred context of its institution, perhaps because any controversial purpose would be strangely out of place in that hour of sacred fellowship'. P. Niewalda, *Sakramentssymbolik im Johannese-vangelium?* (Limburg, 1958), pp. 5f, believed that it would have been absurd for John to report the institution of the Eucharist, since the event itself took place following the sermon. He regarded the farewell discourses as sermons given within the framework of a communal service. (But can this be substantiated?)

21. *Entstehungsgeschichte*, pp. 75f.

22. See C. H. Dodd, *Interpretation*, p. 343, note and text. This idea is fully developed in J. Jeremias, *The Eucharistic Words*, pp. 125–137 ('Protection of the Sacred Formula').

23. See J. Betz, *Die Eucharistie in der Zeit der greichischen Väter* II/1 (Freiburg, ²1964), who insists that John reports the washing of the feet in place of the institution of the Eucharist and refers to 6:51c–58 and the eucharistic overtones of the farewell discourses.

24. *Urchristentum und Gottesdienst*, pp. 102–104. Cullmann also believed that there was an allusion to baptism in 13:9–10.

25. See the survey in H. Klos, *Die Sakramente im Johannesevangelium* (Stuttgart, 1970), pp. 24–37. Klos does not, however, discuss why the account of the institution is absent from John 13.

26. It is possible to ask whether the account of the institution may even have been absent in the Johannine source (an account of the passion). E. Schweizer has gone into this possibility in his 'Das Herrenmahl im Neuen Testament', *Neotestamentica* (Zürich and Stuttgart, 1963), pp. 344–370, especially 356.359; he includes Lk 22:15–18 in his examination of the subject. He regards it as distinctly possible, but has doubts in the light of 1 Cor. 11:23.

27. Bultmann, p. 357, note 5, regarded it as 'grotesque that the Lord's Supper should have been depicted by the washing of the feet, especially as the situation of a meal in fact existed'. This can only hold good if the washing of the feet itself is treated as a symbol of the Eucharist. This interpretation is usually found in connection with v. 10; see *ad loc.*

28. It cannot be denied that the editor had an interest in the Eucharist. This is evident from the eucharistic echoes contained in the meal at Lake Tiberias when the risen Lord appeared (21:9 and 13). If the section 6:51c–58 was the work of an editor, why did that editor not insert an account of the institution of the Eucharist in Chapter 13?

SECTION I: CHAPTER 2: Pages 48–88

1. See F. Büchsel, *op. cit.*, p. 145. J. E. Belser, in *Das Zeugnis des vierten Evangelisten für Taufe, Eucharistie und Geistsendung* (1912), p. 154, interpreted Jn 13:32 as a reference to the institution of the Eucharist which was to follow, but had not been recounted by the evangelist. In his explanation, stressing that the 'glorification' referred to Jesus' previous activity in word and deed, W. Bauer also mistook the meaning of this sentence. For a different interpretation, see W. Thüsing, *Erhöhung und Verherrlichung*, pp. 234f.

2. See Excursus 13 (Vol. 2, pp. 398–410). See also the Johannine presentation of Jesus' passion.

3. V. 32a om. P^{66} B ℵ * C* D al. λ 33 892 al. VL^{pt}sy^s Tert. Ambr. – not included by Westcott and Hort in the text and placed in square brackets by UBS Greek NT.

4. See B. Metzger, *A Textual Commentary, ad. loc.*

5. *Ev. des Joh.*, p. 401, note 5. Bultmann placed 13:31–35 after Chapter 17, which he regarded as a farewell prayer after the meal.

6. See W. Thüsing, *Erhöhung und Verherrlichung*, pp. 235ff; R. Schnackenburg, 'Strukturanalyse von Joh 17', *BZ*, New Series 17 (1973), pp. 67–78.

7. See Bultmann, p. 402, who refers to the 'paradoxical juxtaposition of ἐδοξάσθη (v. 31) and δοξάσει (v. 32)' and to the δόξα 'which is that of the Son and of the Father at the same time'.

8. 'The Glory of God in the Fourth Gospel', *NTSt* 15 (1968/69), pp. 265–277, especially pp. 268–271.

9. Bauer, *Wörterbuch*, p. 405, under δοξάζω 2, who provides other evidence for this.

10. P^{66} B ℵ * H 2148 sy (apart from sy^s, where the phrase is missing) sa bo Orig. The weight of this evidence, in contrast to the volume of other manuscripts, is so great that this version is correctly accorded grade 'B' in UBS Greek NT. The reading αὐτῷ instead of αὑτῷ can hardly be accepted; cf. Mayser, *Grammatik* II/2, pp. 71ff; Blass-Debr §64, 1.

11. See Cyril of Alexandria, *PG* 74, 153, Zahn, Lagrange and G.-M. Behler, *Abschiedsworte*, p. 72.

12. S. Schulz, *Untersuchungen zur Menschensohn-Christologie,* pp. 120–122, believes that the closest parallel is the Ethiopic *Book of Enoch,* 51, 3, and that this apocalyptic prophecy was reinterpreted in a pre-Johannine hymn to the Son of man. In contrast to this, C. Colpe has pertinently observed (in *ThWb* VIII, p. 472) that what is

at issue here is a detailed interpretation of the tradition that was available to the fourth evangelist primarily in the synoptic prophecies of the passion (see also Mk 14:41).

13. See Bauer, *Wörterbuch*, pp. 1031f, under 3.

14. In the Syr. sin. the ἄρτι is included with the following sentence (see Merx, p. 362); similarly P⁶⁶ πλὴν ἄρτι ἐντολήν. Other manuscripts omit ἄρτι and contain πλὴν ἐντολήν: 1 565 pc. This indicates that a reflective process began with P⁶⁶ and later led to the omission of ἄρτι.

15. Bultmann, pp. 403f, made use of this interconnection in his theology of revelation. For the insertion of the commandment to love into this context, see also L. Cerfaux, 'La charité fraternelle et le retour du Christ (Jn 13:33–38)', *EThLov* 24 (1948), pp. 321–332 (=*Recueil L.C.*, II, pp. 27–40).

16. Apart from the commentaries, see R. A. Harrisville, 'The Concept of Newness in the NT', *JBL* 74 (1955), pp. 69–79, especially pp. 78f (where he refers to a 'rule of the new eschatological community'); O. Prunet, *La morale*, pp. 96–107 (dealing with the Christological, ecclesiological and eschatological aspects); C. Spicq, *Agapè* III, pp. 170–180; N. Lazure, *Les valeurs morales*, pp. 220, 229f.

17. Augustine, *In Jo. tr.*, LXV, 1 (*CC* 36, 491); see also John Chrysostom, who pointed to Christ's anticipatory love (*PG* 59, 393f). The Church Fathers (Cyril of Alexandria, Theodore of Heraclea, Ammonius Saccas and Theodore of Mopsuesta) regarded as new the fact that the Christian was not only required to love his neighbour ὡς σεαυτόν, but also had to love him ὑπὲρ ἑαυτόν. Thomas Aquinas (Cai No. 1835) gave three reasons: the effect of renewal (Col 3:9), the source of the Spirit, inflaming the soul to love, and the creation of a new covenant.

18. Blass-Debr § 453, 2; Bauer *Wörterbuch*, p. 773, under 3; Spicq, *Agapè* III, pp. 173f. The relationship between the disciples and Jesus is extended by this καθώς to the relationship between Jesus and his Father; see 6:57; 10:15; 15:10; 17:18, 21ff.

19. See Augustine, *In Jo. tr.*, LXV, 2 (CC 36, 492): 'Ad hoc ergo dilexit, ut et nos diligamus invicem.' See also Bultmann, p. 403, note 6. Most recent exegetes believe that the second ἵνα clause is parallel with the first. See especially Bernard, who explained the construction in the same way as he dealt with those in 17:2 and 17:21, in other words, that the καθώς clause functioned as a parenthesis (p. 560 for 17:2).

20. See Ignatius of Antioch, *Ad Eph.* 4, 1: 'Your unison and your harmonious love are a hymn of praise to Jesus Christ'; Minucius Felix, *Octav.* 9, 2: 'amant mutuo, paene antequam noverint'; Tertullian, *Apol.* 39: 'vide, inquiunt, ut invicem se diligunt'. See also the legend of John in old age repeating again and again: 'My children, love one another!' recorded by Jerome in *Ad Gal.* III, 6, 10 (PL 26, 433).

21. Bultmann, p. 459, placed 13:36–38 after Chapter 16, believing that the question about 'following' Christ was otherwise meaningless. He placed the texts in the following sequence: 13:31–35; 15:1—16:33; 13:36—14:31. But Peter's first question is not about following Jesus, but about where he is going! Bernard's sequence is different again: 13:31a; Chapters 15–16; 13:31b–38; Chapter 14.

22. This question is the origin of the legend of 'Quo vadis?', as narrated in the Martyrdom of Peter 6 (*Acta Apost. Apocr.*, ed. R. A. Lipsius, I, 7f); see also Hennecke and Schneemelcher, II, 218f (German translation).

23. The double name 'Simon-Peter' does not appear in this context. Here the name appears as ὁ (Art. om. א A C θ P pm) Πέτρος. This, however, is the usual procedure of the evangelist whenever the full name was used previously and the narrative continues; cf. 1:41 with 45; 13:5 with 8; 18:10 with 11; 18:15 with 16ff, etc.).

24. For τὴν ψυχὴν τιθέναι as a Johannine phrase (instead of διδόναι), see Vol. 2, p. 296.

25. For the crowing of the cock as a way of describing early morning, see Billerbeck I, p. 993.

26. For the affinity between this text and Luke, see J. Schniewind, *Parallelperikopen*, pp. 28–32; E. Osty, *op. cit.*, p. 147; J. A. Bailey, *op. cit.*, pp. 37–39; C. H. Dodd, *Historical Tradition*, pp. 54–56; R. E Brown, *Gospel* II, pp. 615f. All these scholars agree that John could not have used Luke directly in this text.

Notes

27. See E. Stauffer, 'Abschiedsreden', *RAC* I, pp. 29–35; J. Munck, 'Discours d'adieu dans le Nouveau Testament et dans la littérature biblique', *Aux sources de la tradition chrétienne (Mélanges M. Goguel,* Neuchâtel & Paris, 1950), pp. 155–170; P. Bogaert, *Apocalypse de Baruch* I *(SChr* 144) (Paris, 1969), pp. 121–126 (especially for the apocalypses). A typical farewell discourse is Paul's address to the leader of the community in Miletus (Acts 20:17–38); see J. Dupont, *Le discourse de Milet* (Paris, 1962), pp. 11–21. The discourses addressed by the risen Christ to his disciples are of a different literary genre; see the *Epistles of the Apostles,* Hennecke and Schneemelcher I, pp. 126–155. They were also favoured by the gnostics as revelatory discourses; see the Coptic *Epistles of James,* the *Apocalypses of James,* etc.

28. See the material assembled by E. Stauffer in *Die Theologie des Neuen Testaments* (Stuttgart, ⁴1948), pp. 327–330. There are fewer intermediate comments and dialogues in the earlier texts and, for example, in the Hebrew *TestNaphthali;* see Kautzsch II, pp. 489–492; Riessler, pp. 1213/22; see also A.-M. Denis, *Introduction aux Pseudépigraphes grecs d'Ancien Testament* (Leiden, 1973), p. 53. The objections of the disciples in John are a means of expressing the author's literary style.

29. R. Bultmann, p. 473; Wikenhauser, p. 268; R. E. Brown, p. 623, etc.

30. 'Die Abschiedsreden im Joh-Ev', *ZNW* 61 (1970), pp. 215–246, especially pp. 223–228.

31. See R. Schnackenburg, 'Das Anliegen der Abschiedsrede in Joh 14', *Wort Gottes in der Zeit* (Festschrift für K. H. Schelkle, Düsseldorf, 1973), pp. 89–104, for a critical assessment of this theory.

32. Origen interpreted this sequence of sentences as a hypotaxis: 'Since you believe in God, believe (or: you believe) also in me' (GCS IV, 489). If vv. 1 and 2 are, however, understood as an invitation and as providing motivation, two imperatives are more appropriate here. Bultmann, p. 463, offers another interpretation: 'Do you believe in God? Then believe also in me, since you can only believe in God through me!' This explanation, however, does not take the connection with what follows into account.

33. It is hardly possible to assume that the evangelist is here introducing an idea that he has so far not expressed into a quotation from himself. Some of the other quotations from himself in the gospel are, it is true, formulated in quite a free way or else are difficult to verify (see, for example, 6:35, 65; 10:25, 36; 11:40). As a rule, however, a point of reference that is not too remote can be found. The texts mentioned by Bultmann, p. 464, note 3, are, on the other hand, remote and unconvincing.

34. See J. Becker, *op. cit.,* pp. 221f; he might, instead of this, have inserted an 'and' into the original, traditional saying that he took over.

35. See the discussion in Bultmann, p. 464, note 3, of the various possibilities; see also R. E. Brown, pp. 619f, *ad loc.,* who believes that the best meaning is given by a translation without ὅτι. (But how did the word then find its way into the text?)

36. The change from ὑπάγω to πορεύομαι is clearly intentional since the second verb, which is more strongly orientated towards the goal (cf. 7:35; 10:4, 11:11; 20:17), points more obviously to Jesus' going to the Father (see 14:28; 16:28). Two different aspects are to be found in ὑπάγειν. It is an enigmatic word which non-believers misunderstand (7:33; 8:21f). For believers, on the other hand, it is a revelatory word with a deeper meaning (cf. Mk 14:21). For this question, see H. Leroy, *Rätsel und Missverständnis,* pp. 51–67. See also the two verbs in Hauck and Schulz, *ThWb* VI, p. 575, and Delling, *ibid.,* VIII, pp. 508f.

37. For this, see G. Fischer, *Die himmlischen Wohnungen. Untersuchungen zu Joh 14, 2f* (Berne and Frankfurt, 1975).

38. For the concept 'rest', see O. Hofius, *Katapausis. Die Vorstellung vom endzeitlichen Ruheort im Hebräerbrief* (Tübingen, 1970), who provides further material from non-biblical sources (pp. 59–101). Hofius comes to a very similar conclusion in the case of Jn 14:2f. After referring to *1 Enoch* 39:4; 41:2; 45:3 and the Hebrew *Apocalypse of Elijah* 10:6, he says: 'Jn 14:2f can also be understood in the light of this tradition' (p. 184, note 376).

39. See K. Rudolph, *Die Mandäer* II, pp. 21f and 68. There is need for further reseach to be done into the idea of the *škinas* in the Mandaean literature; it is far more central and more all-embracing than the image of 'dwellings' in Jn 14:2. See G. Fischer, *op, cit.*, pp. 236–273.

40. See W. Bauer, *ad loc.*, and R. Bultmann, *ZNW* 24 (1925), pp. 137f, and *Ev. des Joh.* p. 462, note 3.

41. In addition to other exegetes, see also F. Hauck, *ThWb* IV, pp. 584, 26ff.

42. The rabbis believed that there were seven classes or departments, graded according to merit, in the heavenly Gan Eden (of souls). See, for example, Midrash Ps. 11 § 6: 'Each department has its own dwelling in the Gan Eden and, corresponding to these seven departments, there are seven dwelling-houses for the evil ones in Gehinnom . . . there are seven dwellings for the just and seven dwellings for the unjust; for the unjust, according to the measure of their works and for the just according to the measure of their works' (see Billerbeck IV, p. 1141). Further material can be found n Billerbeck IV, pp. 1138/42. Ideas of this kind were also common in the early Church. Irenaeus speaks of a statement made by the elders: 'They say that there is a distinction between the dwellings of those who have borne fruit a hundred-fold, those who have yielded sixty-fold and those who have yielded thirty-fold; the first will be taken up into heaven, the second shall dwell in paradise and the third shall live in the city. It is for this reason, they claim, that the Lord said: "In my Father's house there are many dwelling-places"' (*Adv. haer.* V, 36; Harvey II, p. 428). See also Augustine, *In Jo. tr.* LXVII, 2 (CC 495): 'Not one of them will be kept out of that house, where each one will be taken into a dwelling on his own merit'. See also Thomas Aquinas, *In Jo. 14 lect.*, I, 3 (Cai No. 1853f).

43. O. Schaefer, 'Der Sinn der Rede Jesu von den vielen Wohnungen in seines Vaters Haus und von dem Weg zu ihm (Joh 14, 1–7)', *ZNW* 32 (1933), pp. 210–217, especially p. 213; J. Heise, *Bleiben*, pp. 93–161, especially pp. 100f; R. H. Gundry, '"In my Father's house are many Μοναί" (John 14:2)', *ZNW* 58 (1967), pp. 68–72, who comes to a similar conclusion, but includes definitive union with Jesus in heaven; see also R. E. Brown, p. 627 (Jesus' body is his Father's house).

44. See J. Becker, *ZNW* 61 (1970), pp. 222f, 228.

45. Many exegetes have thought this until very recently, including Bernard, Schlatter, Tillmann, Strathmann and Morris; similarly W. Michaelis, *ThWb* V, 81ff; or at least as a perspective that cannot be excluded: Schick, Behler and Lindars. C. H. Dodd, *Interpretation*, pp. 395 and 404, held a view that was similar to the one expressed above in the text.

46. The subordinate clause, which is omitted in certain cases (69 pc), has a temporal meaning (= ὅταν); cf. 12:32; 1 Jn 2:28; Bauer, Wb, p. 419, under 1, d.

47. πάλιν is a favourite word in John; it occurs forty-three times in the gospel, as opposed to seventeen times in Mt, eighteen times in Mk, eight times in Lk and Acts, twenty-eight times in Paul and fifteen times in the rest of the NT. Its most characteristic meaning is 'further', but, since it is used here with the common meaning of 'again' or 'a second time', it cannot be regarded as valid for the Johannine style.

48. This verb occurs in Lk 17:34 in the context of the event of the parousia, but in the divine passive as 'being taken' as opposed to 'being left behind'. These verbs can be explained in the light of the figurative situation, whereas Jn 14:3 is barely influenced by it.

49. Materially, 12:32 can be compared with this 'I will take you to myself'. If Jesus' 'coming again' primarily refers to his coming after Easter (see 14:18f), then the personal 'taking to himself' needs to mean no more than the restoration of the personal community, which, in any case, will be completed only in heaven.

50. The longer version is found in P⁶⁶* A D θ 𝔓 λ φ al. VL (apart from a) Vg sy sa Diatess. Cyr. Alex. Chrys.

51 Bultmann, p. 466, called this formula in v. 4 'provoking'; he was followed by J. Becker, *op. cit.*, p. 223, in support of his theory that the evangelist was opposed to a

traditional understanding of the community statement in v. 2f. In maintaining this, however, he has clearly given too little attention to the fact that the verses that follow are subject to the admonition to believe.

52. Codex D contains an explicit reminder of this by adding ὁ λεγόμενος Δίδυμος.

53. For 14:6, see, apart from the commentaries, W. Michaelis, *ThWb* (1954), pp. 80–88; J. Leal, 'Ego sum via et veritas et vita (Jn 14:6)', *VD* 33 (1955), pp. 336–341; I. de la Potterie, '"Je suis la Voie, la Vérité et la Vie" (Jn 14:6)', *NRTh* 88 (1966), pp. 907–942 (this article is rich in material and illuminating).

54. *De bono mortis* 12, 54 (PL 14, 592), quoted by I. de la Potterie, *op. cit.,* p. 908, note 4.

55. See de la Potterie, *ibid.,* p. 909.

56. John Chrysostom, *ad loc.* (*PG* 59, 398); Theophylact, *ad loc.* (*PG* 124, 172); see also Theodore of Heraclea, Fragment 250 (Reuss, p. 130), whose interpretation was similar.

57. See W. Bauer, *ad loc.*; Bultmann, p. 466, note 4, and p. 468, note 4; K. Rudolph, *Die Mandäer* II, pp. 143f.

58. For a critical assessment, see W. Michaelis, *ThWb* V, pp. 86ff (but he is wrong in arguing that the evangelist had the parousia in mind in 14:3); I. de la Potterie, *op. cit.,* pp. 917f (who says, on p. 918, that, in his opinion, an earlier way of speaking was preserved in the Mandaean texts, a form of expression that was derived from Judaism). R. E. Brown, pp. 628ff, does not believe that it is really necessary to go back to gnostic texts, because wide-ranging 'raw material' is provided by the Jewish sources (p. 630).

59. See F. Nötscher, *Gotteswege und Menschenwege in der Bibel und in Qumran* (Bonn, 1958). R. E. Brown, pp. 628f, places too much emphasis, in my opinion, on the significance of the Qumran texts for Jesus' description of himself as 'the way'. De la Potterie, *op. cit.,* pp. 919f, insists on the increasing 'eschatological overtones' of the concept, but even this does not explain why the Johannine Jesus calls himself 'the way'.

60. For this, see S. V. McCasland, 'The Way', *JBL* 77 (1958), pp. 222–230; in his comparison with NT writings, especially the Acts of the Apostles, he correctly does not quote Jn 14:6.

61. I. de la Potterie, *op. cit.,* p. 915, who also quotes M.-E. Boismard, *RB* 78 (1961), pp. 520ff and A. Guilding, *The F.G. and Jewish Worship,* pp. 87f. (The latter author points to Jewish lectionaries for the feast of the New Year, in which such texts are collected. The theme of 'the way' is in fact very suitable for the beginning of a new year, but it is very doubtful whether the Jewish readings for this feast lay behind the use of the concept in the fourth gospel.)

62. Westcott and Hort, B. Weiss, von Soden, Vogels, Merk, Nestlé–Aland and many commentaries are in favour of version I. Tischendorf, Lagrange, Bover, UBS Greek New Testament and, among the more recent commentaries, Bauer, Hoskyns and Davey, Bultmann, Wikenhauser, Barrett, Sanders and Mastin, Lindars and S. Schulz and B. M. Metzger, *Textual Commentary,* p. 243, argue in favour of version II, but K. Aland argues against it in a note of his own. See also my own contribution, 'Johannes 14, 7', in the *Festschrift für G. D. Kilpatrick* (Leiden, 1975).

63. καὶ P⁶⁶ ℵ D Θ P VL al.: Tischendorf, Vogels, Bover, UBS Greek New Testament, in other words, generally speaking those in favour of version II.

64. I believe this, unlike Barrett, Brown, Lindars and others. The ἀπ' ἄρτι only continues to be difficult for as long as it is translated as 'henceforth' or 'from now on'. The meaning of 'now (already)' is confirmed by 13:19; see Bauer, *ad loc.,* Bultmann, p. 470, note 1. The contraction, ἀπαρτί=with certainty, definitely, suggested by A. Debrunner, *ConiNeot* XI (1947), pp. 47f, for Jn 13:19 and 14:7 is not convincing.

65. See Bauer, *Worterbuch,* p. 343, above; H. Schlier, *ThWb* II, p. 28.

66. W. A. Meeks, *The Prophet King,* pp. 304f, note 3, compared this with Moses' request in *Debarim* XI, 8 before his death, but there is no close parallel between the

two. It is more likely that the evangelist was polemicizing as in 5:37 and 6:46 (see *ad loc.*).

67. If these works refer to the signs that took place while Jesus was active on earth, μένων can hardly be seen as prospective in meaning, as J. Heise, *Bleiben*, p. 80 would seem to suggest (God remains with him even during the hour of his abandonment). It should rather be compared with 14:25. Bauer, *Wörterbuch*, p. 996 and *ad loc.*, translated this text as: 'The Father who is permanently (constantly) in me.'

68. This was the interpretation of Augustine (*CC* 505 and 509): 'Tunc igitur verba eius erant opera eius', 'his words were therefore his works', and John Chrysostom (*PG* 59, 401); in more recent exegesis, especially Bultmann, p. 471 and, following him, J. Heise, *op. cit.*, p. 80. Bultmann regarded Jesus' words and works in the fourth gospel as identical in his *Theologie des neuen Testamentes*, p. 413: 'Jesus' works – seen as a single whole: his work – are his words.' W. Wilkens, *Zeichen und Werke*, p. 87, follows Bultmann here, but judges the semeia differently. See also W. Thüsing, *Erhöhung und Verherrlichung*, pp. 58f, who expressed critical reservations in note 28. W. Nicol is critical of Bultmann in his *The Semeia of the Fourth Gospel* (Leiden 1972), p. 119.

69. μοι om. Tat[ar. it. neerl.] 700 291 1820 Vg (non creditis?) sy[P] Tert Didym Chrys. If this is the original reading, the pronoun ought to be included in accordance with the meaning.

70. Instead of αὐτά P[75] B have αὐτοῦ, but this may be an assimilation to the end of v. 10 (where P[75] and other manuscripts have αὐτός).

71. The connection in thought between vv. 13f and 16 has also been observed by other commentators, including, for example, R. E. Brown, p. 644. J. Becker (*op. cit.*, pp. 224f) is of the opinion that Jesus had the function, in v. 13 at least, of a Paraclete with the Father (that is, in heaven) and that this is in accordance with the term 'another Paraclete' in v. 16, thus making the disciples' 'greater works' on earth possible. But Jesus' function as Paraclete does not emerge clearly from the ποιήσω in v. 13, nor is there a clear connection with the 'greater works' in vv. 16f.

72. See J. Becker, *op. cit.*, p. 224, for the two vv. 14 and 15. K. Tomoi, 'Is not John XIV. 15a a Dislocation?', *ExpT* 72 (1960/61), p. 31, who takes a different view and would prefer to place v. 15 between vv. 20 and 21.

73. For Jesus' asking, the gospel of John uses ἐρωτᾶν (14:16; 16:26; 17:9, 15, 20), but when others ask, the same word is used (4:31, 40, 47; 12:21; 19:31, 38). αἰτεῖν is only used in the same gospel in the Samaritan woman's request and in Jesus' reply to her (see 4:9f) and when Martha speaks to Jesus in 11:22.

74. See W. Nicol, *Semeia*, pp. 103f and 117ff.

75. τούτων om. P[66*] (added by a second hand). Augustine, *In Jo. tr.* LXXII, 3 (CC 508f) related the 'greater works' to justification and sanctification. Aquinas followed him, at least to some extent, in his *In Jo. 14*, lect. III, 5 (Cai 1897–1902).

76. In earlier exegesis (that is, in the Fathers and in the Middle Ages), this was usually associated with the miracles performed by the apostles and which accompanied their mission. In later exegesis, it has only been applied to the extension of faith and salvation. A more profound view would have also to include the idea of judgment with regard to the unbelieving world contained in the apostolic preaching (see, for example, Bultmann and Brown).

77. 33 544 Vg complete: τὸν πατέρα.

78. F. Tillmann, *ad. loc.*, and, in the same way, several other exegetes have suggested such a 'mystical' interpretation, in which 'in Jesus' name' is almost equated with 'in Christ' and frequently understood as indicating that the only possible way of praying is for what is necessary for salvation and in accordance with the will of God. The goading words should not, however, be made blunt, but only placed in the right context.

79. This is the view of W. Heitmüller, *Im Namen Jesu* (Göttingen 1903), who traced the formula back to popular Hellenistic linguistic usage.

80. See J. Behm in *ThWb* V, pp. 260f (with an appeal to Deut 18:18f, which was an important text for John). For the rabbinical sources, see *ibid.*, p. 267. For 'asking in

Jesus' name', see Behm, who apeals to A. Schlatter and claims that this means here asking in accordance with his will; later, however, he expresses the opinion that it at the same time means 'appealing to his name' in prayer. He says, for example: 'Such prayer made in Jesus' name is an expression of a faith that he "came from God" and is therefore God's Son' (pp. 275, 43–47). This may be the decisive point of view.

81. See, for example, F. G. Untergassmair, *Im Namen Jesu. Der Namensbegriff im Joh-Ev* (Stuttgart 1974).

82. V 14 om. X λ 565 al. b Vg^mss sy ^s.c.pal Diatess ^Pt. Codex Λ omits the last seven words of v. 13 and the whole of v. 14 (homoioteleuton ποιήσω). See Metzger, *Text. Comm., ad loc.*

83. J. Wellhausen, *Ev. Joh.*, pp. 64f, believed, together with Blass, that v. 13 originally had the Father as subject and that this was corrected in v. 14; F. Spitta, *Joh-Ev*, p. 345, excludes vv. 13–14 from the basic document; E. Hirsch, *Studien*, p. 106, ascribes vv. 13–15 to the editor; W. Heitmüller, p. 150, eliminates v. 14. For J. Becker and K. Tomoi, see p. 412, notes 71 and 72. Bultmann, p. 473, note 1, was critical of these interpretations and believed that the verse came from the 'source'.

84. με om. D P pm VL (apart from c f) sa bo Diatess Aug Cyr Al. Euthym; ἐγώ] τοῦτο: P^75 B A al.

85. See Bultmann, Wikenhauser, Schick, Brown. A favourite division is between the three 'indwellings' of the Spirit (vv. 16f), Jesus (vv. 18–21) and the Father (vv. 23f), but in each case the mode of expression is different. Another division is vv. 1–11, 12–26 and 27–31 (used by Lagrange and Schwank) and a third (favoured by Behler) is vv. 1–11, 12–24 and 25–31.

86. Instead of the future tense, τηρήσετε, other manuscripts have the aorist subjunctive τηρήσητε, while others have the aorist imperative τηρήσατε (see the apparatus in the *UBS Greek New Testament*). The first two formulae are frequently interchangeable. (For the future use of the aorist subjunctive, see Blass and Debr. § 363.) The imperative may be later; it fits less well into the context, and especially into v. 16. It can possibly be explained by the reference to the commandment to love; see 15:7 (μείνατε), 12, 17.

87. This may perhaps have been the editor's idea; 13:34 was probably added by an editor. This, however, is not sufficient reason for rejecting the evagelist's authorship, especially since the thought reappears in vv. 21 and 23.

88. See J. Becker in *ZNW* 61 (1970), p. 225, note 42, and G. Johnston, *The Spirit-Paraclete in the Gospel of John* (Cambridge 1970), pp. 72–75.

89. J. Behm rightly opposed this interpretation in *ThWb* V, p. 799, note 1.

90. G. Johnston, *op. cit.*, p. 84, recognized correctly that the 'Paraclete' is secondary to the 'Spirit of truth', but his suggested translation: 'he will give you, as another Paraclete, . . . the Spirit of truth' is unconvincing, because the ἵνα clause is inserted in between it.

91. Origen, *De princ.* II, 7, 4 (*GCS* 151, 12ff, Koetschau), made a distinction between 'deprecator' (1 Jn 2:1) and 'consolator' (the gospel of John), but Lagrange, p. 382, regarded Rufinus as solely responsible for this. Nevertheless, Lagrange showed, pp. 382f, how the translation became established, first in the case of the Greek Fathers (on the basis of παρακαλεῖν, which can also mean 'to comfort') and then in the case of the Latin Fathers (who previously translated with the word 'advocatus').

92. Augustine, *In Jo. tr.* LXXIV, 4 (CC 515): 'Worldly love does not possess invisible eyes by means of which the Holy Spirit can be seen; it can only act invisibly.'

93. It is probable that μένει and ἔσται are original; for variants (μενεῖ or ἐστίν), see the UBS Greek New Testament. According to δώσει in v. 16, which is future, the verbs should have a future meaning; the present forms can be explained in the light of γινώσκετε.

94. See, for example, Hoskyns and Davey on 14:18: 'This advent of the Christ is not an interpretation of the coming of the Spirit. . . . It is rather a distinct appearance and the primary reference is to the Resurrection appearances', p. 459; see also Barrett, *ad*

loc., who takes a similar view. Boismard, *RB* 68 (1961), p. 519, Wikenhauser, p. 268 and, with some reservations, Brown, pp. 642f, accept the structure of a threefold 'coming'. The Fathers thought about the indwelling of the Trinity partly in connection with v. 23; see Augustine, *In Jo. tr.* LXXVI, 4 (CC 519): 'The Holy Spirit also makes a dwelling with the Father and the Son; he is at home in every way, like God in his temple. The God of the Trinity, the Father, the Son and the Holy Spirit, come to us, when we come to them. . . .' See also Aquinas (Cai 1946).

95. Many of the Greek Fathers found it easy to identify the coming of the Spirit with Jesus' coming. See, for example, Cyril of Alexandria (*PG* 74, 261 A): 'He promised his own coming and showed in this way that the Spirit was not different from what he was himself, because the Spirit of the Father was also his own Spirit. . . . As a weapon and as an indestructible security, then, the Father gave our souls the Spirit of Christ'. Ammonius Saccas (Fragment 494, Reuss, p. 319) stressed that Christ was in the disciples by the indwelling of the Spirit. Most modern exegetes are inclined to the view that John reinterprets Easter, Pentecost and the parousia and points to the presence of Jesus or the Spirit in the community (see Bauer, p. 184). According to Bultmann, p. 477, 'He (Jesus) came himself in the coming of the Spirit. He was himself active as the one who revealed in the Spirit-filled proclamation of the word by the community.' D. E. Holwerda, *The Holy Spirit and Eschatology in the Gospel of John* (Kampen 1959), spoke of an equivalence of function (p. 65) and concluded, after carefully examining the texts, that, in 14:18ff and 16:16ff, Jesus was speaking of his presence, brought about by the Spirit and that Jesus himself was made manifest in the work of the Spirit (p. 76). R. E. Brown, p. 645, thought that Jesus' presence after his return to the Father was fulfilled in and through the Paraclete. It cannot be disputed that John's theological thinking followed this or a similar course, but this does not provide a satisfactory explanation for the juxtaposition of the sayings in vv. 16f and 18ff.

96. This view was suggested especially by H. Windisch, 'Die fünf johanneischen Parakletsprüche', *Festgabe für A. Jülicher* (Tübingen 1927), pp. 110–137; S. Schulz, *Untersuchungen zur Menschensohn-Christologie*, pp. 142–158, who spoke of a 'theme tradition' and accepted this possibility in the case of the sayings about Jesus' coming (pp. 158–173). See also *idem, Das Evangelium nach Johannes*, p. 190: '14:16f and 18ff go back to two different thematic traditions – the promise of the coming of the Spirit-Paraclete and the second coming of Jesus himself – which the evangelist artistically adapted into a prophecy about the redeemer taking his farewell'. See also Lindars on 14:16 and 26.

97. Plato, *Phaed.* 65 (116a), who wrote about the relationship between Socrates' disciples and their teacher who was to leave them, that 'they believed that they had, like children deprived of their father, to lead their future lives as orphans'. Further texts will be found in Bauer, *ad loc.* (p. 184). It is worth noting, however, that the term 'father' does not occur in the fourth gospel and it was for this reason that Bultmann, p. 478, note 1, did not quote such texts from the rabbinical literature, Philo, the mystery religions or the Mandaean documents.

98. θεωρεῖν is used in the gospel of John both for an external seeing that is not sufficient for faith (2:23; 6:2; 7:3, etc.) and for seeing in faith (6:40; 12:45). In 16:16, 17, 19, it means that the disciples will soon no longer see Jesus; for the seeing that follows (after Jesus' resurrection), ὁρᾶν is used (see also 20:20). The use of the verb in 14:19 expresses clearly the fact that the same event (Jesus' departure) leads to not seeing in the case of the world, but to a new kind of seeing for the disciples.

99. Augustine and other church Fathers thought differently, treating the statement about the disciples as an independent sentence relating to the future life of the disciples in heaven. T. Zahn supported this patristic view ('Because I live, you will also live') and Barrett and Brown regard it as possible. It is, however, hardly possible to include the statement about the disciples in the ὅτι clause and to regard the ζήσετε as pointing to the future fulfilment (see Maldonat and Schanz). More recent exegetes have correctly interpreted the 'living' of the disciples as their situation of salvation in the present.

100. ζήσεσθε P⁶⁶ ℵ D Θ 𝒫 pl. This version is to be preferred because of the good evidence in favour of it, at least according to von Soden, Vogels, Lagrange and Merk, but it should be noted that the middle voice is otherwise not used in John.

101. Earlier exegetes (Cyril of Alexandria, Augustine, Rupert of Deutz, Thomas Aquinas and others, as well as Maldonat and Zahn) interpreted 'that day' as indicating the parousia. This is in contradiction to the context and the eschatology of the gospel.

102. Those exegetes who have interpreted v. 20 as pointing to the parousia (see note 101 above) regard this description of community with God as referring to knowledge in the future. Augustine made a distinction between present faith and future knowledge. Although his interpretation of the literal meaning is wrong, what he says is worth bearing in mind: 'now he loved so that we might believe and keep the commandment of faith; then he will love so that we may see. . . . We therefore love now, by believing what we shall see; then we shall love, by seeing what we believe' (CC 517).

103. The use of ἐμφανίζειν in Exod 33:13, 18 (B) LXX is worth considering in this context. In this OT text, Moses asks God to reveal himself and it is possible that 14:8 may be an allusion to it. It is, however, hardly probable that Judas saw in this a fulfilment of Philip's request. See also Mt 27:55 (the appearance of the risen Lord in Jerusalem). For the meaning of the verb, see also Bultmann and Lührman in *ThWb* IX (1969), pp. 7f. In Wis 1:2, ἐμφανίζειν points to an inward, spiritual reality: ἐμφανίζεται δὲ (that is, ὁ κύριος) τοῖς μὴ ἀπιστοῦσιν αὐτῷ. Similarly, Philo, *Leg. all.* III, 27, following Gen 18:17. By adding other texts from the book of Wisdom, such as 6:18 and 6:12, R. E. Brown, p. 646, has come to the conclusion that the sapiential background emerges very strongly in Jn 14:21. I, however, find this very doubtful.

104. καί before τί γέγονεν om. P⁶⁶*, ⁷⁵ A B D Θ 𝒫 33 al. sy sa bo VL (apart from q) Vg. In the UBS Greek Testament it is placed in square brackets; see Metzger, *A Textual Commentary*, ad loc. This καί, however, at the beginning of an interrogatory sentence expresses surprise in Greek; see Kühner and Gerth, *Grammatik* II/2, pp. 247f; Blass and Debr. § 442, 8. It may be original.

105. In *Ep. ad Romanos, Praef.* (GCS VI, 8, Lommatzsch): 'the one whom Matthew called Lebbaeus and Mark called Thaddaeus, Luke wrote as Judas of James'.

106. See J. Blinzler, *Die Brüder und Schwestern Jesu* (Stuttgart 1967), pp. 31–34; in opposition to H. Koester, who defended the Syrian tradition in *HarvThR* 58 (1965), pp. 269f; see also G. Quispel in *NTSt* 12 (1965/66), pp. 380f. See also A. F. J. Klijn, 'John XIV 22 and the Name Judas Thomas', *Studies in John (Festschrift für J. N. Sevenster* [Leiden 1970]), pp. 88–96 (there was an early tradition concerning an apostle with the name 'twin').

107. See T. Zahn, *ad loc.*; *ibid., Brüder und Vettern Jesu (Forschungen zur Geschichte des neutesstamentlichen Kanons* VI [Leipzig 1900]), pp. 344–348; J. Blinzler, in *LexThK* ²V, pp. 1154f; W. Bauer, in Hennecke-Schneemelcher, II, p. 32.

108. In Origen, *Contra Celsum* II, 63–67 (S Chr 132, pp. 430ff).

109. In Macarius Magnes, *Apocritus* II, 14.

110. D e sy^c have, instead of the plural, the singular 'I will come' and 'I will dwell'; it is clear, however, that this is a conscious change, probably in assimilation to v. 21.

111. Cf. Bauer *Wörterbuch*, 1042, under 1.

112. F. Hauck in *ThWb* IV, 584.

113. Used together with λέλαληκα, μένων here has a weaker meaning (cf. 14:10c) and does not point beyond his death. It is not possible to replace or surpass the time when Jesus revealed himself on earth. The disciples have to bear witness later to his words, which the Spirit will bring to their remembrance (cf. 15:27).

114. See O. Betz, *Der Paraklet*, pp. 130–133. According to Betz, the 'teacher of righteousness' was a prophetic interpreter who, as an exegete of the Torah, was able to point to God's will and, as a revealer of prophetic words, preached the approach of the last judgment (p. 132). See also G. Jeremias, *Der Lehrer der Gerechtigkeit*, pp. 316ff. In the revelatory function of teaching, there is an analogy with the Paraclete; the difference, however, is that the Paraclete guides men definitively into all truth (cf.

16:13), whereas the 'teacher of righteousness' in Qumran will be followed at the end of time by another 'teaching righteousness' (Damascus Rule 6:11). See G. Jeremias, *op. cit.*, pp. 275–289.

115. τὸ ἅ γιον has been established by textual criticism; in om. sy^s. Later textual evidence (ℵ^c L X) provides the relative pronoun referring to the Paraclete.

116. Bauer, *Wörterbuch*, 1135, unlike Heitmüller, provides the interpretation: 'whom the Father will send on using my name'; cf., however, H. Bietenhard, *ThWb* V, pp. 273, 33–38.

117. Aquinas simply applied the activity of the Holy Spirit to all believers: 'the effect of the mission of the Holy Spirit is to lead the faithful to the Son' (Cai No. 1958); 'He makes us know all things by inspiring and directing us inwardly and by raising us up to spiritual things' (Cai No. 1959). Lagrange dealt with this question in some detail, pp. 424f, concluding his examination of the problem with the words: 'Generally speaking, it seems to me more probable that the Johannine texts should be understood as pointing to the Holy Spirit's perpetual help of the Church in the order of truth.' F. Mussner, 'Die johanneischen Parakletsprüche und die apostolische Tradition', *Praesentia salutis* (Düsseldorf, 1967), pp. 146–158, especially p. 156.

118. The additional sentence: 'And he said to them: "Peace to you"' (Lk 24:36) was not included by Westcott and Hort, who described it as a 'western non-interpolation'. It has, however, increasingly become regarded as original. See Metzger, *A Textual Commentary*, pp. 186f; K. Aland, *Studien zur Überlieferung des Neuen Testaments und seines Textes* (Berlin, 1967), pp. 157 and 162, who is more decisive (as opposed to Nestlé–Aland).

119. *In Jo. Ev., ad loc.* (PG 74, 305).

120. See, for example, Zahn, p. 573: 'The satisfied and satisfactory state of the soul.' Philo, *De somniis*, II, 250, also strove to attain peace of the soul of this kind: 'The city of God is called Jerusalem by the Hebrews, a name which, when translated, means "the face of peace". Do not therefore look for the city of being in the regions of the earth . . . , but in the clear-sighted soul which is without conflict and which has set as its goal the contemplative and peaceful life'. For Philo, see W. Foerster, *ThWb* II, p, 409, 15–25.

121. Tertullian, *adv. Prax.*, IX, 2 (CC 1168). The fourth-century Fathers were engaged in controversy with Arianism in their exegesis; see Lagrange, p. 395; Hoskyns and Davey, pp. 462f.

122. *In Jo. Ev., ad loc.* (PG 74, 316ff); see also *ibid.*, *De incarn.* (SChr 97, pp. 250f); *Quod unus sit Christus* (*ibid.*, p. 488).

123. *In Jo. tr.* LXXVIII, 2–3 (CC 524f); for the Fathers, see also T. E. Pollard, *Johannine Christology and the Early Church* (Cambridge, 1970), especially pp. 154ff; M. Simonetti, 'Giov. 14:28 nella controversia ariana', *Festschrift für J. Quasten* (Münster, 1970), pp. 151–161; C. K. Barrett, '"The Father is greater than I" (Jn 14:28): Subordinationist Christology in the New Testament', *Neues Testament und Kirche. Festschrift für R. Schnackenburg* (Freiburg, 1974), pp. 144–159.

124. See W. Thüsing, *Erhöhung und Verherrlichung*, pp. 210–212; the same author rejects Bultmann's one-sided exegesis on pp. 486f; H. Conzelmann, *ThWb* IX (1971), pp. 361, 15ff.

125. πολλά om. sy$^{sin.}$; this is regarded by many exegetes (Wellhausen, p. 68; Merx, pp. 383f; Bauer, *ad loc.*; Bultmann, p. 487, note 7; see also Brown, p. 651) as original. This may well apply at the level of literary criticism (an editorial addition; see Spitta, pp. 298f; Hirsch, *Studien*, p. 31; but see the explanation above), but it can hardly be accepted as valid at the level of textual criticism (despite Merx' comment that it is a 'Philistine corruption of the text').

126. See Bauer, Bultmann and Brown (p. 656), *ad loc.*

127. For the rabbinical way of speaking, which had a legal sense, see Billerbeck II, p. 563; for the profane Greek usage, see Bauer, *Wörterbuch*, p. 659 below, who quotes a text from Appian. Deviant readings include: εὑρήσει οὐδέν *KΠ* al f Fathers: οὐκ ἔχει οὐδέν εὑρεῖν D a. These are attempts to clarify; Lindars, *ad loc.*, points to Jn 19:4.

128. For other possibilities, see the *UBS Greek New Testament*. It is not possible to begin a new sentence with καὶ καθώς; this is clear from a comparison with 8:28 (see the commentary above.

129. In this, I disagree with L. Schottroff, *Der Glaubende und die feindliche Welt* (Neukirchen, 1970), pp. 228–296, *passim*. Jn 14:31, unlike 14:30, is not taken into account by the author.

130. See C. H. Dodd, *Interpretation*, pp. 408f., according to whom the call to go means more or less 'Come, let us go to meet the ruler of the world!' Dodd says: 'There is no physical movement from the place. The movement is a movement of the spirit . . .' (p. 409). A similar view is held by H. Zimmermann, 'Struktur und Aussage-absicht der joh. Abschiedsreden (Jo 13–17)', *BuL* 8 (1967), pp. 279–290, who comments, correctly, that the situation before Jesus' departure is presupposed in the first farewell discourse and the situation after the return to the Father is assumed in the second discourse. In my opinion, however, he is wrong to believe that the disciples are urged, in the ambiguous wording, to change the situation spiritually (p. 289). It is, Zimmermann believes, a call to those who have risen to new life and who are in the Father's dwelling (p. 290). This meaning cannot, in my view, be imputed to this formula.

SECTION II: CHAPTER 1; Pages 89–122

1. *Gospel According to St John*, XXVIII–XXXII, pp. 476f. Bernard, however, regarded a transposition or change in the sequence of texts, even without a displacement of pages, on the basis of inner evidence, as probable (Chapter XXX). The same arrangement is also suggested by J. Moffatt, *New Translation of the New Testament* (see Howard, *Fourth Gospel*, p. 303).

2. See Bultmann, p. 350, note 2.

3. *Ev. des Joh.*, pp. 349–351.

4. The only important scholars who believe that there is a second farewell discourse are G. Richter, *Fusswaschung*, pp. 310–313; H. Thyen, *Festgabe für K. G. Kuhn*, p. 342; B. Lindars, *Gospel of John*, p. 486. R. E. Brown, pp. 545ff, brings Chapters 15–16 together under 'Division 2', but divides them up into four 'subdivisions': 15:1–17; 15:18 – 16:4a; 16:4b–15; 16:16–33.

5. For this, see the conspectus in R. E. Brown, pp. 589–593.

6. It is possible that a rather longer exposition written by the evangelist lies behind the figurative discourse of the vine in its present form; cf. 15:1. See also my contribution, 'Aufbau und Sinn von Johannes 15', to the *Festschrift for J. Prado* (Madrid, 1975), pp. 405–420.

7. See R. Schnackenburg, 'Strukturanalyse von Joh 17', *BZ*, new series 17 (1973), pp. 67–78, 196–202.

8. 'Die Abschiedsreden Jesu im Johannesevangelium', *ZNW* 61 (1970), pp. 215–246. Bultmann, pp. 421f, made the following divisions: 15:18 – 16:11; 16:12–33.

9. This observation has been made previously by other exegetes; see especially E. Lohmeyer, 'Über Aufbau und Gliederung des vierten Evangeliums', *ZNW* 27 (1928), pp. 11–36, especially p. 29; J. Schneider, 'Die Abschiedsreden Jesu', *Gott und die Götter. Festgabe für E. Fascher* (Berlin, 1958), pp. 103–112, especially p. 108; R. Borig, *Der wahre Weinstock. Untersuchungen zu Jo 15, 1–10* (Munich, 1967), p. 19.

10. See, among others, Lagrange, Hoskyns and Davey, Bultmann, Wikenhauser, van der Bussche and S. Schulz.

11. In 16:24 too, the idea that the disciples' joy will be full forms a conclusion; cf. 1 Jn 1:4. Bernard, Tillmann and Lindars made an incision after v. 11. R. E. Brown's division of the passage is: vv. 1–6; vv. 7–17 (7–10, 11, 12–17). Other commentators have not provided a division of the text.

12. See Schnackenburg, *Joh-Br*, p. 6. This chain-form connection has often been called a concatenation.

13. J. Wellhausen, pp. 70f; F. Spitta, *Joh.-Ev.*, pp. 314f; W. Bauer, p. 195; H. Windisch, *Die fünf johanneischen Parakletsprüche*, pp. 112 and 117ff; J. Becker, *ZNW* 61 (1970), p. 237; see also B. Lindars, p. 496.

14. The words ἀλλ᾽ in v. 2, which is used here – as it is never used elsewhere in the gospel – to give a rhetorically cumulative effect (see Blass-Debr. § 448, 6), λατρείαν προσφέρειν (in the singular) in v. 2, ἡ ὥρα αὐτῶν (which, from the point of view of textual criticism, should be retained) in v. 4a and the expression of the theme of prophecy which can be contrasted with 13:19 and 14:29 – all these are possible evidence of another hand at work.

15. See R. Borig, *Der wahre Weinstock*, pp. 21ff.

16. The following scholars assumed that there was a written source: Bultmann, p. 406, note 3; H. Becker, *Reden*, pp. 109ff; J. Heise, *Bleiben*, p. 81, note 169, who none the less insists that 'it would be impossible to reconstruct the text of the source completely'.

17. Apart from Borig's monograph, the following specialized works may also be consulted: E. Schweizer, *Ego eimi* . . . , pp. 157–161; G. Johnston, 'The Allegory of the Vine: An Exposition of John 15:1–17', *Canadian Journal of Theology* 3 (1957), pp. 150–158; S. Schulz, *Komposition und Herkunft*, pp. 114–117; B. Schwank, ' "Ich bin der wahre Weinstock" (15, 1–17)', *Sein und Sendung* 28 (1963), pp. 244–258; A. Jaubert, 'L'image de la vigne (Jean 15)', *Oikonomia. Festschrift für O. Cullmann* (Hamburg, 1967), pp. 93–99.

18. See R. Borig, *op. cit.*, pp. 29–33. An important word parallel can be found in Jer 2:21 (LXX), in which God addresses Israel: ἐγὼ δὲ ἐφύτευσά σε ἄμπελον καρποφόρον πᾶσαν ἀληθινόν.

19. For Palestinian practices in this field, see G. Dalman, *Arbeit und Sitte* IV, pp. 312f.

20. For a view which is opposed to the widespread explanation that is summed up under the title of 'life association' (Schweizer, Bultmann, Wikenhauser and others), see R. Borig, *op. cit.*, pp. 26f. The idea of the 'tree of life' may, however, have had an effect here, since this was connected in Judaism with the idea of the vine. See A. Jaubert, *op. cit.*, p. 95.

21. MacGregor, p. 287, and Barrett, p. 393, interpreted it in this sense. For the possible reference to Judas, see Bernard, p. 479, Lightfoot and Evans, p. 282, and R. Borig, *op. cit.*, p. 40. The idea of excommunication from the Church is very unlikely and is a misinterpretation of the Johannine view, which is concerned with the self-willed attitude of those who separated themselves from the community (cf. 1 Jn 2:19) or with God's judgment (cf. Jn 15:6). The whole discourse constitutes an appeal to the disciples, but is not directed towards the community as an institution.

22. This was the view not only of certain church Fathers (Cyril of Alexandria, for example, and John Chrysostom), but of some modern exegetes (Bernard, Loisy, Lagrange, Wikenhauser, Schick and others).

23. See Philo's use of language in this respect: *De Agr.* 10; *de Somniis*, II, 64. The same expression for cleaning the corn of chaff and the soil of weeds is found in Xenophon, *Oecon.*, XVIII, 6 and XX, 11 (see in Barrett, *ad loc.*). For the activity of the vine-dresser, see also in Wettstein, I., pp. 936f, who quotes texts. For the religious language, the NT elsewhere almost always uses the later Hellenistic verb καθαρίζειν.

24. R. Borig, *op. cit.*, pp. 41f, defends this connection between the meanings and therefore the originality of v. 3. In his opinion, v. 3 is a 'necessary link' between vv. 2 and 4, because it directs attention to the disciples and their abiding in Christ (p. 41). V. 4 can, however, also be regarded as a new beginning.

25. A direct reference to 13:10 was assumed (apart from Augustine; see the following note), by MacGregor, *ad loc.* Zahn, on the other hand, p. 578, introduces an inadmissible restriction, claiming that the disciples were 'in a certain sense and to some degree already clean'.

26. Augustine, *In Jo. tr.* LXXX, 3 (CC 529), believed that there was a direct connection with baptism and pointed to Jn 13:10, also to Rom 10:8ff; 1 Pet 3:21 and Eph 5:25f. His statement about this is well-known: 'The Word come to the element and it becomes the sacrament, as though it were the Word made visible.' An interpretation of

Jesus' word so that it refers to the word of the sacrament was not, however, intended by the evangelist or by the editor or editors. Thoughts about the 'purity' of the disciples could be present, however, without any idea of baptism.

27. It would also be wrong to conclude that the author had an anti-sacramental attitude; cf. 13:10 (p. 402, note 62, above).

28. R. Borig, *op. cit.*, pp. 199–236, has written exhaustively about this formula. G. Richter, *ZNW* 60 (1969), p. 40, believed that the formula 'he abides in me and I in him' only occurs in those texts that can be shown by literary criticism to be secondary. The transference of the relationship between the Father and the Son to that between Jesus and the disciples, however, was an obvious step in Johannine thinking; see, for example, the assignation of the mission to the disciples in 20:21; 17:18. The disciple or disciples who edited the text simply developed the evagelist's thought for the community. According to J. Heise, *Bleiben*, p. 85, κἀγὼ ἐν ὑμῖν should not be treated as consecutive, but as providing a motive: 'Abide in me, as and because I abide in you.' He is, however, not sufficiently conscious of the formal character of the expression.

29. The minimal effect of Jesus' figurative language in the gospel of John is quite remarkable; cf. the parables of growth, also Lk 6:43f, par. Mt 7:17f; the parable of the evil vine-dressers, Lk 13:6–9. Matthew in particular made use of the image; see the composition in 7:16–20; 12:33; 21:43. The Johannine discourse on the vine is clearly not dependent on the synoptic tradition. For the idea of fruitfulness, see J. Bommer, *Die Idee der Fruchtbarkeit in den Evangelien* (Rome, 1950); A. Lozeron, *La notion de Fruit dans le Nouveau Testament* (Lausanne, 1957); R. Borig, *op. cit.*, pp. 237–242.

30. See Schlatter, p. 305; Strachan, pp. 289f; Hoskyns and Davey, p. 476; Lindars (for 15:7 and 16); see especially Thüsing, *Erhöhung und Verherrlichung*, pp. 107–114; J. Kuhl, *Die Sendung Jesu*, pp. 205–209. The main arguments are: the wording of 15:16 (see the commentary there), the relationship to the 'greater works' in 14:12 (Schlatter), the same vocabulary in 4:36 and 12:24 and the Johannine idea of mission. The perspective, which is different from that in 14:12f, and the different *Sitz im Leben* of the community must also be borne in mind.

31. This is the opinion of most commentators; see Borig, *op. cit.*, pp. 239ff.

32. According to K. Beyer, *Semitische Syntax*, p. 252, the imperative followed by the future tense (see Jn 15:4a, 7) usually betrays a Semitic influence, but not necessarily and especially not if, as it does here, it contains an admonition in the real sense that has to be carried out. The conditional participle is very frequently used in the gospel, but the construction in Jn 15:5 (with οὗτος) is closer to the Greek practice; see Beyer, *ibid.*, p. 217, note 1.

33. See J. Leal, '"Sine me nihil potestis facere"' (Jn 15:5)', *XI Semana Bíblica Española* (Madrid, 1952), pp. 483–498.

34. These are often interpreted as gnomic aorists; see Blass-Debr. § 333, 1. W. Bauer, *ad loc.*, thought differently: 'they express the sequence that is introduced immediately with absolute certainty' and gave classical examples. Zerwick, *Graecitas Bibl.*, 192, spoke of the 'proleptic use of the aorist', as Moulton and Turner did, III, p. 74. The ἐδοξάσθη in v. 8 should also be interpreted in the same way. The perfect can also be used in such cases (see Jn 3:18; 1 Jn 2:5); see P. Schanz, *ad loc.*; Kühner and Gerth, *Ausführliche Grammatik*, II/1, p. 150.

35. Some manuscripts have the singular form αὐτό here instead of αὐτά: ℵ D L X Δ Π 0141 λ φ 33 al. This, however, is an assimilation to τὸ κλῆμα. A new graphic description begins with the words καὶ συνάγουσιν.

36. See F. Lang, *ThWb* VI, pp. 935–939 for the OT, apocalyptic writings, rabbinical texts and the Qumran literature; pp. 942–946 for the New Testament.

37. P[66] is the only manuscript to have the comparative πλείονα here. The scribe was thinking of v. 2b.

38. The evidence for γένησθε is equally good; see the UBS Greek New Testament, in which this version is included in the text (with 'D'). The future can also follow the aorist subjective in a final clause; see Blass-Debr. § 369, 3. γίνεσθαι can be understood (a) as

having the same meaning as εἶναι (see Bauer, *Wörterbuch*, p. 317, under II, 1); (b) as 'becoming', in which case (as the dative would suggest) it means: 'truly become my disciples' (cf. 8:31); (c) as 'showing' or 'proving oneself to be' (which is W. Bauer's translation, *ad loc.*). This last meaning is worth mentioning (see Bauer, *Wörterbuch*, in earlier editions), but is not sufficiently certain.

39. P⁶⁶ has μου instead of the dative. The dative, however, has a definite function here and, when it is used in similar cases elsewhere in the gospel of John, it has an accent; see 7:23; 10:38; 12:26; 19:10. For the dative of interest, see Mayser, *Grammatik der griechischen Papyri*, II/2, pp. 270–272; Moulton and Turner, III, pp. 238f.

40. The sober use of ἀγάπη and its orientation towards moral action distinguishes Johannine Christianity from Gnosticism. Love does not lead to excessive enthusiasm, as it does, for example, in the *Odes of Solomon*; see 8:1: 'Open, open your hearts to exult over the Lord and your love will grow from your heart (up) to your lips!'; 8:13: 'Love me with the fervour with which you love!'; 8:22: 'Pray for ever and ever and abide in the love of the Lord; (be) beloved in the beloved!' See also *Joh.-Br.*, p. 237.

41. After many expressions of joy in personal piety and in the experience of worship in public, 'eschatological joy' emerges in the OT for the first time as such in the later prophetic books; see Is 25:9; 35:10; 51:3; 61:10; 66:10; Zeph 3:14–17; Zech 9:9f, etc. See H. Conzelmann, *ThWb* IX (1971), pp. 353f. The joy of John the Baptist should perhaps also be seen as a 'fulfilment' of joy in the history of salvation (Jn 3:29); see, however, the next note (42). On the other hand, joy in the gnostic *Odes of Solomon* is also ecstatic and mystical; see, for example, 15:1: 'As the sun is a joy for those who long for their day, so too is the Lord my joy'; 23:1: 'Joy belongs to the saints and who is to put it on, but them alone?'; 31:3: 'He (the Lord) opened his mouth and spoke goodness and joy . . . (31:6) Go out, you who are oppressed, and receive joy!'; 40:4: 'And my face is jubilant in exultation over him and my sprit exults in love for him and my soul radiates in him.'

42. There are rabbinical parallels for the term 'full' or 'perfect' joy; see Billerbeck II, pp. 429f and 566. See also G. Delling, *ThWb* VI, p. 296; H. Conzelmann, *ibid.*, IX, pp. 355 and 361.

43. E. Schweizer, *Ego eimi*, pp. 39–41 (see the idea of 'tree of life'), pp. 157–161 (explanation of the text). See also the same author's collected publications, *Neotestamentica* (Zürich and Stuttgart, 1963), pp. 77f and 260, note 22: 'In contrast to the view that I expressed in *Ego eimi*, pp. 37ff, in 1939, I have recently become convinced by Dodd's argument . . . that the use of the term in the Old Testament and Judaism must be given serious consideration. This is all the more important in view of the fact that, in 10:1ff, the Jewish "shepherds" seem to provide a contrast to the true shepherds.' See also his Foreword to the second edition of *Ego eimi* (1965), pp. 3f.

44. *Komposition und Herkunft*, pp. 114–117; *ibid.*, *Ev nach Joh*, pp. 193f (more strongly expressed, following Bultmann).

45. See Dodd, *Interpretation*, pp. 136f, but extending it to 'a rich background of associations which the vine-symbol had already acquired'. See also Barrett, *John*, pp. 393f; Hoskyns and Davey, pp. 474f; Strathmann, p. 217; R. E. brown, pp. 669–672; L. Morris, p. 668, etc.

46. *Der wahre Weinstock*, pp. 79–128; the author's comments on his method are important in this context, p. 79.

47. The frequent reference to 'cutting off' is particularly striking (about fifty times); see, for example, *JB Mand*, 204, 34f: 'The vine that bears fruit rises up; the one that bears none is cut off'; Ginza, 45, 9f: 'the bad vine that drinks water while fruit, grapes and trees dry up is torn out'. For an interpretation, see Borig, *op. cit.*, pp. 160–162.

48. K. Rudolph, *Die Mandäer*, II, pp. 45f.

49. *Op. cit.*, pp. 138–144. For a description of the redeemer as a vine, see especially Ginza, 429: 8–11 (it is quite different from that in Jn 15).

50. See Borig, *op. cit.*, pp. 162–165. 'Fruit' was originally a mythical representation of the dwelling-place of the supreme being (see Ginza, 65:29ff; 67:17f, etc.). Later, it

changed its meaning, so that 'bearing fruit' came to mean 'learning gnosis'. (This is the meaning in the text mentioned above; see JB Mand, 204:34—205:3.)

51. The Septuagint (79:16) adds the following words: καί ἐπὶ υἱὸν ἀνθρώπου, ὃν ἐκραταίωσας σεαυτῷ. Dodd, *Interpretation*, p. 411, has concluded from this 'that the Vine and the Son of Man are equivalent concepts (cf. v. 18), both standing for the people of God'. See also R. E. Brown, pp. 670f.

52. See Billerbeck, II, pp. 563f.

53. See the material in E. R. Goodenough, *Jewish Symbols in the Greco-Roman Period*, eight volumes (New York, 1953ff), *passim*, but especially Vols V and VI.

54. Following G. Dalman and E. R. Goodenough, see the Excursus in Borig, *Der wahre Weinstock*, pp. 108–111.

55. For Matthew, see W. Trilling, *Das wahre Israel* (Munich, 3rd edn., 1964); for Luke, see G. Lohfink, *Die Sammlung Israels. Eine Untersuchung zur lukanischen Ekklesiologie* (Munich, 1975).

56. See G. Ziener, 'Weisheitsbuch und Johannesevangelium', *Bib* 38 (1957), pp. 396–418; A. Feuillet, *Etudes Johanniques* (Paris, 1962), pp. 72–99; *idem.*, *Le Prologue du quatriéme Evangile* (Bruges and Paris, 1968).

57. The following in particular believe that there is a close relationship between the discourse on the vine and the Eucharist: R. H. Strachan, *Fourth Gospel*, pp. 275–277 (the farewell discourse and the prayer in Jn 17 are derived from a great Christian prophet, who presided at the celebration of the Eucharist); O. Cullmann, *Urchristentum und Gottesdienst* (Zürich, 2nd edn., 1950), pp. 108f (the counterpart to Chapter 6); A. Corell, *Consummatum est*, p. 74; W. Grundmann, 'Das Wort von Jesu Freunden (Joh XV, 13–16) und das Herrenmahl', *NT* 3 (1959), pp. 62–69; A. Feuillet, *Etudes Johanniques*, pp. 83f; R. E. Brown, *New Testament Essays* (Milwaukee, 1965), pp. 72f (he is more reserved in his commentary); B. Sandvik, 'Joh. 15 als Abendmahlstext', *ThZ* 23 (1967), pp. 323–328 (he connects the symbolism of the 'vine' with that of the 'temple' and believes that Jn 15:4a is the Johannine repetition of the commandment); B. Lindars, p. 486f (relationship with Mk 14:25).

58. R. E. Brown, *Gospel*, p. 674.

59. See 1 Jn 3:11, 23; 4:21; 5:3; 2 Jn 6. For the construction, which occurs frequently in *koine*, see Rademacher, *Neutestamentliche Grammatik*, pp. 191f; Blass-Debr. § 394; Zerwick, *Graecitas*, No. 290; Mouton and turner, *Gr* III, pp. 103f.

60. See G. Stählin, *ThWb* IX (1970), p. 151, 19–43.

61. The inclusion of such a general statement was noted by M. Dibelius, 'Joh 15, 13. Eine Studie zum traditionsproblem des Johannes-Evangeliums', *Festgabe für A. Deissmann* (Tübingen, 1927), pp. 168–186, reprinted in *Botschaft und Geschichte* I (Tübingen, 1953), pp. 204–220. He correctly commented that 'the most important statement in the whole of the composition in vv. 13–16 is the saying in 15:13' and regarded the unit of the discourse as a 'digression of the kind found in the midrashim, the centre of which is verse 13' (p. 206).

62. Many articles have been written about this, most recently by G. Stählin, *ThWb* IX, pp. 149–151; K. Treu, 'Freundschaft', *RAC* VIII (1972), pp. 418–424.

63. See the material in Billerbeck, II, pp. 564f; III, p. 682 (on Heb 2:11).

64. I disagree here with W. Grundmann, *NT* 3 (1959), p. 67.

65. For Luke, see G. Stählin, *ThWb* IX, pp. 156–162, who believes that 'early Christian communities seized hold of traditions stemming from the circle of disciples' and that the description of the disciples as friends must therefore go back to Jesus himself (pp. 160f, 11ff). This, however, is very unlikely on the basis of tradition.

66. See Jn 10:11 in the commentary (Vol. 2, pp. 294ff); see also C. Maurer, *ThWb* VIII (1969), pp. 155f.

67. For the idea of 'friendship with God', which also played an important part in the Greek world, see E. Peterson, 'Der Gottesfreund', *ZKG* 42 (1923), pp. 161–202; H. Neumark, *Die Verwendung griechischer und jüdischer Motive in den Gedanken*

The Gospel according to St John

Philons über die Steullung Gottes zu seinen Freunden (Würzburg, 1937); G. Stählin, *ThWb* IX, pp. 165f (origin in the Old Testament and Judaism).

68. Instead of εἴρηχα, P⁶⁶ is the only manuscript with λέγω; this is probably an assimilation with the first λέγω, v. 15a. It is possible that εἴρηχα is purely formally related to v. 14; see the linguistic usage in 4:18; 6:65; 11:13; 14:29, but it is clear from the causal clause that Jesus regarded his revelation to his disciples as the beginning of his friendship with them (ἐγνώρισα).

69. See G. Quell, *ThWb* IV, pp. 156ff. It is only said once of Abraham (Neh 9:7) and once of Moses (Ps 106:23) that they were 'chosen' by God. The idea of election is for the most part connected with the king and the people of Israel in the OT; see *ibid.*, pp. 159–168.

70. τίθημι, with the accusative and εἴς τι or ἵνα, means 'to appoint someone to something'; see Bauer, *Wörterbuch*, p. 1615, under I, 2 b. For this reason, it would be wrong to appeal only or principally to texts dealing with appointments to an office in the Church. (I do not agree here with J. Kuhl, *Die Sendung Jesu*, pp. 142f.) The texts in Paul, especially 1 Thess 5:9; Rom 4:17; see also 1 Thess 3:3; Phil 1:16 (with κεῖμαι), indicate that, generally speaking, a divine appointment ought to be expressed in accordance with its saving intentions. See also C. Maurer, *ThWb* VIII, pp. 157f.

71. Reference has been made here to Lk 10:3 (diff. Mt 10:16), but the basis is too narrow. In Jn 15:16, ὑπάγητε (which is a Semiticism) may correspond to the evocative imperative, which gives greater weight to the following verb; see 4:16; 9:7. See G. Delling, *ThWb* VIII, p. 508, who does not name our text.

72. See Lagrange, p. 408, who sees in this text the key to the discourse, what he called a 'programme for the apostolate'; W. Thüsing, *Erhöhung und Verherrlichung*, pp. 111–114; J. Kuhl, *Die Sendung Jesu*, pp. 205–209, who draws attention to the tension between the statements in vv. 1–8 and v. 16.

73. Instead of the present tense, the scribe of P⁶⁶ first wrote ἐμίσησε, correcting this later to ἐμίσει – an indication that μισεῖ was available to him. The past form can be explained as correlative to πρῶτον. γινώσκετε is certainly an imperative (not an indicative, as is often the case in 1 Jn), because the disciples have to be 'reminded' of the world's hatred of Jesus (see v. 20).

74. ὑμῶν is found in om. ℵ * D 579 e a b c ff² bo. But, since πρῶτος (for πρότερος) with a genitive also occurs in 1:15, 30, it may be original.

75. L. Schottroff, *Der Glaubende und die feindliche Welt*, p. 293.

76. L. Schottroff, *op. cit.*, pp. 284ff, interprets this turning of God to the world in the sense of the dualism of decision between faith and lack of faith. It is 'non-gnostic' that 'John should not safeguard to protect the offer of salvation made to the world from misunderstanding; God or his revealer complied with the world that was hostile to God' (p. 286); this is quite different in 1 Jn. But the 'non-gnostic' pronouncement in Jn 3:16 cannot be argued away and it shows that John is fully within the early Christian tradition of the self-giving of the Son of God (see the commentary on 3:16). It should also be borne in mind that 1 Jn was addressed to a community of believers.

77. See N. H. Cassem's research undertaken on the basis of external viewpoints, 'A Grammatical and Contextual Inventory of the Use of κόσμος in the Johannine Corpus with some Implications for a Johannine Cosmic Theology', *NTSt* 19 (1972/73), pp. 81–91; see also G. Baumbach, 'Gemeinde und Welt im Johannes-Evangelium', *Kairos* 14 (1972), pp. 121–136.

78. L. Schottroff (see above) is certainly right here. The differences resulting from the historical character of Jesus and the statements that have survived from the early Christian tradition must, however, be borne in mind, in which case it is hardly possible to claim that 'Jesus, as the revealer of the Johannine gospel, . . . can, without any reservations, be called a gnostic revealer' (*op. cit.*, p. 289). G. Richter, 'Die Fleischwerdung des Logos im Johannesevangelium', *NT* 13 (1971), pp. 81–126, and 14 (1972), pp. 257–276, has attempted to find a distinctive solution, that the

evangelist was not a gnostic, but that he was partly misunderstood and misused, with the result that an editor or editors introduced anti-docetic additions.

79. The verb μνημονεύειν is remarkable, in that it only occurs here and in 16:4, 21. For 'to remember', the evangelist otherwise uses μιμνήσκεσθαι (2:17, 22; 12:16). Does this indicate that the discourse is not the evangelist's? μνημονεύειν may come from the language of the community. As O. Michel, ThWb IV, p. 686, has observed, 'What Jesus said and did took place as a memory with regard to the community.'

80. τηρεῖν τὸν λόγον is a distinctive Johannine expression, often used with a meaning varying between 'adhere to' or 'preserve' and 'keep' or 'observe' (see 8:51). In 1 Jn, it is a question of 'keeping the commandments' or 'the word' (2:5). In Jn 15:20, the idea is also that of realizing Jesus' word, firstly in faith and then in satisfying moral demands. Many exegetes do not recognize a positive meaning in this context. R. E. Brown, Gospel, p. 687, for example, has commented:'They will keep your word to the extent they have kept mine (and they have not kept mine).' This interpretation, however, marks a falling away from the statement in verse 20b and is also not in accordance with Johannine diction. It is arbitrary to suggest that v. 20c is the completion of a negation.

81. Dodd, Historical Tradition, pp. 408f, pointed to the terminology and Brown, Gospel, p. 694, provides a table with parallels from the synoptic discourse on the end of time. He is right, however, to reject the suggestion that 'because of my name' was taken over directly from Matthew. Both gospels preserved an early tradition independently of each other. This, however, can certainly only be claimed with some reservation.

82. πάντα om. D X 71 251 579; this can perhaps be explained on the basis of reflection.

83. The καί . . . καί may also point to a contrast between opposing ideas, see Mayser, Grammatik II/3, pp. 142f; Blass-Debr § 444, 3. In 6:36 too, ἑωράκατε is possibly without an object (although this is uncertain from the point of view of textual criticism. It is hardly likely that Jesus' enemies would be regarded as able to see Jesus and the Father (cf. 14:9). Bernard, Morris, Lindars and others think differently.

84. I do not accept Bultmann's view here, p. 424, note 1; he suggested that v. 23 should follow v. 24 or that it was the evangelist's addition to the source.

85. Augustine, Tr 89 (CC, pp. 548ff), indulged in speculation about who might plead that he had not known Christ or seen his works and about whether there was not a greater and a lesser guilt. Although he regarded the Jews as the representatives of the world which hated Christ and his disciples, he was reluctant to condemn them universally. In Tr XC, 2 (CC 552), for example, he writes: ' . . . judge, however, that is, hold definite and firm opinions, but do not judge before the time that the Lord comes'.

86. B. Noack, Zur joh. Tradition, has concluded, after investigating the OT quotations in John (pp. 71–89), that the fourth evangelist was not dependent either on the synoptics or on a collection of testimonies, but was fairly isolated in his own tradition (p. 89). B. Lindars, New Testament Apologetic, is more inclined to the view that John should also be included in the common use of Scripture in the early Church (certain chapters of the OT, Psalms and so on), but recognizes certain special aspects, which he traces back to the genius of the evangelist himself (pp. 265–272). The Johannine school may, however, also have contributed a great deal of its own.

87. Several exegetes therefore prefer to accept an allusion to Ps 69; see especially B. Lindars, New Testament Apologetic, p. 103 and ad loc. E. D. Freed, Old Testament Quotations, pp. 94f, who does not commit himself, regards Ps Sol 7:1 as the parallel that is closest to Jn 15:25, at least according to the text. There the Jews say of their enemies: ὅι ἐμίσησαν ἡμᾶς δωρεάν. This would give a special emphasis, but it has to be pointed out that it cannot be established that John knew the Odes of Solomon.

88. See Wellhausen, p. 70; Spitta, Joh-Ev, pp. 314f; Hirsch, Studien, p. 113; W. Bauer, ad loc.,; H. Windisch, Parakletsprüche, pp. 112 and 117f; J. Becker, Abschieds-reden (ZNW, 1970), pp. 237f.

89. See J. Beutler, Martyria, p. 274. Bultmann, p. 425, on the other hand, tried to explain the context: in 15:26f, it is made clear why the disciples are hated by the world; it

is because they bear witness to Jesus. This does not, however, explain the saying about the Paraclete.

90. Bultmann, p. 425, note 4, assumed that there was a saying from the source which the evangelist provided with additions; H. Becker, *Reden,* p. 112, holds a similar view.

91. See S. Schulz, *Untersuchungen,* p. 146, who is opposed to the idea of an interpolation and pleads in favour of a 'tradition in Johannine formulation'. He does not, however, provide any further elucidation.

92. E. Schweizer, *Ego eimi,* pp. 90f (No. 6) on ἐκεῖνος; Ruckstuhl, *Literarische Einheit,* p. 201 (No. 30) on μαρτυρεῖν περί.

93. See Lagrange, Tillmann (who is hesitant), *ad loc.*; J. Huby, *Le discours de Jésus après la Cène* (Paris, 1942), p. 88; Behler, *Abschiedsworte,* p. 202. For a different view, see Schanz; see also J. Kuhl, *Die Sendung Jesu,* pp. 135–137.

94. Theodore of Heraclea reproduces the Greek view very well (Fragment 302, Reuss, p. 144): τὸ πνεῦμα ἐκ τῆς τοῦ πατρὸς οὐσίας ἐκπορεύεται διὰ τοῦ υἱοῦ εἰς ἀνθρώπους καταπεμπόμενον. The Greeks thought of the sending of the Spirit as a dynamic event proceeding from the Father, mediated by the Son and leading to an indwelling of the Spirit in man.

95. Further details will be found in R. Schnackenburg, '"Das Evangelium" im Verständnis des ältesten Evangelisten', *Orientierung an Jesus (Festschrift für J. Schmid)* (Freiburg, 1973), pp. 309–324, especially pp. 311–313.

96. See Dodd, *Historical Tradition,* pp. 410–412; R. E. Brown, pp. 699f, who, however, attributes too little importance to the Paraclete in this historical tradition in his appendix (V) on the Paraclete. G. Johnston, *The Spirit-Paraclete,* does the same, while B. Lindars, *ad loc.* (p. 496), notes that this background (Mt 10:20; Mk 13:11) 'goes some way to explaining why John has chosen this unusual title'. See also my Excursus 16.

97. δέ om. D 565 VL Vg sy. The Latin and Syriac translations must have omitted it in accordance with the meaning.

98. See Blass-Debr § 447, 9. Examples of papyri will be found in Mayser, *Grammatik* II/3, pp. 131f.

99. F. Mussner, *Die johanneischen Parakletsprüche,* goes too far when he claims: 'In this sense, the gift of the Spirit is tied to the apostolic office, but this also means that the Spirit does not speak directly, but only in concrete apostolic testimony' (*Praesentia salutis,* p. 156).

100. See G. Stählin, *ThWb* VII, pp. 345–358, commenting on Jn 16:1, observes that 'Jesus' farewell discourses in John (see 13:19; 14:27, 29), like his last discourses in the synoptics, have the aim of preventing falling away (see, for example, Mt 24:25; Lk 22:31)' (p. 358). For an understanding of this concept in depth, see K. Müller, *Anstoss und Gericht* (Munich, 1969), especially his comments on Rom 16:17, pp. 46–67.

101. See H. Strathmann, *ThWb* IV, pp. 58–66; commenting on Jn 16:2, he says that λατρεία is 'more or less the same as sacrifice'.

102. For ἀλλά in this intensifying sense, see Bauer, *Wörterbuch,* p. 76, under 5; Blass-Debr. § 448, 6 ('introducing something additional in a powerful way').

103. The prototype here is Pinhas (see *Num* 25:6–13). In *Num* r 21, he says: 'Did he make a sacrifice, since expiation is expressed in connection with him? All that it does is to teach you that everyone who sheds the blood of the godless is like one who offers a sacrifice' (quoted in Billerbeck II, p. 565). This 'holy zeal' is fundamental to our understanding of the Jewish movement from the time of the Maccabees onwards; see M. Hengel, *Die Zeloten* (Leiden and Cologne, 1961), pp. 151–234. *Sanh* IX, 6a sheds light on the attitude of the Jewish authorities; the 'zealots' are guaranteed exemption from punishment if they 'set upon' certain religious criminals, that is, kill them.

104. This verse is absent from Syrus Sinait. and is regarded by many exegetes as a parenthesis or a later addition. Many manuscripts have ὑμῖν after ποιήσουσιν (this is attested in the UBS Greek NT.) Here, however, the shorter reading is the better one.

105. It is certainly the more difficult reading; ἡ ὥρα αὐτῶν is found in P⁶⁶ (this is questionable; there is a gap) A B Θ L Π* 33 al. VL (apart from a d ff²) Vg sy^{p.har}.

106. א^c D L ⌀ al. VL (apart from ff²) Vg sy^s sa bo.

SECTION II: CHAPTER 2; Pages 123–137

1. Several exegetes hold this view. J. M. Reese, 'Literary Structure of Jn 13:31—14:31; 16:5–6, 16–33', *CBQ* 34 (1972), pp. 221–331, has put forward his own thesis, suggesting that a pattern of revelation, counter-question and elucidation can be discerned in the farewell discourses, although this was interrupted and obscured by later interpolations. In Chapter 16, the original pattern is preserved, Reese believes, in vv. 5–6, 17–18 and 19–23 (a short separation brings lasting joy) and in vv. 25–28, 29–30 and 31–33 (victory over the world). This is an ingenious hypothesis, but it creates new problems, above all in that it does nothing to explain the existence of the closed units of discourse; see the farewell discourse in Chapter 14.

2. Bultmann made a number of divisions: judgment passed on the world, 16:8–11; the continuation of revelation in the future, 16:12–15, extending the last verses on to 16:12–33, as the future of the believing community as the eschatological situation (pp. 440f). See the discussion in R. E. Brown, p. 709.

3. Zahn, p. 589, says that 'the words of Thomas in 14:5 were not a sympathetic question about Jesus' fate as Jesus himself surveyed it'. Barrett, *ad loc.*, points to the present tense ἐρωτᾷ, as indicating the disciples' immediate reaction. B. Schwank's interpretation, *Sein und Sendung* (1963), p. 341, was that the words should be: 'None of you asks me any more.' This is possible in Hebrew, but the Greek οὐκέτι is also found in 16:10, 16, 21, 25.

4. R. E. Brown, p. 710, believes that the disciples' sorrow is more closely linked with the announcement of persecutions in 15:20ff. If, however, the discourse in Chapter 16 is an independent conception, the sorrow must be interpreted in connection with 16:20ff.

5. 'Telling the truth' (λαλεῖν or λέγειν) means more than ἀληθὲς or ἀληθῆ λέγειν (4:18; 19:35; see also 10:41). There is also a connection between 16:7 and 16:13 ('guide you into all the truth').

6. For οὐ μὴ ἔλθῃ in B L Ψ 33 1071 1819, most manuscripts have the reading οὐκ ἐλεύσεται. This version has therefore been adopted by most editors (including those of the UBS Greek New Testament). The emphatic οὐ μή following ἐαν μή (cf. 4:48) may perhaps be preferable; see Westcott and Hort, and Nestlé–Aland.

7. Bultmann, pp. 430ff, provides an existential interpretation in accordance with his theology of revelation: 'He (Jesus) can only be the revealer as the one who is always smashing the existing order, destroying all security, breaking in from beyond and calling men to the future' (p. 430). But is this what the announcement of the Paraclete really means? See 16:13f, with its emphasis on the continuity of the activity of the Paraclete with Jesus.

8. See F. Büchsel, *ThWb* II, pp. 470ff.

9. See J. Blank, *Krisis*, pp. 332–339.

10. See J. Behm, *ThWb* V, pp. 799ff; the παράκλητος speaks '*for* someone *before* someone' (pp. 801, 37f).

11. This is the opinion of O. Betz, *Der Paraklet*, p. 194.

12. See Bultmann, p. 433: 'The fact that these three concepts have no article shows that they are called into question . . .' He then goes on to say that 'it is at the same time disclosed who is a sinner, who is victorious and who is judged' (p. 434). For the absence of the article, see also O. Betz, *Der Paraklet*, pp. 196f, who points to the linguistic usage in Qumran and the practice in that community of using central theological concepts without the article. It is, however, also possible to point to Paul; see Blass-Debr, § 258.

13. Zahn, p. 591, takes a different view, namely that ὅτι here introduces a causal clause. L. Morris, p. 698, note 21, prefers to translate the second ὅτι as 'because' and the

third as 'that'. Many English commentators have translated ὅτι here as 'because', probably because of the earlier translations, and only the New English Bible has departed from this tradition ('by showing . . .'). Cf. the excellent discussion in Barrett, p. 406.

14. For the view expressed by M. F. Berrouard, I. de la Potterie and others that the Paraclete convinces believers in their consciousness of the truth of these three statements, see Excursus 16.

15. *Der Paraklet,* pp. 192–206. Betz points (p. 202) in addition to the two witnesses in Rev 11.

16. O. Betz, *op. cit.,* p. 196, certainly goes too far here in his interpretation. For the text that he cites, 1 QH 2:14, see G. Jeremias, *Der Lehrer der Gerechtigkeit,* pp. 200f. In this hymn, 'the teacher of righteousness is in the centre of the battles for and against God'.

17. Bultmann, p. 433, note 2, appeals to these texts.

18. See Zerwick, *Graecitas Bibl.,* No. 127: the omission of the article points not to individual sin, but to its quality and nature.

19. See J. Blank, *Krisis,* p. 337.

20. Most modern commentators provide too one-sided a presentation of Jesus' righteousness. According to Hoskyns and Davey, p. 485, Jesus' 'return to the Father is God's imprimatur on the righteousness manifested in the life and death of his Son'. In the same way, Barrett, p. 407, believed that it sets 'the seal on the righteousness of Jesus'. B. Lindars, however, thinks differently and stresses the forensic character of righteousness in this text.

21. See T. Preiss, 'Justification in Johannine Thought', *Life of Christ* (London, 1957), pp. 9–31.

22. The exegesis moves between 'declaring innocent' and 'entering victoriously (the heavenly world)'. According to E. Schweizer, *Erniedrigung und Erhöhung bei Jesus und seinen Nachfolgern* (Zürich, 2nd edn., 1962), p. 106, the text contains the idea of a trial conducted between God and the world. In the case of the second view, an appeal is usually made to gnostic texts; see M. Dibelius and H. Conzelmann, *Die Pastoralbriefe* (Tübingen, 3rd edn., 1955), *ad. loc.* These two views do not, however, necessarily exclude each other, since justice or righteousness and victory were very close to one another both in Judaism and in Gnosticism; see the texts in Bultmann, p. 434, note 7; O. Betz, *Der Paraklet,* pp. 202f.

23. O. Betz, *Der Paraklet,* p. 201.

24. Augustine, *In Jo. tr., XCV,* 3 (CC, 567), applied righteousness to believers in his consideration of the statement: 'you will see me no more': 'It will therefore be, he said, by your righteousness that the world will be proved guilty . . . because in him whom you will not see you will believe in me'. This is, of course, exegetically wrong, but Augustine is right in his conviction that the disciples take over the function of the Paraclete or share in Jesus' 'righteousness' (see also 1 Jn 2:29; 3:7).

25. The same image is also present in other texts in the gospel in which this word occurs (10:31; 19:17; 20:15), apart from 12:6, where it has the special meaning of 'set aside'. The same applies to most of the NT; similarly extended meanings can be found in Gal 5:10 (bearing the judgment of God, taking it on oneself); Rom 15:1 (bearing weaknesses); Rev 2:2 (bearing evil); 2:3 (enduring). See Bauer, *Wörterbuch,* pp. 272f; F. Büchsel, *ThWb* I, pp. 596f; Schlatter, *ad loc.* (parallels in Jewish literature).

26. See G. Johnston, *The Spirit-Paraclete,* pp. 66f.

27. Instead of the present ἀκούει, some manuscripts have the future ἀκούσει: B D E H Θ Ψ 054 579 al. VL Vg sy sa bo; and some editors, Vogels, Bover, the UBS Greek New Testament. This does not, however, change the meaning in any way; cf. the change from λήμψεται in v. 14 to λαμβάνει in v. 15. Discussing the Trinitarian aspect, Augustine regards the saying that the Paraclete will only say what he will hear as a 'difficult, an all too difficult question' (CC 583).

28. Lagrange, p. 423, believes that this classifies the apostles as below the prophets: 'the prophet who has seen the things of the future is above all the author of the Apocalypse'. See also Bernard, p. 511; Wikenhauser, p. 295 (the Paraclete as the one

who gives the gift of prophecy); H. Windisch, *Parakletsprüche*, p. 121 (the inclusion of pre-Johannine ideas that were present in prophetism and in apocalyptic writing). Barrett, p. 408, discusses two possibilities for τὰ ἐρχόμενα: (*a*) from the historical standpoint of Jesus himself, they are the passion and the resurrection; (*b*) 'from the standpoint of the evangelist' they 'must be events still future'. Barrett himself prefers the second possibility, but does not wish to rule the first out (this is hardly possible). Most recent exegetes regard the announcement of future events as a vague and generalized statement. W. Thüsing, *Erhöhung und Verherrlichung*, pp. 149–153, thinks that it refers to everything that is to 'come' at the time of the Paraclete (p. 151), that is, the entire continuation of the work of salvation by the Spirit or the disciples (p. 153).

29. Suggested by P. Joüon in *RSR* 28 (1938), pp. 234f; see also R. E. Brown, *ad loc.* (p. 708). The aspect of proclaiming what has already been heard is indicated less by the word itself than by the context in each case (cf. Jn 4:25; 4:51, v. 1). See also J. Schniewind, *ThWb* I, p. 62, for the use of this word in the Septuagint. F. W. Young, 'A Study of the Relation of Isaiah to the Fourth Gospel', *ZNW* 46 (1955), pp. 215–233, especially pp. 224–227, pointed to the influence of Isaiah's revelation terminology; in connection with our present text, he points particularly to 41:23 and 44:7 (τὰ ἐπερχόμενα ἀναγγέλλειν).

30. W. Michaelis, *ThWb* V, pp. 104–106, assumes that ὁδηγεῖν in Jn 16:13 has the meaning of 'instruct', possibly in contrast to 'guide' or 'accompany'. But ὁδηγεῖν has in itself many meanings. W. Thüsing, *Erhöhung und Verherrlichung*, pp. 146–149, notes in particular 14:4ff as valuable in the exegesis of our present text: the Paraclete makes it possible for the way of 14:6 to be followed or the truth to be known (p. 147). He is right in giving ἀλήθεια a Christological significance, but is too narrow in his view of the relationship between the two texts.

31. Thüsing, *op. cit.*, pp. 150f, points to the connection between this and Jesus' speaking 'openly' (16:25) and the promise that prayer will be heard (16:23f, 26): 'the same reality is at the basis of all these texts'. It is true that the activity of the Paraclete can also be detected in such statements, just as, in Chapter 14, the promises of the coming of the Paraclete (vv. 16f) and of Jesus' coming (vv. 18ff) are juxtaposed. In each case, however, special aspects are emphasized. The exalted Christ is present with his community through the Spirit and is active in it, but he cannot be simply identified with the Spirit.

32. Augustine, *In Jo. tr.* 99 (CC, 581–587).

EXCURSUS 16: Pages 138–154

1. J. Behm, *ThWb* V (1954), p. 802, 2–5.

2. For the earlier literature, see J. Behm, article on παράκλητος, *ThWb* V, pp. 798–812, especially p. 798. Reviews of existing research will also be found in O. Betz, *Der Paraklet* (Leiden and Cologne, 1963), pp. 4–35; R. E. Brown, 'The Paraclete in the Fourth Gospel', *NTSt* 13 (1966/67), pp. 113–132; G. Johnston, *The Spirit-Paraclete in the Gospel of John* (Cambridge, 1970), pp. 80–118; U. B. Müller, 'Die Parakletenvorstellung im Johannesevangelium', *ZThK* 71 (1974), pp. 31–77, especially pp. 31–38. Important works on this subject will be mentioned in the following notes.

3. G. Johnston, *The Spirit-Paraclete*, especially pp. 61–79.

4. U. B. Müller, 'Parakletenvorstellung', pp. 65–77.

5. *ThWb* V, pp. 799–804.

6. See Billerbeck, II, pp. 560–562; S. Mowinckel, 'Die Vorstellungen des Spätjudentums vom heiligen Geist als Fürsprecher und der johanneischen Paraklet', *ZNW* 32 (1933), pp. 97–130; N. Johansson, *Parakletoi. Vorstellungen von Fürsprechern für die Menschen vor Gott in der alttestamentlichen Religion, im Spätjudentum und Urchristentum* (Lund, 1940).

7. According to Lagrange, pp. 382f, the original Latin translations had *advocatus*, but *consolator* gradually took precedence. It is not easy to say precisely how the Greek exegetes originally interpreted the word. The material has been assembled and discussed

by Behm, *ThWb* V, p. 803f. Whenever the word was used in early Christian literature outside the Johannine sayings about the Paraclete, it had the meaning of 'intercessor' or 'counsel' (see *ibid.,* pp. 801, 22–32). In the case of Job 16:2 (A and Θ), Behm, Hastings and Cremer and Kögel have all assumed that these translators decided to use this particular word 'under the influence of a very early exegesis of the gospel of John' (Behm, p. 804, note 39). The active interpretation of παράκλητος suggested itself to the Greek Fathers because the Paraclete in fact exercised active functions. See, for example, Ammonius Saccas, Fragment 488 (Reuss, p. 318), whose interpretation is, however, ambiguous: The Son and the Spirit are called 'Paraclete': ὡς παραμυθίαν ἡμῖν ἐμποιοῦντες καὶ ὡς παρακαλοῦντες ὑπὲρ ἡμῶν τὸν πατέρα. What we have here is obviously a reflection on the term.

8. See Zahn, *Excursus,* pp. 563–572, especially pp. 564f. See also A. Lemonnyer, 'L'Esprit-Saint Paraclet', *RScPhTh* 16 (1927), pp. 293–307; N. H. Snaith, 'The Meaning of "The Paraclete" ', *ExpT* 57 (1945/46), pp. 47–50; J. G. Davies, 'The Primary Meaning of ΠΑΡΑΚΛΗΤΟΣ', *JThSt* New Series 4 (1953), pp. 35–38 (= the Comforter); Barrett, pp. 385f.

9. 'Parakletenvorstellung', pp. 61–65.

10. *ibid.,* pp. 62f.

11. S. Schulz, *Untersuchungen zur Menschensohn-Christologie im Johannesevangelium* (Göttingen, 1957), pp. 142–158. O. Betz, *Der Paraklet,* pp. 11f, is critical of this method.

12. U. B. Müller, 'Parakletenvorstellung', p. 66, who also stresses that 'it is not necessary to eliminate Jn 15:26f from the text as something that has no place in the context' (p. 67, note in text).

13. See J. Blank, 'Die Verhandlung vor Pilatus', *BZ* (1959), pp. 60–81; *ibid.,* Krisis, pp. 332–339. M. F. Berrouard, 'Le Paraclet, défenseur du Christ devant la conscience du croyant (Jo XVI, 8–11)', *RScPhTh* 33 (1949), pp. 361–389, provided an unconvincing interpretation by claiming that the passage does not refer to an external process of proving the world guilty, but to one in which the believers are made conscious and certain. Other French-speaking exegetes have provided similar interpretations. See, for example, I. de la Potterie, 'Le Paraclet', *RScPhTh, op. cit.*; S. Lyonnet, *La vie selon l'Esprit, condition du chrétien* (Paris, 1965), pp. 85–105. especially pp. 102ff. The Johannine community was thinking of a real victory over the world; see Jn 16:33; 1 Jn 4:4; 5:4. Jn 16:8–11 is closely related with 15:26f.

14. J. Becker and U. B. Müller believe that the sayings about the Paraclete in Jn 15 and 16 reveal an understanding of the Spirit that is different from the sayings in Jn 14. According to J. Becker, *ZNW* 61 (1970), pp. 239f, 'the Spirit does not represent Jesus himself, but his teaching, which is obviously the sum-total of several statements . . . "Truth" therefore became a term in the Church's teaching'. The opinion of U. B. Müller, 'Parakletenvorstellung', p. 72, is very similar. 16:13 cannot, however, be understood in this sense if it is remembered that it includes language taken from Wisdom literature.

15. I disagree here with H. Windisch, 'Die fünf johanneischen Parakletsprüche', *Festgabe für A. Jülicher* (Tübingen, 1927), pp. 110–137; S. Schulz, *Untersuchungen,* pp. 143–149. I agree with M. Miguéns, *El Paráclito (Jn 14–16)* (Jerusalem, 1963), pp. 27–44 (although his arguments are to some extent insufficient); G. Johnston, *The Spirit-Paraclete,* pp. 61–79.

16. *Ev-Joh.,* Excursus, pp. 437–440.

17. See W. Michaelis, 'Zur Herkunft des johanneischen Paraklet-Titels', *Coni Neot* XI (1947), pp. 147–162; G. Bornkamm, 'Der Paraklet im Johannesevangelium', *Festschrift für R. Bultmann* (Stuttgart, 1949), pp. 12–35; J. Behm, *ThWb* V, pp. 805–807; G. Johnston, *The Spirit-Paraclete,* pp. 88–92.

18. *Der Paraklet im Joh-Ev* (see note 17 above).

19. R. Bultmann, in the supplementary volume to his *Joh-Kommentar* (2nd edn., 1957), pp. 48f; O. Betz, *Der Paraklet,* pp. 32–35; U. B. Müller, *Parakletenvorstellung,* pp. 35f.

20. *Untersuchungen*, pp. 153f. He also points to the wider framework of the 'farewell discourse' in the apocalyptic authors.

21. *Komposition und Herkunft der Johanneischen Reden* (Stuttgart, 1960), p. 136.

22. *Das Evangelium nach Johannes* (Göttingen, 1972), pp. 188f.

23. See O. Betz, *Der Paraklet*, p. 12 ('the final balance is syncretic').

24. S. Mowinckel, *Vorstellungen*; N. Johansson, *Parakletoi*. J. Behm, *ThWb* V, p. 810, and, with certain modifications, R. E. Brown, *NTSt* 13 (1966/67), pp. 120–124, also believe that the idea of the Paraclete originated with the Jewish notion of the intercessor.

25. *Der Paraklet*, pp. 16–22.

26. See G. Johnston, *The Spirit-Paraclete*, pp. 96–102.

27. *Der Paraklet*, pp. 56–72. F. M. Cross Jr, *The Ancient Library of Qumran* (London, 1958), pp. 159ff, previously held a similar view.

28. *Der Paraklet*, p. 156. Betz also believes that John combined two factors which were apparently kept distinct in Qumran – Michael and the 'Spirit of truth' (*ibid.*).

29. G. Johnston, *The Spirit-Paraclete*, pp. 113–118.

30. U. B. Müller, *Parakletenvorstellung*, p. 34; see also H. Braun, *Qumran und das Neue Testament* II (Tübingen, 1966), pp. 261–264, for the teaching about the Spirit in Qumran.

31. *NTSt* 13 (1966/67), pp. 128–132; *Gospel of John* II, Appendix V: 'The Paraclete', pp. 1135–1144, especially pp. 1142f.

32. See the commentary above, 14:18; see also G. Johnston, *The Spirit-Paraclete*, pp. 92–96.

33. *The Spirit-Paraclete*, pp. 119f.

34. See the material, *op. cit.*, pp. 52–60, and the results, pp. 60f.

35. This is a procedure that Luke often adopted in such cases; see P. Hoffmann, *Studien zur Theologie der Logienquelle* (Münster, 1972), p. 269, with note 111. I would also point here to the close relationship between the reception of the Spirit and the witness borne by the apostles in Luke's theology; see Lk 24;48f; Acts 1:8; 2:32f; 5:32. Acts 5:32, which is a statement made before the Jewish court, makes it seem quite possible that Luke was stimulated by this traditional logion to develop his theology of bearing witness. This would then be a different line of development from the same source.

36. M. Miguéns, *El Paráclito*, pp. 104–151, makes use of other New Testament traditions and tries, on the basis of those traditions, to elucidate the Johannine idea of the Paraclete. His attempt does not, however, go far enough, since he does not try to explain the special and distinctive aspects of the Johannine statements. Unlike Miguéns, I try to find points of departure and contact only in the traditional material.

37. The most resolute representative of this view is a A. Kragerud, who believes that the gospel of John resulted from itinerant prophetism (in contrast with office in the community); see *Lieblingsjünger*, pp. 84–112 (the author refers to the sayings about the Paraclete on p. 92). Other scholars do not go as far as this, but still think that the gospel is within a prophetic tradition. See, for example, E. Käsemann, *Jesu letzter Wille*, p. 71: 'It is all too rarely asserted that John should undoubtedly be seen in the same line as that prophecy, the chief characteristic of which is the present relevance of the Christian message. John teaches, admonishes, consoles and interprets, as the prophets did, the traditional elements in his own time, by which every situation is determined. In this way he brought his gospel to bear on the present with a ruthless and one-sided prophetic insistence. In so doing, he made as much or as little use of tradition as he needed to further his intention.'

38. See H. Bacht, 'Montanismus', *LThK*, 2nd edn., VII (1962), pp. 578–580, especially p. 580. In their interpretation of the sayings about the Paraclete, many of the Church Fathers engaged in polemics against Montanus and Priscilla (his prophetess); see Theodore of Heraclea, Fragments 260, 271, 272 (Reuss, pp. 133f and 136f).

39. See K. Löwith, *Weltgeschichte und Heilsgeschehen* (Stuttgart, 1953), pp. 136–167; J. Ratzinger, *LThK*, 2nd edn., V (1960), pp. 975f.

40. See also K. Haacker, *ThZ* 29 (1973), pp. 197ff, who is opposed to both a (Catholic) claim that the sayings about the Paraclete apply to the Church's office and a (Protestant) disregard of tradition.

SECTION II: CHAPTER 2, CONTINUED: Pages 154–166

33. V. 16+ ὅτι ὑπάγω πρὸς τὸν πατέρα G Θ P 33 al. sy c aur f q Vg georg. The ὅτι was regarded by the versions as causal.

34. Most exegetes correctly include verses 23–24, because an incision is made at v. 25 (ταῦτα . . . λελάληκα). ἐρωτᾶν in v. 23a is connected with v. 19 and the 'perfect joy' of v. 25 also goes back to v. 22. In the continuation of this train of thought, the idea that prayer will be heard is also added (vv. 23b–24) and is taken up again in v. 26. R. E. Brown, p. 728, thinks differently. He believes that there is a turning-point between vv. 23a and 23b, and has therefore arranged the verses before and those after this point in an ascending line. This arrangement is rather artificial.

35. See especially H. Leroy, *Rätsel und Missverständnis*, pp. 57f.

36. In *Jo. tr.* CI, 5–6 (*CC* 592–594). Previously in this treatise, however, Augustine interpreted the two 'little whiles' as applying to the time up to Jesus' death and up to his resurrection (CI, 1). Because of the promises that could not be fulfilled completely on earth, however, he favoured the second interpretation: 'that whole space of time towards which the present age is flying' (CI, 6). Some other exegetes have from time to time followed him (for example, Maldonat).

37. In John, τίνες can fall out after the partitive ἐχ; see 1:24 in the commentary. According to Blass-Debr § 164, 2, 'This usage is rare in classical Greek, but quite usual in Semitic Greek.' This is a striking Semiticism here.

38. Bultmann has considered this, pp. 444f, note 3, ascribing verses 16, 20, 22b to the 'source'.

39. In *koine*, it was common to mix direct and indirect speech, so that ὅτι in this context may represent inverted commas (see, for example, Jn 10:36; 20:18). The word ὅτι may have a similar function in 16:17; see also Blass-Debr § 470.

40. ἔλεγον οὖν om. D VL syˢ; ὁ λέγει om. P⁶⁶ ℵ * D* al. VL; τό before μιχρόν om. P⁶⁶ (?) B L al. (although the article may be there as an anaphora).

41. John also has the article in other comparative images drawn from everyday life; see, for example, 8:35 (slave); 10:10 (thief), 11f (the good shepherd and the hired man); 12:24 (the grain of corn); see also Lk 11:21, etc. It may also possibly be used generically; see Blass-Debr § 263; Moulton and Turner, *Grammar* III, pp. 180f. A Semitic influence is, however, more likely.

42. C. H. Dodd, *Historical Tradition*, pp. 366–387, discusses six or seven relevant texts in the gospel of John, including our present text, pp. 369–373. The use in John is not, in his opinion, radically different from that in the synoptics and the source is to be found in the OT.

43. A. Feuillet, 'L'heure de la femme (Jn 16, 21) et l'heure de la Mère de Jésus (Jn 19: 25–27)', *Bib* 47 (1966), pp. 169–184, 361–380, 557–573, has gone a long way in his recognition of the symbolic character of the woman in labour. See also A. Kerrigan, 'Jn 19: 25–27 in the Light of Johannine Theology and the Old Testament', *Anton* 35 (1960), pp. 369–416, especially pp. 380–387; F. M. Braun, *Jean le Théologien* III/2 (Paris, 1972), pp. 105ff.

44. Apart from the authors mentioned in the preceding note (43), see also W. Thüsing, *Erhöhung und Verherrlichung*, p. 99, who is more cautious in his judgment and does not rule out the possibility that the 'hour' of the woman is no more than an element in the image.

45. W. H. Brownlee, 'Messianic Motifs of Qumran and the New Testament', *NTSt* 3 (1956/57), pp. 12–30, especially p. 29, appealed to 1 QH 3:9ff in connection with Jn 16:21. A different view is taken by O. Betz, 'Die Geburt der Gemeinde durch den

Lehrer', *ibid.*, pp. 314–326, especially pp. 316–320; see also H. Braun, *ThRu* 28 (1962), pp. 229f. G. Jeremias, *Der Lehrer der Gerechtigkeit*, p. 177, note 1, recognizes that 1 QH 3:1–18 as a hymn of the teacher of righteousness, but thinks that the interpretation is so difficult that he has abstained from a discussion. Even in his opinion, however (p. 204, note 1), to interpret it as pointing to the 'birth of the Messiah in the community' is very far from the reality.

46. For the idea of the 'ultimate, evil time' in the apocalyptic writings, see P. Volz, *Eschatologie*, pp. 147–163; for 'distress' or 'tribulation', see H. Schlier, 'Drangsal', *ThWb* III, p. 145. θλῖψις (or the plural form) is also used in the New Testament in an extended sense, that is, as the appearance of Christian existence in this world. The apocalyptic idea of 'great distress' is also mentioned in Rev 7:14 (see also 1:9).

47. The καί is comparative here, like οὕτως (καί); see Jn 3:8; 13:10; 15:4; 1 Jn 2:18; see also Blass-Debr § 453, 1. 48.

48. ἔξετε P⁶⁶ A D L W* Θ Ψ 33 al. a b d e r¹.

49. ἀρεῖ P⁵ B D* T 33 a c d aur ff² r¹ Vg sy sa bo Orig Hilar.

50. The copyist's intention in placing ἐν τῷ ὀνόματί μου first: P²² (?) A D Θ P λ ⊄ pm VL Vg sy bo was probably to connect it with 'ask'.

51. Bauer, *Wörterbuch*, p. 1134 (below) has the translation: 'the Father will give you on the naming of my name (by you)'. Even the linguistic usage found in the Septuagint, however, makes it seem doubtful that the name had to be proclaimed or invoked every time with the formula; see H. Bientenhard, *ThWb* V, p. 262, 30–39. The expression quite often means 'by order', as in the rabbinical way of speaking: 'Rabbi N. said in the name of Rabbi N.' (see *ibid.*, p. 267, 21–27). God cannot, however, grant requests 'by order' or 'on the authority' of Jesus, but, since both are united in action, the Father is able to act in Jesus' place. See the authentic commentary in 16:27, which at least confirms the interpretation suggested above.

52. It is remarkable that the function of overcoming the disciples' perplexity and sorrow is not attributed to the Paraclete, who is (according to 16:13) to guide the disciples into all the truth. He is not, however, mentioned in connection with prayer in John; the assurance that prayer will be heard goes together, in the Johannine school, with prayer to the Father 'in the name of Jesus'. The two aspects are, however, related to each other, since the Spirit has an effect on this prayer by his activity.

53. The παροιμία in 10:1–5 is a figurative discourse (see Vol. 2, pp. 278f),which is cryptic for the outsider. The concept that should have priority, then, is 'cryptic discourse'; W. Bauer's 'figurative way of speaking' is too narrow. See Ecclus 47:17, where it is said of Solomon: 'For your songs and proverbs and parables and for your interpretations, the countries marvelled at you'; LXX: ἐν ᾠδαῖς καὶ παροιμίαις καὶ παραβολαῖς . . . This way of speaking calls for an interpretation, so the LXX added καὶ ἐν ἑρμενείαις.

54. In 16:25, many manuscripts have ἀναγγελῶ instead of ἀπαγγελῶ: Δ Ψ Λ 270 700 pl. and many of the versions. There may have been an influence from 16:13 here.

55. As in the case of v. 23, the possibility that this points to the parousia must be rejected. Even Augustine does not accept this interpretation of v. 25 (CC 595f). A. Oepke, however, speaks in favour of it (*ThWb* V, p. 854f).

56. Above all this Johannine view throws light on the inadequacy for faith of the question of the 'historical Jesus'; this applies to the synoptic gospels, but even more fully to the gospel of John. The fact of Jesus' historicity is theologically important for the Johannine school as the incarnation of the Logos in the person of Jesus, especially in the struggle with the early gnostics (see 1 John). This does not mean, however, that the man Jesus claimed interest as an individual (and especially as a 'personality' and as the head of a group) among his contemporaries. The retrospective question refers to the earthly Jesus, who is, for the community, the mediator of salvation and the living, present Christ after his death. He is that for the community only in his identity with the earthly Jesus and so we are bound to look back at his activity on earth. The question of the 'historical Jesus' arises as the result of our consciousness of a problem that was unknown

in the early Church and therefore, in the sources that are available to us, encounters the greatest difficulties. See F. Hahn, 'Methodologische Überlegungen zur Rückfrage nach Jesus', *Rückfrage nach Jesus*, ed. K. Kertelge (Freiburg, 1974), pp. 11–74.

57. See H. Schlier, *ThWb* V, pp. 877f.

58. For Jesus' 'asking' the Father, the word αἰτεῖν is never used in John. Whenever Jesus himself is speaking and 'praying', the word used is ἐρωτᾶν (14:16; 16:26; 17:9, 15, 20); only Martha uses αἰτεῖν for this (11:22). It is clear, then, that αἰτεῖν is reserved in John for human requests. There must have been an influence on the part of the synoptic and early Christian linguistic usage on petitionary prayer. For possible reasons for this distinction in the use of words, see G. Stählin, *ThWb* I, pp. 192f.

59. See the commentary on 15:15. Although 'friendship' is not directly discussed, this concept is surely obvious because of the use of and the analogy with 15:15. G. Stählin, *ThWb* IX, p. 131, note 190, also stresses that God's love for the disciples is not dependent on their love for Jesus; the love of God is rather always at the beginning (see 1 Jn 4:19). The disciples' love is their response to the love of the one who sent Jesus and God's love for the disciples completes the circle of love around Jesus.

60. Instead of παρὰ τοῦ θεοῦ, παρὰ τοῦ πατρός is found in B C* D L X pc. This change can, however, be easily explained by the context.

61. The first four words are found om. D W b ff² sy^s. This presumption accords with the Johannine style (see my *Joh-Briefe*, p. 5).

62. G. M. Behler, *Abschiedsworte*, p. 246, and B. Schwank, *Sein und Sendung* 28 (1963), p. 398, point to Is 55:10f: God's word does not return empty to God; it returns when it has accomplished the task that he sent it to do.

63. H. N. Bream, 'No Need to Be Asked Questions: A Study of Jn. 16:30', *Search the Scriptures (New Testament Studies in Honour of R. T. Stamm)* (Leiden, 1969), pp. 49–74, point to herm(m) XI, 2–5, and assume that this verse contains polemics against the practice of consulting oracles. The tendency in Jn 2:24f and 16:30 is, however, Christological.

64. ἐν τούτῳ occurs five times in the gospel and fourteen times in 1 John. Bauer, *Wörterbuch*, p. 1183, under οὗτος, 1, b, α, has the translation 'for this reason'; in which case it would be same as ἐκ τούτου; see 6:66; 19:12.

65. This is the opinion of Bernard, Zahn and Schwank, but most commentators and translators prefer a question. Expressed as a question, the faith of the disciples is not thrown entirely into doubt. Their lack of insight and their weakness are, however, exposed. According to Augustine, 'they were still very young in faith and were not yet spiritually resolved' (CC 598).

66. The figure of speech ἔρχεται καὶ ἐλήλυθεν is found only here. In 4:23; 5:25, it appears as καὶ νῦν ἐστιν and, in 12:23; 17:1, simply as ἐλήλυθεν ἡ ὥρα. The comment made about a different linguistic usage (see above, 16:25) is confirmed here: the situation before Easter and that following Easter are contrasted.

67. See C. H. Dodd, *Historical Tradition*, pp. 56ff, who believed that this statement is even closer to Mark and has concluded from the very different presentation in Jn 18:4–9 that a traditional aspect of the passion story was preserved in 16:32.

68. The meaning 'to his own home' is suggested by Est 5:10; 6:12 LXX; 3 Macc 6:27 (cf. 5:21), but see the commentary, Jn 19:27. For a connection with σκορπίζεσθαι, see 1 Macc 6:54: ἕκαστος εἰς τὸν τόπον αὐτοῦ. Zahn, p. 603, note 39, believes that the expression had become an 'ossified idiom'. For the negative tone, see Jn 8:44; 15:19. Liddell and Scott, *Lexicon*, p. 818, under I, 3, gives τὰ ἴδια as 'private interests', with proofs from profane literature. For the entire passage, see E. Fascher, 'Johannes 16, 32', *ZNW* 39 (1940), pp. 171–230 (who provides a history of exegesis, comparison and a history of traditions). See also I. de la Potterie, in *Neues Testament und Kirche. Festschrift für R. Schnackenburg* (Freiburg, 1974), pp. 210–214.

69. This phrase, which at first sight seems to repeat 16:25, looks back, as in 14:25, to the whole discourse and not simply to the announcement of the dark hour, as in 16:4. The conclusion of the discourse (16:25–33) is in many ways influenced by 14:25–31.

Notes

70. νικᾶν also plays an important part in the book of Revelation, occurring sixteen times in all, including seven times in the 'sayings about the victor'. Both as far as the language and the content are concerned, however, there are many distinctive features. The sayings about the victor are a special kind of admonition. The victory of Christ and the victory of Christians are seen in the same line (see 3:21; 12:11), but the characteristic idea that connects Jn 16:33 with 1 John, that is, the victory over the world, is missing. That is why the book of Revelation cannot be mentioned in the same breath, although this has happened quite frequently; see O. Bauernfeind, *ThWb* IV, pp. 943f; Behler, pp. 252f; Brown, p. 738.

SECTION III: Pages 167–202

1. Bultmann, pp. 350f, thought that the 'farewell prayer' (as he called it in a heading on p. 371) was originally placed at the beginning and that Jesus therefore spoke the discourses as the 'glorified' Christ. R. E. Brown, p. 745, and others have written against this view.

2. This term goes back to D. Chytraeus (†1600). The idea of Jesus' high-priestly intercessory prayer can, however, also be found in Cyril of Alexandria, *In Jo* 17:9 (PG 74, 505) and Rupert of Deutz (PL 169, 764). See also, apart from the commentaries: A. George, '"L'heure" de Jean XVII', *RB* 61 (1954), pp. 392–397 (the prayer projects itself at the same time into the present and into the future, into time and eternity); W. Thüsing, *Herrlichkeit und Einheit. Eine Auslegung des Hohepriestlichen Gebetes Jesu* (Düsseldorf, 1962); B. Schwank, *Sein und Sendung* 28 (1963), pp. 436–449, 484–497, 531–546; R. Poelman, 'The Sacerdotal Prayer: John XVII', *Lumen Vitae* 20 (1965), pp. 43–66; C. D. Morrison, 'Mission and Ethic: An Interpretation of John 17', *Interpetation* 19 (1965), pp. 259–273; E. Käsemann, *Jesu letzter Wille nach Johannes 17* (Tübingen, 1966) (this author extends the theme of the prayer to the whole gospel); S. Agourides, 'The "High Priestly Prayer" of Jesus', *St Ev* IV (1968), pp. 137–145; O. Battaglia, 'Preghiera sacerdotale ed innologia ermetica', *Riv Bib* 17 (1969), pp. 209–232 (this author refers to the Hermetic literature: I:31f and XIII:18ff); B. Rigaux, 'Die Jünger Jesu in Johannes 17' *ThQ* 150 (1970), pp. 202–213; *ibid.*, 'Les destinataires du IVᵉ Evangile à la lumière de Jn 17', *RTh Louvain* 1 (1970), pp. 289–319. See also the notes that follow.

3. A. Laurentin, 'We'attah – Kai nun', *Bib* 45 (1964), pp. 168–432, especially pp. 426–432, who in this way has divided the discourse as follows: Introduction, vv. 1–4; transition, vv. 5–6; part 1, vv. 7–12; part 2, vv. 13–23; transition, v. 24; conclusion, vv. 25–26. Even in the traditional subdivision of the passage, there are considerable differences. Several exegetes have, for example, made an incision after v. 8 (Bernard, Loisy, Hoskyns and Davey, van den Bussche, R. E. Brown and others), probably because of ἐρωτῶ in v. 9, although this word (which also occurs in vv. 15 and 20) can hardly be regarded as a factor on which to base a division.

4. G. Malatesta, 'The Literary Structure of John 17', *Bib* 52 (1971), pp. 190–214, who has opted for the following units: vv. 1–5; 6–8; 9–19; 20–24; 25–26. Within these units, he favours an artistic structure: A-B-A' and, in the subsections a-b-c-b'-a'. This structure, however, leads to compressions.

5. J. Becker, 'Aufbau, Schichtung und theologiegeschichtliche Stellung des Gebets in Johannes 17', *ZNW* 60 (1969), pp. 56–83. For a criticism of Becker's structure, see the following note.

6. R. Schnackenburg, 'Strukturanalyse von Joh 17', *BZ*, New Series 17 (1973), pp. 67–78; 196–202. The text is divided and the structural relationships are pointed out (pp. 70–72).

7. Instead of the aorist, the perfect λελάληκεν is found in ℵ W 579, probably as an assimilation with 16:33. Many manuscripts have the article with 'Ιησοῦς. The article appears in most cases in the gospel, but the use is not uniform and there is indeed so

much variety in the manuscripts that it is impossible to formulate any rule or criterion of style.

8. The more recent commentators rightly avoid this question. Schanz (*ad loc.*) remarked, for example, that this attitude of prayer was equally possible indoors and out of doors. Several exegetes have suggested the temple, since the gates were opened on the night of the Passover; see D. F. Westcott, p. 237, and others, including L. Bouyer, in *La Bible et l'Evangile* (Paris, 1951), p. 206. Because there is no indication of the place in the text and the content of the prayer transcends time, it would be wrong to conclude that Jn 17 'is entirely unrelated to history, both in the spatial and in the temporal sense' (A. George, *op. cit.*, p. 394).

9. W. Thüsing, *Erhöhung und Verherrlichung*, pp. 190f, 219ff.

10. On linguistic grounds alone, the second ἵνα clause could be dependent on the καθώς clause ('thou hast given him power so that . . .'), see Lagrange, Barrett, *ad loc.*, but, by analogy with 13:34, the other possibility is preferable; see also 17:21a-c and 17:22b–23b. The accumulation of ἵνα clauses seems to be a feature of the evangelist's style. Bultmann, p. 376, note 1, regarded the καθώς clause (and vv. 2f as a whole) as a 'prosaic clarification' of the source by the evangelist. Other exegetes have seen it as a parenthesis.

11. The aorist does not contradict the fact that the 'glorification' will be accompanied by a giving of power, since Jesus, in prayer, assumes that his glorification has already begun (cf. 13:31). The power in question here is not the power of the Son that has existed from the beginning (see 3:35); it is rather the power given to him when he is sent into the world. This cannot be separated from the perspective of the glorified Christ. The relationship between our present text and Mt 11:27/Lk 10:22 has often been pointed out, but, for Matthew, this statement made in Jesus' 'cry of rejoicing' is more closely related to the statement made by the risen Lord in Mt 28:18 (where ἐξουσία is also used). The common, though remote, background must be Dan 7:14 and the theological basis is the early Church's experience of Easter.

12. The πᾶν κτλ. placed at the beginning can also be regarded as a case of anacoluthia; see Blass-Debr § 466, 3; for the construction *ad sensum*, see *ibid.*, § 282, 3. For δώσῃ αὐτοῖς there are many textual variants: δώσει αὐτοῖς B E H pm (preferred by many editors): ἔχῃ D: δώσω αὐτῷ ℵ* pc: δῷς αὐτοῖς L. The deliberate changes (made to improve the construction) are not difficult to recognize. The future δώσει would be possible in a ἵνα clause (see Blass-Debr § 369, 2), but the aorist subjunctive (see *ibid.* § 95, 1) in ℵᶜ A C G K M S al. is preferable.

13. G. Malatesta, *op. cit.*, pp. 194–198, believes this.

14. See Blass-Debr § 388 ('an intentional or incipient consequence'); cf. the ἵνα clauses after a demonstrative pronoun with εἶναι in Jn 6:39f; 15:12; 1 Jn 3:11, 23; 5:3, in contrast to ὅτι clauses. (Jn 3:19; 1 Jn 5:9, 11). Instead of γινώσκωσιν, γινώσκουσιν is found in A D G L al.

15. For the adjective μόνος, see E. Peterson, *ΕΙΣ ΘΕΟΣ* (Göttingen, 1926), p. 196; for ἀληθινός as an attribute of God, see Bultmann, *ThWb* I, p. 250. For the combination of the two adjectives, it is interesting to note that the Athenians greeted Demetrius Poliorcetes as ὡς εἴη μόνος θεὸς ἀληθινός (*Athenaeus* VI: 62); Philo, *De spec. legibus* I: 332: τὸν ἕνα καὶ ἀληθινὸν θεόν; 1 Clem 43:6: εἰς τὸ δοξασθῆναι τὸ ὄνομα τοῦ ἀληθινοῦ καὶ μόνου. See also Bauer, *ad loc.*; Bultmann, p. 378, note 2.

16. A new aspect of 'knowing God' in the biblical sense is found in Jewish Hellenism in the knowledge of the Creator through his creation; see Wis 13:1ff. This does not, however, change the basic character of knowledge which leads to salvation; see Wis 15:3: 'For to know thee is complete righteousness and to know thy power is the root of immortality.' This is the fundamental aspect of Jn 17:3. It is interesting to compare this with Philo's more vigorous opposition to the Greek understanding of 'knowledge'; see B. L. Mack, *Logos und Sophia* (Göttingen, 1973), pp. 124–130.

17. See John Chrysostom, *Hom* 80:2 (PG 59, 435).

18. *In Jo 17*, Lect I: 3 (Cai 2186): 'Cum ergo intelligentia sit vita et intelligere sit vivere, sequitur quod intelligere rem aeternam sit vivere vita aeterna. Deus est autem res

aeterna, intelligere ergo et videre Deum est vita aeterna. . . . Amor autem est movens ad hanc (scil. visionem), et quoddam eius complementum: nam ex delectatione quae est in fruitione divina, quam facit caritas, est complementum et decor beatitudinis: sed eius substantia in visione consistit.'

19. See Westcott, Lagrange, Barrett and others, *ad loc.*; Dodd, *Interpretation*, pp. 398 and 429 (reference to 19:30); Thüsing, *Erhöhung und Verherrlichung*, pp. 72ff; A. Vanhoye, 'L'oeuvre du Christ, don du Père (Jn 5, 36 et 17, 4)', *Rech Sc R* 48 (1960), pp. 377–419, especially pp. 431f.

20. *Bib* 45 (1964), p. 195.

21. Laurentin, *ibid.*, p. 426, who also thought that καὶ νῦν was always charged with a 'restrained affectivity'. This has, however, to be excluded in the case of Jn 17:5.

22. For the idea of pre-existence, see K. Haacker, *Die Stiftung des Heils*, pp. 116–134; R. G. Hammerton-Kelly, *Pre-Existence, Wisdom and the Son of Man* (Cambridge, 1973), for Jn 17, see pp. pp. 215–224.

23. B. Rigaux occupies a special position in his two articles mentioned above (see note 2). He also recognizes that the idea contained in this verse applies to the later community, but he defines this more precisely, claiming that this community is a closed one, gathered around the spiritual leader ('John'), an élitist group of 'new prophets'; for this see Excursus 17 and 18.

24. This was A. Schlatter's view, *ad loc.*; also H. Bietenhard, in *ThWb* V, p. 271. R. E. Brown's interpretation, pp. 755f, is not convincing; he is of the opinion that by ἐγώ εἰμι was meant the 'name' of God, since this divine revelatory formula is used in a Christological sense in the gospel of John (see Excursus 8, Vol. 2, pp. 79–89). Ought we, however, to be thinking at all of a definite name? See Bultmann, pp. 380f, who thought that the communication of the divine name meant the disclosure of God himself; see also Lindars, p. 521, who speaks of 'the character of the Father'.

25. A reference to this text is rejected by Bultmann, p. 380, note 2, in opposition to H. Bietenhard, *ThWb* V, p. 271, note 197, who acknowledges this reference.

26. R. E. Brown, p. 756, appeals to this in his interpretation of the name as pointing to the formula ἐγώ εἰμι.

27. See the *C Herm* V: 1, 10; Aesculapius 20 and 41; Stobaeus, Exc. VI: 19 (Nock and Festugière III, p. 39); Fragment 3a (Nock and Festugière IV, p. 105); Fragment 11 (Nock and Festugière, p. 110). See also H. Bietenhard, in *ThWb* V, p. 249, 27–41; Nock and Festugière I, pp. 40f, note 20.

28. Aesculapius 41 and P. Mimaut; see Nock and Festugière II, p. 353; Nag Hammadi Codex VI, 7; see K.-W. Tröger's translation, in *ThLZ* 98 (1973), p. 502.

29. *C. Herm* V: 1: (God) φανερῶν αὐτὸς οὐ φανεροῦται; see also V: 9, 11. For the frequency of this verb, see D. Lührmann, in *ThWb* IX, p. 4. On the other hand, it occurs remarkably often in the gospel of John (nine times) and the first epistle (nine times).

30. P. Berol, II, p. 128; see also R. Reitzenstein, *Die hellenistischen Mysterienreligionen* (Leipzig and Berlin, 3rd edn., 1927), p. 296.

31. P. Lugdun, V; see also R. Reitzenstein, *op. cit.*, pp. 295f.

32. The German translation of W. Till, *ZNW* 50 (1959), p. 182, is followed here. For speculation about the name in the *Gospel of Truth*, see F. Untergassmair, *Im Namen Jesu. Der Namensbegriff im Joh-Ev* (Stuttgart, 1974), pp. 245–305.

33. The word ἔγνων ℵ: ἔγνωκα W 579 VL pt in the first person singular is surprising. The words πάντα ὅσα κτλ. ought, after all, to refer to the disciples, but this does not fit well into the context. A 'mature' knowledge would be expected in the light of 10:38 (γνῶτε καὶ γινώσκητε) and 'I am in the Father and the Father is in me' can hardly be materially different in meaning from the idea expressed in 17:7 (cf. also 14:10).

34. I do not agree with R. Laurentin, *op. cit.*, p. 428, here. Together with John Chrysostom, b c ff² (completed with aur) sy³ bo georg, he prefers καὶ νῦν in v. 7. Even then, however, the expression lacks the force that it has in v. 5.

35. J. Becker, in *ZNW* 60 (1969), p. 75, who believes that v. 8 should, as a reiteration of vv. 6f, be excluded. He also cannot accept verse 10a, because its contents are not in accordance with the rest of the scene and the statement is superfluous. In addition, he suspects v. 11a, regarding the half-verse as unnecessary. All the same, he himself recognizes that these exclusions 'cannot be conclusively justified'.

36. In part of the VL (a b ff² q r¹), the verbal form is seen as being in the third person plural and therefore as related to 'words'. According to the other texts, however, this is unlikely; it also disrupts the parallelism with the following clause.

37. See W. Bousset, *Kyrios Christos* (Göttingen, 4th edn., 1935), p. 182; E. Käsemann, *Jesu Letzter Wille*, p. 116, who comments (without referring to Jn 17:9): 'According to John, the Christian mission does not apply to the world as such, but rather to those who were given to Christ in the world by his Father, in other words, those who were chosen and called to faith.' L. Schottroff, *Der Glaubende und die feindliche Welt*, p. 285, believes that there is no contradiction between 3:16 and 17:9 and that the apparent contradictions 'are as interconnected as cause and effect: because of Jesus' offer, the world is seen as hostile to God; he does not therefore pray for that world, but is its judge'.

38. Codex D has ἐδόξασάς με. P⁶⁶ has an error here: τεδοξασμε with a δ written above the first letter; the copyist probably had δεδόξασμαι in mind. This error may, however, explain the unusual reading in Codex D.

39. This may have led to the reading οὐκέτι εἰμὶ ἐν τῷ κόσμῳ, καὶ ἐν τῷ κόσμῳ εἰμί, which precedes 'and they are in the world' in Codex e, but follows 'I am coming to thee' in D r¹.

40. Apart from its use in the combination 'Holy Spirit' (1:33; 7:39; 20:22; see also 14:26), the adjective ὁ ἅγιος, used as a noun, occurs only in Jn 6:69 (+ τοῦ θεοῦ) and 1 Jn 2:20. For the 'sanctification' that comes from God, the verb ἁγιάζειν is employed; see 10:36; 17:17, 19.

41. *Did* 10:2: εὐχαριστοῦμέν σοι, πατερ ἅγιε, ὑπὲρ τοῦ ἁγίου ὀνόματός σου, οὗ κατεσκήνωσας ἐν ταῖς καρδίαις ἡμῶν. . . . There is clearly a close similarity of ideas here, but, because of the special formula in *Did* 10:2 ('which thou hast caused to dwell in our hearts'), the text cannot have been derived from Jn 17:11ff. If it is borne in mind that the two documents are probably very close to each other, both in time (AD 90–100?) and in place of origin (Syria ?), the idea of a liturgical influence here cannot be excluded. This has to be distinguished from the question whether the whole prayer in Jn 17 is liturgical in character or has a liturgical *Sitz im Leben*; for this question, see the reflections that follow the detailed exegesis of Jn 17. For the relationship between the gospel of John and the *Didache*, see Vol. 1, pp. 197f.

42. See O. Procksch, in *ThWb* I, pp. 88–97 and K. G. Kuhn, *ibid.*, pp. 97–101; W. Eichrodt, *Theologie des Alten Testamentes*, 5th edn., I, pp. 176–185; P. van Imschoot, *Théologie de l'Ancien Testament* I, pp. 42–51.

43. J. Huby, 'Un double problème de critique textuelle et d'interprétation', *RechScR* 27 (1937), pp. 408–421, especially pp. 416ff, has advocated this reading.

44. This phrase is missing only in ℵ* sy*. A. Merx, *E. des Joh*, pp. 418ff, has defended the shorter text of sy* in vv. 11f. C. Tischendorf (ed. oct.) believes that it may have been a repetition by another author from v. 11, but correctly observes: 'at nec ab Johanne aliena repititio'. The Latin versions (VL and Vg) have 'quos dedisti mihi' and take it to the following 'custodivi'.

45. See J. Bonsirven, 'Pour une intelligence plus profonde de s. Jean,' *RechScR* 39 (1951), pp. 176–196 (for Jn 17:11b, 12, 26).

46. *In Jo 17*, lect. III, 1 (Cai 2213).

47. om. καί A D Θ 𝔓 pl VL Vg. For the Latin versions, see above, notes 45 and 46.

48. I disagree with Bultmann, p. 385, note 5, here. He believed that the phrase in the source meant each one who is lost and that the evangelist understood the article in the individual sense.

49. This assumption by E. D. Freed, *Old Testament Quotations*, p. 97, must be based

on an error. The words, which are only found in the Septuagint, must undoubtedly be translated as: 'A son, who follows a word (of God or of the king; cf. v. 21), will be outside perdition.' ἀπωλείας does not go with υἱος, but with ἐκτός which it precedes). For the preceding genitive, see Liddell and Scott, *Lexicon*, p. 523.

50. See J. Becker, in *ZNW* 60 (1969), pp. 73f.

51. om. P⁶⁶* D pc b c d e r¹ syˢ. The clause may possibly have come from v. 16, but the shorter reading in the 'western' texts can be more easily explained on the basis of its having the same ending as in v. 16.

52. This is the view held by J. Becker, in *ZNW* 60 (1969), p. 74.

53. Bultmann, p. 389, note 4, regarded v. 16 as a statement found in the source that the evangelist used in v. 14.

54. See R. Asting, *Die Heiligkeit im Urchristentum* (Göttingen, 1930), pp. 308–313, especially p. 313: 'ἀλήθεια points here to the divine reality that is revealed in the divine word.' Asting, however, is too one-sided in his emphasis on the disciples' separation from the world and is not sufficiently conscious of their mission in the world.

55. The article is added in B W 579, but it is often missing in abstracts; see Blass-Debr § 258. Because of the article, it ought to be placed, in these manuscripts, in the first clause, but the truth should not be simply identified with the word of God; the latter is the means by which the disciples are able to enter the sphere of divine truth or possess that truth.

56. This was the opinion of Lagrange, Asting, *Heiligkeit*, p. 313, Bultmann, p. 390, note 1, Wikenhauser and others.

57. See W. Bauer, *ad loc.* The frequently-quoted text from the Mithraic liturgy (Dieterich, S. 4, Z. 22f) ἁγίοις ἁγιασθεὶς ἁγιάσμασιν has a different meaning because of the 'holy consecration'.

58. The purpose of the praise is to introduce a specific commandment that a Jew has to fulfil; see Billerbeck II, pp. 566f.

59. See K. G. Kuhn, in *ThWb* I, p. 100. 'Holiness' is closely connected with the Torah and the scrolls of the Torah. Reading the Torah is a cultic, holy act. This shows that the original meaning of holiness has not been lost.

60. The Greek Fathers' exegesis places great importance on the Holy Spirit as the mediator of holiness and unity. John Chrysostom interpreted the petition for sanctification as: 'Make them holy by the gift of the Spirit and right doctrines!' (*Hom* 82:1; PG 59, 443). For the Greek Orthodox exegesis, see P. Evdokimov, 'L'Esprit saint et la prière pour l'unité', *Verbum Caro* 14 (1960), pp. 250–264.

61. See also the use of tenses in the sending of the disciples at Easter (20:21), where the risen Christ looks back to his own sending in the perfect and sends the disciples in the present tense (πέμπω).

62. Bultmann, p. 390, note 4, who excludes v. 18 from the 'gnostic' source that he assumes existed.

63. C. Spicq, *L'Epître aux Hébreux* I (Paris, 1952), pp. 109–138 (for Jn 17: pp. 122f), was inclined to think this. He certainly believed that the author of the epistle to the Hebrews was dependent on John, not simply on the gospel as we have now, but 'directly on the Johannine catechesis' (p. 109, cf. p. 132). Later, with the Qumran literature in mind, he developed another hypothesis for the emergence of Hebrews, without discussing its possible relationship with the Johannine writings; see *R Qum* 1 (1958/59), pp. 365–390. A different view is held by S. Nomoto, 'Herkunft und Struktur der Hohenpriestervorstellung im Hebräerbrief', *NT* 10 (1968), pp. 10–25 (independently on the basis of early Christian traditions and with the help of typological considerations).

64. Bultmann, p. 391, including note 3, regarded this 'indisputable'. This may be connected with his view that John 'replaces the Lord's Supper with "highly priestly" prayer of Jesus and does this with an unmistakable reference to the sacrament of the Eucharist' (p. 371).

65. *Heiligkeit*, pp. 314f.

66. *Le sacerdoce du Christ et de ses ministres d'après la prière sacerdotale du quatrième évangile et plusieurs données parallèles du Nouveau Testament* (Paris, 1972). For the concept ἁγιάξειν, see I. de la Potterie, 'Consécration ou sanctification du chrétien', *Le Sacré*, ed. by E. Castelli (Paris, 1974), pp. 333–349, in whose view I have subsequently found much to agree with. In the case of v. 19, he stresses above all Jesus' 'total obedience to the Father's will, by the constant offering of himself to the Father throughout the whole of his existence and its fulfilment on the cross' (p. 347).

67. This was Bultmann's interpretation, p. 391, note 5; seen in this light, true holiness rather than cultic holiness is intended here. This, however, is a pure supposition which is, in view of 4:23f, also quite unfounded (see *ad loc.*). The author of Jn 17 might also have put ἀληθῶς here as in v. 8. For the opposite view, see I. de la Potterie, *op. cit.*, p. 347.

68. See Blass-Debr § 255.

69. See, for example, T. E. Pollard, '"That They All May Be One" (John XVII. 21) – and the Unity of the Church', *Exp T* 70 (1958/59), pp. 149f (E. L. Wenger, *ibid.*, p. 333, takes a different view); J.-L. d'Aragon, 'La notion johannique de l'unité', *ScEccl* 11 (1959), pp. 111–119; J. F. Randall, 'The Theme of Unity in John 17, 20–23', *EThLov* 41 (1965), pp. 373–394, especially pp. 393f; R. E. Brown, pp. 775f, etc. It is very difficult to provide a survey of the books and articles written from the contemporary ecumenical viewpoint.

70. See J. Wellhausen, *Ev Joh,* p. 76; F. Spitta, *Das Joh-Ev,* p. 336, who attributes v. 22 to an adaptor; E. Hirsch, *Studien,* pp. 116f.

71. See, for example, J. Becker, in *ZNW* 60 (1969), pp. 74f. Most recent commentators (R. E. Brown, B. Lindars and L. Morris) do not, however, accept this view.

72. J. Becker, *op. cit.,* p. 74.

73. See F. J. Randall, *op. cit.*, p. 389. The Greek construction can hardly be imitated in a modern language. The semicolon in the modern translation is placed there only for this reason and not to mark a separation in the thought.

74. A great number of manuscripts add ἕν: ℵ A Θ 054 𝒫 λ ⏀ 28 33 700 al. aur f q Vg sy^{p.h.pal} bo^{mss} Clem Orig Cyr Cypr Athan Hil. This reading must therefore undoubtedly have been widespread in Egypt. Materially, it stresses the previously expressed idea (πάντες ἕν). The shorter reading, however, is well attested; the manuscripts with this reading include P^{66} probably and B C* certainly and also D W a b c d e sy^s sa. It is clear, then, that this reading is preferable. B. M. Metzger, *Text. Comm.*, p. 250, regards ἕν as a 'pedantic addition'.

75. Bultmann, p. 394, held this view correctly, but it is not necessary to assume that one of the ἵνα clauses was in the source (*ibid.*, note 1). See also J. F. Randall, *op. cit.*, p. 389.

76. In the apocrypha, which provide abundant material for the literary genre of farewell discourses, the admonition to brotherly love and harmony occurs frequently; see *Jub* 7:26 (Noah); 35:20 (Rebekah); 36:4 (Isaac); *Test Zeb* 8:5f; 9:1–4; *Test Jos* 17:2f; *Test Dan* 5:3. See also J. F. Randall, *op. cit.*, pp. 377ff.

77. See E. Käsemann, *Jesu letzter Wille,* pp. 107f. A different view is held by L. Schottrof, *Der Glaubende und die feindliche Welt,* p. 284 and pp. 285f. See also J. Becker, in *ZNW* 60 (1969), pp. 79f: 'The community lived in isolation from the world.'

78. L. Morris, pp. 734f, thinks, in accordance with the Johannine idea, that Jesus' ministry contained within itself, until his death on the cross the 'glory' of the disciples in their imitation of the cross, but δέδωκα αὐτοῖς does not fit in with this idea. W. Thüsing, *Erhöhung und Verherrlichung*, pp. 182f, is more correct in claiming that δόξα is chosen here on account of the aim of unity and defines it for this reason as the 'splendour of Jesus' unity in love'. The essence of this unity in love, Thüsing believes, is already given to them.

79. The reading in Codex D is εἰς τὸ ἕν; also Eusebius and Chrysostom occasionally. An even stronger emphasis is to be found here.

80. In some manuscripts, the two ἵνα clauses are connected by καί: P^{66} ℵ W pc. This equation of the two clauses, however, obscures the idea that the world should recognize Jesus' divine origin by the disciples' unity in love. In fact, the second ἵνα clause is subordinate to the first.

81. The reading in the first person singular is found in D 0141 ≠ al. a b r sy. It is, however, not accepted by any editor in the text. (It is not even taken into consideration by the UBS Greek New Testament.) According to Westcott and Hort, it is a reading that is worth noting, but has to be rejected.

82. There has been a great deal of discussion about this strange name that the Qumran community gave to itself; see especially J. Maier, *Texte vom Toten Meer* II, p. 11; *ibid.*, 'Zum Begriff *yḥd* in den Texten vom Toten Meer', *ZAW* 72 (1960), pp. 148–166. According to Maier, this is a theological concept that was concerned with the form of the communal life of the community, with its strongly cultic and ritual aspect. R. E. Brown, p. 777, believes that the Johannine image of Christian unity had a great deal in common with the *yahad* of Qumran. A. T. Hanson, 'Hodayot XV and John 17: A Comparison of Content and Form', *Hermathena* (Dublin) 18 (1974), pp. 45–58, compares the whole of the prayer in Jn 17 with this hymn in the Qumran literature.

83. E. Käsemann, *Jesu letzter Wille*, p. 102.

84. For forms of address and their function in the prayer, see above: the commentary on v. 1. An intensification is undoubtedly intended in the case of vv. 24 and 25. The prayer becomes more urgent and at the same time warmer towards the end. In v. 25, the address, with its adjective, is to some extent contrasted with v. 24, which contains a distinct prospect. Structurally, v. 24 goes back to v. 2 and v. 25 goes back to v. 11.

85. If the Johannine Jesus says it of his own accord (elsewhere in the gospel, the word only occurs in 5:21 and in the appended chapter, 21:22f), θέλω introduces a majestic statement. G. Schrenk, in *ThWb* III, p. 48, speaks, with Jn 17:24 in mind, of a 'prayerful declaration of Jesus' will'.

86. Instead of the neuter form, many manuscripts here have the plural οὕς: C 𝔓 pl VL (apart from d q) Vg; this is essentially the same manuscripts as in v. 12 (but not D). This reading, however, is only equivalent to a clarification.

87. This applies particularly to earlier commentators such as B. Weiss, B. F. Westcott, T. Zahn, J. H. Bernard; also to O. Michel, in *ZsyTh* 18 (1941), p. 525, Hoskyns and Davey, C. H. Dodd, *Interpretation*, p. 417, and L. Morris. Most recent commentators make a division before v. 24. W. Thüsing, *Herrlichkeit und Einheit*, pp. 7f, summarizes vv. 20–26 as a petition for the whole Church, but at the same time subdivides these verses into vv. 20–23, 24 and 25–26. R. E. Brown also groups the same verses together in the same way, but subdivides them into vv. 20–23 and 24–26.

88. The possessive pronoun is absent from D sy^s, but the text retains a sound meaning even without it.

89. The same expression for the 'foundation of the world' can also be found in Mt 25:34; Lk 11:50; Eph 1:4, Heb 4:3; 9:26; 1 Pet 1:20; Rev 13:8; 17:8. It was probably taken over by early Christians from Judaism (and not from the Septuagint), since the rabbis also speak of divine predestination 'since the beginning of creation'; see F. Hauck, *ThWb* III, p. 623; see also Ass Mos 1:13f.

90. For a possible reference to the parousia, see, among others, Zahn, Barrett, Lindars and, with especial emphasis, Hoskyns and Davey, p. 506: 'There are . . . three epochs in the history of the Church, the time of the manifestation of the glory of God to the original disciples, . . . the time of the manifestation of the name of God to the Church and through the Church to the world . . . and the final and eternal manifestation of the love of God. . . . The last verses of the prayer concern the eschatological hope of the Church, not of the individual believers.' This view, which may be relevant to 1 Jn, has no support, however, in Jn 17. It is not possible to infer a reference to eschatological glory from the mention of Jesus' pre-existent glory, since John only speaks of Jesus' return to his earlier glory (through his exaltation on the cross); see 17:5; see also 3:13; 6:62; 20:17. R. E. Brown, p. 780, believes that the original understanding of 17:24 may perhaps have included an apocalyptic scene such as that described in 5:28f, but that this understanding was put forward in support of the view that eternal life was fulfilled after the believers' death. V. 24 does not, however, contain a future 'apocalyptic' way of speaking as does 5:28f.

91. R. Bultmann, pp. 397ff, has dealt exhaustively with this question. He claims that, for believers, death has 'lost its substance (11:25f), but that it cannot be ignored because of this, that is, because their life on earth would be complete and meaningful without it, but rather because their life is not enclosed within the boundaries of an existence restricted by time and history' (p. 399).

92. J. Becker, *ZNW* 60 (1969), pp. 82f, inclines to this view.

93. See the texts quoted by Bultmann, p. 398, note 2.

94. Cf. 1 Thess 4:17 σὺν κυρίῳ; Phil 1:23 σὺν Χριστῷ; Lk 23:43 μετ᾽ ἐμοῦ; Rev 3:4, 21; 14:1; 20:4, 6. The Christological view that fulfilment consists of community with Christ and participation in his glory can be found in different forms throughout in the NT.

95. See Augustine, *ad loc.*: 'abscedat ab animo omnis imaginum corporalium cogitatio; quidquid menti occurrerit longum, latum, crassum, qualibet luce corporea coloratum, per quaelibet locorum spatia vel finita, vel infinita diffusum, ab his omnibus, quantum potest, aciem suae contemplationis vel intentionis avertat. . . . Sed qui vult quaerere, quaerat potius, ut sum illo sit' (CC 629).

96. See, on the one hand, R. E. Brown, *ad loc.* (p. 773), who claims that this verse describes a judgment, and, on the other hand, B. Schwank, *Sein und Sendung* 28 (1963), pp. 543f, who insists that the connection with 'Father' shows that it is hardly possible to speak here of a strict judge. 'Righteous' here has rather the positive meaning that it has, for example, in Ps 114:5 (LXX). Schwank goes too far, however, in stating that δίκαιος is an intensification of ἅγιος in v. 11 and that Christ intervenes for the world so that it will not be condemned.

97. See Blass-Debr § 444, 3; M. Zerwick, *Analysis philologica Novi Testamenti graeci* (Rome, 1953), p. 244, *ad loc.*

98. See the work by P. Evdokimov mentioned in the commentary on v. 17, note 60.

99. B. Schwank, *op. cit.*, p. 546, cites the exegesis of Rupert of Deutz and believes that the latter was the only one to provide this explanation. But Thomas Aquinas, *In Jo 17 lect.*, VI, 2 (Cai 2270), has supplied a second possible explanation: '. . . sicut tu me dilexisti, ita ipsi participando Spiritum sanctum, diligant'.

100. See the books and articles listed above, p. 409, notes 27 and 28; see also J. F. Randall, *op. cit.*, pp. 375ff.

101. See R. E. Brown, pp. 744f who regards this relationship with Deuteronomy as very important.

102. See also O. Battaglia, 'Preghiera sacerdotale ed innologia ermetica (Giov. 17 – C.H. I, 31–32e XIII, 18–20)', *Rivista Bibl.* 17 (1969), pp. 209–232.

103. See R. Reitzenstein, *Hellen. Mysterienreligionen*, pp. 285–287; Nock and Festugière II, pp. 353f.

104. See W. Bauer, *Joh-Ev*, p. 208; Bultmann, p. 374: 'The prayer is of the kind said by one who is sent and is leaving the world; there are many variations of this kind of prayer in the gnostic literature.'

105. Whether this eucharistic section is ascribed to the evangelist or to an editor or editors is less important in connection with the question that we are considering here. If we assume that it is editorial, then the prayer in Jn 17 might also be the work of an editor, in which case the eucharistic character of Jn 17 would be even more pronounced.

106. Apart from the commentaries, see Teod. da Castel S. Pietro, 'Il sacerdozio celeste di Cristo nella lettera agli Ebrei', *Greg* 39 (1958), pp. 319–334; H. Zimmermann, *Die Hohepriester-Christologie des Hebräerbriefes* (Paderborn, 1964); W. Thüsing, '"Laßt uns hinzutreten . . ." Zur Frage der Kulttheologie im Hebräerbrief', *BZ* 9 (1965), pp. 1–17; S. Nomoto, 'Herkunft und Struktur der Hohepriestervorsstellung im Hebräerbrief', *NT* 10 (1968), pp. 10–25; J. Smith, *A Priest for Ever* (London, 1969).

107. See R. E. Brown, p. 747, who believes that a eucharistic interpretation of the prayer in Jn 17 is no more than one possibility; the hymn may have been used in the liturgy, but this is not important for exegesis.

108. In *ZNW* 60 (1969), pp. 78–83.

Notes

109. *Jesu letzter Wille nach Joh 17*, passim.

EXCURSUS 17: Pages 203–217

1. See E. Käsemann, *Jesu letzter Wille*; L. Schottroff, *Der Glaubende und die feindliche Welt* (dualism and a gnostic Christ); A. Kragerud, *Der Lieblingsjünger* (itinerant prophetism, in contrast with the prophetic office in the community) and others. D. Moody Smith Jr., 'Johannine Christianity: Some Reflections on its Character and Delineation', *NTSt* 21 (1975), pp. 222–248, tries to achieve a certain balance in the research and at the same time his own position is carefully reflected and can be summarized as follows: The Johannine writings are the result of a particular tradition and form of early Christianity. The Johannine 'community' should probably be classified among the special local Christian communities which lived in and from that tradition. The special Johannine form of early Christianity reflects the existence of certain Johannine communities (pp. 236f). Moody Smith also believes that these communities also had a certain sectarian spirit and a tendency towards exclusiveness (p. 224).

2. See the following specialized works: E. Gaugler, 'Die Bedeutung der Kirche in den johanneischen Schriften', *Int. Kirchl. Zeitschrift* (Berne) 14 (1924), pp. 97–117; 181–219; 15 (1925), pp. 27–42; D. Faulhaber, *Das Johannesevangelium und die Kirche* (Kassel, 1935); A. Corell, *'Consummatum est'. Eschatology and Church in the Gospel of St John* (London, 1958); J.-L. d'Aragon, 'Le caractère distinctif de l'église johannique', *L'Eglise dans la Bible* (Bruges, 1962), pp. 53–66; E. Schweizer, 'Der Kirchenbegriff im Evangelium und den Briefen des Johannes', *Neotestamentica* (Zürich and Stuttgart, 1963), pp. 254–271; H. van den Bussche, 'Die Kirche im vierten Evangelium', *Vom Christus zur Kirche* (Vienna, 1966), pp. 79–107; G. Baumbach, 'Gemeinde und Welt im Johannesevangelium', *Kairos* 14 (1972), pp. 121–136; K. Haacker, 'Jesus und die Kirche nach Johannes', *ThZ* 29 (1973), pp. 179–201; S. Pancaro, 'The Relationship of the Church to Israel in the Gospel of John', *NTSt* 21 (1975), pp. 396–405.

3. See F. Hahn, 'Die Jüngerberufung Joh 1, 35–51', *Neues Testament und Kirche (Festschrift für R. Schnackenburg)* (Freiburg, Basle and Vienna, 1974), pp. 172–190.

4. See 2:2, 11, 12, 17, 22; 6:5f; 9:2; 11:54; 12:16, 20–22.

5. The ὄχλος (in the plural in the better reading in 7:12) only follows Jesus outwardly (6:2, 5, 22, 24) or is impressed by his miracles (see 7:31; 12:9, 12, 17f). Opinions on it are divided (7:12, 40–43) or there is a lack of comprehension (see 11:42; 12:29, 34). The word can also have a special meaning – that of pilgrims to a feast and of the ordinary people in Jerusalem; see R. Meyer, *ThWb* V, pp. 587–590, who also observes that 'the response evoked by Jesus in the ὄχλος is in no way unanimous' (p. 589, 3f).

6. In *ThWb* IV, pp. 462f.

7. See C. F. D. Moule, 'The Individualism of the Fourth Gospel', *NT* 5 (1962), pp. 171–190; E. Schweizer, in *Neotestamentica*, pp. 261–263.

8. G. Reim, *Studien zum alttestamentlichen Hintergrund*, pp. 183–186, believes that the chapter on the shepherd in Ezekiel was not used. It is certainly not possible to base one's argument exclusively on this chapter for the Johannine image of the shepherd and the flock, especially not for the idea of the gathering together of those who are scattered, there is undoubtedly a reference back to Ezek 34.

9. See S. Pancaro, 'The Relationship of the Church', *op. cit.* (note 2 above).

10. See, for example, E. Schweizer, in *Neotestamentica*, p. 260: 'Independently of Paul and using a completely different terminology, the gospel here provides a view in which Christ includes all believers as a "corporate personality" within himself.'

11. In *ThZ* 29 (1973), pp. 180ff.

12. *Ibid.*, p. 182.

13. *Ibid.*, pp. 185f.

14. E. Käsemann, *Jesu letzter Wille*, p. 116.

15. *Ibid.*, p. 119.
16. *Stiftung des Heils*, p. 64.
17. G. Schrenk, in *ThWb* IV, pp. 177, 30ff.
18. See B. Olsson, *Structure and Meaning in the Fourth Gospel* (Lund, 1974), who, in his linguistic study of the text of Jn 4:1–42, has confirmed the view expressed above. See especially his Excursus on mission in John (pp. 241–248).
19. See the commentary on Jn 21:15–17 below, and the books and articles cited on the subject of Peter.

SECTION IV: Pages 218–240

1. See above all F. Hahn, 'Der Prozess Jesu nach der Johannesevangelium', *Ev. – kath. Komm., Vorarbeiten Heft 2* (Zürich-Neukirchen, 1970), pp. 23–96; A. Dauer, *Die Passionsgeschichte im Johannesevangelium* (Munich, 1972). Cf. also P. Borgen, 'John and the Synoptics in the Passion Narrative', *NTSt* 5 (1958–59), pp. 246–259; E. Haenchen, 'Historie und Geschichte in den johanneischen Passionsberichten', in: F. Viering (ed.), *Zur Bedeutung des Todes Jesu* (Gütersloh, ³1968), pp. 55–78 (E.T.: *Interpr* 24 [1970], pp. 198–219).
2. Compare the different conclusions of R. Bultmann, R. Fortna (*Gospel of Signs*), F. Hahn, A. Dauer, G. Rein (*Studien zum altestamentlichen Hintergrund des Johannes-Evangeliums*, pp. 209–216). For the Lukan passion narrative, A. Dauer reached, in part, conclusions different from those of G. Schneider, *Verleugnung, Verspottung und Verhör Jesu nach Lukas 22:54–71* (Munich, 1969) – by a rather similar method.
3. On the Johannine arrest-scene, see also the commentaries and the works mentioned further: J. B. Doewe, 'Die Gefangennahme Jesu in Gethsemane', *StEv* (I), pp. 458–480; B. Schwank, 'Jesus überschreitet den Kidron' (18:1–11): *Sein und Sendung* 29 (1964), pp. 3–15; C. H. Dodd, *Historical tradition*, pp. 65–81; G. Richter, 'Die Gefangennahme Jesu nach den Johannesevangelium' (18:1–12), *BuL* 10 (1969), pp. 26–39.
4. The brook is properly called χείμαρρος or χειμάρρους='winter-brook', because it contains water only in the rainy season; thus also in Josephus, *Ant.*, VIII, 17. On its course (in a broad valley to the east of Jerusalem, leading into the Dead Sea), see G. Dalman, *Jerusalem und sein Gelände* (Gütersloh, 1930), pp. 182ff; F.-M. Abel, *Géographie* I, pp. 400f; R. D. Potter, 'Topography and Archaeology in the Fourth Gospel', *StEv* (I), pp. 329–337, particularly 334. Apart from τοῦ Κεδρών A pc Vg VL^(pt) sy^s there are still other readings: τοῦ Κέδρου ℵ* D W a b r¹ sa: τῶν Κέδρων (presumably a misinterpretation as 'cedars') B C Θ 𝔓 pm. Cf. Zahn pp. 617f, n. 3.
5. Cf. G. Dalman, *Orte und Wege*, pp. 340f, E.T.: *Sacred Sites and Ways*, pp. 321f, C. Kopp, *Die Heiligen Stätten*, p. 388, (E.T.: *Holy Places*, p. 336).
6. According to Jn 19:41, Jesus' tomb also is found in a garden. A typological interpretation of the sort favoured by patristic and medieval exegetes (Augustine, Cyril of Alexandria, Thomas Aquinas, Rupert of Deutz) and further represented by Hoskyns-Davey (p. 509), as if the garden of the arrest and of the tomb (and the resurrection respectively) were a counter-type of Paradise with the fall, is certainly not intended by the evangelist, as P. Schanz (*ad loc.*) has already shown. It has been pointed out quite often that Jesus' way recalls David's flight before Absalom (2 Sam 13:23); any intention behind that (at least not the evangelist's) is scarcely demonstrable, cf. Dauer, *Passionsgeschichte*, p. 23.
7. On συνάγεσθαι='to stay' (not 'to gather together') cf. H. Reynen in: *BZ, NF* 5 (1961), 86–90 (points to Acts 11:26).
8. Cf. J. Blinzler, *Der Prozess Jesu*, 4th ed. pp. 95f.
9. Thus Blinzler, *op. cit.*; D. R. Catchpole, *The Trial of Jesus* (Leiden, 1971), pp. 148–150 (against Jewish authors who thrust Jesus' arrest onto the Romans).

Notes

10. Thus also Dauer, *Passionsgeschichte*, p. 27, Doeve, *op. cit.*, p. 466, and Dodd, *Historical Tradition*, p. 81, think that the σπεῖρα was already connected with the Roman military by the source and tradition respectively.

11. Cf. E. Haenchen, *Historie*, p. 60, E.T.: 'History and Interpretation in the Johannine Passion Narrative', *Interpr* 24, p. 201: 'What John offers here and in what follows is not a historical documentary film, but the community's witness to faith . . . the complexion of this witness is taken from the OT.'

11a. D ¢ pc sy⁵ read ἰδών instead of εἰδώς. Only the latter corresponds to the Johannine Christology (6:61; 13:1, 3; 19:28). The supporters of the former were presumably thinking of a (prophetic) foresight (cf. 8:56; 12:41), or they were influenced by Lk 22:49.

12. The expression repeatedly occurs for a hard destiny falling to someone's lot, cf. BauerWb, col. 616.

13. G. Richter, *op. cit.* (*BuL* 1969), draws attention to the objections of the Jew on which Celsus relies (see Origen, *Contra Celsum* II). Among other things it says: 'least of all would he, who was regarded as Saviour, and Son of the greatest God, and an angel, be deserted and betrayed by his associates who had privately shared everything with him and had been under him as their teacher' (II, 9) (Trans. by H. Chadwick, Cambridge, 1953). But when R. thinks that the Johannine presentation is composed and formulated with a view to that, (p. 30), he overlooks the evangelist's positive Christological interest.

14. Cf. especially H. H. Schaeder, *ThWb* IV, pp. 879–884 (E.T.: *TDNT*, IV, pp. 874–879); (the derivation from the name of the city of Nazareth is linguistically and factually irrefutable); B. Gaertner, *Die rätselhaften Termini Nazoräer und Iskariot* (Upsala, 1957) thinks otherwise but, admittedly, recognizes the possibility of the designation of origin, yet reckons with further possibilities for the designation of the Christians as 'Nazarenes'. Critical of this viewpoint, and like Schaeder's, is the approach of C. Colpe, *ThLZ* 86 (1961) 31ff. M. Black, *Aramaic Approach*, 3rd ed., 197f, ignores Schaeder's demonstration (*op. cit.*, p. 882, E.T.: p. 877) that the ω-sound in Ναζωραῖος is also quite possible in the case of a derivation from Nazareth.

15. Cf. Dauer, *Passionsgeschichte*, p. 33.

16. Especially noteworthy is the pluperfect: John seven times, Mark not once, Matthew twice, Luke three times. Cf. Dauer, p. 31, with further observations.

17. See Schlatter, *Der Evangelist Johannes*, p. 328.

18. Dauer, in his Excursus on the parallels in comparative religion (pp. 41–43), assigns special significance to this passage, because Is 11 may also have influenced the evangelist elsewhere (1:32; 8:15f). But the evidence is not so great; cf. G. Reim, *Studien*, pp. 162ff.

18a. C. H. Dodd above all indicates this, *Historical Tradition*, pp. 76f. Behind it he supposes the older idea of Christ as the suffering righteous one, and therefore an already pre-Johannine tradition. But that is improbable according to the wholly Johannine shaping of the scene.

19. Bauer goes too far when he says (*ad loc.*): 'Jesus almost forces himself on those making the arrest.'

20. G. Richter, *op. cit.*, pp. 31f, stresses that too much. Bultmann too expresses doubt on the apologetic tendency.

21. οὕς δέδωκάς μοι is placed first for stress similarly to πᾶν ὃ δέδωκέν μοι in 6:39. That connects these two passages still more closely.

22. The passage 17:12b–c I find suspect as an editorial addition. Cf. also Hirsch, *Studien*, p. 118; Bultmann, p. 640 ('gloss of the redactor').

23. The name is found several times in Josephus and on inscriptions, 'almost only with Gentiles, and as a matter of fact with Nabbatian Arabs', see BauerWb, col. 968. On the spelling and meaning ('king') cf. Zahn, p. 621, n. 12. The definite article probably points to the fact that this (Gentile-born) servant occupied a place of honour among the high priest's servants.

24. Differently Dodd, *Historical Tradition*, pp. 79f; he regards as possible an older, otherwise vanished, tradition. That is entirely possible for Malchus, but hardly for Peter.

25. Cf. Dauer, *Passionsgeschichte*, 44f, with further discussion.

26. Jesus' saying in Mt 26:52: 'All who take the sword will perish by the sword' has been secondarily included in Θ.

27. In the OT it is above all God's cup of wrath which the evil-doers have to drink, cf. Hab 2:16; Is 51:17, 22; Jer 25:15–17; Ezek 23:31–34; Ps 75:8 (74:9). For post-biblical Judaism cf. *Odes of Solomon*, 8:14; 1Qp Hab 11:10–15; for NT cf. Rev 14:10; 16:19; 18:6. The original juridic image may have been transferred to the righteous one in the sense of expiatory suffering: The guiltless one takes the judgment of God's tribunal upon himself for the others; cf. G. Delling, Βάπτισμα βαπτισθῆναι: *NT* 2 (1957), pp. 92–115, especially 110ff: L. Goppelt in: *ThWb* VI, pp. 149–153 (E.T.: *TDNT* VI, pp. 149–153).

28. The narrative of the arrest ends with v. 11. V. 12 already belongs as a link (καὶ ἤγαγον v. 13) to the next account of the hearing by Annas.

29. More recent specialized literature: J. Schneider, Zur 'Komposition von Joh 18: 12–27': *ZNW* 48 (1957), pp. 111–119; P. Benoit, 'Le procès de Jésus', in: *Exégèse et théologie* I (Paris, 1961), pp. 265–289; idem., 'Jesus devant le Sanhedrin': *op. cit.*, pp. 290–311 (both articles in German in: *Exegese und Theologie* [Düsseldorf, 1965], pp. 113–132; 133–148); B. Schwank, 'Petrus verleugnet Jesus' (18:12–27): *Sein und Sendung* 29 (1964), pp. 51–65; A. Mahoney, 'A New Look at an Old Problem' (Jn 18: 12–14, 19–24): *CBQ* 27 (1965), pp. 137–144; J. Blinzler, *Der Prozess Jesu*, 4th ed., pp. 129–136; C. H. Dodd, *Historical Tradition*, pp. 88–96; F. Hahn, *op. cit.* (*EKK* 2), pp. 52–67; A. Dauer, *Passionsgeschichte*, pp. 62–99.

30. In many cases it receives so much attention that literary problems and those of the history of tradition receive too little. For the historical problems cf. especially J. Blinzler, *Prozess*, pp. 129–136; differently, P. Winter, *On the Trial of Jesus* (Berlin, 1961), pp. 33–38 (but he wrongly regards Annas as Ananus II, p. 35); D. R. Catchpole, *The Trial of Jesus* (Leiden, 1971), pp. 8f, 169ff.

31. Despite A. Merx, *Evangelium des Johannes*, pp. 428–431, who energetically defends the text of Syr. sin.

32. For the shifting of v. 24 after v. 13 pleaded: M.-J. Lagrange, pp. 459–462; J. Schneider, *op. cit.*; finally R. T. Fortna (for the source, see below). A. Mahoney, *op. cit*, would offer a text-critical solution: instead of δεδεμένον it is to have been originally δὲ μένον. Annas who remained is supposed to have sent to Caiaphas, who presided over the further hearing until he himself came to the court-room of the Sanhedrin – an imaginative but contrived conjecture which does not help us further.

33. *Gospel of John*, pp. 642ff.

34. *Gospel of Signs*, pp. 117–122. G. Reim, *Studien*, does not deal with the problem more closely, but is obviously thinking of a rival account of the (as he supposes) 'fourth synoptic' (cf. p. 211), who, according to him, ought to be 'older than Mark' (p. 215).

35. Cf. J. Blinzler, *op. cit.*; also Dodd, *Historical Tradition*, pp. 88ff, who, admittedly, does not want to reconstruct the course of historical events but, on the basis of elements of the tradition in Jn 18:12–27, examines only the reliability of the Johannine tradition.

36. Cf. the works of P. Benoit, *op. cit.*

37. *Op. cit.*, pp. 58f and 67: 'We have to do with a reshaping by the editors of the traditional element concerning Jesus' trial before the high council.'

38. *Passionsgeschichte* pp. 69ff.

39. Cf. Blinzler, *Prozess*, pp. 96f.

40. B. Schwank, *op. cit.*, p. 53, finds in the Lord's being bound, an initial instance of the image of the servant of God according to Is 53:7. That certainly does not apply to John, but also scarcely to his source.

Notes

41. On Annas see Blinzler, *Prozess*, pp. 129f; cf. also P. Gaechter, 'Der Hass des Hauses Annas', in: *Petrus und sein Zeit* (Innsbruck, 1958), pp. 67–104. On the justification for the high priest who had been replaced to continue using this title, cf. also J. Jeremias, *Jerusalem zur Zeit Jesu*, II B, pp. 14f.

42. Cf. E. M. Smallwood, 'High Priests and Politics in Roman Palestine', *JThST* 13 (1962), pp. 14–34.

43. Differently, A. Dauer, *Passionsgeschichte*, pp. 69ff, who already attributes the πρῶτον in v. 13a and the whole v. 24 to the source. According to him, this already contained two trials (by Annas and by Caiaphas).

44. On ὑπὲρ τοῦ λαοῦ, cf. the commentary on 11:50; further, B. Schwank, *op. cit.*, p. 55.

45. C Θ P pl. Against that, the oldest mss. witness to the reading without the article: P⁶⁰ᵛⁱᵈ. P⁶⁶ B ℵ* A pc.

46. A. Loisy (p. 459), Hoskyns-Davey (p. 513 'presumably'), H. Strathmann (p. 239), E. Schick (p. 161), W. Wilkens (*Entstehungsgeschichte*, p. 81), especially A. Kragerud (*Lieblingsjünger*, pp. 25f). Yet these authors are not at one in their judgment on the beloved disciple (Kragerud: *symbolic figure*). For criticism, cf. Dauer, *Passionsgeschichte*, pp. 73ff, also Lindars (p. 548). F. Neirynck, who is inclined towards identification, now considers the question extensively: The 'other disciple' in Jn 18:15–16, in: *EThLov* 51 (1975), pp. 113–141.

47. On contrary hypotheses (a connection with priestly circles through his mother Salome or business connections through his father Zebedee), cf. L. Morris, p. 752 n. 32. In a medieval manuscript, *Historia passionis Domini* (14th–15th century), a comment is to be found which is attributed to the *Gospel of the Nazarenes*: 'if he was the son of the poor fisherman Zebedee, he had often brought fish to the palace of the high priests Annas and Caiaphas' (Hennecke-Schneemelcher I, pp. 99f, E.T.: I, p. 152). The remark is also found in the paraphrase of Nonnus (4th century). The hypotheses of more recent exegetes are often hardly novel.

48. Cf. my considerations concerning this in *EKK* 2 (1970) p. 112f.

49. The mode of expression 'acquaintance of the high priest' in v. 16 is presumably only a linguistic variation; not a few manuscripts read here also as in v. 16. The question as to whether the 'acquaintanceship' was only a superficial one or entailed a closer relationship, is to be decided in the latter sense according to the linguistic usage of the LXX. Cf. Barrett, *ad loc.*; C. H. Dodd, *Historical Tradition*, p. 86f.

50. Thus also, Dauer, *Passionsgeschichte*, p. 73, with additional observations on style.

51. syˢ has a special reading in v. 16 'to the door-keeper' and in v. 17 'Maid of the door-keeper', again defended by A. Merx, p. 433f. But the Syr. sin. is already rendered suspect rather often through reflection; that might have caused the alteration here too.

52. The word is also witnessed to elsewhere, but only found here and Jn 21:9 in NT. 21:9 does not need, on that account, to come from the same hand. Glowing pieces of charcoal are meant, cf. Liddell-Scott, *Lex.*, 140; BauerWb, col. 133f.

53. Cf. Bultmann, pp. 642ff and 646. Even Blinzler, *Prozess*, p. 131, who pleads for the historicity of the 'preliminary hearing' by Annas, says: 'The scene may not be regarded as an official preliminary examination; such a procedure was apparently not known to Jewish criminal proceedings.'

54. F. Hahn, *op. cit.*, p. 65.

55. Cf. C. H. Dodd, *Historical Tradition*, p. 92f: 'Probably a constant element in the tradition, which could be introduced in various contexts.' More decided, F. Hahn, *op. cit.*, pp. 58 and 62 ('a usage created from the logion Mk 14:49a').

56. Thus A. Dauer, *Passionsgeschichte*, pp. 80f.

57. Cf. W. Bauer, *ad loc.*, who cites Celsus: 'But what messenger that has been sent ever hid himself when he ought to be delivering the message that he had been commanded to proclaim?' (Origen, *Contra Cels.*, II, 70; trans. by H. Chadwick.) According to Bauer, likewise according to MacGregor p. 331, the thought is rejected as though the religion of Jesus were practised by an obscure sect. But that can hardly be concluded from this.

58. A. Dauer, *Passionsgeschichte*, p. 82, tends to this.

59. Cf. F. Hahn, *op. cit.* p. 67; A. Dauer, *op. cit.*, p. 82ff.
60. *In Jo. tr.*, CXIII, 4 (CC 639).
61. Cf. R. E. Brown, *ad loc.* (p. 827), who compares Acts 22:30.
62. On the historically difficult questions where the meeting of the Sanhedrin took place, cf. the Excursus in J. Blinzler, *Prozess*, pp. 166–170.
63. A question with μή and the indicative expects a negative answer, cf. Blass-Debr § 427, 2; 440. Yet here it expresses not a wholly negative expectation, but a suspicion.
64. Cf. G. Haenchen, *Historie* p. 63, n. 19, E.T.: *History and Interpretation*, p. 205, n. 19.
65. On the question of chicken-rearing in Jerusalem and on the 'cock-crow' as an indication of the early hour, see Billerbeck I, p. 992f; J. Jeremias, *Jerusalem zur Zeit Jesu* I, pp. 53f. Bernard, II, p. 604, R. E. Brown, p. 828, L. Morris p. 760, n. 55 offer further considerations.
66. As against G. Klein, 'Die Verleugnung des Petrus. Eine traditionsgeschichtliche Untersuchung': *ZThK* 58 (1961), pp. 285–328; differently, E. Linnemann, 'Die Verleugnung des Petrus': *ibid.*, 63 (1966), pp. 1–32 (p. 22: 'Peter's denial is the literary concretization of the general failure of the disciples').

SECTION V: Pages 241–267

1. Cf. A. Dauer, *Passionsgeschichte*, p. 103.
2. Apart from the literature mentioned cf. E. Peterson, 'Zeuge der Wahrheit', *Theologische Traktate* (Munich, 1956), pp. 165–224; H. Schlier, 'Jesus und Pilatus', *Die Zeit der Kirche* (Freiburg im Br., 1956), pp. 56–74; J. Blank, 'Die Verhandlung vor Pilatus Jo 18:28—19:16 im Lichte johanneischer Theologie', *BZ NF* 3 (1959), pp. 60–81; E. Haenchen, 'Jesus vor Pilatus (Joh 18:28—19:15)', *Gott und Mensch* (Tübingen, 1965), pp. 144–156; B. Schwank, 'Pilatus begegnet dem Christus (Jo 18, 28–38a)', *Sein und Sendung* 29 (1964), pp. 100–112.
3. Cf. Fortna, *Gospel of Signs*, pp. 122–128; F. Hahn, *Der Prozess Jesu*, pp. 29–52; Dauer, *Passionsgeschichte*, pp. 100–164 (attempts a reconstruction of the pre-Johannine report, pp. 119–132); G. Reim, *Studien*, pp. 209–216 (only cursory; he thinks, p. 214, that John has probably taken over as a whole the reports of the passion and the resurrection corresponding to Mk 14:1ff from the 'fourth synoptic gospel').
4. Wellhausen, *Ev. Joh.*, pp. 83–86, divides into four sections ('Let him who is able find his way'): 18:28–32; 18:33–38a; 18:38b—19:8; 19:9–16; Bultmann, pp. 648f, suggests six scenes in two groups: 18:28—19:7 and 19:8–16a, each of which ends with a presentation of Jesus (19:5 and 19:14). 19:1–7 he takes as a unit. The two presentations are remarkable, but hardly a principle of division. – Most of the commentaries agree on seven scenes; cf. also, A. Janssens de Varebeke, 'La structure des scènes du récit de la passion en Joh., XVIII–XIX': *EThLov* 38 (1962), pp. 504–522, particularly pp. 506–509.
5. Pilate's to-ing and fro-ing may indicate also his wavering position, his being pulled back and forth between the Jews and Jesus. On the symbolic interpretation of the two places cf. Dauer, *Passionsgeschichte* p. 104: 'Outside' the Jews are raging; 'inside' Jesus proclaims the word of revelation.
6. The evangelist narrates (except for the frequent λέγει) generally in the preterite. Yet, sometimes he uses the present historic, especially at the beginning of a scene or in vivid description, so with ἔρχεσθαι 4:5; 12:22; 13:6; 20:1f, 6, 18, 26; with βλέπειν 1:29; 20:1, 5; with ἄγω 9:13.
7. Among others L.-H. Vincent, 'L'Antonia et le Prétoire', *RB* 42 (1933), pp. 83–113; *idem.*, *Jérusalem de l'Ancien Testament* I (Paris, 1954), pp. 193–224; N. Aline de

Notes

Sion, *Le Forteresse Antonia à Jérusalem et la question du Prétoire* (Jerusalem, 1955); R. D. Potter, 'Topography and Archaeology in the Fourth Gospel', *StEv* I (1959), pp. 329–337, particularly pp. 334f; B. Schwank, *BZ NF* 7 (1963) p. 119 (following D. Baldi, *Atlas Biblique*).

8. Among others, G. Dalman, *Jerusalem und sein Gelände* (Gütersloh, 1930), p. 86; P. Benoit, 'Pretoire, Lithostroton et Gabbatha', RB 59 (1952), pp. 531–550; *idem*, *Passion et Résurrection du Seigneur* (Paris, 1966), p. 171, n. 5; C. Kopp, *Die heiligen Stätten*, pp. 412–421 (E.T.: *Holy Places*, pp. 365–373).

9. *Der Prozess Jesus* (⁴1969), pp. 256–259.

10. Seneca, *De ira* II, 7, 3; Macrobius, *Sat.* I, 3 and others. Cf. Sherwin-White, *Roman Society*, p. 45.

10a. This, in contrast to 13:30, often supposed symbolism (J. Blank, *op. cit.*, p. 66: 'The day of fulfilment and victory is dawning'), is not so certain. In the only place where πρωί occurs again in John's gospel, namely, 20:1, σκοτίας ἔτι οὔσης is found with it. The indication of time may simply have been taken over from the source – without any symbolic significance.

11. τὸ πάσχα φαγεῖν means 'to eat the Passover *lamb*', cf. Mk 14:12b, 14 par. τὸ πάσχα has the same meaning in connection with θύειν, see BauerWb 1256 s.v. 2. On the possibility, occasionally suggested, of a reference to the sacrifice at the feast (*ḥagiga*), which could also be eaten in the week of the feast, cf. Billerbeck II, pp. 837–840.

12. A. Dauer, *Passionsgeschichte*, pp. 138–142, is very sceptical of a passover typology in John's gospel. But when the influence of this idea in the rest of the NT is considered and John's distancing of himself from the Jewish Passover is observed ('the feast of the Jews' 2:13; 6:4; 11:55), it is possible that a cultic *Sitz im Leben* is behind it. The evangelist may have found the information in his source (as Dauer reckons); it then inspired him to his understanding of Jesus as the true Passover lamb (cf. 19:36).

13. Billerbeck II, pp. 838f.

14. Cf. Barrett, p. 444; R. E. Brown, p. 846, *ad loc.*

15. Cf. Blinzler, *Prozess*, pp. 260–271; differently, P. Winter in: *ZNW* 50 (1959), pp. 234–249, who traces the gospels' image of Pilate back to Christian apologetic. Yet cf. also, A. N. Sherwin-White, 'The Trial of Jesus', *Historicity and Chronology in the New Testament*, ed. D. Nineham (London, 1965), pp. 97–116.

16. Psychological explanations, e.g., that was difficult for the chief priests to go to the procurator, because that recalled their powerlessness and lost independence (cf. Tillmann, *ad loc.*), are wide of the mark. The evangelist is interested in their claim that Jesus was a criminal, which is shown to be groundless by Pilate's thrice repeated statement: '*I* find no crime in him' (18:38b; 19:4, 6). In 19:6 Pilate reacts exactly as in 18:31: 'Take him yourselves . . .'

17. For κακὸν ποιῶν there are textual variants: κακοποιῶν C* Ψ 33 pc; κακοποιός A θ Ρ λ φ pl. But the first reading is certainly the original; the expression, which does not have to be a Semitism, is perhaps explained by a recollection of a word in the source, similar with Mk 15:14 par., where Pilate asks the Jews: 'What evil has he done?' In Jn 18:35 Pilate asks Jesus: 'What have you done?'

18. That accords with the Romans' practice in the subject provinces. There were special additional privileges for the Jewish people, e.g., freedom from military service and from the emperor cult. The communities of Alexandria and Asia Minor possessed, as can be proved, their own jurisdiction. Cf. Blinzler, *Prozess*, pp. 245f; Sherwin-White, *Roman Society*, pp. 14ff.

19. On the priest's daughter cf. Billerbeck I, pp. 1026f. According to B. the account does not exclude the possibility that the Jewish executions were carried out only after the Roman governor had given his permission. E. Lohse, *ThWb* VII, pp. 863, 20ff (E.T.: *TDNT*, VII, p. 865), supposes that the daughter of the priest was executed during the rule of Herod Agrippa I (AD 41–44).

20. One warning-board was found in 1871, another 1935; see in C. K. Barrett, *Die Umwelt des Neuen Testaments* (Tübingen, 1959), p. 60.

21. Cf. E. Schürer, *Geschichte des jüdischen Volkes,* II, p. 261; Billerbeck I, p. 1027; S. Krauss, *Sanhedrin-Makkot* (Giessen, 1933), pp. 23f, and others. Admittedly, the time is disputed: forty years is taken by some literally, and treated as a round number by others. The latter ought to apply because the *ius gladii* had already been removed from the Jews since the subjection of Judaea to Roman administration (AD 6). Cf. E. Lohse, *ThWb* VII, pp. 863f (E.T.: *TDNT* VII, pp. 865f); H. Balz, *ibid.*, VIII, p. 137:19f (E.T.: *TDNT*, VIII, p. 137). That is also confirmed by a passage in the 'fast roll' (*Megh. Ta'an.* 6), indicating that, after the Romans were driven out of Jerusalem in the year 66, the Jews resumed putting criminals to death. J. Jeremias drew attention to this passage, *ZNW*, 43 (1950–51), pp. 149f.

22. Cf. the extensive discussion in Blinzler, *Prozess,* pp. 229–244; E. Lohse comes to the same result, *ThWb*, VII, pp. 862–864 (E.T.: *TDNT*, VII, pp. 865f).

23. Thus Bultmann, p. 653, who supposes the same for 18:9.

24. Cf. Dauer, *Passionsgeschichte,* pp. 144 and 284.

25. See literature above, p. 446, n. 2. Opinions also diverge on how far John, despite his theological tendency, has also retained historically notable data and perspectives. Cf. on this C. H. Dodd, *Historical Tradition,* pp. 96–120; A. Bajsić, 'Pilatus, Jesus und Barabbas': *Bib* 48 (1967), pp. 7–28. Moreover the theological emphases are not uniformly placed; cf. especially on 18:37; 19:5 and 19:13f.

26. Cf. T. Mommsen, *Römisches Strafrecht* (Leipzig, 1899), pp. 340ff; Sherwin-White, *Roman Society,* pp. 13–23.

27. Cf. Sherwin-White, *Roman Society,* pp. 35ff; Blinzler, *Prozess,* pp. 274f.

28. According to the circumstances (trial), John too is concerned (despite εἶπεν) with a question which in Greek is recognizable only by the tone. The personal pronoun σύ is presumably stressed (cf. Blass-Debr § 277, 1), as also in v. 37a (εἰ σύ). Differently, Moulton-Turner, *Grammar* III, p. 37.

29. Cf. W. Gutbrod, *ThWb* III, pp. 376f (E.T.: *TDNT* III, pp. 375ff).

30. *The Prophet-King,* pp. 63–67.

31. The mss. of the Egyptian text-type (P⁶⁶ also) predominantly read ἀπὸ σεαυτοῦ; against this ἀφ' ἑαυτοῦ W Θ Ρ 33 pl. On account of the weight of the witnesses and of internal probability, most editors prefer the first reading; the second reading appears to be a *lectio difficilior* and is supposed by B. Weiss, Tischendorf and Nestlé–Aland. Yet the more frequent occurrence of ἀφ' ἑαυτοῦ (especially 11:51) could have led the copyists to their reading.

32. Cf. K. L. Schmidt, *ThWb* II, p. 366 E.T.: *TDNT,* II, p. 369 ('ἔθνος . . . without any special sense or characteristics'). Despite the Roman's reserve, it does not necessarily imply hostility to the Jews.

33. Cf. J. Jeremias, *Jerusalem zur Zeit Jesu,* II B, pp. 88–100.

34. On account of the divergent gospel accounts, it is scarcely still possible to determine exactly which 'Jews' played a part in the trial before Pilate. J. Blinzler, *Prozess,* pp. 448f, would apportion the blame between the members of the Sanhedrin and the crowd demonstrating against Jesus – in which case, however, the concern is 'obviously exclusively with the inhabitants of Jerusalem'. John does not mention these either: Luke says, 23:13, that Pilate called together 'the chief priests and the rulers and the people', and in the Barabbas-scene, that 'all together' (παμπληθεί) they demanded the making away with of Jesus (23:18). That accords with his descriptive tendency (cf. Acts 2:36; 3:13 etc.). The thesis of a collective guilt of the Jewish people ought finally to be rejected; cf. also the declaration of the second Vatican Council, which was issued after considerable debate: 'Although the Jewish authorities with their supporters pressed for Christ's death (cf. Jn 19:6), nevertheless, the events of his suffering can be blamed neither on all Jews living at the time without distinction, nor on the Jews of today': *Declaration on the Relation of the Church to the non-Christian religions,* art. 4 (ed. Herder II, p. 493).

35. Cf. on 1:19 (1, pp. 286f). From the more recent literature: C. K. Barrett, *Das Johannesevangelium und das Judentum* (Stuttgart, 1970); F. Hahn, *Der Prozess Jesu,*

pp. 68–89; R. Leistner, *Antijudaismus im Johannesevangelium?* (Berne-Frankfurt/M., 1974).

36. Cf. R. Schnackenburg, *Gottes Herrschaft und Reich,* pp. 230–232. All NT passages which speak of a βασιλεία of Christ, are formulated from the post-Easter viewpoint of the primitive Church.

37. Augustine refuted the misunderstanding that Jesus' 'kingdom' is not of the world on this account. He writes, *tr. CXV*, 2: 'Non ait: Nunc autem regnum non est hic, sed: non est hinc. Hic est enim regnum eius usque in finem saeculi . . . Sed tamen non est hinc, quia peregrinatur in mundo' (CC 644).

38. ὅτι can scarcely be regarded as a causal conjunction ('for I am a king'), as Blass-Debr, § 441, 3, think; cf. the other possibility *op. cit.* 441, 2. The whole sentence is an affirmation, the meaning of which is then explained (so too Bultmann, p. 654 n. 6). B. Lindars, p. 559, *ad loc.*, thinks that it is a rejection of the accusation in the political sense and an affirmation in another sense. That is a correct interpretation but it cannot be deduced from the wording. It must be noted that Pilate here, in contrast to v. 33, asks: 'So you are *a* king?'

39. Cf., on this idea of witness, J. Beutler, *Martyria,* pp. 318–322.

40. Cf. H. Schlier, *Jesus und Pilatus,* pp. 64; 'But Jesus is also witness now before Pilate. Here indeed, where his testimony before the legitimate and public judgment of the cosmos takes place as his final testimony, it reaches fulfilment.' – Often (Schlier too) 1 Tim 6:13 is designated as an echo of Jn 18:37. The text runs: 'Christ Jesus, who in his testimony (μαρτυρήσαντος) before Pontius Pilate made the good confession (ὁμολογία).' N. Brox, *Die Pastoralbriefe* (Regensburg, 1969), p. 216, rightly raises an objection to this: ἐπί does not mean 'before', but 'under'; the direct word of testimony Jn 18:37 is not taken up.

41. In this connection ἀκούειν, with genitive, certainly means 'listen to', attentively taking up, obey. In contrast to this, ἀκ. τὴν φωνήν in 3:8 and 5:37 means hearing in an outward sense. The distinction is not always strictly maintained, cf. on 5:25; ἀκούειν is at least intended in 18:37 as in 5:25 in the dual sense: outwardly receive *and* accept in faith.

42. H. Schlier, *Jesus und Pilatus,* pp. 61f, draws attention to the answer which the grand-children of Judas the Lord's brother gave at a trial before Domitian (according to Eusebius, *Hist. eccles.,* III, 20, 4): 'When they were asked about Christ and concerning the nature of his kingdom and about the place and the time of his appearance, they answered, it is not from this world and not from this earth, it is rather a heavenly kingdom and belonging to the angels, which is only to come at the end of the world.' Such a view seems to have been widespread; cf. Augustine's contradictory statement, above, n. 37.

43. Thus H. Schlier, *op. cit.* p. 63; he then describes the generally 'political' character (now in inverted commas), though admittedly very non-politically. Cf. also his further study: 'Der Staat im Neuen Testament', *Besinnung auf das Neue Testament* (Freiburg im Br., 1964), pp. 193–211, particularly 194–200.

44. *The Prophet-King,* p. 67; cf. also his considerations on the further Johannine presentation of the trial (pp. 67–81).

45. This assessment of the question of Pilate is gaining support, cf. the more recent commentaries (differently, L. Morris, p. 771, *ad loc.*); Schlier, *Jesus und Pilatus,* p. 65; F. Hahn, *Der Prozess Jesu,* p. 42.

46. Dauer, *Passionsgeschichte,* pp. 123–126, tries to reconstruct the text of the source. He thinks: 'The brevity of the report shows the relatively small interest of the evangelist' (p. 123).

47. Cf. J. Schniewind, *Parallelperikopen,* p. 65 (on the Barabbas pericope): 'a special tradition of *oral* narrative'; pp. 69f (on the declaration of innocence); J. A. Bailey, *Traditions Common,* pp. 69ff (assumes knowledge of Luke's gospel by John); R. T. Fortna, *Gospel of Signs,* pp. 124f (from the *semeia*-source which was here similar to Luke); A. Dauer, *Passionsgeschichte,* pp. 123ff (v. 39a is very close to Mt 27:15, the remaining text to Luke).

48. Dauer, *op. cit.,* pp. 124f would attribute Pilate's offer to the source. That might be fitting for the attempt to release Jesus (cf. Lk 23:16); but for the remainder of the passover amnesty that seems doubtful.

49. The dative in connection with εἶναι can, admittedly, also be explained as 'have, possess'; thus Blass-Debr., § 189, 1. But emphasis (ἐστιν) and position of words (ὑμῖν at the end) give the sentence its own character. On the dative referring to a nominative, cf. also Mayser, *Grammatik,* II/2, pp. 145ff. The translation 'among you' is inexact.

50. See in A. Deissmann, *Licht vom Osten* (Tübingen, 4th ed. 1923), p. 229 (plate p. 230).

51. Ch. B. Chavel, 'The Releasing of a Prisoner on the Eve of Passover in Ancient Jerusalem', *JBL* 60 (1941), pp. 273–278. Further discussion in Blinzler, *Prozess Jesu,* pp. 317–320.

52. This πάλιν has already disturbed copyists; they corrected it as πάντες G K 33 al. VL. Many other mss. read πάλιν πάντες P⁶⁶⁽ᵛⁱᵈ⁾ Θ P pm Vg.

53. The origin of πάλιν is variously explained. W. Bauer, p. 217: 'Comes from Mk 15, 13'; likewise Barrett, p. 449 and others. Bultmann, p. 649, thinks that the source must already have mentioned the Jews' κραυγάζειν; but this part of the source has been played down by Jn 18:33–37. Dauer, *Passionsgeschichte,* p. 103, says fittingly, that πάλιν belongs to the evangelist's narrative style, and presumably had already lost much of its meaning.

54. On λῃστής in Josephus, cf. K. H. Rengstorf, *ThWb,* IV, pp. 263f (E.T.: *TDNT,* IV, pp. 258f). Dauer, *Passionsgeschichte,* pp. 125f, likewise attributes λῃστής to the source, but does not consider the possibility that the evangelist understood it differently. Bultmann, p. 657f, sees an irony in the situation in that the Jews denounced Jesus as an alleged political miscreant, but asked for the release of a real political evil-doer. – But that can scarcely be read from the Johannine text.

55. A. Bajsić, *op. cit.,* would assign a key position to the release of Barabbas for the historical course of the trial: Through it Jesus' destiny was sealed. A third part of the trial did not occur any more; in Jn 19 we would still have the Easter amnesty-negotiation before us. – John's theological presentation certainly offers no difficulty for this historical reconstruction; but the reconstruction itself is hardly correct. Cf. against this Blinzler, *Prozess,* p. 310.

56. Differently, J. Blinzler, *Prozess,* pp. 322f and 334f, who concludes from the participle φραγελλώσας in Mk 15:15, that the scourging took place even before the pronouncement of the death-sentence. But the formulation is presumably explained by the context: the point is solely the condemnation to death on the cross (cf. 15:14); the scourging is only mentioned by the way; nothing is said in this about its time. According to the usual Roman practice, everything speaks in favour of the scourging occurring in connection with the crucifixion, cf. Sherwin-White, *Roman Society,* pp. 26f, further the commentaries.

57. Cf. C. Schneider, *ThWb,* IV, p. 523 (E.T.: *TDNT,* IV, p. 517); J. Blinzler, *Prozess,* pp. 321f.

58. Cf. C. H. Dodd, *Historical Tradition,* p. 102 (thinks of OT *testimonia*); A. Dauer, *Passionsgeschichte,* p. 126; differently, P. Borgen, *NTSt* 5 (1958–59), p. 252 (on account of the symmetry with Jn 18:22).

59. P. Benoit, 'Der Prozess Jesu' (*Exegese und Theologie,* Düsseldorf 1965), pp. 117f, would locate the mocking (differently from the scourging) during the trial, before the condemnation, but he also sees the difficulty that the Roman soldiers were subjected to strict discipline. He supposes that the Lukan scene is connected with this: the mocking begun by Herod would have been ended in the Praetorium. Yet the connection with the special Lukan tradition is questionable, see on 19:6 at the end. J. Blinzler, *Prozess,* pp. 335f, would give preference to the Johannine presentation as the more detailed. E. Haenchen, *Historie,* pp. 71f (E.T.: *Interpr* 24 (1970), p. 213), supposes John's knowledge of the synoptic mockery scene: '. . . he [the evangelist] inserted and expanded [this tradition] before the final sentencing of Jesus'. A. Dauer,

Passionsgeschichte, pp. 111 and 126f, offers an exact definition: The tradition comes from the Johannine source, but the moving forward of the scourging and crowning with thorns prior to the judgment is due to the evangelist, who wanted to prepare for the 'proclamation as king' by Pilate.

60. J. Schniewind, *Parallelperikopen*, pp. 62–77, postulates traditions for the special Johannine material in Chapter 19, and sees them as primary, as against Luke (p. 75). Against the use of a common narrative tradition by Luke and John, F. Hahn, *Der Prozess Jesu*, p. 36. A. Dauer, *Passionsgeschichte*, pp. 127f, discover traces of the source, but not for Jesus' presentation as mock-king.

61. The thorn crown woven from a spiky weed is variously understood. H. St J. Hart, 'The Crown of Thorns in John 19:2, 5', *JThSt NS* 3 (1952), pp. 66–75: a shining crown through which Jesus accordingly is deified (*divus radiatus* in imperial manner; but the crown is probably meant to represent only the crown (sign of lordship) of the Roman vassal kings. Also, there is certainly no connection with the crown of victory of war leaders. Cf. R. Delbrueck, 'Antiquarisches zu den Verspottungen Jesu', *ZNW*, 41 (1942), pp. 124–145, especially 129; J. Blinzler, *Prozess*, pp. 326–328; W. Grundmann, *ThWb*, VII, pp. 631f (E.T.: *TDNT*, VII, pp. 632f).

62. According to Mk 15:10/Mt 27:18, Pilate too recognizes that the chief priests have handed Jesus over 'out of envy'. Mt 27:19 adds the special material about Pilate's wife, who begs her husband to desist from 'that righteous man'. This is also a form of declaration of Jesus' innocence.

63. P^{66} a e ff^2 r^1 achm om. καὶ λάγει κτλ., probably, because Pilate has already spoken in v. 4 and these copyists regard the repeated statement as superfluous. They do not regard the *Ecce, homo* as significant!

64. Cf. Blass-Debr § 128, 7; Bauer *Wb*, col. 733, s.v. 2; Mayser, *Grammatik*, II/2, p. 187 under No. 8. More frequent is ἴδε (fifteen times in John; ἰδού only four times), hardly different in meaning, cf. Jn 19:14. Matthew prefers ἰδού, Luke uses it alone, probably under the influence of the LXX. Not a few late mss. read ἴδε, in Jn 19:5 also.

65. J. Blinzler, *Prozess*, p. 329, n. 33, points out that ἄνθρωπος has the meaning 'man' rather often and was apparently usual in judicial language. Accordingly, he suggests: 'There is the man of whom I just spoke . . .'.

66. Cf. C. K. Barrett, *ad loc.* (p. 450): 'ὁ ἄνθρωπος calls to mind those Jewish and Hellenistic myths of the heavenly or primal Man which lie behind John's use of the phrase ὁ υἱὸς τοῦ ἀνθρώπου.' This thesis is, according to more recent religious-historical studies (especially H.-M. Schenke, *Der Gott 'Mensch'*), scarcely tenable, at least not in so undifferentiated a form. Cf. also E. M. Sidebottom, *The Christ of the Fourth Gospel* (London, 1961), who tends to agree with Barrett in regard to Jn 19:5 (p. 96), but in regard to the (gnostic) *anthropos*-myth he is sceptical, thinking rather of the influence of Jewish wisdom-speculation (pp. 99–111).

67. Besides Barrett and Sidebottom (previous footnote), see C. H. Dodd, *Interpretation*, p. 437; J. Blank in: *BZ* (1959), p. 75; I. de la Potterie in: *Bib* 41 (1960), p. 239; A. Dauer, *Passionsgeschichte*, p. 109 (with further views). Cf. also C. Colpe in: *ThWb*, VIII, p. 474 (E.T.: *TDNT*, VIII, p. 470), (the actual meaning of ὁ υἱός τοῦ ἀνθρώπου = 'man' could still have been known to John; but 19:5 is not mentioned).

68. Cf. my contribution to *Jesus und der Menschensohn (Festschrift für A. Vögtle)*, 'Die Ecce-homo-Szene und der Menschensohn' (Freiburg im Br., 1975).

69. See W. A. Meeks, *The Prophet-King*, pp. 69–72; R. E. Brown, p. 876, *ad loc.*, also inclines to this.

70. Thus J. Blank, 'Verhandlung' (*BZ*, 1959), p. 62. He is followed by A. Dauer, *Passionsgeschichte*, pp. 249ff; cf. also F. Hahn, *Prozess Jesu*, pp. 40f.

71. A direct contrast 'man – Son of God', is scarcely intended because Pilate's words are in another context to begin with. Yet the antithesis also appears in the accusation of the chief priests, as a comparison with 10:33 shows.

72. Cf. R. Bultmann, p. 659: 'The declaration ὁ λόγος σὰρξ ἐγένετο has become apparent in its most extreme consequence.' That may in fact apply, but the formulation

does not indicate that – ἄνθρωπος is never found in statements about the incarnation. Likewise, all attempted interpretations are to be rejected, which see an expression of Jesus' humanity in Pilate's words: i.e., the man in his typical human features, or the man who embodies humanity as such.

73. Repetition serves as intensification. The repeated amen in John is comparable. It is noticeable in the passion story that the repetition of the call for crucifixion is only met with in Luke: σταύρου, σταύρου αὐτόν (23:21). The other cry, ἆρον, is repeated in Jn 19:15. Luke alone has it earlier (23:18 αἶρε τοῦτον), but does not repeat it. Admittedly, the *epanadiplosis* is a Lukan stylistic device (cf. 8:24; 10:41; 13:34; 22:31); but John could have decided on repetition independently. J. A. Bailey, *Traditions Common*, p. 77, thinks that John 'is doubtless echoing Luke here'; differently, A. Dauer, *Passionsgeschichte*, p. 160, cf. p. 164, who traces the connections back to the Johannine source.

74. Cf. A. Dauer, *Passionsgeschichte*, p. 128.

75. Assessment from the history of tradition and source criticism of the relationship of Luke and John in the case of the Pilate pericope, is very varied. J. Schniewind, *Parallelperikopen*, pp. 62–77, assumes a common, and as yet unfixed (oral) tradition. J. A. Bailey, *Tradition Common*, pp. 64–77, posits John's knowledge of Luke's gospel. P. Borgen, *John and the Synoptics*, pp. 251f, finds synoptic material blended in John; similarly, A. Dauer, *Passionsgeschichte*, p. 164: 'An intermingling of oral and written tradition, particularly of the synoptic reports', under especially strong influence from the Lukan version. For this he postulates in the further course of his argument a pre-Johannine source.

76. J. Blinzler, *Prozess*, p. 248, speaks of an 'interruption'; the accusation of blasphemy plays no further part (as in the Jewish proceedings). Blinzler regards both proceedings as two self-sufficient trials with different accusations. Another consideration is found in Sherwin-White, *Roman Society*, pp. 46f.

77. On this use of φοβεῖσθαι, cf. Jn 6:19f; Mk 4:41; 5:15 (referring to one possessed by a demon), etc. John expresses outward fear with φόβος with the genitive (7:13; 19:38; 20:19; or by means of the verb with an accusative object (9:22). H. Balz in: *ThWb*, IX (1970), p. 205 (E.T.: *TDNT*, IX, p. 209), sees this kind of fear in connection with epiphany and miracle-motifs, but draws support for this only from the synoptics and Jn 6:19. The motif of epiphany-fear is also found in the Gentile-Hellenistic area, see *ibid.*, p. 191, 1–18 (E.T.: p. 194).

78. Barrett, *ad loc.* would understand μᾶλλον as elative: 'He was very much afraid'; but the examples in Liddell-Scott, *s.v.*, to which he points, hardly apply. The meaning 'much more' (see also BauerWb, col. 967, *s.v.* 3) does not fit our passage. For John, cf. also, 3:19; 12:43 also 5:18 where a similar progression is found (cf. v. 16), see Vol. 2, p. 102, n. 31.

79. Philostratus, *Vita Apollonii* I, 21 (ed. Conybeare I, pp. 58ff): The satrap in Babylon asks Ap.: πόθεν ἡμῖν ἐπιπεμφθεὶς ἥκεις; he then threatens him with torture if he does not answer; but Ap. does not allow himself to be intimidated and the satrap recognizes that he is 'divine'. *Ibid.*, IV, 44 (Conybeare I, pp. 452ff): Ap. behaves similarly before the Roman court of law; the judge Tigellinus finally wants to avoid fighting a god and sets him free. These formally similar presentations, to which G. P. Wetter has drawn attention (*Der Sohn Gottes*, pp. 90f), are instructive in regard to literary genre; John uses the device but does not falsify the result of the trial.

80. Cf. Sherwin-White, *Roman Society*, pp. 1ff. He writes among other things: 'Having the *imperium*, the proconsul had the total power of administration, jurisdiction, defence – in so far as that arose – and the maintenance of public order' (p. 2).

81. The meaning of the term ἐξουσία differs in accordance with the context: freedom of action, actual force, authority, official power, etc., cf. BauerWb, cols. 550f; W. Foerster, *ThWb*, II, pp. 559f (E.T.: *TDNT*, II, pp. 562f). In Jn 19:10 ἐξ, has, in Pilate's terms, the meaning first of (delegated) authority and official power, roughly in the sense of *imperium* (see previous footnote), which, in view of the Roman (military) strength also includes the actual exercise of power. If the above exegesis is correct,

in Jesus' answer this ἐξ, is then restricted to mean freedom and ability to act. W. Foerster mentions our passage only in regard to state relations (p. 562, 13, E.T.: p. 565). The other instance in John's gospel refers throughout to the God-given ἐξ., see 1:12; 5:27; 17:2, or the respective own ἐξ. of Christ (as the Son of God): 10:18. On the use of the term, cf. also on Jn 10:18 (II, pp. 301f).

82. Instead of εἶχες not a few mss. read ἔχεις: ℵ A C D L Ψ 33 565 579 al. The restriction is then still sharper; Pilate's power is denied unless freedom to act is bestowed on him (beforehand, in a specific situation?) 'from above'. For this reading, see Tischendorf, von Soden, Bover; yet the other reading is to be preferred according to the remaining editors. The particle ἄν is dispensable, cf. Blass-Debr § 360, 1.

83. Cf. E. Peterson, *Zeuge der Wahrheit*; H. Schlier, *Jesus und Pilatus* (see p. 446, n. 2); R. Bultmann, *ad loc.* (refers to Rom 13:1); also B. Lindars ('derivative character of all earthly power'). Augustine referred to Rom 13:1 (*In Jo. tr. CXVI*, 5; CC 648).

84. The decisive argument to adopt the above exegesis, which is becoming established, was offered by H. von Campenhausen, 'Zum Verständnis von Joh 19, 11': *ThLZ* 73 (1948), pp. 387–392; further cf. J. Blank, *op. cit.*, p. 79; R. E. Brown, pp. 892f. In the synoptics, the same thought is found in another context (on the arrest of Jesus): Mt 26:53f ('Do you think that I cannot appeal to my Father . . .'); Lk 22:53 ('But this is your hour, and the power of darkness').

85. V. 1. παραδιδούς A D K L M pm. Yet this is the weaker reading.

86. Cf. Bultmann, p. 662, n. 6; 'the [general] singular is occasioned by the quasi-proverbial formulation'. The interpretation as a reference to the devil is quite misleading (Delafosse); in addition, L. Morris refers the passage to Caiaphas alone, p. 797.

87. ἐκ τούτου can have a temporal or a causal meaning, cf. on 6:66. Since there was already talk of Pilate's attempt to release Jesus (declarations of innocence), the explanation 'At these words he tried to release him' seems to be suggested here. R. E. Brown, p. 879, *ad loc.*, prefers the temporal meaning.

88. In Mk 15:9/Mt 27:17, 21 Pilate asks (in the Barabbas scene) only whom he is to release for the Jews. Luke speaks three times of the Roman judge's effort (corresponding to the threefold declaration of innocence). Was the Johannine source close to the third evangelist in this? However, the sentences in Luke show traces of Lukan style, cf. Dauer, *Passionsgeschichte*, p. 162.

89. E. Bammel, Φίλος τοῦ Καίσαρος: *ThLZ*, 77 (1952), pp. 205–210, adduces noteworthy reasons in favour of this. Cf. also Sherwin-White, *Roman Society*, p. 47, n. 1.

90. Cf. J. Blinzler, *Prozess*, p. 265: That was also possible in the time of Sejanus. On the statements of secular historians about Tiberius cf. *ibid.*, pp. 337f. See especially Suetonius, *Tiberius* 58: 'Iudicia maiestatis atrocissime exercuit'; Tacitus, *Ann.* 3, 38: '. . . addito maiestatis crimine, quod tum omnium accusationum complementum erat.'

91. This view was most effectively justified by I. de la Potterie, 'Jésus, roi et juge d'après Jn 19, 13: 'Ἐκάθισεν ἐπὶ βήματος', *Bib* 41 (1960), pp. 217–247. But other exegetes have also expressed themselves in favour, cf. the list in Dauer, *Passionsgeschichte*, pp. 269f, n. 188, among them also A. Loisy, *ad loc.*; E. Haenchen, *Jesus vor Pilatus*, p. 153, and *id.*, *Historie und Geschichte*, pp. 74f, E.T.: *Interpr* 24 (1970), pp. 215f.

92. Cf. Bauer*Wb*, cols. 770f; he prefers the intransitive meaning in Jn 19:13, referring to Josephus *Bellum*, II, 172. Liddell-Scott, p. 854, s.v. (with many proofs from the secular literature). Cf. also C. Schneider in: *ThWb*, III, p. 445, 23–32, E.T.: *TDNT*, III, p. 442 (sitting of the judge).

93. *Jésus, roi et juge*, pp. 223ff (the following numbers also are based on this).

94. Cf. especially the excursus in Dauer, *Passionsgeschichte*, pp. 269–274; further, B. Lindars, p. 570; L. Morris, p. 799.

95. εἰς τόπον does not necessarily speak for the transitive sense of καθ.; εἰς not infrequently replaced ἐν in the *koine*, cf. Blass-Debr § 205. For John, cf. 1:18; for 'sit' with εἰς, Mk 13:3. Perhaps the evangelist wanted to avoid a second ἐπί.

96. The name is Aramaic, but the derivation is uncertain, cf. G. Dalman, *Grammatik des jüdischen-palästinensischen Aramäisch* (Leipzig, ²1905), p. 160, n. 4; *ibid.*, *Jesus-Jeschua*, p. 13 (E.T.: *Jesus-Jeshua*, p. 14), (from *gabbaḥta* = bald forehead); Billerbeck II, p. 572 (from stem *gabbā* = eminence, elevation); L. H. Vincent in: *RB*, 59 (1952), p. 524 ('elevation, hill').

97. The Greek term reproduces an established Hebrew expression; cf. Billerbeck, II, pp. 834–837. Others (especially C. C. Torrey) understand it as 'day of preparation for the sabbath in the passover feast week'; cf. also J. Jeremias, *Die Abendmahlsworte*, pp. 74f (E.T.: *The Eucharistic Words of Jesus*, pp. 54f). This understanding supports the effort to bring the Johannine into agreement with the synoptic chronology.

98. V. 1. τρίτη, א^c D (in the later addition to the Greek, not in d) L X Δ Ψ al. Cf. also the witnesses of early church writers for one or other of the readings in Tischendorf's apparatus (*ed. oct. crit. maior*, reprint, Graz, 1965) I, pp. 940f. But τρίτη might be due to the influence of Mk 15:25 (thus Tischendorf). S. Bartina, 'Ignotum *episèmon* gabex', *VD*, 36 (1958), pp. 16–37, would (like others already before him) understand ἕκτη as a scribal error using the numerical sign *gamma* (= 3) for the similarly written numerical sign *episèmon* or *gabex* (= 6); cf. also C. K. Barrett, *ad loc*. B. Schwank discusses the question in detail, *Sein und Sendung*, 29 (1964), pp. 204–207; he follows Bartina. But all that is speculative because ἕκτη is witnessed to by the oldest and best mss. and the error would hardly have forced its way into all these mss. Cf. also Blinzler, *Prozess*, pp. 417–421, who holds Mk 15:25 to be an interpolation.

99. In favour is above all the (otherwise non-existent) detail of the name Gabbatha, further possibly the 'day of preparation for the passover'. Further arguments in Dauer, *Passionsgeschichte*, pp. 133–136. On the frequently adduced counter-argument that John has altered the details of time on account of the passover-lamb-typology, cf., *ibid.*, pp. 140–142. Dauer emphasizes: 'John's theological considerations can be much better understood if his handed-down account already spoke of Jesus having been nailed to the cross on 14th Nisan, on the day on which the paschal lambs were slaughtered' (p. 142).

100. Thus M. Dibelius, 'Die alttestamentlichen Motive in der Leidensgeschichte des Petrus und Johannesevangeliums', *Botschaft und Geschichte* I (Tübingen, 1953), pp. 221–247, particularly pp. 227–229. According to Dibelius, the Johannine text has its origin in a historicizing reworking of an edifying tradition orientated to the OT, and still preserved in the *Gospel of Peter*. G. Reim, *Studien zum alttestamentlichen Hintergrund*, does not give consideration to a reference to Amos 8:9 (cf. p. 177).

101. Thus J. E. Bruns. 'The Use of Time in the Fourth Gospel', *NTSt*, 13 (1966–67), pp. 285–290, particularly p. 289.

102. If the Johannine account is understood on a historical basis, another intepretation is also permissible; cf. A. Schlatter, *Der Evangelist Joh*; pp. 346f: 'Pilate exploits the situation so as to force the Jews into a renunciation of their own kingdom. Whereas the Jews did not deny messianism, but only wanted to destroy Jesus, Pilate hated messianism . . . He obtained from them unrestricted submission to the emperor.' But that would hardly correspond to the evangelist's representational tendency.

103. Cf. H. Schlier, *Jesus und Pilatus*, p. 73, who also cites Bengel: 'Iesum negant usque eo, ut omnino Christum negent'; J. Blank, *Verhandlung vor Pilatus*, p. 81.

104. The 14th Benediction says, according to the Palestinian recension: 'Have mercy, Yahweh our God . . . on the kingdom of the house of David, the Messiah of your righteousness'; more clearly in the 15th Benediction of the Babylonian recension: 'May David's offspring be born quickly, and his horn arise through your help' (see in Billerbeck IV, p. 213).

105. On παραδιδόναι in judicial language cf. Bauer*Wb*, col. 1219; Liddell-Scott, *Lex.* II, p. 1308, s.v. 3. In the NT cf. also Mt 5:25; 18:34; Acts 8:3; 12:4; 22:4; 28:16f. The sentence in Jn 19:16a agrees rather closely with Mk 15:15b/Mt 27:26b; in the synoptics the comment about the scourging is added, in John αὐτοῖς.

106. Dauer, *Passionsgeschichte*, pp. 131f. The reconstruction is not wholly clear. If 19:2–3 followed 19:16a, as D. assumes, the mention of the soldiers would be expected

Notes

already in 19:16a, not only subsequently. In the table (p. 168) D. has 19:16b following οἱ στρατιῶται 19:2; but then αὐτοῖς 19:16a remains unexplained.

107. In 19:16b, παρέλαβον which corresponds to παρέδωκεν, could take on this emphasis. Luke shows a similar tendency: at the condemnation he says, differently from Mk/Mt: 'But Jesus he delivered up to *their will*' (23:25). Acts 4:10 says: '. . . by the name of Jesus Christ of Nazareth, whom *you crucified*'; in the summary formula, however, that is probably intended causally.

SECTION VI: Pages 268–299

1. R. E. Brown, pp. 910–912, divides the section into five episodes, framed within an Introduction (vv. 16b–18) and a conclusion (vv. 38–42). He arranges these seven units in a descending and ascending line so that they contrast with one another: introduction and conclusion; episode 1 (vv. 19–22) and episode 5 (vv. 31–37); episode 2 (vv. 23–24) and episode 4 (vv. 28–30). At the turning-point in the middle stands episode 3 (vv. 25–27). Brown perceives a theological conception in this; but the arrangement seems artificial, the 'correspondence' of the episodes is not convincing. Admittedly, we can also make two units out of vv. 16b–22 (vv. 16b–18; 19–22) and thus obtain seven units; cf. A. Janssens de Varebeke, *La Structure* (see above p. 446, n. 4), pp. 509ff. But did the evangelist intend a numerically determined or symmetrical arrangement?

1a. Cf. A. Dauer, *Passionsgeschichte*, p. 168 (table).

2. Many mss. extend the text, v. 16b: οἱ δὲ λαβόντες ℵ*: οἱ δὲ παραλαβόντες φ: παραλαβόντες δέ M 700 al; after the participle: ἀπήγαγον (αὐτόν) or similarly: +εἰς τὸ πραιτώριον M 700 al: +ἐπέθηκαν αὐτῷ τὸν σταυρόν φ (Orig). The last two readings are interesting as a reflection of the copyists. The short text witnessed to by the Egyptian text-type obviously caused difficulties early on.

3. βαστάζειν is a word found another four times in John (10:31; 12:6; 16:12; 20:15). Comparative instances: Matthew: 3; Mark: 1; Luke/Acts: 5/4; Paul: 6; Revelation: 2. The verb is only again used for 'carrying the cross' in Lk 14:27; on the way to the cross Luke says φέρειν (23:26). So the word might well be chosen by John.

4. Church fathers (Origen, Hesychius of Jerusalem, see in W. Bauer, *ad loc.*) and many later exegetes harmonize the synoptic and Johannine information: Simon of Cyrene and Jesus carry the cross alternately. C. H. Dodd, *Historical Tradition*, pp. 124f, thinks that John is influenced by Lk 14:27: 'Jesus, bearing his own cross, is an example to his followers'; likewise B. Lindars, p. 574. But these explanations hardly meet the fourth evangelist's intention.

5. The 'binding of Isaac' (*Aqedat Jiṣhaq*) greatly occupied the Jewish Haggadah. In *Gen Rabbah* 56, 3 it says on Gen 22:6: 'And Abraham took the wood of the burnt-offering – like one who carried his on his shoulder.' (Freedman I, p. 493); further: 'And they went both of them together: one to bind and the other to be bound, one to slaughter and the other to be slaughtered' (*ibid.*). Cf. H. J. Schoeps, *Aus frühchristlicher Zeit* (Tübingen, 1950), pp. 229–232; G. Vermès, *Scripture and tradition in Judaism* (Leiden, 1961), pp. 193–227; R. Le Déaut, *La nuit pascale* (Rome, 1963), pp. 198–207.

6. Barn 7:3; *Melito Fragm.*, X (Goodspeed, *Apologists*, p. 312); Tertullian, *Adv. Marc.*, I 18; *Adv. Jud.*, 10 (Isaac, who carried the wood himself, prefigured the death of Christ who bore the wood of suffering); Irenaeus, *Adv. haer.*, IV, 10, 1 (Harvey II, pp. 156f); John Chrysostom, *In Jo. hom.*, 85, 1 (PG 59, col. 459). Cf. further J. Daniélou, *Sacramentum futuri* (Paris, 1950), pp. 97–111.

7. In favour of an allusion to Isaac in Jn 19:17: MacGregor, p. 344; Hoskyns-Davey, p. 527; finally, R. E. Brown, pp. 917f. Other scholars who are in favour of the Isaac-typology in connection with John (see next footnote), do not make reference to 19:17.

8. In favour of the Isaac-typology in the gospel of John, reference is made to a further two passages: 3:16 and 1:29, 36 (the 'Lamb of God'); see G. Vermès *Scripture and Tradition*, pp. 223ff; F.-M. Braun, *Jean le Théologien*, III/1, pp. 157–165; on 3:16 cf.

also Westcott, Bernard, Barrett, Brown *ad loc.*, further G. Reim, *Studien*, p. 105; on the 'Lamb of God', J. E. Wood, 'Isaac Typology in the New Testament', *NTSt*, 14 (1967/68), pp. 583–589, particularly 586f. I have not raised this typological background for these passages and I now still do not regard it as probable since John elsewhere places the emphases more clearly (e.g., for Moses and Abraham). In connection with 3:16, especially, the typical expression ἀγαπητός is missing; μονογενής in John seems to have yet another tone (cf. vol. 1, 399f). In connection with the 'Lamb of God', reference is made to the Jewish speculations according to which the story of Isaac in Gen 22 was interpreted in the light of Is 53 (suffering servant of God), and once again was to give the passover victim the *Aqedat Jiṣhaq* for its strength. But it remains questionable whether John produced such theological combinations.

9. On the Aramaic word-form *golgola*, determ. *golgolta*=(the) skull, see G. Dalman, *Grammatik*, p. 166. 'The lack of the λ in the second syllable serves to avoid the unisonous sound of two syllables following each other' (*ibid.*, n. 1). On the Greek version κρανίου τόπον, cf. J. Jeremias, *Golgotha* (Leipzig, 1926) p 1, n. 1: 'κρανίου is thus an apposite genitive to τόπος.' According to Jeremias, *ibid.*, p. 2, it remains questionable whether the name designated a skull-shaped hill; but this is 'the most likely interpretation'. Cf. A. Parrot, *Golgotha et Saint-Sepulchre* (Neuchâtel-Paris, 1955), pp. 26f. In the East even today, naturally craggy areas, without having to have a human appearance, are called *râs* (head).

10. Origen *In Mt* 27:33 (*GCS* 38, p. 265), tells of a Jewish tradition that Adam's *body* is buried there; Basil, *In Is* 5:1 (*PG* 30, col. 348C), then speaks of Adam's *skull*. According to J. Jeremias, *Golgotha*, p. 2, the legend of Adam's skull is a late Christian extrapolation from the name Golgotha. The interpretation as *locus decollatorum* (Jerome) might be similarly explained. On the situation outside the (second northern) city wall cf., besides the monographs by J. Jeremias and A. Parrot, C. Kopp, *Heilige Stätten*, pp. 422–436, E.T.: *Holy Places*, pp. 374–388.

11. Thus Dauer, *Passionsgeschichte*, pp. 171f.

12. Cf. Suetonius, *Caligula* 32; *id.*, *Domitian* 10; *Dio Cassius* 54, 8. Cf. in BauerWb col. 1624, s.v. τίτλος.

13. Cf. N. A. Dahl, H. Ristow-K. Matthiae (eds), *Der historische Jesus und der kerygmatische Christus* (Berlin, 1960), p. 159: 'The formulation "King of the Jews" originates neither from a fulfilled prophecy nor from the Christology of the Church.' Cf. also P. Winter, *Trial of Jesus*, pp. 107–110, particularly 108 ('bare historical fact').

14. The Latin *titulus* can also assume this meaning, cf. Dauer, *Passionsgeschichte*, p. 175.

15. See the proofs in W. Bauer, *ad loc.* (p. 222).

16. The first perfect has instead an aorist sense, cf. Blass-Debr § 324, 4. The unisonous repetition is Semitizing, cf. Billerbeck II, p. 573; Schlatter, *Evangelist Joh*, p. 349, *ad loc.*

17. That is well demonstrated by Justin, *Dial. with Trypho*. As against the reasoning of his Jewish disputant, Justin is very keen to demonstrate the sufferings of the Messiah witnessed to by Scripture, cf. *Dial.*, 32, 1f; 39, 7; 40; 46, 1; 90, 1; 95; 97, 3f; 111, 3. The last passage is especially instructive: Christ is the passover lamb which was sacrificed; here, Is 53:7 is cited also (the servant of God was like a lamb that is led to the slaughter'), then we have: 'On the day of the passover you took hold of him and likewise crucified him on the passover.'

18. C. H. Dodd, *Interpr.*, p. 437, recalls Ps 96:10 (95:10): 'The Lord reigns! (has become King, LXX ἐβασίλευσεν)' with the old Christian addition 'from the cross', which applies for the Johannine conception. The addition is found in some mss. of the LXX, in the VL and in the *Psalterium Romanum*; it is also taken up in the hymn 'Vexilla regis': 'regnavit a ligno Deus'.

19. Cf. A. Dauer, *Passionsgeschichte*, pp. 183f; G. Reim, *Studien*, p. 48.

20. See, on this, J. Blinzler, *Prozess Jesu*, p. 369, n. 47.

21. Cf. BauerWb, col. 1744, s.v.; Liddell-Scott, *Lex.*, p. 1993.

22. Cf. Col. Repond, 'Le costume du Christ': *Bib* 3 (1922), pp. 3–14; G. Dalman, *Arbeit und Sitte*, V (1937), pp. 126–129.

23. Cf. Bauer*Wb*, col. 913, s.v. 3, with evidence from Ps.-Demosthenes. Blas-Debr § 229, 2 compares the construction with the classical μάχεσθαι περί.

24. Thus E. D. Freed, *OT Quotations*, p. 99, n. 1.

25. Thus especially, F.-M. Braun, *Jean le Théologien*, II, pp. 98–101; cf. also MacGregor, p. 346; C. Spicq, *L'Épître aux Hebreux*, I (Paris, 1952), p. 122; J. Gnilka, *RQum* 2 (1959–60), p. 423; M.-É. Boismard, *Lumière et Vie*, 11 (1962), p. 55; B. Schwank, *Sein und Sendung*, 29 (1964), p. 295. But most of the recent exegetes are critical of this interpretation.

26. Reliance is placed particularly on Jn 6:69 (ὁ ἅγιος τοῦ θεοῦ) and 17:19 (ἁγιάζω ἐμαυτον), see on these passages; but other passages are also brought forward, cf. C. Spicq, 'L'origine johannique de la conception du Christ-prêtre dans L'Épître aux Hébreux', in: *Aux sources de la tradition chrétienne* (Mel. M. Goguel, Paris, 1950), pp. 258–269; F.-M. Braun, *Jean le Théol.*, II, pp. 87–101; M.-É. Boismard, 'La royauté du Christ dans le quatr. év.': *Lum Vie* 11 (1962), pp. 43–63, particularly 49–56. Critically, J. Gnilka in: *RQum* 2 (1959/60), pp. 421–425; rejecting A. Dauer, *Passionsgeschichte*, pp. 188f.

27. Thus already Cyprian, *De cath. eccl. unitate* 7; among the later exegetes Loisy, p. 486; Calmes, p. 180; Hoskyns-Davey, p. 529; Barrett, p. 458. On the interpretation in the Fathers, cf. M. Aubineau, 'La tunique sans couture du Christ. Exégèse patristique de Jn. 19:23', in: *Festschrift für J. Quasten* (Münster, 1970), pp. 100–127.

28. Philo (*fuga* 110–112; *spec. leg.*, I, 84–96; *Mos.*, II, 117–135) interprets the clothing of the high priest in terms of the parts of the universe – which the logos holds together. Cf. also Wis 18:24: 'For upon his [Aaron's] long robe the whole world was depicted.' Such an (in Hellenistic Judaism) obviously widespread cosmic speculation hardly finds support in John. Bultmann also is critical in this regard, p. 671, n. 2.

29. Cf. E. Haulotte, *Symbolique du Vêtement selon la Bible* (Paris, 1966), pp. 86–89 ('nudité et impiété'). On the passion of Jesus cf. pp. 143ff; '. . . the privation of clothing signifies always that the man is a victim of a *spoliation*' (p. 146). The compiler does not specially concern himself with Jn 19:23f.

30. B. Schwank, *Sein und Sendung*, 29 (1964), pp. 294ff, tends in a similar direction: 'When the dying Lord is robbed of his robe, he has taken from him something of his earthly personality' (p. 295); but the author goes beyond this in placing his emphasis on sharing: 'In the clothes Christ shares out something of himself. Jesus gives to us the mystery of his body' (*idem.*). Hence he reintroduces the symbolism of Christ's priesthood and that of the world-wide Church (which he sees symbolized in the quaternary number too). But that surely fails, in that the soldiers share the clothes among themselves.

31. Cf. C. A. Kneller, 'Joh 19, 26–27 bei den Kirchenvaetern (*ZKTh*, 40 (1961), pp. 597–614; T. Koehler, 'Les principales interprétations traditionelles de Jn. 19: 25–27, pendant les douze premiers siècles', *Études Mariales*, 16 (Paris, 1959), pp. 119–155; H. Langkammer, 'Christ's "Last Will and Testament" (Jn 19, 26, 27) in the Interpretation of the Fathers of the Church and the Scholastics', *Anton*, 43 (1968), pp. 99–109; further, the contributions in *Maria in Sacra Scriptura*, V (Rome, 1967). The modern literature on Jn 19:26f, especially outside the narrower exegetical circle, can hardly now be summarily surveyed *in toto*. Only the most important works will be mentioned in regard to specific viewpoints. Up to 1965, cf. also E. Malatesta, *St John's Gospel*, 2089–2118.

32. The alternatives are hardly admissible: historical or symbolic? A historical figure too, in accordance with the remaining persons in the gospel of John, can attain a 'typical' significance. Noteworthy in this respect is the contribution of J. Roloff, 'Der johanneische "Lieblingsjünger" und der Lehrer der Gerechtigkeit', *NTSt* 15 (1968/69), pp. 129–151. He rightly says: 'At the same time, admittedly, the contours of the beloved disciple pass over into the "typical". . . . This tension between the empirical and

"typical" cannot be resolved too quickly, as a contradiction, in one direction . . .'
(p. 141).

33. F. Spitta, *Johannes-Evangelium*, pp. 381ff, attributes v. 26 (but only 'one disciple') and v. 27a to the underlying text and regards v. 25, 'the (disciple) whom Jesus loved' in v. 26, and v. 27b as additions of the redactor. E. Hirsch, *Studien*, pp. 123f, decides the contrary: The women at the cross originate from the evangelist, the mention of Jesus' mother in v. 25 and the following scene from the redactor; behind that he sees the viewpoint 'that in 26 and 27, in historicizing allegory, Jesus entrusts the Church to the beloved disciple'. Cf. also H. Thyen, 'Johannes 13 und die 'Kirchliche Redaktion', p. 352, who regards all beloved-disciple passages in the gospel as editorial interpolations (by the editor with whom Jn 21 originates). But then one asks what purpose the women at the cross fulfilled for the evangelist, why is the mother of Jesus introduced here (allegorically?), and so on.

34. A Dauer, *Passionsgeschichte*, p. 192, rightly draws attention to the fact that an *activity* of the soldiers, but only *standing there* by the women, is spoken of, but the two are connected with μὲν – δέ.

35. Cf. Bultmann, p. 666; Dodd, *Historical Tradition*, pp. 126f; Dauer, *Passionsgeschichte*, p. 193.

36. Cf. J. Blinzler, *Die Brüder und Schwestern Jesu* (Stuttgart, 1967), pp. 111–113.

37. On Magdala, cf. G. Dalman, *Orte und Wege*, pp. 134–136 (E.T.: *Sacred Sites and Ways*, pp. 126–128); C. Kopp, *Heilige Stätten*, pp. 246–251 (E.T.: *Holy Places*, pp. 191–197). According to press reports, two Italian scholars now claim to have determined the exact situation of the old site.

38. Cf. Blinzler, *Brüder und Schwestern Jesu*, pp. 115f.

39. Cf. Blinzler, *ibid.*, p. 118: a valuation of the passage would only be possible with the help of a whole series of unproved suppositions and preconceptions.

40. B. Schwank, *Sein und Sendung*, 29 (1964), p. 299; R. E. Brown, p. 906, and in his *Introduction*, vol. I, p. xcvii.

41. Cf. L. Oberlinner, *Historische Überlieferung und christologische Aussage. Zur Frage der 'Brüder Jesu' in der Synopse* (dissertation, Freiburg im Br., 1973), MS pp. 64–72. He also doubts the very popular supposition, that Salome (according to Mt 27:56) was the mother of the sons of Zebedee; the first evangelist has rather *replaced* the Salome named in Mk 15:40 with the mother of the sons of Zebedee whom he already introduced earlier (20:20) – a plausible ground!

42. Instead of Κλωπᾶ VL Vg bo arm georg read Κλεοπα (Cleophae). These versions probably connect the man with the Emmaus disciple named in Lk 24:18.

43. Cf. J. Wettstein I, p. 955, who cites Lucian, *Toxari* 22 and *Proverb. Plut. adscript. Zenob.*, 564. It is concerned with the provision for surviving mothers without, however, a specific formula. The form of expression in John sounds instead Semitic-Jewish. Cf. E. Stauffer, *Jesus, Gestalt und Geschichte* (Berne, 1957), p. 104; E.T.: *Jesus and his Story*, p. 113: 'Jesus now makes use of this right [to make testamentary dispositions] and with the official formula of the old Jewish family law he places his mother under the protection of the apostle John.'

44. Cf. M. de Goedt, 'Un schème de révélation dans le quatr. év.', *NTSt* 8 (1961–62), pp. 142–150; he finds the same pattern in Jn 1:29–34, 35–39, 47–51. R. E. Brown follows him in this, p. 923.

45. H. Schürmann, 'Jesu letzte Weisung Jo 19, 26–27c': *idem, Ursprung und Gestalt* (Düsseldorf, 1970), pp. 13–29, particularly 20–25. On this account A. Dauer modified his earlier opinion in the essay 'Das Wort des Gekreuzigten . . .', *BZ*, 11 (1967), pp. 222–239; 12 (1968), pp. 80–93, see *Passionsgeschichte*, pp. 326ff.

46. 'Das Wort Jesu "Siehe deine Mutter" und die Annahme der Mutter durch den Jünger' (Johannes 19, 27b), *NT und Kirche (Festschrift für R. Schnackenburg*, Freiburg im Br., 1974) pp. 191–219, especially 204–214. He also compares 16:32: there, εἰς τὸ ἴδια has a negative tone, here in 19:27 a positive one. Further, he underlines the special meaning of λαμβάνειν in John, which means rather 'accept' (pp. 214–216). Hence he

translates: 'From that hour the disciple accepted her (in) among his own' (p. 216). Grateful as one is for this study, which is also instructive on the interesting history of the exegesis of Jn 19:27b (pp. 193–203), the symbolic meaning of Mary for the Church at which the commentator arrives, is not convincing, since it does not precisely fit or goes beyond the inferred meaning of the words.

47. Thus Epiphanius, Hilary, Jerome, Ambrose, cf. T. Koehler, *Principales interprétations,* pp. 120–134. The 'simple' interpretation of the disciple's earthly concern for Mary is represented, without this apologetic interest, by others: e.g., Augustine, *In Jo tr. CXIX,* 2 (CC 658f): Thomas Aquinas, *In Jo 19,* lect. IV, 9ff (Cai 452f); modern Catholic exegetes, such as Lagrange, Tillmann, Wikenhauser and most Protestants.

48. Such an exegesis is not yet evident for the Church Fathers; but in the Middle Ages it is represented by Anslem of Canterbury, Rupert of Deutz, Gerhoh of Reichersberg, Albert the Great and others, cf. H. Langkammer, *op. cit.;* further H. Barré, 'Marie et l'Église. Du Vénérable Bède à S. Albert le Grand', *Études Mariales,* 9 (1952), pp. 59–143. For the present day, see especially F.-M. Braun, *La Mère des fidèles* (Tournai-Paris, 1953), pp. 77–129; *idem., Jean le Théol.,* III/2 (Paris, 1972), pp. 108–115; P. Gaechter, *Maria im Erdenleben* (Innsbruck, 2nd ed., 1954), pp. 201–226; A. Kerrigan, 'Jn. 19, 25–27 in the Light of Johannine Theology and the OT', *Anton,* 35 (1960), pp. 369–416; A. Feuillet, 'Les adieux du Christ à sa Mère (Jn 19, 25–27) et la maternité spirituelle de Marie', *NRTh,* 86 (1964), pp. 469–489; *id.,* 'L'heure de la femme (Jn 16, 21) et l'heure de la Mère de Jésus' (Jn 19, 25–27), *Bib,* 47 (1966), pp. 169–184; 361–380; 557–573; R. E. Brown, pp. 925f; I. de la Potterie, 'La maternità spirituale di Maria e la fondazione della Chiesa (Gv 19, 25–27)', *Gesù Verità* (Turin, 1973), pp. 158–164; further the authors in the following footnotes. On the Protestant side too the symbolic interpretation of the Church is represented occasionally, thus by Hoskyns-Davey, p. 530; M. Thurian, *Maria* (Mainz-Kassel, 1965), pp. 191–200.

49. Cf. A. Kassing, *Die Kirche und Maria. Ihr Verhältnis im 12. Kapitel der Apokalypse* (Düsseldorf, 1958), pp. 67–71; B. Schwank, *Sein und Sendung,* 29 (1964), pp. 301–303 (according to him, John, as the disciple or pupil, represents the position of those who come to the Church from OT Judaism or from the Gentiles). The view that Mary symbolizes the ancient people of God or the believing part of the same, is partly represented on the Protestant side too, cf. MacGregor, pp. 347f; A Loisy, p. 488; W. Bauer, p. 224.

50. See especially the works by P. Gaechter, F.-M. Braun (see above); further, cf. J. Galot, *Marie dans L'Évangile* (Paris-Louvain, 1958), pp. 161–188; T. Gallus, *Die Mutter Jesu im Johannesevangelium* (Klagenfurt, 1963), pp. 27–52.

51. Therefore the Mariologians too rely above all on the tradition. Cf., e.g., J. Gummersbach in his new edition of Pohle, *Lehrbuch der Dogmatik,* II (Paderborn, 10, 1956), pp. 437f, who, after references to the typological interpretation of Jn 19:26f, says: 'In any case the "typical", mystical interpretation of the text is anchored within the doctrine of original sin. . . .' That also applies to the pronouncements of the popes since Leo XIII, up to Pius XII, and to the declaration of Vatican II (*Lumen gentium,* 58) which, compared with many utterances by theologians, is very restrained.

52. *Gospel of John,* pp. 483ff. Almost the same view was already expressed by A. Loisy, p. 488, save that he says further, after 'Jewish Christianity', 'Judaism inasmuch as it produced the Christ and the apostolic Church'. In my opinion, the two are to be distinguished.

53. A. Kragerud, *Der Lieblingsjünger,* p. 28.

54. Thus A. Dauer, *BZ,* 11 (1967), p. 235; *ibid., Passionsgeschichte,* p. 200.

55. That was my notion: 'Der Jünger, den Jesus liebte', *EKK* 2 (1970), pp. 97–117, particularly 107ff and 112f; however, only as a possibility (cf. p. 109). The question must be investigated further (see Excursus 18).

56. Luke refrains from this; he only briefly mentions the drinking of the vinegar, and that in connection with the mocking of Jesus beneath the cross. The soldiers mocked

The Gospel according to St John

him too, and approached 'offering him vinegar' (23:36). That is connected with the fact that this evangelist omits Jesus' cry, 'My God, my God, why have you forsaken me?'

57. On τελέω cf. Bauer *Wb*, cols. 1604f; on Jn 19:28 he adduces a saying of Diagoras of Melos: 'According to the will of God and destiny all is complete.' However, our passage contains not merely the thought of passive completion, but that of completion of the ministry taken over by Jesus, cf. G. Delling in: *ThWb*, VIII, p. 60, 17ff.; E.T.: *TDNT*, VIII, p. 59; Dauer, *Passionsgeschichte*, p. 210. Against watered-down interpretations ('it is over, it is at an end'), see Bultmann, p. 673, n. 6. But when he considers τετέλεσται as explicable from gnostic tradition (p. 674, n. 3), we must contradict him. The personal completion which in the gnostic myth is connected with the completion of the work, and with which the gnostics were decisively concerned, is not expressed in Jesus' cry. Instead of that, the Johannine Christ speaks of his glorification (13:31f; 17:1, 4f).

58. Thus G. Bampfylde, 'John XIX 28. A case for a different translation', *NT*, 11 (1969), pp. 247–260, who draws far-reaching conclusions from it: since the goal is the fulfilment of the Scripture, the concern is with the fulfilment of a great prophecy. He claims to recognize this in the eschatological pouring out of the Spirit, especially according to Zech 14:8 in association with Ezek 47, which begins with Jesus' death (cf. v. 30b; on this, see below).

59. On the moving forward of the ἵνα-clause, cf. Blass-Debr § 478; Moulton-Turner, Gr. III, p. 344; so also G. Delling, *ThWb*, VIII, p. 83, n. 16 (E.T.: *TDNT*, VIII, p. 82, n. 16): 'The thought of the ἵνα-clause is underlined by putting it first.'

60. ἡ γραφή could mean the whole of Scripture; in John the singular generally indicates a single scriptural passage, but now and then Scripture as a whole too (2:22?; 10:35; 20:9). In the source the quotation could mean the conclusion of the prophecy of Scripture about the passion of Jesus, thus, τελειοῦν could yet have a qualified sense after all. There is no other instance of NT evidence for the use of this word in connection with scriptural proof. To this effect not a few commentaries, and G. Reim, *Studien*, pp. 48f. Other exegetes treat πληροῦσθαι and τελειοῦσθαι as synonyms, thus Bultmann, p. 674, n. 1; cf. E. D. Freed, *OT Quotations*, p. 105, who traces the singular usage back to an intention of the evangelist.

61. *Contra*, Freed, *OT Quotations*, pp. 104f. T. Boman makes a case for Ps 63:1 (see below on v. 30).

62. Thus G. Reim, *Studien*, pp. 49 and 161.

63. Cf. H. W. Heidland, *ThWb* V, pp. 288f (E.T.: *TDNT*, V, pp. 288f).

64. Cf. Billerbeck, II, p. 581, who regards as possible the use of the stem of hyssop when it was woody. He mentions several pieces of evidence that hyssop was also used as wood (for burning). However, not a few scholars remain sceptical.

65. M.-J. Lagrange, p. 496, takes ὑσσῷ into his text. A very early copyist did not understand ὑσσωπεριθεντες, because he was unacquainted with ὑσσός (the Romans' javelin), and inserted the ὑσσωπω known to him, in its place. In the same sense, Bernard, II, p. 640; Dodd, *Historical Tradition*, p. 124, n.-text, and others.

66. Critical of such an interpretation Bultmann, p. 673, n. 5; Dodd, *Historical Tradition*, pp. 123f, n. 2; Dauer, *Passionsgeschichte*, p. 208.

67. T. Boman, 'Das letzte Wort Jesu': *StTh*, 17 (1963), pp. 103–119, makes a spirited and interesting attempt by comparison of psalm passages with the expression 'Eli atta' ('you are my God'), which was misunderstood by those standing around as the cry 'Elija ta' ('come, Elijah!'), to discover Jesus' original saying. Among the four psalm passages which come into consideration (22:10; 63:1; 118:28; 140:6), he regards Psalm 118:28 as the historical word on the lips of Jesus; it was a praising and thanking of God (from the Hallel). The primitive Church, which only knew of '*Eli atta*', pointed to other psalm passages: Mk/Mt to the psalm of suffering 22:10, John to Ps 63:1 and Luke to Ps 30:15 LXX (only according to the Greek text). For that reason Boman traces the quotation in v. 28 back to Ps 63:1: 'O God, thou art my God, I seek thee, my soul thirsts for thee . . .', and understands it as Jesus' desire to come to the Father (p. 115). This attractive

theory contains, however, too many points of uncertainty and will hardly do justice to the facts according to the history of tradition; it does not take account, for Jn 19:28f, of the connection with the drinking of vinegar.

68. The manner of speaking is unusual; literal parallels are scarcely to be discovered. Only in the apocryphal apostolic acts is παραδιδόναι τὸ πνεῦμα rather often in evidence (ActJoh, 115; ActPtPl, 83 and others; cf. Dauer, Passionsgeschichte, pp. 214f). A variant of Lk 23:46 (παρατίθεμαι τό πνεῦμα μου) may hardly be supposed; Schlatter, p. 352, would understand the description in Jn 19:30b in line with the picture of falling asleep. Nor is a connection in the history of tradition with Is 53:12 very probable; the passive παρεδόθη is found twice and the idea of the vicarious expiatory death is very distant from Jn 19:30.

69. Cf. Bultmann, p. 673, n. 5; Dauer, Passionsgeschichte, p. 214, thinks: 'The detailed and elaborate description of Jesus' death corresponds to the manner of the source.'

70. See the above-mentioned essay in NT 11 (1969) pp. 247–260. As criticism also the following: apart from the questionable connection of the ἵνα-clause with what precedes it, the translation of τελειοῦν as 'to bring to fruition' (p. 252) is also disputable. The bowing of the head to Mary and the disciple, which is already supposed by Hoskyns, would have to be expressly mentioned because the scene with the drink comes in between. Further theological links which Bampfylde claims to find (with the transfer of the Spirit from Elijah to Elisha, with the Samaria-scene of Chapter 4 and others), remain purely speculative.

71. Dodd, Interpret., p. 437: completion of Jesus' sacrifice (cf. Jn 17:19) for the initiation of believers (cf. CHerm XIII, p. 21 πάντα τελεῖαι); E. Stauffer, Jesus, p. 107, E.T.: Jesus and his Story, p. 117: Jesus prays the Sabbath kiddush in the light of Gen 2:1–3 (God completes his work of creation in the days of salvation); others: the eschatological turning-point. For criticism cf. the excursus in Dauer, Passionsgeschichte, pp. 211–213; Dauer himself sees the point of contact for the evangelist's formulation in Is 55:11.

72. J. Wellhausen, Ev. Joh., pp. 89f: Vv. 34, 35, and 37 are added later; F. Spitta, Johannes-Evangelium, pp. 384ff. The basic document contained only v. 31 (apart from 'since it was the day of Preparation' and the request that the legs be broken). 33–34 (without the crurifragium of the others crucified); E. Hirsch, Studien pp. 125f: vv. 31–34 from the evangelist, vv. 35–37 from the redactor; R. Bultmann pp. 677f: vv. 34b–35 addition of the church redaction; R. T. Fortna, Gospel of Signs, p. 131: vv. 34b–35 'cannot be pre-Johannine'. On what follows cf. also I. Broer, Die Urgemeinde und das Grab Jesu. Eine Analyse der Grablegungsgeschichte im Neuen Testament (Munich, 1972), pp. 201–249 (reconstructs the account of the source just as in the text above, apart from v. 34b, cf. p. 218).

72a. Literally 'dispose of' (αἴρειν); but from the situation the same is intended as expressed by Mk 15:46/Lk 23:53 in καθαιρεῖν. This is seen from 19:38. Bauer translates it in v. 31 with 'dispose of', in v. 38 with 'fetch'; yet, presumably on both occasions, the same linguistic usage of the source is to be found.

73. Cf. Josephus, Ant., XVI, 163; Rabbinic in Billerbeck, I, p. 1053, under e.

74. Thus Bultmann, p. 676, n. 6; he is followed by J. Jeremias, Abendmahlsworte, p. 75 (E.T.: Eucharistic Words, p. 55).

75. Billerbeck II, p. 581, shows only the possibility of which day could be so described. Against that, the accompanying word 'high' seems to have entered into Christian usage; cf. MartPol 8:1; 21.

76. Thus also Bultmann pp. 666f: The source will already have offered the combination before us; the main motif of vv. 31–37 corresponds to the Church's tradition (fulfilling of the Scripture), vv. 38–42 have the character of a didactic-legendary construction. Admittedly, that is also problematical. Fortna, Gospel of Signs, p. 131, attributes the basic form of vv. 31–37 and 38–42 to the source. Further cf. I. Broer, op. cit., pp. 219f; 230.

77. In Christian legend the soldier has received the name Longinus (according to the Greek λόγχη=lance). He has also been identified with the centurion mentioned in the synoptics. J. R. Michaels considers this seriously: 'The Centurion's Confession and the Spear-Thrust': *CBQ*, 29 (1967), pp. 102–109. But with it he ignores problems of the history of tradition.

78. For ἔνυξεν (from νύσσω) was mistakenly read or heard ἤνοιξεν. For further smaller differences (plural instead of singular), see in Tischendorf's apparatus.

79. *In Jo. tr.* CXX, 2 (CC 661). On the symbolic explanations of the Fathers, B. F. Westcott offers a good survey pp. 284–286.

80. There is also discussion whether the thrust was made into the right or left side. B. Schwank, *Sein und Sendung*, 29 (1964), p. 344, thinks that artists under the influence of the vision in Zech 13:1 (the water from the spring of the temple trickled down from the right side) represented the wounds in Jesus' side on the right. On the lance-thrust as a precaution against a possible revival, cf. Quintilian, *Declamationes maiores*, VI, 9: 'cruces succiduntur, percussos sepeliri carnifex non vetat' (cited by W. Bauer, p. 225).

80a. In some mss. the reverse order (water and blood) is also found: 054 579 e bo, further in Church Fathers. M.-E. Boismard, *RB* 60 (1953), pp. 348–350, adduces many patristic witnesses and thinks it is the original reading. But an influence from 1 Jn 5:6 must be supposed. The Boharic papyrus Bodmer III (CSCO 177, p. 42) reads 'blood and water'.

81. Cf. J. Blinzler, *Prozess Jesu*, pp. 382–384, who relies on K.-J. Shulte, 'Der Tod Jesu in der Sicht der modernen Medizin', *Berliner Medizin*, 14 (1963), pp. 177–186; 210–220. J. Massingberd-Ford, *NTSt* 15 (1968–69), pp. 337f (relying on a Talmud passage, *Oholoth* c 3, 5) would understand the double expression in Jn 19:34 as 'mixed blood', with a special allusion to the passover lamb.

82. See the passages in E. Schweizer, *Neotestamentica* (Zürich-Stuttgart, 1963), p. 382.

83. *Lev* r 15 (cited in Billerbeck II, pp. 582f): Man returns the balance; he is one half water and one half blood. Cf. also *4 Macc* 9:20: At the martyrdom of the eldest of the seven brothers not only blood but blood-water flowed over the wheel on which he was stretched.

84. Origen, *C. Celsus*, II, 36 (GCS II, pp. 161f); in more modern times A. Loisy, p. 492 ('miraculous sign'), Lagrange, p. 499, Bauer, p. 226, Hoskyns-Davey, p. 533, Bultmann, pp. 677f.

85. G. Richter, in a thorough examination, 'Wasser und Blut aus der durchbohrten Seite Jesu' (Joh 19:34b), *MueThZ*, 21 (1970), pp. 1–21, opines that from 1 Jn 5:6, Jn 19:34b is to be understood as anti-Docetic. As worthy of attention as his interpretation of 1 Jn 5:6 may be (on this, see in appendix of the fifth edition of my *Johannine Letters*), the starting-point from this passage, as Richter himself sees (op. ·cit., p. 2), is questionable for Jn 19: 34b. That is even more so if v. 34b already comes from the Johannine source. For v. 35 an anti-Docetic intention of the redaction should be mentioned (see *ad loc.*). M. Miguens, 'Salió sangre y agua' (Jn. 19:34), *Studii Bibl. Franc. Liber Annuus* 14 (1963/64), pp. 5–31, explains the passage independently of 1 Jn 5:6 from the passover ritual: The blood of the sacrificial lamb had to flow, no bone was allowed to be broken. In this case, the water remains without explanation.

86. The connection with Jesus Christ is taken up in reliance on 1 Jn 2:6; 3:3, 5, 7, 16; 4:17, among others by Zahn, Lagrange, Tillmann, Strachan, Bauer, Hoskyns-Davey. In John's gospel ἐκεῖνος is also connected with others: in 1:33; 5:19, 37, 38; 6:29 and frequently with God, in 1:8; 5:35 with John the Baptist, in 5:46f with Moses and so on. *Perhaps* there is already a narrower usage in 1 Jn. Reference is made to Iamblichus, *Vita Pyth.*, 255: The students called their master Pythagoras θεῖος during his life, and ἐκεῖνος after his death. If the usage of 1 Jn was similarly established, that explanation would be possible because 19:35 is editorial. Bultmann, pp. 678f, supposes that it originally said: καὶ ἐκεῖνον οἴδαμεν (as Nonnus read); but ἐκεῖνος is scarcely to be doubted from the standpoint of textual criticism.

87. Cf. Blass-Debr § 291, 6 (only his scepticism concerning the textual tradition goes too far); Moulton-Turner, Gr., p. 46.

88. The reading πιστεύητε B ℵ* Ψ Orig is to be preferred as against πιστεύσητε which the remaining textual witnesses read (similarly as in 20:31). An instant of 'coming to believe' is hardly intended. Most editions of the text decide for the reading in the present; differently, B. Weiss, v. Soden (however, reading in the present in the first apparatus), UBS Greek NT.

89. At Jesus' death blood being put first is natural; in 1 Jn 5:6 water being placed first is likewise easily explained if the reference is to the baptism of Jesus. G. Richter, *op. cit.*, pp. 8ff, want to understand the coming 'in water and blood' in relation to the Christ's appearance in the world of men, analogously to 1 Jn 4:2 (ἐν σαρκί). The Docetists had believed that Christ only had a body out of water not out of blood. The proofs are worthy of attention but not compelling. Why then the further emphasis on the πνεῦμα as the one witnessing?

90. The mythical viewpoint that the gods do not have blood in their veins has been referred to E. Schweizer, *Neotestamentica*, pp. 382f, recalls Homer, *Iliad* 5, 34ff: The goddess wounded by a lance-thrust only has blood-water not blood streaming from her because the gods are bloodless. According to Plutarch, *Morals*, 180 e and elsewhere, Alexander said to such as held him to be a god: 'This is blood, as you see, not blood-water as it flows in the blessed gods.' Schweizer doubts that the evangelist thought so substantively, but regards it as possible that these views were an influence on the Gnostics. G. Richter, who only adduces gnostic testimonies, rejects such a connection with mythical thought in the case of the Gnostics (*op. cit.*, p. 13).

91. Above all C. H. Dodd, *According to the Scriptures* (London, 1953), pp. 98f; *idem*, *Historical tradition*, pp. 42–44; 131f; further, Zahn, pp. 663f; C. C. Torrey, JBL 50 (1931), p. 231; M. Dibelius, *Botschaft und Geschichte*, I, p. 237; A. Dauer, *Passionsgeschichte*, pp. 139–141.

92. So G. Reim, *Studien*, p. 52.

93. Thus Bultmann, pp. 676f; in principle (without supposing a source) B. Lindars also, *NT Apologetic*, pp. 95–97, *ibid.*, *Gospel of John*, p. 590.

94. On Zech 12:10, cf. M. Delcor, 'Un problème du critique textuelle, et d'exégèse, Zach., XII, 10', *RB* 58 (1951), pp. 189–199, P. Lamarche, *Zacharie IX–XIV* (Paris 1961), especially pp. 82–84. On Jn 19:37, A. Vergote, 'L'exaltation du Christ en croix selon le quatr. év.', *EThLov*, 28 (1952), pp. 5–23; W. Thüsing, *Erhöhung und Verherrlichung*, pp. 19–22; J. Heer, *Der Durchbohrte* (Rome, 1966), pp. 124–133; R. Schnackenburg, 'Das Schriftzitat in Joh 19, 37', *Wort, Lied und Gottesspruch*, II (*Festschrift für J. Ziegler*, Würzburg, 1972), pp. 239–247.

95. Cf. B. Lindars, *NT Apologetic*, pp. 122–127; E. D. Freed, *OT Quotations*, pp. 114f; C. H. Dodd, *Historical Tradition*, pp. 123f; G. Reim, *Studien*, pp. 55f.

96. Some scholars think that the text of Jn 19:37 is of Christian origin, perhaps coming from a book of 'testimonies'; cf. E. D. Freed, *OT Quotations*, pp. 114f. But a written collection of 'testimonies' is, having regard to Justin, *Dial.*, 14, 8, who mistakenly attributes the citation from Zech 12:10 to Hosea, doubtful. Cf. further my article in the *Festschrift für J. Ziegler*, pp. 241–244.

97. J. H. Bernard, p. 652, Zahn, p. 665, and others connect those 'looking' closely with the Jews; cf. also A. Vergote, *op. cit.*, p. 20. Freed, *OT Quotations*, pp. 115f, explains from Mt 24:30 and Rev 1:7 in the judicial sense, similarly M. Miguens, *op. cit.*, pp. 28ff. R. E. Brown, pp. 954f, thinks of two groups: the Jews now already judged and the believers (represented in the disciple whom Jesus loved), to whom life is given. W. Thüsing and J. Heer especially explain in the sense of salvation (see above).

98. The relation of the two passages to each other is the main thesis of J. Heer; cf. also W. Thüsing, *Erhöhung und Verherrlichung*, pp. 160f and 172; C. K. Barrett, pp. 462f; R. E. Brown, pp. 949f.

99. That does not rule out that in 1 Jn 5:8 the sacraments are intended. The entire passage 5:6f probably looks back to Jn 19:34 and exploits the image further. Bultmann,

Johannesbriefe, p. 83, treats 1 Jn 5:7–8 (Greek text!) as an editorial gloss (with explanation of water and blood in the sense of the sacraments of baptism and the Eucharist as Jn 19:34b).

100. Thus, finally, M. Dibelius, *Botschaft und Geschichte*, I, pp. 236f; against this D. Daube, *ZNW* 48 (1957), pp. 122f; G. Reim, *Studien*, p. 55. On historicity cf. also Barrett, p. 461; Dodd, *Historical Tradition*, p. 133.

100a. Cf. I. Broer, *Die Urgemeinde und das Grab Jesu*, pp. 223–229.

101. J. Wellhausen, *Ev. Joh.*, p. 90, and F. Spitta, *Joh-Ev*, pp. 387f, think that Joseph of Arimathaea and Nicodemus were inserted only later (Spitta: by the one reworking the basic writing). P. Benoit, 'Marie-Madeleine et les Disciples au Tombeau selon Jn 20:1–8', *Judentum, Urchistentum, Kirche* (*Festschrift für J. Jeremias*, Berlin, 1960), pp. 141–152, particularly 147, supposes that v. 38 comes additionally from the synoptic tradition. Similarly, R. Mahoney, *Two Disciples at the Tomb. The Background and Message of Jn 20:1–10* (Frankfurt am Main & Berne, 1974), pp. 121–140, who regards 19:39–42 as the traditional Johannine burial story, before which v. 38 from the synoptic tradition (pp. 127–131) was inserted. This theory would be tenable to some extent, if it were not necessary to suppose a source used by the evangelist. Since there are strong grounds in favour of that, the opposite, that Nicodemus was inserted additionally by John, is more likely; thus also Bultmann, pp. 667f. Cf. also I. Broer, *op. cit.*, pp. 231f.

101a. Fortna, *Gospel of Signs*, p. 132, thinks that Nicodemus already appeared in the source and 3:1 was found originally before 19:39. The evangelist brought forward the remark for use in his story in the third chapter, and then inserted the reference to it in 19:39. This would be somewhat complicated procedure which also does not explain νυκτός. On Nicodemus, cf. vol. 1, p. 365.

102. Cf. J. Blinzler, *Prozess Jesu*, pp. 385–404, who would supplement the short synoptic reports with the more detailed Johannine one. Broer in his above mentioned monograph makes a more critical assessment. He does not doubt the tomb itself; but, in regard to the burial narratives, he states in conclusion that the laying of Jesus in the tomb can no longer be reconstructed in exact detail (p. 294).

103. J. Blinzler, *Prozess Jesu*, p. 393, n. 41, also has to admit that. Cf. also R. E. Brown, pp. 956f.

104. Cf. I. Broer, *Die Urgemeinde und das Grab Jesu*, pp. 139–173 (p. 173 reconstruction of the pre-Marcan tradition).

105. Arimathaea is the ancient Ramah at the western edge of Mount Ephraim, the home and burial place of Samuel (1 Sam 1:1; LXX: Αρμαθαιμ; cf. also 1 Macc 11:34). The present-day location is disputed; in most cases, the village of Rentis, fourteen km northeast of Lod, is suggested. Cf. F.-M. Abel, *Géographie*, II, pp. 427ff; J. Simons, *The Geographical and Topographical Texts of the OT* (Leiden, 1959), p. 572. That Joseph of Arithamaea was resident in Jerusalem is understood from his designation as βουλευτής (on this disputed expression, cf. Blinzler, *Prozess Jesu*, pp. 392f, n. 39) and from his approach to Pilate.

106. In Jn 12:42 the 'authorities' are charged with not confessing their faith in Jesus 'for fear of the Pharisees'. But in 19:38 the comment is hardly intended as a criticism; rather, the difficult situation for Jesus' followers is intended to be obvious (cf. 7:13; 9:22), or the evangelist wants to hint that this man (he is not called an ἄρχων) freed himself from such fear (which still filled the disciples according to 20:19).

107. A noteworthy v. 1 reads at the end the plural ἦλθον . . . ἦραν: א* N W VL (save for f aur q) sa sy^pal Tat^ar. Some scholars regard it as original (thus Bultmann, pp. 679f., n. 9). This is not to be ruled out for the source; but the singular can also be understood causally. Joseph of Arimathaea could not undertake the removal of the body by himself.

108. Cf. R. Mahoney, *Two Disciples*, pp. 127f, who opposes such an argument.

109. μίγμα pl; v. 1 ἐλίγμα (=roll) B א* W: σμίγμα φ pc. No differences in fact result. As to the mixture, some scholars think of the so-called *Aloë medicinalis* in liquid form; but that is unlikely. Cf. J. Blinzler, 'Zur Auslegung der Evangelienberichte über Jesu Begräbnis', *MueThZ* 3 (1952), pp. 403–414, particularly 411–414.

110. Cf. Billerbeck II, p. 53; the view that Abraham was embalmed makes a late appearance (*Ta'an*, 5b). A. Hermann, article '*Einbalmsamierung*', RAC, IV, cols. 803–805, thinks that genuine embalming occurred only in individual cases and by Egyptian influence.

111. Billerbeck II, p. 584, cites a story about the burial of R. Gamliel I (around AD 40–50): A proselyte burnt more than eighty sticks (perfumed substances) and justified this as follows: 'Is R. Gamliel not much better than a hundred kings?' On the sumptuous burial of kings, cf, e.g., 2 Chron 16:14 (king Asa); Josephus, *Ant.*, XVII, 199 (Herod the Great). R. E. Brown, p. 960, thinks that burial in a garden may also indicate this; but he doubts whether the regal motif is intended.

112. On this word, cf. A. Vaccari, '"Ἔδησαν αὐτὸ ὀθονίοις (Johannes 19, 40)', *Miscellanea Biblica B. Ubach* (Montserrat, 1953), pp. 375–386; J. Blinzler, 'Ὀθόνια und andere Stoffbezeichnungen im Wäschekatalog des Ägypters Theophanes und im NT', *Philologus*, 99 (1955), pp. 158–166.

113. J. Blinzler, *Prozess Jesu*, pp. 396f; R. E. Brown, p. 942, who cites A. Vaccari (previous footnote) and C. Lavergne in *Sindon*, III (1961), pp. 1–58 (inaccessible to me).

114. Cf. Billerbeck I, p. 1048.

115. Cf. Blinzler, *Prozess Jesu*, pp. 396f, n. 52.

116. The washing and anointing of a dead person was, according to M. Shabbat XXIII, 5 also allowed on the sabbath. According to Mk 16:1 the women bought ἀρώματα for this purpose. Billerbeck II, p. 53, connects the two passages; he thinks that spices, especially myrrh and aloes, were mixed with the oil, but finds no evidence for this in the rabbinic writings. R. E. Brown, p. 942, regards the ἀρώματα in Jn 19:40 as a third element beside the mixture of myrrh and aloes ('aromatic oils'). But that does not follow from the text. I cannot enter into the problem of Mk 16:1 (Matthew and Luke had already made alterations).

117. Cf. R. E. Brown, p. 943, *ad loc*. In the *Gospel of Peter* 24 it says: 'And he [Joseph] took the Lord, washed him, wrapped him in linen and brought him into his own sepulchre, called Joseph's Garden.' The passage shows how the details in the gospels were combined and supplemented (washing of the body also).

118. N 69 pc read ξένον instead of καινόν, presumably a mis-hearing.

119. Cf. R. E. Brown, p. 959; I. Broer, *op. cit.*, pp. 239f.

120. Cf. G. Dalman, *Orte und Wege Jesu*, pp. 378–402 (E.T.: *Sacred Sites and Ways*, pp. 358–381); J. Jeremias, *Golgotha*, pp. 3–7; 28–33; A. Parrot, *Golgotha et Saint-Sépulcre* (Neuchâtel-Paris, 1955); C. Kopp, *Heilige Stätten*, pp. 436–444 (E.T.: *Holy Places*, pp. 389–394). Certain doubts remain about the course of the 'second wall' cf. Kopp, pp. 425f (E.T.: pp. 380f); but that the church of the Holy Sepulchre lies outside this (at the time of Jesus) existing city-wall is confirmed by Jewish rock-tombs; cf. H. Vincent-F.-M.Abel, *Jérusalem*, II (Paris, 1914), pp. 192f.; A. Parrot, *op. cit.*, pp. 27–34.

121. τῶν Ἰουδαίων om. VL (apart from aur c f q) sy; but that is presumably explained by assimilation to v. 31.

122. On the older hypotheses of C. Guignebert, M. Goguel, G. Baldensperger, cf. F.-M. Braun, 'La sépulture de Jésus', RB 45 (1936), pp. 34–52; 184–200; 346–363 (also published separately, Paris, 1937). Lastly, J. Spencer Kennard Jr, 'The Burial of Jesus', *JBL* 74 (1955), pp. 227–238, represented the hypothesis as follows: before two in the afternoon Jesus was laid in the criminals' grave by the soldiers in the presence of the women; in the evening, however, he was buried in his own tomb by Joseph of Arimathaea. This hypothesis, which arbitrarily explains and combines the various forms of the tradition, has not found any favour.

123. Cf. R. Mahoney, *Two Disciples*, pp. 137–140: On the one hand, the burial represents a conclusion and, on the other hand, prepares for a new beginning. In the Johannine Church the burial was never narrated without the dependent Easter stories; but it was related in such a way that after the darkness the light of Easter morning shone out the more impressively. But can the Johannine burial be described as 'darkness'?

465

The Gospel according to St John

SECTION VII: Pages 300–340

1. The extensive literature on the Easter stories includes: H. Grass, *Ostergeschehen und Osterberichte* (Göttingen, ³1964); H. Frhr von Campenhausen, *Der Ablauf der Osterereignisse und das leere Grab* (Heidelberg, ³1966); J. Kremer, *Die Osterbotschaft der vier Evangelien* (Stuttgart, 1968); U. Wilckens, *Auferstehung. Das biblische Auferstehungszeugnis historisch untersucht und erklärt* (Stuttgart-Berlin, 1970); X. Léon-Dufour, *Résurrection de Jésus et message pascal* (Paris, 1971); R. H. Fuller, *The Formation of the Resurrection Narratives* (London, 1972); B. Rigaux, *Dieu l'a ressuscité* (Gembloux, 1973, with further literature). On Matthew see especially F. Neirynck, 'Les femmes au tombeau. Étude de la rédaction matthéenne' (Mt 28:1–10), *NTSt* 15 (1968/69), pp. 168–190; J. Lange, *Das Erscheinen des Auferstandenen im Evangelium nach Mattaeus* (Wuerzburg, 1973). On Luke cf. P. Schubert, 'The Structure and Significance of Lk 24', *Neutestamentliche Studien für R. Bultmann* (Berlin, 1954), pp. 165–186; E. Lohse, *Die Auferstehung Jesu Christi im Zeugnis des Lukasevangeliums* (Neukirchen, 1961); G. Lohfink, *Die Himmelfahrt Jesu* (Munich, 1971); J. Wanke, *Die Emmauserzählung* (Leipzig, 1974).

2. R. E. Brown, p. 965, divides: A. 1 scene: At the tomb, 20:1–18; 1. episode: Visits to the empty tomb, 1–10, introduction 1–2, main action 3–10; 2. episode: Jesus appears to Mary Magdalene 11–18, link 11–13, main action 14–18. B. 2. scene: Where the disciples are gathered 20:19–29; 1. episode: Jesus appears to the disciples 19–23, introduction and sending; 2. episode: Jesus appears to Thomas 24–29, link 24–25, main action 26–29. Cf. also G. Ghiberti, *I racconti pasquali del capitolo 20 di Giovanni* (Brescia, 1972), pp. 17ff.

3. Cf. P. Benoit, 'Marie-Madeleine et les disciples au tombeau selon Jn 20:1–18', *Judentum, Urchristentum, Kirche (Festschrift für J. Jeremias*, Berlin, 1960), pp. 141–152 (three different traditions, see below); R. E. Brown, p. 996, divides the material as follows: (*a*) Material with parallels in all synoptics, (*b*) contacts with individual synoptics, (*c*) special Johannine material; E. L. Bode, *The First Easter Morning* (Rome, 1970), pp. 72–86; R. Mahoney, *Two Disciples at the Tomb. The Background and Message of Jn 20, 1–10* (Berne-Frankfurt am Main, 1974), pp. 171–227 (criticizes past attempts at tradition- and source-criticism); G. Ghiberti, *I racconti*, pp. 79–99.

4. J. Wellhausen, *Ev. Joh.*, pp. 92f; E. Hirsch, *Studien*, pp. 126f; R. Bultmann, p. 682.

5. 'The Resurrection Narratives in Luke' (XXIV. 12–53): *NTSt*, 2 (1955/56), pp. 110–114 (he regards Lk 24:12 as original).

6. 'The Composition of John XX', *NTSt*, 7 (1960/61), pp. 142–147; cf. *idem, Gospel of John*, pp. 596f.

7. *Op. cit.* (p. 346, n. 101). The author thinks Lk 24:12 presupposes an older state of the Johannine tradition than in Jn 20:3–10 (p. 143).

8. 'Die Vorlage der Osterberichte in Joh. 20': *ZNW* 55 (1964), pp. 197–220.

9. *Gospel of Signs*, pp. 134–141, on the angel-scene, p. 139.

10. *Two Disciples*, pp. 224–226.

11. Cf. R. Mahoney, *Two Disciples*, pp. 202–212.

12. The plural on the lips of an individual is not, to be sure, necessarily a sign that the source told of several persons. Cf. Bultmann, p. 684, n. 1 (a familiar mode of speech); E. L. Bode, *First Easter Morning*, pp. 74f., who recalls 3:2, 11; 9:31; 14:5. However, the instances are differently set. In the event that the source spoke only of Mary, it still acknowledged several women, cf. 19:25.

13. *Gospel of Signs*, pp. 139f.; Fortna strikes out v. 15, because it contains the Johannine theme of misunderstanding, further in v. 16, στραφεῖσα. But is it a 'misunderstanding'? With this Johannine stylistic device no 'explanations' are added.

Surely, it is rather a 'non-recognition', which, in a stylistically appropriate manner, is corrected by Jesus' form of address. Besides, the 'gardener' also fits the source, cf. 19:41.

14. Cf. L. Schenke, *Auferstehungsverkündigung und leeres Grab* (Stuttgart, 1968), who supposes a cultic aetiological legend. But his opinion has received a great deal of criticism; cf. among others E. L. Bode, *First Easter Morning*, pp. 170f; G. Delling, *ThLZ*, 95 (1970), p. 26. On Mk 16: 1–8, cf. further J. Delorme, 'Résurrection et tombeau de Jésus: Marc 16, 1–8 dans la tradition évangélique', *La résurrection du Christ et l'exégèse moderne* (Paris, 1969), pp. 105–151; B. Rigaux, *Dieu l'a ressuscité*, pp. 184–200.

15. On the designation of the first day of the week with μιά τ. σ. (cardinal number instead of ordinal number), cf. Blass-Debr § 247, 1 (already in LXX, influence of the Hebrew); Moulton-Turner, *Grammar*, p. 187. On the comparison with the Easter kerygma see K. Lehmann, *Auferweckt am dritten Tag nach der Schrift* (Freiburg im Breisgau, 1968), pp. 159ff: 355f. L. Schenke, *Auferstehungsverkündigung*, pp. 57–63, regards the detail of the day of the week (Sunday) as cult-orientated; that remains a pure supposition. On the origin of the celebration of Easter on the Sunday, cf. lastly W. Huber, *Passa und Ostern. Untersuchungen zur Osterfeier der alten Kirche* (Berlin, 1969), pp. 49–61.

16. This detail of time is lacking in W a b c; but it is certainly original, cf. 18:28, where it presumably also stood in the source. Is there an intention behind this? The trial which leads to death begins early in the morning; the events which testify to Jesus' resurrection also begin early in the morning.

17. Ephraem, *Comm.*, 21, 27 (Armen. CSCO 145, 235f; Syr. L. Leloir 229) on Jn 20:17. However, R. E. Brown, p. 981, *ad loc.*, is mistaken when he says that the Syr. sin. in 20:1 and 18 leaves out 'Magdalene' and retains only the ambiguous 'Mary'. A. Loisy, p. 504, thinks that Tatian already pointed to Mary the mother of Jesus in the *Diatessaron* and thereby perhaps relied on an older tradition than the Johannine. That is a vague hypothesis, despite the form of address γύναι, which applies to the mother of Jesus in Jn 2:4 and 19:26. She is never mentioned by name in John and her rôle seems to be completed with 19:27, as Loisy himself sees.

18. βλέπειν seems restricted in John's gospel to an external seeing and observing, with one exception, 5:19, which however, perhaps, is explained by the analogy (Son-Father). The alternation of the verbs of seeing in vv. 6 and 8 is striking, but, at most, indicates nuances of meaning, cf. on v. 8. On the word cf. further W. Michaelis, in: *ThWb*, V, p. 317, and more often, especially pp. 343f., E.T.: *TDNT*, V, p. 317, especially pp. 343f.

19. Lk 24:12 om. D a b d e l r[l] sy[pal mss] Marcion Diatessaron Eusebius (once in two quotations). Cf. the apparatus in UBS Greek NT, where the verse is taken up in the text in brackets (degree of certainty 'D'). J. Jeremias, *Abendmahlsworte*, p. 143, n. 2 (E.T.: *Eucharistic Words*, p. 97, n. 1), supposes that in sy[cur. sin] also the verse was only inserted later on.

20. J. Jeremias, *Abendmahlsworte*, pp. 143f (E.T.: *Eucharistic Words*, pp. 97ff); A. R. C. Leaney, *NTSt*, 2 (1955–56) pp. 110–114, and *Gospel Acc. to St Luke* (London, 1958), *ad loc.*; P. Benoit, *Marie-Madeleine*, pp. 142–144 (later addition by Luke himself); K. Aland, 'Die Bedeutung des P[75] für den Text des NT', *Studien zur Überlieferung des Neuen Testaments und seines Textes* (Berlin, 1967), pp. 155–172, particularly 168. Against that again, sceptically, R. Mahoney, *Two Disciples* pp. 41–69. He treats the present historic βλέπει (pp. 54f, 57) as the main argument from the linguistic point of view. J. Muddiman, 'A Note on Reading Luke XXIV. 12', *EThLov*, 48 (1972), pp. 542–548; F. Neirynck, 'The Uncorrected Historic Present in Lk. XXIV. 12': *ibid.*, pp. 548–553, once again defend the primary character of Lk 24:12.

21. This conclusion from R. Mahoney (*op. cit.*, p. 69), after his careful discussion of the pro and contra, must be confirmed.

22. M.-E. Boismard, *RB*, 67 (1960), p. 406, and 69 (1962), p. 202, n.-text, supposes two layers on the basis of the different designations of that disciple; cf. also R. E. Brown, p. 983, *ad loc.*

22a. Some copyists change the plural to the singular οἶδα (cf. v. 13): 028 033 348 477 e sy^s. p arm georg. The testimony of e and sy^s is noteworthy; however, οἴδαμεν is the *lectio difficilior* and very well attested.

23. Cf. Blass-Debr § 135.

24. R. Mahoney, *Two Disciples*, especially pp. 250–260, allows the two disciples no more than a functional significance: Peter, as the link with the Jesus-tradition, determines the facts, and the other disciple, only a literary figure, makes understandable the answer of faith which these facts demand. The evangelist is supposed to have composed in this way without support in the tradition. However, in this, apart from the question of the tradition, the importance of the two persons may be underestimated, cf. Chapter 21.

25. Cf. the reconstructions of E. G. Auer, *Die Urkunde der Auferstehung Jesu* (Wuppertal 1959), and M. Balagué, 'La prueba de la Resurrección (Jn 20, 6–7)', *EstBib*, 25 (1966), pp. 169–192. For criticism, cf. R. E. Brown, pp. 986f, *ad loc.*

26. οὐ μετὰ τῶν ὀθ – ἀλλὰ χωρίς correspond to each other and describe the separate position of the napkin (χωρίς adverb, see BauerWb col. 1760, s.v. 1); ἐντυλίσσω, from 'to wrap up in a cloth' (Mt 27:59; Lk 23:53), is here presumably meant to indicate the rolled-up napkin. Most difficult is εἰς ἕνα τόπον; BauerWb, earlier on in col. 458, refers to Josephus, *Ant.*, VI, 125. This passage can make clear what is meant: The King (Saul) assembles the people in one place (εἰς ἕνα τόπον); he himself appears with his son (Jonathan) at another (κατ' ἄλλο μέρος); (cf. 1 Sam 14:40). Hence a contrast is intended, cf. also Mayser, *Grammatik*, II/1, p. 57, in the middle; the meaning is then 'in a place by itself'.

27. *In Jo hom.*, 85, 4 (PG 59, col. 465). cf. also Theodore of Haraclea, fr. 401 (Reuss, p. 168) and – very similar – Ammonius of Alexandria, fr. 612 (Reuss, p. 348f): 'If he had been abducted by enemies, then, on account of the gain, they would not have left the clothes behind. If it was friends, then they would not have permitted the corpse to be dishonoured in its nakedness. . . . That shows rather that the body which passes over into immortality has no need of clothing in the future'.

28. Billerbeck II, p. 545 (on Jn 11:44 B) adduces a passage from the treatise *Mo'ed Qatan*, 27a, according to which at an early date the faces of the rich remained uncovered but those of the poor were covered. Not to put the poor to shame, it was ordered that all faces should be covered. Thus, the use of the napkin as a head covering was certainly a widespread custom.

29. Christian writers right into the third century answer the accusation that Jesus' body was stolen or removed to another place; cf. the list in W. Bauer, *ad loc.* Like the guards at the tomb in Matthew, the grave-clothes of Jn 20 are given a greater apologetic value in the aprocryphal writings. According to the *Gospel to the Hebrews* cited by Jerome, *De viris ill.*, 2 (Hennecke-Schneemelcher, I, p. 108), the Lord hands over the linen cloth to the servant of the priest. A Coptic fragment, which was published by E. Revillout in *Apocryphes Coptes*, I (1907), pp. 170ff, tells that Pilate himself at the tomb informs the Jewish leaders: if someone had stolen the body he would have also taken the cloths with it; cf. M. R. James, *The Apocryphal New Testament* (Oxford, 1953), p. 151; R. Mahoney, *Two Disciples*, p. 255.

30. Thus G. Ghiberti, *I racconti*, pp. 37f.

31. This is disputed to the present day. G. L. Phillips supposes, similar to G. Ghiberti, a progression: 'Faith and Vision in the Fourth Gospel', *Studies in the Fourth Gospel*, ed., F. L. Cross (London, 1957), pp. 83–96; against that, among others, R. Bultmann, p. 69, n. 2; J.-P. Charlier, *RScPhTh*, 43 (1959), p. 435, n. 6; E. D. Freed, 'Variations in the Language and Thought of John', *ZNW*, 55 (1964), pp. 167–197, particularly 189. In general, a variation of the four verbs must be supposed, with now and then, admittedly, a preference for one or other verb (see above on βλέπειν); the theological differences do not attach to the verbs themselves, but result from the context; C. Traets rightly noted this, *Voir Jésus*, pp. 7–52.

32. Individual mss. read the verbs in the plural: 69 124 sy^s. pal georg. This obviously rests on reflection: Peter also came to believe.

33. Bultmann, p. 685, interprets thus: '. . . till that point the two had not believed since they did not yet understand the Scripture; now they became convinced through the sight of their eyes'. But then it would have to say that both came to faith. On the question whether Peter likewise came to faith (through the discovery in the tomb or through the believing of the other disciple?) there is disagreement. This is affirmed by T. Zahn, p. 674; Bultmann (see above); Wikenhauser, p. 338; H. Grass, *Ostergeschehen*, p. 56; S. Schulz, p. 242; *against* are Hoskyns-Davey, p. 540; Barrett, p. 468; A. Kragerud, *Der Lieblingsjünger*, p. 30, n. 62; Brown, p. 1005 and others. The uncertainty is perhaps intentional (see below).

34. The singular ἤδει 𝕏* b c e ff² q r¹ is obviously a simplified reading.

35. Thus Bultmann, p. 685, who also cites Wellhausen and Schwartz in favour. Wellhausen, *Ev. Joh.*, p. 92, only says: 'Verse 9 obtrudes in this location.' Bultmann in fact has to slip in an intermediate remark, ('. . . till that point the two had not believed') which is not found in the text.

35a. Cf. also G. Reim, *Studien*, p. 49: 'The reference to Scripture in Jn 20:9 comes from the tradition and John obviously knows neither its wording nor its source'.

36. Cf. on this K. Lehmann, *Auferweckt am dritten Tag*, pp. 205–230.

37. Against, A. Kragerud, *Der Lieblingsjünger*, pp. 29f, 144f.

38. Cf. my 'Der Jünger, den Jesus liebte' (*EKK* 2, 1970), pp. 97–117, particularly 102–105.

39. ἔξω om. 𝕏* A VL (save for aur d f q) sy^{s. p} Diatess.

40. *The Gospel of Peter*, dating from around the middle of the second century or from only about 170, takes up features from all canonical gospels and develops them further. It hardly has a value of its own for tradition. The motif of the womens' lamenting and weeping which is adduced several times, comes from Jn 20. Cf. M. G. Mara, 'Évangile de Pierre' (*SChr*, 201, Paris, 1973), pp. 56–64, and commentary, pp. 197–208. Another development is found in the *Epistula Apostolorum*, 10: The Lord appears to three women and twice sends one of them to the apostles, see H. Dünsing, Hennecke-Schneemelcher, I, pp. 130f.

41. Here is the difference from the presentation in Mt 28. There, the angel proclaims to the women Jesus' resurrection and gives them the commission to go to the disciples; on the way Jesus appears to them and repeats the commission. On this development cf. F. Neirynck, 'Les femmes au tombeau: Étude de la redaction matthéenne', *NTSt,* 15 (1968–69), pp. 168–190. In Jn 20 the main weight is shifted from the beginning: Jesus' appearance to Mary is the decisive experience. For that reason a further development from Mt 28:9f, in the way Neirynck supposes it (pp. 184–190), is not probable.

42. That speaks for the supposition that the plural in v. 2 is not only a device of the writer in place of the singular. In Mary's answer ὅτι is not recitative but gives the reason, precisely as the answer to the question.

43. The phrase cannot be used as a stylistic criterion. It is found again in John's gospel in 6:66 and 18:6. Fortna, *Gospel of Signs*, p. 140, regards it as pre-Johannine, related to Mt 13:16; Lk 9:62. But the basis is too narrow; an editor could also have used the expression.

44. Cf. F. Schnider – W. Stenger, 'Beobachtungen zur Struktur der Emmausperikope (Lk 24, 13–35)', *BZ NF,* 16 (1972), pp. 94–114; J. Wanke, '. . . wie sie ihn beim Brotbrechen erkannten'. Zur Auslegung der Emmaus-erzählung Lk 24, 13–35, *BZ NF,* 18 (1974), pp. 180–192.

45. βαστάζειν, evidenced elsewhere for disposing of a corpse (Josephus, *Ant.*, III, 210; VII, 287, see BauerWb, col. 272), is here only a stylistic variation for αἴρειν. But the context shows clearly that Mary is not thinking of any evilly intended removal.

46. Tertullianm *De spect.*, 30, 6 (CC I, 253). In the later Jewish polemic 'Juda the gardener' plays a part: He had removed the body and then, as the disciples proclaim Jesus' resurrection, he brings it back again. Cf. S. Krauss, *Das Leben Jesu nach jüdischen Quellen* (Berlin, 1902), pp. 170ff; M. Goldstein, *Jesus and the Jewish Tradition* (New York, 1950), pp. 153 and 158f.

47. Represented with emphasis by H. von Campenhausen, *Der Ablauf der Osterereignisse,* pp. 32f.

48. The name is given differently in the mss. in the other verses also. In v. 16 B ℵ L N *Π* 050 1 33 565 sa bo pc read Μαριάμ. In this passage the Semitic tone corresponding to Rabboni may be intended; in v. 18 the form of the name is retained in the same mss. (additionally P⁶⁶). Most editors prefer this reading in v. 16 apart from von Soden, Vogels and UBS Greek NT. Μαριαμ is also what the LXX uses for the name in the OT: Exod 15:20f and frequently.

49. στρέφεσθαι can mean not only 'to turn' but 'to turn to', cf. e.g. Lk 7:44; 10:23; 22:61; 23:28. The frequent participle may already have appeared in the source. Therefore it is unnecessary to suppose that the reading of Sy^sin, 'she recognized him', is the original and to suspect a wrong translation, as M. Black, *Aram. Approach,* 3rd ed., pp. 255f, proposes.

50. 'In Hebrew' means, as more often, 5:2; 19:13, 17, 20, the Aramaic. Rabboni is evidenced by the pal. Pentateuch-Targum as the usual form of address of the time. G. Dalman, *Worte Jesu,* pp. 267, 279f, was not yet able to use this Targum, but P. Kahle could do so in the fragments from the Cairo Geniza (cf. finally in *ZNW,* 49 [1958], pp. 111, 115); now it is found in Cod. Neofiti 1. Cf. E. Lohse, in: *ThWb,* VI, pp. 962f, n. 15; p. 965 (E.T.: *TDNT,* VI, p. 962, n. 15); pp. 964f (no difference in meaning to Rabbi); M. Black, *Aram. Approach,* 3rd ed., pp. 23f, 46 (pronunciation).

51. At the beginning of v. 17 +καὶ προσέδραμεν ἅψασθαι αὐτοῦ ℵ³ Θ Ψ ϕ sy^s sa bo. In point of fact the addition is caused by Mt 28:9, but formulated independently. The verb προστρέχειν (cf. Mk 9:15; 10:17; Acts 8:30) was suggested by the situation.

52. F. Neirynck, *Les femmes,* pp. 187f, regards the alternation of the verbs as only a variant translation; he indicates Mt 8:15, where Matthew replaces Mark's κρατήσας with ἥψατο. However, there still remains the exhortation not to touch, which has no parallel in Matthew. Neirynck would explain this from Johannine theology in connection with the 'ascent' of Jesus (p. 188). Whether v. 17a comes from the source or from the evangelist, is hard to decide; cf. C. H. Dodd, *Historical Tradition,* pp. 146f; G. Hartmann, *ZNW,* 55 (1964), pp. 207ff; R. T. Fortna, *Gospel of Signs,* p. 140. The conjecture proposed by Bernard, pp. 669ff, μὴ πτόου, does not fit what follows and is rightly rejected by more recent commentaries.

53. Cf. Blass-Debr § 336, 3; Moulton-Turner, *Grammar,* p. 76; BauerWb, col. 203.

53a. The absolute τὸν πατέρα will be the original text; the addition μου is, admittedly, widely attested: P⁶⁶ P Θ pl; cf. particularly the apparatus in UBS Greek NT and B. M. Metzger, *Textual Comm.,* p. 255.

54. Thus Augustine, who finds a mystery here and explains it figuratively: In that woman, the Church from among the Gentiles was represented, which could only believe in Christ when he had ascended to the Father (*In Jo. tr. CXXI,* 3; CC 666); after him, Aquinas and others. Also the explanation that Mary is still thinking in an earthly way (cf. Bultmann, p. 687) will scarcely do justice to the text. P. Schanz, p. 572, is correct already 'Jesus is not speaking of his subsequent union, but of his going to the Father.'

55. Thus, among others, W. Michaelis, *Die Erscheinungen des Auferstandenen* (Basle, 1944), pp. 77ff; P. Benoit, 'Die Himmelfahrt', *Exegese und Theologie* (Düsseldorf, 1965), pp. 182–218, particularly 195 and 213; A. Wikenhauser, pp. 339f. Critical of this: R. E. Brown, pp. 1014f; G. Lohfink, *Die Himmelfahrt Jesu,* pp. 117f.

56. 'Continuous' form of action, cf. Blass-Debr § 318; 312, 3. Cf. R. E. Brown, p. 994, *ad loc.*

57. On the Lukan Ascension, cf. G. Lohfink, *Die Himmelfahrt Jesu,* especially pp. 245–250.

58. Cf. also W. Thüsing, *Erhöhung und Verherrlichung,* pp. 263–269, who tries to explain the difficulty in the texts by the 'two stages' of Jesus' ministry (earthly and heavenly) (p. 266).

59. This theory is held by G. Richter, 'Der Vater und Gott Jesu und seiner Brüder in Joh 20, 17', *MueThZ,* 24 (1973), pp. 95–114. The supposition that, in the tradition

which lies behind Mt 28:10 and Jn 20:17, originally by Jesus' 'brethren' were meant his physical relatives, was already previously asserted by C. H. Dodd, *Historical Tradition,* pp. 147 and 324. But we cannot go beyond a supposition. In some mss. μου is lacking after ἀδελφούς: א* D W e, perhaps in assimilation to the absolute πατέρα. The omission is hardly significant for the facts.

60. The text variants, ἀπαγγ. P⁶⁶ᶜ 𝔓 D Θ pm; ἀναγγ. E G 33 al, may be traceable to the fact that the simple form is only found in the NT again in Jn 4:51 v. 1 (text-critically uncertain); against that ἀπαγγ. forty-six times, ἀναγγ. thirteen times.

61. Cf. W. Michaelis, in: *ThWb,* V. p. 358 and p. 360, n. 214 (E.T.: *TDNT,* V, p. 358 and p. 359), n. 214. R. Pesch, 'Zu Entstehung des Glaubens an die Auferstehung Jesu', *ThQ* 153 (1973), pp. 201–228, particularly 214–218, would understand the formula ὤφθη + dative as a legitimation formula 'which has the function of legitimating the one named as experiencing the appearance, as the authority' (p. 217). But, having regard to the alternation with 'ἑώρακα τὸν κύριον' the exclusion of actual visions by R. Pesch (*ibid.*) is to be contested.

62. The direct speech in the first statement was predominantly altered: ἑώρακεν A D L Θ 𝔓 λ ⌀ pl; but the alteration of the second statement into direct speech is also to be found: ταῦτα εἶπεν μοι aur b ff² Vg sa boᵖᵗ. The text attested by the best mss., ἑώρακα and αὐτῇ, is certainly the original.

63. Cf. Blass-Debr § 470; Moulton-Turner, *Grammar,* pp. 325f. The evangelist also uses indirect speech in 5:15.

64. Differently, C. H. Dodd, 'The Appearances of the Risen Christ: An Essay in Form-Criticism of the Gospels', *Studies in the Gospels* (in Memory of R. H. Lightfoot, Oxford, 1957), pp. 9–35, particularly 31f; R. E. Brown, p. 1003. But the crowded list, which now looks different with regard to form-criticism, in the light of *history of tradition* relies, however, on the narratives of the canonical gospels. For Mary Magdalene it also draws upon Lk 8:2.

65. Against F. Neirynck, *Les femmes,* pp. 176–184 (editorial work of Matthew), with R. E. Brown, p. 1002.

66. Thus R. E. Brown, p. 1003; further cf. G. W. Trompf, 'The First Resurrection Appearance and the Ending of Mark's Gospel': *NTSt,* 18 (1971–72), pp. 308–330 (heaping up hypotheses).

67. The two genitive absolutes following one another are abnormal in the Johannine style (the redaction has probably taken a hand in 13:2); εἰς τὸ μέσον; πνεῦμα ἅγιον without an article (cf. against this 7:39a; 14:26; in 7:39b we have πνεῦμα without the article, but without ἅγιον). Words found here only: ἐμφυσάω, ἀφιέναι and κρατεῖν.

68. Differently, Wellhausen, *Ev. Joh.,* p. 94 (v. 20 is inserted); cf. Bultmann pp. 691f: v. 20a is unmotivated within the narrative as we have it, presumably retained from the source on account of the story of Thomas.

69. Fortna, *Gospel of Signs,* pp. 141f and 245, has the source closing with v. 20.

70. Cf. Lk 24:36–49; Mt 28:16–20; canonical Mark-ending: Mk 16:14–20. The linking of these appearances to commission and sending has often been confirmed, cf. C. H. Dodd, *The Appearances,* pp. 11ff; A. George, 'Les récits d'apparitions, aux Onze à partir de Luc 24:36–53', *La résurrection du Christ et l'exégèse moderne* (Paris, 1969), pp. 75–104, particularly 91ff; U. Wilckens, *Auferstehung,* 69–91; G. Ghiberti, *I racconti pasquali,* pp. 100ff; B. Rigaux, *Dieu l'a ressuscité* (Gembloux, 1973), pp. 253–277.

71. A striking feature is the participle placed first in the genitive absolute, which is abnormal for John, cf., against this, 4:51; 5:13; 7:30; 12:37; 13:2; 20:1. The genitive absolute in 6:23 is probably an editorial addition.

72. Many mss. add συνηγμένοι: א ᶜ Θ Ψ 𝔓 al VL Vg. There is no indication at all that it is the same room in which the last supper took place. There is no more exact localization in Lk 24:33, 36. This evangelist names 'the eleven and those who were with them'. In the history of tradition there is certainly a connection with Lk 24:36–43, cf. especially ἔστη ἐν μέσῳ αὐτῶν and the showing of the hands and feet; but so strong are the divergences that the most that can be supposed is contact between the specific sources.

A. George, *op. cit.*, p. 93, suggests a common source for Lk 24:36–43; otherwise, J. A. Bailey, *Traditions Common*, pp. 92f, who here regards Luke as the source of John.

73. It is disputed whether the eirenic greeting in Lk 24:36 originally belonged to the text; codex D and most mss. of the VL leave it out ('western non-interpolation'). UBS Greek NT takes it up in the text in brackets; cf. Metzger, *Textual Comm.*, pp. 186f. However, there is here a strong suspicion of a borrowing from John.

74. That already happens in Ignatius of Antioch in the *Letter to the Smyrnians*, cf. especially 2 against false teachers who assert that Jesus only apparently suffered: ἀληθῶς ἔπαθεν, ὡς καὶ ἀληθῶς ἀνέστησεν ἑαυτόν; further 3:1: ἐγὼ γὰρ καὶ μετὰ τὴν ἀνάστασιν ἐν σαρκὶ αὐτὸν οἶδα καὶ πιστεύω ὄντα. The following quotation (in 3:2) seems to draw on the *Gospel of the Hebrews*, cf. Jerome, *De viris ill.*, 16 (cited in Aland, *Synopsis*, p. 503).

75. The participle ἰδόντες is presumably not to be understood as the content of their joy ('that they saw the Lord' – classical, after verbs of emotion), but as a detail regarding time ('when they saw'), cf. Blass-Debr § 415; differently Moulton-Turner, *Grammar*, p. 160.

76. Normally the aorist is used for Jesus' sending by the Father; only in 5:36 is the perfect found, and supported by textual criticism: the works of Jesus are a continual testimony to his being sent. As in v. 1. the perfect is found in 7:29. In so far as Jesus is returning (ὑπάγω or πορεύομαι) to the Father, his earthly mission is fulfilled; but in so far as he is coming to the disciples again (cf. 14:3, 18, 28), or sends them the Spirit, his mission continues through the disciples. Cf. J. Kuhl, *Die Sendung Jesu und der Kirche*, pp. 145–147 (distinguishes more sharply between the 'two phases' of the work of salvation).

77. Some exegetes even think that the formula ὤφθη with dative was a legitimation formula for the authoritative envoys of Christ (the 'apostles'); cf. U. Wilckens, *Auferstehung*, p. 147; R. Pesch, 'Zur Entstehung des Glaubens an die Auferstehung Jesu', *ThQ* 153 (1973), pp. 201–228, particularly 212–218. For a critical view of this approach, see A. Vögtle, 'Wie kam es zu Artikulierung des Osterglaubens?' (II), *BuL*, 15 (1974), pp. 16–37, particularly 31f; cf. *idem.*, in the concluding summing-up, *ibid.*, p. 192.

78. In *ThWb*, I, p. 404 (E.T.: *TDNT*, I, p. 405).

79. In all eleven times; those passages are important which are concerned with giving life or reviving. Gen 2:7; 1 Kings 17:21 (reviving of the youth by Elijah); Wis 15:11 (of God: ἐμφυσήσαντα πνεῦμα ζωτικόν); Ezek 37:9. – 'breathing on' can also have an exorcistic significance or indicate the transfer of the power of office, cf. Bultmann p. 692, n. 6; H. Thyen, *Studien zur Sündenvergebung* (Göttingen, 1970), p. 248. But the connection with the spirit of life is closer; on the question of a transfer of office, see below.

80. J. Schmitt, 'Simples remarques sur le fragment Jn., XX, 22–23', *Mélanges en l'honneur de Monseigneur Michel Andrieu* (Strasbourg, 1956), pp. 415–423, drew attention to this passage and similar notions in Qumran.

81. Thus also J. E. Yates, *The Spirit and the Kingdom* (London, 1963), pp. 213–219; G. Johnston, *The Spirit-Paraclete*, pp. 49f; B. Lindars, *ad loc.* (p. 612).

82. Thus, following others, H. Thyen, *Studien zur Sündenvergebung*, p. 248. His reliance on the material from the history of religion in W. Staerk, *Erlösererwartung*, pp. 312ff, is confusing; for the rich evidence from Egyptian and Babylonian religion all has to do with 'the conception of the divine power of the πνεῦμα ἅγιον as that of the potency which lies behind creation' (p. 308, emphasized); the spirit is the breath of life, the power to bring to life (Egyptian texts, pp. 314f; Accadian texts, pp. 326f). In the exegesis of the early Church and in Catholic exegesis up to our time the imparting of the Spirit has been treated, it is true, mostly as a special gift to the apostles, cf. P. Schanz, F. Tillmann, E. Schick and others, *ad loc.*

83. On the Lukan Pentecost event (Acts 2:1–13) cf., besides the commentaries, E. Lohse, *Die Bedeutung des Pfingstberichtes* im Rahmen des Lukanischen Geschichtswerkes, *EvTh*, 13 (1953) pp. 422–436; *idem.*, *ThWb*, VI, pp. 50–52, E.T.: *TDNT*, VI, pp. 50–52; further especially J. Kremer, *Pfingstbericht und Pfingstgeschehen* (Stuttgart,

1973). He supposes a specific occurrence drawing on an early experience of the Spirit by the apostles in Jerusalem which became significant for the entire primitive Church (p. 261), but which otherwise is heavily overlaid in the presentation with theological motifs (cf. pp. 261–267). On Jn 20:22–23 see Kremer, pp. 224–228 (an assessment similar to that in the commentary above). The Orthodox theologian A. Cassien, *La Pentecôte Johannique* (Valence, 1939), attempted to bring it closer to the Lukan Pentecost.

84. The view of Theodore of Mopsuestia, that the Spirit was only symbolically given to the disciples when they were breathed on, was condemned by the fifth Ecumenical Council (Constantinople, 553), (Denz., p. 224). John Chrysostom says that the Holy Spirit was not given to the disciples for general effectiveness but for a specific purpose, namely, for the forgiveness of sins (*PG*, 59, col. 471). Thomas Aquinas: 'Super Apostolos autem primo descendit in flatu, ad designandam propagationem gratiae in sacramentis, cuius ipsi ministri erant . . . secundo vero in igneis linguis ad significandam propagationem gratiae per doctrinam' (*In Jo XX lect.*, IV, 5; *Cai*, no. 2539). But the restriction of Jn 20:22f to a special equipping of the apostles is also found in Protestant exegesis, see J. Jeremias, *ThWb*, III, p. 753, 8ff (E.T.: *TDNT*, III, p. 753); D. E. Holwerda, *The Holy Spirit and Eschatology in the Gospel of John* (Kampen, 1959), pp. 23f.

85. This viewpoint has found ever stronger support from Catholics too, cf. X. Léon-Dufour, *Résurrection de Jésus et message pascal* (Paris, 1971), pp. 239f; R. E. Brown, pp. 1041–1044; J. Kremer, *Pfingstbericht*, pp. 224–228; B. Rigaux, *Dieu l'a ressuscité*, pp. 266–270.

86. κρατεῖν, here affected by the contrast with ἀφιέναι, thus = not loosen, keep hold of, is unique in this sense in the NT, cf. BauerWb, col. 887, s.v. at the end; but also, according to the general lexica, scarcely any further examples may be adduced. Sirach 28:1 says, that God διατηρῶν διατηρήσει the sins of those seeking revenge: that is to say, retains (in his memory). The next verse, also noteworthy, is: 'Forgive (ἄφες) your neighbour the wrong he has done, and then your sins will be pardoned (λυθήσονται) when you pray.' Thus, here ἀφιέναι – λύειν stand next to each other as synonyms; λύειν in Mt 16:19; 18:18 is comparable, although δέειν – λύειν is an already existing juxtaposition, cf. Billerbeck I, pp. 738–741; F. Büchsel, in: *ThWb*, II, pp. 59f (E.T.: *TDNT*, II, pp. 60f). On the passive of κρατεῖν cf. Lk 24:16: the eyes of the Emmaus disciples were 'kept' (ἐκρατοῦντο), so that they did not recognize Jesus.

87. On the link in the history of tradition with Mt 18:18, cf. C. H. Dodd, *NTSt*, 2 (1955–56), pp. 85f; *idem.*, *Historical Tradition*, pp. 347–349. A. Vögtle offers further clarification, 'Ekklesiologische Auftragsworte des Auferstandenen', *Das Evangelium und die Evangelien* (Düsseldorf, 1971), pp. 243–252, particularly 246–248 and 250–252. He understands Jn 20:23 as the 'presumably already pre-Johannine decisive variant of the tradition of the original form attested in Mt 18:18' (p. 251), and he thinks 'that the primitive Church influenced the shape of Jn 20:23 while striving for an explanation of the extent and content of the power to bind and loose in accordance with a specific aspect which was very important to salvation' (p. 252).

88. The perfect form is not attested by all mss.; divergent readings: ἀφίονται (B*) Ψ; ἀφίενται Θ P pm aur b c f Vg bo Orig Euseb Basil al; ἀφεθήσεται א* q (d ff² r¹ in the plural) sy sa al; ἀφίεται 69* 127. But the perfect is certainly original, as the following κεχράτηνται and presumably also ἔσται δεδεμένα in Mt 18:18 suggest; cf. Blass-Debr § 97, 3. According to Metzger, *Test Comm.*, p. 255, *Vaticanus*, which in the first version gives ἀφεῖονται, is perhaps also evidence of the perfect, since ιο is written for ω.

89. Cf. H. Frhr. von Campenhausen, *Kirchliches Amt*, p. 152; H. Thyen, *Sünden-vergebung*, pp. 248f.

90. H. Thyen, *Sündenvergebung*, p. 249; cf. also E. Schweizer, *ThWb* VI, pp. 440f (E.T.: *TDNT*, VI, p. 442), ('power of proclamation'); *idem.*, *Neotestamentica* (Zürich-Stuttgart, 1963), p. 265 (the Christ is the κρίσις in the preaching of the disciples). We may distinguish between the logion handed down and the understanding of the evangelist (so

H. Thyen, p. 249, n. 2); but as far as the evangelist is concerned, we must also ask whether he referred the logion to the proclamation alone. If we do not wish completely to sever his connection with 1 Jn, he cannot be denied an interest in the further necessary forgiveness of sins in the Church. Von Campenhausen perceived more clearly in this respect: 'John sees in the power of forgiveness something which the Church must value above everything, because it lives from the power of forgiveness. Not only individual, specific sinners but all Christians need forgiveness and are increasingly dependent on truly receiving it. The power of the keys is the primal authority of the Christian Church as a whole' (p. 152, cf. also 153f).

91. Thus G. Richter, 'Die Fleischwerdung des Logos im Johannesvangelium', *NT*, 13 (1971), pp. 81–126, particularly 123f. In stylistic criticism it is not necessarily possible to rely on words found only once, such as $\check{\alpha}\pi\iota\sigma\tau\sigma\varsigma$ and $\pi\iota\sigma\tau\sigma\varsigma$.

92. Cf., for the older literary criticism, J. Wellhausen, *Ev. Joh.*, p. 93 (excludes from the basic writing all appearances after 20:18), further pp. 94f (on 20:24–29); F. Spitta, *Joh-Ev*, pp. 398ff, who assumes an apologetic tendency; differently, E. Hirsch, *Studien*, pp. 128: assimilation to the Lukan resurrection account. M.-E. Boismard goes still further, *RB*, 69 (1962), pp. 200–203, and regards as probable a reworking by Luke himself of Jn 4:46–53 and the related Thomas pericope. Against that L. Erdozáin, *La función del signo en la fe según el cuarto evangelio* (Rome, 1968), pp. 39–42. In detail: A. Dauer, 'Die Herkunft der Thomas-Perikope Joh 20, 24–29', *Biblische Randbemerkungen* (*Schülerfestschrift für R. Schnackenburg*, Würzburg, 1974), pp. 56–76 (secondary from the evangelist; however, vv. 25b, c and 27, in the plural and referring to the disciples, were originally in the account of the tradition on which 20:19–23 is based).

93. G. Richter, *Fleischwerdung*, pp. 121–124. Cf. his conclusions in the second part of his study: *NT*, 14 (1972), pp. 257–276, particularly 275f.

93a. Cf. A. Dauer, *Herkunft*, pp. 68–71.

94. The article is lacking with ᾽Ιησοῦς in P⁵ B ℵ* D; this, in contrast to the mass of the later mss., ought to be the original reading, which most of the newer editions of the text also prefer (apart from Vogels, Merk and Bower). On account of the text-critically dubious nature of many passages with (ὁ) ᾽Ιησοῦς, no stylistic criterion may be obtained from this (differently, J. Jeremias, *ThBl*, 20 [1941], pp. 44f). ᾽Ιησοῦς without article also 19:26; 20:15–17 (similar text-critical doubt). Cf. Abbott, *Joh. Grammar*, p. 57; Blass-Debr § 260, 1; R. C. Nevius, 'The Use of the Definite Article with "Jesus" in the Fourth Gospel', *NTSt*, 12 (1965–66), pp. 81–85.

95. ἄλλοι om. ℵ* syᵖ bo.

96. The imperfect is hardly iterative in intent, as some exegetes opine. For ἔλεγον and εἶπον can alternate, cf. Blass-Debr § 329.

97. There is a confusion in the mss. between τύπον and τόπον; but most read τύπον in the first case, and τοὺς τύπους P⁶⁶ 565 is also noteworthy in this regard, because originally this reading would presuppose the same word in the singular. τύπος = mark (of a wound) also fits 'see' better. In the second case, τόπον is to be preferred, despite B D P pl; these mss. have obviously been made to coincide with the preceding τύπον.

98. Future indicative and aorist subjunctive alternative without any apparent reason, cf. Blass-Debr § 329.

99. Cf. here the work of L. Erdozáin, *Fonción del signo*.

100. Cf. Augustine, *In Jo. tr.*, CXXI, 5 (CC 668); 'Quoniam generalis quodammodo sensus est visus. Nam et per alios quatuor sensus nominari solet . . .'

101. The Syr. Sinait. expressly adds: 'on the first day of the week'; hence, according to Merx, p. 454, it leaves out the πάλιν.

102. Cf. W. Rordorf, *Der Sonntag. Geschichte des Ruhe- und Gottesdiensttages im ältesten Christentum* (Zürich, 1962), pp. 213–233, who also discusses critical objections (p. 217). For Jn 20:26, he also supposes 'that the evangelist allowed his precise information to be influenced by contemporary liturgical practice' (p. 231). On Barn 15:9, cf. G. Lohfink, *Die Himmelfahrt Jesu* (Munich, 1971), pp. 121–125.

103. On γίνομαι in the sense of 'to be', cf. BauerWb, cols. 317f, s.v. II, 1. The meaning 'to show oneself, to prove' is attested in papyri, see E. Mayser, *Grammatik*, II/3, p. 15; a good comparison on a Leipzig papyrus (Lips. I, 104, 27): ἄλοιποι (= ἄλυποι) γίνεσθε περὶ ἐμοῦ (*ibid.*, line 36f). Codex D reads ἴσθι for it.

104. C. H. Dodd, *Historical Tradition*, pp. 354f, considers a reminder of the parable of the steward Lk 12:42–46 par. Mt 24:45–51; but in Lk 12:46 μετὰ τῶν ἀπίστων cf. J. Jeremias, *Die Gleichnisse Jesu* (Göttingen, ⁶1962), p. 54, n. 6. Apart from the feature of the doubt and unbelief (cf. Lk 24:11, 41) in the Easter stories, the evangelist certainly does not use any tradition; ἄπιστος is formed *ad hoc*, nor does it have, as in Paul, the settled meaning 'non-Christian' (Gentile).

105. In general the older commentaries assume contact and the newer ones are cautious, cf. Lindars p. 614: 'The believing disciple does not need to touch him.' The evangelist hardly sensed any contradiction cf. 20:17 (Wellhausen, p. 93); that passage comes under another emphasis (*q.v.*). We may not invoke 1 Jn 1:1 because it is not specifically the risen but the incarnate one who is in mind (see *Joh-Briefe*, p. 53 and *ad loc.*).

105a. To this effect, especially R. E. Brown, p. 1046: '. . . the evangelist would not have considered Thomas' faith adequate if the disciple had taken up Jesus' invitation and would never have put on Thomas' lips the tremendous confession of v. 28.'

106. The Fathers found Jesus' humanity and divinity attested but not necessarily in the two predicates, cf. Augustine (CC 667): 'Videbat tangebatque hominem, et confitebatur Deum, quem non videbat neque tangebat.' Thomas apportions humanity and divinity between the two predicates (*In Jo XX lect.*, VI, 3; Cai no. 2562). This view has been represented again by G. Richter, *op. cit.*, p. 123, in support of his explanation (anti-Docetic tendency). The use of the Thomas narrative by later writers for the purposes of anti-Docetic contention (Irenaeus, cf. Richter, p. 124) is no argument for the same tendency in the original narrative.

107. The vocative is possible, since the address in the nominative, especially under Semitic influence, occurs frequently in the NT, cf. Blass-Debr § 147, 3, almost in the same form Rev 4:11, further cf. Jn 13:13. However, the vocative κύριε is available for κύριος, cf. Rev 15:3. If κύριε is being avoided in the confession of Thomas, that is an indication that more is intended by the expression than the address of the earthly Jesus.

108. Against G. Richter, *op. cit.*, p. 124. For 1 Jn 5:20 we must consider whether a comma should not be placed after ὁ ἀληθινός: Jesus Christ is 'the true' (namely) God and eternal life (cf. similarly on 1:18 with the reading θεός). On Jn 20:28 C. K. Barrett says, p. 477, and rightly: 'The difference between the present verse and 1.1 (where θεός is anarthrous) cannot be pressed; here the articular nominative is used for vocative.'

109. Cf. O. Cullmann, *Christologie*, pp. 316f and 336, if an implied statement on being is not denied. Cf. also on 1 Jn 5:20 (*Komm.*, pp. 291f).

110. The addresses to God are closest, thus Ps 34:23 LXX ὁ θεός μου καὶ ὁ κύριός μου; further Ps 29:3; 87:2; 85:15 LXX. The confession is less comparable, because ὁ Κύριος in LXX is the rendering of Yahweh, cf. 2 Kings (LXX) 7:28; 3 Kings 18:39; Jer 38:18; Zech 13:9. In Jn 20 ὁ κύριος becomes the designation for the risen Lord; from the viewpoint of the history of tradition the primitive Christian transfer of the title Κύριος from Yahweh to the exalted Jesus (cf. Phil 2:11; Rom 10:9, 13, etc.) is at best, far in the background; cf. F. Hahn, *Christologische Hoheitstitel*, pp. 123f. In fact John has not adopted this use of the Κύριος-title (enthronement at the right hand of God, lordship and so on); in the Johannine letters it is wholly lacking (different again in Revelation). It is best to suppose that the Johannine usage comes from the formula ἑώρακα τὸν κύριον (see on 20:18).

111. The designation claimed by the Emperor Domitian is well-known: 'Dominus et Deus noster' (Suetonius, *Domit.* 13). On the application to rulers cf. further

W. Foerster, in: *ThWb* III, pp. 1052/56 (E.T.: *TDNT*, III, pp. 1054/58). The different $K\acute{u}\rho\iota o\varsigma$-predication in Revelation, which certainly depends in part on the emperor-cult, makes the distance from John clear. Other possibilities of comparison with similar locutions among the Gentiles (cf. W. Bauer, *ad loc.*, Bultmann, p. 695, n. 2) have scarcely any significance for our passage.

112. Westcott-Hort, Nestlé-Aland, Bover; Bernard, Loisy, Tillmann, Lagrange, Schick, Lindars, Schulz. Many minuscules also read a question.

113. Cf. G. Bertram-F. Hauck, *ThWb* IV (1942) pp. 365–373 (E.T.: *TDNT*, IV, pp. 362–370); A. George, 'La "forme" des béatitudes jusqu'à Jésus', *Mel. Bibl. en l'honneur de A. Robert* (Paris, 1957), pp. 398–403; E. Lipinski, 'Macarismes et psaumes de congratulation', *RB* 75 (1968), pp. 321–367; J. Dupont, *Les Béatitudes II* (Paris, 1969), pp. 324–338 (detailed, with much material).

114. Cf. W. Bieder, 'Die sieben Seligpreisungen in der Offenbarung des Johannes', *ThZ*, 10 (1954), pp. 13–30; he sees them as an intermediary form between words of declaration and exhortation (pp. 25f), and attributes a missionary character to them. Further cf. H. Kraft, *Die Offenbarung des Johannes* (Tübingen, 1974), 22f.

115. *Historical Tradition*, p. 354.

116. Now and then there is doubt, cf. Hoskyns-Davey, p. 550: The concluding comment 20:30f refers only to the appearances; Chapter 21, on account of the missionary viewpoint, belongs essentially to John's gospel. On the origin of Chapter 21 see *ad loc*.

117. Cf. the material assembled by Bultmann, pp. 697f n. 2.

118. Cf. M.-É. Boismard, *RB*, 69 (1962) pp. 201ff. He found stylistic grounds are one reason for regarding Luke as the editor of Jn 20:24–31.

119. Om. A B K Δ Π 0250 al. Most text editors strike it out, because they presumably hold the *lectio brevior* to be original. UBS Greek NT puts $\alpha\dot{u}\tau o\tilde{u}$ in brackets.

120. The personal pronoun is also lacking in 4:31, 33; 11:7f, 54, 13:5, 22; 20:18, 19, 20. In several places the evangelist leaves out the pronoun if the disciples of Jesus (with pronoun) were mentioned previously; that would apply here also (v. 25). Yet, apart from this, he occasionally also writes only $o\acute{\iota}$ $\mu\alpha\theta\eta\tau\alpha\acute{\iota}$, e.g., 11:7f.

121. Cf. vol. 1, pp. 515f; K. H. Rengstorf offers the same opinion, *ThWb*, VII, pp. 253f (E.T.: *TDNT*, VII, pp. 254f). R. T. Fortna, *Gospel of Signs*, thinks that the resurrection of Jesus was not a 'sign' for the evangelist (p. 197, n. 3), but certainly for the source which even saw in it the sign *par excellence* (p. 198, n. 4). That corresponds to his view that Jn 20:1–20 comes, in basic substance, from the *semeia*-source.

122. Thus, R. E. Brown, p. 1058.

123. W. Nicol, *The Sēmeia in the Fourth Gospel* (Leiden, 1972), p. 115.

124. Fortna, *Gospel of Signs*, p. 198, also ascribes $\acute{o}$ $\chi\rho\iota\sigma\tau\grave{o}\varsigma$ $\acute{o}$ $u\acute{\iota}\grave{o}\varsigma$ $\tauo\tilde{u}$ $\theta\varepsilon o\tilde{u}$ to the source and regards the continuation ($\varkappa\alpha\grave{\iota}$ $\acute{\iota}\nu\alpha$ . . .) as only an addition by the evangelist; likewise, J. Becker, 'Wunder und Christologie', *NTSt*, 16 (1969/70), pp. 130–148, particularly 135–139.

125. W. Oehler. *Das Johannesevangelium eine Missionsschrift für die Welt* (Gütersloh, 1936); *idem., Zum Missionscharakter des Johannes-Evangeliums* (Gütersloh, 1941); E. D. Freed, 'Did John write his gospel partly to win Samaritan converts?', *NT*, 12 (1970), pp. 241–256; K. Bornhäuser, *Das Johannesevangelium, eine Missionsschrift für Israel* (Gütersloh, 1928); W. C. van Unnik, 'The Purpose of St John's Gospel', *StEv* (Berlin, 1959), pp. 382–411; J. A. T. Robinson, 'The Destination and Purpose of St John's Gospel', *NTSt*, 6 (1959/60), pp. 117–131.

126. On the Johannine $\acute{\iota}\nu\alpha$-clauses: *StTh*, 19 (1965), pp. 213–220.

127. H. Leroy, *Rätsel und Missverständnis*; B. Olsson, *Structure and Meaning in the Fourth Gospel. A Text-Linguistic Analysis of John 2:1–11 and 4:1–42* (Lund, 1974). He writes: 'My conclusions as regards the character of the texts as a whole, therefore, confirm Leroy's thesis of a Johannine "Sondersprache", and Meek's description of Jn as a book for insiders and, to some extent also, de Jonge's designation of Johannine theology as "a typical in-group theology"' (p, 282).

Notes

128. Cf. my essay: 'Die Messiasfrage im Johannesevangelium', *Neutestamentliche Aufsätze* (*Festschrift für J. Schmid*, Regensburg, 1963), pp. 240–264; further M. de Jonge, 'Jewish Expectations about the "Messiah" according to the Fourth Gospel', *NTSt*, 19 (1972/73), pp. 246–270 (on the purpose of the fourth gospel see pp. 263–266).

129. G. Richter says in an essay, 'Die Deutung des Kreuzestodes Jesu in der Leidensgeschichte des Johannesevangeliums (Jo 13–19)', *BuL*, 9 (1968), pp. 21–36, particularly 34, that the evangelist writes 'a document defending and confessing the endangered faith in Jesus' messiahship'. That is apt; but I cannot agree with his restriction to this aim and his attribution of all material which does not strictly accord with it to one or several editorial layers (so also in further works).

130. Thus, J. Becker, *Wunder und Christologie*, pp. 140f; also E. Schweizer, who questions this, *ThWb*, VIII, pp. 389f (E.T.: *TDNT*, VIII, pp. 386f). Cf., with this, Vol. 2, pp. 180f. So Hellenistic an explanation of the title 'Son of God' would obscure the theology of the *semeia*-source with which J. Becker is concerned.

EDITORIAL CONCLUSION: Pages 341–374

1. See especially W. G. Kümmel, *Einleitung* (17th ed., 1973), pp. 173f, 201 (E.T.: *Introduction to the New Testament* ([17]1975), pp. 207f, 235f); Wikenhauser-Schmid, *Einleitung*, pp. 323f (E.T.: *New Testament Introduction*, pp. 290f); M.-E. Boismard, 'Le chapître XXI de s. Jean: Essai de critique littéraire', *RB* 54 (1947), pp. 473–501; R. Bultmann, pp. 700–706; Cassian, 'John XXI', *NTSt* 3 (1956–57), pp. 132–136; O. Merlier, *Quatr. Ev.*, pp. 149–174; S. B. Marrow, *John 21 – An Essay in Johannine Ecclesiology* (Rome, 1968); R. E. Brown, pp. 1077–1085; R. Mahoney, *Two Disciples*, pp. 12–40. Further the special literature cited in the following notes on individual sections.

1a. Thus M. J. Lagrange, pp. 520f; Hoskyns-Davey, p. 550.

2. In the German scholarly literature, Jn 21 is mostly designated as 'Nachtrag' [postscript, *translator*]; in the English as 'appendix'. 'Epilogue' is favoured by S. B. Marrow, *op. cit.*, pp. 43f, and R. E. Brown, p. 1079 ('gives balance to the presence of a prologue at the beginning'; he thinks that prologue and epilogue were added by the same hand. That is very open to question).

3. Jn 21 plays an important part in theories about the editorial layers in the fourth gospel; cf. D. M. Smith Jr., *The Composition and Order of the Fourth Gospel* (New Haven, 1965), pp. 234–237; H. Thyen, *Tradition und Glaube* (*Festgabe für K. G. Kuhn*, Göttingen, 1971), pp. 344f. But the conclusion of Jn 21 is also the one place which gives us a direct insight into a situation within the Johannine Church (death of the disciple whom Jesus loved). Therefore, the chapter also plays a significant part in the discussion about the historical background, cf. e.g., A. Kragerud, *Der Lieblingsjünger*, pp. 15–19.

4. R. Pesch, *Der reiche Fischfang (Lk 5–11/Jo 21, 1–15). Wundergeschichte – Berufungsgeschichte – Erscheinungsbericht* (Düsseldorf, 1969). On the history of research concerning Jn 21:1–14, pp. 42–52. Cf. further S. S. Smalley, 'The Sign in John XXI', *NTSt* 20 (1974), pp. 275–288; he appears not to know Pesch's work.

5. *Op. cit.*, pp. 148f.

6. *Gospel of Signs*, pp. 87–98. Fortna's book appeared in 1970, one year after Pesch's; but, apparently, Fortna could not yet make use of it.

7. *Op. cit.*, p. 97.

8. C. H. Dodd, *Appearances of the Risen Christ* (see above on 20:18), pp. 13–15; *idem.*, *Historical Tradition*, p. 143, places Lk 24:13–35 and Jn 21:1–14 form-critically together as examples of the 'circumstantial' type of appearance story (in contrast to the 'concise type'). That is seen, yet very superficially. On the relationship of the Lukan and Johannine narratives, cf. further U. Wilckens, *Auferstehung* (Stuttgart, 1970), pp. 78–85 ('recognition narratives', p. 85); similarly on the Emmaus story

F. Schnider-W. Stenger, 'Beobachtungen zur Struktur der Emmausperikope' (Lk 24, 13–35): *BZ NF* 16 (1972), pp. 94–114. J. Wanke, *Die Emmauserzählung. Eine redaktionsgeschichtliche Untersuchung zu Lk 24, 13–35* (Leipzig, 1973), pp. 102–105, lays stronger emphasis on the meal-scene in both narratives. He thinks that the one already recognized (v. 7) gives the bread and the fish. If the figure of the beloved disciple is meant to be secondary in v. 7, then an initial recognition by Peter must presumably have been mentioned (p. 104 and n. 741).

9. R. Pesch, *Der reiche Fischfang*, p. 151, objects that allegorical fish cannot serve as a meal. But the saying of Jesus: 'Bring some of the fish that you have just caught' (v. 10) has another function; according to Pesch himself, it is an editorial bracketing together of fishing story and appearance report. The detail about the 153 large fish only follows later (v. 10). The large amount is already stressed earlier (v. 6). With an inclination to a symbolico-allegorical interpretation (Pesch also explains the seven in v. 2 in that way), an allusion is not excluded to the great number of the believers (less so to positive missionary activity). The Johannine Church is entirely open to such an attitiude, cf. Jn 12:20–24.

10. Cf. Bultmann, pp. 712f; Brown, pp. 1088f; H. Thyen, *Studien zur Sündenvergebung* (Göttingen, 1970), p. 230; A. Vögtle, 'Zum Problem der Herkunft von "Mt 16, 17–19"', *Orientierung an Jesus* (*Festschrift für J. Schmid*, Freiburg, 1973), pp. 372–393, particularly 379; *Peter in the New Testament*, eds. R. E. Brown, K. P. Donfried and J. Reumann (Minneapolis-New York, 1973), p. 144.

11. On this much-discussed problem, cf. A. Vögtle, *Problem der Herkunft* (previous footnote), pp. 377–383, in discussion with other viewpoints.

12. Such a one is assumed by not a few scholars, among others H. Grass, *Ostergeschehen und Osterberichte*, p. 76; Bauer, p. 237; Bultmann, pp. 705f; Brown, p. 1070 (on v. 4) and pp. 1093ff; R. Mahoney, *Two Disciples*, p. 35. Although much speaks in favour of this, it is not certain because the exposition of the appearance narrative was crowded out by the fishing narrative. Formerly it was often supposed that the story stood in the broken-off conclusion of Mark (cf. Bauer, p. 237). The combination of a first appearance before Peter during a fishing scene and a first appearance to the disciples during a meal-scene, as Brown suggests as a hypothesis, pp. 1094f, is, according to the above analysis, not possible. Cf. the critical reserve in B. Rigaux, *Dieu l'a ressuscité*, p. 241, with n. 53 (p. 252).

13. Cf. the works already mentioned by M.-E. Boismard, O. Merlier, R. Pesch as well as those cited in the following footnotes.

14. Boismard, *op. cit.*, p. 501. Here he withholds his later viewpoint that Luke is the editor.

15. *Literarische Einheit des Joh-Ev*, pp. 146–149 and 218.

16. *Two Disciples*, pp 17–32.

17. Thus P. Parker, 'Two Editions of John': *JBL*, 75 (1956), pp. 303–314, particularly 305f.

18. *Two Disciples*, pp. 38f.

19. Cf. R. Pesch, *Fischfang*, p. 88; Bultmann–Lührmann, *ThWb* IX (1973), pp. 5f (E.T.: *TDNT*, IX, pp. 5f).

20. Most mss. give the article; it is lacking in B C, and D M e Chrys omit the name altogether. Of the editors, Merk, Bover, UBS Greek NT take up the article. A similar uncertainty prevails in vv. 5, 13, 14; Vaticanus also leaves out the article in vv. 10 and 12.

21. Often with εἰς, also with δύο Lk 24:13; Mk 16:12, with πέντε Mt 25:2. Cf. Bauer*Wb*, col. 467, s.v. 4, a, α; Blass-Debr § 164; Mayser, Gramm. II/3 II/2, p. 352.

22. That is inferred with difficulty from 2:1–11; cf. besides on 1:45. The suspicion that Nathanael and Thomas were scarcely fishermen at all, is strong. That is, of course, not expressed; why should not other disciples accompany Peter on his fishing? Yet, it can be an indication that those mentioned do not belong to the original fishing story.

23. Cf. H. Grass, *Ostergeschehen*, pp. 77, 80ff; H. von Campenhausen, *Ablauf der*

Osterereignisse, pp. 16f; U. Wilckens, *Auferstehung*, p. 81 (a combination of motifs from older and younger traditions); R. E. Brown, p. 1094. The two Galilean stories (appearance before Simon Peter and before the twelve during the meal) 'seem to have survived in John XXI in a more consecutive form than anywhere else in the NT'. Cf. also R. Mahoney *Two Disciples*, p. 35. Differently, R. Pesch, *Fischfang*, p. 133: 'from the viewpoint of history of tradition, young'.

24. Cf. the literature adduced at the beginning of Chapter 20.

25. γινομένης B C* A L 21 pc] γενομένης ℵ D Θ P pm. The reading in the present is preferred by most editors; favouring the second UBS Greek NT, also Barrett, p. 482. The present could suggest the morning break of day. The same text-critical uncertainty in 13:2 (q.v.).

26. *Fischfang*, pp. 93f and 131.

27. Cf. Blass-Debr § 427, 2; such questions introduced with μή are frequent in John (about seventeen times). The question ἔχεις τι is evidenced as seeking information concerning success or failure as to catching, cf. Wettstein I, p. 962, *ad loc.*

28. Evidence in BauerWb, col. 1426; Liddell-Scott, *Lex.* p. 1529.

29. Cf. Pesch, *Fischfang*, p. 95.

30. E. Schweizer, *Ego eimi*, p. 93, and Ruckstuhl, *Literar. Einheit*, p. 204 (under No. 38), have taken up ἑλκύω among the criteria of Johannine style. The verb is used figuratively in Jn 6:44; 12:32, in 18:10 (as also in Acts 16:19) in the proper sense. Since the verb (present-stem ἕλκω) is not unusual (cf. BauerWb, cols. 498f), it must disappear, in my view, as a criterion of Johannine style.

31. Cf. G. Dalman, *Arbeit und Sitte*, VI (1939), pp. 346–351. He distinguishes between a net which is cast (about four metres, thrown by hand), a trawl-net and one stretched out (in deep water). For Jn 21 only the trawl-net comes into question; cf. *op. cit.*, p. 349: 'On the Sea of Tiberius the trawl-net (*ǧarf*) was spread out from a boat and was dragged from the shore with cables on poles. When this was not possible, men went into the water stripped, drove the fish together with nets and drew the trawl-net on to the boat in sections.' This description does not apply fully to the situation in Jn 21; here the boat is somewhat more distant from the shore. The traditionally indicated spot at the 'Seven Wells' on the north-west shore of the lake (Church of the Appearance of the Risen One) is not a bad choice. C. Kopp, *Heilige Stätten*, p. 277 (E.T.: *Holy Places*, p. 224): 'The warm torrent of water from Seven Wells with its plant debris attracts fish, and the little bay forms a sheltered harbour for boats.'

32. Pesch, *Fischfang*, pp. 60–64, shows that the Lukan and Johannine story are variants of a like tradition. On the analysis of Lk 5:4b–7, see *op. cit.*, pp. 76–84.

33. Cf. 13:25 in relation to 13:23. The redaction of Jn 21 specially has the scene at the supper in mind, cf. v. 20. Yet it will have introduced the scene in v. 7 also in reference back to 20:2–8, because that disciple at the tomb likewise excels on account of his believing recognition. 'It is the Lord' also makes a link with 20:18, 20, 25, 28.

34. ἐπενδύτης is a piece of clothing worn over other clothing; cf. BauerWb, col. 563; Liddell-Scott, *Lex.*, p. 617, s.v. The comment that he was naked can then be understood in such a way that he wore no other clothing under the over-garment; the fishermen had, namely, under some circumstances, to jump into the lake, to deal with the net. Here Peter keeps on his garment but puts a belt round it and thus holds it together, so as to be able to swim better. Thus the explanation of M.-J. Lagrange, p. 525, cf. also R. E. Brown, p. 1072, who rejects other explanations. G. Dalman, *Orte und Wege*, p. 145 (E.T.: *Sacred Sites and Ways*, pp. 135f), thinks against this that Peter found himself naked in the boat and threw a short shirt over himself. But that would be doing less justice to the expression διεζώσατο; besides, Peter will not have been without clothing in the cold night.

35. It is, after all, presupposed in the story of the catch of fish, that the disciples know who stands on the shore. It is then understandable for them as well that Peter should keep his cloak on 'as the oriental sense of decency demands, almost even more than our own' (Dalman, *Orte und Wege*, p. 145, omitted in E.T.).

36. ἀπό with detail of distance also 11:18, presumably from the source (cf. Vol. 2, p. 329). Cf. BauerWb, col. 172, s.v. III.

37. The verb frequently expresses an act of force, cf. Acts 8:3; 14:19; 17:6; concerning fishing also Plutarch, *Mor.*, 977f, cf. BauerWb, col. 1572; Liddell & Scott, *Lexicon*, p. 1733.

38. The v. 1. καιομένην, which is presupposed in the VL rendering, 'incensos', can hardly depend only on a hearing lapse, but also on reflection. Vg d e f read 'positos'.

39. Cf. the discussion in R. E. Brown, pp. 1073f, who is himself of the opinion that Peter boarded the boat. Presumably the same viewpoint is presupposed in the reading ἐνέβη ℵ L W Ψ 1 565 al. However, this is improbable for the situation; it is to be noted: εἰς τὴν γῆν. Even if Peter is standing on firm ground, considerable strength is attributed to him. If the addition of οὖν after ἀνέβη in a group of mss. (B ℵ C L W λ 33 al.) is secondary (with Tisch., Nestlé–Aland), then it is an example of how copyists adjusted to the tricks of speech of an author. However, in accordance with external textual criticism, οὖν is possibly to be retained (thus also UBS Greek NT).

40. *In Ezek* 47:6–12: PL 25, col. 474C. Jerome's information is contradicted by R. M. Grant, *HarvThR* 42 (1949), pp. 273ff.

41. *In Jo. tr.*, CXXII, 8 (CC 673f). More recent authors who hold or adduce this explanation are in part ignorant that it goes back to Augustine.

42. *In Jo. lib.*, *XII, ad loc.* (PG 74, col. 745).

43. Cf. J. A. Emerton, 'The Hundred and Fifty-three Fishes in John XXI. 11', *JThSt NS* 9 (1958), pp. 86–89; (objection) P. R. Ackroyd, *ibid.*, 10 (1959), p. 94; (answer) J. A. Emerton, *ibid.*, 11 (1960), pp. 335f.

44. H. Kruse, 'Magni Pisces Centum Quinquaginta Tres', *VD*, 38 (1960), pp. 129–148. But the designation which he works out from the Hebrew q^{e}hal ha-ahabah= *ecclesia amoris* (p. 143) is never found elsewhere.

45. Cf. H. Kruse, *ibid.*, p. 130; again, R. E. Brown, p. 1076, inclines to this view.

46. *Literar. Einheit*, pp. 194f.

47. Cf. BauerWb, col. 211 (but translated in his commentary as 'have breakfast'); R. Pesch, *Fischfang*, p. 101. The LXX uses the word in Gen 43:25; 1 Kings (Sam) 14:24; 3 Kings (1 Kings) 13:7, not for the morning meal; cf. also Tob 2:1S.

48. B. Schwank, in: *Sein und Sendung* 29 (1964), p. 497.

48a. Cf. also A. Shaw, 'The Breakfast by the Shore and the Mary Magdalene Encounter as Eucharist Narratives', *JThSt* 25 (1974), pp. 12–26. The writer also recognizes the 'typical' relationship with the Emmaus story. But the explanation of Jn 20:11–18 in terms of the eucharistic fellowship is not convincing.

49. R. E. Brown, pp. 1111 and frequently.

50. Cf. H. Schürmann, *Das Lukasevangelium* I (Freiburg im Breisgau, 1969), p. 270 (Peter experiences his creaturely nothingness; in the choice of words 'all possible arguments' for the later fall and the conversion of Peter are, admittedly, also anticipated); R. Pesch, *Fischfang*, pp. 117f (reaction of the one experiencing the miracle, of the sinner, before the holy one; further views, *ibid.* in n. 31).

51. τούτων is certainly not to be understood neutrally ('more than these things'; namely, nets and catch of fish), as Bernard pp. 704f and some others suggest; it is also not to be referred to the object: 'More than you love these (other disciples)', as A. Fridrichsen interprets in: *SvExA* 5 (1940), pp. 152–162, because no basis exists for such a question. Rather, with most exegetes, the elliptical mode of speech must be supplemented thus: Do you love me more than these love me? A similarly abbreviated mode of expression in Jn 5:36 (see *ad loc.*), cf. Blass-Debr § 185, 1.

52. Cf. Bultmann, p. 711, n. 4 (considers a gloss); R. E. Brown, p. 1104. Several mss. omit πλέον τούτων: 1 565 al. VL (except d f) sy^s. But that is surely due to reflection.

53. πλέον alternates with πλεῖον (cf., e.g., Lk 3:13 with 7:42; Acts 15:28 with 20:9). John uses for other inflexions πλειο- (4:1, 41; 7:31; 15:2); it cannot be concluded from this that πλέον (adverb) is non-Johannine style. Cf. Blass-Debr § 30:2.

54. The reading Ἰωνᾶ in many later mss. is clearly an assimilation to Mt 16:17;

Ἰωάννου is read by B אᶜ C* D L W Tatᴾᵗ VL (except c) Vg cop. The picture is similar in 1:42 (on Cod. Θ see there).

55. Cf. Th. Zahn, p. 695: '. . . especially emphatic reminder of that which this disciple is in origin, in contrast to that to which Jesus had called him and what he wanted to make out of him'; Lightfoot-Evans, p. 340; Brown, p. 1102: 'Jesus is treating him less familiarly and thus challenging his friendship.' Against that Lagrange, p. 529, and Lindars, p. 633, see in the form of address a specially solemn occasion.

56. B. F. Westcott, p. 303 (ἀγαπᾶν is a higher love); Trench, *Synonyma*, pp. 30f (φιλεῖν expresses warmth of affection); E. Evans, 'The verb ἀγαπᾶν in the Fourth Gospel', *Studies in the Fourth Gospel* (London, 1957), pp. 64–71 (φιλεῖν is a higher love); C. Spicq, *Agapè* III, pp. 230–237 (with a survey of the representatives of the distinction since Origen p. 232, n. 1).

57. φιλεῖν is also used in 16:27 for the disciples' love for Jesus; if Chapter 16 does not come from the evangelist, this parallel is noteworthy. In Chapter 14 the evangelist uses ἀγαπᾶν throughout for the disciples' love of Jesus. The differences in meaning which Spicq, *Agapè*, III, pp. 219–230, claims to discover for the other φιλεῖν – passages, are only convincing in part.

58. Cf. G. Stählin in: *ThWb*, IX, pp. 128–134 (E.T.: *TDNT*, IX, pp. 129–136), and most of the newer commentaries. Cf. for the English-speaking world C. F. D. Moule, *An Idiom Book of New Testament Greek* (Cambridge, 1953), p. 198; Lindars, p. 634.

59. *Det. pot. ins.*, 25 in an allegorical exegesis of Gen 37:15f.

60. πρόβατα C* D VL (except f ff²) could be an assimilation to v. 16 and v. 17.

61. Cf. J. Jeremias, *Gleichnisse Jesu*, p. 69.

62. Against E. Ruckstuhl, *Literarische Einheit*, p. 201 (no. 37). πάλιν + δεύτερος is only found twice in John: 4:54; 21:16; compare besides Mt 26:42; Acts 10:15 (π. ἐκ δευτέρου). An example from a papyrus see in BauerWb, col. 1203, s.v. 2. In individual mss. one of the two words is lacking: πάλιν om. e c; δεύτερον om. א* VL (except e c) Vg syˢ Tatⁱᵗ. Such a pleonasm is unusual in Latin.

63. Cf. J. Jeremias, in: *ThWb*, VI, p. 493 (E.T.: *TDNT*, VI, pp. 493f) (on 1 Pet 2:25: 'the One who provides for and watches over His people') and p. 497 (E.T.: pp.497f).

64. Cf. *BauerWb*, col. 1636, s.v. 3; Blass-Debr § 248, 4. Differently, Spicq, *Agapè* III, p. 234, n. 4; O. Glombitza, *NT* 6 (1963), p. 280.

65. 'Das dreifache "Weide meine Lämmer"': *ZKTh*, 69 (1947), pp. 328–344; also in: *idem.*, *Petrus und seine Zeit* (Innsbruck, 1958), pp. 11–30.

66. *ThWb*, IX, p. 132, n. 194 (E.T.: *TDNT*, IX, p. 134, n. 194).

67. Among the most recent ecumenical discussions, cf. the contributions in *Zum Thema Petrusamt und Papsttum* (Stuttgart, 1970); Schnackenburg, 'Das Petrusamt. Die Stellung des Petrus zu den anderen Aposteln', *Wort und Wahrheit* 26 (1971), pp. 206–216; W. Trilling, 'Zum Petrusamt im Neuen Testament', *ThQ*, 151 (1971), pp. 110–133; R. Pesch, 'Die Stellung und Bedeutung Petri in der Kirche des Neuen Testaments': *Conc.*, 7 (1971), pp. 240–245; R. E. Brown, K. P. Donfried, J. Reumann (eds), *Peter in the New Testament* (Minneapolis and New York, 1973, with bibliography).

68. The Fathers generally regarded the commission to Peter as a pastoral office for all believers; only occasionally is a pronouncement made concerning his primacy over the other apostles, according to P. Schanz, *ad loc.*, by Chrysostom, Eusebius of Emesa and Euthymius. Thomas Aquinas refers the office of Peter to all believers (Cai. 2623) and sees the reason for the threefold commission as 'quia in Ecclesia sunt tria genera hominum, scilicet incipientium, proficientium et perfectorum' (no. 2625). For the now relevant idea of the office of Peter as the office of unity, the words of Cyprian are noteworthy: 'Quamvis apostolis omnibus post resurrectionem suam potestatem tribuat . . . (Jn 20:21–23), tamen, ut unitatem manifestaret, unitatis eiusdem originem ab uno incipientem sua auctoritate disposuit. Hoc erant utique et ceteri apostoli quod fuit Petrus, pari consortio praediti et honoris et potestatis, sed exordium ab unitate proficiscitur, ut ecclesia Christi una monstretur' (*De unit. eccl.*, 4; CSEL, III/1, p. 212). On the explanation of Vatican I, *Const. de Ecclesia*, Cap. 1 (Denz. 1822), which is not a

dogmatic determination of the explanation of our passage, cf. R. E. Brown, p. 1116, who cites a work by V. Betti (Rome, 1961).

69. Bultmann, pp. 712f, supposes a source and sees in the fragment as Mt 16:17–19 the 'commission for leadership of the community'; the fragment 'might well be derived from early tradition'. Further cf. O. Cullmann, *Petrus* (2nd ed., 1960) pp. 209–214 (E.T.: *Peter: Disciple, Apostle, Martyr* (trans., F. von Filson), 1962, pp. 186–191) (assumes that Mt 16:17ff; Lk 22:31ff; Jn 6:66ff and 21:15–17 have a common source behind them; he transfers the origin of the tradition into the supper-room; but that is extremely questionable); Lindars, p. 633 (entrusting with the pastoral authority over the church); L. Morris, p. 875; S. Schulz, p. 252.

70. Cf. O. Cullmann, *Petrus*, pp. 71f (E.T.: Peter, pp. 64f); R. E. Brown, p. 1113 ('apostolic mission').

71. O. Glombitza, 'Petrus – der Freund Jesu', *NT* 6 (1963), pp. 277–285, would read the notion: 'Love of the Lord is expressed in this loving care for the world which has been entrusted' (p. 281); but that strains the text.

72. It is no longer necessary to perceive the comparative in νεώτερος, cf. BauerWb, col. 1060, s.v. 1, b, β; Blass-Debr § 244, 2. The objection which some exegetes take to the change of viewpoint ('young' from being old, 'old' from being young), disappears, if a middle age is attributed to Peter.

73. Cf. on ζώννυμι Acts 12:8; περιζ. Lk 12:35; Eph 6:14. The last passages show that the picture was also used metaphorically.

74. Thus Bultmann, p. 713, without being able to give further proof.

75. W. Bauer, *ad loc.*, p. 239; refuted by Wellhausen who also already knew this explanation as 'antiquarian sophistry'.

76. *Scorpiace* 15, 3 (CC, II, 1097) with consideration of Jn 21:18: 'Tunc Petrus ab altero cingitur, cum cruci adstringitur'. The explanation goes still further, that Peter was crucified head down, cf. Eusebius, *Hist. eccles.*, III, 1, 2; *ActPetr*, 36–41. A prophecy of the death on the cross is also supposed by E. Dinkler, in: *ThRu* 25 (1959), p. 203; O. Cullmann, *Petrus*, p. 98.

77. Cf. A. Schulz, *Nachfolge und Nachahmen*, pp. 167f.

78. ἀκολοθοῦντα om. ℵ* W ff² bo.

79. Cf. Hoskyns-Davey, p. 558; Barrett, p. 488 (even thinks that he follows Jesus to death); Lightfoot-Evans, p. 342 (on 21:7); Sanders-Mastin, p. 456. Different A. Kragerud, *Der Lieblingsjünger*, pp. 38–40: The 'beloved disciple' is a follower, but he was already a follower *before* Peter and is superior to Peter. But that cannot be read from the passage; Kragerud arrives at this on the basis of his overall understanding.

80. Bultmann, p. 714, n. 6, regards the entire reference back as a secondary interpolation; to link the relative clause the interpolator added on ἀκολοθοῦντα and took up the thread again with τοῦτον οὖν ἰδών in v. 21. But before such an explanation is resorted to, we must ask whether the narrator cannot be pursuing some intention in making the reference.

81. Thus R. E. Brown, p. 1121; cf. also B. W. Bacon, 'The Motivation of John 21, 15–25' *JBL* 50 (1931), pp. 71–80.

82. Cf. Bauer, *ad loc.*; Blass-Debr § 299, 2.

82a. B. Schwank, *Sein und Sendung* 29 (1964), pp. 538f interprets thus: Peter asks out of a friend's love, because he sees that the other disciple also wants to follow. But that is also not to be found here.

83. Cf. R. Schnackenburg, 'Der Jünger, den Jesus liebte' (*EKK* 2), pp. 106f.

84. This has often been considered, cf. Bauer, p. 239; Bultmann, p. 716, no. 2; Barrett, p. 488; Brown, p. 1118; Lindars, p. 639, and others.

85. Cf. the monograph by J. Heise, Bleiben. However, the writer attributes 21:22f, following Bultmann, to everyday usage (p. 50).

86. Here again the closeness to the main letter is shown. The Church regards itself as a fellowship of brethren, who address one another as such amongst themselves.

Cf. Excursus 5 in Joh-Br. (pp. 117–121). In the gospel only 20:17 could point to a narrower circle of Jesus' disciples; but cf. *ad loc.*

87. The demonstrative pronoun οὖτος cannot be referred to the preceding saying in v. 22, on account of the continuation with the ὅτι-clause as Zahn, pp. 700f, wants. He has then to describe the addition of the ὅτι-clause as 'careless brevity'. But then something would have had to be added as actually happens in D: καὶ ἔδοξαν. Whether οὖτος is placed first (so the better MSS) or tacked on (many later MSS), signifies nothing, cf. Blass-Debr § 292.

88. This argument constantly recurs, from Zahn, p. 701, to L. Morris, p. 879.

89. There are some textual variants, which, however, only betray the writer's reflection on the difficult saying. Most Latins already make alterations in v. 22: ἐάν] sic aur b c r¹ Vg^pt Tat^fin.; si sic d ff² Vg^pt. Codex D likewise adds after μένειν a οὕτως. The *sic* then also appears with similar attestation in v. 23; it betrays a reflection concerning the 'remaining'. In v. 23 several mss. leave out τί πρὸς σέ: ℵ* 565 al. a e sy^s.

90. Cf. Bultmann, p. 715: 'Now v. 23 of course affirms that the saying of Jesus was not a prophecy but only a hypothetical statement'; further Wikenhauser, Schick, S. Schulz and others. Admittedly Bultmann would give another original meaning to the saying in v. 22, namely, 'that the beloved disciple in a way takes Peter's place, and that the authority assigned to Peter has passed over to him' (p. 717). But that remains a mere supposition.

91. Cf. already Augustine, *In Jo. tr.*, *CXXIV*, 5 (CC 686): 'Perfecta me sequatur actio, informata meae passionis exemplo; inchoata vero contemplatio maneat donec venio, perficienda cum venero.'

92. Cf. Blass-Debr § 373, 1; Moulton-Turner, *Grammar* III, p. 114.

93. Cf. Hoskyns-Davey, p. 559: 'Perhaps the opinion may be hazarded that the reader is meant to understand that that perfect discipleship of which the Beloved Disciple is the type and origin will never fail the Church.' Barrett, p. 486: The disciple was meant to be the continuing guarantor of the Church's tradition through the written gospel. Kragerud goes farthest of all, in accordance with his hypothesis, *Der Lieblingsjünger*, pp. 120–129: the continuing existence of charismatic-prophetic speech (in peripatetic prophetism) is hinted at.

94. Cf. M.-J. Lagrange, pp. 520 and 534: Only when others, probably the elders of Ephesus, added 21:24f, was the original conclusion (20:30f) restored. Differently, L. Vaganay, *La finale du Quatrième Évangile*, *RB*, 45 (1936) pp. 512–528, who would place 20:30f between 21:24 and 21:25. But then v. 25 would really be a wholly meaningless addition. That the connection between v. 24 and v. 25 is extremely loose was recognized by early copyists who accommodated the pericope of the adulteress (7:53—8:11) at this point; but they are few in number: the Lake-minuscule group and MSS of the Armenian version (cf. *UBS* Greek NT, p. 413).

95. The same writer who first left out v. 25 and affixed his scroll and his signature, deleted them again and added v. 25. Cf. H. J. M. Milne – T. C. Skeat, *Scribes and Correctors of the Codex Sinaiticus* (London 1938) p. 12; see also Brown p. 1125.

96. Bultmann, pp. 715f, considers whether vv. 23–24 are not an addition of a further editor, but then rejects this possibility again. In fact vv. 23–24 belong together in any case. Their omission would make the scene of vv. 20–22 easier; but the editorial Chapter 21 cannot easily be thought to have closed with v. 22. V. 25, because of its style, does not come into question as the original conclusion. Besides, Bultmann (*ibid.*, n. 6) rightly sees that then the interest of the redactor in what is narrated would not be clear.

97. Cf. further on this point, J. Beutler, *Martyria*, pp. 59f., 223–227, 282f.

98. Thus C. H. Dodd, *JThSt*, *NS*, 4 (1953), pp. 212f, and *Historical Tradition*, p. 12.

99. Cf. Zahn, p. 705; indirectly, the closing comment refers admittedly also to the whole, now finally concluded gospel.

100. Cf. Bernard, p. 713; A. Dauer, *BZ*, *NF*, 12 (1968), p. 91. This possibility is considered by other exegetes but then thrown out (cf. Barrett, Morris *ad loc.*). To regard the words καὶ ὁ γράψας ταῦτα as an addition by another hand, as a later gloss (cf. Sanders-Mastin, p. 48), is rightly rejected by most commentators as arbitrary.

101. The textual tradition wavers somewhat: καὶ ὁ B D VL sy; ὁ καὶ Θ ᵠ 33 pc; καί without an article ℵ* A c 𝔓 pl. The first reading is probably the original; it commends itself anyway on account of the tense change. That gives a special emphasis, but there is also a certain contrast with the bearing witness (in the present).

102. Bultmann thinks that the disciple whom Jesus loved is a symbolic figure in the gospel and was understood as an historical person only by the redactor (p. 484). The editor of 21:23 'by this means . . . had gained a person who was acknowledged to be a witness from the earliest time as a guarantor for the worth of the Gospel, and indeed as its author. That by this time the man had already died . . . was no real obstacle to his procedure; the only thing that mattered to him was to set the present Gospel under the authority of the oldest witness' (716). H. Thyen, *Johannes 13 und die 'Kirchliche Redaktion'*, p. 352, regards all beloved disciple passages in the gospel as interpolations of the editor of Chapter 21. 'He wants in this way, on the one hand, to set up a memorial to the honoured "disciple" of his circle, and, on the other hand, to bestow on his gospel the authority of the beloved eye-witness'; cf. *ibid.*, p. 345. R. Mahoney also, *Two Disciples*, pp. 295f, holds, at the very least, that a mistake is not ruled out. Differently, Kragerud attempts (*Der Lieblingsjünger*, pp. 115–119) to solve the problem of ὁ γράψας ταῦτα: The expression refers to the entire circle behind the gospel; the beloved disciple and the Johannine circle are identical. But, according to the context, that is impossible; reliance on 1 Jn 1:4 does not help, because of the plural.

103. Most commentaries refer οἴδαμεν to the Church or to the editors as its mouthpiece. Lindars, p. 641: '. . . it represents the imprimatur of the Church in which it originated'. Differently, Hoskyns-Davey, pp. 559f: the original apostles of the Lord.

104. G. D. Kilpatrick, *Bible Translator*, 11 (1960), pp. 173–177, and *JThSt*, 12 (1961), pp. 272f, claims to observe that in John ἀληθής is used predicatively and ἀληθινός is used attributively with the same meaning. But this distinction does not apply to Jn 19:35 and 21:24.

105. Cf. Blass-Debr, § 294, 5.

106. B C* ℵᶜ 1219 read χωρήσειν; it must presumably be retained as the *lectio difficilior* (differently, UBS Greek NT). Cf. Blass-Debr § 350.

107. A series of examples from the Hellenistic and Jewish area is collected in Wettstein I, p. 966. Cf. especially Philo, *poster.*, 144; *Moys.* I, 213.

Excursus 18: Pages 375–388

1. We should dispense with the expression 'Lieblingsjünger' (favoured disciple). 'Der geliebte Jünger' follows the usual designation in English 'the Beloved Disciple'.

2. *Der Jünger, den Jesus liebte*, EKK, *Vorarbeiten, Heft 2* (Zürich-Neukirchen, 1970), pp. 97–117.

3. N. E. Johnson, 'The Beloved Disciple in the Fourth Gospel', *Church Quart. Review* 167 (1966), pp. 278–291; L. Johnson, 'Who was the Beloved Disciple?', *ExpT* 77 (1965–66), pp. 157f; D. G. Rogers, *ibid.*, p. 214; A. Dauer, *BZ* 12 (1968), pp. 88–93; J. Roloff, 'Der johanneische "Lieblingsjünger" und der Lehrer der Gerechtigkeit', *NTSt* 15 (1968–69), pp. 129–151; J. Colson, 'L'énigme du Disciple, que Jésus aimait' (Paris, 1969); T. Lorenzen, *Der Lieblingsjünger im Johannesevangelium* (Stuttgart, 1971); H. Thyen, in *Festgabe für K. G. Kuhn* (1971), pp. 352–355; B. Lindars, *Gospel of John* (1972), pp. 31–34; L. Morris, *Gospel acc. to John* (1972), pp. 8–30; B. de Solages, 'Jean, fils de Zébédée et l'énigme du disciple que Jesus aimait', *Bull. de Littér. Ecclés.*, 73 (Toulouse, 1972), pp. 41–50; O. Cullmann, *Der johanneische Kreis* (Tübingen, 1975), pp. 74–88; F. Neirynck, 'The "Other Disciple" in Jn 18, 15–16': *EthLov*, 51 (1975), pp. 113–141.

4. *Gospel of John,* pp. 483ff, on Jn 13:23–26; further p. 701 on Jn 21: 'In this passage the beloved disciple is not the representative of Gentile Christianity, but a definite historic person.' His opinion is followed by S. Schulz, *Ev nach Joh.*, p. 176, making Peter the representative of Jewish Christianity.

Notes

5. *Gospel of John*, p. 716.
6. *Der Lieblingsjünger*, p. 14.
7. *Op. cit.*, pp. 113–129.
8. Cf. Th. Lorenzen, *Der Lieblingsjünger*, particularly pp. 76f, 108f; similarly W. G. Kümmel, *Einleitung* (new edition, 1973), pp. 200–204.
9. In *NTSt*, 15 (1968–69), especially pp. 143–150. Roloff also determines like functions for both figures: '*Both are neither revelators nor transmitters of tradition but primarily interpreters and exegetes,* who bear witness from a special understanding of the divine saving act' (p. 148). But he overlooks the fact that the master of the Johannine school also wants to present the Jesus-tradition thus: he is a bearer of tradition. It scarcely suffices to say: 'With the beloved disciple, so to say, the place of the Torah and the word of the prophets is taken by the word and way of Jesus' (*ibid.*).
9a. Cf. the authors mentioned by A. Kragerud, *op. cit.*, pp. 11f. J. Roloff also expresses himself cautiously in this direction, *op. cit.*, p. 134: 'Something in any case could speak in favour of the beloved disciple passages in Chapters XIII–XX, also going back to that last stage in the editing, which is also the cause of the "post-script" chapter.'
10. H. Thyen in the *Festgabe für K. G. Kuhn*, p. 352.
11. *Two Disciples at the Tomb*, pp. 82–103; 237–277. Cf. especially p. 282: In none of the three passages 'is the disciple given characteristics attaching to him as a person and making him personally into a model. . . . If the point be pressed, the disciple is less a model than a mannequin.'
12. On Jn 21 see Mahoney, *op. cit.*, pp. 287–297; quotation p. ˙295.
13. Cf. *Gospel of John*, p. 484: 'The more detailed interpretation of the relevant passages must start with 19:26f.
14. According to Mahoney, *op. cit.*, pp. 95–103, Jn 19:25–27 has a certain anti-Docetic tendency. By means of the scene under the cross is shown that Jesus really wants to die and is putting his earthly affairs into order. But this explanation certainly does not do justice to the scene.
15. Cf. E. Krafft, 'Die Personen im Johannesevangelium: *EvTh* 16 (1956), pp. 18–32; J. Roloff, *op. cit.*, p. 141; T. Lorenzen, *Der Lieblingsjünger*, pp. 80–82.
16. This argument is frequently adduced, cf., e.g., J. Roloff, *op. cit.*, p. 140; T. Lorenzen, *Der Lieblingsjünger*, pp. 77f; W. G. Kümmel, *Einleitung* (1973), p. 203.
16a. On earlier hypotheses, for instance, the assertion of one province of the Church against the claims of another, cf. Kragerud, *Lieblingsjünger*, pp. 48f; G. Hartmann also holds such a view in his unpublished dissertation on the Easter accounts in Jn 20 (Kiel, 1963) according to T. Lorenzen, *op. cit.*, p. 80, n. 18. But it is not necessary to go so far. I have expressed the view in *EKK2* (1970), pp. 105 and 107, that the beloved disciple through the bringing together with Peter is meant to be strengthened in his position ('revaluation-motif'). Cf. also the commentary on the passages concerned.
17. Thus Bultmann p. 484; similarly other scholars.
18. Cf. the introduction to Chapter 21 under 4.
19. *Gospel of John*, p. 641.
20. *EKK* 2 (1970), pp. 114f.
21. 'Jesu letzte Weisung Jo 19; 26–27a,' in: *idem., Ursprung und Gestalt* (Düsseldorf, 1970), pp. 13–29, particularly 25. Cf. the commentary on 19:26–27.
22. *L'énigme du disciple* (see above p. 484, n. 3). The writer compares the evidence in John's gospel with the witnesses of church tradition in the second century; on these see also F.-M. Braun, *Jean le Théologien et son évangile dans l'église ancienne* (Paris, 1959).
23. *Jean, fils de Zébédée* (see above, *loc. cit.*). The author compares the grouping of the apostles in the synoptics, especially in Luke, and thinks the convergence permits the conclusion that in John the beloved disciple refers to the apostle John.
24. L. Morris, *Studies in the Fourth Gospel* (Grand Rapids, 1969), especially pp. 139–214; *idem., Gospel acc. to John*, pp. 8–30 (the assessment of the change of view in Britain, p. 8).
24a. N. E. Johnson, *Church Quart. Rev.*, p. 167 (1966), pp. 278–291, attributes to the beloved disciple (= John, son of Zebedee) a document with eye-witness reports

concerning the passion story (QJ), which was then incorporated into the gospel written by a friend or disciple.

25. Cf. A. Wikenhauser-J. Schmid, *Einleitung* (^{6}1973), p. 314.

26. Cf. B. Lindars, *Gospel of John,* pp. 28f.

27. J. N. Sanders, 'Those whom Jesus Loved' (John XI. 5), *NTSt* 1 (1954–55), pp. 29–41, particularly 33f; *idem., Commentary* (ed., B. A. Mastin 1968), pp. 31f. Admittedly, he distinguishes the beloved disciple (= Lazarus) from the evangelist, whom he identifies with John Mark (*Comm.,* pp. 50f).

28. See especially P. Parker, John and John Mark': *JBL* 79 (1960), pp. 97–110; L. Johnson, in: *ExpT* 77 (1965–66), pp. 157f (against him D. G. Rogers, *ibid.,* p. 214, who favours John the son of Zebedee).

29. Cf. C. Kopp, *Heiligen Stätten,* pp. 377–387 (E.T.: *Holy Places,* pp. 323–334); W. Baier, *Haag, BibLex* (^{2}1968) pp. 299f.

29a. F. Neirynck, *op. cit.* (*EThLov,* 1975), now urges in favour of this in detailed discussion. He also points to predecessors in the last century of the theory that the beloved disciple was a Jerusalem supporter of Jesus, especially H. Delff (pp. 121ff).

30. Cf. A. von Harnack, *Die Mission und Ausbreitung des Christentums in den ersten drei Jahrhunderten,* I (Leipzig, ^{4}1924, pp. 411f (E.T.: *The Expansion of Christianity in the First Three Centuries,* I: London, 1904, trans. J. Moffat, pp. 437f): see also on the 'apostles', who can be shown to have existed in Asia Minor, T. Zahn, 'Apostel und Apostelschüler in der Provinz Asien' (*Forschungen* VI/1, Leipzig, 1900). Cf. also J. Roloff, *NTSt,* 15 (1968–69), pp. 141f; R. Schnackenburg, *EKK,* 2 (1970); pp. 115–117.

BIBLIOGRAPHY OF CITED WORKS

(Containing only those works not listed in the general bibliography in Volumes I and II)

I. SOURCES AND TRANSLATIONS

Flavius Josephus, De Bello Judaico, ed. and trans. O. Michel and O. Bauernfeind, 2 vols. (Bad Homburg, 1959/68).
Pseudepigrapha Veteris Testamenti Graece, ed. A.-M. Denis and M. de Jonge (Leiden, 1970ff):
    Vol. III: Apocalypsis Henochii Graece. ed. M. Black; Fragmenta Pseudepigraphorum quae supersunt Graece, coll. A.-M. Denis (1970).
Judische Schriften aus hellenistisch-römischer Zeit, W. G. Kümmel (Gütersloh, 1973ff):
    Vol. I, 1: H. Bardtke, Zusätze zu Esther; O. Plöger, Zusätze zu Daniel (1973).
    Vol. II, 1: E. Hammershaimb, Das Martyrium Jesajas; N. Meisner, Aristeasbrief (1973).
    Vol. 2, 2: Ch. Dietzfelbinger, Ps.-Philo: Antiquitates Biblicae (1975).
    Vol. III, 1: J. Becker, Die Testamente der zwölf Patriarchen (1974).
    Vol. III, 2: A. H. J. Gunneweg, Buch Baruch, Brief Jeremias; E. Janssen, Testament Abrahams; N. Walter, Fragmente jüdisch-hellenistischer Exegeten (1975).
    Vol. IV, 1: E. Oßwald, Gebet Manasses; A. S. van der Woude, Die Fünf syrischen Psalmen (1974).
    Vol. V, 1: W. Hage. Griechische Baruch-Apk; K. G. Eckart, Apokryphon Ezechiel (1974).
Maier, J./Schubert, K., Die Qumran-Essener. Texte der Schriftrollen und Lebensbild der Gemeinde (München-Basel, 1973).
Levey, S. H., The Messiah: An Aramaic Interpretation (Hebrew Union College, 1974).
Wacholder, Ben Zion, Eupolemus. A Study of Judaeo-Greek Literature (Hebrew Union College, 1974).
The Facsimile Edition of the Nag Hammadi Codices (Leiden, 1972ff). Codex VI (1972); Codex VII (1972); Codex XI, XII and XIII (1973); Codex II (1974).
The Coptic Gnostic Library (Institute for Antiquity and Christianity, Claremont, USA). Nag Hammadi Codices III, 2 and IV,2: The Gospel of the Egyptians, ed. A. Böhlig and F. Wisse (Leiden, 1975).
Deutsche Übers. der Schriften aus Nag Hammadi Codex VI mit Einleitung von Mitgliedern des Berliner Arbeitskreises für koptisch-gnostiche Schriften, in: ThLZ 98 (1973); also from Codex VII, in: ThLZ 100 (1975).
The Odes of Solomon, ed. with translation and notes by J. H. Charlesworth (Oxford, 1973).
Évangile de Pierre. Introduction, texte critique, traduction, commentaire et index par M. G. Mara (SChr 201) (Paris, 1973).
Eusebius von Caesarea, Kirchengeschichte, H. Kraft (München, 1967).

II. GENERAL BIBLICAL LITERATURE

Ökumenisches Verzeichnis der biblischen Eigennamen nach den Loccumer Richtlinien (Stuttgart, 1971).
Metzger, B. M., A Textual Commentary on the Greek New Testament. A Companion Volume to the UBS Greek NT (London – New York, 1971).

The Gospel according to St John

A Complete Concordance to Flavius Josephus, Vol. 1: A–△. ed. K. H. Rengstorf (Leiden, 1973).

Kümmel, W. G., Einleitung in das Neue Testament, völlig neu bearbeitete Aufl. (Heidelberg, 1973).

Wikenhauser, A./Schmid, J., Einleitung in das Neue Testament (Freiburg, ⁶1973).

Denis, A.-M., Introduction aux Pseudépigraphes Grecs d'Ancien Testament (Leiden, 1970).

Jongeling, B., A Classified Bibliography of the Finds in the Desert of Judah, 1958–1969 (Leiden, 1971).

Kieffer, R., Essais de méthodologie néo-testamentaire (Lund, 1972).

Stock, A., Umgang mit theologischen Texten (Zurich, 1974).

III. COMMENTARIES

Rupertus Tuitiensis, Commentaria in Ev. S. Johannis, ed. R. Haacke (CC IX) (Turnhout, 1969).

Catholic

Huby, J., Le discours de Jésus après la Cène (Paris, 1942).

Van den Bussche, H., Le discours d'adieu de Jésus (Tournai, 1959).

Behler, G. M., Die Abschiedsworte des Herrn (Salzburg, 1962).

Thüsing, W., Herrlichkeit und Einheit. Eine Auslegung des Hohepriesterlichen Gebetes Jesu (Johannes 17) (Düsseldorf, 1962).

Schwank, B. (Erklärung von Joh 13–21 in Einzelaufsätzen) in: Sein und Sendung 28 (1963) und 29 (1964).

Vawter, B., The Gospel according to John, in: The Jerome Biblical Commentary (London, 1968) II, pp. 414–466.

Russell, R., St John, in: A New Catholic Commentary on Holy Scripture (London, 1969), pp. 1022–1074.

Protestant

de Boor, W., Das Evangelium des Johannes. 2 Vols. (Wuppertal, 1968/70).

Barcley, W., Johannesevangelium (translated from English). 2 Vols. (Wuppertal, 1969/70).

Fenton, J. C., The Gospel of John (London, 1970).

Lindars, B., The Gospel of John (London, 1972).

Morris, L., The Gospel according to John (London, 1972).

Schulz, S., Das Evangelium nach Johannes (NT Deutsch 4) (Göttingen, 1972).

IV. SELECTED LITERATURE ON THE GOSPEL OF ST JOHN

Barrett, C. K., "The Father is greater than I" (Joh 14.28): Subordinationist Christology in the New Testament, in: Neues Testament und Kirche (Festchr. f. R. Schnackenburg) (Freiburg – Basel – Wien, 1974), pp. 160–171.

– The Gospel of John and Judaism (London, 1975).

Baumbach, G., Gemeinde und Welt im Johannes-Evangelium, in: Kairos 14 (1972), pp. 121–136.

Becker, J., Aufbau, Schichtung und theologiegeschichtliche Stellung des Gebets in Johannes 17, in: ZNW 60 (1969), pp. 56–83.

– Die Abschiedsreden Jesu im Johannesevangelium, in: ZNW 61 (1970), pp. 215–246.

– Wunder und Christologie. Zum literarkritischen und christologischen Problem der Wunder im Joh-Ev, in: NTSt 16 (1969/70), pp. 130–148.

Berger, K., Die Amen-Worte Jesu (Berlin, 1970), pp. 95–130.

Bibliography of Cited Works

Betz, O., Der Paraklet. Fürsprecher im häretischen Spätjudentum, im Johannes-Evangelium und in neu gefundenen gnostischen Schriften (Leiden – Köln, 1963).

Beutler, J., Martyria. Traditionsgeschichtliche Untersuchungen zum Zeugnisthema bei Johannes (Frankfurt a. M., 1972).

Blank, J., Die Verhandlung vor Pilatus Joh 18.28 – 19, 16 im Licht johanneischer Theologie, in: BZ NF 3 (1959), pp. 60–81.

Boice, J. M., Witness and Revelation in the Gospel of John (Paternoster Press, 1971).

Boismard, M.-E., Le lavement des pieds (Jn 13, 1–17), in: RB 71 (1964), pp. 5–24.

Borgen, P., God's Agent in the Fourth Gospel, in: Religions in Antiquity (in mem. of E. R. Goodenough) (Leiden 1968), pp. 137–148.

Borig, R., Der wahre Weinstock. Untersuchungen zu Jo 15, 1–10 (München, 1967).

Braun, F.-M., Jean le Théologien III/2: Le Christ, notre Seigneur (Paris, 1972).

Cadman, W. H., The Open Heaven. The Revelation of God in the Johannine Sayings of Jesus (Oxford – New York, 1969).

Charlesworth, J. H. (ed.), John and Qumran (London, 1972).

– and Cullpepper, R. A., The Odes of Solomon and the Gospel of John, in: CBQ 35 (1973), pp. 298–322.

Cribbs, F. L., St Luke and the Johannine Tradition, in: JBL 90 (1971), pp. 422–450.

Cullmann, O., Der johanneische Kreis (Tübingen, 1975).

Dauer, A., Das Wort des Gekreuzigten an seine Mutter und den "Jünger, den er liebte", in: BZ NF 11 (1967), pp. 222–239; 12 (1968), pp. 80–93.

– Die Passionsgeschichte im Johannesevangelium. Eine traditionsgeschichtliche und theologische Untersuchung zu Joh 18.1 – 19.30 (München, 1972).

– Die Herkunft der Tomas-Perikope Joh 20.24–29, in: Biblische Randbemerkungen, hrsg. von H. Merklein u. J. Lange (Würzburg 1974), pp. 56–76.

De Jonge, M., Jewish Expectations about the "Messiah" according to the Fourth Gospel, in: NTSt (1973), pp. 246–270.

De la Potterie, I., Jésus, roi et juge d'aprés Jn 19, 13, in: Bib 41 (1960), pp. 217–247.

– "Je suis la Voie, la Vérité et la Vie" (Jn 14, 6), in: NRTh 88 (1966), pp. 907–942.

– Das Wort Jesu 'Siehe, deine Mutter' und die Annahme der Mutter durch den Jünger (Joh 19,27b), in: Neues Testament und Kirche (Festschr. f. R. Schnackenburg) (Freiburg – Basel – Wien 1974), pp. 191–219.

– Consécration ou sanctification du chrétien, in: Le Sacré, éd. E. Castelli (Paris 1974), pp. 333–349.

Fenton, J. C., The Passion according to John (London, 1961).

Feuillet, A., L'heure de la femme (Jn 16,21) et l'heure de la Mére de Jésus (Jn 19,25–27), in: Bib 47 (1966), pp. 169–184, 361–380, 557–573.

– Le sacerdoce du Christ et de ses ministres d'après la prière sacerdotale du quatrième évangile et plusiers données parallèles du Nouveau Testament (Paris, 1972).

Fischer, G., Die himmlischen Wohnungen. Untersuchungen zu Joh 14,2f (Bern – Frankfurt a.M., 1975).

Fischer, K. M., Der johanneische Christus und der gnostische Erlöser, in: Gnosis und Neues Testament, hrsg. von K.-W. Tröger (Gütersloh, 1973), pp. 245–266.

Forestell, J. T., The Word of the Cross. Salvation as Revelation in the Fourth Gospel (Rome, 1974).

Fortna, R. T., From Christology to Soteriology. A Redaction-Critical Study of Salvation in the Fourth Gospel, in: Interpr 27 (1973), pp. 31–47.

Ghiberti, G., I racconti pasquali del cap. 20 di Giovanni (Brescia, 1972).

Haacker, K., Die Stiftung des Heils. Untersuchungen zur Struktur der johanneischen Theologie (Stuttgart, 1971).

– Jesus und die Kirche nach Johannes, in: ThZ 29 (1973), pp. 179–201.

Haenchen, E., Historie und Geschichte in den johanneischen Passionsberichten, in: Die Bedeutung des Todes Jesu, ed. F. Viering (Gütersloh, 1967), pp. 55–78.

– Jesus vor Pilatus (Joh 18,28 – 19,15), in: F. Viering, Gott und Mensch (Tübingen, 1965), pp. 144–156.

Hahn, F., Der Prozeß Jesu nach dem Johannesevangelium, in: EKK 2 (Zürich – Neukirchen, 1970), pp. 23–96.

– Sehen und Glauben im Johannesevangelium, in: Neues Testament und Geschichte (Festschr. für O. Cullmann) (Tübingen, 1972), pp. 125–141.

Hartmann, G., Die Vorlage der Osterberichte in Joh 20, in: ZNW 55 (1964), pp. 197–220.

Ibuki, Yu, Die Wahrheit im Johannesevangelium (Bonn, 1972).

Johnston, G., The Spirit-Paraclete in the Gospel of John (Cambridge, 1970).

Klos, H., Die Sakramente im Johannesevangelium (Stuttgart, 1970).

Leistner, R., Antijudaismus im Johannesevangelium? (Bern – Frankfurt a.M., 1974).

Lindars, B., Behind the Fourth Gospel (London, 1971).

Lorenzen, Th., Der Lieblingsjünger im Johannesevangelium (Stuttgart, 1971).

Mahoney, R., Two Disciples at the Tomb. The Background and Message of John 20,1–10 (Bern – Frankfurt a.M., 1974).

Marrow, S. B., John 21 – An Essay in Johannine Ecclesiology (Rome, 1968).

Martyn, J. L., Source Criticism and Religionsgeschichte in the Fourth Gospel, in: Perspective (Pittsburgh) 11 (1970), pp. 247–273.

Meeks, W. A., The Man from Heaven in Johannine Sectarianism, in: JBL 91 (1972), pp. 44–72.

Miranda, J. P., Der Vater, der mich gesandt hat (Bern – Frankfurt a.M., 1972).

Moody Smith, D., Jr., Johannine Christianity: Some reflections on its character and delineation, in: NTSt 21 (1974/75), pp. 222–248.

Morrison, C. D., Mission and Ethic: An Interpretation of John 17, in: Interpr 19 (1965), pp. 259–273.

Müller, U. B., Die Parakletenvorstellung im Johannesevangelium, in: ZThK 71 (1974), pp. 31–77.

– Die Bedeutung des Kreuzestodes Jesu im Johannesevangelium, in: KeDog 21 (1975), pp. 49–71.

Nicol, W., The Sēmeia in the Fourth Gospel. Tradition and Redaction (Leiden, 1972).

Olsson, B., Structure and Meaning in the Fourth Gospel. A Text-Linguistic Analysis of John 2:1–11 and 4:1–42 (Lund, 1974).

Pancaro, S., The Relationship of the Church to Israel in the Gospel of John, In: NTSt 21 (1974/75), pp. 396–405.

Panimolle, S. A., Il dono della legge e la grazia della veritá (Gv 1,17) (Rome, 1973).

Pesch, R., Der reiche Fischfang Lk 5,1–11; Jo 21,1–14 (Düsseldorf, 1969).

Porsch, F., Pneuma und Wort. Ein exegetischer Beitrag zur Pneumatologie des Johannesevangeliums (Frankfurt a.M., 1974).

Randall, J. F., The Theme of Unity in John 17.20–23, in: EThLov 41 (1965), pp. 373–394.

Reim, G., Studien zum alttestamentlichen Hintergrund des Johannesevangeliums (Cambridge, 1974).

Rengstorf, K. H. (ed.), Johannes und sein Evangelium (Wege der Forschung 82) (Darmstadt, 1973).

Richter, G., Die Deutung des Kreuzestodes Jesu in der Leidensgeschichte de Johannesevangeliums (Jo 13–19), in: BuL 9 (1968), pp. 21–36.

– Die Fleischwerdung des Logos im Johannesevangelium, in: NT 13 (1971) 81–126; 14 (1972), pp. 257–276.

Riedl, J., Das Heilswerk Jesu nach Johannes (Freiburg – Basel – Wien, 1973).

Rigaux, B., Les destinataires du IVᵉ Evangile à la lumière de Jn 17, in: RThLouv 1 (1970), pp. 289–319.

Robinson, J. M., Die johanneische Entwicklungslinie, in: Entwicklungslinien durch die Welt des frühen Christentums, von H. Köster und J. M. Robinson (Tübingen, 1971), pp. 223–250.

Ruckstuhl, E., Die johanneische Menschensohnforschung 1957–1969, in: Theol. Berichte 1 (Zürich, 1972), pp. 171–284.

Bibliography of Cited Works

Ruckstuhl, E., Das Johannesevangelium und die Gnosis, in: Neues Testament und Geschichte (Festschr. für O. Cullmann (Tübingen, 1972), pp. 143–156.

Sabugal, S., *XPIΣTOΣ*. Investigación exegética sobre la cristologia joannea (Barcelona, 1972).

Sakkos, St N., "*Ο πατήρ μου μείζων μού εστιν*", 2 Vols. (Thessalonica, 1968).

Schlier, H., Zur Christologie des Johannesevangeliums, in: Das Ende der Zeit (Freiburg i.Br., 1971), pp. 85–101.

Schnackenburg, R., Der Jünger, den Jesus liebte, in: EKK 2 (Einsiedeln – Neukirchen, 1970), pp. 97–117.

– Das Anliegen der Abschiedsrede in Joh 14, in: Wort Gottes in der Zeit (Festschr. für K. H. Schelkle) (Dusseldorf, 1973), pp. 89–104.

– Strukturanalyse von Joh 17, in: BZ NF 17 (1973), pp. 67–78; 196–202.

– Aufbau und Sinn von Johannes 15, in: Homenaje a Juan Prado (Madrid, 1975), pp. 405–420.

Schnider, F. – Stenger, W., Johannes und die Synoptiker (München, 1971).

Schürmann, H., Jesu letzte Weisung Jo 19, 26–27a. in: idem., Ursprung und Gestalt (Düsseldorf, 1970), pp. 13–28.

Smalley, S. S., Diversity and Development in John, in: NTSt 17 (1970/71), pp. 276–292.

– The Sign in John XXI, in: NTSt 20 (1974), pp. 275–288.

Talavero, S., Problemática de la unidad en Jn. 18–20, in: Salm 19 (1972), pp. 513–575.

Teeple, H. M., The Literary Origin of the Gospel of John (Evanston, 1974).

Thyen, H., Johannes 13 und die "kirchliche Redaktion" des vierten Evangeliums, in: Tradition und Glaube (Festgabe für K. G. Kuhn) (Göttingen, 1971), pp. 343–356.

– Aus der Literatur zum Johannesevangelium, in: ThRu 39 (1974/75), pp. 1–69, 222–252, 289–330.

Untergaßmair, F., Im Namen Jesu. Der Namensbegriff im Johannesevangelium (Stuttgart, 1974).

Wead, D. W., The Literary Devices in John's Gospel (Basel, 1970).

Wind, A., Destination and Purpose of the Gospel of John, in: NT 14 (1972), pp. 26–69.

Zimmermann, H., Struktur und Aussageabsicht der johanneischen Abschiedsreden (Jo 13–17), in: BuL 8 (1967), pp. 279–290.

V. OTHER LITERATURE

Benoit, P., Exegese und Theologie. Gesammelte Aufsätze (Düsseldorf, 1965).

Bode, E. L., The First Easter Morning (Rome, 1970).

Bornkamm, G., Geschichte und Glaube I und II (München, 1968–1971).

Broer, I., Die Urgemeinde und das Grab Jesu (München, 1972).

Catchpole, D. R., The Trial of Jesus (Leiden, 1971).

Conzelmann, H., Grundriß der Theologie des Neuen Testaments (München, 1967).

Cullmann, O., Urchristentum und Gottesdienst (Zurich,[2] 1950).

Dalman, G., Arbeit und Sitte in Palästina, 7 Vols. (Gütersloh, 1928–1942).

Feneberg, R., Christliche Passafeier und Abendmahl (München, 1971).

Fuller, R. H., The Formation of the Resurrection Narratives (London, 1972).

Grass, H., Ostergeschehen und Osterberichte (Göttingen,[3] 1964).

Haenchen, E., Gott und Mensch. Gesammelte Aufsätze (Tübingen, 1965).

Hamerton-Kelly, R. G., Pre-Existence, Wisdom, and the Son of Man (Cambridge, 1973).

Hengel, M., Nachfolge und Charisma (Berlin, 1968).

– Der Sohn Gottes. Die Entstehung der Christologie und die jüdisch-hellenistische Religionsgeschichte (Tübingen, 1975).

Huber, W., Passa und Ostern. Untersuchungen zur Osterfeier der alten Kirche (Berlin, 1969).

Jeremias, J., Golgotha (Leipzig, 1926).

Kümmel, W. G., Die Theologie des Neuen Testaments nach seinen Hauptzeugen Jesus. Paulus, Johannes (Göttingen, 1969).

Le Déaut, R., La nuit pascale (Rome, 1963).

Léon-Dufour, X., Résurrection de Jésus et message pascal (Paris, 1971).

Lohfink, G., Die Himmelfahrt Jesu (München, 1971).

Lohse, E., Gründriß der neutestamentlichen Theologie (Stuttgart, 1974).

Mack, B. L., Logos und Sophia (Göttingen, 1973).

Mußner, F., Praesentia salutis. Gesammelte Studien (Düsseldorf, 1967).

Neues Testament und Geschichte. O. Cullmann zum 70. Geburtstag. ed. H. Baltensweiler und B. Reicke (Zürich – Tübingen, 1972).

Neues Testament und Kirche. Für R. Schnackenburg, ed. J. Gnilka (Freiburg, 1974).

Parrot. A., Golgotha et Saint-Sépulcre (Neuchâtel – Paris, 1955).

Peter in the New Testament, ed. by R. E. Brown, K. P. Donfried, J. Reumann (Minneapolis – New York, 1973).

Richter, W., Exegese als Literaturwissenschaft (Göttingen, 1971).

Rigaux, B., Dieu l'a ressuscité (Gembloux, 1973).

Rudolph, K., Gnosis und Gnostizismus (Wege der Forschung 262) (Darmstadt, 1974).

Schelkle, K. H., Theologie des Neuen Testaments, 4 Vols. (Düsseldorf, 1968–1974).

Schnackenburg, R., Schriften zum Neuen Testament (München, 1971).

Sherwin-White, A. N., Roman Society and Roman Law in the New Testament (Oxford, [3]1969).

Thyen, H., Studien zur Sündenvergebung (Göttingen, 1970).

Tradition und Glaube. Das frühe Christentum in seiner Umwelt, Festgabe für K. G. Kuhn, ed. G. Jeremias, H.-W. Kuhn und H. Stegemann (Göttingen, 1971).

Vermès, G., Scripture and Tradition in Judaism (Leiden, 1961).

Vögtle, A., Das Evangelium und die Evangelien. Beiträge zur Evangelienforschung (Düsseldorf, 1971).

Wilckens, U., Auferstehung. Das biblische Auferstehungszeugnis historisch untersucht und erklärt (Stuttgart – Berlin, 1970).

INDEX OF BIBLICAL REFERENCES

The names and order of the books are those adopted in the Revised Standard Version Common (Ecumenical) Bible

I OLD TESTAMENT

II APOCRYPHA/DEUTEROCANONICAL BOOKS

III NEW TESTAMENT

IV   EARLY CHRISTIAN WRITINGS

V JEWISH WRITINGS

VI MANDAEAN WRITINGS

VII CLASSICAL AND HELLENISTIC WRITINGS

INDEX OF AUTHORS

Index of Authors

Index of Authors

Index of Authors

Index of Authors

Index of Authors

Index of Authors

Index of Authors